THE GARDENER'S GUIDE TO PLANTING AND GROWING

SHRUBS, TREES AND CLIMBERS

THE GARDENER'S GUIDE TO PLANTING AND GROWING

SHRUBS, TREES
AND CLIMBERS

AN ILLUSTRATED ENCYCLOPEDIA OF THE BEST GARDEN
VARIETIES WITH OVER 1250 BEAUTIFUL PHOTOGRAPHS

JONATHAN EDWARDS AND MIKE BUFFIN

LORENZ BOOKS

Contents

Introduction

A beautiful garden, no matter what its size, shape and aspect, usually contains an assortment of well-placed, visually pleasing shrubs, trees and climbers. While the hard landscaping of lawn, patio, paths, walls and fencing provide the framework for the garden, it is the plants that add the dazzle of colour, texture and delicious scent. These are the furnishings that soften our immediate land-scape, and as the seasons change so too does the planting focal point. The yellows, whites and blues of spring give way to the myriad hues of summer, which in turn become a blaze of autumn gold, red and orange. Together the shrubs, trees and climbers ensure that the garden becomes an ever changing panorama throughout the year.

Trees often form the backdrop around which other shrubs are planted. Not only do trees provide leaf cover, flowers and fruits, they introduce structure and height to the garden. They are usually home to a vast array of beneficial birds and insects too. A well-chosen tree, with a height, spread and growth rate that is appropriate for the size of the garden and its location helps the garden to look established. Since their shape and size

usually dictate what can be planted beneath and around them, trees are a good starting point from which to plan the rest of the garden.

Climbers, like trees, create height, making them an astute addition to the boundaries of very small gardens. While providing greenery and colour, they help to mask noise, clean the air, and can help to deter uninvited guests. With regular nurturing and maintenance climbers can be coaxed to cover great amounts of bare walls and fencing.

Shrubs are the mainstay of the garden. From tiny evergreens that provide year-round colour, to large herbaceous specimens that produce showy flowers, then die back at the end of the season, shrubs are available in every size, shape and colour

imaginable. There are varieties that will suit every soil type and garden aspect, as well as every gardener. Many shrubs are low maintenance once established, and will thrive contentedly for many years. Others will need more regular maintenance to train and contain them within the required space.

This beautiful book contains all you need to know to plan, nurture and maintain your garden to its peak. There is advice on choosing plants, how to propagate them, which tasks to do and when. In addition there are three A–Z directories of the most popular shrubs, climbers and trees to help identification in an already established garden. The key features of each species are listed as well as ultimate growth and spread.

Left: Clematis 'Perle d'Azur'

Right: Shrubs and trees in a myriad hues of green blend together and provide a restful environment.

The naming of plants and trees

All plants are named according to a universally acknowledged system of classification, which was developed by Carl Linnaeus, a Swedish botanist.

Naming names

The North American tulip tree is universally known as *Liriodendron tulipifera*. However, in various countries it has an array of common names, such as tulip poplar, tulip tree, yellow wood and canary whitewood. Some of these common names are used for other trees as well. For example, *Magnolia* x *soulangeana* is sometimes known as tulip tree. For this reason, botanical Latin is used as the definitive name.

Plant names are based on the relationships between plants and other nearby relatives. For example, the genera *Magnolia* and *Liriodendron* (tulip tree) belong to the same family, Magnoliaceae (which also includes the genera *Manglietia* and *Michelia*). The flowers in the family

Liriodendron tulipifera – otherwise known as tulip poplar, tulip tree, yellow wood or canary whitewood.

are distinguished by the arrangement of petals, anthers, ovaries and styles. It is these shared traits that put them in the same family. Although their flowers look similar, the plants' leaves, bark,

trunk (if appropriate), size and habit may be quite different. This means that, even though magnolias and tulip trees both belong to the Magnoliaceae family, they are distant cousins rather than direct relatives.

Trees such as *Liriodendron chinense* (Chinese tulip tree) and *Liriodendron tulipifera* (tulip tree) are classified as being directly related because they both belong to the Magnoliaceae family and because they look similar. The only differences are their overall height and distribution; one being found in China and Vietnam and the other along the eastern seaboard of North America.

In addition to these species, there are numerous other plants in the Magnoliaceae family, and these are found in both temperate and tropical zones of the world.

Families

Plant families are large, generalized groups, whose members have some similar traits, such as susceptibility to particular diseases. Some, however, contain only a single genus. The names of plant families can be easily distinguished as most end in 'aceae'. For example, Rosaceae, Fagaceae and Magnoliaceae are, respectively, the rose, beech and magnolia families.

Genera

Below the botanical rank of family is genus (plural: genera) – a large grouping of plants but with a higher number of shared characteristics than the family.

Within the family Fagaceae are the genera *Castanea* (chestnut), *Castanopsis*, *Chrysolepis* (golden chestnut), *Fagus* (beech), *Lithocarpus* (tan oak), *Nothofagus* (southern beech) and *Quercus* (oak), even though beech trees look different from oak trees.

Magnolia grandiflora 'Goliath' has a highly descriptive name – both the species and cultivar names suggest the flower's large size.

Species

The second part of a plant's botanical name designates the species (sp.). Species names are generally more informative for the gardener and usually indicate a major identifying feature of that particular group of plants, examples include: 'purpureus' (purple), 'macrophylla' (small leaved), 'nana' (dwarf), and 'glauca' (blue). Variety and cultivar names are extremely variable, often commemorating breeders, their family members and friends or famous people, but some are more helpful because they emphasize a particularly desirable feature of the plant, such as 'Golden Showers' – an excellent description of the flowers. Although each species within a genus has a different specific name, the same species name can be used in different genera: for example, *Quercus alba* (white oak) and *Abies alba* (European silver fir).

Occasionally, two plants have similar traits but still appear different, and an additional name may be required. This often occurs in the wild to distinguish individual populations. For example, the widely planted Australian species *Eucalyptus pauciflora* (snow gum) is distinguished from *E. pauciflora* subsp. *niphophila* (alpine snow gum), which grows at a higher altitude, is much hardier and has slightly narrower leaves. Because of these differences, it is designated as a subspecies of the snow gum.

Two other such subdivisions also exist. They are form or forma (f.) and variety (var.), both of which occur naturally in wild populations.

Hybrids

Many plant species that grow close together, both in their wild habitats and in towns and gardens, will breed with different species of plants and create offspring that are intermediate between both parents. These hybrids, signified by a multiplication sign (x), are usually of the same genus but different species. For example, hybrids between the deciduous *Quercus cerris* (Turkey oak) and the evergreen *Quercus suber* (cork oak) were named *Quercus* x *hispanica* (lucombe oak). A number of different forms have arisen and these tend to have intermediate leaf shapes between both parents and are also semi-evergreen.

Cultivars

Trees and shrubs that have originated in gardens, nurseries and among plant breeders are termed cultivars or cultivated varieties. Their names are given after the species name and are distinguished by single quotation marks. For example, *Quercus rubra* 'Aurea' is a selection of the red oak with leaves that are butter yellow when they emerge in spring but fade slowly to light green. It is similar in all other respects to the type species, *Quercus rubra*.

A cultivar name can also occur when a tree has been hybridized and one, but not both, of the parents is known. In these cases no species name is used. *Malus* 'John Downie', for example, is a hybrid crab apple of unknown parentage.

Groups

In recent years various propagation methods have resulted in the production of a number of similar-looking plants that are not identical clones (as happens with cultivars). These are known as Cultivar Groups. In such cases the plant name includes the word Group, which can result in some unwieldy names – for example, *Acer palmatum* var. *dissectum* Dissectum Atropurpureum Group and *Magnolia campbellii* (Raffillii Group) 'Charles Raffill'.

By convention, plants have their Latin names in italics, with a capital letter for the genus, lower case for the species and their cultivar name in a roman font surrounded by single quote marks – hence the plant above is called *Viburnum opulus* 'Xanthocarpum'.

How to use the directories

With so many thousands of varieties of shrubs, climbers and trees to choose from, selecting the right plants for your garden, its aspect and size, can be a bewildering exercise. To help with this selection process, this book contains three separate directory sections on shrubs, trees and climbers: Plants are arranged alphabetically within each directory, by genus. Each main entry features a general introduction to that genus, plus specific useful information such as tips on propagation and which hardiness zone the genus belongs to. This is followed by a selection of plants from that genus, also arranged alphabetically according to their most widely accepted names. One of these entries might be a species, a hybrid, a variety, form or cultivar. Each has a useful description that includes height and spread, together with any other salient features.

Sarcococca confusa

Photograph

Each entry features a full-colour photograph that makes identification easy.

Caption

The full botanical name of the plant in question is given with each photograph.

Genus name

This is the internationally accepted botanical name for a group of related plants.

Common name

This popular, non-scientific name applies to the whole of the plant genus, but can be different in other countries.

Cultivation

This section gives the level of sun and shade that the plant either requires or tolerates, advice on the best type of soil in which it should be grown and other helpful tips, as appropriate.

Pruning

Pruning details specific to each plant are included. The type of pruning and the correct season in which to prune are given.

Propagation

This section gives essential information on how and when to increase the plant – from seed, cuttings or layering.

Individual plant entry

This starts with the botanical name of the plant in bold. This can refer to the species, subspecies, hybrid, variant or cultivar. If a synonym (syn) is given, this provides alternative names by which the plant is known.

SARCOCOCCA
Sweet box
A genus of around 15 species, including the dense-growing, evergreen shrubs featured here, grown for their neat habit and sweet vanilla-scented winter flowers. An ideal choice for a dark, shady corner where nothing else will grow. Well suited to urban gardens as it is pollution tolerant.
Cultivation Grow in a moisture-retentive, well-drained garden soil that is reasonably fertile and in dappled or deep shade.
Pruning No routine pruning is necessary. Remove any damaged growth in mid-spring.
Propagation Take hardwood cuttings in mid-autumn.

Sarcococca confusa
A dense, evergreen shrub with glossy dark green leaves that bears clusters of sweetly scented white flowers from early winter to early spring.
H 2m (6ft) S 1m (3ft).
Aspect: Semi-shade to deep shade
Hardiness: ❀❀❀ Zones: 7–8

Genus introduction

This provides a general introduction to the genus. Other information featured here may include general advice on usage, preferred conditions and plant care, as well as sub-species, hybrids (indicated by an 'x' symbol in the name), varieties and cultivars (featuring names in single quotes) that are available.

Plant description

This gives a description of the plant's key features, along with any other information that may be helpful.

Size information

The average expected height and spread of a genus or individual plant is given, although growth rates may vary depending on location and conditions. Average heights and spreads are given as H and S.

Plant hardiness and zones

The plant's hardiness and appropriate zones are given at the end of this section (see page 512 for details of hardiness and zones, as well as a zone map).

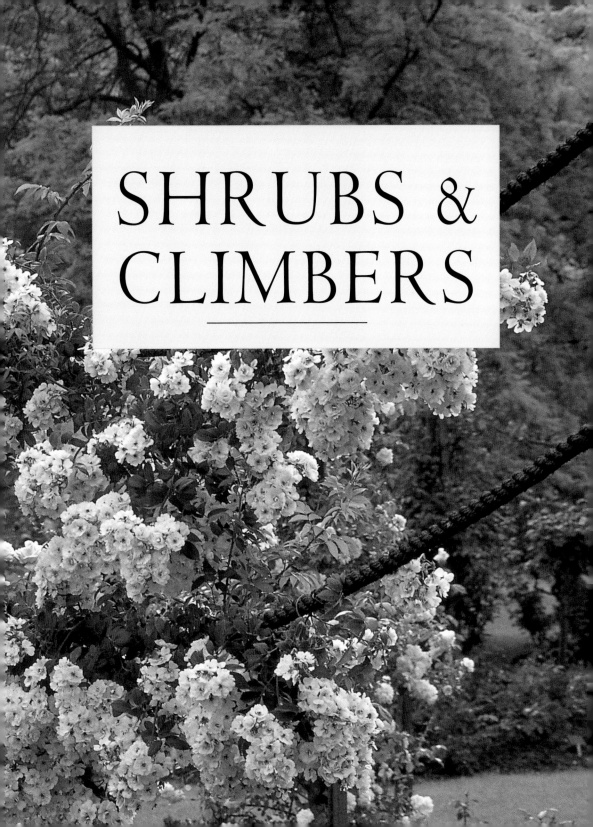

SHRUBS & CLIMBERS

What are shrubs and climbers?

Shrubs and climbers are the mainstay of the garden, providing structure and an ever-changing tapestry of colour throughout every month of the year. Their variety is both a delight and a dilemma – with so many to choose from there's almost certainly one to suit you and your garden, but the choice is so vast it can be totally bewildering.

Enjoying plants

Even if you stick to the basic fare offered by most garden centres, you may have 400 varieties of shrubs and nearly as many climbers to consider. So where do you start?

Well, not with an empty trolley at the garden centre, because impulse buys almost always lead to disappointing results. If you are planting a new border from scratch, buying all the plants in this way at best leads to a border that looks good at one time of year. The safest way to buy the right plant for your garden is to ask yourself the following questions while standing in your garden viewing your plot:

A garden only really comes together with maturity. This means that thought should be given to the eventual size and staying power of the plant when you are setting out your design.

Where is it to be planted?

Consider the amount of direct sun the plot gets; the type of soil and its condition; and the plot's exposure to wind, rain and cold. It is also worth noting the space available.

What will the plant's role in the garden be? Is it to fill a gap, add height and/or colour, extend the period of interest, cover the ground or a fence, hide an eyesore, act as a barrier or backdrop or is it to be used as a specimen or focal point?

How quickly must it perform?

Do you want results in a year or two, or are you prepared to wait a little longer? Bear in mind that many fast-growing plants will continue to get bigger and so will either need regular pruning or moving. Others, such as *Lavatera*, are short-lived and will need replacing after a few years.

Any special requests?

In certain circumstances you might want to avoid certain plants. For example, if your gardening time is

very limited or unpredictable, you might want to avoid high-maintenance plants that require a lot of pruning or training. On the other hand, if you have young children or young visitors, you should avoid or remove any poisonous plants that you have in your garden. With this

Climbers can be grown up exterior walls to hide eyesores such as outdoor pipes.

Clematis 'Comtesse de Bouchard' is ideal for growing against a sunny wall.

Rosa 'Queen of Denmark' is one of the finest old-fashioned shrub roses and is ideal for an open, sunny site. It is a vigorous, disease resistant plant.

Learning the ropes

There is no need to worry overly much about gardening techniques. Most gardening is common sense, and if you do make a mistake, you can always put it right the following year. Having said that, there are, of course, a few basic, sensible and effective practices that have been developed over many generations, and all of these are clearly outlined in the book.

Choosing your plants

Plants form the basis of all good gardens, and none more so than the backbone of the garden, the shrubs and climbers. We have therefore produced two directories to introduce you to the best shrubs and climbers available.

However, there are far, far more than can be featured in any one book and there are always many new varieties being introduced. As you develop your garden, you will become more interested in certain plants and will go to greater lengths to seek out more and more of them.

information in mind, you are then in a position to draw up a shortlist of potential plant candidates. You can follow the same procedure when planning a whole border from scratch. The first three questions apply to the border as a whole, then the last can be considered for each individual element.

Working with colour

Many beginners are worried about combining colours, but the key is simply to go for plants and effects that you like, without worrying about what other people do.

Remember, we all have some ability where colour is concerned: we choose what goes with what when we get dressed every morning, and we choose colours for decorating and furnishing our home. Planning a garden is really no different. In the same way that there are fashion and style magazines to advise you about these areas of your life, there is no shortage of different types of gardening magazines to browse

through for inspiration – and there is nothing more enjoyable for the enthusiastic gardener than being able to wander around other people's gardens, horticultural displays or the grounds of stately homes in search of new ideas and planting styles.

Shrubs provide a multitude of different shapes, colours, textures and sizes. Blending them together, as shown by the variety of green backdrop foliage plants and trees above, allows the stunning hues of the *Daboecia cantabrica* 'Atropurpurea' pride of place in the foreground.

Choosing shrubs and climbers

To establish quickly, grow well and perform superbly, a new shrub or climber needs to be in the best possible condition when you buy it. However, even a top-quality plant will languish if it does not suit the conditions you have in your garden. For this reason, it is essential that you choose the right plant for the position you have in mind.

It is also worth considering how the plant will fit in with your existing garden residents. Some plants produce a spectacular but brief display, while others give a more restrained performance over a much longer period of time. A few plants are of particular value in the garden because they offer more than one season of interest, with summer flowers, autumn berries and foliage as well as colourful winter stems. It is also worth choosing reliable shrubs and climbers that are not susceptible to pest and disease.

If you are filling a new garden with shrubs and climbers, try to include a proportion of quick-growing plants, such as forsythia and buddleja, to give an instant display while the others are getting established.

The careful choosing, nurturing and siting of shrubs and climbers can produce the most stunning effects in the garden.

Buying shrubs and climbers

How well a new plant performs in your garden will depend largely on the quality and condition of the plant you buy. The following will provide a useful guide to choosing the best possible new candidate for your garden.

Choose the healthiest looking plants. Opt for those with a strong, bushy habit (centre) and avoid those with any signs of leaf yellowing (right). Plants with stunted, straggly growth (left) should be rejected, as should those with premature leaf fall.

Check out the supplier

The most important advice to any would-be planter is to go to a reputable plant supplier. If they are known for offering good quality, well-looked-after and reasonably priced plants, the chances are you will not be disappointed.

However, even reputable garden centres, nurseries and internet suppliers can have their off days, particularly towards the end of a busy spring, when many essential tasks are put off, as well as towards the end of summer, when unsold stock has become pot-bound and running short of nutrients. The best time to visit a garden centre is early in the season, when they are up to date with their maintenance and stock. Ideally, find out which days they get their deliveries so that you will have the best choice possible.

One drawback with most garden centres is that they tend to have a very limited range of the most

Garden centres tend to stock the most popular and commonly available shrubs and climbers and will offer growing advice.

popular and easy-to-propagate varieties, so if you want something a little unusual or are after a particular variety, you would be better off going to a specialist nursery.

If you are trying a new garden centre for the first time, walk around the plant beds and take an overall view. Look at plants you know, to check that the labels are correct and not faded – a tell-tale sign that the plant has been hanging around the outlet for too long.

Inspect the plant

Pots should be weed and moss free, and there should not be excessive roots coming out of the bottom of the pot – a tell-tale indication that the plant has been in the pot too long. On the other hand, a plant with loose compost is likely to have been potted only recently, which means it will need to be grown on in its pot until well established, before it is ready to plant out. If you are

unsure, ask if you can see the rootball to make certain the plant's roots have filled the pot but are not pot-bound.

Check the label before you buy, to see if the plant has any special soil requirements, then check to see if it needs to be planted in sun or shade. Also bear in mind that only fully hardy plants will survive outside all year round in cooler climates. If the information on the label is unclear or ambiguous, don't be afraid to ask for advice, or check out the information for yourself here, or in another reputable plant reference book.

Buying a climber

When bought during the growing season, the ideal climber should have several new stems that are putting on vigorous growth. New shoots should also be coming from near the base. Grafted climbers such as wisteria and budded climbers such as roses

Rootballed plants have a ball of soil around the roots and are protected by a covering of net or hessian.

Bare-rooted plants are usually sold covered with plastic wrapping. Keep the wrap intact until you are ready to plant.

foliage. If you are buying bare-rooted plants, the roots should be moist and well covered.

Getting your plants home

Once you have chosen your top-quality plants, don't destroy all your good work by damaging them on the way home. If you are transporting plants in cold weather, wrapping them in a blanket or bubble wrap not only provides good padding but also protects the plant from getting over-chilled. When buying in hot weather, avoid leaving plants in the car for any length of time, as the inside can turn into a furnace in sunny weather and may destroy the plants. Protect from direct sun by throwing a cover over them and make sure you drive them straight home, giving them a good drink of water when you arrive.

Small shrubs and climbers can be easily transported by car but tall plants need to be transported lying down. Cover them to stop the soil escaping and secure them to stop them from rolling around in the car.

should have a strong, well-healed union with all the stems coming from above it. Check that the shoots of all climbers are in good condition and not broken or damaged.

Another important point is that they should not be showing any signs of pest or disease attack. In particular, watch out for colonies of tiny insects in the growing tips (aphids) and white (mildew) or brown (leaf spots) patches on the leaves. On roses also look out for orange spots (rust) on the undersides of leaves.

Buying a shrub

A well-grown deciduous shrub should be roughly symmetrical, with vigorous, well-branched shoots. Evergreen shrubs should have healthy-looking foliage right down to the compost level.

Do not be seduced by buying big, as a small, vigorous shrub will establish itself more quickly than a larger shrub, and it will soon catch up in size when it is planted in the border. By buying small, you'll save money, too. The only exceptions to this rule are for very slow-growing

shrubs, such as acers, which are worth buying larger, and flowering shrubs that you want for providing an instant display in a prominent container on the patio.

As with climbers, you should check for any signs of pests or disease and watch out for all-green shoots on variegated varieties. Avoid shrubs with withered or yellow

Specialist nurseries carry a wider range of shrubs and climbers. Plants can also be ordered from catalogues or bought via the Internet. This is especially helpful if you are after a plant that is unusual or not carried by your local garden centre.

Right plant, right place

Before you decide which plant to buy for your garden, make sure that it is suited to the growing conditions available. It should be hardy enough to survive the winter and will have particular soil and sun requirements.

Sun or shade?

All plants need sunlight to enable them to photosynthesize. This is a process by which plants use energy from sunlight to produce food. However, some have adapted to thriving on the forest floor, where light levels are low and diffused, while others thrive at the wood's edge or in open country, where they get full sun for at least part of the day.

To make choosing plants easier, labels carry symbols for three levels of light: full sun; partial shade; and full shade. Full sun represents an open site that gets direct sunlight for at least half of the day during the growing season, with little shade from nearby buildings, fences or

trees. Most areas in south-facing gardens and parts of east- and west-facing gardens will be in full sun. Partial shade includes areas with reduced light levels, as well as areas that are shaded for much of the day. All gardens have some areas of partial shade. Full shade describes areas that are shaded permanently by trees, hedges or buildings throughout the year. All gardens have at least one shaded corner or north-facing wall or fence, but north-facing plots are the worst affected.

What type of soil?

You need to understand your soil both physically and chemically before you can choose suitable plants. All soils are made up of sand, clay, silt and loam in various proportions, which determine its physical make-up. Sand particles are large and irregularly shaped and so do not pack together tightly. This means that they have lots of air spaces between them. Clay particles are tiny and pack together tightly, leaving

very few air spaces between them. This means that a soil with a high proportion of sand will drain freely in winter, warm up quickly in spring and be prone to drought in summer. Conversely, a soil with more clay particles will be poorly drained in winter, cold and difficult to work in spring, and liable to severe shrinkage and cracking in a dry summer. The best soils have a balance of the different-sized particles.

The important chemical considerations are how acid or alkaline a soil is as well as the nutrients it contains. How acid or alkaline your soil is will determine which types of plants you can grow well. The acidity of a soil can be measured on the pH scale, on which the mid-point is 7 (neutral). Anything higher than this is increasingly alkaline and anything lower is increasingly acid. The pH of a soil also can affect the amount and types of nutrients a plant can take up from the soil. So, even if your soil contains a lot of essential plant nutrients, such as potash (K), phosphate (P) and magnesium (Mg), if it is very acid or alkaline the plants will not be able to absorb them. Most plants prefer a neutral (pH7) to slightly acidic soil (pH6). A few plants, including azaleas and rhododendrons, need a slightly acidic soil to thrive, while other plants, such as lilacs, prefer slightly alkaline conditions (*see also*, Know your soil, page 86).

How hardy?

Hardiness indicates the ability of a plant to cope with winter cold. Fully hardy plants can cope with temperatures down to -15°C (5°F), frost hardy plants can withstand frosts down to -5°C (23°F), half-hardy plants can't cope with

This *Rhododendron macabeanum*, like almost all rhododendrons and azaleas, is an acid-loving plant and so will thrive on ericaceous (lime-free) soil when grown in containers.

For shady sites, the variegated evergreen *Euonymus fortunei* 'Emerald Gaiety' (shown in the background) will add colour and depth.

temperatures below 0°C (32°F) and tender plants need a minimum night temperature of 5°C (41°F). However, also bear in mind how exposed the garden is because wind-chill will need to be taken into consideration, so always err on the side of caution when choosing plants for your garden.

Plants for difficult areas

Although it is a worthwhile exercise trying to find a shrub or climber that is recommended for growing in the conditions you have in your garden, there are certain areas that are so demanding that even the toughest of plants would struggle to survive. In these circumstances it is important to choose plants with real survival skills, and although they won't perform to their full potential, they will provide useful cover where it would otherwise be bare.

Shady corners Every garden has a shady corner at the foot of a north-facing wall or fence. Here the soil is often dry so that plants struggle to get established. If the soil is impoverished, replace it with fresh

soil. The best way to give dark, shady areas a lift is to use shade-loving plants with shiny or variegated leaves. These will reflect the available light and help lift the display. Shrubs such as *Fatsia japonica*, with huge, glossy, palm-shaped leaves, are particularly useful for these areas or you could try one of the decorative large-leaved ivies, such as *Hedera colchica* 'Dentata Variegata' or 'Sulphur Heart'. Add interest with colourful evergreen shrubs, such as *Euonymus fortunei* 'Emerald 'n' Gold' or 'Emerald Gaiety'.

Deep shade This lighting is usually found under trees and large shrubs. Low light is compounded by dry soil that is found in this area, so you will have to improve the soil environment by clearing fibrous roots from planting areas and adding plenty of moisture-holding organic matter, such as well-rotted farmyard manure or garden compost (soil mix). Take care not to damage the roots of suckering shrubs, such as robinia and rhus, because they will respond by throwing up a thicket of suckers.

It is often tempting to raise the soil level around trees by adding topsoil, but this can have serious implications for the trees – and may

kill them. If you want to plant an under-storey of choice, non-vigorous specimens, you may have to create special planting sanctuaries by digging out large planting holes and lining the sides with old, untreated timber that will eventually rot away. In the meantime, the wood will help to prevent tree roots invading the planting holes, giving the new plants extra time to get established. Under trees with a dense canopy, you can try the real survivors, such as periwinkle and variegated ivy.

Wind tunnels Shade and a constant buffeting from winds that are being funnelled between buildings is a common problem in urban and city gardens. Good wind-resistant shrubs and climbers for shade include cotoneaster, *Hydrangea petiolaris*, ivies and periwinkles. In sunny but windy spots, try berberis, *Cistus x corbariensis*, *Helianthemum nummularium*, *Lavandula angustifolia*, *Salvia officinalis* and *Spartium junceum*.

Growing plants in containers

If the conditions are simply too much in your problem area, you can always grow plants in pots and move them in and out of the 'dead' spot so they can recover.

The fragrant and wind-resistant English lavender (*Lavandula angustifolia*) is a good choice for planting in a sunny site by the coast, as the wind will not damage it.

Plant selector: multi-season interest

The following Plant Selector has been structured to make choosing the right plants for your garden as easy as possible. There are Selectors for each season and colour, as well as for scent. However, we must first look at those plants that offer particular garden value, because they provide a range of different ornamental features that enable them to spread their period of interest over two or more seasons.

Location, location

Shrubs and climbers are permanent additions to your garden, so it is important that you not only choose the right plant for a particular spot but also select a good variety that can justify itself. Over the next few pages some of the best garden shrubs and climbers for every season have been outlined, but first we must consider the few highly rated shrubs and climbers that offer two, three or even four seasons of interest.

The impressive coral-bark maple, *Acer palmatum* 'Sango-kaku', provides year-round interest in this way and is an ideal choice for small gardens. The brilliant coral-red young shoots dramatically set off the emerging palm-shaped, orange-yellow leaves in spring. Then the leaves gradually turn green in summer, before taking

Multi-season shrubs and climbers to try

Shrubs
Acer palmatum 'Osakazuki' (leaves, fruits, autumn colour)
Acer palmatum 'Sango-kaku' (leaves, stems, new shoots, autumn colour)
Amelanchier lamarckii (leaves, flowers, autumn colour)
Berberis darwinii (leaves, flowers, berries)
Cornus alba cultivars (leaves, stems, flowers, autumn colour)
Cornus sanguinea 'Midwinter Fire' (leaves, stems, flowers, fruits, autumn colour)
Corylus maxima 'Purpurea' (leaves, flowers, nuts)
Cotinus coggygria 'Royal Purple' (leaves, flowers, autumn colour)
Cotoneaster horizontalis (leaves, flowers, fruit)
Daphne mezereum (leaves, flowers, berries)
Fatsia japonica (leaves, flowers)
Hamamelis mollis 'Pallida' (flowers, leaves, autumn colour)
Hydrangea quercifolia (leaves, flowers, autumn colour)
Mahonia japonica (leaves, flowers, fruits)
Rhamnus alaternus 'Argenteovariegata' (leaves, flowers)
Rhododendron luteum (leaves, flowers, autumn colour)
Rhus typhina 'Dissecta' (leaves, stems, new shoots, autumn colour)
Rosa 'Blanche Double de Coubert' (leaves, flowers, hips, autumn colour)
Rosa rugosa 'Rubra' (leaves, flowers, hips, autumn colour)

Skimmia japonica 'Rubella' (leaves, flower-buds, flowers)
Viburnum opulus 'Roseum' (leaves, flowers, fruit, autumn colour)
Viburnum plicatum 'Mariesii' (leaves, flowers, fruit, autumn colour)

Climbers
Akebia quinata (flowers, foliage)
Aristolochia macrophylla (flowers, foliage, autumn colour)
Clematis alpina cultivars (leaves, flowers, seed-heads)
Clematis 'Bill MacKenzie' (leaves, flowers, seedheads)
Clematis tangutica (leaves, flowers, seed-heads)
Hedera helix 'Green Ripple' (leaves, winter colour)
Hydrangea petiolaris (leaves, flowers, seed-heads, autumn colour)
Parthenocissus henryana (leaves, autumn colour)
Passiflora caerulea (leaves, flowers, fruit)
Rosa filipes 'Kiftsgate' (flowers, hips)
Rosa 'Madame Grégoire Staechelin' (flowers, hips)
Rosa 'Rambling Rector' (flowers, hips)
Sollya heterophylla (flowers, foliage, fruit)
Vitis coignetiae (leaves, autumn colour, fruit)
Vitis vinifera 'Purpurea' (leaves, autumn colour, fruit)
Wisteria floribunda (leaves, flowers, pods, autumn colour)

Viburnum opulus 'Roseum' produces big, white, snowball-like blooms in May.

on fabulous shades of yellow in autumn, falling to reveal the coloured stems through winter.

Another deciduous shrub that provides year-round interest is the dogwood *Cornus sanguinea* 'Midwinter Fire'. This relatively new cultivar bears clusters of tiny, creamy-white flowers during early summer, against green leaves that transform in autumn, when they take on orange-yellow hues and when spherical

bluish fruits are also produced. But it is in winter that it really comes to the fore, revealing spectacular glowing, red-tipped, orange and yellow winter stems that shine out in the winter garden.

In a larger garden, the snowy mespilus, *Amelanchier lamarckii*, provides excellent value. It is a spectacular shrub at both ends of the growing season and is covered in a profusion of star-shaped, white flowers accompanied by bronze-tinted emerging leaves during spring. In autumn, the dark-green foliage transforms into a beacon of orange and red. Sweet and juicy dark red fruits are also produced during early summer.

The purple-leaved smoke bush, *Cotinus coggygria* 'Royal Purple' makes an impressive specimen in any size of garden as it responds particularly well to hard pruning each spring. Airy plumes of pale pink flowers that darken with age are produced from mid-summer. The rich, red-purple leaves offer a colourful point of focus in the summer shrubbery or mixed garden border before turning brilliant scarlet in autumn.

Although the stag's horn sumach, *Rhus typhina*, has developed a troublesome reputation for suckering, the named cultivar 'Dissecta' is less of a problem and has the bonus of more finely cut, decorative foliage. Like the species, it also offers velvet-covered, red winter shoots as well as foliage that turns fiery shades of orange-red in the autumn. Spectacular bristly fruits

The Japanese *Acer palmatum* 'Osakazuki' will brighten up any garden, particularly during the autumn when its leaves turn a rich, vibrant red.

The autumn leaf colours of *Cotinus obovatus* can be yellow, red, orange or reddish-purple.

follow insignificant mustard flowers on conical spikes during the summer. The ornamental buckthorn *Rhamnus alaternus* 'Argenteovariegata' is worth a mention for its year-round white-edged evergreen foliage and red fruits that ripen to black in autumn.

The oak-leaved hydrangea, *Hydrangea quercifolia,* is a good garden shrub, offering attractive oak-leaf-shaped foliage that turns shades of bronze-purple in autumn. But it is the named cultivar 'Snow Queen' that steals the show, with its brilliant white conical flower clusters, produced in summer, that fade to pink as they age.

Another deciduous favourite that provides good colour is the Japanese snowball bush *Viburnum plicatum* 'Mariesii'. This produces tiered branches that carry white, lacecap-like flowers throughout late spring over toothed, prominently veined, dark-green leaves that turn red-purple in autumn.

A few climbers also offer year-round interest. Evergreens, such as ivy, are more or less ubiquitous, but for real garden value you want ever-changing displays like that offered by the climbing hydrangea, *Hydrangea petiolaris,* which bears huge, flat heads of creamy, lacecap flowers that stand out against a backdrop of dark green leaves from late spring. Then in autumn, the leaves turn butter-yellow before falling to reveal attractively flaking brown bark.

Clematis 'Bill MacKenzie' and *C. tangutica* are worth mentioning in this respect, too. The former produces butter-yellow, bell-shaped flowers in succession from mid-summer against ferny, mid-green leaves, followed by large, fluffy seed-heads, while the latter offers small, nodding, yellow, lantern-shaped flowers with waxy-looking lemon peel-like petals from mid-summer, again followed by fluffy seed-heads later on.

Plant selector: early spring

The weather in early spring is very variable, with wide fluctuations in temperature from day to night, from day to day and from year to year.

Keep an eye on the weather

The contrast in the weather is often at its greatest the further north you go and also on higher, more exposed locations. Rain can be heavy and the winds strong, although the sun is increasing in strength as the garden moves out of its winter slumbers.

Early spring is often less wet than the winter and this provides good opportunities to get on with some planting and other winter garden tasks that you have been unable to complete because soil conditions were not suitable. However, be wary of cold north-easterly winds. These can be very damaging at this time of the year, as they can burn vulnerable blossom and scorch the tips of emerging leaves.

Frosty welcome

Frost can also be a problem throughout early spring in most areas. It can be very penetrating if it is accompanied by northerly winds,

Early spring shrubs and climbers to try

[Note: each variety is in season when it starts flowering. Check individual entries for finish flowering times.]

Shrubs
Abeliophyllum distichum
Abeliophyllum distichum Roseum Group
Acer palmatum 'Sango-kaku'
Amelanchier lamarckii
Amelanchier x grandiflora 'Ballerina'
Camellia japonica 'Adolphe Audusson'
Camellia japonica 'Hagoromo'
Camellia japonica 'Lady Vansittart'
Camellia japonica 'Mikenjaku'
Camellia 'Leonard Messel'
Camellia japonica 'Nobilissima'
Camellia x williamsii 'Anticipation'
Camellia x williamsii 'Donation'
Camellia x williamsii 'E.G. Waterhouse'
Camellia x williamsii 'J. C. Williams'
Camellia x williamsii 'Jury's Yellow'
Camellia x williamsii 'Mary Phoebe Taylor'
Chaenomeles speciosa 'Geisha Girl'
Chaenomeles speciosa 'Moerloosei'
Chaenomeles speciosa 'Nivalis'
Chaenomeles x superba 'Crimson and Gold'
Chaenomeles x superba 'Nicoline'
Chaenomeles x superba 'Pink Lady'
Chimonanthus praecox

Chimonanthus praecox 'Grandiflorus'
Chimonanthus praecox 'Luteus'
Coronilla valentina subsp. glauca
Coronilla valentina subsp. glauca 'Citrina'
Corylus avellana 'Contorta'
Corylus maxima 'Purpurea'
Daphne mezereum
Forsythia 'Beatrix Farrand'
Forsythia x intermedia 'Spring Glory'
Forsythia x intermedia 'Week-End'
Kerria japonica 'Golden Guinea'
Kerria japonica 'Picta'
Kerria japonica 'Pleniflora'
Leucothoe 'Scarletta'
Magnolia stellata
Magnolia stellata 'Rosea'
Magnolia stellata 'Royal Star'
Magnolia stellata 'Waterlily'
Mahonia aquifolium 'Apollo'
Pieris japonica 'Valley Valentine'
Prunus tenella 'Fire Hill'
Prunus triloba
Rhododendron 'Cilpinense'
Skimmia japonica 'Rubella'
Skimmia x confusa 'Kew Green'
Spiraea prunifolia

Climbers
Akebia quinata
Clematis armandii 'Apple Blossom'
Clematis armandii 'Snowdrift'

Rhododendrons are good-value shrubs to have in the garden. Their glossy green leaves last all year, with a huge range of different coloured blooms.

so keep tender plants well protected until late spring. Try to take advantage of any spells of good weather during early spring to carry out essential seasonal tasks, such as rose pruning or planting hardy shrubs and climbers.

Although many garden plants will still remain dormant throughout early spring, those that do break through will offer some of the most spectacular flowering displays – all the more welcome after a long, grey winter. Spring-flowering bulbs, such as snowdrops and early daffodils, are traditionally the harbingers of spring, but there are many hardy shrubs and climbers that are even more dramatic. Just take a look around local gardens in your area and you'll find breathtaking displays of both evergreen and deciduous varieties. Who can fail to be impressed by the spectacular magnolias? Star of the show must be *Magnolia stellata* and its varieties, with their silky buds that open on bare branches during early spring to reveal lightly scented, white or pink flushed, star-shaped flowers. For classical goblet-shaped flowers consider 'Heaven Scent' (pale pink), 'Susan' (purple) or, slightly later, the white or pink blooms of the larger *Magnolia x soulangeana*.

Pink, white and red camellias shine out against their leathery evergreen foliage, including the peony-shaped, yellow-centred, white flowers of 'Nobilissima', the large, semi-double, bright red flowers of 'Adolphe Audusson' and the ever-flowering and ever-popular semi-double, sugar-pink 'Donation'. Covering the ground, swathes of winter-flowering heathers are still in bloom: *Erica carnea* 'Myretoun Ruby' offers masses of urn-shaped, large

Ceanothus 'Dark Star' produces small but profuse flowers that appear in spring, which are a vivid dark blue to blue-violet colour.

ruby-red flowers that mature to crimson against dark green foliage, the pure white 'Springwood White' is still going strong, while 'Pink Spangles' adds a splash of shell-pink to the scene. Rose-pink is also offered by highly fragrant daphnes, including *Daphne bholua* 'Jacqueline Postill', *Daphne mezereum* and *Daphne odora* 'Aureomarginata'.

Yellow is an even more eye-catching colour, especially when light

levels are low. Mahonias keep the garden glowing well into early spring with their elegant sprays of fragrant, flowers, such as pale yellow 'Bealei', the deeper shade of 'Apollo' and the lemon-yellow 'Charity'. Later, the early spring garden lights up with the ever-popular forsythias, such as the golden-yellow 'Lynwood', pale yellow 'Spring Glory' or the rich yellow flowers of 'Week-End'. For something a little more unusual, try the orange-yellow 'Beatrix Farrand'.

Reluctant climbers

Although there are few climbers putting on a show during early spring, those that do are worth seeking out. The chocolate vine *Akebia quinata* is a real gem, offering pendent clusters of maroon-chocolate flowers that have a sweet and spicy fragrance against lobed, purple-tinged, dark green foliage.

As a complete contrast, the massed pale pink, fragrant flowers of *Clematis* 'Apple Blossom' or *C.* 'Snowdrift' are a sight to behold in the early spring garden.

Daphne bholua 'Jacqueline Postill' produces clusters of scented, deep purple-pink flowers early in the year, accompanied by lance-shaped, dark green leaves.

Plant selector: late spring

In some years, spring can be delayed for several weeks so keep an eye on local weather forecasts and gauge the temperature. Use these as a guide to your gardening activities, rather than doing things just because it is the season to do them.

Protect your plants

By late spring, the threat of frost recedes and in milder areas it's safe to plant out tender shrubs and climbers, but always keep a sheet of garden fleece to hand to cover vulnerable plants if an unseasonally late frost is forecast after planting has taken place.

Variations in weather conditions are generally less marked as the spring progresses, so there are fewer sharp frosts and the weather generally becomes calmer. In cooler areas, however, you will have to be a good deal more cautious and should wait until early summer to put tender plants outside.

Growth spurts

In the garden, shrubs and climbers are making up for lost time as they break into growth and compete for your attention.

Camellia x williamsii 'Jury's Yellow' has creamy-yellow, anemone-flowered blooms.

Late spring shrubs and climbers to try

Shrubs
Berberis darwinii
Berberis linearifolia 'Orange King'
Berberis thunbergii 'Atropurpurea Nana'
Berberis thunbergii 'Aurea'
Berberis x stenophylla
Berberis x stenophylla 'Crawley Gem'
Berberis x stenophylla 'Irwinii'
Calluna vulgaris 'Spring Cream'
Camellia japonica 'Adolphe Audusson'
Camellia japonica 'Elegans'
Camellia japonica 'Lady Vansittart'
Camellia 'Leonard Messel'
Camellia x williamsii 'Debbie'
Camellia x williamsii 'Donation'
Camellia x williamsii 'E.G. Waterhouse'
Camellia x williamsii 'J. C. Williams'
Camellia x williamsii 'Jury's Yellow'
Ceanothus 'Puget Blue'
Chaenomeles speciosa 'Geisha Girl'
Chaenomeles speciosa 'Moerloosei'
Chaenomeles speciosa 'Nivalis'
Chaenomeles x superba 'Crimson and Gold'
Chaenomeles x superba 'Nicoline'
Chaenomeles x superba 'Pink Lady'
Choisya 'Aztec Pearl'
Choisya 'Goldfingers'
Choisya ternata
Choisya ternata 'Sundance'
Cytisus multiflorus
Cytisus x praecox 'Allgold'
Cytisus x praecox 'Warminster'
Drimys winteri
Exochorda x macrantha 'The Bride'
Forsythia x intermedia 'Lynwood'
Fothergilla major
Leucothoe fontanesiana 'Rainbow'
Magnolia 'Heaven Scent'
Magnolia stellata 'Royal Star'
Magnolia x loebneri 'Leonard Messel'
Magnolia x soulangeana
Osmanthus delavayi
Osmanthus x burkwoodii
Paeonia delavayi
Paeonia lutea var. *ludlowii*
Paeonia suffruticosa 'Duchess of Kent'
Paeonia suffruticosa 'Duchess of Marlborough'
Paeonia suffruticosa 'Mrs William Kelway'
Paeonia suffruticosa 'Reine Elisabeth'
Pieris formosa var. *forrestii* 'Wakehurst'

Pieris 'Forest Flame'
Pieris japonica 'Purity'
Pieris japonica 'Variegata'
Prunus laurocerasus 'Otto Luyken'
Prunus laurocerasus 'Rotundifolia'
Prunus laurocerasus 'Zabeliana'
Prunus lusitanica
Rhododendron 'Blue Diamond'
Rhododendron 'Glowing Embers'
Rhododendron 'Grumpy'
Rhododendron 'Koster's Brilliant Red'
Rhododendron 'Persil'
Rhododendron 'Pink Drift'
Rhododendron 'Pink Pearl'
Rhododendron 'Sapphire'
Rhododendron 'Scarlet Wonder'
Ribes sanguineum 'Brocklebankii'
Ribes sanguineum 'King Edward VII'
Ribes sanguineum 'Pulborough Scarlet'
Salix lanata
Skimmia japonica subsp. *reevesiana*
Skimmia japonica subsp. *reevesiana* 'Robert Fortune'
Sophora microphylla
Sophora microphylla 'Sun King'
Spiraea 'Arguta'
Spiraea thunbergii
Viburnum carlesii
Viburnum 'Eskimo'
Viburnum x burkwoodii
Viburnum x carlcephalum
Viburnum x juddii
Vinca major
Vinca minor 'Illumination'

Climbers
Clematis alpina 'Frances Rivis'
Clematis alpina 'Frankie'
Clematis alpina 'Pamela Jackman'
Clematis alpina 'Pink Flamingo'
Clematis 'Early Sensation'
Clematis 'Helsingborg'
Clematis macropetala 'Markham's Pink'
Jasminum polyanthum
Lonicera japonica 'Halliana'
Lonicera japonica 'Hall's Prolific'
Lonicera japonica var. *repens*

Rhododendron 'Pink Pearl' is a delightful plant, bearing huge trusses of beautiful soft pink, funnel-shaped flowers that eventually fade to white as they age.

Many of the early flowering shrubs, including camellias and magnolias, are still going strong, but they are joined by equally impressive displays from popular plants such as peonies and rhododendrons. Perhaps the best peony of all is 'Ludlowii', which looks magnificent when furnished with large bright yellow flowers against bronze-tinted, bright apple-green lush foliage. If you are looking for a red, consider *Paeonia delavayi* instead, for its single, cup-shaped, blood-red flowers. Pale pink peonies are always popular, and the flamboyant 'Duchess of Marlborough', with its double, crinkle-edged flowers, is hard to beat.

Dramatic plants

There's a huge array of dramatic rhododendrons to choose from that will to add flower power to a late spring garden. Evergreen rhododendrons include the unusual violet-blue shade of 'Blue Diamond', which bears masses of funnel-shaped, flowers that age to lavender-blue. 'Grumpy' offers attractive pink-flushed, cream flowers in flat-topped trusses, while the compact 'Pink Drift' blooms are a rose-lavender shade – a good choice for small gardens. Well liked for good reason are the white-edged, soft pink, funnel-shaped flowers of 'Pink Pearl'.

Vivid azaleas

Deciduous azaleas come into bloom during late spring, too. The aptly named 'Glowing Embers' shows off its flaming, reddish-orange, funnel-shaped flowers, while 'Koster's Brilliant Red' offers vivid, orange-red blooms. For large clusters of orange-flushed, white flowers, look no further than the brilliant 'Persil'.

The appeal of flowering quince can be an acquired taste, but they'll never let you down with their startling flowers on a twiggy framework, often followed by aromatic, yellow-tinged green fruit. Good names to look out for at this time of the year are the apricot-pink and yellow, double flowers of 'Geisha Girl', the large white, apple blossom-like blooms of 'Moerloosei', the snow-white 'Nivalis' or the scarlet 'Nicoline'. But, perhaps the pick of the bunch is the compact and easy to grow 'Crimson and Gold'. This offers vivid red flowers with contrasting golden anthers.

Another late spring stalwart if you have an acid soil is the lily-of-the-valley shrub, pieris. It's particularly remarkable because it bears its pendent clusters of fragrant, urn-shaped flowers just when the glossy, brilliant-red young foliage emerges – a startling contrast that works perfectly together. 'Wakehurst', 'Forest Flame' and 'Purity' are all good white cultivars, while 'Valley Valentine' is dark pink.

Spring climbers

Popular climbers that are on display in the late spring garden include the many forms of alpine clematis, which bear small, nodding, bell-shaped flowers, often with contrasting centres. Look out for 'Frances Rivis' (blue), 'Helsingborg' (deep purple) and 'Pink Flamingo' (pink). Other floriferous early clematis that are at their best right now are: 'Early Sensation', which bears a single flush of small, green-centred, white, bowl-shaped flowers, and the semi-double 'Markham's Pink', which offers pink flowers with creamy-yellow centres.

Pieris 'Forest Flame' has glorious red leaves that fade to a pale pink and then dark green.

Plant selector: early summer

By early summer a westerly airflow dominates the weather, but winds are lighter and rain is less frequent. Dull days can be humid, while on sunny days temperatures can soar.

Propagation and pruning

Many shrubs and climbers can be propagated from early summer and it's the right time to start routine spraying of roses to prevent outbreaks of disease through the summer months.

Early flowering shrubs should be pruned to improve displays in subsequent years, while repeat-flowering plants can be enhanced by regular deadheading throughout the summer months.

In the garden, scented shrubs and climbers come to the fore. Lilacs are among the best of the scented shrubs, with their gloriously fragrant flowers. There are many cultivars but few can beat 'Superba' (rose-pink), 'Palibin' (purple-pink), 'Charles Joly' (dark purple), 'Katherine Havemeyer' (lavender-purple), 'Madame Lemoine' (white) or 'Michel Buchner' (rose-mauve).

Rosmarinus officinalis

Other very fragrant shrubs are the mock orange (*Philadelphus*) and *P. coronarius* 'Aureus', which has golden-yellow leaves that turn greenish-yellow in summer. Also enjoyed for their aroma are the single, cup-shaped, white flowers of 'Belle Etoile' or the double white 'Virginal'. In milder gardens, French lavender is worth considering for its tufted

Clematis 'Mrs Cholmondeley'

Abelia x grandiflora 'Gold Spot'

Buddleja alternifolia

Early summer shrubs to try

Shrubs

Abelia 'Edward Goucher'
Abelia x grandiflora
Abutilon 'Kentish Belle'
Azara dentata
Banksia coccinea
Berberis julianae
Berberis thunbergii 'Dart's Red Lady'
Brugmansia suaveolens
Buddleja alternifolia
Buddleja globosa
Callistemon citrinus 'Splendens'
Camellia japonica 'Elegans'
Carpenteria californica
Carpenteria californica 'Ladhams' Variety'
Ceanothus arboreus 'Trewithen Blue'
Ceanothus 'Concha'
Ceanothus 'Italian Skies'
Ceanothus thyrsiflorus var. repens
Chaenomeles speciosa 'Geisha Girl'
Chaenomeles speciosa 'Nivalis'
Chaenomeles x superba 'Pink Lady'
Choisya 'Aztec Pearl'
Choisya 'Goldfingers'
Choisya ternata
Choisya ternata 'Sundance'
Cistus 'Silver Pink'
Cistus x aguilarii 'Maculatus'
Cistus x corbariensis
Cistus x dansereaui 'Decumbens'
Cistus x purpureus 'Alan Fradd'
Cistus x skanbergii
Convolvulus cneorum
Cornus florida 'Cherokee Chief'
Cornus florida 'Rainbow'
Cornus florida f. rubra
Cornus kousa var. chinensis
Cotoneaster conspicuus 'Coral Beauty'
Cotoneaster dammeri
Cotoneaster frigidus 'Cornubia'
Cotoneaster horizontalis
Cotoneaster salicifolius 'Gnom'
Cytisus 'Boskoop Ruby'
Cytisus multiflorus
Cytisus x praecox 'Allgold'
Cytisus x praecox 'Warminster'
Daboecia cantabrica f. alba
Daboecia cantabrica 'Atropurpurea'
Deutzia gracilis
Deutzia x elegantissima 'Rosealind'
Diervilla x splendens
Enkianthus campanulatus
Enkianthus cernuus f. rubens

Erica cinerea 'Pink Ice'
Escallonia 'Apple Blossom'
Escallonia rubra 'Crimson Spire'
Euonymus europaeus 'Red Cascade'
Fremontodendron 'California Glory'
Fuchsia 'Mrs Popple'
Gaultheria mucronata 'Mulberry Wine'
Gaultheria mucronata 'Wintertime'
Gaultheria procumbens
Genista lydia
Genista pilosa 'Vancouver Gold'
Genista tinctoria 'Royal Gold'
Grevillea juniperina f. sulphurea
Grevillea 'Robyn Gordon'
Halesia monticola
Halesia tetraptera
Hebe pinguifolia 'Pagei'
Hebe rakaiensis
Hebe 'Red Edge'
Hebe 'Rosie'
Helianthemum 'Chocolate Blotch'
Helianthemum 'Wisley Primrose'
Helianthemum 'Wisley White'
Hypericum calycinum
Hypericum x moserianum 'Tricolor'
Indigofera heterantha
Jasminum humile 'Revolutum'
Kalmia angustifolia f. rubra
Kalmia latifolia 'Ostbo Red'
Kolkwitzia amabilis 'Pink Cloud'
Lantana camara 'Radiation'
Lantana camara 'Snow White'
Lavandula 'Helmsdale'
Lavatera x clementii 'Barnsley'
Leptospermum scoparium 'Red Damask'
Nerium oleander
Olearia ilicifolia
Philadelphus 'Beauclerk'
Philadelphus 'Belle Etoile'
Philadelphus coronarius 'Variegatus'

Rhododendron 'Marty'

Syringa x josiflexa

Philadelphus x lemoinei 'Lemoinei'
Phlomis fruticosa
Phlomis italica
Phygelius x rectus 'Moonraker'
Phygelius x rectus 'Salmon Leap'
Potentilla fruticosa 'Abbotswood'
Potentilla fruticosa 'Goldfinger'
Potentilla fruticosa 'Primrose Beauty'
Prostanthera cuneata
Rhododendron 'Blue Danube'
Rhododendron 'Blue Peter'
Rhododendron 'Cunningham's White'
Rhododendron 'Debutante'
Rhododendron 'Dopey'
Rhododendron 'Geisha Red'
Rhododendron 'Gibraltar'
Rhododendron 'Homebush'
Rhododendron 'Klondyke'
Rhododendron luteum
Rhododendron 'Marty'
Rhododendron 'Purple Splendour'
Rosmarinus officinalis
Rosmarinus officinalis 'Majorca Pink'
Rosmarinus officinalis 'Miss Jessopp's Upright'
Rubus odoratus
Salvia officinalis 'Icterina'
Salvia officinalis 'Tricolor'
Spartium junceum
Spiraea nipponica 'Snowmound'
Syringa x josiflexa
Syringa vulgaris 'Charles Joly'
Syringa vulgaris 'Katherine Havemeyer'
Viburnum davidii
Viburnum opulus 'Roseum'
Viburnum plicatum 'Mariesii'
Weigela florida 'Foliis Purpureis'
Weigela 'Florida Variegata'

spikes of fragrant flowers. Of the many different varieties, 'Helmsdale' offers dark purple flowers topped by purple wing-like bracts; 'Papillon' bears lavender-purple flowers, with matching bracts; 'Fathead' has broad, almost rounded midnight-purple flowerheads with plum-purple feathers; and 'Snowman' bears slender spikes of white flowers, topped by snow-white flags.

New introductions

Excellent new introductions include 'Kew Red', with plump, fragrant, cerise-pink flower heads topped by pale-pink bracts, and 'Rocky Road' – goblet-shaped purple flower spikes topped by large, pale-violet wings.

The earliest roses start to bloom as spring turns into summer. The first to show include the shrub roses, such as 'Cornelia', with its very fragrant, double, apricot-pink flowers; 'Fantin-Latour', which offers slightly fragrant, double, pale pink blooms; 'Felicia', with its sweetly fragrant, double, apricot-yellow flowers that are flushed with pale pink; and 'William Lobb', which bears wonderfully fragrant, semi-double, purple-magenta flowers that age to lavender. Some plants offer

Hydrangea petiolaris

Early summer climbers to try

Climbers

Actinidia kolomikta	*Eccremocarpus scaber*
Ampelopsis aconitifolia	*Hibbertia scandens*
Aristolochia littoralis	*Hoya carnosa*
Aristolochia macrophylla	*Hydrangea petiolaris*
Berberidopsis corallina	*Jasminum beesianum*
Billardiera longiflora	*Jasminum officinale*
Bougainvillea glabra	*Jasminum x stephanense*
Bougainvillea glabra 'Snow White'	*Lonicera henryi*
Bougainvillea glabra 'Variegata'	*Lonicera periclymenum* 'Belgica'
Bougainvillea 'Miss Manila'	*Lonicera x americana*
Bougainvillea 'Raspberry Ice'	*Lonicera x heckrottii* 'Gold Flame'
Bougainvillea 'Scarlett O'Hara'	*Lonicera x italica* 'Harlequin'
Clematis 'Barbara Jackman'	*Lonicera x tellmanniana*
Clematis 'Bees' Jubilee'	*Plumbago auriculata*
Clematis 'Belle of Woking'	*Rosa* 'Albéric Barbier'
Clematis 'Doctor Ruppel'	*Rosa* 'Albertine'
Clematis 'Duchess of Edinburgh'	*Rosa* 'American Pillar'
Clematis 'Fireworks'	*Rosa* 'Climbing Iceberg'
Clematis florida var. *sieboldiana*	*Rosa* 'Emily Gray'
Clematis 'General Sikorski'	*Rosa* 'Guinée'
Clematis 'Gillian Blades'	*Rosa* 'Madame Grégoire Staechelin'
Clematis 'Lasurstern'	*Rosa* 'Maigold'
Clematis 'Marie Boisselot'	*Rosa* 'Paul's Scarlet Climber'
Clematis 'Miss Bateman'	*Rosa* 'Veilchenblau'
Clematis montana var. *rubens* 'Elizabeth'	*Rosa* 'Zéphirine Drouhin'
Clematis montana var. *rubens* 'Pink Perfection'	*Solanum crispum* 'Glasnevin'
	Solanum jasminoides 'Album'
Clematis montana var. *rubens* 'Tetrarose'	*Sollya heterophylla*
Clematis 'Mrs Cholmondeley'	*Stephanotis floribunda*
Clematis 'Mrs N.Thompson'	*Wisteria floribunda*
Clematis 'Multi Blue'	*Wisteria floribunda* 'Alba'
Clematis 'Nelly Moser'	*Wisteria floribunda* 'Macrobotrys'
Clematis 'The President'	*Wisteria floribunda* 'Royal Purple'
Clematis 'Vyvyan Pennell'	*Wisteria sinensis*
Clerodendrum thomsoniae	*Wisteria sinensis* 'Alba'
Clianthus puniceus	*Wisteria x formosa*
Cobaea scandens	

aromatic foliage too. Rosemary shouldn't be missed for its strongly aromatic evergreen foliage that forms a dense and rounded bush and bears purple-blue flowers.

Early summer bloomers

Many unsung heroes of the shrub border start to flower during early summer. If you have got room for only a few, choose from escallonia, hebe, helianthus, kolkwitzia,

lavateras, potentilla, salvia, viburnums and weigela. Or opt for the brilliant, if short-lived, display provided by broom: the golden-yellow flowers of *Genista lydia* festoon prickly, arching, grey-green leaves; *G. pilosa* 'Vancouver Gold' is a spreading shrub with masses of golden-yellow flowers; while the extremely long-flowering *Genista tinctoria* 'Royal Gold' bears golden-yellow blooms until late summer.

Quick-growing shrubs

Quick-growing shrubs, such as lavatera, can be used to provide instant colour at this time of the year. 'Barnsley' bears large, white blooms, each with a red eye, which are produced in succession from now onwards. Other cultivars to consider are 'Burgundy Wine' (dark pink flowers), 'Kew Rose' (frilly, dark pink) 'Peppermint Ice' (pure white) and 'Rosea' (dark pink).

If you're looking for something more unusual, consider the crimson bottlebrush, which bears its distinctive flower-spikes at the tips of stiffly arching branches, or flowering dogwood such as 'Eddie's White Wonder', which offers insignificant purplish-green flowers, each surrounded by striking white, petal-like bracts.

Another sought-after dogwood that is well worth seeking out is *Cornus kousa* var. *chinensis*, which bears conspicuous, creamy-white flower bracts that fade to white before turning red-pink.

Climbers to watch

Climbers to look out for at this time of the year include the huge array of clematis. Among the best are 'Barbara Jackman' (pale purple), 'Bees' Jubilee' (dark pink), 'Belle of Woking' (silvery-mauve), 'Doctor Ruppel' (dark pink), 'Duchess of Edinburgh' (white), 'Fireworks' (purple with red bars), var. *sieboldiana* (white with a central boss of deep purple stamens), 'Gillian Blades' (mauve-flushed, white), 'Lasurstern' (cream-centred, purple-blue), 'Elizabeth' (fragrant, pale pink), 'Mrs Cholmondeley' (chocolate-centred, lavender-blue), 'The President' (red-centred, purple) and 'Vyvyan Pennell' (golden-centred, mauve, violet and purple).

Bougainvillea

Clematis 'Bees' Jubilee'

Rosa 'Climbing Iceberg'

Rosa 'Albertine'

Wisteria sinensis

Solanum jasminoides 'Album'

Plant selector: late summer

Calm weather patterns continue
through the summer months,
although prolonged periods of rain
are possible. However, there's still
time to take cuttings and it is the
ideal time to prune many early
summer-flowering shrubs and
climbers to keep them flowering
well, year after year.

Glorious roses

In the garden, roses are at their best
throughout the summer and will
produce long-lasting displays if
regularly deadheaded. The most
impressive large-flowered bushes
include: 'Alexander', which has
double, slightly fragrant, vermilion-
red flowers with scalloped petals;
'Congratulations', which bears
double, slightly fragrant, rose-pink
flowers on long stems; the unusually
coloured 'Just Joey', with fragrant,
double, coppery-red flowers with
wavy-margined petals; 'Peace', which
is covered in double, pink-flushed,
deep yellow, slightly fragrant flowers;
'Royal William', which carries
double, deep-crimson flowers with a
spicy fragrance; and 'Silver Jubilee',
which bears fragrant, double, rose-
pink flowers, flushed salmon-pink.

If you're looking for a cluster-
flowered bush rose that produces
masses of flowers throughout the
summer, consider the aptly named

Clematis 'Jackmanii Superba'

Rosa 'Ingrid Bergman'

'Amber Queen', with fragrant,
double, amber-yellow flowers;
'Arthur Bell', with large, semi-double,
very fragrant, golden-yellow flowers
that age to cream; 'Mountbatten',
which carries large, fragrant,
double, golden-yellow flowers;
'Southampton, which is covered in
large, double, slightly scented, red-
flushed apricot flowers with ruffled
petals; and 'Queen Elizabeth', which
offers double, slightly fragrant, pale
pink flowers.

Patio varieties

Other roses looking their best right
now are the celebration patio
varieties, which make ideal gifts and
can be grown in containers or at the

front of the border. Check out
'Golden Anniversary', with large,
semi-double, slightly fragrant,
apricot-pink flowers; 'Happy
Anniversary', which bears sweetly
fragrant, deep-pink flowers; 'Happy
Birthday', with double, creamy-white
blooms; and 'Pearl Anniversary' – a
semi-double, pearl-pink variety.

Groundcover roses

You can also have roses covering the
ground at this time of the year and
the county series are among the best:
'Kent', with slightly fragrant, semi-
double, white flowers; 'Suffolk', a
slightly fragrant cultivar with single,
golden-centred, deep-scarlet flowers;
'Surrey', which bears cup-shaped,

Late summer shrubs to try

Shrubs
Abelia 'Edward Goucher'
Abelia x *grandiflora*
Aloysia triphylla
Ballota acetabulosa
Buddleja davidii 'Black Knight'
Buddleja davidii 'Dartmoor'
Buddleja davidii 'Nanho Blue'
Buddleja davidii 'White Profusion'
BBupleurum fruticosum
Callistemon citrinus 'Splendens'
Callistemon rigidus
Calluna vulgaris 'Alicia'
Calluna vulgaris 'Silver Knight'
Calluna vulgaris 'Silver Queen'
Calluna vulgaris 'Spring Cream'
Calluna vulgaris 'Wickwar Flame'
Caryopteris x *clandonensis*
Caryopteris x *clandonensis* 'First Choice'
Ceanothus 'Autumnal Blue'
Ceanothus 'Burkwoodii'
Ceratostigma griffithii
Ceratostigma willmottianum
Ceratostigma willmottianum 'Desert Skies'
Cistus x *aguilarii* 'Maculatus'
Cistus x *argenteus* 'Peggy Sammons'
Cistus x *corbariensis*
Cistus x *skanbergii*
Colutea arborescens
Colutea x *media* 'Copper Beauty'
Cotinus coggygria 'Royal Purple'
Cotinus 'Flame'
Cotinus 'Grace'
Cytisus battandieri
Desfontainia spinosa
Escallonia 'Iveyi'
Eucryphia x *nymansensis* 'Nymansay'
Hebe 'Great Orme'
Hebe 'Midsummer Beauty'
Hibiscus rosa-sinensis 'The President'
Hibiscus syriacus 'Blue Bird'
Hibiscus syriacus 'Woodbridge'
Hydrangea arborescens 'Annabelle'
Hydrangea aspera Villosa Group
Hydrangea macrophylla 'Blue Wave'
Hydrangea macrophylla 'Mariesii'
Hydrangea macrophylla 'Veitchii'
Hydrangea paniculata 'Floribunda'
Hydrangea 'Preziosa'
Hydrangea quercifolia 'Snow Queen'
Hydrangea serrata 'Bluebird'
Hypericum 'Hidcote'

Buddleja davidii 'Dartmoor'

Indigofera amblyantha
Itea ilicifolia
Justicia carnea
Lavandula angustifolia 'Hidcote'
Lavandula angustifolia 'Royal Purple'
Lavandula stoechas 'Rocky Road'
Lavandula x *intermedia* 'Grappenhall'
Lavandula x *intermedia* 'Grosso'
Leycesteria formosa
Myrtus communis
Myrtus communis subsp. *tarentina*
Nandina domestica 'Fire Power'
Olearia macrodonta
Olearia x *haastii*
Osmanthus heterophyllus 'Goshiki'
Romneya coulteri
Romneya coulteri 'White Cloud'
Rosa 'Amber Queen'
Rosa 'Arthur Bell'
Rosa 'Ballerina'
Rosa 'Blanche Double de Coubert'
Rosa 'Blessings'
Rosa 'Boule de Neige'
Rosa 'Buff Beauty'
Rosa 'Charles de Mills'
Rosa 'Congratulations'
Rosa 'Fragrant Cloud'
Rosa 'Golden Anniversary'
Rosa 'Golden Wedding'
Rosa 'Happy Anniversary'
Rosa 'Happy Birthday'
Rosa 'Heritage'
Rosa 'Iceberg'
Rosa 'Ingrid Bergman'

Rosa 'Just Joey'
Rosa 'Loving Memory'
Rosa 'Mary Rose'
Rosa 'Masquerade'
Rosa 'Peace'
Rosa 'Pearl Anniversary'
Rosa 'Polar Star'
Rosa 'Queen of Denmark'
Rosa 'Queen Elizabeth'
Rosa 'Rose de Rescht'
Rosa 'Roseraie de l'Haÿ'
Rosa 'Ruby Anniversary'
Rosa 'Ruby Wedding'
Rosa rugosa 'Rubra'
Rosa 'Silver Jubilee'
Rosa 'Southampton'
Rosa 'Suffolk'
Rosa 'Surrey'
Rosa 'Sussex'
Rosa 'Sweet Dream'
Rosa 'The Times Rose'
Rosa 'Winchester Cathedral'
Rubus 'Benenden'
Rubus biflorus
Rubus cockburnianus
Santolina chamaecyparissus 'Lambrook Silver'
Santolina chamaecyparissus var. *nana*
Spiraea japonica 'Anthony Waterer'
Spiraea japonica 'Golden Princess'
Tamarix ramosissima
Tamarix ramosissima 'Pink Cascade'
Tamarix ramosissima 'Rubra'
Tibouchina urvilleana

fragrant, double, rose-pink flowers; and 'Sussex', the slightly fragrant, double, apricot version.

Beneficial insects

Many other late-summer flowering shrubs provide a rich source of food for beneficial insects. Perhaps the most well known is the butterfly bush, *Buddleja davidii*, which bears dense terminal spikes of fragrant flowers that are a magnet to butterflies: 'Black Knight' (dark purple), 'Nanho Blue' (lilac-blue), 'Pink Delight' (orange-eyed, bright-pink flowers), 'White Profusion' (white) and the variegated 'Harlequin'(reddish-purple).

English lavenders are also covered in insects at this time of the year when they bear their very fragrant flowers in dense spikes. Cultivars to look out for include: 'Hidcote' (dark violet), 'Hidcote Pink' (pale pink), 'Lady' (mauve-blue) 'Nana Alba' (white) and 'Royal Purple' (bluish-purple).

Unusual shrubs

Slightly more unusual shrubs that are looking their best right now include the hare's ear, *Bupleurum*

Hydrangea macrophylla

fruticosum, which bears greenish-yellow, ball-shaped clusters of star-shaped flowers on a dense and spreading evergreen shrub with dark green leaves that are silvery on the underside. Another excellent choice is the bladder plant, *Colutea arborescens*, which has racemes of bright yellow flowers followed by green seed-pods that become bloated and translucent as they mature. Highly recommended is hibiscus, particularly the delightful 'Blue Bird', which bears violet-blue, trumpet-shaped flowers, each with a maroon eye, in succession throughout late summer.

Finally, consider the white, tissue paper-like flowers, each with a golden-yellow centre, of *Romneya coulteri* 'White Cloud'.

Flowering structures

Walls and fences can be covered in flowers at this time of year, many of them sweetly fragrant. You can choose from a huge range of late-

Olearia x haastii

Rosa 'Golden Showers'

Rosa 'Gloire de Dijon'

flowering, large-flowered clematis, climbing and rambler roses and sweetly fragrant honeysuckles, such as: 'Graham Thomas', with large, tubular white flowers that age to yellow; 'Dropmore Scarlet,' which bears a succession of long, trumpet-shaped, bright-scarlet flowers; and 'Serotina', the late Dutch honeysuckle, which bears tubular, purple-streaked, creamy-white blooms.

Late summer climbers to try

Campsis grandiflora	*Mandevilla boliviensis*
Campsis radicans 'Flamenco'	*Mandevilla splendens*
Campsis x *tagliabuana* 'Madame Galen'	*Mandevilla* x *amabilis* 'Alice du Pont'
Clematis 'Alba Luxurians'	*Passiflora caerulea*
Clematis 'Betty Corning'	*Passiflora caerulea* 'Constance Elliot'
Clematis 'Bill MacKenzie'	*Passiflora* 'Eden'
Clematis 'Comtesse de Bouchaud'	*Pileostegia viburnoides*
Clematis 'Ernest Markham'	*Rosa* 'Aloha'
Clematis 'Etoile Violette'	*Rosa* 'Bantry Bay'
Clematis flammula	*Rosa* 'Breath of Life'
Clematis 'Gipsy Queen'	*Rosa* 'Climbing Iceberg'
Clematis 'Hagley Hybrid'	*Rosa* 'Compassion'
Clematis 'Henryi'	*Rosa* 'Danse du Feu'
Clematis 'Huldine'	*Rosa filipes* 'Kiftsgate'
Clematis 'Jackmanii'	*Rosa* 'Gloire de Dijon'
Clematis 'Jackmanii Superba'	*Rosa* 'Golden Showers'
Clematis 'Niobe'	*Rosa* 'Handel'
Clematis 'Perle d'Azur'	*Rosa* 'Laura Ford'
Clematis 'Polish Spirit'	*Rosa* 'Madame Alfred Carrière'
Clematis 'Prince Charles'	*Rosa* 'Mermaid'
Clematis 'Princess Diana'	*Rosa* 'New Dawn'
Clematis 'Rouge Cardinal'	*Rosa* 'Rambling Rector'
Clematis tangutica	*Rosa* 'Schoolgirl'
Clematis 'Ville de Lyon'	*Rosa* 'Warm Welcome'
Clematis viticella 'Purpurea Plena Elegans'	*Rosa* 'Wedding Day'
Fallopia baldschuanica	*Schizophragma hydrangeoides*
Jasminum officinale 'Devon Cream'	*Schizophragma integrifolium*
Lapageria rosea	*Trachelospermum asiaticum*
Lonicera periclymenum 'Graham Thomas'	*Trachelospermum jasminoides*
Lonicera periclymenum 'Serotina'	
Lonicera x *brownii* 'Dropmore Scarlet'	

Clematis viticella 'Purpurea Plena Elegans'

Trachelospermum asiaticum

Passiflora caerulea

Plant selector: autumn

Although the summer can continue into early autumn in some years, this time of the year usually sees a dramatic change in both the weather and the appearance of the garden.

Shorter days and cool, longer nights are certain, causing plants to slow down and gradually become dormant. The autumn garden is briefly dominated by the fiery displays of many deciduous shrubs and climbers.

The acers

Some of the most spectacular autumn hues are offered by Japanese maples. Cultivars such as *Acer palmatum* 'Atropurpureum' make a graceful and slow-growing maple, with attractive palm-like, deeply lobed, dark purple leaves that are eye-catching all summer before turning brilliant shades of red in autumn. Another purple-leaved cultivar worth seeking out is 'Bloodgood', which turns brilliant red before falling. The startling red autumn colour of 'Osakazuki' is equally spectacular and would make a dramatic addition to any garden. If you prefer one of the cut-leaved varieties of Japanese

Abutilon megapotamicum 'Variegata'

maples, look out for *Acer palmatum* var. *d.* 'Dissectum Atropurpureum' Group, which makes a neat dome covered in particularly fine, deeply cut, red-purple, ferny foliage that turns fiery shades in autumn. 'Garnet' is similar, but the foliage is darker purple. Both these cultivars look good after leaf fall, too, as they reveal a tracery of fine twigs that provide winter interest.

Others that offer excellent autumn shades are the barberry (*Berberis*) cultivars, such as 'Atropurpurea Nana', which is grown for its dark purple leaves that turn a brilliant red in autumn accompanied by glossy red fruits; by contrast 'Aurea' offers brilliant acid-yellow spring growth that turns orange-red in autumn with conspicuous glossy red fruit; 'Bagatelle' is compact and easy to grow, with dark purple leaves that transform into a stunning red in autumn; 'Dart's Red Lady' is equally suitable for a confined space and has plum-red foliage that turns brilliant shades of red at this time of the year. If you're looking for a columnar version, try 'Helmond Pillar', which is clothed in plum-purple leaves that take truly eye-catching shades of red in autumn.

Brilliant autumn foliage is also the main ornamental feature of *Cotinus*, the smoke bush. Excellent purple-leaved versions include 'Grace' and 'Royal Purple', which spectacularly turn fiery shades of red and orange during the autumn.

Enkianthus perulatus

Cotinus coggygria 'Golden Spirit' is a
relatively new and compact cultivar
with golden-yellow leaves that take
on eye-catching pink, orange and red
coloration at this time of the year.
The hardy plumbago, *Ceratostigma
willmottianum*, is also worth
considering because it makes a neat
mound covered in clusters of pale
blue summer flowers and brilliant
fiery foliage effects in autumn. Look
out for 'Forest Blue', which turns
flaming shades of red and orange at
the end of the growing season.

Fruits of autumn

Autumn is also a time for bountiful
fruit production and few plants can
match the startling displays offered
by the beauty bush, *Callicarpa bodinieri*
var. *giraldii* 'Profusion', which bears
astonishingly vibrant violet, bead-like
berries. *Hippophae rhamnoides* is equally
dramatic, forming a large, bushy
plant with sharp spines and silvery
lance-shaped leaves that fall in
autumn to reveal the clusters of
bright orange berries, that last well
into winter. Don't overlook
cotoneasters as they produce
long-lasting, glossy, brightly
coloured berries. *C.* 'Coral Beauty'
makes excellent ground cover for
sun or semi-shade and is covered
in glossy, bright-orange berries
during the autumn.

The popular herringbone
cotoneaster, *Cotoneaster horizontalis*,
is encrusted with spherical, bright-
red berries during the autumn.
C. 'Cornubia' is an upright,
evergreen cultivar that is often
trained as a single-stemmed tree and
is covered in spherical, bright-red
berries just as the leaves become
bronze-tinted for the winter; while
'Hybridus Pendulus' is lower
growing and produces glossy, bright
red berries at this time of the year.

Autumn shrubs and climbers to try

Shrubs
Acer palmatum 'Atropurpureum'
Acer palmatum 'Bloodgood'
Acer palmatum 'Orange Dream'
Acer palmatum 'Osakazuki'
Acer palmatum var. d. Dissectum
Atropurpureum Group
Acer palmatum 'Garnet'
Amelanchier lamarckii
Amelanchier x grandiflora 'Ballerina'
Aucuba japonica 'Rozannie'
Aucuba japonica 'Variegata'
Berberis julianae
Berberis thunbergii 'Atropurpurea Nana'
Berberis thunbergii 'Aurea'
Berberis thunbergii 'Bagatelle'
Berberis thunbergii 'Dart's Red Lady'
Berberis thunbergii 'Helmond Pillar'
Berberis thunbergii f. *atropurpurea*
Callicarpa bodinieri var. *giraldii*
'Profusion'
Callistemon rigidus
Calluna vulgaris 'Alicia'
Calluna vulgaris 'Amethyst'
Calluna vulgaris 'County Wicklow'
Calluna vulgaris 'Dark Star'
Calluna vulgaris 'H. E. Beale'
Calluna vulgaris 'Silver Knight'
Calluna vulgaris 'Spring Cream'
Camellia sasanqua 'Narumigata'
Caryopteris x clandonensis
Caryopteris x clandonensis 'First Choice'
Caryopteris x clandonensis 'Heavenly
Blue'

Caryopteris x clandonensis 'Worcester
Gold'
Ceanothus 'Autumnal Blue'
Ceratostigma griffithii
Ceratostigma willmottianum
Ceratostigma willmottianum 'Desert
Skies'
Ceratostigma willmottianum 'Forest
Blue'
Clerodendrum trichotomum var. *fargesii*
Colutea arborescens
Colutea x media 'Copper Beauty'
Cornus alba 'Spaethii'
Cornus 'Eddie's White Wonder'
Cornus sanguinea 'Midwinter Fire'
Cotinus coggygria 'Golden Spirit'
Cotinus coggygria 'Royal Purple'
Cotinus 'Flame'
Cotinus 'Grace'
Enkianthus perulatus
Fothergilla gardenii
Gaultheria mucronata 'Mulberry Wine'
Gaultheria mucronata 'Wintertime'
Gaultheria procumbens
Hippophae rhamnoides
Viburnum x bodnantense 'Dawn'
Viburnum x bodnantense 'Charles
Lamont'

Climbers
Although many summer-flowering
climbers continue to bloom into
autumn, none starts blooming at this
time, so no entries are shown.

Foliage climbers

Some climbers also offer glorious
autumnal foliage displays. For
example, the ornamental grape vine,
Vitis 'Brant' has apple-green leaves
that turn rust-red between the main
veins in autumn, while the crimson
glory vine, *Vitis coignetiae*, is absolutely
spectacular when its dark green
leaves turn fiery shades of red during
the autumn.

On the other hand, Chinese
Virginia creeper, *Parthenocissus henryana*,
offers handsome, deeply divided,
dark green leaves with distinctive

white and pink veins that turn fiery
shades before falling at the end of
the growing season. The related
Virginia creeper (*P. quinquefloia*) is
clothed in deeply divided, slightly
puckered green leaves that transform
themselves during the autumn when
they take on brilliant shades of
crimson and purple.

Other named varieties of creeper
to look out for include 'Robusta'
and 'Veitchii', both of which
transform themselves at this time of
the year and develop a spectacular
cloak of red and purple.

Plant selector: winter

Winter-flowering shrubs and climbers are the gems of the garden during the dormant season. Although the flowers are not as spectacular as those produced by many spring- and summer-flowering plants, their intricate markings and delightful fragrance more than make up for it.

The Wintersweet, *Chimonanthus praecox*, is a prime example, with its waxy-looking, fragrant, sulphur-yellow flowers, often with a contrastingly tinted throat, that smother bare stems throughout this period. Named varieties worth seeking out include 'Grandiflorus', which is larger and of a darker yellow colour, as well as 'Luteus', with its clear yellow flowers. The winter-flowering shrubby honeysuckle, *Lonicera x purpusii* 'Winter Beauty' or the equally fragrant *Lonicera fragrantissima* are both a delight at this time of the year, bearing creamy-white flowers on naked stems during mild spells. Winter-flowering viburnums, such as *Viburnum tinus*

Winter shrubs and climbers to try

Shrubs

Acer palmatum 'Sango-kaku'
Bupleurum fruticosum
Calluna vulgaris 'Amethyst'
Calluna vulgaris 'Blazeaway'
Camellia japonica 'Nobilissima'
Camellia sasanqua 'Narumigata'
Chimonanthus praecox
Chimonanthus praecox 'Grandiflorus'
Chimonanthus praecox 'Luteus'
Cornus alba 'Aurea'
Cornus alba 'Kesselringii'
Cornus alba 'Sibirica'
Cornus alba Spaethii'
Cornus sanguinea 'Midwinter Fire'
Cornus stolonifera 'Flaviramea'
Corylus avellana 'Contorta'
Daphne bholua 'Jacqueline Postill'
Daphne odora 'Aureomarginata'
Erica carnea 'Ann Sparkes'
Erica carnea 'Challenger'
Erica carnea' December Red'
Erica carnea 'Foxhollow'
Erica carnea 'King George'
Erica carnea 'Myretoun Ruby'
Erica carnea 'Pink Spangles'
Erica carnea 'Springwood White'
Erica x darleyensis 'Furzey'
Erica x darleyensis 'Darley Dale'
Garrya elliptica

Garrya elliptica 'James Roof'
Hamamelis mollis
Hamamelis x intermedia 'Arnold Promise'
Hamamelis x intermedia 'Diane'
Hamamelis x intermedia 'Jelena'
Hamamelis x intermedia 'Moonlight'
Hamamelis x intermedia 'Pallida'
Jasminum nudiflorum
Lonicera fragrantissima
Lonicera x purpusii 'Winter Beauty'
Mahonia japonica Bealei Group
Mahonia x media 'Buckland'
Mahonia x media 'Charity'
Mahonia x media 'Lionel Fortescue'
Mahonia x media 'Winter Sun'
Rubus cockburnianus
Salix hastata 'Wehrhahnii'
Sarcococca confusa
Sarcococca hookeriana var. *digyna*
Sarcococca hookeriana var. *humulis*
Viburnum tinus 'Eve Price'
Viburnum tinus 'French White'
Viburnum tinus 'Gwenllian'

Climbers

Clematis cirrhosa 'Freckles'
Clematis cirrhosa 'Jingle Bells'
Clematis cirrhosa var. *balearica*
Clematis cirrhosa 'Wisley Cream'

Jasminum nudiflorum

'Eve Price', 'French White' or 'Gwenllian' bloom on bare, twiggy stems, producing highly fragrant flowers in dense clusters. Witch hazel, *Hamameli*s, is a winter essential for its bizarre sprays of sweetly scented, spidery flowers that are produced on bare stems. 'Arnold Promise' is a traditional favourite with golden flowers; 'Moonlight' is equally impressive when covered in its pale yellow blooms; or you could go for the coppery-red blooms of 'Diane' or 'Jelena'.

A dense, evergreen shrub that is covered in clusters of sweetly scented white flowers throughout the winter is *Sarcococca confusa. S. hookeriana* var. *digyna* and *S. hookeriana* var. *humulis* both have small, creamy-white or pink-tinged flowers. Another fragrant evergreen is the late-winter-flowering daphne. Cultivars worth looking out for include *Daphne bholua* 'Jacqueline Postill', with rose-pink flowers, and *D. odora* 'Aureomarginata', which also has attractive yellow-edged, glossy, dark green foliage.

Stem colours

Brightly coloured stems are also of great ornamental value in the winter garden. The red-barked dogwoods, *Cornus alba* 'Sibirica' or 'Spaethii', are hard to beat when they both reveal brilliant red stems that look particularly impressive (especially adjacent to water features) when grown alongside the contrasting yellow-stemmed variety 'Flaviramea'. If you've only got room for one dogwood, go for the relatively new cultivar 'Midwinter Fire', which produces glowing red-tipped, orange and yellow winter stems that shine out in the winter gloom.

Berries

Most berries have been eaten by birds or shed by shrubs and climbers by the winter, but the hermaphrodite variety of *Skimmia japonica* called *reevesiana*, as well as its cultivar 'Robert Fortune', buck the trend by carrying their startling bright red berries throughout the winter. You can find them in garden centres as fully berried miniature shrubs and they are ideal for adding winter-long colour to containers and prominent borders around the garden.

At the back of a shrubbery or against a wall, the subtle charms of *Garrya elliptica* will be appreciated in the winter. While its lustrous, leathery leaves provide a year-round backdrop at other times, during the coldest months it becomes decorated

Sarcococca confusa

with elegant, grey-green catkin tassels. Those of the cultivar 'James Roof' are impressive, with each silvery catkin up to 20cm (8in) long.

Clematis

Not to be forgotten are the clematis. Winter-flowering *Clematis cirrhosa* var. *balearica* will also provide winter

interest when carrying its fragrant, creamy-white, bell-shaped, waxy-looking flowers that are heavily blotched with maroon inside the petals. Look out for the named cultivars, such as 'Freckles', with its distinctive red speckles, and 'Wisley Cream', which has attractively bronze-tinted leaves.

Hamamelis x intermedia 'Pallida'

Colour selector: orange

Colour is a critical ingredient in an overall garden design. Not only must the balance and blend of colours suit the plan you have in mind, but they will also have an impact on the final atmosphere that will be created.

Using colour in the garden

Knowing that different colours are perceived in particular ways enables the garden designer to reinforce the underlying mood – or even create illusions. For example, very strong, vibrant colours, such as oranges, reds and golden yellows, stand out like beacons in the border, seeming much nearer to the eye than they really are.

You can use these confident colours to create a more intimate atmosphere, even in a large garden. Plant them in bold groups at the furthest point of the vista to act as points of focus. From a distance, bright colours will have very much more impact than softer shades, such as blue and grey, which seem to recede into the background. You can also use this to your advantage in a small garden by planting bright colours close to the house and misty

HOW TO USE THE COLOUR WHEEL

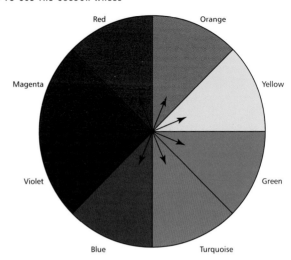

Colours that are next to each other on the colour wheel are complementary and will blend together well. Colours that are opposite are contrasting and will either look garish or stand out together. For example, orange and blue make a striking contrast but can't claim to blend with each other. It is usually wise to pick colours that are next to each other on the wheel. Select two or three colours and stick to plants within this range, knowing that they will harmonize well.

tones further afield to increase the sense of space and make the garden seem bigger than it really is.

There are many ways you can use hot colours in border schemes, creating a range of different effects.

You can combine them in a single scheme for a fiery display that will attract the eye. If you add lush foliage plants to the combination, the effect suddenly becomes more tropical, almost as if you were creating a steamy atmosphere. An even more dramatic effect can be achieved by combining these brilliant colours with complementary purple-leaved companions – producing a rich, sensual tapestry of texture and colour on which to feast the eye. You can also use contrast to add impact to hot colour schemes by combining a paler shade of a bright colour with a darker shade of a complementary dark colour, such as bright red with dark purple.

Brilliant orange

Orange is an intense colour that can be difficult to place in a border, as it tends to dominate all those colours

Attractive for much of the year, *Berberis linearifolia* 'Orange King' has spectacular deep orange flowers in spring, with a smaller flush of flowers appearing in late summer.

around it. Sitting between red and yellow in the colour wheel, it can be successfully combined with both these colours in a hot border scheme, or used in isolated blocks as a contrast to a soothing sea of green or silver, for example.

When used in mixed colour schemes, orange is much more difficult to accommodate and so is often avoided by gardeners. However, if flanked by less intense shades of peaches and cream, or apricot and bronze, it can help to create some harmony where otherwise there would be discord.

Striking orange

The range of orange-flowered shrubs and climbers is fairly limited, but most of them are strikingly orange and really do make a dramatic impact in the garden.

In spring, the deciduous azalea 'Gibraltar' is a beacon of colour, as the eye-catching, funnel-shaped flowers become the centre of attention. During early summer, *Berberis darwinii* and *Berberis linearifolia* 'Orange King' come to the fore, lighting up the border with their

Orange shrubs and climbers to try

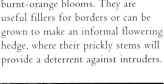

Shrubs
Abutilon indicum 'Kentish Belle'
Acer palmatum 'Orange Dream'
Acer palmatum var. *dissectum* 'Green Globe'
Acer palmatum var. *dissectum* 'Inaba-shidare'
Amelanchier lamarckii
Amelanchier x grandiflora 'Ballerina'
Banksia coccinea
Berberis darwinii
Berberis linearifolia 'Orange King'
Berberis thunbergii 'Rose Glow'
Berberis x stenophylla 'Crawley Gem'
Berberis x stenophylla 'Irwinii'
Buddleja globosa
Cornus sanguinea 'Midwinter Fire'
Cotoneaster conspicuus 'Coral Beauty'
Fothergilla major
Hamamelis x intermedia 'Jelena'
Helianthemum 'Chocolate Blotch'
Hippophae rhamnoides
Lantana camara 'Radiation'
Nandina domestica 'Fire Power'
Parrotia persica

Parrotia persica 'Pendula'
Phygelius x rectus 'African Queen'
Phygelius x rectus 'Salmon Leap'
Potentilla fruticosa 'Sunset'
Potentilla fruticosa 'Tangerine'
Pyracantha 'Golden Charmer'
Pyracantha 'Orange Glow'
Pyracantha 'Saphyr Orange'
Rhododendron 'Gibraltar'
Rhododendron 'Glowing Embers'
Rhododendron 'Koster's Brilliant Red'
Rhododendron 'Persil'
Rhus typhina
Rhus typhina 'Dissecta'
Rosa 'Remember Me'
Rosa 'Southampton'
Stephanandra incisa 'Crispa'
Stephanandra tanakae

Climbers
Ampelopsis aconitifolia
Campsis grandiflora
Lonicera x heckrottii 'Gold Flame'
Lonicera x tellmanniana

burnt-orange blooms. They are useful fillers for borders or can be grown to make an informal flowering hedge, where their prickly stems will provide a deterrent against intruders.

Coppery orange

Later in the summer you can enjoy the large, fragrant, double, coppery-orange, flushed-yellow flowers of the rose 'Remember Me', as well as the large, double, slightly scented, red-flushed apricot clustered blooms of 'Southampton', with its distinctive ruffled petals.

By autumn, startling clusters of orange pyracantha berries, such as the cultivars 'Saphyr Orange' and 'Orange Glow', last well into winter and shine out against a backdrop of glossy, dark green leaves. There can be splashes of orange to see in the garden in even the coldest months, with the glowing bare stems of *Cornus sanguinea* 'Midwinter Fire', as well as the fragrant, coppery-orange, spidery flowers of *Hamamelis x intermedia* 'Jelena', which are borne on bare stems from Christmas onwards.

The many shades of orange combine to produce the lovely rose 'Miss Pam Ayres' – a very vigorous plant to have in the garden.

Colour selector: yellow

Warm and inviting, yellow is many a gardener's favourite flower colour. It seems to shine out in all weathers and at all times of the year.

Welcome yellow

In the spring, autumn and winter, yellow is a welcome relief on dreary days, radiating its cheerful disposition to all its neighbours. Then, in summer, it can be used to light up borders in both sun and dappled shade – contrasting the dark shadows where the sun is at its most fierce and reflecting light all around where it is not.

All yellows are fairly easy to accommodate into border schemes, combining well with oranges and reds to create hot, fiery displays, as well as providing startling contrasts to purples, violets and black. Yellow also partners browns and bronze shades to good effect, while white is a natural bedfellow.

Any yellow will happily partner green, which lies adjacent to it on the colour wheel, and some shades of yellow can be successfully added to schemes predominantly based on blue and silver tones. Even a monochrome display using a variety

Hypericum 'Hidcote'

of yellow hues can work particularly well. Choose two or three distinct, but complementary shades, such as the palest lemon-yellow, a clear butter-yellow and a rich bronzy-yellow. Being so accommodating, yellow is easy to take for granted. If it is used too liberally it dominates the whole garden display. However, there are so many shades of yellow that allow you to create subtly different effects around the garden without the effect being monotonous.

Yellow variegated foliage

Another way to introduce yellow into your garden is by using shrubs and climbers with yellow-variegated foliage. The effect you achieve will depend on the plants you choose and the plants that surround them. Yellow-variegated foliage ranges from the subtle greenish shades to the dramatic eye-catching tones of some all-yellow foliage plants. It is tempting to include yellow-variegated plants in monochrome schemes of yellow flowers, but this seldom works in practice because displays lack contrast and the various elements tend to cancel each other out. However, you can add a few pale yellow flowers to an all-yellow foliage scheme to good effect if you are aiming for a soothing, low-key combination.

Warm yellow

There is a huge range of plants that produce yellow flowers or foliage. You can start the year with the densely packed, arching spikes of the fragrant butter-yellow flowers of *Mahonia aquifolium* 'Apollo', which appear above the holly-like leaves that have a reddish tinge in winter. The stunning flower power of forsythias light up the spring with

Berberis 'Goldilocks'

their brilliant blooms produced *en masse* on bare stems. Among the best varieties are 'Beatrix Farrand' (orange-yellow), 'Lynwood' (golden-yellow), 'Spring Glory' (pale yellow), and 'Week End' (rich yellow). The deciduous azalea, *Rhododendron luteum*, is worth seeking out for its spectacular early summer, sweetly scented, yellow, funnel-shaped blooms. Another sought-after yellow is produced by *Fremontodendron* 'California Glory', which bears eye-catching, saucer-shaped, butter-yellow, waxy-looking flowers from late spring to autumn against a backdrop of leathery, lobed, dark green leaves.

Butter yellow

A spectacular seasonal highlight is produced by *Genista lydia*, when its arching stems are festooned in golden-yellow flowers throughout early summer. For larger, bright-yellow flowers at this time of year, you could opt for *Potentilla fruticosa* 'Goldfinger', which bears a crop of blooms against a mound of small, dark green leaves. You could also try *Hypericum* 'Hidcote', which bears impressive cup-shaped, golden-yellow flowers in succession from mid-

Yellow shrubs and climbers to try

Shrubs

Abelia x grandiflora 'Francis Mason'
Abelia x grandiflora 'Gold Spot'
Abutilon megapotamicum 'Variegatum'
Acer palmatum 'Sango-kaku'
Acer palmatum var. dissectum 'Ornatum'
Aucuba japonica 'Crotonifolia'
Aucuba japonica 'Picturata'
Azara dentata
Berberis aristata
Berberis thunbergii 'Aurea'
Berberis thunbergii 'Helmond Pillar'
Berberis x stenophylla
Berberis x stenophylla 'Claret Cascade'
Berberis x stenophylla 'Corallina
Compacta'
Brachyglottis compacta 'Sunshine'
Buddleja davidii 'Harlequin'
Bupleurum fruticosum
Calluna vulgaris 'Wickwar Flame'
Caryopteris x clandonensis 'Worcester
Gold'
Chimonanthus praecox
Chimonanthus praecox 'Grandiflorus'
Chimonanthus praecox 'Luteus'
Choisya 'Goldfingers'
Choisya ternata 'Sundance'
Colutea arborescens
Cornus alba 'Aurea'
Cornus stolonifera 'Flaviramea'
Coronilla valentina subsp. glauca
Cotinus coggygria 'Golden Spirit'
Cytisus battandieri
Cytisus x praecox 'Allgold'
Cytisus x praecox 'Warminster'
Diervilla x splendens
Elaeagnus pungens 'Maculata'
Elaeagnus x ebbingei 'Gilt Edge'
Elaeagnus x ebbingei 'Limelight'
Enkianthus campanulatus
Euonymus fortunei 'Emerald 'n' Gold'
Euonymus fortunei 'Sunspot'
Forsythia 'Beatrix Farrand'
Forsythia x intermedia 'Spring Glory'
Forsythia x intermedia 'Week End'
Fremontodendron 'California Glory'

Berberis aristata

Genista lydia
Genista pilosa 'Vancouver Gold'
Genista tinctoria 'Royal Gold'
Hamamelis x intermedia 'Moonlight'
Hamamelis x intermedia 'Pallida'
Hebe ochracea 'James Stirling'
Helianthemum 'Wisley Primrose'
Hypericum calycinum
Hypericum 'Hidcote'
Hypericum x moserianum 'Tricolor'
Ilex aquifolium 'Golden Queen'
Ilex x altaclerensis 'Golden King'
Jasminum nudiflorum
Kerria japonica 'Golden Guinea'
Kerria japonica 'Pleniflora'
Lantana camara 'Goldmine'
Lonicera nitida 'Baggesen's Gold'
Mahonia aquifolium 'Apollo'
Mahonia japonica Bealei Group
Mahonia x media 'Buckland'
Mahonia x media 'Charity'
Mahonia x media 'Lionel Fortescue'
Paeonia lutea var. ludlowii
Phlomis fruticosa
Phygelius aequalis 'Yellow Trumpet'
Potentilla fruticosa 'Abbotswood'
Potentilla fruticosa 'Goldfinger'
Pyracantha 'Soleil d'Or'
Rhododendron luteum
Rhododendron macabeanum
Ribes sanguineum 'Brocklebankii'
Rosa 'Felicia'

Rosa 'Golden Wedding'
Rosa 'Graham Thomas'
Rosa 'Masquerade'
Rosa 'Peace'
Rosa xanthina 'Canary Bird'
Salix lanata
Salvia officinalis 'Icterina'
Sambucus racemosa 'Plumosa Aurea'
Sambucus racemosa 'Sutherland
Gold'
Santolina chamaecyparissus var. nana
Sophora microphylla 'Sun King'
Spartium junceum
Spiraea japonica 'Golden Princess'
Spiraea japonica 'Goldflame'
Viburnum rhytidophyllum

Climbers

Campsis radicans 'Flamenco'
Celastrus orbiculatus
Clematis 'Bill MacKenzie'
Clematis tangutica
Hedera colchica 'Sulphur Heart'
Hedera helix 'Buttercup'
Hedera helix 'Goldheart'
Hibbertia scandens
Humulus lupulus 'Aureus'
Jasminum officinale 'Fiona Sunrise'
Lonicera japonica 'Halliana'
Lonicera japonica 'Hall's Prolific'
Lonicera x americana
Lonicera x italica 'Harlequin'

Rhododendron macabeanum

summer onwards. Yellow roses are another popular choice and cultivars to look for include 'Amber Queen' (amber), 'Arthur Bell' (gold), 'Canary Bird' (clear yellow), 'Chinatown' (pink-edged yellow), 'Felicia' (apricot-yellow), 'Golden Wedding' (gold), 'Graham Thomas' (clear yellow), 'Masquerade' (clear yellow), 'Mountbatten' (gold) and 'Peace' (pink-flushed, deep yellow). Clematis tangutica and 'Bill MacKenzie' are two of the best yellow-flowered climbers, producing their blooms in succession from mid-summer.

Colour selector: white and green

Green is the predominant colour in most gardens and usually forms the canvas upon which all the other colours are added. However, you can create a garden using greens alone because there is such a wide range of shades and textures.

Atmospheric greens

The amazing variations of the tones of green and its variety of finishes, ranging from matt, through silk to high gloss, means that a real tapestry can be achieved with this colour.

Green also harmonizes with yellows and blues, which lie on each side of it on the colour wheel, so you can safely combine these, creating a calming atmosphere.

Alternatively, you can combine greens with contrasting reds and oranges, which lie opposite the green sector on the colour wheel. Green is an excellent foil for these strong colours, which would otherwise dominate the display.

In spring and summer, *Prostanthera cuneata* produces clusters of broadly tubular, pure white flowers.

Variegated green

Many ornamental shrubs and climbers have attractively variegated leaves: striped, splashed or edged with contrasting shades of green, yellow or white. These are particularly useful for adding light to darker corners and for providing interest all around the garden when other plants are out of season.

Monochrome plantings need a backdrop of green or silver to act as an effective foil, but they can also be used to striking effect in full sun, be eye-catching in dappled shade and glowing in full shade.

White

Like green, the importance of white within the garden palette is often overlooked. It is the universal colour that can be used in conjunction with any other colour in the colour wheel, or on its own.

When backlit in the twilight hours, white flowers can seem almost ghostly, shimmering above the border. Few flowers are pure white all over; most have a hint of green, pink, yellow or blue that makes them even more intriguing, while others may have pure white petals but combine with a contrasting colour, such as a splash of golden stamens. Even the purest of white flowers open from coloured buds that change the whole perception of the display.

There is a huge range of garden-worthy shrubs that bear brilliant white flowers in profusion. Among the best is *Amelanchier lamarckii*, a spectacular shrub in spring when smothered in star-shaped, white flowers accompanied by bronze-tinted emerging leaves. The flowering Chinese dogwood, *Cornus kousa* var. *chinensis*, is even more conspicuous when covered in its creamy-white flower bracts that fade

Choisya ternata

to white before turning red-pink during early summer, followed by strawberry-like fleshy fruit.

The star magnolia, *Magnolia stellata*, is equally dramatic, producing silky buds that open on bare branches in early spring to reveal stunning, lightly scented, white, star-shaped flowers. For sheer visual power, few shrubs can equal the floriferous *Exochorda x macrantha* 'The Bride', which produces elegant arching branches smothered in brilliant white flowers during late spring.

Roses should not be overlooked either, including 'Blanche Double de Coubert' (pure white), 'Boule de Neige' (pure white), 'Happy Birthday' (creamy-white), 'Ice Cream' (ivory), 'Iceberg' (pure white), 'Kent' (pure white) and 'Polar Star' (pure white).

Several climbers are noted for their sparkling white flowers. The *Clematis armandii* varieties 'Apple Blossom' and 'Snowdrift' bear their fragrant, star-shaped blooms in early spring against leathery, evergreen leaves. For early summer, *Solanum jasminoides* 'Album' is hard to beat, with its clusters of jasmine-scented flowers and glossy, dark green leaves.

White and green shrubs and climbers to try

Shrubs

Amelanchier lamarckii
Amelanchier x grandiflora 'Ballerina'
Brugmansia suaveolens
Buddleja davidii 'White Profusion'
Buxus sempervirens 'Suffruticosa'
Buxus sempervirens 'Elegantissima'
Calluna vulgaris 'Alicia'
Calluna vulgaris 'Spring Cream'
Camellia japonica 'Nobilissima'
Camellia x williamsii 'Jury's Yellow'
Carpenteria californica
Chaenomeles speciosa 'Nivalis'
Choisya 'Aztec Pearl'
Choisya 'Goldfingers'
Choisya ternata 'Sundance'
Cistus x aguilarii 'Maculatus'
Cistus x corbariensis
Clethra alnifolia
Clethra alnifolia 'Paniculata'
Colutea arborescens
Convolvulus cneorum
Cornus 'Eddie's White Wonder'
Cornus kousa var. chinensis
Cotoneaster salicifolius 'Gnom'
Cytisus multiflorus
Daboecia cantabrica f. alba
Deutzia gracilis
Drimys winteri
Erica carnea 'Springwood White'
Escallonia 'Iveyi'
Eucryphia x intermedia 'Rostrevor'
Eucryphia x nymansensis 'Nymansay'
Euonymus 'Emerald Gaiety'
Exochorda x macrantha 'The Bride'
Fatsia japonica 'Variegata'
Garrya elliptica

Philadelphus 'Manteau d'Hermine'

Gaultheria mucronata 'Wintertime'
Gaultheria procumbens
Griselinia littoralis
Hebe cupressoides 'Boughton Dome'
Hebe pinguifolia 'Pagei'
Helianthemum 'Wisley White'
Hydrangea arborescens 'Annabelle'
Ilex aquifolium 'Silver Queen'
Itea ilicifolia
Lantana camara 'Snow White'
Lavandula angustifolia 'Nana Alba'
Lavandula stoechas 'Snowman'
Ligustrum lucidum 'Excelsum Superbum'
Lonicera fragrantissima
Lonicera x purpusii 'Winter Beauty'
Magnolia stellata
Nerium oleander
Olearia ilicifolia
Olearia macrodonta
Olearia x haastii
Osmanthus delavayi
Osmanthus x burkwoodii
Pachysandra terminalis
Philadelphus 'Beauclerk'
Philadelphus 'Belle Etoile'
Philadelphus x 'Lemoinei'
Philadelphus 'Manteau d'Hermine'
Philadelphus microphyllus
Philadelphus 'Virginal'
Phoenix roebelenii
Phygelius x rectus 'Moonraker'
Pieris 'Forest Flame'
Pieris formosa var. forrestii 'Wakehurst'
Pieris japonica 'Purity'
Pieris japonica 'Variegata'
Pittosporum 'Garnettii'
Pittosporum tenuifolium 'Variegata'
Potentilla fruiticosa 'Abbotswood'
Rhododendron 'Cunningham's White'
Rosa 'Blanche Double de Coubert'
Rosa 'Boule de Neige'
Rosa 'Happy Birthday'
Rosa 'Ice Cream'
Rosa 'Iceberg'
Rosa 'Kent'
Rosa 'Polar Star'
Rubus 'Benenden'
Ruta graveolens 'Jackman's Blue'
Santolina chamaecyparissus var. nana
Sarcococca confusa
Sarcococca hookeriana var. digyna
Sarcococca hookeriana var. humilis
Spiraea 'Arguta'

Rosa 'Boule de Neige'

Spiraea nipponica 'Snowmound'
Spiraea prunifolia
Spiraea thunbergii 'Albovariegatum'
Syringa vulgaris 'Michael Buchner'
Viburnum davidii
Viburnum tinus 'French White'
Viburnum x burkwoodii
Viburnum x carlesii
x fatshedera lizei 'Variegata'

Climbers

Bougainvillea glabra 'Snow White'
Cissus antartica
Cissus rhombifolia
Clematis 'Alba Luxurians'
Clematis armandii 'Snowdrift'
Clematis 'Belle of Woking'
Clematis cirrhosa 'Wisley Cream'
Clematis 'Duchess of Edinburgh'
Clematis florida 'Seiboldii'
Clematis 'Henryi'
Clematis 'Huldine'
Clematis 'Lasurstern'
Clematis 'Marie Boisselot'
Clematis 'Miss Bateman'
Fallopia baldschuanica
Jasminum officinale
Jasminum officinale 'Clotted Cream'
Mandevilla boliviensis
Passiflora caerulea 'Constance Elliot'
Philodendron scandens
Solanum jasminoides 'Album'
Stephanotis floribunda
Trachelospermum jasminoides
Wisteria floribunda 'Alba'
Wisteria sinensis 'Alba'

Colour selector: pink

Pink is perhaps the most common flower colour, coming in a huge variety of shades, ranging from the most subtle of blush-whites to the quite startling shocking pinks.

Complex pink

Pink is the mongrel of the colour world and its complexity means it is not included on the colour wheel because pinks are viewed as a sort of watered-down red, with various amounts of other colours thrown in for good measure.

In fact, pinks are so varied that they could make up a colour wheel all of their own, with the purest clear pink at the core, made up of a splash of red and lots of white, flanked by heart-warming yellowish-pinks (including warm apricot-pink and vibrant salmon-pink) on one side and breezy bluish-pinks (such as shell-pink and lilac-pink) on the other, with white filling in between.

Pink is a chameleon colour too, as it seems to change with the intensity of light and the colours that surround it. The perception of pink also varies from one observer to another, so consider this when planning a planting scheme. Fortunately, pink is very easy to combine with other colours, provided you avoid saturated reds, with which it clashes terribly. As a rule, try to choose a shade of pink on the side of the spectrum from which its companions are derived. For example, if you want a pink to go with blue or purple, choose a cool lilac-pink or a clear pink as a companion. Similarly, if you want a pink to accompany a colour from the warmer side of the colour wheel, go for a yellowish-pink. Best of all, combine pink with white for a fool-proof partnership that cannot fail to look impressive, as it offers a sense of romance and fun. Both these colours also combine well with other pastel shades and can be highlighted with splashes of deeper hues.

Soft pink

Pink looks its best in spring when light levels are not so intense. Early flowering plants are ideal choices for small gardens, such as *Rhododendron* 'Pink Pearl', with its white-edged, soft-pink, funnel-shaped flowers that age to white, 'Pink Drift', which bears rose-lavender flowers, and 'Homebush', which offers pretty pink, semi-double blooms.

Camellias come into their own at this time of the year, too, and there are many excellent pink-flowered forms, including *Camellia japonica* 'Elegans', 'Hagoromo' and 'Lady Vansittart', 'Leonard Messel', 'Debbie', 'Donation' and 'J. C. Williams'. Peonies are one of the features of early summer, including 'Duchess of Kent', with tulip-shaped buds that open in to reveal deep rose-pink, semi-double, cup-shaped flowers, and the exquisite 'Duchess of Marlborough', which bears huge, double, pale pink flowers with crinkle-edged petals that fade to silvery-white at the margins.

Rhododendron 'Pink Pearl'

The blush-pink to white sweetly scented blooms of *Rosa* 'Stanwell Perpetual'.

Other early summer favourites are the lavaterias, such as 'Burgundy Wine', 'Kew Rose' and 'Rosea', which all offer a succession of large, dark pink blooms.

Candy-floss pink

Of course, summer wouldn't be summer without the succession of candy-floss pink roses. Among the best are 'Ballerina' (white-centred, pale pink), 'Blessings' (coral-pink), 'Congratulations' (rose-pink), 'Fantin-Latour' (pale pink), 'Fru Dagmar Hastrup' (light pink), 'Happy Anniversary' (deep pink), 'Heritage' (pale pink), 'Louise Odier' (clear pink), 'Madame Pierre Oger' (pale silvery-pink), 'Mary Rose' (rose pink), 'Oxfordshire' (pale pink), 'Pearl Anniversary' (pearl-pink), 'Penelope' (pale creamy-pink), 'Queen Mother' (clear pink), 'Queen of Denmark' (deep to light pink) and 'Silver Jubilee' (rose-pink).

Early flowering clematis worth seeking out include 'Pink Flamingo', then later in the season the pinkish blooms of 'Bees' Jubilee', 'Doctor Ruppel', 'Markham's Pink', 'Pink Perfection', 'Tetrarose' and the flamboyant 'Nelly Moser' come to the fore. For a sun trap, consider the luminescent, cerise-pink *Bougainvillea* 'Raspberry Ice'.

Pink shrubs and climbers to try

Shrubs

Abelia 'Edward Goucher'
Abelia x grandiflora 'Confetti'
Abeliophyllum distichum Roseum Group
Buddleja alternifolia
Buddleja davidii 'Pink Delight'
Calluna vulgaris 'Blazeaway'
Calluna vulgaris 'County Wicklow'
Calluna vulgaris 'H. E. Beale'
Calluna vulgaris 'Silver Queen'
Camellia japonica 'Elegans'
Camellia japonica 'Hagoromo'
Camellia japonica 'Lady Vansittart'
Camellia 'Leonard Messel'
Camellia x williamsii 'Debbie'
Camellia x williamsii 'Donation'
Camellia x williamsii 'J. C. Williams'
Camellia x williamsii 'E.G. Waterhouse'
Chaenomeles speciosa 'Geisha Girl'
Chaenomeles x superba 'Pink Lady'
Cistus 'Silver Pink'
Cistus x pulverulentus 'Sunset'
Clethra alnifolia 'Pink Spire'
Clethra alnifolia 'Rosea'
Cornus florida 'Rainbow'
Cornus florida f. rubra
Daboecia cantabrica 'Bicolor'
Daphne bholua 'Jacqueline Postill'
Daphne odora 'Aureomarginata'
Deutzia x elegantissima 'Rosealind'
Deutzia x hybrida 'Mont Rose'
Erica carnea 'Foxhollow'
Erica carnea 'King George'
Erica carnea 'Pink Spangles'

Hebe 'Great Orme'

Erica cinerea 'Pink Ice'
Erica x darleyensis 'Darley Dale'
Erica x darleyensis 'Furzey'
Grevillea 'Robyn Gordon'
Hebe 'Great Orme'
Hebe 'Midsummer Beauty'
Hebe 'Red Edge'
Hebe 'Rosie'
Hibiscus syriacus 'Woodbridge'
Hydrangea macrophylla 'Veitchii'
Hydrangea paniculata 'Floribunda'
Justicia carnea
Kalmia latifolia 'Ostbo Red'
Kolkwitzia amabilis 'Pink Cloud'
Lantana camara 'Fabiola'
Lavandula angustifolia 'Loddon Pink'
Lavandula angustifolia 'Rosea'
Lavatera x clementii 'Barnsley'
Lavatera x clementii 'Burgundy Wine'
Lavatera x clementii 'Kew Rose'
Magnolia 'Heaven Scent'
Magnolia stellata 'Royal Star'
Magnolia x loebneri 'Leonard Messel'
Magnolia x soulangeana
Paeonia suffruticosa 'Reine Elisabeth'
Phlomis italica
Phygelius x rectus 'Pink Elf'
Pieris japonica 'Valley Valentine'
Potentilla fruticosa 'Royal Flush'
Prunus tenella 'Fire Hill'
Prunus triloba
Rhododendron 'Debutante'
Rhododendron 'Grumpy'
Rhododendron 'Homebush'
Rhododendron 'Pink Drift'
Rhododendron 'Pink Pearl'
Rosa 'Buff Beauty'
Rosa 'Congratulations'
Rosa 'Cornelia'
Rosa 'Fantin-Latour'
Rosa 'Fru Dagmar Hastrup'
Rosa glauca
Rosa 'Golden Anniversary'
Rosa 'Happy Anniversary'
Rosa 'Heritage'
Rosa 'Louise Odier'
Rosa 'Madame Pierre Oger'
Rosa 'Many Happy Returns'
Rosa 'Mary Rose'
Rosa 'Oxfordshire'
Rosa 'Pearl Anniversary'
Rosa 'Queen of Denmark'
Rosa 'Sharifa Asma'

Rhododendron 'Homebush'

Rosa 'Silver Jubilee'
Rosa 'Surrey'
Rosa 'Sussex'
Rosa 'Sweet Dream'
Rosmarinus officinalis 'Majorca Pink'
Rubus odoratus
Salvia officinalis
Spiraea japonica 'Anthony Waterer'
Symphoricarpos x chenaultii 'Hancock'
Syringa vulgaris 'Madame Lemoine'
Viburnum tinus 'Eve Price'
Viburnum tinus 'Gwenllian'
Viburnum x bodnantense 'Dawn'
Viburnum x juddii
Weigela florida 'Foliis Purpureis'
Weigela 'Florida Variegata'

Climbers

Actinidia kolomikta
Bougainvillea 'Miss Manila'
Bougainvillea 'Raspberry Ice'
Bougainvillea glabra
Bougainvillea glabra 'Variegata'
Clematis alpina 'Pink Flamingo'
Clematis armandii 'Apple Blossom'
Clematis macropetala 'Markham's Pink'
Clematis montana var. rubens 'Elizabeth'
Clematis montana var. rubens 'Tetrarose'
Clematis 'Nelly Moser'
Clematis 'Princess Diana'
Hoya carnosa
Jasminum x stephanense
Mandevilla splendens
Wisteria floribunda 'Macrobotrys'

Colour selector: red

Plants with scarlet and vermillion flowers are often seen as the showgirls of the border, demanding attention as they cry out from the chorus of other more subtle shades all around them.

Hot reds

Reds fall on the hot side of the colour wheel, and so sit particularly happily alongside oranges and yellow in fiery combinations. However, reds have much more going for them than that.

The most saturated reds, which fall in the middle of the spectrum, have the most intense colour and can hold their own in any display. However, if they are used too liberally, they will dominate all the other colours surrounding them. For this reason, saturated red flowering plants with large blooms need to be used with care and reserved for creating distinctive points of focus in a border of more subtle shades, such as pale green.

Shrubs with scattered, small red flowers are much easier to accommodate in mixed planting schemes because their effect is moderated by the intermittent

Pieris 'Forest Flame'

backdrop of foliage that peeks through from behind the vibrantly coloured flowering display.

Velvet-reds

Rich velvet-reds that have just a hint of blue will add sensuality to a planting scheme and are particularly well suited to combining with plants of a purple tone. Many flowers offer plum-purple shades, which are now very popular. More subtle than the saturated reds, velvet-reds tend to add warmth and intimacy to a planting scheme.

Brilliant reds

Shades of red also can be introduced into the border by including plants with purple or red foliage. This can be a seasonal highlight, such as the brilliant red, glossy young leaves of *Photinia x fraseri* 'Red Robin' or, for longer-term display, *Berberis thunbergii* 'Atropurpurea Nana', with its dark purple leaves that turn a brilliant red in autumn, or *Cotinus coggygria* 'Royal Purple', another red-purple-leaved, bushy shrub that turns brilliant scarlet in autumn.

Japanese maples such as 'Atropurpureum', 'Bloodgood' and 'Garnet' make excellent specimens for small gardens, with their attractive palm-like, lobed or deeply cut dark purple leaves that look spectacular all summer before turning brilliant shades of red at the end of the growing season.

Crimson and scarlet

The ever-popular crimson and scarlet roses, such as 'Alec's Red' (crimson), 'Alexander' (vermilion), 'Charles de Mills', 'Fragrant Cloud' (deep-scarlet), 'Ingrid Bergman' (deep red), 'Just Joey' (coppery-red), 'Loving Memory' (dark red), 'Rose de Rescht' (deep mauve-red), 'Royal

Rosa 'Danse du Feu'

William' (deep-crimson), 'Ruby Anniversary' (ruby-red), 'Ruby Wedding' (ruby-red), 'Suffolk' (golden-centred, deep-scarlet) and 'The Times Rose' (dark-crimson), shouldn't be overlooked.

However, there are many other red-flowering shrubs worth considering, including the vermillion-red *Potentilla fruticosa* 'Red Ace', which blooms from late spring to autumn, or the stunning *Paeonia delavayi*, which bears single, cup-shaped, blood-red flowers from spring into early summer.

Red also makes a splash at the end of the growing season as shrubs and climbers take on their autumnal hues. Few sights are more spectacular than the blood-red foliage of the crimson glory vine, *Vitis coignetiae*, when its huge, heart-shaped leaves turn fiery shades, accompanied by bunches of small, blue-black, inedible grapes.

Equally impressive are the deeply divided, slightly puckered green leaves of the Virginia creeper, *Parthenocissus quinquefolia*, which transform in autumn as they take on brilliant shades of crimson and purple. When autumn turns to

Red shrubs and climbers to try

Shrubs
Abutilon megapotamicum
Acer palmatum 'Bloodgood'
Acer palmatum 'Fireglow'
Acer palmatum 'Osakazuki'
Acer palmatum 'Sango-kaku'
Acer palmatum var. dissectum
'Atropurpureum'
Amelanchier lamarckii
Amelanchier x grandiflora 'Ballerina'
Aucuba japonica 'Rozannie'
Aucuba japonica 'Variegata'
Berberis thunbergii 'Atropurpurea Nana'
Berberis thunbergii 'Bagatelle'
Berberis thunbergii 'Dart's Red Lady'
Berberis thunbergii 'Harlequin'
Berberis thunbergii 'Helmond Pillar'
Berberis thunbergii 'Red Chief'
Callistemon citrinus 'Splendens'
Calluna vulgaris 'Dark Star'
Calluna vulgaris 'Wickwar Flame'
Camellia japonica 'Adolphe Audusson'
Camellia japonica 'Mikenjaku'
Camellia x williamsii 'Anticipation'
Ceratostigma griffithii
Chaenomeles x superba 'Crimson and
Gold'
Chaenomeles x superba 'Nicoline'
Colutea x media 'Copper Beauty'
Cornus 'Eddie's White Wonder'
Cornus alba 'Sibirica'
Cornus alba 'Spaethii'
Cotinus 'Flame'
Cotinus 'Grace'
Cotoneaster dammeri
Cotoneaster frigidus 'Cornubia'
Cotoneaster horizontalis
Cotoneaster 'Hybridus Pendulus'
Cotoneaster salicifolius 'Gnom'

Cytisus 'Boskoop Ruby'
Daboecia cantabrica 'Bicolor'
Desfontainia spinosa
Enkianathus cernuus f. rubens
Erica carnea 'Ann Sparkes'
Erica carnea 'Challenger'
Erica carnea 'December Red'
Erica carnea 'Myretoun Ruby'
Escallonia rubra 'Crimson Spire'
Euonymus europaeus 'Red Cascade'
Fothergilla gardenii
Fuchsia 'Mrs Popple'
Fuchsia 'Pumila'
Fuchsia 'Riccartonii'
Gaultheria mucronata 'Mulberry Wine'
Gaultheria procumbens
Helianthemum 'Ben Heckla'
Helianthemum 'Ben Hope'
Helianthemum 'Henfield Brilliant'
Hibiscus rosa-sinensis 'The President'
Ilex aquifolium 'J.C. van Tol'
Leptospermum scoparium 'Red Damask'
Leucothoe 'Scarletta'
Leycesteria formosa
Paeonia delavayi
Photinia x fraseri 'Red Robin'
Potentilla fruticosa 'Red Ace'
Pyracantha 'Saphyr Rouge'
Rhamnus alaternus 'Argenteovariegata'
Rhododendron 'Dopey'
Rhododendron 'Geisha Red'
Rhododendron 'Klondyke'
Rhododendron 'Lord Roberts'
Rhododendron 'Mother's Day'
Rhododendron 'Scarlet Wonder'
Ribes sanguineum 'King Edward VII'
Ribes sanguineum 'Pulborough Scarlet'
Rosa 'Alec's Red'
Rosa 'Alexander'

Viburnum betulifolium

Rosa 'Charles de Mills'
Rosa 'Fragrant Cloud'
Rosa 'Ingrid Bergman'
Rosa 'The Times Rose'
Rosa moyesii 'Geranium'
Skimmia japonica subsp. reevesiana
Virburnum betulifolium
Weigela 'Bristol Ruby'

Climbers
Berberidopsis corallina
Bougainvillea 'Scarlett O'Hara'
Campsis x tagliabuana 'Madame Galen'
Clematis 'Ernest Markham'
Clematis 'Niobe'
Clematis 'Rouge Cardinal'
Clematis 'Ville de Lyon'
Clianthus puniceus
Eccremocarpus scaber
Lonicera x brownii 'Dropmore Scarlet'
Parthenocissus quinquefolia
Parthenocissus tricuspidata 'Robusta'
Vitis 'Brant'
Vitis coignetiae

winter, sparking red stems stand out
from the dormant borders, with the
red-barked dogwood *Cornus alba*
'Sibirica' taking centre stage with its
brilliant red winter stems.

Coral
If you are looking for a shrub that
offers year-round interest then
seriously consider the coral-bark
maple, *Acer palmatum* 'Sango-kaku'.

This magnificent, ever-changing
plant offers startling coral-red young
shoots that dramatically set off the
emerging palm-shaped, orange-yellow
leaves in spring. The leaves gradually
turn green in summer, before taking
on fabulous shades of yellow in
autumn. When these lovely leaves
eventually fall, they reveal their
brilliantly coloured stems
throughout the winter.

Clematis reds
Clematis with flowers in shades of
red include the semi-double, reddish-
purple blooms of *Clematis viticella*
'Purpurea Plena Elegans', which are
produced *en masse* from mid-summer
onwards, and the ever-popular 'Ville
de Lyon', which offers large, cherry-
red flowers with contrasting golden
centres through the summer and into
the autumn.

Colour selector: purple, black and blue

Lying on the cool side of the colour wheel, purple, blue and black are all recessive colours and as such seem to sink back into the border — creating a subdued, almost brooding, edge to the garden atmosphere.

Purple

Despite its apparent richness and associations with opulence, purple is surprisingly calming and soothing. However, it doesn't take to competition all that well and will tend to get lost if it is included in a mixed scheme.

The best way to use purple is in isolated blocks, surrounded by greens and silvers, or combined with bluish-pinks such as lilac. Purples also associate well with cool blues and greens as well as hot reds, which lie either side of the purple sector in the colour wheel. For colour contrast, go for yellow, which lies opposite the purple sector on the colour wheel, or startling whites, which will help lift the mood and provide sensational highlights.

Softer mauves and lavenders are also part of the purple group and are even more subdued than their more vibrant, violet counterparts. They

Vitis vinifera 'Purpurea'

benefit from being used in bold swathes of single colours that lead the eye from one part of the garden to another, such as a lavender hedge alongside a path or a wisteria cascading over a boundary fence.

Black

By contrast, black (actually the darkest shade of purple) can be used for focal point plants when it is dotted within a planting of pale foliage plants. They look even better against a backdrop of silver or intermingled with the purest of whites. In blocks, black is too austere and will get overwhelmed in mixed colour schemes. Good examples of black plants include the lovely *Sambucus nigra* 'Black Lace' and *S. nigra* 'Black Beauty'.

Blue for illusion

Blue is perhaps the most tranquil colour in the garden palette, associating well with water and seating areas where its peaceful ambience can be best appreciated.

Although one of the least prominent colours, blue is also useful for creating illusions in a small garden where you want to increase the sense of space.

Like purple, blue associates well with white flowers and silver foliage, as these complement its introverted nature. It also harmonizes with other cool colours, such as bluish-purples and bluish-greens — both tones making an ideal antidote to the more flamboyant colour combinations often found elsewhere.

True blue

Pure blue flowers have a wonderfully luminescent quality about them, which means they often look their most spectacular at dusk and dawn, when other dominant colours seem

Cotinus coggygria

to recede and allow the blues to shimmer magnificently.

Perhaps the most reliable and impressive blue flowering shrub is the late spring-blooming Californian lilac (*Ceanothus*). Excellent varieties include: 'Burkwoodii', which bears clouds of sky-blue flowers above a compact evergreen shrub with bright green glossy leaves; 'Concha', which makes a dazzling mound of dark blue flowers; and the relatively new 'Italian Skies', which is covered in dense clusters of brilliant blue flowers. Other blue flowers that should not be forgotten are the popular 'Puget Blue' (dark blue) and 'Trewithen Blue', which bears fragrant, rich blue blooms. For a late show, go for 'Autumnal Blue', which bears clouds of bright blue flowers.

Vivid blue

Other shrubs that produce piercing, vivid blue flowers include the Chinese plumbago *Ceratostigma willmottianum* 'Forest Blue' and the ground-hugging periwinkles *Vinca major* (deep blue) and *Vinca minor* (pale blue). Alternatively, you might like to try *Caryopteris* x *clandonensis*

Purple, black and blue shrubs and climbers to try

Shrubs
Acer palmatum 'Atropurpureum'
Acer palmatum 'Garnet'
Ballota acetabulosa
Berberis thunbergii 'Atropurpurea Nana'
Berberis thunbergii 'Bagatelle'
Berberis thunbergii f. atropurpurea
Buddleja davidii 'Black Knight'
Buddleja davidii 'Nanho Blue'
Calluna vulgaris 'Amethyst'
Caryopteris x clandonensis
Caryopteris x clandonensis 'First Choice'
Ceanothus arboreus 'Trewithen Blue'
Ceanothus 'Autumnal Blue'
Ceanothus 'Burkwoodii'
Ceanothus 'Concha'
Ceanothus impressus 'Puget Blue'
Ceanothus 'Italian Skies'
Ceanothus thyrsiflorus var. repens
Ceratostigma griffithii
Ceratostigma willmottianum
Ceratostigma willmottianum 'Forest Blue'
Cistus x argenteus 'Peggy Sammons'
Clerodendrum trichotomum var. fargesii
Cordyline australis 'Atropurpurea'
Cordyline australis 'Purple Tower'
Cordyline australis Purpurea Group
Cordyline australis 'Red Star'
Cornus alba 'Kesselringii'
Corylus maxima 'Purpurea'
Cotinus 'Grace'
Cotinus coggygria 'Royal Purple'
Daboecia cantabrica 'Atropurpurea'
Fuchsia 'Mrs Popple'
Hibiscus syriacus 'Blue Bird'
Hydrangea macrophylla 'Blue Wave'
Hydrangea macrophylla 'Mariesii'
Hydrangea serrata 'Bluebird'
Hydrangea villosa
Indigofera heterantha
Lavandula angustifolia 'Hidcote'
Lavandula angustifolia 'Lady'
Lavandula angustifolia 'Munstead'
Lavandula angustifolia 'Royal Purple'
Lavandula 'Fathead'
Lavandula 'Helmsdale'

Lavandula stoechas 'Papillon'
Lavandula stoechas 'Rocky Road'
Lavandula x intermedia 'Grappenhall'
Lavandula x intermedia 'Grosso'
Magnolia 'Susan'
Magnolia x soulangeana 'Lennei'
Photinia x fraseri 'Birmingham'
Rhododendron 'Blue Danube'
Rhododendron 'Blue Diamond'
Rhododendron 'Blue Peter'
Rhododendron 'Purple Splendour'
Rhododendron 'Sapphire'
Rosa 'Cardinal de Richelieu'
Rosa 'Roseraie de l'Haÿ'
Rosa 'William Lobb'
Rosa rugosa 'Rubra'
Rosmarinus officinalis 'Severn Sea'
Salix hastata 'Wehrhahnii'
Salvia officinalis 'Purpurascens'
Salvia officinalis 'Tricolor'
Sambucus nigra 'Black Beauty'
Sambucus nigra 'Black Lace'
Syringa meyeri var. spontanea 'Palibin'
Syringa vulgaris 'Charles Joly'
Tamarix 'Rubra'
Tibouchina urvilleana
Vinca major
Vinca minor
Vinca minor 'Argenteovariegata'
Vinca minor 'Atropurpurea'
Vinca minor f. alba 'Gertrude Jekyll'

Climbers
Akebia quinata
Ampelopsis megalophylla
Aristolochia littoralis
Billardiera longiflora
Clematis alpina
Clematis alpina 'Frances Rivis'
Clematis alpina 'Frankie'
Clematis alpina 'Pamela Jackman'
Clematis 'Barbara Jackman'
Clematis 'Comtesse de Bouchaud'
Clematis 'Etoile Violette'
Clematis 'Fireworks'
Clematis 'General Sikorski'

Solanum laciniatum

Clematis 'Jackmanii'
Clematis 'Jackmanii Superba'
Clematis 'Mrs Cholmondeley'
Clematis 'Mrs N.Thompson'
Clematis 'Multi Blue'
Clematis 'Perle d'Azur'
Clematis 'Polish Spirit'
Clematis 'Prince Charles'
Clematis 'The President'
Clematis viticella 'Purpurea Plena
Elegans'
Clematis 'Vyvyan Pennell'
Cobaea scandens
Lonicera henryi
Lonicera japonica var. repens
Lonicera periclymenum 'Belgica'
Parthenocissus henryana
Parthenocissus tricuspidata 'Veitchii'
Passiflora caerulea
Plumbago auriculata
Solanum laciniatum 'Glasnevin'
Sollya heterophylla
Vitis vinifera 'Purpurea'
Wisteria floribunda
Wisteria floribunda 'Royal Purple'
Wisteria sinensis
Wisteria x formosa

'Heavenly Blue', for its impressive dark blue flowers, or *Hibiscus syriacus* 'Blue Bird', for its exotic-looking, violet-blue, trumpet-shaped summer blooms, each with a maroon eye.

Blue clematis
Finally, there are a couple of clematis that are worth mentioning in the blue category. These are 'Perle d'Azur', for its beautiful yellow-centred, lilac-blue flowers, produced in succession from mid-summer onwards, and 'Prince Charles', which offers pale mauve-blue flowers with green centres.

Scent selector

Fragrance is an elusive quality that is almost impossibly difficult to define. Not only does each person's perception of scent vary from day to day, but atmospheric conditions, location and the blend of scents in the air all have an impact.

The fragrant garden
Although scent is a bonus to the gardener, its reason for existence is to attract insects for pollination. For this reason, many winter-flowering plants are aromatic. However, there are not many pollinators around at this time of year, so the flowers have to work particularly hard to attract them – and they do.

Some plants throw out their scent with gay abandon, and can be smelled over long distances. Others are much more discreet and can only be appreciated when you get up very close to them. Some are only noticable during the evening, as the light fades. Generally, a warm, sunny day brings out the scents of shrubs and climbers, but there are some that are much more noticable during or after a fall of rain.

Summer scent: *Rosa* 'Zéphirine Drouhin'.

Many gardeners believe that modern-day flowers have lost their delicate fragrance when compared to old-fashioned varieties. In a lot of cases, this is true. As breeders develop more and more hybrid plants, particularly roses, for even larger blooms, a wider range of colours and disease resistance, it is sometimes at the expense of their aromatic charms. However, breeders are now aware of this and are taking more care to preserve the other beauty that satisfies the gardener's senses – that of smell.

Fragrance or odour?
It is essential that you check out a plant's fragrance in person before you buy – because one gardener's pleasing fragrance is another gardener's bad odour.

Subtle fragrances are often the worst offenders: it seems the more delicate the scent, the greater the range of reactions it receives, with unusual scents the most likely to be perceived completely differently by different people.

The main reason for this is that a particular fragrance is made up of various layers. The first layer is the ephemeral part of the scent that the nose picks up initially and its influence on the appreciation of the whole scent varies from one person to another. This is the part of the scent that grabs your attention, for good or for bad.

Spring scent: *Viburnum x juddii*

Soon the nose becomes aware of a more representative part of the fragrance, which is the main body of the scent. Then finally, the experience transforms as you appreciate the underlying part of the fragrance that stays with you.

Scent structure

Perhaps the best way to picture the structure of a scent is as a pyramid, as described by the leading French rose breeder, Henri Delbard.

In his pyramid, the top is the 'spirit' of the fragrance and includes the citrus scents and more aromatic elements, such as aniseed and lavender. In the middle is the 'heart' of the scent, which includes floral, fruity, spicy and earthy fragrances. At the bottom is the 'base' scent, which comprises the woody elements. Examples of this are cedar or balsam.

Universal scents

There are some fragrances that are more or less universally liked. Vanilla is a case in point, with the spicy vanilla scent of the chocolate vine (*Akebia quinata*) or the sweet vanilla fragrance of *Clematis* 'Elizabeth' and *C. armandii*, as well as that of wisteria, very widely rated.

By contrast, other sweet scents, such as honey, are loved by some and despised by others. For example, the strong honey scent of most varieties of Butterfly bush (*Buddleja*) or that of *Viburnum carlesii* are not universally appreciated, nor is the sweet honey scent of the Californian lilac (*Ceanothus*).

Many floral scents, such as jasmine, honeysuckle and lily-of-the-valley, are also widely acclaimed, as are those with fruity scents such as the peachy scents of *Coronilla glauca*, the fresh pineapple aroma of *Cytisus battandieri*, the spicy orange of

Spartium junceum and the perky lemon of *Eucalyptus citriodora*. Many roses have quite complex aromas, including the bananas-and-oranges smell of *Rosa* 'Bobbie James' and *R.* 'Polyanthus Grandiflorus'; the mix of lemon, peach, apricot and pears of

R. 'Nahema'; or very complex fragrance of mandarin, lemon, hyacinth, lilac, mango and lychee of *R.* 'Chartreuse De Parme'.

Many other climbers and shrubs have aromatic foliage, too, which can be resinous-smelling. Examples

---

Spring-scented shrubs and climbers to try

Shrubs	
Abeliophyllum distichum	*Syringa vulgaris* 'Charles Joly'
Aloysia triphylla	*Syringa vulgaris* 'Katherine Havemeyer'
Choisya ternata	*Syringa vulgaris* 'Madame Lemoine'
Choisya ternata 'Aztec Pearl'	*Syringa vulgaris* 'Michael Buchner'
Choisya ternata 'Goldfingers'	*Viburnum* x *burkwoodii*
Choisya ternata 'Sundance'	*Viburnum* x *carlcephalum*
Cytisus x *praecox* 'Warminster'	*Viburnum* x *carlesii*
Daphne mezereum	*Viburnum* x *juddii*
Drimys winteri	
Fothergilla gardenii	**Climbers**
Fothergilla major	*Akebia quinata*
Magnolia 'Heaven Scent'	*Clematis armandii* 'Apple Blossom'
Magnolia stellata	*Clematis armandii* 'Snowdrift'
Magnolia stellata 'Rosea'	*Clematis* 'Betty Corning'
Magnolia stellata 'Royal Star'	*Clematis flammula*
Magnolia stellata 'Waterlily'	*Clematis montana* var. *rubens* 'Elizabeth'
Osmanthus delavayi	*Clematis montana* var. *rubens* 'Pink
Pieris formosa var. *forrestii* 'Wakehurst'	Perfection'
Rhododendron luteum	*Clematis montana* var. *rubens* 'Tetrarose'
Skimmia japonica 'Rubella'	*Clematis* 'Mrs Cholmondeley'
Syringa meyeri var. *spontanea* 'Palibin'	*Hoya carnosa*
Syringa pubescens subsp. *microphylla*	*Jasminum polyanthum*
'Superba'	*Stephanotis floribunda*

Spring scent: *Choisya ternata*

Summer scented shrubs and climbers to try

Shrubs
Abelia x grandiflora
Abelia x grandiflora 'Confetti'
Abelia x grandiflora 'Francis Mason'
Abelia x grandiflora 'Goldspot'
Aloysia triphylla
Azara dentate
Brugmansia suaveolens
Buddleja 'Lochinch'
Buddleja alternifolia
Buddleja davidii 'Black Knight'
Buddleja davidii 'Nanho Blue'
Buddleja davidii 'White Profusion'
Buddleja globosa
Carpenteria californica
Carpenteria californica 'Ladhams Variety'
Caryopteris x clandonensis
Ceanothus arboreus 'Trewithen Blue'
Clethra alnifolia
Clethra alnifolia 'Paniculata'
Clethra alnifolia 'Pink Spire'
Clethra alnifolia 'Rosea'
Cytisus battandieri
Cytisus x praecox 'Warminster'
Deutzia gracilis
Escallonia 'Iveyi'
Eucryphia x intermedia 'Rostrevor'
Eucryphia x nymanensis 'Nymansay'
Itea ilicifolia
Jasminum humile 'Revolutum'
Lavandula 'Helmsdale'
Lavandula angustifolia 'Munstead'
Lavandula angustifolia 'Hidcote Pink'
Lavandula angustifolia 'Hidcote'

Lavandula angustifolia 'Lady'
Lavandula angustifolia 'Loddon Pink'
Lavandula angustifolia 'Nana Alba'
Lavandula angustifolia 'Rosea'
Lavandula angustifolia 'Royal Purple'
Lavandula stoechas 'Papillon'
Lavandula stoechas 'Fathead'
Lavandula stoechas 'Kew Red'
Lavandula stoechas 'Rocky Road'
Myrtus communis
Myrtus communis subsp tarentina
Olearia ilicifolia
Philadelphus 'Beauclerk'
Philadelphus 'Belle Etoile'
Philadelphus 'Manteau d'Hermine'
Pittosporum tenuifolium 'Silver Queen'
Rosa 'Alec's Red'
Rosa 'Alexander'
Rosa 'Bantry Bay'
Rosa 'Blanche Double de Coubert'
Rosa 'Blessings'
Rosa 'Boule de Neige'
Rosa 'Buff Beauty'
Rosa 'Cardinal de Richelieu'
Rosa 'Charles de Mills'
Rosa 'Chinatown'
Rosa 'Congratulations'
Rosa 'Cornelia'
Rosa 'Felicia'
Rosa 'Fragrant Cloud'
Rosa 'Happy Anniversary'
Rosa 'Heritage'
Rosa 'Ice Cream'
Rosa 'Ingrid Bergman'

Rosa 'Just Joey'
Rosa 'L.D. Braithwaite'
Rosa 'Louise Odier'
Rosa 'Madame Pierre Oger'
Rosa 'Many Happy Returns'
Rosa 'Mary Rose'
Rosa 'Queen of Denmark'
Rosa 'Rosa de Rescht'
Rosa 'Roseraie de L'Hay'
Rosa 'Royal William'
Rosa 'Ruby Wedding'
Rosa 'Silver Jubilee'
Rosa 'Surrey'
Rosa 'Sussex'
Rosa 'Sweet Dream'
Rosa moyesii 'Geranium'
Rosa rugosa 'Rubra'
Rosa xanthina 'Canary Bird'
Rubus odoratus
Sambucus nigra 'Black Beauty'
Spartium junceum

Climbers
Actinidia kolomikta
Bougainvillea 'Raspberry Ice'
Cobaea scandens
Jasminum beesianum
Jasminum officinale
Jasminum officinale 'Clotted Cream'
Jasminum x stephanense
Lonicera japonica 'Halliana'
Lonicera japonica 'Halls Prolific'
Lonicera japonica var. repens
Lonicera periclymenum 'Belgica'
Lonicera periclymenum 'Serotina'
Lonicera x americana
Lonicera x heckrottii 'Goldflame'
Mandevilla x amoena 'Alice du Pont'
Passiflora caerulea 'Constance Elliot'
Rosa 'Alberic Barbier'
Rosa 'Albertine'
Rosa 'Aloha'
Rosa 'Bantry Bay'
Rosa 'Breath of Life'
Rosa 'Climbing Iceberg'
Rosa 'Compassion'
Rosa 'Emily Gray'

Rubus odoratus

Rosa 'Bantry Bay'

include cistus and escallonia; some can be camphorous, such as lavender, perovskia, and eucalyptus; while others are simply pungent, as with rue and ribes.

Siting fragrant plants
Aromatic plants are usually best positioned near places where you sit and relax. This could be in containers on the patio, by garden

seats or by windows and doors, so that the scent wafts into the house during a warm day or evening. If you have a table and chairs for outdoor eating in the summer months, you

Summer scent: *Lavandula angustifolia*

Autumn- and winter-scented shrubs and climbers to try

Autumn Shrubs
Camellia sasanqua 'Narumigata'
Clerodendrum trichotomum 'Fargesii'
Jasminum nudiflorum
Mahonia x *media* 'Lionel Fortescue'
Mahonia x *media* 'Winter Sun'

Winter Shrubs
Abeliophyllum distichum
Chimonanthus praecox
Chimonanthus praecox 'Grandiflorus'
Chimonanthus praecox 'Luteus'
Coronilla valentia subsp. *glauca*
Coronilla valentia subsp. *glauca* 'Citrina'
Daphne bholua 'Jacqueline Postill'
Daphne odora 'Aureomarginata'
Hamamelis mollis
Hamamelis x *intermedia* 'Arnold Promise'
Hamamelis x *intermedia* 'Diane'

Hamamelis x *intermedia* 'Jelena'
Hamamelis x *intermedia* 'Pallida'
Hamamelis x *intermedia* 'Moonlight'
Lonicera fragrantissima
Lonicera x *purpusii* 'Winter Beauty'
Mahonia japonica 'Bealei'
Mahonia x *media* 'Buckland'
Sarcococca confusa
Skimmia x *confusa* 'Kew Green'
Viburnum x *bodnantense* 'Dawn'
Viburnum x *bodnantense* 'Charles Lamont'

Winter Climbers
Clematis cirrhosa 'Freckles'
Clematis cirrhosa var. *balearica*

may want to grow shrubs in containers so that you can site them nearby on the patio.

Fragrant foliage

Scent is not limited to the flowers of course, as several plants offer wonderfully aromatic foliage, including many herbs such as thyme, rosemary and bay. And not to be forgotten is the citrus-rich smell of lemon verbena (*Aloysia triphylla*).

In some cases, as with flowers, warmth brings out the fragrance, although in most cases it is necessary to crush the leaves or stems so that their aroma is released.

With scented foliage plants, it is best to site them near to a path so that you can run your fingers through them as you walk.

It is easy to run away with the idea of a fragrant garden. However, caution should be taken when planting, as some scents will vie with each other for attention, overwhelm their companions and not allow you to appreciate their individual fragrances. For this reason, when you are planning your purchases, try to smell your plants before you buy them, as some may not be as scented as you wish. Another reason for trying out scents, either in the garden or the plant nursery, is simply that you may not like the fragrance.

Summer fragrance: *Philadelphus*

Autumn: *Mahonia* x *media* 'Lionel Fortescue'

Winter fragrance: *Hamamelis mollis*

Using shrubs and climbers

Shrubs and climbers can be used in a number of different ways, depending on the effect you are trying to create. Over the following pages their various roles and uses are explored. Unlike bedding and perennials, the biggest challenge when selecting shrubs and climbers is to be able to visualize what they might look like five or ten years later and how you can take this into account when planning a new border.

Shrubs and climbers are permanent additions to the garden's overall design and so extra care must be given to placement and combinations. Many can be used to make strong points of focus in the garden that can draw the eye and add impact to the overall design, while others provide a much more subtle, but no less important, role as building blocks in the border that offer a suitable contrast to their more flamboyant neighbours. Bear in mind both the ultimate size and growth rates of the various shrubs and climbers you choose to combine in a single border to ensure that they continue to complement each other and the rest of the garden over time.

Even the most beautiful plants can benefit by being displayed well. Showing off plants relies on planting them in sympathy with their surroundings so that both landscape and plant are in harmony.

Specimens and focal points

There are many shrubs and climbers that make superb specimens and focal points in the garden. Some provide a constant point of reference, with their bold outline or foliage colour, while others offer a seasonal splash when in flower or take on autumnal hues when the blooms have finished.

Positioning specimens

The most attractively designed gardens use plants and structures to guide the visitor and casual viewer. Eye-catching features help to draw the attention to a particular spot or vista, and can also achieve the opposite by distracting the eye from less aesthetically pleasing aspects, such as a vegetable patch or a bed of spent daffodils.

A series of well-spaced and carefully positioned points of focus lead the eye around the garden and even subconsciously entice the visitor to explore further.

Good plants to try

Flowers	Bold foliage
Buddleja	Eucalyptus
Camellia	Fatsia
Carpenteria	Hedera
Ceanothus	Mahonia
Cistus	Paulownia
Clematis	Philadephus
Cytisus	Phormium
Forsythia	Sambucus
Genista	Vitis
Helianthemum	Yucca
Hibiscus	
Hydrangea	Autumn colour
Magnolia	Acer
Paeonia	Amelanchier
Rhododendron	Berberis
Syringa	Cornus
	Cotinus
	Cotoneaster
	Euonymus
	Rhus
	Viburnum

Create a blend of colours by planting different varieties of roses together. Here, the lovely soft red of *Rosa* 'American Pillar' and the gentle pink of *Rosa* 'Kew Rambler' grow up a supporting structure. Another growing season will see them mingling together at the top of the post.

When choosing a specimen shrub or climber, your first consideration should be its backdrop. If it is to stand out it needs to contrast in some way with its surroundings – by either its height, colour, form or texture. However, don't be tempted to overdo the contrast, as the specimen could result in totally dominating the scene, rather than simply drawing the eye. If the attractive feature is only temporary, you should consider what the plant will look like when it is out of season. This is particularly important for specimens in prominent positions, such as next to the patio or set into a lawn.

When positioning a focal point or specimen, consider where it will be viewed from: windows overlooking the garden, the patio and seating areas or the entrance into the garden, for example. Specimens and focal points should be at home in their surroundings. The style of the plant should not be at odds with its neighbours, and should look like an intrinsic part of the overall design, rather than an after-thought. It should be sited so that it looks prominent among nearby features but not isolated from them.

Shape, colour and texture

Some plants have such a dramatic shape or outline that they provide a permanent focal point throughout the year. Others undergo dramatic makeovers with the changing of the seasons and so can be used to great effect within a garden design. You can even use seasonal specimens in pots and position them in different parts of the garden to change the point of focus from month to month, thereby constantly altering how the garden is viewed.

Bear in mind that colours vary in the way they are perceived. Hot, vibrant colours, such as red, orange and yellow, make a bigger impact on the eye and so the plant seems bigger, closer and larger than it really is. Conversely, cooler blues, greens and greys are more recessive to the eye and so have the opposite effect.

Texture also has an impact. Although much more subtle than using colours, plants with bold or glossy leaves create a more intimate atmosphere, while those plants with finely cut and matt foliage can help create the illusion of space.

Position trellis above a wall and grow a vigorous climbing rose to provide privacy as well as a beautiful backdrop to a border.

An enticing vista has been created by training *Rosa* 'Seagull' to drape over a hanging structure made of rope to provide a stunning focal point.

Beds and borders

Shrubs and climbers are the building blocks of the garden, providing a permanent framework that holds the design together in harmony. Try to use them in carefully considered groups rather than dotting them around individually. This will ensure that they provide structure and backbone to the overall design.

Using shrubs in borders

The usual way shrubs are used in the garden is in beds and borders — either in a special, dedicated shrubbery or combined with other types of plants, such as perennials and bulbs.

Shrubs that are being added to an existing display are the easiest to select because you already have a fixed reference point provided by the surrounding plants. You might want to choose a new addition to add height, form, texture or seasonal interest to the existing planting

The secret to planting a beautiful border is to design it with layers of colour and different textures, as well as planting shrubs and climbers that will grow at different heights.

The addition of the vibrant red perennial Maltese Cross (*Lychnis chalcedonica*) makes this combination of foliage shrubs come alive.

scheme, or it could be that you just want a more anonymous border plant to use as a background filler that doesn't upset the display.

New border planting

When planning a new shrub border from scratch, the options are seemingly endless. Unless you have a clear idea of what you want to achieve, you could spend a lot of time trying to make up your mind about the best plan to follow.

First-time planters and old gardening hands alike can be a bit nervous about border design, but a simple and effective method is to use a graduated growing scheme. Select small plants for the front of the border, medium-sized ones in the centre and tall shrubs at the back. This provides a slope effect, allowing the plants to be seen in all their glory.

Garden centres and plant nurseries can be very seductive places. One common pitfall is buying all your favourite shrubs and then trying to fit them into a border plan when you get home. This will inevitably end in disappointment. It is far better to decide what effect you are trying to achieve before you buy the plants and then draw up a list of potential candidates for each position in the border.

Factors that you need to take into account include the heights, spreads and growth rates of the larger specimen shrubs that are to go at the back. Also consider the same factors for the smaller ones that will go near the front. However, try not to over-regiment the border by size as this will look unnatural. As a rule of thumb, don't select any shrub that grows taller than the width of the border.

Next to consider are the foliage colours and textures of the plants on your shortlist. Successful planting is achieved when there is a combining of contrasting elements that provide a dramatic appearance or, conversely, a blend of similar elements that provide a soothing, mellow affect.

Combining plants

Combine evergreen and deciduous varieties in the ratio of about two to one, to give a continuity in the display, and mix different forms and outlines for added interest. Finally, consider the seasonal variations, including flowering periods, changes in foliage, berries, bark and scent.

Good plants to try

Backbone	Kolkwitzia
Abelia	Lavatera
Berberis	Leycesteria
Callicarpa	Perovskia
Carpenteria	Rubus
Ceanothus	Sambucus
Cotoneaster	Syringa
Deutzia	Tamarix
Erica	
Escallonia	**Dome shapes**
Euonymus	Buxus
Fuchsia	Calluna
Genista	Cotoneaster
Hebe	Daboecia
Helianthemum	Daphne
Hydrangea	Erica
Hypericum	Euonymus
Kerria	Gaultheria
Lavatera	Genista
Lavandula	Hebe
Pachysandra	Helianthemum
Potentilla	Hypericum
Ribes	Lavandula
Skimmia	Potentilla
Spiraea	Santolina
Weigela	Senecio
Fountains	**Spiky plants**
Buddleja	Cordyline
Itea	Phormium
Kerria	Yucca

The design of a bed or border will be largely influenced by the shape and size of the garden as well as the effect you are trying to achieve. Unless you are aiming to create a very formal design, most borders look best with sweeping curves rather than fussy shapes or sharp corners and straight lines.

If there is space, you may allow some of the border to form a peninsula so that part of the garden is hidden from view. This achieves the effect of sub-dividing the design and creating a sense of mystery. However, in smaller gardens it is usually best to keep the centre of the plot uncluttered, either laid to lawn or some form of hard landscaping. The deeper the bed, the more plants it will be able to accommodate, but try to avoid very deep beds over 4m (13ft) as they will be more difficult to maintain. On the other hand, very narrow beds (less than 1m/3ft) limit the scope for planting design.

Layering borders

Most borders can be designed in layers. The back layer should comprise most of the tallest plants: wall shrubs and climbers. It is best to choose plants that will provide an attractive, if somewhat plain, backdrop when out of season, so that they can set off the plants in the foreground to better effect.

If the plants are being used to cover ugly walls, fences or other structures, try to choose ones with evergreen foliage so that the disguise lasts all year round. Back-of-the-border plants shouldn't spread too much, otherwise they will tend to dominate the design. Avoid plants that need a lot of maintenance because pruning, spraying and deadheading will be more difficult to carry out in this area.

The low-growing bright blue flowers and dark foliage of *Lithodora diffusa* combine with *Salix repens* for spectacular ground cover.

The front layer should comprise most of the smallest plants. The job of this layer of planting is to provide a transition from the border to the lawn or path that runs along the front. If you choose the right plants, they can also be used to cover up the shortcomings of more spectacular but short-lived displays provided by plants behind. The middle layer of plants should offer most of the seasonal highlights, with colourful flowers at different times of the year and dramatic autumn colours to sustain the display.

Choose a few taller plants to break the regimented effect and give the design a more natural feel. You may prefer to choose plants that flower together in the most spectacular way, or combine plants that flower at different times to create a longer period of interest.

If space is restricted, try to choose plants that offer at least two seasonal features, as well as plants that flower for weeks or months, rather than days, so that the border can continue looking good for a longer period of time.

The silvery leaves of the shrub *Elaeagnus* 'Quicksilver' provide a beautiful foil for the showy flowers of *Erysimum* 'Bowles' Mauve'.

Using shapes for structure

A border simply made up of layers can be attractive, but often the effect seems to lack impact and contrast. For this reason it a good idea to take some time to consider what role each individual plant is to play in the border so that you can combine them to their best effect.

A few will be focal points that act as anchors to the overall display; other plants will be there to provide a backdrop and act as a foil for the more showy plants. They also help define boundaries and are essential in-between fillers that add structure and are generally restful on the eye. You can only have so many drama queens that provide flower power, eye-catching foliage and colourful berries or winter stems in your border, so don't underestimate the value of the less showy shrubs.

Making shapes

Another factor essential to consider is how all the different shapes of your chosen plants will work with each other, as well as the overall appearance of the border. For example, tall and columnar shapes

draw the eye like living exclamation marks, while low-spreading shapes have the opposite effect. Add a sense of movement and gracefulness to a static border using fountain shapes, such as grasses. Further back, try weeping shapes, which tend to harmonize with their neighbours, or spiky shapes for added drama.

To get an impression of how these different shapes will work together, draw an outline of the plants and then cut them out and move them around as if you were designing a stage set until you achieve a combination that appeals to you.

Use the lists on the previous page and the opposite page to help you decide which plants to try. Bear in mind that the plants will grow and change shape over time, so ensure that you give them enough space to spread and develop their true outline. If you don't want it to spread, choose plants that will take well to being pruned.

Year-round interest

Unless you are trying to create a seasonal splash, try to combine plants to provide interest throughout the year. In a small garden it is particularly important that every plant contributes to the display during more than one season. Also, make the most of available space by under-planting shrubs with ground cover and bulbs that flower at other times.

The easiest way to visualize how these different plants will work together is to make a calendar of the plants and their main periods of interest. Use coloured pencils to indicate when their decorative features are on show so that you can see how the colours combine. You can also check how they overlap to achieve continuity in the display.

When planning your beds and borders, try to include a few plants that will add a bold splash at certain times of the year so that the border

A mix of the pink *Rosa* 'Zéphirine Drouhin', the purple *Clematis* 'Lady Betty Balfour' and the large-leaved *Vitis coignetiae* grow happily together in a border.

Great border design combines plants of different heights, textures and colours together to make a pleasing, unifying whole.

design ebbs and flows with the seasons. Equally, don't overlook the value of evergreens and variegated evergreens, as these will provide reliable winter interest as well as a constant setting for the more flamboyant jewels that sparkle at other times.

Using climbers in borders

Climbers are versatile plants that can be used in all three layers of the border design. At the back, they are a space-saving way of covering walls and fences (*see also* page 72); when planted in the middle, they can be trained over structures to add height to borders (*see* page 76) as well as through established plants (*see* page 78). For the front of the border, there are many climbers that will scramble over the ground between shrubs to provide attractive, weed-suppressing groundcover (*see* page 80). Climbers grown across the ground are also a useful way of disguising eyesores such as manhole covers, immovable rubble and old tree stumps.

Climbers for all situations

There are climbers and wall shrubs that can be grown in nearly every position in the garden. They not only take up very little space, but allow you take advantage of vertical surfaces that would otherwise remain bare. Perhaps the most challenging aspect is walls that face north and east, which remain cool in summer and cold in winter – bitterly so if exposed to northerly gales. The soil is usually dry because the wall casts a rain shadow over the area from the majority of rain-bearing weather systems that move in from the south and west.

Fences are less of a problem because water percolates naturally through the soil under the fence. However, walls do have the advantage in that they store warmth from the sun and improve a microclimate for the climbers and wall shrubs attached to it. Walls are also permanent structures and can generally carry a greater weight, which can be an issue over time as the plant matures and grows.

Shrubs and climbers for a north aspect must be very tough, able to cope with constant shade as well as biting winds during the winter months. Easterly aspects get more sunlight, but the plants must be able to withstand rapid thaws on sunny mornings after a severe frost. Shrubs to try for these planting positions include Japanese flowering quince (*Chaenomeles*), climbing hydrangea (*Hydrangea petiolaris*), *Cotoneaster horizontalis*, *Garrya elliptica*, winter jasmine (*Jasminum nudiflorum*) and firethorn (*Pyracantha*), which are all as tough as old boots and provide valuable seasonal interest.

Climbers to try include varieties of *Clematis macropetala*, *C. montana*, *C. orientalis* or *C. tangutica*; ivy such as *Hedera colchica* 'Dentata Variegata'; and Virginia creeper (*Parthenocissus henryana*). Easterly vertical surfaces that get some sun can be improved with the planting of climbing and rambler roses such as 'Albertine', 'Madame Alfred Carrière' and 'Maigold', as well as *Schizophragma hydrangeoides* and *Vitis coignetiae*.

Seasonal sensations

Colourful		
Acer	Hibiscus	Choisya
Amelanchier	Hippophae	Convolvulus
Azalea	Magnolia	Elaeagnus
Berberis	Nandina	Escallonia
Camellia	Olearia	Euonymus
Chaenomeles	Paeonia	Fatsia
Cistus	Pieris	Griselinia
Cornus	Pyracantha	Hebe
Cotinus	Rhododendron	Mahonia
Cytisus	Rhus	Myrtus
Enkianthus	Romneya	Olearia
Eucryphia	Rosa	Osmanthus
Exochorda		Pachysandra
Forsythia	**Evergreens**	Photinia
Fothergilla	Aucuba	Pittosporum
Genista	Azalea	Pyracantha
Hamamelis	Camellia	Rhododendron
	Ceanothus	Skimmia

Shrubs and climbers in containers

Many shrubs and climbers make excellent container plants and can be used to transform a patio, decorate a bleak wall or extend the range of plants you can grow in your garden. However, it is essential to choose the right plants, container and compost (soil mix) to ensure success.

Why grow in containers?

Growing shrubs and climbers in permanent containers allows you to grow plants that otherwise would not thrive in your garden soil. For example, if your soil is chalky, you can grow acid-loving shrubs such as pieris and azaleas in containers filled with a lime-rich ericaceous compost (soil mix). Similarly, plants that are too tender to survive outside in the garden during the winter months can be grown in containers and given protection or moved somewhere frost-free during the coldest weather.

Growing in containers also allows you to keep your plants where they'll get noticed so that you are able to see their delicate or intricately marked foliage and flowers close up. In addition, shrubs in containers make excellent mobile focal points,

Containers allow you to combine shrubs for colour and texture, such as this lavender and *Euonymus fortunei* 'Emerald Gaiety'.

Fuschias cope with being potted very well and make beautiful container plants. Tender varieties can be overwintered inside.

If cut to the base each year, *Sambucus racemosa* 'Plumosa Aurea' will produce a stunning display of colourful foliage.

as they can be moved into a prominent position when they are looking their best. Once their season has finished, place them in a less noticeable position. You can also use pots to grow living screens to provide natural cover and privacy on the patio when you need it. Container-grown plants are also ideal for taking the limelight away from fading bedding plants.

As the seasons and the sun's position changes, you can move your plant to a sunnier or shady spot to prolong its flowering.

Choosing suitable plants

Before you choose the plants for your containers, you need to consider where they are to be positioned. If exposed to wind and cold on a roof garden, say, your choice of suitable candidates will be different than for a pot destined for a sheltered corner on a sunny patio. Unless the container is to be moved under cover in winter, it is the conditions during the coldest months that are most crucial.

All container plants need to be able to cope with a restricted root growth, periods of drought between waterings and exposure to wind. Choose something that will look good for most of the year, either with attractive evergreen foliage and a neat silhouette, or a deciduous candidate that has attractive bark or outline when out of leaf. Slow-growing Japanese acers are a good example: many have colourful emerging spring foliage that is decorative all summer, before the leaves turn brilliant shades in autumn and then fall to reveal an appealing tracery of stems that last all winter long.

Growing tips

If you want to grow shrubs and climbers in pots for a long period, the pot will need to be quite large. Choose one with a circumference of at least 45cm (18in), as this will hold a sufficient amount of compost (soil mix) to allow for good root development. It will also provide a buffer against problems such as winter cold and inconsistent watering and feeding. The container also needs to be frost proof and should have drainage holes. The drainage holes should be covered with crocks and then about 3cm (1in) of stones or other drainage material can be added on top. Fill up the rest of the pot with either a loam-based compost (soil mix), which is suitable for most shrubs and climbers, or a lime-rich ericaceous compost (soil mix) for acid-loving plants, such as rhododendrons and camellias.

Watering pots

Plants in containers tend to dry out much quicker than those planted in the garden. For this reason, watering is critical. Expect to water at least once a week in spring and summer (maybe daily during warm spells) and occasionally during dry spells at other times. Use collected rainwater for acid-loving plants if you live in hard-water areas.

It is important to remember that frequent watering will wash the plant food out of the soil and the plant will use up the nutrients in the

Shrubs benefit from being grown in pots if the garden soil is unsuitable. Acid-loving plants such as rhododendrons (*above*) can be successfully grown in pots in ericaceous compost.

limited amount of soil you have in the pot quite quickly. For this reason, regular feeding is essential. Do this by either inserting slow-release fertilizer pellets, which will last a whole season, into the compost (soil mix) in spring or add liquid feed to its weekly watering.

Good plants to try

Shrubs for containers
Acer japonica
Aucuba
Azalea (acid-loving)
Camellia (acid-loving)
Choisya
Convolvulus cneorum
Elaeagnus
Euonymus
Hebe pinguifolia 'Pagei'
Hydrangea macrophylla
Lavandula
Magnolia stellata
Nandina domestica
Pieris (acid-loving)

Phlomis fruticosa
Phormium tenax
Rhododendron (acid-loving)
Rosa, miniature
Santolina chamaecyparissus
Skimmia japonica 'Rubella' (acid-loving)
Viburnum davidii
Vinca
Weigela florida

Climbers for containers
Clematis
Hedera
Jasminum officinale
Passiflora

Pot-grown plants have their growth curtailed. This *Cornus mas* 'Aureoelegantissima' could grow to 6m (20ft) in garden soil.

Fragrant walkways and entrances

Climbers and shrubs are an ideal
way of adding colour and scent to
the air around a path or entrance,
making what would normally be a
functional area into a delightful
visual and aromatic experience.

Scented climbers

You can make garden visitors feel
really welcome by planting the
entrance with deliciously scented
varieties of climbers. Like other parts
of the garden, the plants you choose
will depend on how much sun the
area gets, as well as how exposed it is
to buffeting winds. The growing
space available as well as the size of
the support are also important
factors to consider.

In sunny positions, there are many
options. An early sweet-vanilla
fragrance can be provided by *Clematis
armandii* cultivars such as 'Snowdrift'
or 'Apple Blossom', followed by the
familiar and appealing scent of
summer jasmine, which will last for
much of the summer. Another
jasmine-scented climber for a well-lit
spot is *Trachelospermum jasminoides*,
which bears its creamy flowers from
mid-summer onwards. Alternatively,
you could try the spicy vanilla
fragrance of the chocolate vine
(*Akebia quinata*), which thrives in full
sun or partial shade, and bears its
unusual maroon-coloured flowers
during early summer.

If you have space, you could try
the wonderful fresh aroma of *Wisteria
sinensis* cultivars, which put on a
spectacular display at the same time.

Scented roses

If roses are your preference, there are
quite a number you could try. 'New
Dawn' offers a summer-long display
of pale pink flowers with a sweet
aroma as well as attractive foliage,
while 'Gloire de Dijon' is peachier in

While the vivid red flowers of *Rosa* 'American Pillar' attempt to hog the limelight, the delicate
Clematis 'Alba Luxurians' manages to make a highlighting contrast.

Good plants to try

Scented climbers
Actinidia chinensis
Akebia quinata
Clematis (many species/cultivars)
Jasminum officinale
Lonicera (many species/cultivars)
Rosa (many species/cultivars)
Trachelospermum jasminoides
Wisteria

Fragrant shrubs
Ceanothus
Chimonanthus praecox
Choisya ternata
Clerodendrum trichotomum
Corylopsis pauciflora
Cytisus battandieri
Daphne x burkwoodii
Daphne mezereum
Daphne odora
Elaeagnus x ebbingei
Lonicera fragrantissima
Osmanthus delavayi
Ribes odoratum
Sarcococca confusa
Syringa vulgaris
Viburnum x bodnantense
Viburnum carlesii
Viburnum fragrans

colour and has a rich tea fragrance. However, you may prefer near-thornless roses such as the very fragrant 'Blush Rambler' or the creamy-white aromatic 'Madame Alfred Carrière', which will flower reliably in sun or shade.

Insects and bees

Honeysuckles are another option, offering their heady, intoxicating fragrance wherever they are grown. Try combining the early red- and purple-flowered 'Belgica' with the later purple, red and cream blooms of 'Serotina' for a continuous display from late spring to mid-autumn. Honeysuckles are prone to aphid attack and so tend to drip

sticky honeydew over everything – including paths, seats and doorsteps. For this reason, you might prefer to site the plants at the back of a nearby border instead.

Also, all scented flowers will tend to attract hoards of pollinating insects – including bees – that might become a nuisance if they are lured by plants near a doorway or window.

Fragrant shrubs all year

Bring in the New Year with style by planting the very sweetly scented, yellow-flowered *Chimonanthus praecox*, following on with *Daphne odora* and *Sarcococca confusa*. Later on, add a bit of spice and zest in mid-spring with the aptly named Mexican orange blossom (*Choisya ternata*), followed by the heady perfume of the lilac varieties. For a mid-summer treat, add the honey-scented *Ceanothus* 'Gloire de Versaille', with the pungent *Clerodendrum trichotomum* following on. Next, blend in the

Golden hop (*Humulus lupulus* 'Aureus') and honeysuckle (*Lornicera periclymenum*).

autumn-flowering and sweetly fragrant *Elaeagnus x ebbingei*, and complete the year with the delicious perfume of *Viburnum fragrans*.

During the summer, the fragrance of the roses tumbling over the archway will intermingle with the scent of newly mown grass, providing the perfect garden perfume.

Hedging and screening

There are a number of shrubs that make excellent hedging plants, and which you choose should depend on how big you want it to grow and the amount of time you want to spend keeping it in shape.

Choosing a hedge

The choice of hedging is far wider than the ubiquitous privet. You can choose from flowering, fragrant and fruiting ones, to dwarf, herb and topiary hedges. However, before you choose a variety that meets your requirements, you can reduce the options available by asking yourself the following three questions:
• Do you want a deciduous or evergreen hedge? Evergreen hedges provide constant cover throughout the year, but are more susceptible to winter cold and some soil-borne diseases. Deciduous hedges offer a changing backdrop and are more wildlife friendly.

Before purchasing plants, bear in mind that deciduous shrubs will drop their leaves in the autumn, so if privacy is your main consideration for a hedge, you would be better off choosing an evergreen shrub, as they provide good all-year screening.
• Do you want a formal or flowering hedge? Formal hedges provide a neat backdrop and complete privacy, but require regular trimming. Informal flowering hedges require little maintenance, but take up more space and aren't as dense.
• Do you want it to grow quickly? Quick-growing hedges provide privacy in a short period of time but will require more trimming once they have reached the desired height.

You also need to consider whether you want a secure boundary or simply a decorative screen. Hedging plants that make dense growth and are covered in vicious thorns make the best impenetrable boundary hedges, while evergreen hedges are an excellent backdrop for other garden features. Available space will also affect the choice you make. Most hedges occupy a strip at least 60cm (2ft) wide, while a few, including

A formal beech (*Fagus sylvatica*) hedge makes a neat garden boundary. Beech is a slow-growing plant and needs little attention.

beech and privet, can be kept half this width with regular trimming. Also consider that evergreen hedges tend to cast deep shade so that few plants will grow at the base on the north-facing side.

Wildlife hedges

Hedges can provide nesting and roosting sites for birds, and their flowers and berries are vital food sources for insects and butterflies.

Although all hedges offer some benefit to garden birds and other wildlife, a mixture of deciduous species, such as beech, hawthorn, hazel, holly and hornbeam, would be a good choice. Not only will they provide shelter and safe breeding sites, but if you get the mixture right, the hedge can also offer a year-

Low-growing hedges can be successfully made out of lavender bushes. Here, two rows of lavender border a narrow path. As you brush past, the aroma is spectacular.

Buying hedging

Deciduous hedging plants are usually sold as barerooted plants in bundles, while evergreen varieties are available as young plants in small pots. Even though you can get much larger plants in containers, you will save a lot of money if you buy smaller ones. Such plants, about 30–45cm (12–18in) high, will establish themselves more quickly and soon catch up with the larger versions. Shop around, as prices can vary considerably between suppliers.

Good plants to try

Evergreen hedges
Aucuba japonica 'Variegata'
Berberis darwinii
Buxus sempervirens
Chamaecyparis lawsoniana
Elaeagnus pungens
Escallonia rubra var. macrantha
Griselinia littorialis
Hebe pinguifolia
Lavandula
Lonicera nitida
Olearia x haastii
Prunus laurocerasus
Pyracantha rogersiana
Taxus baccata
Thuja plicata
Viburnum tinus

Deciduous hedges
Berberis thunbergii
Carpinus betulus
Chaenomeles japonica
Corylus maxima 'Purpurea'
Crataegus monogyna
Fagus sylvatica
Forsythia x intermedia
Fuchsia magellanica
Ligustrum ovalifolium
Philadelphus coronarius
Potentilla fruticosa
Ribes sanguineum
Rosa rugosa
Weigela florida

Flowering hedges
Camellia x williamsii
Chaenomeles japonica
Escallonia rubra var. macrantha
Forsythia x intermedia
Fuchsia magellanica
Hebe pinguifolia
Lavandula
Philadelphus coronarius
Potentilla fruticosa
Pyracantha rogersiana
Ribes sanguineum
Rosa rugosa
Weigela florida

Hedges in shade
Aucuba japonica 'Variegata'
Buxus sempervirens
Chaenomeles japonica
Euonymus japonicus
Ilex aquifolium
Lonicera nitida
Taxus baccata
Viburnum tinus

Thorny hedges
Berberis darwinii
Berberis thunbergii
Crataegus monogyna
Olearia x haastii
Pyracantha rogersiana

round larder of food for birds, butterflies and other beneficial insects looking for sustenance.

Garden dividers

Hedges can also be used to sub-divide a garden or provide a neat edging to beds and borders. Although any type of hedge can be used in a large garden, for small gardens slow-growing, dwarf forms are best, such as the evergreen box, grey-leaved flowering lavender, potentilla, hebe and the red-leaved *Berberis thunbergii* 'Atropurpurea Nana'.

Planting hedges

Often, hedges are expected to thrive when planted in poor soil – or even subsoil dug up during house construction or renovation. Many hedges are planted too close to, or underneath, trees, making it difficult for them to get their fair share of nutrients from the soil as they compete with larger roots.

Preferably, hedges should be planted in spring or autumn when the plants are resting. They can be planted in exactly the same way as

PLANTING HEDGES

1 Start by digging a trench where you wish to plant the hedge. Turn over the soil and dig in some manure or compost (soil mix).

2 Fix a line taut across the centre of the trench and lay out the plants at regular intervals so they have equal growing space.

3 Remove the plants from their pots and position them in the trench, checking that they are accurately spaced.

4 Fill in the trench, firming the soil around each plant. Water throughly and mulch with well-rotted organic matter.

shrubs, but it is easier to excavate a trench along the line of the hedge, rather than digging individual planting holes.

The autumn before planting, dig a strip 60–90cm (2–3ft) wide, double-digging down its entire length. For less vigorous hedges and step-over hedges, you can get away with single digging. Plant each hedging plant as you would for shrubs, using a taut line as a guide to keep the hedge straight.

Hedges can be planted in single or staggered double rows. Unless you want a very thick, impenetrable hedge for security reasons, a single row should be sufficient. Planting distances depend on the vigour of your chosen hedge (see Hedge planting distances chart, below).

High or low maintenance?

Another essential consideration is how much time you are prepared to spend on keeping your hedge looking good. Formal hedges will need to be pruned several times a year if they are to remain attractive.

If you prefer a low-maintenance option, you would do better if you went for an informal, more natural-looking hedge. For the more ambitious gardener, topiary hedges look fantastic, but you really must be realistic. Are your pruning and trimming skills up to it?

Hedges should be cut in mid-summer and mid-winter, although if they need a little tidying up in between seasons, you can do this safely at any time. If more severe pruning is required, it is best done in late autumn.

The most common mistake when pruning is not cutting the plant back far enough, or cutting it too narrow at the base. This is especially true for young, growing plants. This condition becomes worse as the top grows and shades the lower portions. Cutting back is the only solution.

When to prune evergreen hedges

Name	when to prune
Berberis	late spring
Buxus sempervirens	early summer
Calluna	after flowering
Chamaecyparis lawsoniana	early summer and early autumn
Erica	after flowering
Escallonia	early summer
Euonymus	mid-summer
Griselinia	early summer
Ilex	mid-summer
Lavandula	early autumn
Ligustrum	late spring and late summer
Lonicera nitida	early summer
Prunus lusitanica	early summer
Rosmarinus	late-summer
Taxus	mid-summer
Thuja	mid-summer
x Cupressocyparis leylandii	early summer

Pruning and feeding your hedge

If you begin trimming hedges when they are first planted, they will respond well to shaping and training. Cut a few centimetres off the top of a hedge plant as soon as it has been planted to help form healthy, bushy plants. Try to shape the hedge so that it is wider at the bottom than it is at the top. This will allow sunlight to reach the lower leaves. Follow the steps on the right for maintaining hedges – these instructions will ensure you get an even-looking side, top and edge to your hedge.

Fast-growing hedges may require trimming two or three times a season to keep their shape. It is unwise to allow a hedge to grow rapidly to its desired height before you prune, as it will develop a thick top and open sides.

Prune your hedge during the active growing season, but only give it a light trimming at the end of the

Hedge planting distances

Deciduous hedges	vigour	planting distance
Beech	medium	60cm (2ft)
Hawthorn	medium	30cm (1ft)
Hornbeam	medium	45cm (18in)
Privet	high	25cm (10in)
Ribes	medium	45cm (18in)
Rose	medium	45cm (18in)
Evergreen hedges	vigour	planting distance
Berberis	medium	45cm (18in)
Box	low	25cm (10in)
Elaeagnus	low	45cm (18in)
Escallonia	medium	45cm (18in)
Holly	low	45cm (18in)
Lavender	low	30cm (1ft)
Laurel	medium	45cm (18in)
Lawson's cypress	high	45cm (18in)
Leyland cypress	high	60cm (2ft)
Photinia	medium	45cm (18in)
Portugal laurel	medium	45cm (18in)
Western red cedar	medium	45cm (18in)
Yew	low	45cm (18in)

growing season to keep your hedge looking good throughout the winter months. Evergreen hedges, such as juniper and cypress, should never be trimmed below the foliage because they will not grow back, so take care and clip only a few inches off the previous year's growth.

It should also be remembered that although your hedge may look like a room-divider or a screen, it is also a living shrub. Your hedge should be fed at least once a year, preferably in the early spring. Scatter the fertilizer along both sides of the hedge and work it well into the soil with a fork. A layer of mulch will help keep weeds at bay.

Good neighbours

The final factor to take into consideration when you are choosing a hedge is to take great care about where you site it. Will your hedge grow so big that it affects your neighbour's view, as well as their garden's light and shade? Do your research first, so you don't end up in a legal dispute, as a few unhappy owners of fast-growing *Leylandii* hedges have.

When buying your shrubs, choose those that will grow to the desired height – and no further. Planting a tall-maturing shrub where a short, informal hedge is desired creates unnecessary work.

Hedging alternatives

A solid barrier, such as a wall or fence, may seem like a good way to protect an exposed garden, but the wind is simply deflected over the top, creating damaging turbulence on the side that you are trying to protect. Hedges make excellent windbreaks because they filter the wind, rather than block it. However, you can also use other shrubs to achieve the same effect. Try tough, fast-growing shrubs such as berberis, viburnum, cotoneaster and elaeagnus in a mixed planting for a small garden, or combine un-pruned hedging plants such as laurel, photinia, holly and escallonia if there is enough space.

MAINTAINING HEDGES

1 Before you start trimming the hedge, lay down a cloth or plastic sheet under the area to make gathering up the clippings easier.

2 If you are using shears to trim the hedge, keep the blades flat against the plane of the hedge to achieve an even cut.

3 The top of a formal hedge looks neater if it is regularly trimmed flat. Stretch string against two poles to get an even cutting guide.

4 When cutting the top of a hedge, keep the blades flat. If it is a tall hedge, you will probably need steps to reach the top.

5 The job is done much quicker if you use a power trimmer – but things can go wrong much quicker, too. Always mind the cord.

6 Untidy growth on informal hedges is easier to trim to shape using secateurs (pruners). Large-leaved hedges are pruned this way.

Covering walls and fences

Climbers are an obvious choice for covering all types of vertical surfaces, from boundary fences to garage walls, but there are several wall shrubs that are worth considering, too.

Wall shrub or climber?

There are a number of factors to consider when choosing what to plant next to a particular wall or fence. The first is how much available space you have. Climbers generally require less border space than wall shrubs, but usually need a lot more wall space. So, for example, if you have a border under a window, a wall shrub would probably be the best option. But if you want to cover a large fence or wall in just a few seasons, there are quick-growing climbers that will fit the bill.

Some climbers also need to be given support, at least until they get established, whereas wall shrubs gradually cover the space with a framework of woody branches that are completely self-supporting. Different climbers hold on in

Climbing roses not only cover the walls well, but have the added bonus of lovely fragrance.

The combination of boundaries – the wooden fence supported on a low brick wall – is greatly softened in visual effect by an escallonia flowering hedge growing through it. The density of the hedge provides privacy and security.

different ways (see How climbers climb box, below). Twining climbers, such as the chocolate vine, need a support all the way up the vertical surface being covered, while self-clinging climbers, such as ivies, can scramble up the smoothest of surfaces without assistance.

Maintenance time can also vary. Most wall shrubs and some climbers need to be pruned annually to keep them neat and flowering well. If you want to avoid this, choose an easy-care variety. Furthermore, vigorous climbers that outgrow their allotted space may need trimming several times a year to keep them within bounds, so bear this in mind before you plant.

Planting next to walls and fences

The microclimate next to a vertical surface can be completely different to the surrounding garden, which offers a unique combination of challenges and opportunities. For

example, against a sheltered, south-facing wall you will be able to grow borderline hardy plants that wouldn't survive elsewhere. But to thrive, they will need to be able to cope with scorching summer days and water

How climbers climb

Different climbers cling on to their support in various ways. Some are self-clinging and are able to scramble up a vertical surface without any assistance. Ivies and climbing hydrangeas, for example, hold on to the wall or fence using modified roots along their stems that attach themselves to rough surfaces such as brick or wood. A few climbers, such as Virginia creeper, produce tiny suckers that will stick to any surface – even glass. Most climbers climb by twining stems (e.g. wisteria), leaf stalks (e.g. clematis) or tendrils (e.g. sweet peas) that literally wrap themselves around a support as the plant grows upwards.

Good plants to try for different aspects

South-facing aspect	North-facing aspect	East- or west-facing aspects
Acacia dealbata	Chaenomeles	Actinidia chinensis
Actinidia kolomikta	Clematis montana	Escallonia
Campsis grandiflora	Cotoneaster horizontalis	Holboellia coriacea
Carpenteria californica	Garrya elliptica	Humulus lupulus
Ceanothus	Hedera helix	Leptospermum
Cytisus battandieri	Hydrangea petiolaris	scoparium
Eccremocarpus scaber	Jasminum nudiflorum	Lonicera x tellmanniana
Fremontodendron	Parthenocissus	Myrtus communis
Hibiscus syriacus	Pyracantha	Phygelius capensis
Jasminum officinale		Ribes speciosum
Passiflora caerulea		Solanum crispum
Sollya heterophylla		Trachelospermum
Wisteria floribunda		jasminoides
		Vitis vinifera

Climbers and shrubs can help to soften the edges of brickwork and take the angularity away from modern structures.

shortages. On the other hand, plants on a north-facing wall will face the challenge offered by constant shade, cooler summers and colder winters than will be found in nearby borders.

Make sure you treat wooden fences and supports with preservative and repair loose mortar on walls before planting your chosen climber or wall shrub. Also, put up any supporting trellis, wires or netting at this stage. The soil at the base of walls and fences is usually dry and impoverished, so it needs to be improved before you plant by digging in plenty of well-rotted organic matter.

Making a feature

Although the standard advice is to put up trellis or wires as a support for climbers so that the trained plants eventually provide a complete cover-up, an alternative method is to use an attractively shaped trellis, such as a perspective panel, that creates the illusion of a tunnel. You can then train the climber tightly to the frame so that the overall shape is maintained. Not only is the trellis attractive in its own right, but the

eventual effect will be a living replica of the trellis and it will form an unusual and attractive garden feature all year round. This method works particularly well with small-leaved evergreen climbers such as ivies, and wall shrubs such as firethorns (Pyracantha). On a larger

scale, you can use twining climbers such as wisteria or a large-leaved ivy.

Another option is to create the pattern yourself using wires, so that the feature you design will fit the available space exactly. You can also design your structure to complement an existing feature in the architecture of the house or in a neighbouring part of the garden – helping to provide a linking theme to the garden's overall design.

Once established, most climbing roses like nothing better than to be given free rein over structures, weaving themselves in and out to face the sun.

Pergolas and arches

These structures make stunning garden features when covered in colourful climbers – and also provide the practical benefits of shade and privacy.

Using pergolas and arches

Pergolas and arches can be used in a variety of ways around the garden. Pergolas are ideal for providing a secluded hideaway halfway down the garden, or they can be combined with a sunny patio to create a shady retreat on hot sunny days.

Despite their size, they are also a handy design device for use in smaller gardens, where they can be positioned at an angle in a far corner to help disguise the boundary and create the illusion that the garden is bigger than it really is.

Arches have even more uses. Apart from framing an entrance over a gate or at the start of a garden path, they can also be used to highlight a particular feature, such as a bird bath or urn, to dramatically increase its impact. Similarly, if you have a particularly interesting view from your garden, for example an attractive church steeple, a stream or beautiful countryside, bring it to the attention of visitors by framing with an arch. In a small garden, an arch covered in scented climbers or surrounded by scented plants can be used to create an intimate and intoxicating atmosphere around a garden bench.

Arches are also ideal for linking different elements within a garden together. For example, two borders separated by a path become a single feature with a central point of focus when linked by an arch. If you have an uninspiring straight path in your garden, add interest by spacing several identical arches at intervals. Cover them with the same climber and they will seem as one, like an old-fashioned arbour.

Good plants to try

Rambler roses
'Albéric Barbier'
'Albertine'
'American Pillar'
'Emily Gray'
'Rambling Rector'
'Veilchenblau'

Climbing roses
'Bantry Bay'
'Climbing Iceberg'
'Gloire de Dijon'
'Guinée'
'Madame Alfred Carrière'
'Madame Grégoire Staechelin'
'Mermaid'
'Zéphirine Drouhin' (thornless)

MAKING A HOOP FOR CLIMBERS

1 In early spring, make a series of hoops from pliable hazel (*Corylus avellana*) and push each end firmly into the ground.

2 As you bend the hazel, take care that you do not force the curve too sharply. If you do, the hazel might snap.

3 Tie in the long shoots of the climber (a climbing rose is shown here) along the length of the hoop.

4 The leaves of the plant will turn to face the light and new buds will be produced on the upper edges of the curved stems.

5 The plant will have filled out and produced blooms by mid-summer. Remove some of the older stems and tie in new ones annually.

GROWING CLIMBERS UP A TRIPOD

1 Dig a hole big enough to contain the roots of the climber. Position the plant in front of the tripod, not inside.

2 Fan out the stems of the plant and tie them in to the lowest rungs of the tripod, spreading them out to get an even coverage. Water well.

3 In another season the tripod will be covered in foliage and blooms. The structure will also weather down and look less obvious.

Plants for pergolas and arches

All but the biggest and most vigorous climbers can be used to cover pergolas and arches. However, it should be remembered that although leafy growth overhead will provide shade on sunny days, at other times the area may seem gloomy, and persistent drips falling on you after a rain shower can be a big nuisance.

Some climbers such as honeysuckle should be avoided as they are prone to pests that exude honeydew as they feed, resulting in everything underneath being covered with a sticky coating.

You can create the impression that a pergola is completely covered with climbers by training them up and over the outside edges, but leaving the hidden central portion free. Children will love being able to hide in it. Alternatively, you could grow smaller climbers that just cover the uprights and allow a glimpse inside.

The plants you select are a matter of choice and preference, but you do need to consider when you are most likely to use or view the structure, so that the climber is looking its best at that time. You can also combine different varieties to double the impact or plant pairs of plants that flower at different times in order to extend the show.

Temporary cover

When you first put up a pergola or arch, you will have to wait several seasons before the climbers provide dense cover. During this interim period, use quick-growing annual climbers to decorate the structure. Plants you could try include the cup-and-saucer plant (*Cobaea scandens*), sweet peas (*Lathyrus odoratus*) or black-eyed Susan (*Thunbergia alata*). If you have sited your structure in a sheltered spot, have a go with Chilean glory flower (*Eccremocarpus scaber*).

A welcome retreat from the sun is achieved by including the *Vitis vinefera* 'Purpurea' for foliage and grapes at the end of autumn and *Clematis montana* for colour in spring and early summer.

Adding height to borders

Whether you are planting a new garden or enhancing a more established one, simple garden structures, such as posts, obelisks and tripods, can add height and instant interest to borders – and are also ideal for transforming lifeless displays in tired borders.

Lifting displays

Although shrubs can grow to significant heights, sometimes borders need a little extra something to rejuvenate their appearance. This is where climbers show their true value: they can be used to either twine around existing shrubs, add colour when evergreens are not flowering, or provide structure within the garden.

As with trees and other tall focal points, structures have an important impact on the way a garden is viewed, instantly altering the garden's perspective.

Annual and perennial climbers can also be used to cloak obelisks, posts and tripods to obscure an

unattractive sight, such as a bed awaiting planting or one undergoing renovation. Even eyesore garden items – compost bins, water butts, oil storage tanks and the like – can be cunningly concealed with climber-clad structures.

When carefully sited, these structures can help to create a sense of intrigue, enticing the visitor to explore further. By combining these features with sweeping paths and peninsular borders, you can emphasize the effect, introducing a welcome sense of movement and purpose to the design.

Essential maintenance

The main drawback to growing climbers in the middle or the back of a border is that access for essential maintenance can often be made difficult. For example, repeat-flowering roses need to be pruned and long shoots will need tying in to the support. Clematis may need pruning, depending on the variety you choose, and any wayward stems should be removed or tied in periodically throughout the growing season. Self-clinging ivies are the exception to this rule, as they require attention only when they start to outgrow their allotted space.

The advantage of growing climbers up a pergola is that you can site the structure wherever you choose in your garden, ensuring that it has maximum impact.

Scrambling evergreen *Solanum jasminoides* 'Album' bears star-shaped white flowers.

The vigorous climber *Clematis* 'Lasurstern' is frost hardy. In summer it produces beautiful lavender-blue single flowers.

Simple posts can be used singly or in pairs, like sentries on duty at the entrance to the garden or at the end of a path, reinforcing the starting point or a change in direction. Further back in the border, a climber-clad post will draw the eye, providing height, colour and a change in pace. Several at intervals in a large border pull the viewer along as the eyes move from one vertical element to the next.

In a large garden, you can reinforce the sense of formality by using wrought-iron obelisks, which have the added advantage of providing a striking appearance even

after the climber has retreated from view for the winter months.

At the back of a border, posts can be linked with lengths of rope to form a traditional colonnade. Once trained with climbers, the loops of rope will become festooned with flowers during the summer but also provide a strong, decorative backdrop at other times.

An even more powerful effect can be created by linking the posts with timber, rather like a one-dimensional pergola. This produces a look that can be relaxed and rustic or more ornate and regimented, depending on the style of the structure and the plants you use to decorate it.

Selecting a climber

If you are looking for a cheap and cheerful transformation, there are several vigorous annual climbers that will give any lacklustre border a makeover for the price of a packet of seeds. Try sweet peas (*Lathyrus odoratus*), black-eyed Susan

(*Thunbergia alata*), morning glory (*Convolvulus major*), canary creeper (*Tropaeolum canariensis*) or annual hop (*Humulus japonicus*).

For a permanent display, choose a climber that will not get too big. The variegated forms of common ivy (*Hedera helix*) provide year-round appeal, while flower power can be supplied by *Clematis alpina* or *C. macropetala* early in the season, with *C.* 'Marie Boisselot' and *C.* 'Niobe' later on. Summer jasmine (*Jasminum officinale*) should be close to the patio or seating area where you can appreciate the heady scent.

Climbing roses are useful in the middle or back of the border. Choose repeat-flowering varieties, such as 'Paul's Scarlet Climber', 'Handel', 'Compassion' and 'Madame Alfred Carrière'. For autumn tints, try Virginia creeper (*Parthenocissus quinquefolia*) and the early summer flowering potato vine (*Solanum jasminoides* 'Album'), which will continue on until early winter.

Good plants to try

Climbing roses for pillars
'Aloha'
'Compassion'
'Golden Showers'
'Handel'
'Madame Alfred Carrière'
'New Dawn'
'Zéphirine Drouhin'

Shrubs are the backbone of a border and here you can see how the plants are positioned higher at the back and trail down to the lawn, making a beautiful vista along the path.

Combining climbers

Climbers are very sociable plants. They combine just as well with each other as they do with shrubs and hedges, which helps create an eye-catching display as well as extending the flowering season.

Choosing a perfect partner

When selecting a climber to combine with another plant, it is essential that you match the vigour of the climber with the host or companion plant you have in mind. If it is too vigorous, the climber will soon swamp its partner and need regular cutting back, but if it is not vigorous enough, the climber will never put on a decent show and may disappear without trace. Also bear in mind the climber's maintenance requirements. For example, it is a good idea to pair clematis that have the same pruning requirements, so they can be tackled at the same time and in the same way. Similarly, if you are planning to plant a clematis to scramble through a tall, inaccessible tree, choose one that needs the minimum of pruning.

Clematis are probably the most versatile climbers, combining well with both climbing and rambler roses as well as honeysuckles and other climbers. You can pair up clematis that will bloom at the same time for added impact or create a succession of colour by combining climbers with overlapping flowering periods. Flowers that are produced at the same time should blend or contrast, but not clash in colour. Of course, this is a matter of personal preference, so choose colour combinations that you find pleasing to the eye, but bear in mind how scented plants will intermingle.

On a large structure, such as a pergola, you could combine several different plants and varieties to provide colour and interest for much of the year. You can even achieve this with clematis alone (*see* Clematis all year box, below). Alternatively, you could plan the display so that it is at its best when you are most likely to be in the garden – during the summer and Easter holidays, for example.

In a shady spot, try combining a variegated ivy, such as *Hedera helix* 'Goldheart' or *H. colchica* 'Paddy's Pride', for year-round interest, with a shade-tolerant flowering climber, such as *Jasminum nudiflorum* (winter jasmine), which will combine to give an excellent winter display. For summer flowers, you could add a rose or vigorous clematis that can cope with partial shade.

Getting quick results

Climbers are an excellent way to improve the look of a new garden and to cover eyesores in an

GROWING A CLIMBER THOUGH A SHRUB

1 Choose a shrub that flowers at a different time to the climber. Here, a relatively low *Salix helvetica* will be planted with *Clematis alpina*.

3 Use a cane to train the clematis into the shrub (remove when established). Spread the climber's shoots through the shrub's foliage.

2 Next to the shrub, start digging a planting area and add some well-rotted manure. For clematis, plant on the shady side of the shrub.

4 Once planted, give both shrub and climber a good watering. Keep an eye on the climber's watering needs until it is established.

Clematis all year

Winter into spring: *Clematis alpina, C. armandii* and *C. macropetala*
Spring into summer: *Clematis montana* and early-flowering hybrids
Summer into autumn: *Clematis orientalis, C. tangutica, C. viticella* and large-flowered hybrids
Autumn into winter: late-flowering hybrids and *Clematis cirrhosa*.

Clematis climbing partners

Try combining the following clematis with roses for beautiful effects:
C. 'Mrs Cholmondeley', which bears chocolate-centred, lavender-blue flowers (late spring–early summer), with R. 'New Dawn', which produces fragrant, double, pink flowers (early summer–early autumn). C. 'Marie Boisselot', which bears white flowers with golden centres (mid-summer–early autumn), with R. 'Madame Alfred Carrière' for its fragrant, double, pink-flushed white flowers from (mid-summer–early autumn). C. 'Niobe', which produces golden-centred, dark ruby-red flowers (mid-summer–early autumn) in combination with R. 'Zéphirine Drouhin', which has strongly fragrant, double, deep pink flowers (mid-summer–early autumn). C. 'Jackmanii Superba', which offers red-flushed, dark purple flowers with cream-coloured centres (mid-summer–early autumn), with R. 'Golden Showers', adding double, rich-yellow flowers (mid-summer–early autumn). C. 'Gipsy Queen', which bears red-centred, bright purple flowers (mid-summer–early autumn), alongside R. 'Climbing Iceberg',with its double, white flowers from (mid-summer–early autumn). C. 'Perle d'Azur', with yellow-centred, lilac-blue flowers (mid-summer–early autumn), paired with C. 'Purpurea Plena Elegans', which bears semi-double, reddish-purple flowers (mid-summer–early autumn).

established one. Fast-growing climbers will soon cover fence panels and walls with a cloak of foliage that softens the appearance and helps disguise the line of a boundary. In a small garden this will help to create the illusion of space, while in a larger one the effect can be the opposite – giving an area a sense of seclusion. Honeysuckles, such as 'Belgica' and 'Serotina', with their fragrant, tubular, reddish-purple flowers, are always worth considering, as are the vigorous clematis, such as C. montana and C. tangutica, which never disappoint with their masses of lantern-like flowers. Then there are the repeat-flowering climbing roses, such as Rosa 'Aloha', with its large, double, fragrant, rose-pink flowers; the double, rich-yellow blooms of 'Golden Showers'; and 'New Dawn', which bears fragrant, double, pink flowers in clusters. All bloom from mid-summer onwards.

Annual climbers are another option for small walls and garden dividers, especially if you are on a tight budget. They are an ideal stop-gap measure to provide colour and interest while slower-growing, more permanent climbers are getting established. Sow them under cover in the greenhouse, conservatory or kitchen windowsill to give them an early start or buy young plants in pots from garden centres in late spring. Nasturtiums are old favourites that are now back in vogue. The latest varieties offer more refined colour schemes than their rather garish predecessors. The related Canary creeper (Tropaeolum peregrinum) is also worth a try for its attractive foliage and brilliant yellow, tubular flowers produced from mid-summer onwards.

The beautiful Clematis 'Marie Boisselot' combines with a small apple tree to provide a stunning display from early summer to late autumn.

Ground cover, edging and banks

Low-growing, well-behaved shrubs and some climbers are ideal for growing under the skirt of larger shrubs and trees to provide a weed-suppressing carpet of attractive foliage and colourful flowers. They are also useful elsewhere in the garden and for planting up problem areas where little else will grow.

Genista lydia

What makes good ground cover?

A good ground cover shrub should be easy to look after, have a ground-hugging, uniform habit and should be quick to establish after planting. It should form a dense carpet of foliage over the ground, so there is no space for the weeds to grow. On the other hand, it should not be too invasive otherwise it will become the weed rather than the weed suppressor. Most good ground cover plants are evergreen and have attractive foliage, providing year-round cover, but there are one or two very good deciduous candidates worth considering. Ideally, the ground cover should bear colourful flowers, followed by berries as well as autumn and winter colour – but that's probably asking too much!

There are many shrubs and climbers recommended in books and catalogues for use as ground cover, but few actually make the grade in most situations. Ground cover roses are a good example. Although they do sprawl attractively across the ground and put on an excellent show during early summer, they don't produce enough leaf cover early in the season to smother the first flush of weed growth – and weeding between the thorny stems is a practical impossibility.

Using ground cover plants

While ground cover plants are ideal for filling in the gaps between large shrubs and trees, while providing a carpet of attractive foliage and suppressing weeds, they can also be used in other ways around the garden. Problem areas, such as narrow borders along the side of the house or under windows can be filled with suitable ground cover, as can that difficult-to-plant strip along evergreen hedges, where the soil is dry and there is almost constant shade. Similarly, some ground cover plants are an ideal way of covering

awkward banks that would be difficult, if not dangerous, to mow if covered in grass. They can also be used to hide eyesores, such as manhole covers, ugly tree stumps, the footings of dismantled walls and old buildings that are too difficult to remove.

In the centre of the garden, ground cover plants make an easy-care alternative to grass, which can be particularly useful in areas that are well away from the main lawn or even in the front garden. Here, they will be on display, so you will need to choose plants that put on a show.

Planting ground cover

When you use plants as ground cover, plant them closer together than is usually recommended. This will ensure a complete cover more quickly, although it will cost more to achieve. The best time to plant is autumn or spring, so the plants will establish quickly. Ideally, plant through a sheet of landscape fabric into weed-free soil to prevent any new weeds appearing until the plants have carpeted the soil.

Vinca minor 'Aureovariegata'

Budget ideas

Planting ground cover on any scale requires a great number of plants. As most ground cover plantings use swathes of the same variety, you can save money by propagating your own plants or buying in bulk direct from the grower.

Propagating plants doesn't mean waiting for years to get an effective cover on the ground, as many of the shrubs and climbers recommended here produce quick results if planted slightly closer.

If you know what type of ground cover you want, you could buy a large, well-established plant and divide it into many others. For example a 2-litre (3½ pint) pot of a periwinkle, such as *Vinca minor* 'Gertrude Jekyll', could yield up to five plants, while a 5-litre (9-pint) pot could produce ten new plants. Look for a stock plant that is well established in the pot and which has plenty of shoots and buds.

Other ground cover shrubs and climbers are easier to propagate from cuttings. Evergreen shrubs such as *Euonymus fortunei* 'Emerald 'n' Gold', conifers such as *Juniperus x media* 'Pfitzeriana Aurea' and climbers such as *Hedera helix* and its cultivars can all be increased easily in this way.

It is also worth visiting nurseries in your area or going to gardening shows to see if they will supply plants in bulk at a reduced cost. Small plants, known as liners, will be a fraction of the cost of a potted plant from the garden centre and will establish quicker. If you want larger plants, some nurseries will offer these at wholesale prices.

Using climbers as ground cover

Many climbers are as happy scrambling over the ground between shrubs and trees as they are covering walls and fences. If you match the vigour of the climber to the space available, it will also be largely maintenance free – requiring no tying in, pruning or training.

For example, in a large space between trees, a variety of the vigorous *Clematis montana* or a honeysuckle, such as 'Halliana', would be ideal. If the space is more restricted, for example in a shrubbery, then ornamental ivies or a less vigorous large-flowered clematis such as 'Lasurstern' or 'Perle d'Azur' would suit. Between flowering shrubs such as roses, choose a groundcover climber that will flower in early spring before the roses open. This will extend the season of interest. Alternatively, choose a variety in a complementary colour that will bloom at the same time as the roses to create a really stunning floral display.

Climbers are often the best option for covering steep slopes or narrow borders at the base of a wall. The climber can be planted in the most favourable position at the top of the slope or at one end of the wall and allowed to cover the ground with its trailing stems. Ornamental vines such as the Boston Ivy (*Parthenocissus tricuspidata* 'Veitchii') will cover slopes with a neat bed of evergreen foliage, while varieties of the Alpine clematis look delightful scrambling along the front of a wall.

Good plants to try

Under shrubs
Clematis macropetala (cultivars)
Cotoneaster dammeri
Euonymus fortunei (varieties)
Gaultheria procumbens – acid-loving
Hebe pinguifolia 'Pagei'
Hedera colchica (varieties)
Hedera helix (varieties)
Stephanandra incisa 'Crispa'
Vinca major (varieties)
Vinca minor (varieties)

Under trees
Berberis thunbergii 'Atropurpurea Nana'
Clematis montana (varieties)
Cotoneaster conspicuus 'Coral Beauty'
Cotoneaster salicifolius 'Gnom'
Euonymus fortunei (varieties)
Hedera colchica (varieties)
Hedera helix (varieties)
Hypericum calycinum
Rubus cockburnianus
Santolina chamaecyparissus (varieties)

Over sunny banks
Calluna vulgaris (varieties) – acid-loving
Ceanothus thyrsiflorus 'Repens'
Eccremocarpus scaber
Erica carnea (varieties) – acid-loving
Genista lydia

Hedera colchica (varieties)
Hedera helix (varieties)
Rubus cockburnianus
Santolina chamaecyparissus (varieties)
Tropaeolum tuberosum

Alternative to lawns
Calluna vulgaris (varieties)
Erica carnea (varieties)
Hedera helix (varieties)
Vinca major (varieties)
Vinca minor (varieties)

Hiding eyesores
Clematis macropetala (varieties)
Cotoneaster conspicuus 'Coral Beauty'
Cotoneaster horizontalis
Cotoneaster salicifolia 'Gnom'
Euonymus fortunei (varieties)
Humulus lupulus
Vitis coignetiae

In deep shade
Euonymus fortunei (varieties)
Hedera colchica (varieties)
Hedera helix (varieties)
Lonicera pileata
Pachysandra terminalis
Sarcococca hookeriana var. *humilis*
Vinca major (varieties)

Conservatory plants

A conservatory offers you the opportunity to grow a wide range of plants that would not thrive outside in the garden or in the relative gloom of indoor rooms.

Choosing the right plants

Many tropical and Mediterranean plants will appreciate the good light levels and high temperatures found in most conservatories. However, unless dedicated to plant raising, the conditions within the conservatory are usually a compromise between the needs of the plants and those of the owners.

For example, if you want to use your conservatory as an extension of the house and fill it with furniture and fabrics, you will not be able to provide the high humidity levels demanded by many tropical plants. Instead, you will have to confine your choice to climbers such as passion flowers, plumbago and

monstera, as well as flowering shrubs such as brugmansia and hibiscus, which can cope with the lower air-moisture levels and fluctuating temperatures in a conservatory that is in constant use. However, you will still need to heat your conservatory in winter in colder climates, with a minimum temperature of 8°C (45°F).

In a sunny conservatory, temperatures can rocket unless sufficient shade and ventilation are provided. Try to ensure there are opening vents in the roof and at the sides, so that a constant cooling flow of air can be achieved. This will also help prevent disease problems. In cool and damp weather, when the vents are closed, air movement can be maintained using an extractor fan.

By late spring, ventilation alone will not keep the temperature under control on sunny days, so you will need to provide shade. This can be achieved using internal or external

blinds, but internal blinds can easily become tangled with climbing stems. Instead, you might like to consider training a sun-loving climber, such as bougainvillaea, on wires inside the roof, so that it provides the shade for the other occupants and helps prevent sudden temperature rises.

Another option is to apply a shade wash to the roof of the conservatory, but this will cut down light levels severely on gloomy days.

In a cool conservatory that is just kept frost-free in winter, you can try a wide range of houseplants, as well as palms, bay, myrtle, olives and citrus, which can be placed outside during the summer months, plus half-hardy climbers such as *Jasminum polyanthum* and bougainvillaea.

Looking after plants

Watering All plants need to be regularly watered – possibly every day if they are in small pots. An alternative is to grow the plants in larger containers, such as raised beds or large troughs, so that they have a greater root run. You can also grow them in self-watering containers, which have in-built reservoirs that can be topped up regularly. There is also a range of automatic watering devices that you can use.

Misting Invest in a hand mister to spray the leaves of plants from time to time. It is also worth standing plants in groups on trays of moist gravel so that the air around the plants is kept as humid as possible. Wet the gravel periodically.

Feeding All actively growing conservatory plants need regular feeding. You can do this using a slow-release fertilizer stick pushed into the soil at planting time and at the beginning of each growing season, or you can add a houseplant liquid feed to the weekly waterings.

A year in the conservatory

Spring
Increase watering as necessary and feed only those plants growing strongly. Keep the conservatory glass clean to allow as much light in as possible. Clean leaves and remove yellowing and dead ones.

Summer
Maintain an even temperature by careful ventilation and use of shading. Water and feed all actively growing plants as necessary. Propagate from cuttings and layering. Mist plants and moisten gravel trays daily to maintain sufficient humidity around the plants. Pinch out trailing plants when they reach the floor and tie in new growth on climbers to their supports. Move plants outdoors for their summer holiday. Deadhead repeat-flowering shrubs, such as azaleas, to keep them blooming strongly.

Keep an eye open for signs of pest and disease attack and take the appropriate action to control it. Cut back permanent plants that outgrow their allotted space.

Autumn
Reduce watering and stop feeding all but strongly growing plants such as jasmine. Bring in shrubs and climbers from the summer break in the garden, but check them carefully for pests and diseases. Put up insulation. Clean glass to maximize light penetration. Keep an eye open for spider mite in a heated environment.

Winter
Water sparingly and feed only those plants that are actively growing. Routinely remove dead flowers and leaves and watch out for grey mould (botrytis) on leaves.

Good plants to try

Warm conservatory (min. temp. 5°C/41°F)

Abutilon megapotamicum
Aristolochia littoralis
Bougainvillaea glabra
Cissus antarctica
Cobaea scandens
Hoya carnosa
Jasminum polyanthum
Nerium oleander
Passiflora caerulea
Tibouchina urvilleana

Hot conservatory (min. temp. 10°C/50°F)

Brugmansia suaveolens
Clerodendrum thomsoniae
Hibiscus rosa-sinensis 'The President'
Justicia carnea
Lantana camara
Mandevilla x amabilis 'Alice du Pont'
Phoenix roebelenii
Rhapis excelsa

Problems Look out for any signs of pests and diseases and treat them immediately. Use suitable biological controls or chemical sprays as necessary. Check new plants carefully before adding them to your display, as this is the most likely way new pests and diseases are introduced.

Displaying conservatory plants

Plants in the conservatory look their best when displayed in groupings. Not only does this appear more natural than individual specimens, but there are practical benefits of keeping them in tight-knit communities, too: they are easier to look after and the microclimate surrounding each plant will be more humid, reducing the need for constant misting. Keep a display looking fresh and attractive by moving the plants within each group and between groups as they come in and out of flower.

Similarly, plants that are resting or are in less than pristine condition can be partially hidden behind those that are looking their best.

It is important to group plants with similar cultural requirements so that they will all need watering at the same time and be content with the common growing environment.

The best conservatory plant displays usually look natural in their setting and with the plants that surround them. You can bring out the best in neighbours by choosing complementary but contrasting features so that one emphasizes the attributes of the other. For example, a plain foliage plant is the perfect foil for a brash flowering plant.

You can also group plants to provide a bold splash at a particular time of the year, such as a colourful display of winter-flowering heathers at Christmas. Include props, such as wicker baskets and cast-iron planters, to highlight the plants that are looking their best. Plant stands, such as a tiered French *étagère*, are worth considering for large numbers of

plants in containers. Many modern versions come with built-in gravel trays to make providing a humid atmosphere easy. Stands are also ideal for showing off the cascading foliage of trailers and climbers to their best advantage, as well as bringing small plants and those with intricate makings closer to the eye.

On a table display, use a large container to provide a temporary home for plants as they come into flower. A basic planting of foliage trailers or a fern can be given a lift by introducing flowering plants as temporary bedfellows while they are in full bloom. Grow the seasonal highlights in one size of pot so that they are easy to slot in and out of the main display.

Some plants are worth using as solo specimens. Choose a suitable ornamental container to complement the plant's main features. As a rule of thumb, go for simple designs to show off vibrant and fussy shrubs and climbers and more ornate containers for feature plants with a strong but subtle appeal.

Having a conservatory or a greenhouse allows the gardener to grow shrubs and climbers that would not survive outside. It also allows you to prolong the season of others.

Gardening techniques

To get the best from your shrubs and climbers you will need to understand a few basic principles of gardening and master a number of straightforward techniques. In this section we guide you through all the essential tasks, using easy-to-follow instructions and clear, stage-by-stage photography and illustrations.

Before you can take steps to create a new garden or improve the appearance of an existing one, it is worth getting to know a little about your soil. Basic information such as pH and soil type are just two critical factors that will help determine which shrubs and climbers will thrive in your garden – as well as those that are likely to fail. Knowing more about your soil also enables you to take effective steps to improve it by adding well-rotted manure and, where appropriate, applying fertilizers.

Once the soil is in good heart, you will need to learn a few basic techniques, such as planting, watering, weeding and mulching, so that your new shrubs and climbers get off to the best possible start. You will find plenty of tips and advice here for improving the performance of established plants, too.

Beautiful, disease-resistant blooms are the pride and joy of every gardener, as they show that love, care and the proper gardening techniques have been successfully used.

Know your soil

The health of your soil is crucial to the types and quality of the plants you can grow. It is therefore essential that you have some understanding of the type of soil you have, and its advantages and limitations, before you can choose the correct plants for your garden. Once you know the basic facts about your soil, you can also set about improving it.

Identifying your soil

The quickest and easiest way to find out what type of soil you have in your garden is to handle it. Wet a small amount of soil and rub it between your finger and thumb and literally feel its consistency. By wetting the soil you will be able to assess more easily the types of particles it contains.

• **Gritty** If it feels gritty and the particles easily separate, then the soil has a high sand content. Then try rolling a small ball of the soil in the palm of your hand so you can estimate how much sand it contains: the easier the ball falls apart the greater the proportion is sand.
• **Gritty and cohesive** If the sample feels gritty but the particles hold together well, then it contains sand and loam. The ball of soil should hold together when rolled in the palm of the hand, but will break up when rolled into a sausage shape.

• **Gritty and sticky** If it feels gritty but is slightly sticky to the touch, it contains sand and clay particles. If the ball of soil becomes shiny when rubbed and can be rolled into a sausage shape and bent like a horseshoe without cracking or breaking, it contains sand, clay and also loam.
• **Smooth and silky** If the sample feels smooth and silky between finger and thumb and moulds into a ball and a sausage, but breaks when bent into a horseshoe shape, then it contains mainly loam and silt.
• **Sticky and malleable** If it feels sticky to the touch and the ball of soil is shiny and easy to roll into a sausage, but cracks when bent into a ring shape, then it contains mainly clay with some loam.
• **Very sticky** If the sample literally sticks your finger and thumb together and the ball of soil is shiny, easy to roll into a sausage and bend into a ring shape without breaking or cracking, then it contains mainly clay.

Soil types

All soils are made up of the same basic ingredients: sand, loam, clay, silt and organic matter. The proportions of each ingredient will determine the type of soil you have and how good the soil is for growing different plants. Sandy soil contains

Daphne bholua 'Darjeeling' prefers a well drained but not dry soil that is slightly alkaline.

a high proportion of large, irregularly shaped particles that have air spaces between them. This means that water drains freely so they tend to dry out quickly, which is a bonus in spring as they are easier to work and warm up earlier than other soils, but they are a problem in summer when they are more prone to drought during dry spells. Free-draining soils also tend to have essential soil nutrients washed out, known as leaching, leaving the soil impoverished unless given a regular application of fertilizer.

Clay soil contains a high proportion of tiny soil particles that pack very closely together, leaving very few air spaces. This prevents water from draining through the soil so it remains wet for longer. Clay soils are also heavy and sticky, and so very difficult to cultivate. They are easily damaged if walked on when wet, causing compaction of the surface, which just exacerbates the drainage problems. They are also slow to warm up in spring, and so planting has to be delayed. In

Soil type at-a-glance

Gritty to touch	Sticky to touch	Shines when rubbed	Rolls into ball	Rolls into sausage	Bends into ring	What's in your soil
√	x	x	x	x	x	Sand
√	x	x	√	x	x	Sand and loam
√	√	√	√	√	x	Sand, clay and loam
x	√	√	√	√	x	Clay and loam
x	√	√	√	√	√	Clay

Viburnum 'Eve Price' is easy going, but does best on clay or silty soil.

Plants for different soils

Sandy, chalky or alkaline soil	Peaty or acid soil	Clay or silty soil
Ceanothus	Calluna	Abelia
Ceratostigma	Camellia	Alnus
Clematis	Corylopsis	Bergenia
Cytisus	Cryptomeria	Choisya
Daphne	Desfontainia	Corylus
Euonymus	Enkianthus	Crataegus
Euphorbia	Fothergilla	Kerria
Genista	Gaultheria	Laburnum
Hypericum	Halesia	Malus
Ligustrum	Hamamelis	Philadelphus
Mahonia	Kalmia	Potentilla
Rosmarinus	Larix	Pyracantha
Spiraea	Leucothoe	Pyrus
Stachyurus	Pieris	Rhamnus
Weigela	Pinus	Sedum
Wisteria	Rhododendron	Sorbus
	Sarcococca	Symphoricarpos
	Skimmia	Taxus
	Staphylea	Viburnum
		Vinca

summer, clay soils can dry out to form a concrete-hard crust with a distinctive cracked surface as the soil shrinks. Clay soils are usually fertile.

Silty soil contains mainly medium-sized particles, and so tends to drain well in winter but retain soil moisture in summer. It is also usually fertile. Silty soils are easily damaged if walked on when wet, causing a compaction of the surface, known as 'capping'.

Loamy soil contains a mixture of particle sizes and so has the advantages of all the other soils, without the disadvantages. Loamy soils are usually easy to cultivate and have a robust and stable structure that drains well in winter and is still fairly moisture retentive in summer. They also generally warm up quickly in spring and are usually fertile.

Soil-testing laboratories

For really accurate soil analysis you will have to send off a soil sample to a specialist laboratory for testing. Set up for the agricultural and horticultural industries. Some local authorities also offer a soil analysis service for gardeners, for which there may be a nominal charge. Not only will they test your soil accurately for pH, but many will provide an analysis of the main plant nutrients: potassium, phosphate and nitrogen as well as some trace elements (magnesium, calcium, manganese, iron, copper and zinc, for example), and information about the organic matter content. The most comprehensive soil analysis services will give some recommendations for fertilizer and lime application rates in order to improve your soil.

This sort of professional analysis may be worth considering if you have just moved to a new house and don't know anything about the garden's history, or where you've had difficulties in the past and suspect the problem lies in the soil. You can also use this sort of soil analysis to test deliveries of topsoil to make sure they are up to standard, but bear in mind that results can take anything from a week to a month to get the results, so you may have to hold back on planting.

Hamamelis mollis prefers peaty or acid soil.

Assessing your soil

Once you are familiar with your soil type, there are two other key factors you need to find out so that you can take steps to improve the soil before planting: how acid the soil is and which nutrients it contains.

Testing your soil

Although the best way to find out about your soil in detail is to send a representative sample off to a specialist laboratory to have it analysed, you can find this out with reasonable certainty by carrying out a simple set of tests yourself.

There are cheap and reliable soil-testing kits widely available from garden centres and DIY stores that will tell you your soil's pH level as well as indicate the nutrient balance in your soil.

The pH level is a measure of your soil's acidity or alkalinity. Each plant has an ideal pH range in which it will thrive, which varies from plant to plant. To make the most of your plants' growing potential, it is

The rock rose (*Helianthemum*) is a dwarf shrub that is able to thrive on almost any soil that is reasonably fertile and well drained.

Checking drainage

Another important factor to establish when planting a new area is how well it drains. If the soil is poorly drained, you may wish to take steps to improve it before planting. To check how well your soil drains, dig several holes about 30cm (12in) deep spaced randomly across the plot. Fill each hole with water and see how quickly it drains. If there is still water in the hole after 24 hours, you may have a drainage problem. This can usually be overcome by digging deeply and incorporating plenty of well-rotted organic matter and grit into the soil, otherwise you will have to consider installing land drains, or building raised beds to improve drainage around the roots of the plants.

---

essential that you test a soil sample that's representative of the whole area you are planning on planting up. Make sure that you do not test contaminated areas, such as where a compost heap has been, otherwise the results will be invalid.

The easiest and most reliable way to select a representative soil sample is to lay out four canes on the soil surface in a large 'W' shape. Use a hand trowel to dig five small holes about 15cm (6in) deep at the points of the W. Scoop out a little soil from the bottom of each hole and place this in a sieve over a bucket. This will remove stones, pieces of chalk and organic matter that might skew the results. Mix the sieved soil samples together before testing.

Altering acidity

The best range of nutrients are provided when the soil has a pH value of about 6–7. It is possible to temporarily reduce the acidity of the soil by applying lime several weeks before planting. Choose either garden lime or ground

chalk that has been made for the purpose. The amount of lime you apply will be determined by the type of soil and its pH. For example, to change a clay soil from pH5 to pH6 will require about 1,200g of lime per square metre, while you would need only 800g per square metre on loamy soil and 400g per square metre on a sandy soil.

It is essential that you follow the guidance notes on the soil test kit and the instructions on the lime

A more high-tech soil-testing device is an electronic meter. When the probe is inserted in the soil, a reading of its pH level is given.

packaging to work out exactly how much you need to apply to your soil.

The best time to apply lime is during the autumn or early winter when soil conditions allow. Wear gloves and apply lime only in still, non-windy conditions. Rake the lime roughly into the surface after application. Bear in mind that liming is only a temporary solution, and so you will need to check the soil acidity every few years.

If you intend to add organic matter to your soil before planting, do this during early spring at least two months after liming to prevent the two reacting together and producing ammonia. Use acidic well-rotted farmyard manure on alkaline soil to help lower the pH and alkaline mushroom compost on acid soils to help raise the pH.

Tricky situations

Climbers and wall shrubs are often planted in borders next to walls where the soil is impoverished. In new gardens, the soil can be full of builders' rubble and so needs digging out to a depth of at least 30cm (12in) and replacing with good-quality topsoil from elsewhere in the garden or from a garden supplier. The soil will also be dry because the wall draws water from it via capillary action and, more often than not, prevents rain falling on the border. The best way to counteract this is to add lots of well-rotted organic matter to the soil before planting and to cover the soil surface with an organic mulch afterwards.

In the dappled shade under trees and the dense shade along evergreen hedges, ground cover shrubs can be difficult to establish. Give new plants the best start by planting in spring into well-prepared soil cleared of roots and mulching the soil surface after planting. Pay particular attention to all new plants in difficult situations to make sure they are kept weed-free and well watered through their first growing season.

TESTING YOUR SOIL FOR ITS NUTRIENT VALUES

1 Collect a soil sample from 10cm (4in) below the surface. Take several different samples and mix together for a representative test.

2 Follow the instructions on the kit. Usually, you mix 1 part soil with 5 parts water. Shake well and then allow the water to settle.

3 Using the pipette provided with the kit, draw off some of the settled liquid from the top of the jar.

4 Having drawn off about 5cm (2in) of the solution, transfer the sample to the test chamber in the plastic container.

5 Select a colour-coded capsule (one for each nutrient). Put the powder in the chamber, replace the cap and shake well.

6 After a few minutes, you can compare the colour of the liquid with the shade panel shown on the side of the container.

Improving your soil

If you know what your soil type is and have a good idea about its acidity and nutrient content, you can take steps to improve it by thorough cultivation as well as the application of well-rotted organic matter and fertilizers.

Soil conditioners

No matter whether your soil is predominantly clay, sand, loam or silt, it will benefit from the application of well-rotted farmyard manure or garden compost. In fact, all but peaty soils, which are already high in organic matter, can be improved in this way.

The organic matter works in different ways for different soils. In heavy clay, the fibrous organic particles improve the structure – creating air spaces and allowing water to drain more freely. In sandy soil, the same fibrous particles collectively act like a sponge, holding on to soil moisture so plants are less prone to drought.

In all soils, the organic matter provides food for plants and beneficial soil-borne creatures, such as ground beetles and earthworms,

which help break it down slowly, releasing more essential plant nutrients. The soil-borne creatures also help aerate the soil as they move around their subterranean habitat.

Well-rotted organic matter can be added to the soil when it is cultivated at planting time, and after planting as a mulch on the soil surface. Whenever it is applied it must be well rotted – tell-tale signs include a dark brown, even, crumbly structure that is practically odourless. If it is put on the soil before reaching this stage, it will continue to rot down once applied, and the soil-borne micro-organisms will use up nitrogen from the soil in the process. This could lead to plants running short of this vital nutrient.

Cultivating your soil

Soils are cultivated to remove weeds and to improve the soil structure and nutrient content by incorporating well-rotted organic matter. There are several ways this can be achieved:

Forking Light sandy soils and other soils that have been well cultivated in the recent past can be broken up

easily with a garden or border fork. Weed the area by hand, then cover the surface of the soil with a layer of organic matter. Cultivate the soil by simply plunging the fork to the full depth of its prongs and turn the soil over in more or less the same position so that the organic matter is roughly buried.

Digging There are three levels of digging with a spade. Which you choose should depend on how thoroughly and how deeply you want the cultivation. Simple digging is the most basic, with the soil being turned over and deposited in roughly the same place. Any annual weeds are buried and will rot down, while perennial weeds can be removed by hand. Repeat this process, moving across the plot. When the other side is reached, move back about 15cm (6in) and repeat, until the whole area has been cultivated. Organic matter can be incorporated at the same time or simply spread over the surface afterwards to allow earthworms and other beneficial soil-borne creatures to incorporate it for you.

Single digging is the best way to tackle heavier loamy, silty and clay soils, as it ensures that the organic matter is thoroughly incorporated into the upper soil layer. Excavate a trench about 30cm (12in) wide right across the plot, leaving the soil to one side. Fill the bottom of the trench with a 7cm- (3in-) deep layer of well-rotted organic matter.

Move back 30cm (12in) and dig another trench – using the excavated material to fill the previous trench with topsoil. Repeat until the entire plot has been dug. The excavated soil from the first trench can then be used to fill the last trench. Double digging cultivates the soil to about a depth of 30cm (12in) and is a

Autumn is the best time for digging over the soil. Fork in some organic matter afterwards, such as well-rotted garden compost or farmyard manure, to help improve the soil's structure.

useful way of preparing soil with a compacted or poorly draining subsoil. After excavating each trench of soil (as for single digging), use a garden fork to break up the subsoil at the bottom of the trench and incorporate some well-rotted organic matter as you go. If you are trying to improve the drainage, add plenty of grit, too. Fill up the trench with topsoil from the next trench (as for single digging).

Feeding your soil

In nature, there is a continuous recycling of organic matter as plants die and rot down, but in the garden, not all the plant material stays so you may need to top up the nutrient levels artificially.

You can improve the fertility of your soil by adding well-rotted organic matter, such as composted bark or farmyard manure, as well as adding suitable fertilizers. Which fertilizers you choose and how much you apply should depend on your soil and the plants you intend to grow. There are three main (or primary) plant nutrients: nitrogen (N), phosphorus (P) and potassium (K), the proportion of which is expressed as a ratio of N:P:K on the fertilizer packaging.

Each of these nutrients promotes a different type of growth: nitrogen encourages leafy growth; phosphorus is essential for healthy root development; and flowering is encouraged by potassium. Other nutrients (namely calcium, sulphur and magnesium) are just as essential, but are needed in less quantity and so are called secondary nutrients. Seven more (boron, chlorine, copper, iron, manganese, zinc and molybdenum) are required in very small amounts. These are known as micro-nutrients or trace elements.

ORGANIC FERTILIZERS

Blood

Bonemeal

Seaweed

Fish, blood and bone

INORGANIC FERTILIZERS

Balanced general fertilizer

Sulphate of ammonia

Potash

Superphosphate

Fertilizers

Fertilizers are grouped according to their origin. Organic fertilizers are derived from naturally occurring organic materials and include bonemeal, fishmeal and seaweed. They are generally slow acting because they have to be broken down by micro-organisms before their nutrients can be absorbed by plants. Inorganic fertilizers are made either in a factory or mined as naturally occurring minerals (in the case of rock potash). They are generally concentrated and quick acting. Check the packaging to make sure you buy one containing levels that suit your soil and plants.

Planting shrubs

Shrubs and hedges are designed to be long-term additions to the garden, so it is essential that the ground is prepared properly before planting so that they are able to establish quickly, thrive in their allotted space and require only the minimum of aftercare.

Ground preparation

Successful planting of all shrubs and climbers depends on thorough ground preparation beforehand, so that the soil is in good heart and there is no competition for moisture and nutrients from surrounding plants – and weeds.

Thereafter, the key to success is to keep the new addition well watered, otherwise all your good work will result in failure.

When to plant

Container-grown shrubs and hedges can be planted at any time of the year, provided the soil is not waterlogged or frozen solid. However, they will establish more quickly if they are planted when the soil is warm and moist, which is usually in spring or autumn.

Autumn planting is the best option if your soil is light and prone to drying out, since the plants will have more time to get established before their first summer. Spring planting is a better option in colder areas and on exposed sites because it gives the new addition a chance to get established before the winter.

Bare-rooted shrubs and those that are field-grown and potted up before sale are best planted during the dormant season when soil conditions allow. However, all evergreens are best planted during late spring, so that they have time to establish before the onset of winter.

Where to plant

Choose shrubs that naturally suit the soil and conditions in your garden, so that they are easier to look after and will perform better after planting. Shrubs can be planted anywhere in the garden, but bear in mind their ultimate height and spread when planning a new border. Check the plant label for recommended planting distances or look up the information in a plant encyclopaedia. However, they can be more closely spaced for instant impact if you are prepared to carry out regular pruning to keep them within bounds.

How to plant

Clear the planting area of weeds and other potential competition. If you are planting in a lawn, remove a 1m- (3ft-) wide circle of turf. Dig a hole about twice as wide as the rootball of a container-grown shrub, or sufficiently wide to accommodate a bare-root specimen when its roots are spread out. Place the excavated soil on a plastic sheet or old compost bag next to the hole. The hole should be as deep as the container or rootball, so that the specimen will be planted at the same depth as it is in the pot.

If necessary, you can check this by standing the pot in the planting hole and laying a bamboo cane across the hole. Remove or replace soil as necessary until the correct planting depth is achieved. Then, fork over the bottom of the planting hole. If your soil is poor, you can augment the excavated soil and the soil in the

PLANTING A POTTED OR ROOTBALLED SHRUB

1 Clear the planting area of weeds and dig a sufficiently large hole. Add garden compost or well-rotted manure to improve the soil.

2 Having soaked the rootball in water, tease out some of the curling roots from the plant to encourage them to grow out into the soil.

3 Once you have made sure that the hole is big enough to take the rootball, backfill with soil and press down firmly with your foot.

4 Feed with a general garden fertilizer. Sprinkle it around the plant, keeping away from the stem. Water the plant well.

planting hole with well-rotted organic matter and a little bonemeal, but in most gardens this is unnecessary. It is far more important to use the precious organic matter as a mulch on top of the soil after you have planted to help prevent competition from weeds and to retain soil moisture around the establishing roots.

Water container-grown plants thoroughly before planting and leave to drain. Bare-root specimens should have their roots plunged into a bucket of water. If the soil is dry, fill the hole with water too and allow to drain. Remove the pot from container-grown specimens and tease out the roots from around the rootball before planting. This will encourage the roots to spread into

This planting makes the most of the different shapes, textures and heights that shrubs have.

PLANTING A BALLED OR ROOT-WRAPPED SHRUB

1 Check the the hole is the correct depth for the balled or root-wrapped shrub by placing a level over the hole.

2 When the plant is in position, untie the plastic or hessian and slide it out from underneath. Avoid disturbing the root soil.

3 Replace the soil and firm well with your foot. Sprinkle fertilizer around the plant, avoiding the stem, and water well.

4 Mulch the ground after planting to conserve moisture. This not only keeps down weeds but looks attractive, too.

the surrounding soil. Place the plant in the centre of the hole and then step back to check that it is upright and that you have the best 'face' at the front. Backfill the first few centimetres (1in) around the rootball of bare-root specimens before gently shaking the plant to get the soil particles to trickle down between the fine roots. All new shrubs should then have the hole filled in layers, carefully firming each layer to remove air pockets before repeating the process, until the hole is filled.

After planting, level the surface and then water the shrub thoroughly before applying a generous 8cm- (3in-) deep organic mulch around the plant, taking care not to pile it up against the stem. If your garden is exposed, protect new shrubs after planting by putting up a windbreak barrier. This is particularly important for evergreens. If rabbits are a pest in your garden, you will need to protect stems with special spiral rabbit guards, too.

Planting climbers

Most climbers are planted in the same way as described for shrubs, although the technique varies slightly depending on the type of support they are being grown against. Clematis are the main exception to this rule, since they are planted deeper than other climbers as a precaution against disease (*see* box opposite).

Planting next to walls and fences

Thorough soil preparation is the key to success when planting next to vertical surfaces, especially if they have foundations. The soil at the base of a wall or fence is usually dry because the border is in the rain shadow of the solid barrier and is often shallow and impoverished. Therefore, it is essential to improve the moisture-holding capacity of the soil by incorporating well-rotted organic matter before planting. Clear all weeds and debris from the soil as you go. If the soil is particularly poor, it may be worth replacing it with fresh soil from elsewhere in the garden or buying it (*see* pages 90-91). Also make sure any supporting wires or trellis that is to be attached to the vertical surface is put up before planting (*see* pages 96-9).

You can also aid establishment of the climber by planting it away from the vertical surface so that its roots can spread out in all directions. Dig a hole about 30–45cm (12–18in) away from the wall or fence about twice as wide as the rootball of a container-grown climber. Place the excavated soil on a plastic sheet or old soil bag next to the hole. Unless you are planting a clematis (*see* below), the hole should be as deep as the container or rootball, so that the specimen will be planted at the same depth as it is in the pot. If necessary, you can check this by standing the pot in the planting hole and laying a bamboo cane across the hole. Remove or replace soil as necessary until the correct planting depth is achieved. Then, fork over

PLANTING A CLIMBER

1 Start by digging a hole twice the size of the rootball. The centre of the plant should be at least 30cm (12in) from the wall.

2 Dig in a generous amount of rotted manure or garden compost. This will help retain moisture around the roots.

3 Put the rootball in the hole, having teased out some of the roots to aid growing. Firm the soil around the plant.

4 Loosen the stems if they have been tied to a cane, spread them out, high and low, and tie them onto the trellis.

5 Water in well and regularly. Climbers need more water as they are usually planted where walls or other plants shield them from rain.

6 Apply a mulch at least 5cm (2in) deep around the plant to help reduce water loss and supress weeds. Don't pile over the stem.

the bottom of the planting hole. Improve the excavated soil and the soil in the planting hole with well-rotted organic matter and a little bonemeal. Water the climber thoroughly before planting and fill the planting hole with water and allow to drain. Remove the pot and tease out the roots from around the rootball before planting to encourage the roots to spread into the surrounding soil. Place the climber in the centre of the hole and angle it backwards at 45 degrees towards the support. Then backfill the excavated soil around the rootball in layers, carefully firming each layer to remove air pockets. Repeat the process until the hole is filled. After planting, level the surface and then water the climber thoroughly before applying a generous 8cm (3in) deep organic mulch around the plant, but take care not to pile it up against the stem.

Planting next to arches and pergolas

Freestanding supports should be erected and the soil allowed to settle before climbers are planted,

Ideal for growing up supports, *Clematis* 'Jackmanii' is a sun-seeker and will thrive in sunny spots.

Plant clematis deep

Clematis should be planted deeper than other climbers so that the base of their stems are underground. This means making the planting hole about 8cm (3in) deeper then normal. This technique is a precaution against clematis wilt disease, which is a serious problem with clematis – killing all the top-growth. However, any shoots underground are unaffected, so that any deeply planted clematis that suffer from this disease can recover by producing new shoots the following year from healthy buds that form at the base of the stems underground.

following the technique described above. You can plant right next to the support if space is limited, unless foundations were laid under the soil to support the structure. Once planted, untie the climber from its supporting cane in the pot and spread out the stems. Carefully tie them into the support. If there is only one stem, tie the cane into the support and pinch out the tip of the climber to encourage new side shoots to be produced.

Planting near shrubs and trees

Climbers can also be planted alongside established shrubs and trees that can be used as a natural support. The soil is likely to be dry and full of roots, so choose a planting position at the edge of the host plant's canopy, where water will naturally run off when it rains – this is known as the 'drip zone'. Carefully excavate a hole and cut off any fibrous roots that have become exposed. If large roots are in the way, move the planting hole to another position. Improve the soil as before, then line the sides of the planting hole with old pieces of softwood. This will help prevent the surrounding roots from the host plant competing with the climber while it becomes established. In time, the timber will rot away.

Providing support: vertical surfaces

Although some climbers can scramble up, over and through supports without any assistance, all wall shrubs and some climbers require a helping hand. By providing wires, trellis or mesh supports, you can also train the climbers and wall shrubs to go exactly where you want them to grow.

Supporting climbers and wall shrubs

There are a number of ways you can support climbers and wall shrubs up a vertical wall or fence. It is essential that you choose a support that's robust and sufficiently large to match the vigour of the climber or wall shrub. For example, annual sweet peas can be supported on plastic mesh or wire netting loosely anchored to the vertical surface, while a vigorous clematis will need a substantial trellis that's been securely screwed into place. Indeed, some climbers, such as wisteria, can reach tree-like proportions and need a heavy-duty support to match. The support system you choose should

Some climbers can cling to brick, stone or wood by putting out modified roots.

Vigorous clematis varieties are ideal for clothing the walls, particularly if you want to hide eyesores, such as compost bins.

also be in keeping with its surroundings. For example, on a decorative wall, you may prefer to use a series of parallel wires that are invisible to the naked eye from a short distance. On the other hand, a less attractive structure can be camouflaged or enhanced by adding prominent decorative trellis as a support for a new climber.

Using wires

Most climbers and wall shrubs can be supported using wires. Wires are the most versatile support, covering any shape or size of surface. Choose a strong galvanized or plastic-coated wire, say 10 to 14 gauge. The wire needs to be held 5–8cm (2–3in) away from the wall or fence using special wall fixings called vine-eyes. This gap will allow air to flow around the plant and help prevent the wall remaining damp for long periods. There are two types of vine-eye: triangular pegs that are hammered into the mortar between courses, or screw-in eyelets that are

Clinging plants will cover any vertical surface without needing any support, as seen with this *Hydrangea petiolaris*.

secured in holes drilled into the wall and filled with wall plugs. Space parallel wires every 30cm (12in) up the wall for most climbers and wall shrubs, but use a fan-shaped or even vertical arrangement of wires for twining climbers. When training and tying in new growth to the support, make sure that it is in front of the wires, so that it helps to hide the wires, the plants are easy to prune and, if necessary, can be detached and lowered from the wall without removing the support system.

Using trellis

Wooden trellis is available in a range of decorative shapes and sizes, but you can also make your own from inexpensive wooden lathes, which can be bought from builders' merchants. These will have been pressure-treated against rot, so just need to be cut to length and fixed with screws. Making your own trellis won't work out any cheaper than buying ready made, but it can be tailored to fit any size or shape of wall or fence.

All types of trellis need to be attached to battens or wooden blocks on the wall so that the trellis is held 3–4cm (1–1½in) away from the vertical surface. Ready-made trellis may look attractive, but the battens are actually spaced too close together. If you make you own, aim to space them 30cm (12in) apart for most climbers and wall shrubs. Expanding trellis is even worse. It isn't as strong as ready-made panels and is usually more expensive. However, it is easy to transport and can be expanded to fit the space available, so is worth considering for very restricted areas and lightweight climbers.

Ready-made trellis is also useful for extending the height of your boundary fence. Special post extensions are available, or you can make your own using 8cm- (3in-) wide exterior quality plywood. There is a wide range of trellis styles available, from simple squares to a diamond pattern or basket weave, so you can select one to suit your garden design.

Trellis can be used to break up the appearance of large walls and fences, too. For example, eye-catching perspective panels effectively draw the eye to the centre of the trellis and the climber it supports. Alternatively, use strips of standard trellis panels to hide a prominent downpipe or other eyesore or paint decorative trellis as an effective way of disguising ugly walls or fences, or even a garden shed. Choose from a wide range of coloured stains made for the purpose, or make your own by diluting oil-based exterior gloss paint in the colour of your choice with white spirit in the ratio of 1:3.

Using mesh

Plastic-coated wire mesh or plastic mesh panels are also available in a limited range of colours. They are easy to cut to size and can be shaped around doorways or windows, used

GROWING CLIMBERS UP WIRES

1 Drill holes where you want the vine-eyes, which will support the plant, to go. You can hammer them in, but a drill makes it easier.

2 If you are using vine-eyes with a screw fixing, insert a plastic plug into the wall first. Then screw the eye into the plug.

3 If you are using wedge vine-eyes, hammer them into the masonry .

4 Thread the wire through the hole in the vine-eye and then wrap the excess back on itself to keep it taut and secure.

5 Arrange the longest stems to the wire and tie in with plastic ties or string. Ensure that the stems lie flat against the wall.

6 The stems should be fanned so the plant can cover the wall as it grows and produce more buds on the top edges of the stems.

to cover downpipes or to fill in gaps in freestanding structures such as arches.

Like wires and trellis, they will also need supporting away from the wall using vine-eyes or wooden battens. However, mesh is less pleasing on the eye than trellis and plastic mesh isn't strong enough for vigorous climbers.

Access for maintenance

Both the vertical support and the trellis attached to it will need maintenance from time to time. Although most ready-made trellis has been pressure-treated against rot, which should protect it for at least

ten years, the trellis may need repairing every now and then as the staples may become loosened by wind-rock and the weight of the climber pulling on it.

Some climbers can be cut back to near ground level to free the trellis, which can be removed so that the supporting wall or fence can be maintained. With sufficient space and a flexible climber, you might prefer to unscrew the trellis and lay it down on the ground with the climber still attached while you carry out repairs. However, if the wall requires regular maintenance, painting for example, you can make the whole job easier if you attach the

Some climbers hold on by twining up their support as they grow, and so do not require routine tying in through the growing season.

ERECTING A TRELLIS

1 Start by digging a hole at least 60cm (2ft) deep. If your soil is light, you may need to dig an even deeper hole to secure the trellis.

2 Put the post in the hole and partly fill with a dry-mix concrete. Check the upright, adjust if necessary and then continue filling the hole.

3 When you fill the hole with concrete, make sure to ram it down very firmly. Once the concrete has 'cured' it will be solidly secure.

4 Lay the trellis next to the ground to work out where the next hole should be. Dig the next hole as for the first.

5 You now have two posts at the right position for the trellis. Offer up the trellis and nail the panel on to the supporting posts.

6 As you progress putting up the panels, stop and check the uprights regularly, ensuring they are level and at the right angle.

bottom of the trellis panel to the lower batten using galvanized hinges. You can then can lower the top of the panel away from the wall and replace it in exactly the right position in just a few seconds.

Next to doors and windows

Climbers and wall shrubs can look delightful when trained to frame a doorway or window and, as long as you choose the right plants, it is as easy to achieve as growing them against other vertical surfaces.

Aim to choose a plant that will provide year-round interest. This effect can be formal or informal, depending on the type of plant you choose. For example, a small-leaved evergreen could be used to create neat, leafy pillars if they are positioned on either side of the door, while a languid, scrambling clematis or rose can offer garlands of colour and scent throughout the summer months.

Plants to avoid around doors and windows include anything that is very vigorous, because it will need constant cutting back. Also steer clear of thorny climbers and wall shrubs, opting for the spineless varieties instead, as children and unaware visitors could get nasty scratches if they brush against them.

Plants that are prone to being attacked by sap-sucking insects, such as honeysuckle, are also worth avoiding, because the resultant honeydew excreted by such pests will make a mess on your windows, as well as making the ground around a doorway sticky underfoot.

Train your selected plants up the wall to the side of the window or doorway by tying them into a support. To do this, either use strong horizontal wires spaced 30cm (12in) apart up the wall, held taut

A fragrant honeysuckle will take just one or two seasons to clothe supporting trellis. The plant is ideal for growing up structures, as it is not too heavy and spreads well.

between vine-eyes, or install a trellis by screwing it to a series of battens. This will ensure good air circulation between the wall and the plant, helping to prevent disease problems. Make sure the battens are made from pressure-treated timber to prevent rot and that they are fixed with rust-resistant screws. You can either plant the climber or wall shrub straight into the soil at the base of the wall

or you may prefer to set it into a large, permanent container. Before you begin planting, make sure the soil has been improved with well-rotted organic matter and keep the plant well watered until it has become established.

Position the climber or wall shrub at least 18in (45cm) away from either side of the doorway so that there is room for growth.

Providing support: freestanding structures

Climbers can be used to cover vertical structures all around the garden. They are an ideal way of adding height to borders as well as creating living focal points that attract the eye.

Arches and pergolas

Although attractive features in their own right, arches and pergolas can be used to enhance the overall design of the garden: framing an entrance or feature; leading the eye farther down the garden; connecting separate elements within the garden; or creating the illusion of space by emphasizing an attractive view outside the garden. Pergolas are useful for creating secluded seating areas or a shady refuge in a hot sunny garden. Both pergolas and arches can also be used to create covered walkways.

Arches and pergolas are available in a wide range of styles and materials, so there should be one to suit your garden. For example, metal structures look most at home in modern or formal garden settings, while rustic wooden pergolas and

This metal archway provides medium support. The Golden hop (*Humulus lupulus* 'Aureus') plant covers the arch with a mass of yellow leaves, which support themselves with curling stems.

arches are perfect for a more relaxed cottage-style garden. For best effect, choose a structure that fits in with its surroundings and select a combination of climbers to suit the position you have in mind as well as the size of the structure. Bear in mind what the structure will look like in winter. An ornate metal structure will tend to stand out and

Creating a living arch

If you have hedges on either side of a pathway, you can create a living arch by training them together. To do this, first select two or three upright growing shoots on the hedging plants adjacent to the path, trimming the rest of the stems back. Insert a 3m (10ft) cane into the ground next to the stems so that they can be trained up vertically. Each year, trim the hedge as usual, leaving the selected stems un-pruned.

When the un-pruned shoots reach about 2.5m (8ft), remove the canes and tie a hoop of wire to the stems on either side of the path, so that the top of the hoop is about the right height for the arch. Then, bend the selected stems over the hoop and tie them in using soft string. If they are long enough to touch at the top of the hoop, tie them together.

Continue to tie in new shoots in subsequent years until the arch is thick enough and the desired shape has been achieved. In following years, keep in shape by regular trimming when you cut back the rest of the hedge. Any type of hedging plant can be trained in this way.

To help climbers get a good coverage, tie in their stems, spreading them out so that they are near horizontal, to encourage flowering.

Repeat-flowering roses are ideal for growing up archways, as they will provide colour and cover for a longer season.

Even when it is not in flower, wisteria makes a good covering for structures because its foliage is abundant even when its characteristically beautiful lavender-coloured drooping blooms are over.

This simple arch is constructed using rustic poles and is covered with variegated ivy.

become a feature in its own right, while one made from wood is likely to blend in more with the rest of your garden.

Metal structures Metal arches and pergolas can be practically maintenance-free if well made. Make sure they are coated completely to prevent corrosion, especially around joints, welds and drilled holes. The structure should seem sturdy and rigid, with strong joints and welds. Have a small tin of matching exterior paint to hand to touch up any chips or unprotected areas after erection to ensure protection.

Wooden structures Most softwood arches and pergolas are pressure-treated to prevent rot, but if you have bought one from a local supplier it's worth checking this before you buy. If the wood was treated before it was cut, then untreated wood will be exposed to the elements and will need painting with preservative before you put the structure together. All wooden arches and pergolas should have strong joints and should not be warped.

Check that the structure is well braced with cross-members so that it will be rigid once put together.

Pergolas and arches are available in kit form, usually flat-packed, and are relatively easy to construct. However, it may require two people to put them together. The key to success is to make sure that the posts are vertical and spaced correctly before securing them and that the crossbars are horizontal. The structure will have to bear the weight of the climbers it supports, which can be considerable after heavy rain. Climber-clad arches and pergolas

Sited in the middle of a wildflower meadow, this wonderfully romantic arch serves no purpose other than to support some roses and provide an absolutely beautiful scene.

A combination of sweet-scented roses, clematis and an overhanging fig makes an intimate, shady area for sitting and relaxing in the summer months.

A newly planted arbour will eventually be smothered in foliage and blooms, creating a tranquil spot for sitting.

also put up a lot of wind resistance when the climbers are in leaf, so check how rigid the structure is before you buy. All types of arches and pergolas need to be well anchored to keep them secure.

Mid-border structures

Simple garden structures such as single posts and tripods are much underrated and under-used. They are ideal for adding instant and inexpensive points of focus to a garden. There are many decorative obelisks now available that look attractive all year round without the need for a climber. Pots and tripods also make effective markers at the ends of paths – acting like sentries to emphasize a change in direction or a meeting point. Posts can also be effective when linked with timber crossbars or wire at the back of the border to provide a backdrop. When festooned with climbers, the simple structure becomes a cascade of colourful flowers and foliage that will add height to your borders and help provide privacy. Making mid-

border plant supports is very straightforward. For example, you can create an attractive obelisk from inexpensive wooden roofing laths, available from builders' merchants, which come pressure treated against rot. First construct four 2.5m (8ft) high triangular frames that are 45cm (18in) wide at the base, then attach

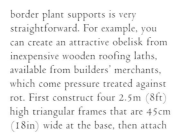

horizontal battens on each triangle using the same wood, spacing them about 15cm (6in) apart. Fit the four sides together, securing them with weather-proof screws. Finally, add a fence post finial to the top as a finishing touch. You can also make a traditional colonnade out of posts and rope or lengths of plastic chain

A large arbour, built for entertaining, is covered by a variety of climbers, including a purple grapevine (*Vitis vinifera* 'Purpurea'), which needs a strong trellis or pergola to support it.

– an ideal way to make a feature out of your favourite climbing rose. You can also combine trellis with posts within the garden to divide the growing area into separate 'rooms' or to add height to beds and borders. The trellis needn't be a continuous screen – you can create the impression of separate areas using just a couple of matching screens on either side of a pathway and they won't make the garden seem too small or the divisions too claustrophobic. Ornate screens that have been stained in a colour that complements or contrasts with the colour scheme of the surrounding

A secluded spot tucked away in the garden allows you to view your gardening efforts in peace and quiet after a hard day of digging, weeding and pruning.

Growing climbers into established shrubs

Climbers look their most natural when climbing through other shrubs and trees. It is important that you match the vigour of the climber to its host plant and try to choose one that flowers at a different time so that the climber extends the period of interest. The host plant needs to be well established, but not so old that it is no longer growing vigorously.

Position the climber on the side of the prevailing wind so that any gusts will blow the climber as it grows into the host plant rather than away from it. After planting the climber (see pages 94–5), hammer a short stake into the ground nearby and attach a rope to the stake. The other end of the rope should be attached to a suitable low branch of the host plant. Untie the climber from its supporting cane, then tie it to the rope, and if the stems are long enough, train them into the canopy of the supporting plant. Do not, as is sometimes recommended, loop the bottom end of the rope under the rootball of the climber when planting, because the climber is likely to be pulled out of the ground by the first strong gust of wind.

plants are the most eye-catching. However, in a small garden you may prefer to give the screen a more neutral or rustic finish so that it is recessive on the eye and blends naturally into the garden. For those who have smaller gardens, siting a mirror surrounded by climbing

foliage will give the illusion of more space. Combine this with an arch and the optical effect is one of leading the viewer into another part of the garden, hitherto unseen. A similar effect can be achieved by siting a sculpture at the end of a vista to give a sense of space.

A romantic walkway is created from a series of arches along a path cut through long grass. The arches provide a tunnel effect, leading the eye to the end, where a statue completes the view.

Watering and mulching

Watering is one of the most important and time-consuming tasks around the garden. It makes sense, therefore, to be water-wise and use this increasingly precious resource as efficiently as possible.

Watering efficiently

How often your garden will need watering will be determined by the following factors: the type of plants you have (each plant grows at a different rate); the plant's absorption rate and ability to retain moisture; the site's exposure to sun and wind; the depth and type of mulch you use (if any); the amount of recent rainfall; the amount of hot, drying sunshine; and the amount of organic matter in the soil. Each of these factors will affect how quickly your garden dries out.

Plants lose water through their leaves all the time so it is essential to water regularly to make sure they have enough moisture to replenish the roots, otherwise they will die. Plants growing next to walls and fences tend to dry out more easily and so need extra watering.

Saving water

You can collect your own water to use in your garden. A water butt plumbed into a downpipe off the house or an outbuilding can be in exactly the right place to water climbers and wall shrubs in dry borders alongside. There are many decorative versions now available, some shaped like terracotta pots and urns, so there is no need to hide them away. The butt should also be easy to use. Make sure it is raised so that you can get a watering can or hose to the drainage tap at the base. Choose a butt with a cover to keep the water 'sweet' and clean.

If you live in a hard-water area, saving rainwater is a good idea as it's slightly acidic and so is perfect for watering acid-loving shrubs and climbers grown in ericaceous soil. Waste water from washing or bathing can also be recycled in the garden. Known as 'grey-water', it is suitable for applying to established shrubs and climbers.

That said, most shrubs and climbers do not need regular watering once they are established. However, on well-drained and shallow soils, and elsewhere during drought periods, it is a good idea to water judiciously.

Newly planted shrubs and climbers should be kept well watered throughout their first growing season until they have become well established. You might need to water them for longer if your soil is dry, which is often the case at the base of a wall or on a sunny slope.

Efficient watering

The key to watering efficiently is to water thoroughly when and where it is needed.

Watering a little and often is a common mistake made by novice gardeners. This not only wastes a lot more water through evaporation, but it means that only the surface layer of the soil is moistened. This encourages shallow rooting, which exacerbates the problems you will have during dry spells. Aim to apply the equivalent of 2.5cm (1in) of water to drought-affected borders. It is best to water during the evening, especially in summer, as this will prevent unnecessary water loss through evaporation caused by the sun drying out the water you have just applied. Also, the hot sun acts like a magnifying glass on the watered leaves and can scorch them.

Rain is slightly acidic, so ericaceous plants like rhododendrons benefit from being watered with rainwater. Collect it in a water butt.

Watering systems

Apart from using a watering can, there are several different watering systems available to make the tedious task of watering plants easier.

Perforated hosing This consists of plastic tubing punctured with tiny holes through which the water slowly leaks out. This type of system can be quickly removed when it is no longer needed.

Seep or soak hosing A flexible, porous hose made from rubber is buried in the ground and left in for a season or more.

Drip irrigation This is a system professional growers use. One or more drip nozzles deliver water to individual plants or containers. It can be designed to cover any size and shape of garden.

Sprinklers Although mainly used by gardeners to water their lawns, sprinklers can be very helpful for dowsing beds and borders.

When watering, aim the water directly to the root areas of the plants rather than spreading it liberally all over the garden. You can avoid wetting the surface altogether by sinking a pot or pipe filled with gravel next to the plant and applying the water through this. If the soil surface remains dry, there is the added benefit of fewer weeds to deal with.

Applying a mulch

You can reduce the need for watering still further by applying a loose mulch or laying a proprietary mulch mat. These methods will stop water evaporating out of the soil surface and also help to prevent weed seeds germinating. They are best applied in spring when the soil is moist and also weed-free.

There are two main methods of mulching plants:

Loose mulches These are organic or inorganic mulches, and are the most popular because they not only help to reduce water loss and prevent weed competition, but they also provide food for soil-borne creatures such as ground beetles and earthworms.

These creatures incorporate the humus into the soil and improve its structure and fertility. However, the mulch will need to be topped up each year to remain effective. Aim to apply the mulch of organic matter at a thickness of 5–8cm (2–3in). Use a mulch of well-rotted garden compost, composted bark or cocoa shells and remember to keep topping it up each spring.

Inorganic loose mulches, such as pea gravel and pebbles, also reduce water loss and prevent weeds, but they do not help to feed the soil. On the plus side, however, they look attractive and do not require topping up each spring, so offering an easy-care alternative to organic mulches.

Sheet mulches When you are planting up specimen shrubs and climbers, specially made sheet mulches are an option that is well worth considering.

Also known as mulch matting or landscape fabric, these sheets are all weed-proof. They are more effective weed barriers than loose mulches, but do not look as attractive. However, they can be disguised with a thin layer of soil or mulch if used in a prominent position.

To apply a sheet mulch, lay it over the prepared soil and cut cross-shaped slits in the sheet for the climber to be slotted into. For planted shrubs, place the sheet around the bottom of the plant, surrounding the base of the plant by an area of at least 1 sq m (1 sq yard) of sheeting.

USING DIFFERENT TYPES OF MULCH

1 Bare soil is prone to weeds and loses water through evaporation. Before applying a mulch, remove any weeds in the bed.

2 Avoid using grass clippings as a mulch as they deplete the nitrogen in the soil. They may also root, causing a weed problem.

3 Composted bark is attractive as a mulch. However, don't use fresh bark as it may deplete the soil of nitrogen as it decomposes.

Weeding and feeding

Weeds not only spoil the display but they also compete with your plants for soil moisture and nutrients. Most gardeners find weeding a chore, but there are ways you can keep weeding to a minimum without sacrificing the appearance of your garden.

Keeping weeds at bay

The best way to prevent weeds becoming a problem is to thoroughly clear soil of all weeds, including the entire root system of perennial weeds such as dock, bindweed and couch grass, before planting. Thereafter, you can go a long way to prevent new weeds colonizing your garden by preventing them gaining a foothold. In practice, this means keeping bare soil to a minimum and tackling weeds as soon as they are noticed. You can cover bare soil by planting up all beds and borders, filling any gaps with ground cover plants or mulches (see page 105). Between well-established woody plants such as in a shrubbery, you can use a special chemical to treat the soil surface that inhibits any weed seed from germinating. However, such products cannot be used in borders with bulbs or herbaceous plants

since the new growth will be damaged as it pushes through the chemically treated soil.

Controlling weeds

Even in the best-kept gardens, weed problems can occur from time to time. The best strategy is to tackle them early, before they have a chance to flower and set seed. The old saying 'one year's seed means seven years' weed' is as true today as it has ever been.

Annual weeds, such as groundsel and chickweed, are easy to tackle, either by ripping them out by hand or hoeing them off between shrubs. Take care not to hoe too deeply and avoid hoeing between shallow-rooted shrubs or those prone to suckering, such as rhus.

Perennial weeds are more difficult, because you have to remove the whole of the root system from the soil to prevent it regrowing from below ground. With tap-rooted perennial weeds, such as dandelions and thistles, this can be difficult enough, but with brittle-rooted perennial weeds, such as couch grass and bindweed, it's nigh-on impossible! Indeed, if you have a widespread problem with the latter,

Use a spade to dig out large, unwanted plants and weeds before you prepare the ground for your shrubs and climbers.

you might be better off digging up all the plants so that you can painstakingly clear the soil of every bit of weed root, before replanting. If you do this, make sure there are no weed roots hidden in the rootball of the shrub or climber, otherwise all this effort will have been in vain.

Another method you can try is to kill perennial weeds by constantly cutting them back to ground level each time they re-sprout. Over time, they will gradually weaken and eventually die if they are unable to photosynthesize. However, you will have to be as tenacious as they are and be very thorough about removing them at all times.

The final option is to tackle the weeds using a chemical weedkiller. There are two types available: contact weedkillers, which kill the parts of the weed they touch; and systemic weedkillers, which are taken up by the weeds and transported inside it, killing all parts.

Take care when applying weedkillers as they will kill anything that they come into contact with – and that could mean your ornamental plants as well. For this reason, you will have to either use a dab-on-the-spot treatment, which you apply directly to the weed leaves by hand, or cover ornamental plants

Removing weeds by hand is a laborious task, but it is necessary when weeding larger annual weeds and perennial weeds.

Hoeing is a quick and simple weeding method. It is an ideal way of removing weed seedlings that have just emerged.

with plastic before spraying the weeds between them. Leave the plastic in position until the weedkiller has dried completely to avoid accidentally affecting the nearby shrubs or climbers.

Feeding shrubs and climbers

All plants need nutrients to keep them healthy and enable them to produce a magnificent display of blooms. Unfortunately, they have to compete with each other to get their fair share of food. This is especially true when the plants are crowded into beds and borders to make a lush display. The more crowded they are, the more they have to compete, particularly those that have been newly planted and are in need of extra care and support.

Get new shrubs and climbers to establish quickly by applying a slow-release fertilizer, such as blood, fish and bonemeal, over the rooting area during early spring. Thereafter, if your soil is in good condition, most well-established shrubs and climbers will need no regular feeding.

However, hungry shrubs, such as roses and lilacs, and floriferous climbers, such as clematis, do

Before planting, prepare the soil and then sprinkle a balanced fertilizer evenly over the planting area.

Granular fertilizer can be applied by hand. Apply it as a top dressing according to the manufacturer's instructions.

perform better if given an annual feed. On poor soils, use a general balanced fertilizer containing a 7-7-7 balance of NPK nutrients – nitrogen (N), phosphorus (P) and potassium (K) – to promote healthy growth throughout the garden (*see* page 91). These ready-made preparations are widely available at garden centres and DIY stores.

Apply the general fertilizer over the root area during early spring. Double this amount for hungry shrubs, such as roses. During the early summer months, you can also give your shrubbery a fillip by applying a foliar feed using a hose-end diluter, but do not feed after

mid-summer, otherwise you will promote soft new growth that won't have time to ripen before winter and will be liable to frost damage.

If your plants are already established, choose a slow-release or controlled-release fertilizer so that the plants will receive all the nutrients they need throughout the summer months.

Feeding container plants

Liquid feed is suitable for container-grown shrubs and climbers. Add the feed to the water and give to the plant every 1–3 weeks, depending on the type of plant and the manufacturer's recommendations.

FEEDING YOUR PLANTS

1 Add fertilizer at the rate recommended by the manufacturer. Use a controlled release fertilizer if planting in the autumn.

2 Gently hoe the fertilizer into the soil. This will help it penetrate the soil more easily and provide nutrients for the plant more quickly.

3 Water around the plant thoroughly to ensure the nutrients are taken down into the root system area.

Protecting vulnerable plants

Frosts, wind, heavy snowfalls and excessive rain can all kill vulnerable shrubs and climbers during the winter months, so take steps to protect them in autumn before the onset of the coldest weather.

Preventing weather damage

Frosty weather can cause water in plants' cells to freeze. When this happens, the cell walls of the plant are damaged. This makes the plants limp and they become distorted, with their leaves and stems wilting and blackening. If the ground is frozen, water lost through the leaves of evergreens cannot be replaced and so the leaves become scorched and unsightly. In severe cases, the whole plant can be killed.

Wind damage is also a problem. Evergreens in particular are susceptible to wind during the winter months. Newly planted evergreens are most at risk, so make sure these are protected with a screen of windbreak netting or hessian sacking material held taught between stout, securely anchored posts. Some deciduous shrubs are also susceptible

to wind damage. Japanese maples, for example, often suffer die-back at the tips of branches. Also, their emerging leaves in spring can be scorched before they have had a chance to unfurl. However, they can be protected in exactly the same way as evergreens.

Groups of susceptible low-growing shrubs, such as ground cover plants or dwarf shrubs such as hebes, are easier to protect by laying the windbreak netting directly over the top. If your garden gets a lot of snow in winter, lift the material clear of the shrubs using hoops or bamboo canes.

Climbers and wall shrubs can be protected by attaching a double sheet of fine-mesh netting or garden fleece on either side above the vulnerable plant and then stuffing between the sheets with insulating material for protection.

Preventing root damage

Many borderline-hardy shrubs, such as hardy fuchsia, *Phygelius* and *Romneya*, as well as borderline-hardy climbers, such as passionflower and

Climbers that are vulnerable to temperature damage can be protected by covering them with netting during the worst of the weather.

solanum, will produce new shoots from the crown in spring even if all the top-growth is killed over the winter. The best way to protect these is to insulate the roots with a layer of insulation material before the cold weather starts. You can either pile on a 15cm- (6in-) deep layer of dry leaves, straw or bark chippings, or use prunings cut from evergreen hedges. If using dry leaves, ideally choose ones that don't rot down too quickly, such as oak, beech or chestnut tree leaves. In exposed gardens, keep the leaves in position by pegging down netting over the top or create a low fence around each plant with a piece of plastic or wire mesh. If your soil is very well drained, you can even protect vulnerable plants by mounding soil over the crowns in winter, clearing it away again before new shoots appear in spring.

To protect a tender shrub, you can provide a shield for it. To do this, insert three stout stakes firmly into the ground around the plant. Wrap bubble wrap, plastic sheeting or several layers of horticultural fleece around the outside of the stakes. Tie securely and peg down the bottom.

Avoiding winter wet

A few shrubs, such as *Convolvulus cneorum* and sage, are susceptible to winter wet, particularly if the soil is not well drained. Put an up-turned pot, slightly raised on stones to allow good air circulation, over the top to keep off the worst of the rain. Alternatively, you could use open-ended barn cloches. Another option is to grow these plants in containers and move them into a protected area, such as underneath the eaves of the house, for the winter.

Insulating containers

Even hardy plants in containers may need protection during the winter months. During spells with sub-zero temperatures the rootball is liable to freeze solid, damaging fine roots and preventing the plant from taking up any moisture.

   You can help to prevent this by planting in frost-proof containers so that the pots don't crack when the temperature drops. Once the cold well and truly sets in, move small plants to a sheltered position at the base of a hedge or beside the house.

Conifers are particularly susceptible to damage caused by the weight of heavy snow, which can pull the plant out of shape or break its boughs. Prevent damage by tying up the shrub before winter. If you are too late and the snow has fallen, knock it off before any damage is caused.

A temporary method of protecting plants is to cover them with a large plastic bag or horticultural fleece sleeve.

Another method is to plunge them rim-deep into the border soil.

   The easiest method is to insulate the pot with bubble wrap packaging material or improvise a protective 'duvet' made from a plastic bag stuffed with dry leaves or crumpled newspaper. Tie the insulating material securely right around the pot. If the plant is only borderline hardy for your area, you could protect this using bubble wrap or a double layer of garden fleece. Make sure there is an access flap to the pot, so the plant can be watered if necessary and allowed to breathe. If there isn't sufficient air, the plant will rot and die from condensation building up inside the plastic.

   Vulnerable shrubs grown as standards, such as bay, can have their stem protected using a foam pipe insulating tube. Move them out of windy areas where they could be knocked over by high winds.

   Despite all your efforts, excessive cold or chill, drying winds will almost certainly kill off one or two of your plants – but wait until spring before getting rid of them, as they could well surprise you and come back to life.

Moving established plants

No matter how good you are at planning your garden, at some stage you may change your mind about where a shrub or climber should go. Another reason for moving shrubs or climbers is that sometimes, despite your regular pruning efforts, a plant outgrows its allotted space and threatens to overwhelm the other plants. If a plant outgrows its welcome, it is time to move it on.

The best time to move

Moving established plants is hard work and requires careful planning. Rootballs will be difficult to dig up and heavy to move, so you will probably need help.

The best time to move established deciduous plants is during the dormant season (late autumn to early spring). Choose a time when the soil is not frozen or waterlogged. The transplants will establish more

quickly if the soil is warm and moist, so the depths of winter are best avoided.

Evergreens, including conifers, are best moved in mid-spring when the soil is moist and warm so that they have time to re-establish themselves before the onset of winter. On heavy soils, delay moves until the soil dries out in late spring.

How to move established plants

Before you start, you should prepare the planting site to receive the transplanted plant. To do this, dig a hole about twice as wide and as deep as the rootball. Fork over the bottom of the hole and incorporate a bucketful of grit to improve drainage on heavy soils. If the rootball is large, make sure there is an easy access route to the new hole, so that the rootball can be dragged into position if necessary.

When preparing the rootball, first clear any weeds and loose soil from under the canopy of the plant. Then, use a sharp spade to mark out the circumference of the rootball. Cut a slit-trench, using the line as a guide, by pushing the spade in vertically to its full depth all the way round the established plant, severing any roots as you go. Move away about 30cm (12in) and make a second slit-trench running parallel to the first.

Dig out the soil between the two to create a moat-like trench right around the plant being moved. This trench should be as deep as the rootball you are trying to create.

Use the spade at an angle to undercut all the way around the rootball from the bottom of the trench, again severing any roots that are encountered. This should be sufficient to free rootballs under 45cm (18in) in diameter. The

Once you are happy about where your shrubs have been planted and they have enough room to reach their best growth and shape, you can relax and enjoy a spectacular display for years to come.

MOVING AN ESTABLISHED SHRUB

1 If possible, root-prune the shrub a few months before moving to encourage the formation of fibrous roots.

2 Dig a trench around the plant, leaving the rootball completely uncovered. Sever any roots, if necessary, to remove the rootball.

3 Dig under the shrub as far as you can. It may be necessary to cut through any tap roots that are stubbornly holding it in place.

4 Tilt the plant to one side and insert a sheet of sacking or plastic. Push several folds of the material under the rootball.

5 Rock the rootball in the opposite direction and pull the material through, so that it is completely underneath the plant.

6 Pull the material around the rootball to enclose the soil and tie it securely. The plant is now ready for moving.

7 Heavier plants require a joint effort. Slide a pole through the material. With one person on each end, lift the shrub out of the hole.

8 Having prepared the ground at the new site, follow the reverse procedure for planting the shrub in its new home.

rootball can then be carefully wrapped and secured with string. Larger rootballs may need further excavation to reveal any vertical roots at the centre of the rootball.

Wrap large rootballs by rocking the rootball over to one side and placing a folded piece of heavy-duty plastic or sacking underneath. By rocking the rootball the other way you can release the leading edge of the material, which can then be pulled through. Securely tie the corners of the material together over the rootball and tie these to the main stem. To keep the soil in position, use strong string to wrap up the rootball tightly on all sides as well as underneath.

Move the rootball by slipping a sturdy post or pole through the wrapping. Do not lift the rootball by the trunk because the soil will not be supported and it will crumble away. Very large rootballs are easier to drag from one place to the other. Create a ramp out of the hole using short, smooth planks to make it easier and lay plastic sacks over rough, level surfaces so that the rootball slides easily.

Once positioned in the new hole, carefully remove the wrapping and string, then backfill the excavated soil in layers, firming each layer to remove air pockets. Water thoroughly and cover the rootball with a thick organic mulch.

Aftercare
Spray the foliage of newly transplanted evergreens every few days to help prevent scorching. Provide shade if the weather is sunny and warm. On exposed sites, put up a windbreak to prevent wind scorch. With all transplanted shrubs, keep well watered during any dry spells throughout the first growing season.

Pruning shrubs and climbers

One of the most common questions asked by a gardener when they buy a new shrub or climber is 'How do I prune it?' As there is often more than one correct answer to this simple query, pruning has gained an undeserved reputation for being a difficult and risky operation – especially for those new to gardening.

Fortunately, you can prune successfully to the standard of your gardening expertise without any risk to the plant. By being a little bit bolder, you can take the art of pruning a step farther by learning a little about each individual plant, so that you can tailor the pruning to suit them and keep them vigorous, looking natural and problem free. If you take a further step forwards, you can become an expert pruner, using your craft to increase the ornamental performance of a particular shrub or climber.

To show your plants off to their best advantage, pruning is essential. It need not be an arduous task, and many gardeners find it both rewarding and creative.

Pruning made easy

Pruning is an essential part of growing shrubs and climbers successfully. Although initially all shrubs and climbers will grow perfectly well without pruning, eventually the appearance and overall flowering performance of many will decline.

At its most basic, pruning is all about cutting out the three Ds: dead wood, diseased wood and damaged wood. Provided you do this using a suitable pruning tool that's been kept clean and sharp, you will only do good to your garden plants. Basic pruning also includes cutting back plants to keep them within bounds. The aim here should always be to maintain the plant's overall natural shape, not cutting back all wayward shoots to exactly the same length.

Shredder

When to prune

Some plants are best pruned at certain times of year because they have a tendency to 'bleed' sap or are particularly vulnerable to airborne diseases, so this is also worth knowing before you start. Initial pruning after planting, often called formative pruning, is important to get right since this sets up the shrub or climber for life. This involves the removal of damaged and weak shoots as well as creating a balanced framework to the desired shape for the plant. Thereafter, pruning should be confined to maintaining the health of the shrub or climber.

Pruning encourages larger and better flowering displays that last for longer as well as bigger, more dramatic and lush foliage. Shrubs and climbers that offer attractive bark, autumn colour or crops of eye-catching berries can all be enhanced by choosing the right pruning technique.

Creative pruning

You can graduate to be a master pruner by employing more creative pruning techniques that alter the plant's overall appearance. For example, you can have fun creating hedges on legs, known as pleaching, or lollipop trees, known as pollarding, trim suitable shrubs into intricate topiary shapes or train climbers to form screens, unusual ground cover or standards.

Pruning isn't essential, of course, as native shrubs and climbers in their natural habitat cope admirably without human intervention. Indeed, there are many shrubs and some climbers that don't require any routine pruning in the garden either, and these are often the ones recommended for beginner gardeners. The need for pruning can

Hand shears with wavy blade

Hand shears with straight blade

also be reduced by planting shrubs at the correct spacing and matching the vigour of the climber to the space available and size of support. Overcrowded plants not only have to compete for light, soil moisture and nutrients with their neighbours but will also be under more stress and less able to shrug off pest and disease attacks, as well as being more vulnerable in periods of drought.

After any significant pruning, always water your shrub or climber thoroughly and cover the ground with a 8–10cm (3–4in) thick organic mulch, keeping the immediate area around the trunk clear. The mulch will not only help to insulate the root area and prevent soil moisture from evaporating but will help prevent competition from weeds. The mulch will slowly rot down and add nutrients to the soil. In spring, it is also worth feeding the pruned plants with a balanced, slow-release fertilizer to promote new growth in the growing season.

BASIC TOOLS AND EQUIPMENT

Most gardeners manage with the minimum of equipment – a pruning saw and a pair of secateurs (pruners). However, to do the job more efficiently and more effectively, it really does make sense to invest in the proper tools, particularly if you have a large garden.

Long-arm pruners

Curved saw with hook for removing cut-off branches

Straight-bladed pruning saw

Long-handled pruners

Electric hedge trimmer

Secateurs (pruners)

Petrol hedge trimmer

Curved pruning saw

Petrol chainsaw

How and when to prune

Many gardeners find pruning daunting, but it is actually very straightforward, provided you follow a few simple rules that are easy to understand and put into practice in your garden.

How to prune

All pruning cuts should be made in the same way, whatever you are pruning. If you are shortening a stem, the cut should be made cleanly just above a healthy-looking bud, preferably facing outwards from the centre of the plant so that new growth does not increase congestion. If you are using secateurs (pruners) or loppers with just a single cutting blade, this should be cutting into the stem on the opposite side from the bud. Pruning cuts should be made at a slight angle, with the lowest point on the side opposite from the bud. If the stem produces pairs of buds that are opposite each other on the stem, make the cut square to the stem as close to the buds as possible, but without damaging them.

Always make sure your pruning tools are sharp and clean. They will cut more easily and so cause less bruising and other damage to the part of the plant left behind. This, in turn, ensures that the potential

for disease infection is reduced. If you are cutting out diseased material, minimize the risk of spreading the infection to other healthy branches by cleaning the pruning blade between cuts with a suitable garden disinfectant. Large cuts can also be treated with special wound sealants to help prevent disease spores gaining access through the cut. Small pruning cuts do not need covering because they will soon heal naturally.

When to prune

It is essential that pruning is carried out at the right time. The exact timing will depend on which shoots the shrub or climber flowers on. Early flowering shrubs and climbers tend to produce their blooms on stems produced the previous year, and so need to be pruned directly after flowering is over. This will allow them sufficient time to produce new shoots that will mature and ripen sufficiently to bear flowers the following year. On the other hand, later-flowering shrubs and climbers, tend to produce the blooms on stems produced during the current season and so are best pruned before new growth is put on during early spring. This will

maximize the number of flowering stems on the plant. There are exceptions to this rule, such as many repeat-flowering plants producing a first flush of blooms on the old wood and a second flush later in the season on older wood. Other plants produce flowers on spurs, like fruit trees, so the aim here is to promote as many spurs as possible on a permanent framework of branches. To check when specific plants need pruning, use the month-by-month pruning guide in the Calendar of Care section on pages 252–57.

Which pruning tool to use

If you buy good-quality pruning tools and keep them well maintained, they will make pruning easier and the tools will last a lot longer. Make sure that you find the handles comfortable before you buy and that the fully open position for secateurs (pruners) is not too wide for your hand. Do not use pruning tools for other jobs around the garden, such as cutting string or wire, because you will damage the blades. Also, avoid letting the blades come into contact with the soil, as this can dull the cutting edge. It is also important to choose the right tool for the specific pruning job.

A good pruning cut is made about 2mm (⅛in) just above a strong bud. If the stem has pairs of buds, make a horizontal cut (right).

If you use blunt secateurs (pruners), you will get an unhealthy, ragged cut (left). Instead, make sharp cuts not too far from the bud.

Cutting too close to the bud can damage it or allow disease to enter. Do not slope the cut backwards (right), as this could cause die-back.

Deadheading not only improves the appearance of the plant, but will encourage repeat-flowerers to produce more blooms later in the season.

start pruning, make sure your tetanus protection is up to date. If you haven't had a booster jab in the last ten years, make an appointment at your local doctor's surgery.

When pruning, always wear suitable clothing that won't get caught up in the plant or equipment. Thick, thorn-proof gloves are useful when pruning roses and other prickly plants, but it's wise to protect your forearms and eyes too. If you are dealing with stems above head height, consider investing in a pair of long-handled pruners. When cutting back plants that are high off the ground, such as trimming a large hedge or reducing the spread of a tall climber, make sure you work from a sturdy platform rather than balancing on a ladder.

Pruning new plants

Most shrubs and climbers do not need pruning during the first few years. However, a few benefit from being pruned during the first year after planting to encourage branching from low down the main stem and to establish more quickly.
Improved shape Shrubs, such as aucuba, box, elaeagnus, evergreen euonymus, griselinia, holly, bay, Portugal laurel and evergreen buckthorn, can be encouraged to produce a bushy, balanced shape by pruning back the previous year's growth by about one-third after planting. The shape of mahonias can also be enhanced by removing the uppermost rosette of leaves on each stem after flowering.
Quick establishment Shrubs such as buddleja, deciduous ceanothus, kerria, dogwoods, hypericum, lavatera, leycesteria and sambucus will establish quickly if the previous season's growth is cut back to within 5cm (2in) of the main framework during the early spring after planting.

• Use garden shears for trimming off wispy stems on climbers and flower-heads from shrubs such as lavender and heather.
• Use a pair of secateurs (pruners) for cutting woody stems up to 1cm (½in) thick.
• Use a pair of long-handled loppers for stems 1–3cm (½–1¼in) thick. Don't be tempted to cut stems larger than this with these pruning tools because you will end up damaging the plant you are pruning, leaving bruised tissue behind that is open to disease infection.
• Use a pruning saw for stems more than 3cm (1¼in) thick. Choose a curved Grecian saw with teeth on the lower edge, because this is easier to use and less likely to cause damage to other parts of the plant than other types of pruning saw. Don't use carpentry saws because their teeth will soon clog up with sawdust and sap and the blade will stick in the cut. A pruning knife with a curved blade is also useful for tidying up larger pruning cuts.

Prune safely

All pruning tasks should be carried out with safety in mind. Even deadheading can be hazardous if there are unprotected canes sticking out of the border that could poke you in the eye. Before you make a

Pruning popular deciduous shrubs

Most shrubs will flower reasonably well without pruning, but problems such as diseased wood, congested growth and non-flowering shoots will build up with time. This can all be rectified by pruning, but it must be carried out at the correct time of the year.

Pruning early-flowering shrubs

Many of the most popular deciduous garden shrubs, including deutzia, philadelphus, forsythia, flowering currant, some flowering spiraeas and weigela, flower in spring or early summer – producing their blooms on wood produced the previous year. This means you have to wait until after flowering before you can prune.

No-prune shrubs

You can reduce the amount of time you spend maintaining your garden by choosing shrubs that flower perfectly well without routine annual pruning. They may need pruning to remove broken or dead stems or if they outgrow their allotted space, however. These include:

Abelia
Berberis
Choisya
Corylopsis
Cotoneaster (many)
Daphne
Elaeagnus
Euonymus (most)
Fatsia
Genista
Hamamelis
Hibiscus
Ilex
Mahonia
Olearia
Osmanthus
Phormium
Sarcococca
Skimmia
Viburnum (most)
Yucca

It is important to prune directly after flowering so that the shrub has plenty of time to put on new growth and flower buds for the following season. If you prune later in the year, you risk losing the flowering display for the following season.

Prune out any dead or diseased material as well as crossing or rubbing branches that are congesting growth in the centre of the plant. Then cut out one in three stems, starting with the oldest, to a new side shoot lower down or a plump outward-facing bud. Most shrubs in this group do not need pruning every year – once every two or three years is ideal and will not noticeably reduce their overall performance. The exception is forsythia, which can become woody at the base and flower less well if it not pruned each year.

Pruning late-flowering shrubs

Deciduous shrubs that flower from mid-summer onwards, such as *Buddleja davidii*, hardy fuchsia, *Caryopteris*, *Hydrangea paniculata*, lavatera, *Potentilla fruiticosa* and late-flowering spireas, produce blooms on wood produced during the current season. These must be pruned before

HARD PRUNING

Several plants that have attractive coloured bark in the winter are best cut right back to the ground in the spring.

the new growth is produced during early spring. During mild years, especially with the impact of global warming, pruning may be required earlier than many traditional gardening books suggest. Be guided by the state of the shrubs in your garden and start pruning as growth buds start to break. All shrubs in this group are vigorous and should be pruned back every year. Some, such as hardy fuchsias, will shoot from below soil level and should be cut back to the ground. Others should have all the previous season's growth cut back to a low, stubby framework of stems.

1 Late-flowering shrubs that bear blooms on new growth perform better if pruned back hard during early spring.

2 Cut the shoots back almost to the ground to encourage the maximum new stems, which will bear blooms during the current season.

Pruning for colourful stems and foliage

Several deciduous shrubs, such as dogwoods, willows, white-stemmed brambles, cotinus, eucalyptus, *Sambucus nigra* and *Spiraea japonica* 'Goldflame', are grown more for their brightly coloured juvenile stems or enlarged, decorative foliage than for their flowers. To promote the type of growth you want, these shrubs need to be pruned in a different way from those that are grown for their flowers. Shrubs in this group do not need to be pruned every year, but annual pruning will produce the most dramatic displays.

Cut back all the previous growth to near ground level or to a low framework of woody stems during early spring. This will produce bright-coloured stems and larger, more brightly coloured foliage. Indeed, if you leave *Eucalyptus gunnii* without pruning, you will be disappointed by the rather lacklustre adult foliage that results rather than the plant producing dramatic elliptic foliage that is so sought-after by flower arrangers.

PRUNING FOR COLOURFUL STEMS

1 If left unpruned, the winter stems of *Salix alba* subsp. *vitellina* will produce its colourful new stems higher up where they cannot be seen – eventually forming a small tree.

2 To prune, cut back some of the older wood and any congested branches. This will allow the shrub to rejuvenate from the base of the plant. Use a saw on the thicker wood.

3 Remove any of the dead branches and shoots, cutting or sawing off until you reach healthy wood. Use a saw for thicker wood and clean up the cuts.

4 When you have finished thinning out the old and straggly wood, you are left with the basic framework of the shrub. This will give you an idea of how it will look next year.

5 Cut back any remaining shoots from last year's growth to a good, strong bud. This may seem very drastic but it will encourage strong and vigorous new growth.

6 If the shrub is planted at the front of the border or has another shrub situated behind it, try to ensure that the cutting back is sufficiently low so other plants can be seen.

Pruning popular evergreen shrubs

Most evergreens do not need routine pruning but can be cut back to restrict their overall size or as part of a remedial programme to restrict the spread of a pest attack or disease infection. Evergreens come in a huge variety of forms, from the dapper, dome-shaped shrubs to dramatic drama queens that dominate a garden with their huge flowers and monster foliage. Fortunately for the gardener, they can be grouped according to their pruning requirements.

Pruning small evergreen shrubs

Most small evergreens, such as cistus, heathers, hebe and rosemary, do not need regular pruning, unless grown as a hedge. In this situation, use shears to clip off spent flower-heads and to trim new growth to shape. Trim summer-flowering hedges in mid-autumn and winter-flowering hedges in mid-spring. Specimen plants do not need any serious pruning unless they have suffered die-back as the result of harsh winter weather. Inspect the shrubs during late spring or early summer to look for signs of growth on apparently dead stems before deciding what needs to be pruned out. If you need to cut back hard, aim to cut back to a healthy side shoot lower down on the branch. Do not cut back into old wood as this is unlikely to re-sprout.

Pruning large-flowered evergreens

Rhododendrons, camellias and evergreen azaleas all fall into this group. They are all acid-loving shrubs that require no routine pruning other than the removal of the seed-pods of spent flowering heads to tidy up the shrub after flowering. Removing the seed-pods before they swell also avoids the

The foliage of *Pieris japonica* alters its colour as it matures, providing a constantly changing appearance. This evergreen will grace any garden with acid soil.

shrub wasting energy producing seeds. This should be carried out very carefully since the next year's flower buds are carried just below this year's fading flowers. The best technique is to hold the bottom of the seed-head between finger and thumb, twist it and pull sharply.

Specimen shrubs with dead or diseased growth should have these cut out to a healthy side shoot lower down. Straggly shrubs can be cut back after flowering during mid-spring before new growth is put on.

Pruning large-leaved evergreens

Large-leaved evergreens, such as laurel, aucuba and holly, make excellent specimen shrubs as well as robust hedges. Specimen plants require little or no routine pruning, other than the removal of dead or diseased stems. In this situation, aim to cut back to a healthy side shoot lower down on the branch. However,

large-leaved evergreens grown as hedges will need annual pruning to maintain their neat shape and dense habit (see below). Ornamental forms with attractive variegated foliage can sometimes produce all-green reverted shoots. These should be cut out completely as soon as they are noticed to prevent them spoiling the overall appearance of the shrub.

Pruning grey-leaved evergreens

Many grey-leaved shrubs, such as artemesia, helichrysum and santolina, are grown solely for their attractive foliage. For this reason many gardeners trim the shrubs to prevent flowering stems being produced so that they do not detract from the overall appearance of the display. Other grey-leaved shrubs, notably lavenders, are valued for their flowering display, so these should not be trimmed until after flowering is over. All grey-leaved shrubs can be kept neat and compact by trimming new growth to within a couple of leaves of the main shrub during spring. Do not cut back into old wood, as this is unlikely to re-sprout.

Repairing weather damage

Evergreens are particularly susceptible to severe weather damage because they remain in full leaf throughout the winter months, when most storms occur. The weight from heavy snow, for example, can build up on the foliage, pulling the shrub out of shape and, in severe cases, causing branches to break. Even branches that remain intact do not 'close-up' again to the original position when the snow melts, exposing the brown areas underneath their dense outer covering of evergreen foliage. This is most noticeable on upright conifers that normally have a neat columnar habit.

Icy winds can be equally troublesome because they dry out the foliage through evaporation, just when the roots find it most difficult to draw water from the frozen ground. This leads to exposed conifers becoming scorched on the windward side. Fortunately, both these problems are easy to avoid. Protect particularly vulnerable plants by wrapping them in a straitjacket of fine mesh netting for the winter months. You can prevent scorch by protecting exposed conifers with a barrier of windbreak netting held up on stout posts fixed firmly into the ground. (*see* Protecting vulnerable plants, page 108).

Where damage does occur, you can persuade wayward branches back into their normal position by wrapping the plant in fine green or black netting. The netting can either be removed after a season or left in place, since the new foliage will grow

through it and hide it completely within a couple of years. Small, partially broken branches on other evergreen shrubs can be repaired by putting on a splint of bamboo canes and binding the break together with tape. The fracture will take at least two full growing seasons to mend and be strong enough for you to remove the splint. If the branches

are badly broken they will have to be removed. If this makes the evergreen shrub lopsided, try balancing it by removing a similar-sized unbroken stem from the other side. Where a hole has developed in the canopy of the evergreen, use soft string to pull neighbouring branches towards each other to fill it in and repair the look of the plant.

PRUNING EVERGREEN SHRUBS

1 Evergreen shrubs generally need little pruning. However, on occasion, as with this bay (*Laurus nobilis*), they may need to have their shape checked or smartened up.

2 Remove any dead or damaged wood and cut back any straggly stems at the top of the shrub to improve the overall shape. Keep stepping back to check on the shape.

3 The best time to carry out any pruning is during the spring, just before new growth appears. However, during the growing season they can be trimmed at any time.

4 Prune evergreens with secateurs (pruners) to avoid leaving damaged leaves on the plant. Make pruning cuts within the foliage so they do not detract from the shrub's appearance.

Pruning roses

Despite having a reputation for being complicated, rose pruning is no more difficult than pruning other garden shrubs. Indeed, recent research has suggested that the precise traditional methods might be a waste of time. So, how should you treat your roses?

Why do you need to prune roses?

Roses are so floriferous that after a few years of growing and flowering, an old stem becomes exhausted and flowering declines. The old shoot is more prone to pest and disease attack and often suffers from die-back. This prompts a newer shoot nearer the base to break and grow, eventually replacing the older shoot as it withers. Pruning is a good way of managing this natural process of renewal, helping to prevent any serious health problems while promoting vigorous new shoots that flower more profusely and for longer. Annual pruning also keeps large roses to a manageable size.

How to prune roses

If you follow all the basic rules of pruning you won't go far wrong:

Most gardeners would claim that without exception, there is no other plant to match the beauty of the rose. With careful pruning and nurturing, roses will reward you with beautiful blooms.

Pruning newly planted roses

Rose bushes should be pruned after planting to encourage them to establish quickly and produce a well-balanced shape. If too many shoots are left on the plant, the limited root system will not be able to cope.

Prune new roses by removing any dead or diseased stems completely. Then reduce the length of the shoots on bush roses and standard roses by about half their length. The top growth on miniature roses and shrub roses should be cut back by about a quarter at this stage.

- use clean tools with a sharp blade
- prune to just above a healthy, outward-facing bud
- make the cut sloping to help protect the bud and shed water from the cut
- keep the centre of the shrub clear of crossing, weak and diseased stems

Wearing thorn-proof gloves and eye-protection is also a good idea when dealing with roses. Deadhead all repeat-flowering roses throughout the growing season to get better and longer-lasting flowering displays.

Miniature roses These require little or no pruning other than to keep growth neat and compact. On well-established plants you should remove all dead, damaged or weak growth to thin out the centre. Miniature roses

are a bit of a novelty and do not match the best of the other forms of roses for scent, colour and disease resistance. However, since they grow well in containers, miniature roses are becoming increasingly popular. See the 'Roses to try' box on page 125 for miniature cultivars to try.

Patio and polyantha roses The patio rose is a compact, small bush that is usually covered in wide clusters of flowers throughout the summer. Polyantha roses are also small bushes and have a graceful habit. Pruning of these roses is easy. After planting, cut back the stems to 8–10cm (3–4in) above ground to a strong bud. Once established, the rose can be pruned to remove any dead, damaged or diseased wood. Also, cut

To cut out crossed stems, try to do it when they are still young (before they start rubbing against each other) and free from damage and disease, as this will make it a lot easier. Use secateurs (pruners) to cut the stem at the base where it joins the main stem.

The tips of stems often die back and should be cut out to prevent the shoot dying. Cut back to good wood, just above a strong bud.

back all stems to about half to two-thirds of their length to an outward facing bud or a strong shoot. Every few years, take out one or two of the oldest stems to promote new growth.

Bush roses The traditional method of pruning bush roses is probably still the most reliable. Cut back all the stems of large-flowered (hybrid tea) roses by about half their length.

Cut back old stems of cluster-flowered (floribunda) roses to their base. The remaining younger stems of cluster-flowered roses should be pruned back to about 45cm (18in).

PRUNING A MINIATURE ROSE

Remove all dead and damaged wood on miniature roses, along with any weak growth. Deadhead to prolong flowering. Well-established miniatures require little or no pruning, other than to keep their growth neat and compact.

PRUNING A PATIO ROSE

Patio roses are initially pruned in the same way as miniature roses. Once established, they are generally pruned in the spring. Pruning involves removing any dead or weak wood and cutting back any remaining stems by up to two-thirds. Deadhead throughout the summer.

You should also remove all dead, damaged or weak growth and thin out the centre of the plant. Pruning should be carried out annually during early spring.

Rough pruning

There has always been a bit of a debate about pruning roses. Should you go carefully, or just hack away? It is now known that although the results won't be quite as good, all bush roses can be pruned roughly, cutting all stems back to 15–20cm (6–8in) once every few years without worrying about cutting to just above a bud. You can even use a hedge trimmer if you have a lot of roses and time is short.

Shrub roses

These comprise various roses that do not fit easily into other classes. This mix includes everything from hybrid rugosas and musks to floribundas and the modern landscape roses. They also include single-flowering and repeat-flowering roses.

That said, the advice is to give shrub roses a light prune each year or once every other year. Remove between a quarter and a half of the new growth and cut out any dead, diseased or congested stems. This will increase blooming and decrease disease and pest problems.

Standard roses always look impressive, particularly when placed on either side of an entrance or doorway. These plants require the support of a stout stake, held with a tree or rose tie. Miniature roses planted in containers should be held secure with a cane.

Disbudding

If you want to grow roses for a flower arrangement or for showing, you may want to encourage larger flowers on longer stems by removing the smaller side buds from hybrid tea roses. Remove the side buds by pinching them out between finger and thumb when they are small, taking care not to damage the main terminal bud.

Ground cover roses Prune repeat-flowering and creeping rambler ground cover roses to keep them within bounds by removing the growing tips of spreading stems. Remove upright shoots completely.

Rambler roses Cut out poor-flowering old stems to encourage floriferous new stems. If the growth is congested, cut out one old shoot for every new one being produced from the base. Cut back any side-shoots that have flowered to two or three leaves. Tie in all stems to their supports.

Standard roses Prune standard roses lightly, since cutting back severely will encourage over-vigorous shoots

Removing rose suckers

Vigorous new shoots from the base of the plant below the union on budded or grafted roses or emanating from roots underground, will produce flowers and foliage of inferior quality to the ornamental variety. Suckers are usually more vigorous and, if left to grow, will eventually swamp the desired variety, spoiling the overall appearance. Suckers should not be pruned off at soil level, since they will re-grow even more vigorously. Instead, excavate a hole to find the point at which the sucker is attached to the rootstock and then rip it off by hand as cleanly as you can. If this is not possible, cut it off at this point.

HOW TO PRUNE A STANDARD ROSE

1 When pruning, start by removing any dead, damaged or diseased growth. You also need to take out any weak stems.

2 Cut out any stems that cross over others, especially if they are rubbing and causing wounds. This will also reduce congestion.

3 Reduce the remaining shoots by about half to two-thirds of their length. Patio standards should just be tip-pruned.

4 You are now left with the basic framework of the standard rose. Aim for an open, tulip shape that is not too crowded with stems.

that may spoil the shape. Shorten the main stems in the head of the standard as well as any side shoots. Prune standards during late winter or early spring, but prune weeping standards after flowering in summer.

Deadheading

It is not essential to deadhead roses but it is desirable if you want to maximize the number of flowers produced by repeat-flowering versions. If you don't deadhead, the rose will tend to put some of its energies into making seeds at the expense of new flowers. To ensure a

succession of blooms, remove the fading flowers as soon as the petals start to fall. Pinch out the fading flower between finger and thumb for miniatures or use secateurs (pruners) to cut back the flowering stem to just above the next leaf joint, where new flowering shoots will emerge to bloom later in the

season. It is also worth deadheading roses that have suffered from balling – where flower-buds fail to open after becoming waterlogged and infected with botrytis. Deadheading will not only improve the overall appearance of the rose but will also help to reduce the incidence of this disease.

Roses to try

Shrub	Miniature		Polyantha
'Cardinal de Richelieu'	'Amber Sunset'	'Red Bells'	'Ballerina'
'Chaucer'	'Angela Rippon'	'Robin Redbreast'	'Bashful'
'Constance Spry'	'Apricot Sunblaze'	'Sweet Magic'	'Cameo'
'Duc de Guiche'	'Baby Masquerade'		'Gloria Mundi'
'Fantin-Latour'	'Blue Peter'	**Patio**	'Lovely Fairy'
'Madame Hardy'	'Little Flirt'	'Amber Hit'	'Perle d'Or'
'William Lobb'	'New Penny'	'Bright Smile'	'White Pet'
	'Peach Sunblaze'	'Conservation'	
	'Peter Pan'	'Festival'	
		'Fond Memories'	

Pruning climbing and rambling roses

There are hundreds of varieties of climbing and rambler roses that have been bred from a wide range of rose hybrids and species, which means they vary greatly in how they grow and when they flower. Before you can prune your plant successfully, you really need to know a little bit about it.

Know your climbing rose

When it comes to climbing roses, terms such as 'climber', 'rambler' and 'repeat-flowering' are used very loosely in nursery catalogues, gardening magazines and books, so bear this in mind when deciding which way you are going to prune

When well cared for and pruned, climbing roses will reward you with spectacular displays of eyecatching – and often deliciously fragrant – blooms.

PRUNING A CLIMBING ROSE

1 When pruning a climbing rose, you can either prune it in situ or untie it, prune it and then tie it back up to the support.

2 Cut out dead and damaged wood and reduce one or two of the oldest stems to a point just above a new shoot.

3 After pruning, tie in the remaining shoots using rose ties or soft garden string. Tie the stems in firmly but not too tightly.

4 To keep your climbing rose tidy, deadhead any faded blooms. Do this by cutting the stem back to a leaf, shoot or bud.

your rose. For this reason, it is worth taking a little time to get to know your rose to see how vigorous it is, where new growth is produced (from underground, around the base or part-way up older stems), when it flowers and whether the blooms are produced on new growth or stems produced during previous seasons. Use the climbing rose checker (opposite) if you are unsure.

Pruning climbing species roses

Climbing species roses and their varieties, such as 'Bobbie James', 'Kiftsgate', 'Seagull', 'Wedding Day' and 'Rambing Rector', are extremely vigorous roses that need a lot of space, so they are not really suitable for most gardens. Sometimes known as wild roses, they can be trained to cover a large wall or even left to scramble through a well-established, healthy tree. They bloom during early summer in a single flush, producing sprays of cream, pink or white single flowers, often strongly fragrant. Flowers are borne on stems produced during previous seasons. Pruning is a matter of clearing out dead and damaged stems and thinning out congested growth during early spring. Tie in all stems to their supports.

Pruning rambler roses

Varieties such as 'American Pillar', 'Crimson Shower', 'Dorothy Perkins' and 'Sander's White Rambler', have a single flush of blooms during the summer, which are produced on growth that was formed the previous year. They produce long new shoots from the base. For each vigorous new young shoot, prune out an unproductive old one back to ground level after flowering. Do not prune out an old shoot unless there is a new one to replace it, but remove completely any very old, dead or diseased wood. Also cut back flowered side shoots on the remaining stems to two or three leaves. You can cut out poor-flowering old stems to encourage floriferous new stems. If growth is congested, cut out one old shoot for every new one being produced from the base. Tie in all stems securely to their supports.

Pruning single-flowering climbing roses

This group includes some of the best-loved varieties of climbing roses including 'Albéric Barbier', 'Albertine', 'Gloire de Dijon', 'May Queen', 'Madame Grégoire Staechelin', 'Paul's Scarlet Climber' and 'Veilchenblau', which produce large flowers in a single flush during early summer. Prune after flowering by removing up to one-third of the stems, starting with the oldest. Cut back to near to the base or to a new side shoot produced low down. If there isn't much new growth, cut back older branches to 30–45cm (12–18in) to encourage more next

Climbing rose checker

What is the growth habit of your rose?				
very vigorous	√	√	√	x
flowers once	√	√	√	x
flowers more than once	x	x	x	√
small flowers	√	√	x	x
large flowers	x	x	√	√
flowers on new wood	x	x	x	√
flowers on old wood	√	√	√	x
new shoots from the base	x	√	√	x
new shoots part-way up	√	x	√	√
What you've got:	species rose	rambler rose (single-flowering)	climbing rose	climbing rose (repeat-flowering)

year. Trim back flowered side shoots on the remaining stems to two or three leaves.

Pruning repeat-flowering climbing roses

Flowering on and off all summer long, producing large blooms on new side shoots, these include some of the best value climbing roses such as 'Aloha', Bantry Bay', 'Climbing Iceberg', 'Compassion', 'Danse du Feu', ' 'Dublin Bay' and 'Golden Showers'. Little structural pruning is needed, but they benefit from regular deadheading to encourage further

flushes of flowers. Further pruning is best done in winter, when the weakest and oldest stems can be removed. It is also necessary to cut back flowered side shoots on the remaining stems to two or three leaves. Since these roses tend to put all their energies into flowering after they have become established, rather than extension growth, light pruning and deadheading to remove the faded blooms will encourage further flower production. During the dormant season, dead, damaged or congested growth should be removed completely.

PRUNING CLIMBING ROSES

Cut out one or two of the oldest stems to just above a new shoot at the base of once-flowering climbers

PRUNING RAMBLING ROSES

Ramblers are easy to prune. Cut out old stems that have flowered, taking them back to a point where there is a replacement shoot.

Pruning clematis

Clematis are often thought to be difficult to prune because they are not all tackled in the same way, which leads many gardeners to neglect their plants so that they become a tangled mass of stems with the flowers out of sight at the top of the support. In fact, clematis are very easy to prune, provided you know when they flower.

Early spring-flowering varieties (Pruning Group 1)

Clematis that flower during the winter and into early spring bear their flowers on shoots produced during the previous growing season.

They produce single, nodding, bell-shaped flowers with ferny foliage or leaves divided into three leaflets. Some are deciduous, many are evergreen, but not all of them are fully hardy. Cut back vigorous species as necessary to keep them in check, but others in this group need

Group 1 clematis can largely be left alone in terms of pruning, apart from those that grow too vigorously for their allotted space.

Remove straggly new growth to keep your clematis under control and looking good. Prune harder if it is overgrowing its position.

little pruning other than the removal of dead, damaged or diseased stems. Prune back unwanted stems immediately after flowering (during late spring) to their point of origin

or to a pair of plump buds near to ground level. Keep mature plants flowering well and growing vigorously by cutting old stems back hard to encourage new growth from the base.

Early summer-flowering varieties (Pruning Group 2)

Clematis that flower during early summer do so on growth produced during the previous season and include many popular showy varieties with deciduous foliage.

The flowers are generally large, open, sometimes saucer-shaped and can be single, semi-double or fully double. Many also produce a second flush during late summer and early autumn of smaller flowers on the new wood produced during the current season.

They need little pruning other than the removal of dead, damaged or diseased stems. Congested growth can be thinned out by pruning back stems to their point of origin or to a pair of plump buds near to ground level. Alternatively, you can cut half

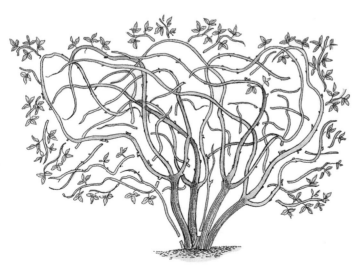

The flowers in this group are formed on the previous year's wood, so severe pruning will remove these – and its ability to flower in the current year. This group requires very little pruning other than that required to keep the plant under control and to remove any dead wood that has accumulated, which tends to build up and make the plant very congested.

PRUNING CLEMATIS GROUP 2

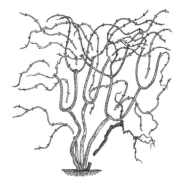

Pruning Group 2 Clematis require little or no pruning. However, the flowering wood tends to get higher and higher, as well as more congested, so it is better to prune lightly to keep them at bay. Take back the shoots to the topmost pair of strong buds. Damaged or dead wood should be removed.

the stems back to a pair of buds before growth starts to increase the number of blooms produced later in the year. Overgrown varieties can be cut back hard to a plump pair of buds about 30cm (12in) from the base immediately after the first flush of flowers.

Mid- and late-summer-flowering varieties (Pruning Group 3)

Flowering after mid-summer, this group of deciduous clematis includes varieties with flowers in a variety of shapes from open, pendulous bells, such as 'Bill MacKenzie', tight, tulip-shaped flowers, such as 'Gravetye Beauty', to open saucer-shaped flowers, such as those of 'Etoile Violette'. Many varieties continue to bloom well into the autumn. All flower on wood produced during the current season. Cut back all new growth during the winter or early spring to the lowest pair of buds. Group 3 clematis mainly flower on new wood produced in the current

PRUNING CLEMATIS GROUP 3

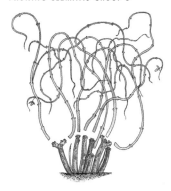

The previous year's growth of can often look like a tangled mess, but Group 3 Clematis is easy to prune. Cut all the stems back in late winter to the first pair of strong buds above where you cut the previous year. Cut out dead stems. New growth is almost immediate.

year and should be pruned back severely every year in late winter, when they are completely dormant.

Clematis Pruning Groups

Pruning group 1	Pruning group 2	Pruning group 3
Clematis alpina	Clematis 'Barbara Jackman'	Clematis 'Abundance'
Clematis alpina 'Constance'	Clematis 'Bees' Jubilee'	Clematis 'Betty Corning'
Clematis alpina 'Frances Rivis'	Clematis 'Belle of Woking'	Clematis 'Bill MacKenzie'
Clematis alpina 'Frankie'	Clematis 'Carnaby'	Clematis 'Comtesse de Bouchaud'
Clematis alpina 'Pamela Jackman'	Clematis 'Daniel Deronda'	Clematis 'Duchess of Albany'
Clematis alpina 'Pink Flamingo'	Clematis 'Doctor Ruppel'	Clematis 'Ernest Markham'
Clematis alpina 'Ruby'	Clematis 'Duchess of Edinburgh'	Clematis 'Etoile Violette'
Clematis alpina 'Willy'	Clematis 'Elsa Späth'	Clematis flammula
Clematis armandii	Clematis florida var. sieboldiana	Clematis 'Gipsy Queen'
Clematis armandii 'Apple Blossom'	Clematis 'General Sikorski'	Clematis 'Gravetye Beauty'
Clematis armandii 'Snowdrift'	Clematis 'Gillian Blades'	Clematis 'Hagley Hybrid'
Clematis cirrhosa	Clematis 'Guernsey Cream'	Clematis 'Huldine'
Clematis cirrhosa 'Freckles'	Clematis 'Henryi'	Clematis 'Jackmanii'
Clematis cirrhosa var. balearica	Clematis 'Lasurstern'	Clematis 'Jackmanii Superba'
Clematis 'Helsingborg'	Clematis 'Lincoln Star'	Clematis 'Lady Betty Balfour'
Clematis macropetala	Clematis 'Lord Nevill'	Clematis 'Perle d'Azur'
Clematis macropetala 'Jan Lindmark'	Clematis 'Marie Boisselot'	Clematis 'Polish Spirit'
Clematis macropetala 'Markham's Pink'	Clematis 'Miss Bateman'	Clematis rehderiana
Clematis montana	Clematis 'Mrs Cholmondeley'	Clematis 'Rouge Cardinal'
Clematis montana var. rubens	Clematis 'Nelly Moser'	Clematis 'Star of India'
Clematis montana var. rubens 'Elizabeth'	Clematis 'Niobe'	Clematis tangutica
Clematis montana var. rubens 'Pink Perfection'	Clematis 'The President'	Clematis 'Victoria'
	Clematis 'Vyvyan Pennell'	Clematis 'Ville de Lyon'

Pruning wisteria and honeysuckle

Wisteria and honeysuckle tend to become unruly, tangled masses of stems if they are allowed to grow unchecked. Wisteria need to be pruned twice annually, but honeysuckles can be left for two or three growing seasons before requiring attention.

Pruning and training wisteria

Wisterias are beautiful, dramatic and vigorous climbers that require a lot of space and a very sturdy support – as well as regular pruning – to be seen at their best.

Perhaps the most striking of wall-trained climbers, they're also an excellent choice for growing over a robust archway or pergola and can even be trained as an unusual and eyecatching standard.

Training wisteria

Against walls, wisteria should be trained rather like an espalier fruit tree on strong galvanized or plastic-coated horizontal wires (about 10–14 gauge) and spaced 25–30cm

To ensure successful flowering of wisteria, it needs to be pruned twice a year, in summer and winter. Careful pruning of a wisteria diverts its energies to flower production, rather than the ever-expanding new growth of stems and shoots, and will reward you with a magnificent display.

(10–12in) apart up the wall. The wire needs to be held 5–8cm (2–3in) away from the wall using vine-eyes. These allow air to flow around the plant and so help prevent the wall from becoming damp for long periods (see page 96).

PRUNING WISTERIA

1 In spring and early summer, wisteria produces long, tendril-like new growth. Cut back leaving 4–6 leaves on each shoot.

2 In early- to mid-winter, cut back summer-pruned shoots even further to about half their length, leaving 2–3 buds on each shoot.

Grow a standard wisteria

Wisteria can also be trained as an eye-catching focal point in the middle of a border. Although spectacular and unusual, it is surprisingly quick and easy to accomplish. After planting, insert a sturdy stake about 15cm (6in) shorter than the eventual height of the desired standard wisteria. Tie in the main shoot to the stake and cut off any side shoots completely. Keep tying in the leader as it grows and removing all side shoots each winter. When the main stem reaches beyond the top of the stake, cut it back to a plump bud. The following winter, select four or five well-spaced side shoots around the top of the main stem to form the head of the standard, then cut out completely all other side shoots lower down the stem. Also cut back the selected side shoots by about one-third – pruning to a healthy bud. Each summer thereafter trim the head of the standard to shape and shorten the side shoots to two or three buds from the main framework.

WISTERIA PRUNING CUTS

Cut back the new growth of wisteria each summer to about 4–6 leaves and reduce this even further with a winter pruning.

After planting the wisteria, cut back the main stem to a plump, healthy-looking bud about 90cm (36in) from the ground. Any side shoots should be completely removed. This will encourage new, vigorous side shoots to be produced.

During the first summer, tie in the top side shoot vertically to the horizontal wires to form the new leader. Also tie in the strongest side shoots on either side of the plant at about 45 degrees. Remove all other new side shoots.

During the second winter, untie the two side shoots and lower them to 90 degrees so they can be tied along the first horizontal wire on each side of the plant. Tip-prune the shoots back by about one-third, cutting just beyond a healthy bud. Also, cut the new leader back to a plump, healthy-looking bud about 90cm (36in) above the first tier of branches. Repeat this process until there are sideshoots trained along each of the horizontal wires.

Pruning wisteria

Once the main framework of the plant is complete, wisteria will continue to require pruning twice a year: during late summer and in winter. Any shoots that are required to extend the range or shape of the

wisteria should be left unpruned. The pruning is straightforward: cut back all the whippy new growth to four to six leaves during late summer and, when the leaves have fallen and it easier to see what you are doing, cut the same stumps to just two or three buds from the main framework.

Pruning honeysuckle

Honeysuckles are vigorous twining climbers that can be divided into two groups, according to their pruning requirements. The first group bear their flowers in pairs on wood produced during the current season, for example *Lonicera japonica*. They do not need regular pruning, unless the climber outgrows its allotted space. In this case, cut back all stems during the winter to allow for new growth the following season. Congested specimens can have one in three stems cut back to near ground level, starting with the oldest. The second group, which includes most of the popular varieties such as *Lonicera* x *italica*,

L. periclymenum, *L. tellmanniana* and *L. tragophylla*, bear their flowers in whorls on stems produced during the previous season. These should be cut back after flowering, pruning out all flowered stems to a newer shoot lower down on the stem.

Aftercare

Pruning inevitably removes part of the climber that provides the plant with energy, so it is a good idea to help the plant recover, especially after severe pruning. Feeding and watering are the most important factors because the climbers will need to put on new growth to replace what it has lost. Choose a balanced fertilizer that contains similar amounts of the main plant nutrients (nitrogen, potassium and phosphorus) as well as other trace elements. Feed in spring after pruning and mulch the ground with a generous layer of well-rotted organic matter to help keep the soil moist and prevent weeds. Water thoroughly during dry spells.

PRUNING HONEYSUCKLE

1 In late winter to early spring, when the stems are bare and you can see what you are doing, cut out any dead and congested stems.

2 Cut just above strong buds. You can be quite brutal when thinning, as honeysuckles are vigorous plants that will thrive on it.

Pruning and training other popular climbers

Provided you match the vigour of a climber to the size of the support and space available, little pruning should be necessary other than the removal of dead or damaged stems and thinning out congested growth. However, a few popular climbers do benefit from more routine pruning.

Climbing hydrangea

The climbing hydrangea, *Hydrangea petiolaris*, needs to be tied into its support until its self-clinging stems get a grip, which may take two or three years. Thereafter, it will climb happily without any help. No routine pruning is necessary unless you want to train the climber to a particular

shape, such as around a door frame or keep it on a fan-shaped trellis. Once established, to get the best flowering display, cut back about a quarter of the oldest flowering shoots that grow out horizontally from the support. Do this each year during the winter or early spring. Once the climber has filled its allotted space, it can be kept within bounds by cutting individual stems back to a healthy bud or to their point of origin on the main framework. Overgrown and neglected plants can be rejuvenated by cutting back all stems hard during early spring to the main framework. This is best done over a three-year

Climbers are born to reach for the sky, so make sure you prune them before they do damage to gutters, eaves and roof tiles.

period so that you don't miss out on the flowering display while the climber recovers.

Kolomikta vine

Unless the specimen is already well branched, *Actinidia kolomikta* benefits from being cut back after planting in spring to 30–45cm (12–18in). This encourages side shoots lower down that can then be trained up the support to form the main framework. Space these side shoots about 15cm (6in) apart up the support. During subsequent summers, side shoots can be cut back each year to an outward-facing bud about 15cm (6in) from the framework. In winter, shorten the same shoots to just two buds of the main framework. Once the climber has filled its allotted space, control it by cutting back new growth by about a half its length – cutting individual stems back to a healthy bud or to their point of origin on the main framework. Rejuvenate overgrown and neglected plants by cutting back all stems hard during early spring to the main framework.

REJUVENATING A CLIMBER

1 Climbing plants tend to grow with enthusiasm, criss-crossing their leaves and stems into densely tangled forms.

2 Untangle the old wood and trim away dead and excess shoots until you can see the basic structure of the climber.

3 Cut back the older wood to a strong shoot lower down to encourage strong, vigorous growth from the base.

4 Dead wood or stems that have died back should be cut back to a healthy shoot. This will encourage new growth.

Honeysuckles

Neglected honeysuckles become a huge mass of tangled, spindly, poorly flowering shoots that are prone to pest and disease attack. Often the new growth and the flowers are produced out of sight at the top of the plant. The best way to tackle an overgrown honeysuckle is to give it a hair cut with a pair of shears, removing most of the tangled top-growth. Then, when you can see the framework of stems underneath, identify which of the younger and vigorous stems you want to keep for a balanced shape and remove the rest. Alternatively, you can cut all the stems back to younger side shoots or plump pairs of buds about 30cm (12in) from the ground, but you will miss out on the flowering display for a year or two.

If neglected, honeysuckles will tend to become a tangled mess of stems with their flowers out of sight at the top of the plant.

Passion flower

Varieties of passion flower (*Passiflora caerulea*) all require careful training and pruning to get the best results. These evergreen or semi-evergreen tendril climbers are woody stemmed. The aim with pruning is to develop a permanent framework of branches that will produce a succession of flowering side shoots. If training against a flat surface such as a wall or fence, choose a plant with several stems that can be spaced about 15cm (6in) apart across the support. Unbranched specimens can be encouraged to produce side shoots by cutting back to 30–45cm (12–18in) after planting. If you are training the plant up the post of a pergola or arch, two or three stems will be sufficient. Tie in the stems until they reach the top of the support and then pinch out the growing tip to encourage the side shoots to grow.

On pergolas and arches, trim back all side shoots except those near the top, which can be trained over the support until the framework is completely covered, then simply cut back shoots that have flowered and fruited to two buds of the main framework. Overgrown and neglected plants can be rejuvenated by cutting back one or two of the older branches in the framework each year, to a younger side shoot lower down.

Actinidia kolomikta

Solanum crispum 'Glasnevin'

Potato vine

Solanum crispum 'Glasnevin' and the white form, *S. laxum* 'Album', which have just one or two stems, benefit from being cut back after planting in spring to encourage side shoots to be produced lower down which can then be trained up the support to form the main framework.

These should be spaced out and tied into the support as they grow. Once the climber is established, simply prune all the new growth to just two or three buds of the main framework during late spring after the threat of frost has passed.

Overgrown and neglected plants can be rejuvenated by cutting back one or two of the older branches in the framework each year.

Trumpet vine

Encourage *Campsis radicans* to bush out and produce new shoots from low down on the climber by pruning back to buds about 15cm (6in) from the ground during the spring after planting. If more than three or four side shoots are produced, remove the weakest first, before spreading out the rest and tying them into their support to form the main framework. Thereafter, once the climber is established, simply prune all new growth to two or three buds of the main framework during late winter or early spring. Overgrown and neglected plants can be rejuvenated by cutting back all stems hard in the winter.

Ornamental vines

Vigorous ornamental vines, such as *Vitis* and *Parthenocissus*, require very little routine pruning, other than the removal of any dead or damaged stems. If they outgrow their allotted space, cut back about half of the oldest shoots to the main framework and trim the remainder to keep them within bounds. Where space is very restricted, cut all new growth back to within two or three buds of the main framework each winter.

Ampelopsis

An increasingly popular climber, *Ampelopsis brevipedunculata* is a vigorous self-clinging plant that can be left to its own devices if you have the space. In a smaller garden it makes a lovely climber over a pergola, where it can be trained to produce a curtain of handsome leaves and attractive berries. Train the main stem along the pergola cross beam and allow the new shoots to cascade. Cut back all new growth to this framework each winter to keep it neat.

Chocolate vine

One of the 'must-have' plants of recent years, the chocolate vine (*Akebia quinata*) bears maroon-chocolate flowers with a hint of vanilla during late spring and early summer. Although regular pruning is not necessary, if they do need cutting back, do it in late spring after flowering – cutting back with shears to encourage fresh growth. Old plants can be rejuvenated by cutting back one or two of the oldest stems.

Dutchman's pipe

Easy to keep within bounds, the Dutchman's pipe (*Aristolochia*) responds well to hard pruning. If there is no need to keep it within bounds, let its twining stems spread freely. Prune either after flowering during summer or before buds break in early spring.

Coral plant

Do not hard-prune the Coral plant, *Berberidopsis corallina*, because it does not respond well to severe treatment. Instead, tidy it up by regular trimming to keep it within bounds. Prune in spring after the threat of frost has passed, removing only dead, damaged or wayward stems.

PRUNING ESTABLISHED CLIMBERS

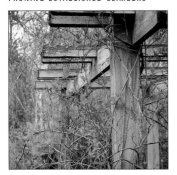

1 Late autumn or early winter are the ideal times to prune overgrown deciduous climbers. Without the leaves, you can see the shape.

2 The first task is to remove all the dead and damaged wood so that you can regain a good shape and form to the climber.

3 Cut dead wood back to the healthy shoot or, if congested, take it back even farther, but always towards a shoot.

4 Once you have cut out the dead wood, take away congested wood, preferably the weakest and oldest growth.

5 Select some of the strongest and healthiest growths. These are most likely to be the youngest growth. Train them up the structure.

6 Tie in the healthy shoots to the supporting structure using garden twine. Distribute the younger shoots throughout the structure.

Virginia creeper

When the rampant growth of Virginia creeper, *Parthenocissus quinquefolia*, reaches the guttering or the roof, it is time to prune back hard to keep it under control. It climbs up surfaces by using its adhesive tendrils, so you may have to pull it away from its supporting structure to prune it. When established, this creeper can send out new growth up to 6m (20ft) in a year. Plants are very tolerant of trimming and can be cut right back to the base if required to rejuvenate the plant. Any pruning is best carried out in the spring.

Virginia creeper (*Parthenocissus quinquefolia*)

Pruning overgrown shrubs and climbers

If left unpruned for many years, most climbers will become woody and ugly at the base, with most of the ornamental flowers and leaves out of sight at the top of the plant. Fortunately, most climbers respond well to hard pruning and will produce vigorous new shoots that flower better if pruned in the right way and at the right time.

Getting started

Renovation pruning is best carried out during the dormant season when the sap is flowing slowly and there are no leaves in the way.

Choose a dry, mild day and arm yourself with a pair of secateurs (pruners), loppers for thicker stems and a pruning saw for woody growth over 3cm (1¼in) in diameter. A pruning knife is also useful for tidying up large cuts and if you are tackling thorny plants, wear stout gloves and goggles to protect your hands and eyes before you start.

Clematis

You can leave clematis unpruned for a few years, but if neglected for longer periods, it will gradually become a mass of unproductive woody stems at the base, with few flowers and little leaf cover. Any flowers that are produced tend to appear right at the top of the plant.

Clematis have a reputation for being difficult to prune (see page 123), but they all respond well to hard pruning. Clematis that flower on shoots produced during the current season respond to pruning back very severely to within 30cm (12in) of the base – cutting back to a newer side shoot or a pair of plump, healthy buds. Those that flower on older wood can also be cut back as severely, but you will miss out on the flowering display for a

HOW TO PRUNE OVERGROWN SHRUBS AND CLIMBERS

1 Tangled, congested stems need cutting out to encourage new, more vigorous and free-flowing growth.

2 Cut out the dead wood and take away congested growth, preferably the weakest and oldest, to allow new stems to flourish.

year or two. For this reason, you may prefer to cut them back over a three-year period, removing one in three of the stems during early spring, starting with the oldest.

Roses

Climbing and rambler roses will become less productive if they are left unpruned for many years. Large climbing roses can reach almost tree-like proportions, with large, gnarled, woody bases and sparse leaf cover, with all the green growth and flowers high up on the plant. They will have lost their vigour and often be plagued with diseases during the summer months. Fortunately, all but the most aged of climbing roses can be successfully renovated by severe pruning carried out during the early spring. When the stems are clear of leaves, it is easier to plan where to make the pruning cuts to maintain some sort of balanced shape. Aim to cut out one in three of the oldest stems – either right back to the base or to a younger side shoot close to the ground. Repeat over a three-year period to reinvigorate the plant.

Rambler roses are treated differently as they readily produce new shoots from underground or

very low down on the plant. This means that if they are neglected over a period of time, they will form an impenetrable thicket of stems that gradually lose their vigour. Improve flowering and reduce the overall size of the plant by cutting all the older stems right back to ground level during the dormant season.

Honeysuckles

Neglected honeysuckles can quickly become a huge mass of tangled, spindly, poorly flowering shoots, which makes them more prone to pest and disease attack when they are in this state. As for the blooms, the new growth and the flowers tend to be produced out of sight at the top of the plant.

The best way to tackle honeysuckle is to give it a haircut with a pair of shears, removing most of the tangled top growth. When you can see the framework of stems, identify which of the younger and vigorous stems you want to keep for a balanced shape and remove the rest.

You can cut all the stems back to younger side shoots or plump pairs of buds about 30cm (12in) from the ground, but you will miss out on the flowering display for a year or so.

Pruning other neglected shrubs

Vigorous shrubs can soon outgrow their space and will need trimming on a regular basis. If you haven't been able to carry out pruning for some years, you'll need to know which respond well to severe pruning and those best discarded.

Abelia
Responds well to severe pruning. Cut all the stems back to near ground level during early spring.

Artemesia
Responds well to severe pruning, so cut all the stems back to near ground level after the last frost in mid-spring.

Aucuba
Spotted laurels that have got too large or bare at the base can be cut back hard in spring. Remove one in three stems, starting with the oldest.

Berberis
Protect yourself with gloves and goggles before cutting back hard in early spring.

Buddleja
Responds well to severe pruning, so cut all the stems back to near ground level during early spring.

Camellia
Cut back oldest stems to a stubby framework 50cm (20in) from the ground after flowering in spring.

Ceanothus
Evergreen varieties are best replaced, but deciduous varieties can be cut back hard during spring.

Chaenomeles
Flowering quince can be cut back hard in spring after flowering. Remove one in three stems, starting with the oldest.

Choisya
Responds well to severe pruning, so cut all the stems back to near ground level during spring, after flowering.

Cistus
These do not respond well to severe pruning and so are best replaced.

Cornus
Dogwoods grown for stems and leaves can be cut back hard during early spring.

Corylus
Hazels respond well to severe pruning, so cut all the stems back to near ground level during winter.

Cotinus
Cut back to a stubby framework 50cm (20in) from the ground.

Cotoneaster
Fishbone cotoneaster (*C. horizontalis*) does not respond well to severe pruning, but individual shoots can be removed back to the main stem. Others can be cut back hard during spring.

Elaeagnus
Responds well to severe pruning, so cut all the stems back to near ground level during spring.

Escallonia
Responds well to hard pruning, so cut all the stems back to the main framework during spring.

Forsythia
Plants that are too large or bare at the base can be cut back hard in spring. Remove one in three stems, starting with the oldest.

Fuchsia
Hardy varieties respond well to severe pruning, so cut all the stems back to near ground level during early spring.

Garrya
Responds well to pruning over a period of three years, so cut one-third of the oldest stems back to the main framework each year during spring.

Hamamelis
These can struggle after hard pruning, with the more vigorous rootstock throwing up new shoots. Cut back during spring over three or four years and remove any new shoots from beneath the graft.

Helianthemum
These are short lived plants and are best replaced.

Kerria
Responds well to severe pruning, so cut all the stems back to near ground level during early spring.

Kolkwitzia
Responds well to severe pruning. Cut old stems to near ground level after spring flowering, leaving the youngest stems intact.

Lavender
Trim after the last frost in mid-spring, but don't cut back into bare wood.

Lavatera
Responds well to severe pruning. Cut stems back to near ground level during early spring.

Leycesteria
Responds well to hard pruning, so cut all the stems back to withing a few centimetres of the ground during spring.

Magnolia
Cut back oldest stems to 50cm (20in) from the ground after spring flowering.

Mahonia
Responds well to hard pruning, so cut all the old stems back to near ground level after flowering in spring, leaving the youngest to replace them.

Olearia
Responds well to severe pruning, so cut all the stems back to near ground level after flowering.

Osmanthus
Responds well to severe pruning, so cut all the stems back to near ground level after flowering.

Philadelphus
Mock oranges can be cut back hard by removing the oldest stems to ground level and cutting the youngest back by about half.

Photinia
Severe pruning is fine, so cut the stems back to near ground level during spring.

Pieris
Cut back oldest stems to 50cm (20in) from the ground after spring flowering.

Potentilla
Cut back hard to a stubby framework, but old plants are best replaced.

Rosemary
Cut back all stems by half or replace with a new one.

Sambucus
Can be cut back hard, but best replaced.

Santolina
Cut back hard to a stubby framework, or replace old plants with new ones.

Skimmia
Cut back hard to a stubby framework, but old plants are best replaced.

Weigela
Responds well to severe pruning, so cut all the stems back to near ground level during early spring.

Propagating shrubs and climbers

One of the joys of being a gardener is to grow your own plants from seed, cuttings or layering. Growing them on until they can be planted and become established in the beds or borders provides a tremendous sense of satisfaction.

Some gardeners, however, are put off or intimidated by growing plants from such an early stage, or have been unsuccessful in their attempts and prefer to spend much more money at a garden centre or nursery on plants that they believe they can grow more successfully.

If you follow the simple rules of propagation carefully and remember to water and shade plants as appropriate, your beds and borders will be flourishing with your own homegrown shrubs and climbers.

Growing your own plants from the beginning – either from seeds, cuttings or layering – is immensely satisfying. It isn't at all hard to do once you have learned a few basics.

Propagating plants

Many shrubs and climbers are easy to propagate and you can use a variety of different methods. Whichever technique you choose will depend on the type of plant you want to increase.

Raising your own shrubs and climbers from seed can be a worthwhile exercise if you want a lot of plants of the same type, such as for a hedge or for ground cover. It's also worth trying for plants, such as daphne, which are difficult to propagate in other ways. However, it is worth bearing in mind that you can raise only species from seed – results from named cultivars will be variable, with few being of real garden value.

Some plants are easy to raise using any one of a range of different methods, while others can only be propagated easily using only a single technique. Your success when propagating your own plants will also depend on timing and the equipment you have. It is very important to propagate plants at the right time of the year. Softwood cuttings taken in spring, for example,

If you don't have a propagator, cover a pot with a plastic bag. Inflate it to ensure that the bag is not in contact with the leaves. Remove the bag when the plants have rooted.

will often root in a matter of weeks, but delay that until the summer and some cuttings might not root at all.

Seeds will germinate and cuttings will root much more quickly if you can provide the right environment. It is essential that they do not run short of moisture and are kept at the optimum temperature for the plant you are trying to propagate.

Equipment

You don't need a lot of expensive equipment – a simple plastic bag cover and a snug spot on a warm, shaded windowsill will be sufficient for many shrubs and climbers. Others will germinate and root successfully in a coldframe or a basic border propagator made from old coat hangers and a supermarket carrier bag! Slightly more sophisticated versions of this can be made from kits or by buying the correct equipment (*see* Making a tunnel cloche, opposite).

However, for the best results it is worth investing in a thermostatically controlled, heated propagator if you want to raise plants from seeds or cuttings that germinate or root better in warm conditions.

Before you start propagating plants, it is worth thinking about where and how you are going to look after them once they have started to grow. There can be nothing more frustrating than raising a batch of new plants from seed or cuttings, only to find that you do not have sufficient shelf space in the greenhouse or enough room in the coldframe to accommodate them all.

You will also need to have the time to water, feed and pot the new plants on periodically so that they don't receive a check in growth, so bear this in mind before you start.

Harvesting seed from berries

Seeds in berries are often lost to the birds. It is, therefore, worthwhile protecting one or two selected branches with netting before the berries start to ripen. Although most harvested ripe berries can be sown as they are, you may prefer to clean the seed before sowing. The simplest way to do this is to place the berries in a polythene bag, squashing them thoroughly before tipping the pulp into a bowl of water and mixing well. The berry flesh will float and the seeds will sink. Collect the seed and sow or treat as necessary before sowing.

Collecting your own seed

It is perfectly possible to collect your own seed from shrubs and climbers. It is important to collect the seed as soon as they are ripe, but before they are eaten by birds and rodents. Ripe seed from your garden will often germinate more readily than shop-bought seed, but, depending on the plant, you may have to treat it first to overcome in-built germination inhibitors (see below).

Temperature treatments

Cold Many hardy shrubs and climbers that are native to areas prone to cold winters will germinate readily only after they have received a period of cold.

You can do this naturally by sowing during the autumn in a shaded position outside and waiting for seedlings to appear during the spring, but you will run the risk of some winter losses.

Alternatively, you can trick the seed into germinating more quickly by giving it a period of time at a temperature of $1-3°C$ ($35-7°F$).

The easiest way to do this is to place the seed in a sealed container with some moist peat or sand and put them in the crisper drawer at the bottom of the refrigerator for six to eight weeks before sowing. Some seed may require exposing to two 'fake' winters before germinating, so you will have to repeat this process before sowing the seed.

Hot and cold A few plants that come from areas that have warm autumns and cold winters produce seed that requires a period of warmth before the cold treatment. You can achieve this by placing the sealed container in a propagator set at 18–20°C (64–8°F) for about a month before subjecting it to the cold treatment.

Hard seed coats

Seeds with hard seed coats often take many years to germinate because they are unable to take up water until the seed coat has started to break down. However, you can speed up this process in several different ways, depending on the strength of the seed coat you are trying to breach.

Soaking Most seed can be encouraged to take up water by soaking them in tepid water for 24 hours. As a general rule of thumb, any seed that sinks after this period will be ready to sow.

Boiling If all the seed remains on the surface, try soaking in boiling water for 24 hours by placing the seed in a thermos flask and adding boiling water from the kettle. Again, any seed that sinks after this period will be ready to sow.

Rubbing Some seed has such a thick coat that soaking isn't sufficient to break down the seed coat. In this case, the coats can be worn away by rubbing. The easiest way to do this

is to line a jar with some fine-grade abrasive paper. Place the seed inside the jar, screw on the lid and shake or roll the jar for up to ten minutes. After this, give the seed the soaking treatment. Repeat the process, if necessary.

Nicking Larger seed can be tackled individually by cutting through the seed coat by using a sharp knife or scuffing them with an old nail file. Make the cut or abrasion on the opposite side of the seed from the scar.

Leave it to nature A few plants, such as crataegus, do not respond to these treatments and so have to be stratified naturally outside, which helps to break down their seed coat so that they can absorb moisture and germinate. This may take two winters to achieve.

To keep the seed safe while this happens, place them on layers of moist sand in a robust but ventilated container that is both bird- and rodent-proof. Place in a cool spot outside in permanent shade.

MAKING A TUNNEL CLOCHE

1 Prepare the soil thoroughly by digging over and removing all weeds. Lay out the cloche and space the supports along the plastic.

2 Carefully insert the hoops into the soil, ensuring that they are spaced sufficiently to hold the plastic taut over the prepared bed.

3 Pull the plastic sheeting taut over the frame. Gather the ends together and secure with sticks or pegs.

4 Heap a low bank of soil over the edge of the plastic sheeting to secure it in place and to stop any draughts getting inside.

Sowing seed

For successful plants, it is essential to provide the right conditions at the earliest possible moment – and that means when sowing.

Basic methods

How you sow your seed will depend on how many plants you are trying to raise. If you want a lot of shrubs for a hedge or are planning to run a charity stall at your local fair, you may be better off sowing into a prepared seedbed outside during the autumn, provided your soil is well drained.

You will need to protect the bed from birds and rodents. You also need to be prepared to protect early emerging seedlings during early spring with a floating mulch of garden fleece. Alternatively, sow medium quantities of seed in a coldframe, where they are easier to

look after and protect. Many shrubs and climbers will germinate and grow on more quickly if raised indoors, and all tender and borderline plants should be protected in this way.

Large seed can be sown individually during autumn in holes about 10cm (4in) apart, deep enough so that they are covered with about 1–2cm (½in) of soil.

Smaller seed is best left until late winter, when it should be scattered over the surface and lightly raked into the soil or covered in a thin layer of sharp sand. Very fine seed is best sown in spring on the surface and misted regularly to keep moist.

Small amounts of seed and all fine seed are easier to sow in pots or trays filled with potting mix and placed in the coldframe. Most spring-sown seed need a temperature of 15°C (60°F) to germinate and should be

sown in a container in a thermostatically controlled propagator or covered with plastic and placed on capillary matting in a heated greenhouse.

Once the seeds reach sufficent growth, they need to be thinned and potted on, a process called pricking out. This may be the first spring after an autumn sowing or during the following autumn, depending on how the seedlings are developing. Spring-sown seed should be pricked out into individual pots when large enough to handle.

All seedlings need a well-lit spot, out of direct sunlight, and need to be kept moist. All seed raised indoors or in a coldframe will need weaning off the warmer and more protected environment very gradually before planting outside, known as 'hardening off'.

SOWING SEED IN A POT

1 You will need a clean pot, sowing mix, seeds (your own or from a packet), plastic sheeting or a glass cover, a leveller and labels.

2 Fill the pot with the sowing mix. This mix deliberately has few nutrients, which could damage the little seedlings.

3 When the pot is full, level it off and then firm it down, either with a wooden block or the bottom of another pot.

4 Sprinkle the seeds over the top of the sowing mix very thinly. Very small seeds can be mixed with fine sand to make this easier.

5 Spread a fine layer of sowing mix or vermiculite over the surface of the pot. You can use a sifter to do this.

6 Label and lightly water them carefully. Cover with the plastic or glass. Keep inside or place in a heated propagator.

Shrubs and climbers to raise from collected seed

Abutilon Collect dry seed from seed-pods and sow immediately. No treatment necessary.

Amelanchier Pick ripe berries, remove seed and sow immediately. A warm and cold period is necessary for germination; alternatively, sow in spring.

Aucuba Pick ripe berries, remove seed and sow immediately. No treatment necessary.

Berberis Harvest ripe berries and sow after cold treatment to break dormancy; alternatively, leave outside during winter in a coldframe.

Callicarpa Collect seed from ripe fruits and sow immediately in a coldframe outside; alternatively, keep seed until spring and sow then.

Callistemon Collect seed and keep dry until spring. Sow on the surface of the potting mix.

Camellia Seed should be pre-soaked in warm water and its hard covering should be filed down to leave a thin covering. It usually germinates in 1–3 months at 23°c. Prick out into pots when they are large enough to handle. Grow them on in light shade in the greenhouse for at least their first winter.

Caryopteris Collect fruits and remove seed. Keep dry until spring and sow then. No treatment necessary.

Ceanothus Collect seed and soak in hot water before sowing to help break down the hard seed coat. Give cold treatment to break dormancy.

Chaenomeles Collect seed from ripe fruits and sow immediately in a coldframe outside, or keep seed to sow in spring.

Clematis Harvest seed and sow after cold treatment to break dormancy; alternatively, leave outside over winter in a coldframe.

Clianthus Collect dry seed from seed-pods and rub the seed coat or soak in water to break it down.

Leycesteria formosa

Colutea Collect dry seed from seed-pods and rub the seed coat or soak in water to break it down.

Cotinus Collect ripe seed and sow immediately outside or in a coldframe.

Cotoneaster Pick ripe berries, crush and remove seed. A warm and cold period is necessary for germination. Sow in spring.

Cytisus Collect seed and sow immediately outside or in a coldframe. Or store dry until spring, then soak in hot water before sowing to break down the hard seed coat.

Daphne Collect ripe fruit, remove seed and sow immediately after cold treatment to break dormancy. Some species may require two cold winters to germinate.

Enkianthus Surface-sow seed on lime-free potting mix immediately after collection and place in a heated propagator set at 15°C (60°F). Cover seed tray with clear film (plastic wrap) to prevent the seed from drying out.

Euonymus Collect ripe seed and sow immediately outside or in a coldframe.

Fatsia Collect ripe fruits and remove seed before sowing immediately. Place in a heated propagator set at 15°C (60°F).

Forsythia Harvest seed and sow after cold treatment to break dormancy, or leave outside during winter in a coldframe

Fuchsia Collect ripe fruits and remove seed and store for sowing in spring. Place in a heated propagator set at 20°C (68°F).

Genista Collect seed-pods and store dry until spring. Remove seed and sow after

rubbing or soaking in hot water to break down the hard seed coat.

Hibiscus Collect seed-pods and store dry until spring. Extract seed and sow. No treatment necessary.

Hypericum Collect seed-pods and store dry until spring. Extract seed and sow. No treatment necessary.

Kalmia Surface-sow seed on lime-free soil mix immediately after collection and place in a heated propagator set at 15°C (60°F). Cover seed tray with clear film to prevent the seed from drying out.

Lavandula Collect and dry seedheads, remove seed and give cold treatment before sowing to break dormancy.

Leycesteria Collect ripe seed and sow immediately outside or in a coldframe.

Lonicera Harvest ripe berries, remove seed and sow after cold treatment to break dormancy; alternatively, leave outside during winter in a coldframe.

Paeonia Sow after two periods of cold treatment to break dormancy; alternatively, leave outside during winter in a coldframe for two years.

Philadelphus Collect ripe seed and sow after cold treatment to break dormancy; alternatively, leave outside during winter in a coldframe.

Pieris Surface-sow seed on lime-free compost immediately after collection and place in a heated propagator set at 15°C (60°F). Cover seed tray with clear film to prevent seed from drying out.

Euonymus alatus 'Compactus'

Seedling aftercare

Seeing your seedlings grow is a very satisfying experience. There is great pleasure to be had from seeing a tiny seed develop into a big plant that can climb up the side of a house or grow into a fully mature shrub, covered in beautiful flowers.

Seedling care

Growing shrubs from seed requires more patience than propagating climbers, as many shrubs take a number of years between sowing and growing to reach flowering size.

Once the seedlings emerge, they should be allowed to grow on in situ, provided there is sufficient room, and should be watered regularly. When the first set of true leaves appear, they are ready for pricking out. True leaves are usually the first set of leaves that emerge after the original germination leaves. The seedlings are ready for potting on when they have two or more sets of leaves large enough to handle. Pot up individually into pots that will provide plenty of root depth. However, it is important to water the seedlings an hour or so before pricking them out to make the roots easier to separate.

The most important aftercare task is to check how much watering your seedlings require so that you can keep them thriving.

Always handle the seedlings carefully by their leaves, never by the fragile stem that is so easily bruised or damaged.

Transfer the seedlings one by one into their own individual pots. You can do this by either filling a pot half way, holding the seedling in position and then filling up the pot with the remaining compost (*see* Pricking out seedlings, opposite), or you can hold the seedling gently by its leaves and loosen it from the seed tray with a dibber or just a pencil. Make a hole with your tool in the compost to accommodate the seedling, insert the seedling and gently push the compost towards the hole to fill it. Firm lightly with the dibber afterwards.

When to prick out seedlings

Prick them out as soon as possible, as the sowing mix is not very rich in nutrients and the seedlings will soon become starved. This may be the first spring after an autumn sowing or during the following autumn, depending on the rate of development of the seedlings.

Spring-sown seed should be pricked out into individual pots as soon as they are large enough to handle. Keep all seedlings in a well-lit position that is out of direct sunlight and never let them run short of moisture.

If the seedlings are left for any length of time, they will become overcrowded and consequently spindly and unable to grow properly.

Most seedlings are best pricked out into individual plant pots rather than seed trays as they will need to have space to grow. If they are overcrowded, the seedlings will fail to make sturdy young plants. As is more than likely, you will have many more seedlings than you need, so

some will have to be disposed of – either on to the compost heap for recycling or given to friends.

Compost types

Use a good potting compost (soil mix) that doesn't contain too much fertilizer. You can use a stronger one when you pot the seedlings on at a later stage.

Seed and potting composts are available in soil-based and soilless forms. Whichever you use will be a matter of personal preference. Seeds seem happy in either, but different composts seem to suit different regimes. Try some of each to see which suits your seeds.

Soilless composts are planting mixes that are based on fibrous material, such as peat or coir. The advantages are that they are lightweight and moisture-retentive, but they are a bit too easy to overwater and difficult to rewet if allowed to dry out.

Soil-based composts are heavier than soilless ones, are well-draining, difficult to overwater and absorb moisture easily when dry.

Damping off

If your seedlings keel over and wilt, this could be due to a condition known as damping off. This is caused by a range of soil- and water-borne fungi that attack the stem base of the seedling, making it become thin and brown. A white, fluffy fungus may also appear. This same fungus may also attack in the soil, causing the seed to fail to germinate. The disease is encouraged by cool, humid conditions and also by overwatering.

To prevent damping off, always be scrupulously vigilant about cleanliness. Use clean containers, fresh compost and clean water.

Creating a seedbed

Choose a sheltered site that does not suffer unduly from late or early frosts. Dig over the soil carefully and remove any weeds, including the roots of perennial weeds. Incorporate sharp sand into the soil if the ground is not free draining. Create a raised bed about 20cm (8in) higher than the surrounding soil to improve the drainage further. Level the top of the bed and remove any lumps by raking both along the bed and across it until the surface has a fine breadcrumb-like structure. Allow the soil to settle, then rake again before sowing.

Aftercare

Turn the plant pots every few days to stop the seedlings growing lopsided as they try to head towards the light. Water the compost when needed to stop them drying out. You might want to use a mist gun rather than a watering can to avoid accidentally washing out the seedlings. Keep the seedlings out of direct sunlight for a day or two after pricking out and water when needed.

Hardening off

Hardening off is a process that gradually acclimatizes the seedling to life outside. All seed raised indoors or in a coldframe will need weaning off the warmer and more protected environment very gradually before they can be planted outside.

Plants raised in protected environments need acclimatizing to cooler temperatures and increased air movement. If they are not, the shock at planting out can kill them. The time it takes to harden off plants varies, but generally it takes between two to six weeks. You will have to slowly increase ventilation

PRICKING OUT SEEDLINGS

1 Half fill the pot with a suitable potting compost (soil mix). Take care to hold the individual seedling only by the leaves, not the stem or the root. Suspend the seedling over the centre of the pot, resting your hand on the edge of the pot to steady it. With the other hand, fill the pot with more compost.

2 Gently tap the pot on the table to settle the compost mix and lightly firm it down with your thumbs, levelling off the surface. If you have had any problems in the past with seedlings rotting, add a 1cm (½in) layer of fine grit to the surface of the pot. Once potted up, water the seedlings well.

and reduce the ambient temperature. Greenhouse-raised plants will need to be moved to a cool coldframe. A couple of weeks before you want to move them outside, reduce the amount of water the seedlings get. You should not be keeping them constantly moist – let the soil become a bit dry-looking between waterings. This has the effect of making the roots more efficient at

extracting water from the soil, a trait the plant will find very beneficial when it is planted in garden soil.

About a week before planting out, let the seedlings get used to the outdoors by leaving them out during the day. If the weather is suitable, you may be able to leave them out overnight – but check the weather forecast first. When the soil outside is warm enough, you can plant away.

Camellias can be grown from seed with success, as this *Camellia* 'Cornish Spring' bush shows. Grow the pricked out seedlings on in light shade in the greenhouse for at least their first winter.

Propagating from cuttings

Most shrubs and climbers can be propagated from cuttings. Many will root perfectly well from softwood cuttings, which are taken in spring when the plant is actively growing, but some will root better during the summer from material that has started to ripen at the base, or even in winter from fully ripened wood.

Taking softwood cuttings

Softwood cuttings are cut from new sappy growth taken from shrubs and climbers that are still in active growth. This is usually in mid- to late spring. Collect material while it is turgid and showing no signs of wilting – ideally choose an overcast day or collect early in the morning. Select healthy-looking material that shows no signs of pest or disease attack and is representative of the plant you are trying to propagate. Ideally, choose material that is not flowering or about to flower.

If this is not possible, remove any flowering stems from the material before trimming it into cuttings. When you remove the material from the parent plant, use a clean, sharp knife or pair of secateurs (pruners), cutting just above a leaf joint. Make a clean cut, which will help minimize the chance of infection, and then place the material directly into a labelled plastic bag to prevent them from wilting. You must keep the cuttings out of direct sunlight until you are ready to prepare them.

Prepare the cuttings

• Trim the stems using a clean sharp knife just below a leaf joint, so that the cuttings are 2.5–8cm (1–3in) long, depending on the type of growth that the plant produces.
• Remove the lowest pair of leaves from all the cuttings and the growing tip from longer cuttings. Most cuttings should then have two to four leaves.
• Dip the bottom cut end of the cuttings into a pot of hormone

TAKING ROSE CUTTINGS

1 Select a side shoot that is still green but beginning to turn woody at the base. Cut just above an outward-facing bud.

2 From the removed stem, trim an individual cutting from the base, making the cut just below a leaf joint.

3 Having made your lower cut, now trim back the soft tip to leave a length of stem about 10cm (4in) long.

4 Remove the lower leaves and thorns of the cutting and dip the base in hormone rooting powder. Tap off any excess.

5 Using a dibble or a pencil, make a hole in the rooting medium and put the cutting into it, inserting it to two-thirds of its length.

6 Label the cutting and cover with a plastic bag 'tent' to ensure moisture retention. Don't allow the bag to touch the cutting.

POTTING UP AND POTTING ON CUTTINGS

1 Pot up the cuttings as soon as they have formed strong growth. Use an 8–10cm (3–4in) pot and a potting mix suitable for the young plants. Water thoroughly and keep out of direct sunlight for a couple of days while they recover from the root disturbance.

2 Cuttings that rooted earlier and have already been potted up for a month or more may need moving into larger pots. Check that the roots have filled the compost (soil mix) before you transfer them. If the compost has lots of white roots, pot on into a larger size.

3 When potting on, use a container a couple of sizes larger and put some compost in the bottom. Put the unpotted plant into the new container and trickle the same type of compost around the root ball. Firm well to remove air pockets.

rooting compound (also available as a gel), shaking off any excess, before inserting the prepared cuttings around the edge of a pot filled with moist, fresh cuttings compost.

• It is important to prevent softwood cuttings from wilting, so cover the container with a plastic bag, but make sure it is held clear of the cuttings by inserting short sticks or hoops of wire to hold it proud of

the cutting. Secure the bag in position around the pot using an elastic band. Alternatively, you can place the uncovered pot in a propagator with a lid.

• Place the pots of prepared cuttings in a warm, well-lit position that is out of direct sunlight. When the cuttings show signs of healthy growth, puncture the plastic bags to allow some air to enter and

surround the plant, or open the vents if they are being raised in a propagator.

• Gradually harden off the rooted cuttings by increasing ventilation and lowering the temperature. Once hardened off, they can be planted up individually into larger containers and filled with fresh, moist potting compost (soil mix) (*see* Potting on cuttings steps, above).

Avoiding disease problems

Softwood cuttings and the foliage of semi-ripe cuttings are susceptible to rot before the cuttings have had a chance to root. Apart from choosing healthy cuttings material, ensure that the propagation tools and equipment are clean and the compost fresh and sterile. You can help to prevent disease outbreaks by drenching the cuttings in a fungicidal solution once they are prepared. Check the information on the packaging for dilution rates and whether the fungicide can be used in conjunction with hormone rooting preparations.

ENCOURAGING BUSHY PLANTS

1 Bushy shrubs, such as the fuschia shown here, usually respond well to early 'pruning'. As soon as the cuttings have three pairs of leaves, pinch out the growing tip if you want a bushy shape.

2 New shoots will form after a few weeks. For really bushy plants, pinch out the tips of the side shoots as well. Repeat this process several times throughout the spring to encourage bushiness.

Summer cuttings

Many shrubs and climbers can be propagated from cuttings taken as growth slows down and new shoots start to ripen – turning woody at the base. Although rooting may take a little longer, the cuttings are generally easier to look after.

Types of cutting

Taking semi-ripe cuttings is largely the same as taking a softwood cutting (see below), except that the material is no longer growing vigorously and is starting to turn woody at the base. Where you make the bottom cut depends on the type of shrub or climber you are trying to propagate.

Nodal cutting Many shrubs and climbers can be raised from semi-ripe cuttings that are trimmed just below a leaf joint (or node). Simply make a straight cut across the stem just below the leaf joint so that the resulting cutting is about 8–10cm (3–4in) long. The leaves should then be trimmed off cleanly from the bottom half of the cutting.

Internodal cutting With this type of cutting, you will need to make a straight cut across the stem midway between leaf joints, so that the cutting is about 10cm (4in) long.

Stem cutting This an internodal or nodal cutting taken from part-way down a stem with the top of each cutting trimmed just above a leaf joint.

Basal cutting Trim off the cutting right at the base where it joins the previous year's growth – look for a slight swelling that is often present. Use a sharp knife or razor-blade to make the cut as close to the base of the material as possible.

Heeled cutting The cutting is removed from the parent tearing a short piece of woody material at the base from the previous year's growth – so that the cutting is 5–10cm (2–4in) long. Simply tidy up the 'heel' using a sharp knife so that it is 1–2cm (½–¾in) long before dipping in rooting hormone and inserting in compost.

Leaf-bud cutting A few shrub species, such as camellia, fatsia and mahonia, and many climbers, including campsis, clematis (see opposite), ivy and honeysuckle, root best if the cutting is simply a leaf joint. Make the top cut just above the leaf joint and the bottom cut about 3–5cm (1–2in) below it, using a straight cut made with a sharp knife. You should be able to get several cuttings from a single stem. These cuttings are best taken during the late summer.

TAKING SOFTWOOD CUTTINGS

1 Typically, a stem is taken from the new shoots produced in the current year. Cut off below the third or fourth pair of leaves.

2 Trim or pull off the lowest pair of leaves. Trim the base of the stem with a sharp knife, cutting just below a leaf joint.

3 Dip the end of the cutting into hormone rooting powder. Although not necessary, the powder will speed up rooting.

4 Make a hole in the compost with a dibber and insert the cutting, firming round it. Don't force the cutting, as you may damage it.

5 Water and place in a propagator or, as here, cover with a plastic bag – but don't let it touch the leaves. Secure with a tie twist.

Clematis cuttings

Clematis are easiest to root from double leaf-bud cuttings taken during early to mid-summer. Trim the top of the cutting just above a pair of leaves and the bottom cut about 3–5cm (1–2in) below it. If you are trying to get a lot of new plants from a single climber, you can double the number of cuttings by carefully cutting down through the middle of the main stem vertically so that each cutting has a half-thickness stem and one leaf.

Rooting summer cuttings

Although you can root summer cuttings in pots covered with plastic or in a heated propagator, they are just as easy to root in a simple border propagator in the garden.

Choose a position in a sheltered spot that is in light shade for most of the day. Dig a trench 5cm (2in) deep and about 25cm (10in) wide and fill it with sharp sand. Make hoops over the bed out of stiff wire such as an old coat hanger. Insert the prepared cuttings into the sand and water well. Push the wire hoops in every 15cm (6in) along the bed and cover with an opaque piece of plastic – such as an old supermarket carrier bag. This should be buried in the soil on one side and held down with bricks or stones at the ends and along the other side.

Check to see if the cuttings need watering from time to time and remove and discard any that show signs of disease.

Once most of the cuttings have rooted, cut some ventilation slashes in the cover to help harden them off, removing the cover completely after a couple of weeks. After this, you can then pot up or plant out the rooted cuttings.

Propagate clematis from double leafbud cuttings taken during early to mid-summer. You can also root cuttings later in the year but they will need to be kept humid and will take longer to root.

Autumn and winter cuttings

Many deciduous and a few evergreen shrubs can be propagated from hardwood cuttings using stems produced during the most recent season's growth. A few difficult-to-propagate shrubs can be increased from root cuttings taken during the dormant season.

Harwood cuttings

Once the current season's shoots have ripened fully and the leaves have fallen, it is an ideal time to take hardwood cuttings from many clump-forming deciduous shrubs. Select vigorous and healthy stems that are about the thickness of a pencil and typical of the plant you are trying to propagate. Remove the stems from the parent plant using secateurs (pruners), just above a bud. Trim the cutting to about 20–30cm (8–12in) with a straight

cut just below a bud at the base and a sloping cut just above a bud at the top. This will help you identify which way up to insert the cuttings later on. Wound difficult-to-root subjects and dip the straight-cut ends in rooting hormone (see Improving box, right).

Hardwood cuttings are usually easy to root, but you will have to be patient as it can take up to a year. The simplest way to root them is in a slit trench 15–20cm (6–8in) deep that's been lined with sharp sand. Space the cuttings 8–10cm (3–4in) apart along the row, inserting each cutting into the sand so that about one-third is still above ground when the trench is refilled. Water and weed the area around the cutting throughout the following year and plant out the rooted cuttings or pot them up the following autumn.

Difficult-to-root subjects, such as this *Rhododendron* 'Loder's White', can be encouraged to root by cutting a thin sliver off the base of the stem of the prepared hardwood cutting.

Improving your chances of success

Some shrubs and climbers can be reluctant to root from softwood, semi-ripe and hardwood cuttings, but you can improve your chances of success with many by increasing the size of the cut and applying a specially formulated hormone to the cut surface.

Wounding Difficult-to-root subjects, such as rhododendrons and magnolias, can be encouraged to root by cutting a thin sliver off the base of the stem of the prepared cutting. Use a sharp knife on one side of the cutting a few centimetres (1in) from the base to remove a thin piece of material.

Rooting hormone Rooting hormone products are available as powders, liquids and gels that are simply applied to the base of the prepared cutting before it is inserted into the compost. They contain special chemicals that stimulate rooting, making difficult-to-root subjects easier to propagate and getting quicker results for most other cuttings. To avoid contaminating the hormone, tip a small amount into a saucer and use this. Throw away any unused rooting hormone that's left in the saucer once all cuttings have been completed. Bear in mind that rooting hormone deteriorates rapidly, so buy fresh stocks each year to make sure of its effectiveness.

Root cuttings

A few shrubs, including aralia, chaenomeles, clerodendron, rhus, romneya and rubus, can be increased from root cuttings taken during the dormant season. Excavate around the base of one side of the shrub to expose a few suitable large, fleshy roots. Select vigorous, healthy roots of about drinking-straw thickness if possible and sever them from the parent plant. Prepare the cuttings using a sharp knife so that they are

TAKING HARDWOOD CUTTINGS

1 Select healthy, blemish-free pieces of wood about the thickness of a pencil. Cut each of these into sections about 20–25cm (8–10in long), angling the top cut.

2 Moisten the bases of the cuttings in water and then dip them in hormone rooting powder. Although not essential, the powder should increase the success rate.

3 Prepare a narrow slit-trench deep enough for the cuttings. Dig down enough so that the top 2.5–5cm (1–2in) of the cuttings will be proud of the earth surface.

4 Loosely fill the trench to about two-thirds with sharp sand or fine grit. This allows the passage of air around the bases of the cuttings and will help prevent rotting off.

5 Insert the cuttings about 8–10cm (3–4in) apart, making sure that the angled cut is uppermost, leaving about 5–10cm (2–4in) above the ground.

6 Firm the soil around the cuttings, ensuring that they are not over-compacted. Leave the cuttings for a whole growing season before lifting and planting out the next winter.

about 5–10cm (2–4in) long, making a straight cut nearest the end of the root nearest the crown and a sloping cut at the other end.

Dip the cuttings in a fungicidal solution to prevent rot setting in. Then, either insert the cuttings around the edge of a pot filled with a well-drained sowing compost (soil mix), with the straight cut just proud of the surface, or lay the cuttings horizontally on a tray of compost.

Cover the compost surface in either case with a thin layer of grit before watering well and allowing to drain. Place the prepared cuttings in a cool, sheltered spot, such as a cold frame or under a cloche in the garden.

Cornus kousa cuttings are taken in the dormant season after the leaves fall in autumn. However, it can be more successfully propagated by using seed, as this produces more vigorous plants.

Layering

Layering is perhaps the most underrated – and yet one of the easiest and most successful – methods of propagating many shrubs and climbers. There are several variations on a theme to layering, all of which involve wounding and partially covering a vigorous, healthy shoot to encourage it to root while it is still attached to the parent plant.

Layering explained

Some plants, notably magnolia and cornus, are very difficult to propagate by taking cuttings. Fortunately, layering is a very simple way of making new plants from old

ones. It involves promoting the development of new roots from a plant's stem, with the stem still attached to the plant. Once it has rooted, it is then severed from the main plant and planted up on its own. Layering can occur spontaneously, when branches of a plant touch the ground and decide to take root.

As the technique of layering is an asexual one, the plants that are produced always have the same flowers, foliage and fruit as the parent plant, which is very beneficial if you want to keep an old and favourite plant going. There are six different methods of layering:

Which method suits which shrub or climber

Simple layering Abelia, aucuba, azalea, camellia, carpenteria, choisya, hamamelis, magnolia, rhododendron, syringa and viburnum.
Serpentine layering Clematis, lonicera, magnolia, rhododendron, viburnum and wisteria.
French layering Acer, chimonanthus, cornus, corylopsis, corylus, cotinus, fothergilla and hydrangea.
Tip layering Rubus and jasminum
Mound layering Amelanchier, calluna, cotinus, daboecia, erica and pernettya.
Air layering Hamamelis, magnolia, rhododendron and wisteria.

LAYERING

1 Select a low-growing young stem and remove any side leaves. Clear the ground beneath the stem.

2 Bend it until it touches the ground at 15–30cm (6–12in) from the branch tip.

3 Dig a small hole where the stem meets the soil, about 5–8cm (2–3in) deep, and bend the stem into the hole.

4 Anchor the stem in place with a peg. Bend the branch tip to as near vertical as you can, taking care not to snap it.

5 Cover the bent section with soil and support in an upright position with a cane. The young plant will be well rooted after two years, and can be transported to a new home.

simple, serpentine, French, tip, mound and air, although simple and air are the most commonly used.

Simple layering

First, select a suitable vigorous, healthy stem low down on the plant. It should be flexible enough to bend down to ground level without snapping. If there are no suitable candidates, prune back one or two of the lowest branches to encourage new shoots in spring. These can be layered the following autumn.

Thoroughly dig over the area of soil under the potential layer and remove any weeds. If the soil is poor, incorporate old potting compost (soil mix) and grit. Use a pair of secateurs (pruners) to trim off any side shoots from the layer and then remove any leaves on the part of the shoot that is to be buried. Pull the layer down to the soil and make a

Layering naturally

Many climbers, including ivies and ornamental vines as well as some thicket-forming shrubs, spread by producing roots on shoots that touch the ground. With climbers, the trailing shoots scramble horizontally, rooting as they grow, until they come across something to climb, while shrubs produce long pliable stems that arch out and root where the tip touches the ground. If this happens in your garden, use the self-layered shoots to propagate your plants. Simply cut off the rooted layer from the parent plant and then pot it up using fresh compost (soil mix) and cut back the top growth to a bud about 15cm (6in) from the ground. If the layer is established and has started to form a new plant, lift it with as much soil around the roots as possible and move it to a suitable position in the garden where it has room to grow and develop.

Cotinus coggygria 'Royal Purple'

shallow depression in the soil using a trowel along the line of the layer, about 30cm (12in) behind the tip of the layer. Carefully bend the stem to form a right-angle about 20cm (8in) behind the growing tip. Secure it into the bottom of the hole using a bent piece of stiff wire. Next, tie the growing tip vertically to a bamboo cane.

With difficult-to-root shrubs and climbers you can improve your chances of success by wounding the stem of the layer on the underside where it will be in contact with the soil using a sharp knife. You then dust the cut surface with rooting hormone before pegging the layer into position, as before.

Cover the portion of the layer that has been pegged to the soil with more soil and firm lightly before watering thoroughly. Water and weed as necessary during the following year, also checking that rooting is taking place. It will take anything from 6–18 months for the layer to root, depending on the species you

are layering, which can then be separated from the parent plant and moved to a suitable position elsewhere in the garden.

Serpentine layering

There are several variations on the layering theme, one of which is serpentine layering. This method is suitable for propagating climbers, such as clematis, wisteria and honeysuckle, which all produce long flexible shoots that can be layered several times along their length.

During early spring, bury a stem at intervals so that it loops in and out of the soil, making sure it has the growing tip poking out of the ground (as for simple layering). It is essential that each of the loops that are out of the ground has at least one leafbud so that it can produce new shoots once rooted.

By autumn of the same year, each of the loops should have rooted and can then be separated and planted out or potted up. Propagating in this way means that a single stem can produce several new plants in a single growing season.

Magnolia aquifolium 'Apollo'

You can grow new plants of the *Amelanchier* species by mound layering. The *Amelanchier lamarckii* shown here produces coppery-red leaves that turn green in summer and then red, orange or yellow in autumn.

French layering

A few vigorous shrubs, such as cotinus, cornus and willow, can be layered by shallowly burying the whole shoot.

Prepare the selected shoot in autumn by pegging it into position. This will encourage all the buds along its length to break at the same time in spring. Once this happens, prepare the soil as for simple layering and then peg the stem to the ground and carefully earth it up so that the stem is just below the surface and the top 5cm (2in) of the new side shoots can be seen.

As the side shoots grow, earth them up periodically to increase the depth of soil over the layered stem, until the ridge of soil is about 15cm (6in) high.

By the autumn, roots will have been produced along the length of the layered stem and each side shoot can be separated with its own portion of rooted layer.

Tip layering

A few shrubs, notably ornamental blackberries and winter jasmine, can be propagated by rooting the tips of their long, flexible shoots into the ground. This is how they would spread naturally if left to their own devices.

Heathers, such as *Calluna vulgaris* 'Wickwar Flame', are propagated by mound layering.

Mound layering

Also known as stooling or burying, this method of layering is suitable for small bushy shrubs, such as heathers, provided you have a well-drained soil.

As the name suggests, the whole plant is gradually covered in a 5–10cm (2–4in) deep mound of free-draining soil so that the roots are encouraged to form on the buried portion of each of the main stems. These can then be separated from the parent plant and potted up or replanted the following autumn.

Air layering

Air layering, often associated only with the propagation of house plants, is also a useful way of propagating some shrubs, such as rhododendron, magnolia, witch hazel and hydrangea, as well as woody climbers such as wisteria.

Air layering, also known as Chinese layering, as the technique was first devised by the Chinese

Layering aftercare

Once the newly rooted layers have been removed from the parent plant, they can either be replanted in the garden or potted up in a container and kept in the greenhouse until they are strong enough to survive being planted outside.

When they are ready to plant out in the garden, they are also ready to be pruned to promote new growth. Prune so that the leaf area is reduced to about one-third.

Plants outdoors should be shaded lightly through their first season. However, after the first winter the screens can be removed as the plants should be robust enough at this stage to survive outside without any additional protection.

many centuries ago, is a useful way of layering woody shrubs and climbers that don't produce pliable stems near to the ground that can be layered by other more conventional techniques. The best time to air layer is during the spring when new growth starts and sap rises.

Choose a healthy and vigorous stem that is representative of the plant as a whole. Trim off all its side shoots for about 30cm (12in) from the tip. Using a sharp knife, make a clean, shallow cut that is slanting upwards, towards the tip. The cut

should be about 5cm (2in) long and reach about halfway through the stem. Use a matchstick to hold the cut open while you dust both the cut surfaces with a hormone rooting compound.

Next, slide in a little moist sphagnum moss, peat or fresh cuttings compost into the cut before removing the matchstick. Tie a piece of black plastic around them, about 5cm (2in) below the cut, so that it can form a sleeve over the layer. Pack the plastic sleeve with moist sphagnum moss so that it forms a

5–8cm- (2–3in-) diameter bulge around the cut stem. Secure the tip end of the moss or the cuttings compost ball by tying the other end of the plastic to the stem and sealing it with tape. This will prevent any water running down the stem and waterlogging the moss or compost. It is important to use black plastic, rather than the clear type, because it will exclude any light and encourage rooting, while keeping the moss/compost moist but not too wet.

Inspect the layer every few months to see if it has rooted. The time this takes varies from plant to plant and with the time of year – taking anything from just three to 18 months. If there are insufficient roots, recover it after moistening, if required. Leave it for another period before inspecting again.

Once sufficient roots have formed, use a pair of secateurs (pruners) to sever the stem just below the roots. Remove the plastic and carefully tease out the roots before potting up into a container, using fresh potting mix. Don't forget to give it a good drink of water afterwards and to keep it well watered until well established.

AIR LAYERING

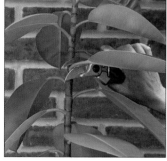

1 Layer the plant above the bare area of the stem, just below the leaves. If you are using the technique on a multi-stemmed plant to increase stock, remove a few leaves from the point where you want to make the cut.

2 Carefully make an upward slit about 3cm (1in) long, below the leaf joint. Use a sharp knife, particularly on woody plants, to get a clean cut. Do not cut more than halfway through the stem or the shoot may break.

3 Make a sleeve out of a sheet of black plastic, wrapping it around the stem (clear plastic is shown here to make the process easier to see). Fix the bottom of the sleeve using a twist tie or waterproof adhesive tape.

4 Brush a small amount of rooting hormone (either powder or gel) into the wound to speed up the rooting process. Pack a bit of sphagnum moss into the wound to keep it open, or just use a matchstick.

5 Pack plenty of damp sphagnum moss around the stem to enclose the wound. Cover with the plastic and secure at the top, as before. Keep the moss moist and check for rooting after a few months.

Common problems

Once well established and growing vigorously, shrubs and climbers will shrug off most pest and disease attacks. However, if they have recently been planted or are not growing well, they can fall victim to a wide range of problems. The most common pests to affect the ornamental garden are slugs and snails, aphids, whiteflies, caterpillars and vine weevils, while the most common diseases are blackspot, mildew, grey mould and rust. With the exception of blackspot, which attacks only roses, all the others can attack a wide range of garden plants.

Whether you want to take any steps to prevent and control pests and diseases on ornamental plants is largely a matter of personal choice. Some gardeners like to maintain a balance between pests and their natural predators, allowing a constant, low level of problems so that there is always sufficient food for the predators to keep them in the garden. Alternatively, you may prefer setting aside an area of the garden for this purpose – a wild corner where you can cultivate plants that are loved by common pests to act as a living larder for predatory birds and insects. You can also encourage natural predators to stay in your garden by providing them with shelter and suitable places to breed.

No matter how good a gardener you are, insects and diseases will affect your plants at some time. The best way to fight them is to understand what these invaders are and how they affect the plants.

Dealing with pests

The most common pests in most gardens are slugs and snails, but they do not cause any serious damage to established shrubs and climbers, so are not covered here. They can devastate new plants.

Catch them early

If a prominent or prized plant is attacked, you may prefer to take action to prevent the problem from spreading further. If you catch it early, you simply have to prune out the disease-affected parts of the plant or pick off individual pests, but if the problem becomes established, you may have to sacrifice affected plants to help protect their neighbours – either by cutting the affected plants back hard or removing them altogether. If you grow a lot of one plant in the same area, such as in a rose bed, pest and disease outbreaks are usually worse because the problem can spread easily from one plant to another. You can avoid this by mixing up plants in

Aphids appear quickly and in legions. They suck the sap out of the plants and spread viruses, causing plants to lose vigour or die.

Caterpillars attack a wide range of plants. Pick them off leaves, let their natural predators deal with them, or use a pesticide.

The evidence of slugs and snails, which eat their way through stems. They are particularly troublesome during wet weather in spring.

borders or, in the case of roses, growing disease-resistant varieties. However, the following pests are all worth watching out for.

Aphids

Green, black, pink or brown insects attack actively growing shoot tips, quickly forming large colonies. Like other sap-sucking insects, aphids can transmit debilitating virus diseases. Be vigilant and pick off small colonies as soon as they are noticed. Where this is not possible, use a jet of water from a hose to dislodge them. Control with a suitable systemic insecticide.

Caterpillars

Voracious eaters of fresh new leaves, several common moth caterpillars can attack a wide range of ornamental plants. Caterpillars of the Angle Shades moth are green with V-shaped markings; Buff-Tip caterpillars are black and yellow; and grey-green caterpillars indicate that you have got the Small Ermine moth in residence. However, if silk webbing can be seen, you might have caterpillars of the web-forming Lackey moth or Hawthorn Webber moth. Fortunately, you don't need to identify the caterpillars to get rid of them. Simply pick off any that you

see before they do too much damage. Those that produce webbing should have their 'tents' cut from the plant and opened out for birds. Severe infestations can be controlled using a biological control containing the bacterium *Bacillus thuringiensis*.

Vine weevil

Vine weevils seem to attack anything and everything. They can be a significant problem for anyone who grows a lot of shrubs and climbers in containers. Watch out for the tell-tale sign of notched leaves, which indicate the adult female is about, but it is the white grubs up to 8mm (⅜in) long that cause the real damage – feeding unnoticed on the roots. Vine weevils are flightless and so move around quite slowly. They

Mammals

Mice, rabbits and deer can all be troublesome in some gardens. Although they are not widespread pests, where they do occur they can cause serious damage to shrubs and climbers. Mice are mainly a problem with new plants and seedlings; rabbits eat young shoots and strip bark from shrubs; while deer will cause similar damage higher up the plant. The best way to deal with mice is to set traps around vulnerable plants, such as in the coldframe or greenhouse. For rabbits, you'll need to erect a boundary barrier at least 90cm (3ft) high, with a further 30cm (12in) buried under the ground; while deer will require a fence at least 1.8m (6ft) high to keep them out of your garden.

Pest-free shrubs and climbers

Abelia	Griselinia
Actinidia	Hebe
Aucuba	Hibiscus
Choisya	Jasminum
Cistus	Kerria
Cornus	Kolkwitzia
Corylus	Leptospermum
Cytisus	Myrtus
Deutzia	Parrotia
Escallonia	Phlomis
Euonymus	Photinia
Fatsia	Pittosporum
Fothergilla	Rosmarinus
Garrya	Santolina
Gaultheria	Skimmia

are usually introduced to an unaffected garden on new plants. Since vine weevils reproduce parthenogenically, it takes just a single female weevil to start off an infestation. Control is by catching the slow-moving adults at night, squashing any grubs that you find or applying biological controls. If you prefer to sleep at night, there is also a chemical control for vine weevil grubs that is applied as a drench to the compost of container plants.

Vine weevil larvae attack the roots while the parents eat holes in the leaves. They are becoming a big pest of shrubs and climbers.

Scale insects

These sap-sucking insects are immobile once they have found a suitable plant. Looking like round, raised spots on the stem or bark, they appear and hold on like miniature limpets.

Small numbers can be prised off individually. If you have a bad infestation, you can gain some control by rubbing over the affected stems with some soft soap. You can also use a suitable systemic insecticide to control these pests.

Galls

Many shrubs and climbers can be affected by galls, which appear as raised lumps on the upper or lower leaf surface and are caused by insects. The plant itself is stimulated by the insect to produce the odd-looking growths that can be either brightly coloured or well camouflaged. The main groups of insects that cause plants to produce galls are gall-wasps, gall-midges and gall-mites. They generally lay eggs inside the gall so that the hatching grub is protected by the plant as it feeds. In one particular type of attack by gall-mites, witches brooms are produced.

Control is unnecessary. If the galls are unsightly, cut off the affected foliage. On deciduous plants, rake up and bin the leaves at the end of the season in question.

Leaf-cutter bees

Semi-circular notches in the leaves of roses, privet and laburnums can be attributed to the activities of leaf-cutter bees, which collect material to build their nests.

The females get busy in early summer building individual cells out of pieces cut from suitable foliage.

The pest is a solitary bee that doesn't swarm or sting, and so is otherwise perfectly harmless. Little damaged is caused and no control is necessary. Unsightly leaves can be picked off if required.

Leaf miners

Tunnels, blotches and other leaf blemishes are caused by the grubs of certain insects. Different insects attack different types of plants. For example, the holly leaf miner causes unsightly tunnelling and brown areas in the fleshy leaves of this plant, which are caused by the grub of a fly. This can be a particular nuisance on hedges and hollies cut for indoor arrangements.

Different species of moth caterpillar cause similar damage to laburnums, gorse, lilac and other ornamental plants during early summer. Control is rarely called for because the plants are largely unaffected. However, if you want to stop further damage to hedges and prominent plants, dispose of hedge clippings and fallen leaves carefully, clear weeds that can harbour these pests and spray with a suitable systemic insecticide.

Box and bay sucker

These are two similar problems that affect two particular plants.

Box sucker attacks the *Buxus* species, causing the stunting of new growth so that the tips of the shoots often look like tiny cabbages.

Bay (*Laurus nobilis*) is attacked by tiny sap-sucking insects that cause the leaves to thicken and distort, often with yellow leaf margins.

In both cases, the control is a matter of removing the affected foliage or, in severe attacks, spraying with a suitable systemic insecticide.

Dealing with diseases

The most prevalent diseases affect a wide range of different plants. Their spread depends both on the vigour of the shrub or climber being attacked and also on the prevailing weather conditions.

Plant health

There are many different diseases that can affect your plants. Most of these are quite rare but every garden will suffer from its share of diseases at some point. In the main, most of these diseases are relatively easy to deal with, if you have made the correct diagnosis. As ever, it is best to be able to prevent disease rather than allowing it to take hold and spread in your garden.

The best way to control pests and diseases is to stay one step ahead of them and prevent them from becoming a problem in the first place. Stay vigilant at all times, so that when they do occur, you will be able to take decisive action quickly and effectively.

How to prevent pests and diseases

Practise good garden hygiene and you will go a long way to preventing outbreaks of pests and diseases. Clearing away fallen leaves and other debris and consigning any diseased material to the dustbin or bonfire, will help to prevent these problems carrying over from one year to the next.

It is also a good idea to keep weeds under control, which often act as a sink of infection. Always keep your eyes open for the first signs of pest and disease attack. When you are moving among your plants when watering, weeding or feeding, for instance, stay vigilant for tell-tale signs and symptoms of disease. Check them at night, too, since some serious pests, including slugs and vine weevils, are more active at night than they are at other times.

If you see anything untoward, take action quickly so that you can nip stop any problems before they spread and become more serious. Individual pests can be picked up and destroyed, while isolated outbreaks of disease can be pruned off the plant. Similarly, initial colonies of small insects such as aphids can be rubbed out between you finger and thumb. You can also stay one step ahead of the pests and diseases by putting down traps and barriers.

Powdery mildew

These are white, dusty-looking deposits that can be found on the young leaves and stems of plants, usually on the upper surface, causing their growth to become stunted and discoloured. It is caused by a range of fungi. Attacks are most acute during long, dry spells.
Treatment Remove and destroy any affected foliage and keep susceptible plants well watered during drought. Weed carefully, as the disease can be spread by weeds. Spray with a suitable systemic fungicide.

Downy mildew

Usually seen as yellow patches on the leaves, with grey or purple mould growing on the undersides, downy mildew is most prevalent in mild and damp weather.
Treatment Pick off and destroy any of the affected stems and try to encourage more air flow to flow between the plants by spacing them more widely. Spray healthy looking leaves with a suitable systemic fungicide to prevent a recurrence.

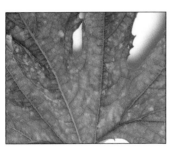

Powdery mildew looks like a dusty white-grey coating. It causes stunting and distortion of leaves, buds, growing tips and fruit.

Rust is a common fungal disease. Rusty patches or spots appear on the leaves, distorting growth and causing leaf drop.

Blackspot is a fungal disease that particularly affects roses. Black spots appear, primarily on the leaves, but sometimes on the stems.

The distinctive pinkish pustules of coral spot. The fungus enters through small wounds in the plant, usually caused by careless pruning.

Nutrient deficiencies

When plants run short of one or more particular nutrients, it can show up as leaf symptoms that are easy to confuse with disease symptoms. Magnesium and manganese deficiencies, for example, both cause yellowing between the leaf veins, while potash deficiency often causes the leaf edges to yellow or leaf tips to scorch.

The other two main plant nutrients, nitrogen and phosphorus, are more difficult to spot, causing poor, often pale, growth with small leaves that are sometimes discoloured. Fortunately, all these problems are easy to put right by feeding: use a balanced general fertilizer for the three main nutrients and one containing trace elements to supply your plants with extra magnesium and manganese.

Blackspot

This disease causes dark spots on the leaves, often with a yellow edge, which can lead to premature leaf drop. It is a serious disease when it affects roses, as it can severely weaken the plant if it is allowed to flourish year after year.

Treatment To control it, remove and destroy any affected foliage and clear fallen leaves in autumn to help prevent the continuation of the disease. This may mean hard-pruning infected plants. Spray healthy-looking leaves with a suitable systemic fungicide.

Rust

This is a common fungal disease that causes distinctive bright orange to brown spots on the undersides of leaves, with yellow flecks on the upper surface. The spots will eventually darken to black and the symptoms can sometimes spread to nearby plant stems.

Different species of rust attack different plants, with roses being particularly affected.

Treatment To control rust, remove and destroy any affected foliage and clear fallen leaves in autumn to help prevent the disease continuing. Try to avoid overhead watering, as the rust spores can be carried back up to the plant by the splashing water. Instead, apply the water at the base of the plant. Spray healthy-looking leaves with a suitable systemic fungicide as necessary.

Leaf spots

There are several types of leaf spot, some with dark green, brown or black spots, sometimes round, sometimes angular, on leaf surfaces. Coral spot, for example, has distinctive small, coral-coloured pustules. A host of fungi can be responsible, but the problem will only be temporary.

Treatment Prune out affected growth if you find it unsightly and feed the plant to encourage vigorous new shoots. Generally, it is not usually worth spraying for these spots, but if you want you can tackle them by using a suitable systemic fungicide.

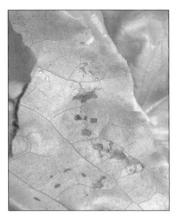

Downy mildew appears as a white coating over leaves and causes distended growth, browning and wilting.

Grey mould

Also known as botrytis, this disease causes fluffy grey mould to appear on buds, flowers, leaves or stems and can occur on nearly any garden plant. However, it can be problematic with large flowers that 'ball' in wet weather and rot, as well as leaves and stems that have been damaged before the attack.

Treatment Pick off affected flowers and shoots and clear fallen ripe fruit, which can also be attacked. Make sure the plants are well spaced and ventilated to prevent a recurrence.

The tell-tail sign of powdery mildew is a dusty-looking coating appearing on the plant. It is often associated with humid conditions.

Keep plants well watered. Cut off any affected shoots and improve air circulation around the plant. Spray with a systemic fungicide.

Methods of control

All pests are preyed upon by natural predators in the garden, including birds, small mammals, amphibians, spiders and insects. One of the best ways of keeping pests under control is to encourage these natural predators to set up home.

Encourage natural predators

Welcome nature's way of controlling pests to your garden. For example, you can get frogs and toads, which feed on a wide range of insects, to remain by providing them with suitable places to hide and a small pond where they can breed. Similarly, many beneficial insects, such as hoverflies and lacewings, will be attracted by nectar-rich plants, such as buddleja, hawthorn and viburnum, and can be encouraged to overwinter by putting up bundles of bamboo where they can hibernate.

Other creatures to encourage include ladybirds (ladybugs), which eat aphids, scale insects, mealy bugs and caterpillars; ground beetles, which consume slugs, troublesome flatworms, vine weevils and spider mites; and centipedes, which eat slugs and snails.

The following are good predators to invite into your garden.

Ladybirds (Ladybugs) A single ladybird larva is able to eat more than 500 aphids while it is developing, so for this reason alone, ladybirds can have a dramatic impact on these pest numbers. Ladybird larvae look nothing like the familiar black-spotted red adult but look like a cross between a beetle and a caterpillar – so make sure you know what they look like so that you don't inadvertently think it's another pest to control.

Lacewings These are green flying insects that have translucent green wings, long antennae and bright,

Not all insects are pests in the garden. The ladybird is one of many that feed on garden problem pests and help keep their damaging populations under control.

golden eyes. Both the adults and larvae feed on aphids. The larvae are similar to ladybird larvae, but they are lighter in colour and often have dead aphids stuck to their bodies to act as camouflage.

Hover flies These are insects that mimic the appearance of wasps but are smaller and able to hover in one spot. They don't sting. As their name implies, they are true flies and their larvae eat aphids and other small sap-sucking insects.

Ground beetles Some beetles are troublesome in the garden, but the big black beetles that scurry about at night are ground beetles and they are definitely worth encouraging as they are voracious eaters of slugs and other insects.

Centipedes Often confused with millipedes, which can damage plants, centipedes eat insects and are worth encouraging into the garden. One simple way to tell them apart is to touch them: a centipede will scuttle away as fast as possible, while a millipede will tend to roll itself up for protection.

Amphibians Frogs, toads and newts are all useful predators in the garden,

as they gobble up slugs and insects. You will need a pond to encourage them into your garden, with suitable access and cover to provide a safe haven and breeding ground.

Hedgehogs Under the cover of darkness, hedgehogs are busy clearing gardens of slugs, caterpillars, beetles and other problem pests. Provide food and winter shelter to encourage them to set up home in your garden.

Birds Many garden birds eat pests. Starlings will eat worms and grubs; sparrows eat insects and weed seeds; thrushes love slugs and snails; robins favour spiders and weed seeds; and blue tits like caterpillars and aphids. Encourage them to stay in your garden by providing a plentiful supply of seed- and berry-producing plants, sheltered areas where they can build nests safely and rear their young, and a source of food and water during the winter months for resident species.

Using pesticides

If you choose to use pesticides to control pest and disease outbreaks, you must read the instructions carefully to ensure that the pest you are trying to control is featured on the label. Garden chemicals are broadly divided into three groups: fungicides, which control disease; insecticides, which control pests; and herbicides, which control weeds.

Some chemicals, called contact pesticides, work only when they are applied to the target. For this reason, if you are using contact insecticides it is essential that they are applied, sprayed or dusted where the pests are lurking – often in the shoot tips and on the undersides of the leaves. Some contact pesticides will remain active for a period of time to control pests and diseases that try to attack the plant for up to a fortnight after being applied. Others, known as systemic chemicals, are absorbed by the plant and transported throughout its structure via the sap. Such chemicals can be applied anywhere on the plant to control the pests and diseases attacking it. This means you can spray less accurately and do not need to cover all the foliage completely. A few chemical fungicidal sprays can be applied to

Using chemicals as a last resort

If all else fails and your plants are plagued by a damaging attack, you may want to resort to using a chemical spray. It is essential that you choose the right spray for the job and apply it exactly as described in the information on the packaging. However, you may also want to keep a few chemicals to hand, locked away safely in the garden shed or garage, that can be used in an emergency. It's worth having a packet of slug pellets if you want to protect vulnerable new plants, and a general systemic insecticide is handy for combating insect pests.

plants before the disease has attacked to provide protection. These are known as preventative fungicides. Like contact chemicals, they have to be applied thoroughly to give complete protection. Check the label carefully for instructions about how often the product should be reapplied and follow this diligently if you want it to be effective. Roses are a good example of how using a combined pesticide and fungicide produces healthy blooms.

Applying chemicals

Garden pesticides are available in various forms. Ready-to-use sprays that are already diluted are the most convenient form and, as their name suggests, can be applied immediately. They are an expensive way to buy pesticides, but they are useful if you are trying to control a small outbreak quickly, such as a pest outbreak in the greenhouse.

In the longer term, it might be preferable to invest in a small hand-pumped pressure sprayer in which to dilute concentrated chemicals. These work out much cheaper if you are applying a lot of the same chemical over the course of a season. Sprayers with a lance will also apply the chemical more quickly and accurately to border plants. For really large gardens, consider investing in a knapsack sprayer, which is much larger and enables you to spray for longer between refills.

Weedkillers are applied differently, depending on where the seeds are located. On a gravel path, for example, you could water the weedkiller using a watering can fitted with a dribble bar, but in the border you would be better off using a sprayer fitted with a spray hood to prevent any spray drift affecting neighbouring plants. Simply place

Healthy roses

The best way to keep roses healthy is to grow disease-resistant roses (see below). However, you can prevent the three common rose diseases of blackspot, mildew and rust on less robust varieties by following a regular spraying programme. If you use a combined pesticide and fungicide that is designed for the purpose, you can prevent outbreaks of pests such as aphids, too. Roses also benefit from a foliar feed containing trace elements to keep the foliage green and healthy.

The following varieties have all shown some resistance to blackspot, mildew and rust:

Large-flowered bush roses 'Alec's Red', 'Alexander', 'Blessings', 'Congratulations', 'Just Joey', 'Peace', 'Polar Star' (not rust), 'Remember Me', 'Royal William' and 'Silver Jubilee'.

Cluster-flowered bush rose 'Amber Queen', 'Mountbatten', 'Queen Elizabeth' (not blackspot) and 'Southampton'.

Climbing roses 'Aloha', 'Compassion', 'Golden Showers' and 'New Dawn'.

the hood over the weed, with the rim on the ground, before pressing the trigger to release the chemical spray. Set the spray nozzle to produce a coarse spray to minimize any airborne droplets.

Safety first

Always read the label carefully before you buy or use a garden pesticide to make sure it will do what you want. Take great care to apply it at the right dilution and observe any precautions that are recommended. Always wear the protective clothing suggested when handling chemicals. Dispose of unwanted garden chemicals at your local authority's waste disposal centre.

Diagnosing problems

Most common pests and diseases are possible to diagnose from the tell-tale symptoms they cause. Use the following guide to help you identify the problem affecting the plants in your garden.

Identifying the problem

A pest is any living creature that causes damage to garden plants. Some are highly visible and easily recognized, while others can be microscopically small and therefore very difficult to spot and identify.

Recognizing that a pest or disease exists is the first stage in learning how to eradicate or control it. The damage created by insects can be infuriating, particularly if you are a gardener who has put many hours of work into the garden in order to enjoy watching your plants blossom and thrive.

Once you establish which plants are being attacked, you are on the way to recognizing the conditions in which the pests thrive. When this happens, you can take steps to remove them. However, many insects look similar, even though the damage they create can vary dramatically. Learning to recognize a beneficial insect from a pest is important. However, it is not just pests that attack plants. Other fungal conditions can develop in plants and stunt or ruin their growth. Bacteria is another important problem group. However, they are never seen and usually function within a plant's tissue. Many can be beneficial, and play an important role in breaking down dead plant material in order to return valuable nutrients to the soil. Most gardeners manage to control or live with a host of pests and diseases, but being able to produce strong and healthy plants is what gardening is all about.

The greyish-white spores of powdery mildew cover the leaves, making it look like a coating of powder. The problem is usually associated with humid conditions and root dryness.

Rhodendron leafhoppers have distinctive reddish markings on their backs. They suck sap from the leaves and cause little harm, but it is thought they contribute to bud blast.

The distinctive pink pustules of coral spot indicate that this troublesome fungus has entered the plant through small wounds, usually caused by careless pruning.

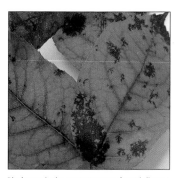

Black spot is the most common fungal disease of roses. It causes the rose to become lacking in vigour. It can be identified by the round brownish-black spots with ragged margins.

Capsid bugs damage leaves at the shoot tips. They suck sap and also secrete a toxic saliva that kills plant cells. Forsythias, fuchsias, roses and hydrangeas are susceptible.

These disfiguring masses are known as galls and they commonly affect forsythia plants. Cut back the affected growth, pruning to ground level. A good recovery should result.

Identifying common problems

LEAF SYMPTOMS

Are there spots on the leaves?
- Silver spots on privet = privet thrip
- White powdery covering = powdery mildew
- Dark green/brown scabby patches = pyracantha scab
- Grey or brown circular spots = fungal leaf spot
- Black spots with yellow edges on roses = blackspot
- Orange spots on leaf undersides = rust
- Transparent spots on roses = rose slugworm
- Yellow spots on rhododendron = rhododendron lacebug
- Translucent patches, often with darker spots = leaf miner

Are the leaves discoloured?
- Yellow leaves, brown spotting = chlorosis
- Yellow patches between veins = magnesium deficiency
- Pale green small leaves = nitrogen deficiency
- Purple small leaves = phosphorus deficiency
- Brown leaf edges = potash deficiency
- Pale green patches between the veins = manganese deficiency
- Furry white covering = downy mildew
- Silvery-grey sheen = silver leaf
- Discoloured leaves, wilt and die = eelworm

Are there holes in leaves?
- Semicircular cuts in leaf edges = leaf-cutter bee
- Small holes = shothole canker

Leaf-cutting bees take neat pieces from leaves, which they use to build their nests.

- Holes and notches = vine weevil
- Ragged holes with evidence of slime trails = slugs and snails

Are there misshapened leaves?
- Rough, often coloured lumps = galls
- Leaf surface grazed off on willow = willow leaf beetle
- Thick leaves, yellow margins = bay sucker
- Tightly rolled leaves on roses = leaf rolling sawfly
- Rolled or webbed leaves = caterpillars
- Distorted leaf clusters on box = box sucker

Are there insects on the leaves?
- Green, black, pink or brown insects = aphids
- White insects on rhododendron = rhododendron whitefly

Have variegated leaves turned green?
- Variegated leaves turn green = reversion

FLOWER SYMPTOMS

Were no flowers produced?
- No flowers = growing conditions (*see* pages 104–111)
- No flowers – incorrect pruning (*see* pages 112–137)

Did the flowers fail to open?
- Flowers fail to open and fall in early spring = frost damage
- Flower buds dry and harden on rhododendron = rhododendron leaf hopper
- White or brown fuzz on withered flowers = grey mould (botrytis)
- Withered flowers = blossom wilt

Are the flowers distorted?
- Flowers open unevenly = capsid bug

Are the flowers discoloured?
- Petal blight

Are there holes in the flowers?
- Holes at the base of flowers = bumble bee
- Irregular holes = moth caterpillars
- Ragged holes = earwigs

Whiteflies suck the sap of the plant and excrete honeydew.

Are the flowers covered in insects?
- Green, black, pink or brown insects = aphids
- Shiny black insects = pollen beetles

Did the flowers disappear?
- Flower buds scattered under plant = birds, squirrels and other wildlife

STEM AND TRUNK SYMPTOMS

Have stems and shoots wilted and died?
- Shoots wilt and die on clematis = clematis wilt
- Shoot tips dying back slowly = die-back
- Shoot tips dying back from flowers = fireblight

Are the stems broad and flattened?
- Flattened stems or flowers = fasciation

Are there spots or lumps on stems?
- Brown spots on bark = scale insects
- Pink or red spots on bark = coral spot
- Rough lumps on forsythia stems = gall
- Rough lumps on stems = crown gall
- Rough patches, sometimes concentric rings on bark = canker
- Unusually flat patches of bark = bacterial canker

Has the bark been stripped?
- Bark removed from right around the trunk = squirrels or rabbits
- Wood stems removed, leaving ragged edge = deer

Is the whole plant distorted?
- Stunted and distorted growth = virus

A directory
of shrubs

This directory offers a comprehensive array of
shrubs – including all the familiar favourites
plus some rarer specimens. The selection here
will help gardeners of all levels find the shrubs
that will make the most of their garden space.
The initial introduction for each entry is either
for the whole genus or the main species grown.
Beyond this, the entry is split between more
common species and cultivars and those that are
less common. The advent of the internet has
meant that it is often possible to obtain rare
shrubs from around the world. Growing rarer
species can be rewarding, as they are often
particularly beautiful.

However, there is also a joy in growing less
exotic plants. If your garden centre does not
have the ones you want, you can always try mail-
order catalogues – and the internet – to find
the perfect plant for your garden.

Shrubs are often viewed as the backbone of the garden, allowing other plants to
look their best. However, shrubs in their own right make a delightful addition to
beds and borders, with their stunning blooms, fruits, foliage and scents.

Abelia x grandiflora

ABELIA

A genus of about 30 species with a long flowering season that make excellent compact, garden plants. Their pretty, trumpet-like flowers are produced on arching stems throughout summer and into early autumn. Although hardy in milder areas, they will need protection elsewhere.
Cultivation They will grow in well-drained garden soil that is reasonably fertile. They need full sun and protection from cold winds. Most are not reliably hardy in colder areas and need the protection of a sheltered, south-facing wall or fence.
Pruning Prune established plants after flowering to encourage new growth. In colder areas, treat as a herbaceous plant and cut down the whole plant in autumn and protect roots with a layer of dry leaves or bark chippings held in place with wire netting.

Abelia x grandiflora 'Gold Spot'

Propagation Take softwood cuttings during early summer, semi-ripe cutting in late summer or hardwood cuttings in mid-autumn.

Abelia 'Edward Goucher'
Purple-pink trumpets are produced from early summer to early autumn along arching stems. The glossy, bronze-green leaves mature to dark green. H 1.5m (5ft) S 2m (6ft).
Aspect: sun
Hardiness: ✿✿ Zone: 9

Abelia x grandiflora (syn. A. rupestris)
Scented, trumpet-shaped, pale pink and white flowers are borne on arching stems from early summer to mid-autumn. Vigorous and long-flowering, this semi-evergreen shrub with glossy leaves makes a perfect focal-point plant for a well-drained border in sun. This plant is orderline frost hardy. H 3m (10ft) S 4m (13ft).
Named varieties: 'Confetti', with very compact, pink-tinged white flowers. Frost hardy. H 1m (3ft) S 1m (3ft). 'Francis Mason', variegated, glossy, yellow-edged leaves. More tender than other varieties. H 1.5m (5ft) S 2m (6ft). 'Gold Spot' (syn. 'Gold Strike', 'Aurea'), bright yellow foliage. H 1.5m (5ft) S 2m (6ft).
Aspect: sun.
Hardiness: ✿✿ Zone: 9 (some borderline).

ABELIOPHYLLUM

A genus of just one species, that is grown for its masses of fragrant flowers borne on bare branches during late winter and early spring. A good alternative to forsythia, they can be grown in the border or trained against a wall or fence. To fully appreciate the almond-scented flowers, plant close to an entrance or path.
Cultivation Abeliophyllum will grow in well-drained garden soil that is reasonably fertile and in full sun.
Pruning No routine pruning is necessary. Neglected plants can be rejuvenated by cutting back one stem in three to near ground level after flowering, starting with the oldest stems.
Propagation Take softwood cuttings during early summer, semi-ripe cuttings in late summer or hardwood cuttings in mid-autumn.

Abeliophyllum distichum
White forsythia
A much underrated, forsythia-like shrub that bears masses of fragrant, star-shaped, pink-tinged white flowers on bare branches during late winter and early spring. H 1.5m (5ft) S 1.5m (5ft).
Named varieties: 'Roseum Group', pale pink flowers on dark stems. H 1.5m (5ft) S 1.5m (5ft).
Aspect: sun
Hardiness: ✿✿✿ Zone: 9+

ABUTILON

A genus of about 150 species of graceful shrubs, many with spectacular, lantern-like flowers. Most are tender, but a few can be grown against a warm, sheltered wall or fence in mild areas, in a container on the patio or in the conservatory in colder areas.
Cultivation In the garden they will grow in well-drained garden soil that is reasonably fertile and in full sun. Indoors, grow in a soil-based compost (soil mix). Water freely during the spring and summer and sparingly at other times. Feed every fortnight during the growing season.
Pruning In the garden, prune out frosted shoots in early spring or mid-spring. Indoors, prune back established plants by half in mid-spring to restrict their size.
Propagation Take softwood cuttings in late spring or semi-ripe cuttings from early summer to late summer. They can also be raised from seed in mid-spring.

Abutilon 'Kentish Belle'
Chinese lantern
This is a lax and graceful evergreen shrub with toothed, three- or five-lobed green leaves and delightful, long, pendent, bell-shaped flowers with pale yellow petals and burnt-orange base that are borne from late spring to mid-autumn. H 2.5m (8ft) S 2.5m (8ft).
Aspect: sun
Hardiness: ✿✿ Zone: 9+

Abutilon x suntense

Abutilon x suntense 'Geoffey Gorer'

Abutilon megapotamicum
Brazilian bell-flower, trailing abutilon

This is a graceful, frost-hardy evergreen shrub with slender stems that carry red and yellow lantern-like flowers from late spring to mid-autumn. The toothed, three-lobed bright green leaves form an attractive backdrop at other times. H 2m (6ft) S 2m (6ft).
Named varieties: 'Variegatum' (variegated trailing abutilon), wonderful yellow-blotched leaves on self-layering branches means that it can be grown as deep ground cover in mild areas, but it also makes an attractive shrub if trained against a warm, sheltered wall or fence in cooler areas. H 2m (6ft) S 2m (6ft).
Aspect: sun
Hardiness: ✸✸ Zone: 9+

ACER
Maple

This genus of about 150 species of deciduous trees and shrubs contain many that are grown for their ornamental bark and foliage, as well as brilliant autumnal tints. Only the shrubs are covered here.
The 'palmatum' group have distinctively lobed leaves and attractive bark, while the 'dissectum' group are generally more compact and have leaves that are much more deeply cut. Both are slow growing and make superb garden specimens – creating spectacular seasonal focal points in spring, summer and autumn. They also make excellent specimens in containers.
Cultivation In the garden, grow in well-drained garden soil that doesn't dry out in summer and is reasonably fertile. Acers will grow in sun or partial shade, where they are sheltered from cold winds and late frosts that can scorch the emerging leaves. In containers, grow in a soil-based compost (soil mix). Feed every fortnight throughout the growing season and water as necessary.
Pruning No routine pruning is necessary. Neglected plants can have any wayward branches removed to balance the overall shape of the canopy.
Propagation Can be raised from seed in mid-autumn, but results are variable. Named varieties must be grafted in early spring or budded in late summer on to seedling stock of the same species.

Acer palmatum 'Atropurpureum' (syn. *A. palmatum* f. *atropurpureum*)
Japanese maple

This is a graceful and slow-growing maple that makes an excellent specimen for a small garden or for growing in a large container. The plant's attractive palm-like, deeply lobed, dark purple leaves look spectacular through all of the summer before turning brilliant shades of red in autumn. H 8m (26ft) S 8m (26ft).
Aspect: semi-shade
Hardiness: ✸✸✸ Zone: 4+

Acer palmatum 'Bloodgood'
Japanese maple

This is one of the best purple-leaved varieties. It has attractive deeply lobed, palm-like leaves that are sumptuous all summer long, turning brilliant red in autumn. This is an ideal specimen or accent plant for a partially shaded spot. The autumn hues are particularly long lasting, making it the perfect choice for a seasonal display. When its leaves fall, dark purple twigs and stems add winter interest. Can be grown in a container. H 5.5m (18ft) S 5.5m (18ft).
Aspect: semi-shade
Hardiness: ✸✸✸ Zone: 5+

Acer palmatum var. *dissectum* 'Atropurpureum' (syn. *A. palmatum* var. *dissectum* 'Atropurpureum Group')
Japanese maple

Ideal for growing in a container or as a specimen plant on the patio, this compact Japanese maple has a neat dome-like habit and particularly fine, deeply cut, red-purple, ferny foliage. In autumn the leaves turn dramatic fiery shades. Protect from cold winds and late frosts. Its delicate foliage can burn in full sun. H 2m (6ft) S 3m (10ft).
Aspect: semi-shade
Hardiness: ✸✸✸ Zone: 4+

Acer palmatum 'Garnet'
Japanese maple

A popular form of Japanese maple with a mound-like habit and dark

Acer palmatum 'Orange Dream'
Japanese maple

A wonderful new variety that forms an attractive specimen for a

purple, finely cut leaves. It makes an excellent specimen or focal point in a small garden that gets some sun. In autumn the leaves turn brilliant red before falling to reveal a tracery of fine twigs that provide winter interest. Protect from cold winds and late frosts, which can burn the delicate foliage. H 5.5m (18ft) S 5.5m (18ft).
Aspect: sun to semi-shade
Hardiness: ✸✸✸ Zone: 4+

Acer palmatum 'Sango-kaku'

Acer palmatum 'Osakazuki'

Acer palmatum var. dissectum
'Crimson Queen'

small garden. The foliage emerges
golden-yellow with pink edges in
spring, slowly taking on a
greenish hue in summer before
transforming into a brilliant
orange in the autumn. This plant
is a good choice for a large
container as its growth rate will
be restricted. H 6m (20ft)
S 1.5m (5ft).
Aspect: semi-shade
Hardiness: ✿✿✿ Zone: 5

Acer palmatum 'Osakazuki'
Japanese maple
Startling red autumn colour
makes this slow-growing Japanese
maple a dramatic addition to any
garden. The large, palm-shaped
leaves are rich green at other
times and set off the hanging
brilliant red fruits in summer.
H 6m (20ft) S 6m (20ft).
Aspect: sun to semi-shade
Hardiness: ✿✿✿ Zone: 4+

Acer palmatum 'Sango-kaku'
(syn. *A. palmatum 'Senkaki'*)
Japanese maple, coral-bark
maple
Perhaps the best maple for year-
round interest, it is an ideal
choice for small gardens. The
brilliant coral-red young shoots
dramatically set off the emerging
palm-shaped, orange-yellow leaves
in spring. The leaves gradually
turn green in summer, before
taking on fabulous shades of
yellow in autumn. The leaves then
fall to reveal the beautifully
coloured stems that can be seen
throughout the winter. Stem
coloration is less pronounced on

mature specimens. H 6m (20ft)
S 5.5m (18ft).
Aspect: semi-shade
Hardiness: ✿✿✿ Zone: 4+

ALOYSIA
A genus of about 35 species of
deciduous or evergreen flowering
shrubs, only one of which is
commonly cultivated for its
distinctive lemon-scented foliage
that is widely used for culinary
purposes. Plant it in a convenient
location in full sun, such as next
to a path or outside the kitchen
door, where you can harvest the
leaves for adding to dishes,
making lemon tea or pot-pourri.
Cultivation In the garden, grow in
well-drained, poor, dry soil in full
sun – the base of a sunny wall is
ideal. Indoors, grow in a soil-
based compost (soil mix). Water
freely during the spring and
summer, sparingly at other times.

Pruning In mild areas where the
plant can form a permanent
framework of branches, prune in
mid-spring to keep within
bounds. Elsewhere, cut back in
autumn and protect roots with a
layer of dry leaves or bark
chippings held in place with
wire netting.
Propagation Take softwood
cuttings in mid-summer.

Aloysia triphylla (syn. *A.
citriodora, Lippia citriodora*)
Lemon verbena
An upright, deciduous shrub with
narrow, lemon-scented leaves, that
is covered in clusters of pale lilac
flowers from mid-summer to late
summer. Tolerates poor, dry soils.
H 3m (10ft) S 3m (10ft).
Aspect: sun
Hardiness: ✿✿ Zone: 5+

AMELANCHIER
Juneberry, snowy mespilus
A genus of over 25 species of
deciduous multi-stemmed trees
and shrubs that offer pretty
spring flowers, attractive felted
leaves that turn dramatic shades
in autumn, accompanied by juicy
fruit that are loved by birds.
They make ideal specimens or
seasonal focal points for use at
the back of a mixed border in full
sun or partial shade.
Cultivation Amelanchier will grow
in any neutral to acid garden soil
provided that it is reasonably
fertile and positioned in full sun
or partial shade.
Pruning No routine pruning is
necessary. Neglected plants can

have wayward branches removed
to open the canopy and maintain
the overall balance.
Propagation Layer suckers in early
spring and separate when well
rooted in mid-autumn. Take
softwood cuttings during mid-
spring or semi-ripe cuttings in
mid-summer. Sow seed as soon
as ripe in summer.

Amelanchier x grandiflora
'Ballerina'
This compact and free-flowering
deciduous shrub produces
clouds of white, star-shaped
flowers from early spring to
mid-spring. Emerging bronze-
tinted, the foliage matures to
dark green before turning
brilliant shades of red and orange
during autumn. Sweet and juicy
dark red fruits are produced in
early summer. H 6m (20ft)
S 8m (26ft).
Aspect: sun or semi-shade
Hardiness: ✿✿✿ Zone: 4+

Amelanchier lamarckii
A spectacular shrub in spring and
autumn, that is covered in a
profusion of star-shaped, white
flowers during early spring and
mid-spring accompanied by
bronze-tinted emerging leaves.
By summer the leaves mature to
dark green and then transform
into a beacon of orange and red
in autumn. Sweet and juicy dark
red fruits are produced in early
summer. H 10m (33ft) S 12m
(40ft).
Aspect: sun or semi-shade
Hardiness: ✿✿✿ Zone: 4+

Aloysia triphylla

Amelanchier lamarckii

Aucuba japonica

Azara dentata

AUCUBA

A genus of three species of evergreen shrubs that offer robust, glossy foliage that is incredibly tough. Able to grow almost anywhere, including dry shade and wind tunnels found between buildings. Their tolerance of dry soil and urban pollution means they are widely used by landscapers in towns and cities. Their ability to cope with salt-laden air makes them ideal filler or hedging shrubs in coastal gardens. On female plants, bright red autumn berries are sometimes produced.

Cultivation Plant in almost any soil (except waterlogged soil), in sun or shade. To enhance berry production, plant one male to every five female plants. In containers, grow in a soil-based soil mix. Feed every fortnight throughout the growing season and water as necessary.

Pruning Prune in mid-spring to maintain the size and shape you require. Leave hedges until mid-summer or late summer. Use secateurs (pruners) so that you can avoid damaging any foliage that remains on the plant after trimming.

Propagation Take semi-ripe cuttings in late summer or hardwood cuttings in early autumn. Sow seed in early autumn or mid-autumn.

Aucuba japonica
Japanese laurel
Tough as old boots, this easy-to-please evergreen shrub is perfect for heavily shaded areas and wind tunnels found between buildings where little else will grow. However, its neat, domed habit and densely packed lustrous, dark green leaves means it is a bit on the boring side. On female plants, bright red autumn berries follow insignificant late spring flowers. H 3m (10ft) S 3m (10ft).

Named varieties: 'Crotonifolia' is the best spotted laurel with leathery, yellow-speckled, dark green leaves. Although female, it rarely produces fruit. H 3m (10ft) S 3m (10ft). 'Picturata' (spotted laurel), is the male variety, with yellow-splashed, dark green leaves that are yellow-speckled at the margins. H 3m (10ft) S 3m (10ft). 'Rozannie' is very compact, with glossy dark green leaves and large, bright red berries. H 1m (3ft) S 1m (3ft). 'Variegata' (spotted laurel) has yellow-speckled, dark green leaves and bright red berries. H 3m (10ft) S 3m (10ft).
Aspect: sun or deep shade
Hardiness: ✿✿✿ Zone: 4+

Azalea – see Rhododendron

AZARA

A genus of about 10 species of evergreen trees and shrubs, only one of which is widely grown. Frost-hardy, it should be given a sheltered position against a sunny wall or fence or among other hardier shrubs in the garden. In colder areas, try growing in a tub on the patio and move it into a cool greenhouse where the fragrant flowers can be best appreciated.

Cultivation Grow in any moist, garden soil that is reasonably fertile, in full sun or partial shade.

Pruning No routine pruning is necessary unless it is grown as a wall shrub, where selected shoots should be trained in a fan shape and subsequent side shoots thinned as necessary to maintain the overall shape.

Propagation Take semi-ripe cuttings in mid-summer.

Azara dentata
Unusual early summer-flowering evergreen shrub with serrated, glossy green leaves. It produces masses of fragrant, golden-yellow spidery flowers during early summer. H 3m (10ft) S 3m (10ft).
Aspect: sun or semi-shade
Hardiness: ✿✿ Zone: 5+

BALLOTA

Ballota comprises a genus of over 30 species of shrubs and also perennials but only one of the shrubs is featured here. This borderline hardy shrub has evergreen foliage covered in woolly hairs that give it a grey sheen. It is an ideal choice for a gravel or Mediterranean garden where it will appreciate the good drainage and full sun. Grow in a container on a sunny patio elsewhere.

Cultivation In the garden, grow in well-drained, poor, dry soil in full sun – the base of a sunny wall is an ideal spot for this plant. In containers, grow in a soil-based soil mix. Feed monthly throughout the growing season and water as necessary.

Pruning To promote a neat habit, established plants should be cut back by about half each mid-spring.

Propagation Take softwood cuttings in mid-spring or semi-ripe cuttings in late summer.

Ballota acetabulosa
A compact, aromatic, evergreen, drought-tolerant shrub that is generally pest- and disease-resistant. This grey-stemmed, evergreen shrub has felty, sage-green, heart-shaped leaves and silvery shoot tips. A bonus of pretty purple-pink flowers are produced in whorls during mid-summer and late summer. H 60cm (24in) S 75cm (30in).
Aspect: sun
Hardiness: ✿✿ Zone: 5+

Ballotta acetabulosa

Banksia coccinea

BANKSIA
Named after the botanist Sir Joseph Banks, who discovered this genus at Botany Bay, the plant is now known to contain about 70 species of evergreen shrubs and trees. The one featured here is grown for its dramatic dome-like flower-spikes produced from late spring and into summer. Ideal for cutting for use in indoor flower arrangements.
Cultivation Grow in neutral to acid, well-drained, poor, dry soil in full sun. In frost-prone areas, grow under glass in containers filled with a half-and-half mixture of ericaceous compost and a soil-based compost (soil mix). Feed every fortnight in the growing season and water as necessary.
Pruning Deadhead plants after flowering.
Propagation Raise from seed in mid-spring.

Banksia coccinea
Scarlet banksia
Wonderful spikes of bright orange-red flowers are produced in late spring and early summer from the tips of an open, upright shrub. The serrated, heart-shaped, dark green leaves have a felty covering underneath and make an excellent foil for the conspicuous flowers that appear from late spring to mid-summer. Can also be cut to use in flower arrangements. H 5m (16ft) S 3m (10ft).
Aspect: sun
Hardiness: ❀ Zone: 9+

BERBERIS
Barberry
A genus of over 450 species of evergreen or deciduous shrubs. Most are hardy, easy to grow and have vicious thorns and autumn berries. Deciduous species are also grown for their yellow-orange flowers and dramatic autumn colours, while the evergreen species have year-round, dense, glossy foliage, with some species offering eye-catching, spring flowers, too. They can be grown as border fillers and some make excellent hedging plants.
Cultivation They will grow in almost any well-drained garden soil that is reasonably fertile in full sun or partial shade. Deciduous varieties are best planted in a sunny position to get the best of their autumn colour and berries.
Pruning No routine pruning necessary, but you can trim lightly after flowering to maintain the overall shape.
Propagation Can be raised from seed in late autumn, but the results can be variable. Take softwood cuttings from evergreen varieties in mid-summer or semi-ripe cuttings of deciduous varieties in early autumn.

Berberis darwinii
An upright, evergreen shrub with prickly, holly-like leaves, which produces a profusion of pendent burnt-orange coloured flowers during mid-spring and late spring, followed in autumn by purple

fruit with a bluish bloom. It is a useful filler for the shrub border or for growing as an informal flowering hedge where its prickly stems will provide a deterrent against intruders. H 3m (10ft) S 3m (10ft).
Aspect: sun or semi-shade
Hardiness: ❀❀❀ Zones: 7–8

Berberis julianae
This upright-growing, evergreen berberis has glossy, dark green leaves that turn red in autumn. A bonus of yellow flowers is produced during late spring, followed by black fruit with a bluish bloom. Although not as ornamental as some berberis, its dense growth and upright habit means it makes an excellent screen or hedge where its spiny leaves will provide an intruder deterrent to intruders. H 3m (10ft) S 1.2m (4ft).
Aspect: sun or semi-shade
Hardiness: ❀❀❀ Zones: 7–8

Berberis linearifolia 'Orange King'
This is an upright, carefree, evergreen shrub with viciously spiny, glossy, dark green leaves. Profuse burnt-orange coloured flowers are produced in clusters along stiffly arching stems during mid-spring, followed by rounded, blackish fruits. This vigorous evergreen makes an informal flowering hedge, as viciously thorny leaves provide a deterrent against intruders.

Berberis aristata

H 2.7m (9ft) S 2.7m (9ft).
Aspect: sun or semi-shade
Hardiness: ❀❀❀ Zones: 7–8

Berberis x *stenophylla* (syn. *B. darwinii* x *B. empetrifolia*)
The spiny, dark green leaves of this vigorous, evergreen barberry are the perfect foil for its dark yellow, double flowers, which are produced in arching clusters during mid-spring and late spring. A bonus of rounded, black fruits are produced in autumn. Easy to grow, it makes an excellent screen or hedge, where its spine-tipped leaves will provide a deterrent against intruders. H 3m (10ft) S 5m (16ft).
Named varieties: 'Claret Cascade', red shoots with bronze-green foliage, dark yellow flowers and

Berberis thunbergii f. *atropurpurea*

Other berberis plants to look out for:

Berberis thunbergii f. *atropurpurea*, purple leaves turn brilliant red in autumn; red-flushed pale yellow flowers are followed by glossy red fruit. H 1m (3ft) S 2.5m (8ft).
Berberis thunbergii 'Golden Ring', yellow-edged purple leaves turn brilliant red in autumn; red-flushed pale yellow flowers are followed by glossy red fruit. H 1m (3ft) S 2.5m (8ft).
Berberis thunbergii 'Red Chief', purple leaves turn fiery orange and red in

autumn; purple stems provide winter interest. H 1.5m (5ft) S 1.5m (5ft).
Berberis thunbergii 'Red Pillar', purple leaves turn fiery orange and red in autumn; red-flushed pale yellow flowers. H 1.5m (5ft) S 1.5m (5ft).
Berberis thunbergii 'Rose Glow', pink-mottled, reddish-purple leaves turn fiery orange and red in autumn; red-flushed pale yellow flowers are followed by glossy red fruit. H 1m (3ft) S 2.5m (8ft).

black fruits. H 1.2m (4ft) S 1.2m (4ft). 'Corallina Compacta', very compact and slow growing with red-flushed yellow flowers that open from red buds. H 30cm (12in) S 30cm (12in). 'Crawley Gem', compact and very free flowering. Its orange blooms open from red buds. H 60cm (24in) S 60cm (24in). 'Irwinii', compact with spiky leaves and orange flowers. H 1.5m (5ft) S 1.5m (5ft). 'Lemon Queen' (syn. *B. x stenophylla* 'Cornish Cream', *B. x stenophylla* 'Cream Showers'), dark green leaves, creamy-white flowers and black fruits. H 3m (10ft) S 5m (16ft).
Aspect: sun or semi-shade
Hardiness: ✿✿✿ Zones: 7–8

Berberis thunbergii 'Atropurpurea Nana' (syn. *B. thunbergii* 'Crimson Pygmy', *B. thunbergii* 'Little Favourite')
Grown for its dark purple leaves, which turn a brilliant red in autumn, this compact deciduous shrub also bears pale yellow flowers with reddish highlights during mid-spring and late spring, followed by glossy red fruit in autumn. It is a useful filler for the front of a shrub border in sun or partial shade or for growing as a low, informal flowering hedge. It also makes an excellent foliage plant for containers. H 60cm (24in) S 75cm (30in).
Aspect: sun or semi-shade
Hardiness: ✿✿✿ Zones: 7–8

Berberis thunbergii 'Aurea'
Brilliant acid-yellow spring foliage is the main feature of this deciduous berberis with a neat rounded habit. The foliage colour deepens as the season progresses, eventually turning orange-red in autumn. Pale yellow flowers pass almost unnoticed during mid-spring and late spring, followed by more conspicuous glossy red fruit in autumn. An excellent choice for illuminating a shady corner. Avoid planting in full sun as it can scorch the foliage. H 1.5m (5ft) S 2m (6ft).
Aspect: semi-shade
Hardiness: ✿✿✿ Zones: 7–8

Berberis thunbergii 'Bagatelle'
Compact and easy to grow, this dwarf deciduous berberis has dark purple leaves that turn a brilliant red in autumn. It is ideal at the front of a border in sun or partial shade. The pale yellow flowers with reddish highlights are produced during mid-spring and late spring and are followed by glossy red fruit in autumn. H 30cm (12in) S 40cm (16in).
Aspect: sun or semi-shade
Hardiness: ✿✿✿ Zones: 7–8

Berberis thunbergii 'Dart's Red Lady'
This compact deciduous berberis has plum-red foliage that turns brilliant shades of red in autumn. The foliage is a perfect foil for the red-flushed, pale yellow flowers that are produced during mid-spring and late spring, followed by glossy red fruit in autumn. It is a useful specimen for a shrub border in sun or partial shade. H 1m (3ft) S 2.7m (9ft).
Aspect: sun or semi-shade
Hardiness: ✿✿✿ Zones: 7–8

Berberis thunbergii 'Harlequin'
An unusual deciduous berberis that has beetroot-red foliage marbled with pink and white, which turns pale crimson in the autumn. A bonus of pale yellow flowers with reddish highlights are produced during mid-spring and late spring, followed by glossy, red fruit in autumn. This compact, variegated

Berberis jamesiana

shrub makes a useful specimen for a shrub border in sun or partial shade. Lightly prune each winter to get the best foliage coloration. H 1.5m (5ft) S 2m (6ft).
Aspect: sun or semi-shade
Hardiness: ✿✿✿ Zones: 7–8

Berberis thunbergii 'Helmond Pillar'
A columnar, deciduous shrub with plum-purple leaves that take on brilliant shades of red in autumn. A bonus of red-tinged, pale yellow flowers are produced during mid-spring and late spring. This upright berberis makes a useful focal point or specimen for a shrub border in sun or partial shade, where it will add vertical interest to the planting scheme. H 150cm (5ft) S 60cm (2ft).
Aspect: sun or semi-shade
Hardiness: ✿✿✿ Zones: 7–8

Berberis 'Georgii'

Berberis valdiviana

Brachyglottis compacta 'Sunshine'

Brugmansia suaveolens

BRACHYGLOTTIS

A genus of about 30 species, including several evergreen shrubs. The one featured here has felty grey leaves that show off its brilliant yellow, daisy-like flowers during early summer. This sun-loving shrub is also tolerant of salt-laden air, so is an ideal choice for coastal gardens.

Cultivation It will grow in almost any well-drained garden soil that is reasonably fertile in full sun. It makes a suitable addition to a gravel or 'dry' garden, where it will appreciate the open site and well-drained soil.

Pruning No routine pruning is necessary, but you can trim it lightly after flowering to maintain overall shape.

Propagation Take semi-ripe cuttings in mid-summer.

Brachyglottis compacta 'Sunshine' (syn. Senecio 'Sunshine')

A popular evergreen, grey-leaved shrub that bears bright yellow, daisy-like flowers on wiry stems during early summer and mid-summer. The attractive felty leaves emerge silvery-white and mature to a darker green as the hairs are shed. H 1m (3ft) S 2m (6ft).
Aspect: sun
Hardiness: ✿✿ Zone: 9

BRUGMANSIA
Angels' trumpet

A genus of five species that includes the vigorous shrub featured here, which produces conspicuous, night-scented trumpets. Ideal for adding an exotic touch to a sheltered patio. Bear in mind that all parts of the plant are highly toxic if eaten, so it is not suitable if young children are around.

Cultivation In the garden, moisture-retentive, well-drained garden soil that is reasonably fertile suits this plant. It also prefers full sun. In containers, grow in a soil-based compost (soil mix). Feed every month throughout the growing season and water as necessary. The plant should be moved to a warm spot under cover when the temperature falls below 7°C, and watered sparingly throughout the winter.

Pruning No routine pruning is necessary, but you can trim lightly after flowering to maintain its overall shape. Neglected plants can be rejuvenated by cutting back one stem in three to near ground level after flowering, starting with the oldest stems.

Propagation Take semi-ripe cuttings in late summer or sow seed in mid-spring.

Brugmansia suaveolens

This night-scented tender shrub bears stunning, 30cm-(12in-) long, trumpet-shaped, white, yellow or pink flowers from early summer to early autumn, which appear against leathery, wavy-edged, mid-green leaves. H 5m (16ft) S 3m (10ft).
Aspect: sun
Hardiness: tender Zone: 10

BUDDLEJA

Over 100 species are in this genus, which includes the popular deciduous shrubs featured here. They are grown for their profusion of flowers, usually produced in terminal spikes, which are loved by butterflies and other beneficial insects. Buddlejas are also quick growing and easy to please and so are an ideal choice for a new garden.

Cultivation Grow in any well-drained, dry soil in full sun.

Pruning For best flowering displays, most should be cut back hard in early spring to encourage new, vigorous and free-flowering shoots from the base during early spring. The exceptions are *B. alternifolia* and *B. globosa*, which, once established, should have their flowered shoots cut back to a healthy shoot or a bud lower down in order to maintain a compact shape and encourage new flowering shoots. This should be done directly after flowering.

Propagation Take semi-ripe cuttings in late summer or hardwood cuttings during late autumn.

Buddleja alternifolia

An open, deciduous shrub with stiffly arching branches that are covered in dense clusters of very fragrant, lilac flowers during early summer. The gracefully arching branches look particularly effective when the shrub is grown as a standard to make a striking seasonal focal point in a sunny border. Train a single stem to 1.5m (5ft), then pinch out the growing tip. Progressively remove sideshoots from the base to create attractive weeping heads on a clear stem. The leaves also turn butter-yellow in autumn. H 4m (13ft) S 4m (13ft).
Aspect: sun
Hardiness: ✿✿✿ Zones: 7–8

Buddleja alternifolia

Buddleja davidii 'Black Knight'

Buddleja davidii 'Black Knight'
Butterfly bush
A dramatic, deciduous shrub that bears dense terminal spikes of fragrant, dark purple flowers from mid-summer to early autumn that are highly attractive to butterflies and other beneficial insects. The leaves also turn butter-yellow in autumn. H 3m (10ft) S 5m (16ft).
Aspect: sun
Hardiness: ✿✿✿ Zones: 7–8

Buddleja davidii 'Harlequin'
Variegated butterfly bush
Many gardeners would say that this is probably the best variegated version of this popular deciduous summer-flowering shrub. The lance-shaped, grey-green leaves are edged with yellow, maturing to cream, and provide added interest before the flowers appear. The dense spikes of fragrant, reddish-purple flowers are produced at the end of shoots in succession from mid-summer to early autumn and are a magnet for butterflies and other beneficial insects. H 3m (10ft) S 5m (16ft).
Aspect: sun
Hardiness: ✿✿✿ Zones: 7–8

Buddleja davidii 'Nanho Blue'
(syn. B. davidii 'Nanho Petite Indigo')
Butterfly bush
Slender, densely packed spikes of lilac-blue flowers are produced on the tips of gracefully arching branches on this deciduous shrub from mid-summer to early autumn. The fragrant flower spikes, up to 15cm (6in) long, are loved by butterflies and other beneficial insects. The leaves also turn butter-yellow in autumn. H 3m (10ft) S 5m (16ft).
Aspect: sun
Hardiness: ✿✿✿ Zones: 7–8

Buddleja davidii 'Pink Delight'
Butterfly bush
This splendid deciduous shrub bears densely packed, fragrant flower-spikes up to 30cm (12in) long at the end of arching shoots in succession from mid-summer to early autumn. Each flower-spike is made up of thousands of tiny orange-eyed, bright pink flowers that are a magnet for butterflies and other beneficial insects. The leaves are butter-yellow in autumn. H 3m (10ft) S 5m (16ft).
Aspect: sun
Hardiness: ✿✿✿ Zones: 7–8

Buddleja davidii 'White Profusion'
Butterfly bush
The best white form of the popular butterfly bush, this produces densely packed, fragrant terminal flower-spikes up to 40cm (15in) long in succession from mid-summer to early autumn. Each flower-spike is made up of thousands of tiny yellow-eyed, pure white flowers that become smothered in butterflies and other beneficial insects. The leaves also turn butter-yellow in autumn. For best displays, deadhead fading flower-spikes as they turn brown. H 3m (10ft) S 5m (16ft).
Aspect: sun
Hardiness: ✿✿✿ Zones: 7–8

Buddleja globosa
Orange ball tree
This is an unusual, semi-evergreen early summer-flowering shrub that bears ball-shaped clusters of fragrant, dark-orange and yellow flowers at the end of stiff stems from late spring to early summer. Although the plant is frost hardy (to –5°C/23°F), it prefers to be grown in the shelter of a warm wall or fence, where the deeply veined, dark green leaves are often retained over winter in mild areas. More protection will be required for this shrub in very cold areas. H 5m (16ft) S 5m (16ft).
Aspect: sun
Hardiness: ✿✿ Zone: 9+

Buddleja davidii 'Nanho Blue'

Buddleja 'Lochinch'
Butterfly bush
This is a popular compact form of the butterfly bush that bears densely packed spikes of honey-scented flowers on arching stems in succession from mid-summer to early autumn. Each flower-spike is made up of thousands of tiny orange-eyed, lavender-blue flowers that are loved by butterflies and other beneficial insects. The fresh-cut flowers are popular in floral arrangements. The downy, grey-green leaves turn butter-yellow in autumn. For best displays, deadhead the fading flower-spikes to encourage further flowering. H 2.5m (8ft) S 3m (10ft).
Aspect: sun
Hardiness: ✿✿✿ Zones: 7–8

Buddleja davidii 'Dartmoor'

Camellia japonica 'Elegans'

CAMELLIA

This is a very large genus of over 250 species that includes many evergreen shrubs with beautiful, flamboyant blooms during the spring that stand out against the dark, glossy foliage. Generally slow growing and long lived, they make excellent border fillers, while some compact varieties are also suitable for growing in large containers.
Cultivation In the garden, grow in any well-drained acid soil in dappled shade, but in colder areas provide shelter and plant in a position that gets afternoon sun. Add plenty of organic matter (but not alkaline mushroom compost/soil mix) before planting. In pots, grow in ericaceous compost and keep well watered. Wherever the camellia is planted, bear in mind that the flowers are susceptible to damage by a frost that is followed by a rapid thaw, so avoid positioning in east-facing areas that get early morning sun in spring.
Pruning Deadhead after flowering. Prune straggly branches of established plants to maintain the overall shape during late winter or early spring.
Propagation Layer low branches in early spring or take semi-ripe cuttings in late summer.

Camellia japonica 'Adolphe Audusson'
A compact evergreen shrub that bears masses of large, semi-double, bright red flowers intermittently from early spring to late spring against a backdrop of glossy, dark green foliage. Reliable and free-flowering, it offers great garden value. H 5m (16ft) S 4m (13ft).
Aspect: semi-shade
Hardiness: ✿✿✿ Zones: 7–8

Camellia japonica 'Elegans' (syn. *C. japonica* 'Chandleri Elegans')
Superb, sugar-pink, anemone-like flowers are produced during mid-spring and late spring against a backdrop of lustrous, wavy-edged, dark green leaves. H 3.5m (12ft) S 3m (10ft).
Aspect: semi-shade
Hardiness: ✿✿✿ Zones: 7–8

Camellia japonica 'Nobilissima'
This is one of the earliest flowering camellias, bearing peony-shaped, yellow-centred, white flowers from mid-winter to early spring against a backdrop of glossy, dark green leaves. This tough evergreen shrub will survive cold and windy conditions and so is an ideal choice for colder areas. H 5m (16ft) S 3.5m (12ft).
Aspect: semi-shade
Hardiness: ✿✿✿ Zones: 7–8

Camellia x williamsii 'Anticipation'
This is a handsome evergreen camellia that is deservedly popular for its large, peony-like, bright red flowers during late winter and early spring. Its narrow habit makes it an ideal container camellia or for use as an informal flowering hedge. Fast growing. H 4m (13ft) S 2m (6ft).
Aspect: semi-shade
Hardiness: ✿✿✿ Zones: 7–8

Camellia x williamsii 'Debbie'
An excellent camellia that bears dark rose-pink, peony-shaped flowers during mid-spring and late spring that are reputed to have good weather resistance. This free-flowering, vigorous evergreen has a dense mound of

Camellia williamsii 'Anticipation'

Camellia williamsii 'Debbie'

Camellia x williamsii 'Donation'

glossy, bright green foliage and tends to drop its blooms as they fade, so it always looks attractive. H 3m (10ft) S 2m (6ft).
Aspect: semi-shade
Hardiness: ❊❊❊ Zones: 7–8

Camellia x williamsii 'Donation'
A very long-flowering evergreen camellia, it produces its large, semi-double, sugar-pink flowers from late winter to late spring against lustrous, bright green leaves. Its compact, yet upright shape makes it an ideal choice for growing in a large container filled with ericaceous compost. H 5m (16ft) S 2.5m (8ft).
Aspect: semi-shade
Hardiness: ❊❊❊ Zones: 7–8

Camellia x williamsii 'J. C. Williams'
Beautiful single, rose-pink flowers are produced in early spring and mid-spring on open evergreen branches that can be trained effectively against a semi-shaded wall or fence. This free-flowering, fast-growing evergreen covered in lustrous, bright green foliage tends to drop its blooms as they fade and so always looks attractive. H 5m (16ft) S 3m (10ft).
Aspect: semi-shade
Hardiness: ❊❊❊ Zones: 7–8

CARPENTERIA
A genus of just one species of frost-hardy shrubs with beautiful, scented summer flowers. This

upright, spreading evergreen is ideal for growing in the middle of a border in mild areas, but needs a sheltered wall or fence if grown elsewhere. Carpenteria can also be trained to grow effectively as a fan-shaped wall shrub.
Cultivation Grow this shrub in any well-drained, but moisture-retentive, soil in a sheltered spot in full sun.
Pruning Established plants can have one stem in three removed after flowering in late summer, starting with the oldest, to promote better flowering and a more compact shape.

Carpenteria californica

Propagation Take softwood cuttings from new growth or semi-ripe cuttings in mid-summer, or sow seed in mid-spring.

Carpenteria californica
Brilliant white and fragrant anemone-like flowers, each with a pronounced central boss of yellow stamens, are produced in succession throughout early summer and mid-summer against a backdrop of lustrous, dark green leaves. H 2m (6ft) S 2m (6ft).
Named varieties: 'Ladhams' Variety' has brilliant white flowers up to 8cm (3in) across. H 2m (6ft) S 2m (6ft).
Aspect: sun
Hardiness: ❊❊ Zone: 9+

CARYOPTERIS
A genus of over five species, including deciduous shrubs with aromatic foliage and late-summer flowers. The misty profusion of fragrant blooms are a magnet to bees and butterflies and provide much-needed colour to the late summer display. Ideal for growing alongside other shrubs or in a mixed border.
Cultivation Grow in any well-drained soil that is reasonably fertile and situate in full sun. In very cold areas, grow by a south-facing wall or fence.

Caryopteris x clandonensis

Pruning Once established, prune the shrub by cutting back to 5cm (2in) of the ground in early spring. This will help promote more vigorous flowering.
Propagation Take softwood cuttings from new growth in mid-summer or semi-ripe cuttings in late summer, or sow seed in early autumn.

Caryopteris x clandonensis Bluebeard
This is a mound-forming shrub that has grey-green, lance-shaped, aromatic leaves covered in silvery hairs on the underside. The leaves form the perfect foil for the whorls of purplish-blue flowers that are borne throughout late summer and early autumn and which are a valuable source of nectar for butterflies and other useful insects.
Named varieties: 'First Choice', a new variety bearing dark blue buds that open to reveal a haze of rich, cobalt-blue flowers. H 1m (3ft) S 1m (3ft). 'Heavenly Blue', upright deciduous variety with dark blue flowers. H 1m (3ft) S 1m (3ft). 'Worcester Gold' (golden bluebeard), glowing yellow, aromatic foliage and dense clusters of lavender-blue flowers. The fragrant flowers act almost as a magnet to beneficial insects such as bees and butterflies. H 1m (3ft) S 1m (3ft).
Aspect: sun
Hardiness: ❊❊❊ Zones: 7–8

Ceanothus 'Concha'

Ceanothus 'Julia Phelps'

CEANOTHUS

This genus of over 50 species includes both deciduous and evergreen shrubs that are covered in masses of blue flowers in either late spring or late summer. Quick growing, they make effective border fillers, or can be trained against walls and fences in colder areas, where they will help to extend the flowering season. The deciduous varieties tend to be hardier than the evergreen.

Cultivation Grow in any well-drained soil that is reasonably fertile in full sun, but sheltered from cold winds. In very cold areas, grow in the protection of a south-facing wall or fence.

Pruning Once the plant has become established, prune deciduous varieties in early spring by cutting back the previous year's growth to an outward-facing side shoot within a few centimetres of the base. Evergreen varieties should be pruned only lightly after flowering. Do not cut back into old wood as it is reluctant to resprout.

Propagation Take semi-ripe cuttings from deciduous varieties in early autumn, or take stem cuttings from evergreen varieties in mid-summer.

Ceanothus arboreus 'Trewithen Blue'
Blueblossom

This is a large, vigorous evergreen shrub with notched, dark green leaves that is smothered in fragrant, rich blue flowers from late spring to early summer. It is

less hardy than some other varieties and so is not a good choice for colder regions. H 6m (20ft) S 8m (26ft).
Aspect: sun
Hardiness: ❈❈ Zone: 9+

Ceanothus 'Autumnal Blue'
California lilac

A useful evergreen filler shrub with apple-green glossy leaves, and clouds of bright blue flowers borne from late summer to mid-autumn. Although it is hardier than other forms, it still needs protection in colder areas. H 3m (10ft) S 3m (10ft).
Aspect: sun
Hardiness: ❈❈❈ Zones: 7–8

Ceanothus 'Burkwoodii'
California lilac

Clouds of sky-blue flowers provide a dramatic seasonal accent to sunny beds and borders from late summer to early autumn above a compact evergreen shrub with bright green glossy leaves. H 1.5m (5ft) S 2m (6ft).
Aspect: sun
Hardiness: ❈❈ Zone: 9+

Ceanothus 'Concha'
California lilac

This dense, evergreen shrub with lustrous dark green foliage transforms into a dazzling mound of dark blue flowers during late spring and early summer. The flowers emerge dramatically from purple buds borne in dense clusters along arching stems to smother the entire shrub in a cloak of colour.

H 3m (10ft) S 3m (10ft).
Aspect: sun
Hardiness: ❈❈ Zone: 9+

Ceanothus 'Italian Skies'
California lilac

This is a relatively new variety with a spreading habit that is covered in dense clusters of brilliant blue flowers during late spring to early summer above glossy evergreen foliage. It is less hardy than some other varieties and so is not a good choice for colder regions. H 1.5m (5ft) S 3m (10ft).
Aspect: sun
Hardiness: ❈❈ Zone: 9+

Ceanothus 'Puget Blue'
Santa Barbara ceanothus

A vigorous spreading, evergreen shrub that is covered in masses of dark blue flowers from mid-spring to early summer above heavily veined, dark green leaves. Protect from cold winds as the leaves are easily scorched. H 3m (10ft) S 3m (10ft).
Aspect: sun
Hardiness: ❈❈ Zone: 9+

Ceanothus thyrsiflorus var. repens
(syn. *C. repens*)
Creeping blueblossom

A steadfast, mound-forming, evergreen shrub that is excellent for covering sunny banks in mild areas where its profusion of pale blue flowers can be seen at their best during late spring and early summer. Although it is hardier

than other forms, it still needs protection in colder areas. H 1m (3ft) S 2.5m (8ft).
Aspect: sun
Hardiness: ❈❈ Zone: 9+

CERATOSTIGMA

A genus of eight species, including both deciduous and semi-evergreen shrubs with vivid late-summer flowers and brilliant autumn foliage colours. These spreading shrubs are perfect for a sunny, sheltered site positioned in a prominent position in the garden where they can be appreciated most.

Cultivation In the garden, grow in a moisture-retentive, but well-drained soil in full sun. Add plenty of organic matter to the soil before planting. When grown in containers, use a soil-based

Ceanothus thyrsiflorus 'Millerton Point'

Ceratostigma griffithii

compost (soil mix) and site on a sunny patio. Keep well watered.
Pruning In early spring, cut back straggly stems to a plump bud or side shoot near to ground level.
Propagation Take semi-ripe cuttings in mid-summer.

Ceratostigma griffithii
Excellent for autumn colour, this small, rounded semi-evergreen with purple-edged green leaves turns brilliant red in autumn and lasts well into winter. From late summer to mid-autumn the shrub is transformed by terminal clusters of large, purple-blue flowers. An ideal choice for the front of a sunny, sheltered border. H 1m (3ft) S 1.5m (5ft).
Aspect: sun
Hardiness: ❀❀ Zone: 9+

Ceratostigma willmottianum
Hardy plumbago
A spreading deciduous shrub that bears terminal clusters of pale blue flowers from late summer to mid-autumn over a mound of purple-edged, dark green leaves. The attractive foliage then turns brilliant fiery shades in autumn. H 1m (3ft) S 1.5m (5ft).
Named varieties: 'Desert Skies' (golden plumbago, syn. *C. willmottianum* 'Palmgold'), a new variety with brilliant yellow foliage that forms a dramatic foil for the cobalt-blue flowers

produced throughout late summer and early autumn. Slightly less hardy than the other varieties, so grow as a container plant in colder areas. H 1m (3ft) S 1.5m (5ft). 'Forest Blue' (Chinese plumbago), vivid blue flowers are produced in clusters over a mound of purple-edged, dark green leaves that turn flaming shades of red and orange in autumn. H 1m (3ft) S 1.5m (5ft).
Aspect: sun
Hardiness: ❀❀❀ Zones: 7–8

CHAENOMELES
Flowering quince
A genus of just three species that includes the deciduous, spring-flowering shrubs featured here. The yellow-tinged green fruit that follow the flowers are edible when cooked, and the flowering stems are valued in early spring and autumn by flower arrangers. The neat habit of these shrubs makes them particularly useful in the border or trained against a wall or fence. They are also ideal for growing as an informal flowering hedge in sun or shade, where their thorny branches form an impenetrable thicket.
Cultivation Grow in any well-drained soil that is reasonably fertile in full sun or dappled shade. Flowering and fruiting is reduced if planted in full shade.

Chaenomeles x superba 'Crimson and Gold'

Pruning In the border, no routine pruning is necessary. Informal hedges can be pruned after flowering to keep within bounds. You can also prune established shrubs grown against a wall or fence to enhance the overall display. Cut back all new stems to just after the main cluster of flower buds in early spring, then prune again after flowering in late spring by cutting back the shoots to two or three buds from the main framework.
Propagation Take softwood cuttings in early summer or layer shoots in early autumn.

Chaenomeles speciosa 'Geisha Girl'
Apricot-pink and yellow double flowers add subtle charm to this compact, deciduous shrub from early spring to late spring, followed by aromatic, yellow-tinged green fruit. The twiggy, thorn-covered branches form a thicket, covered in lustrous, oval, dark green leaves. H 2m (6ft) S 1.2m (4ft).
Aspect: sun or semi-shade
Hardiness: ❀❀❀ Zones: 7–8

Chaenomeles speciosa 'Moerloosei' (syn. C. speciosa 'Apple Blossom')
Many gardeners consider this plant to be one of the most outstanding cultivars of this popular species. Beautiful large, white, apple blossom-like flowers that are delicately flushed with

pink cover the twiggy branches of this vigorous flowering quince and appear from early spring to late spring. H 2.5m (8ft) S 5m (16ft).
Aspect: sun or semi-shade
Hardiness: ❀❀❀ Zones: 7–8

Chaenomeles speciosa 'Nivalis'
Brilliant, snow-white flowers smother the twiggy, spine-covered stems of this vigorous flowering quince from early spring to late spring. H 2.5m (8ft) S 5m (16ft).
Aspect: sun or semi-shade
Hardiness: ❀❀❀ Zones: 7–8

Chaenomeles x superba 'Crimson and Gold'
Compact and easy to grow, this popular variety bears striking crimson flowers with contrasting golden anthers along twiggy, spine-covered branches from early spring to late spring. The aromatic, yellow-tinged, green fruit that follow are edible when cooked. H 1m (3ft) S 2m (6ft).
Aspect: sun or semi-shade
Hardiness: ❀❀❀ Zones: 7–8

Chaenomeles x superba 'Nicoline'
Striking scarlet flowers are produced in profusion along twiggy, thorn-covered stems from early spring to late spring. The branches form a thicket, covered in lustrous, oval, dark green leaves. H 1.5m (5ft) S 2m (6ft).
Aspect: sun or semi-shade
Hardiness: ❀❀❀ Zones: 7–8

Chaenomeles speciosa 'Geisha Girl'

Chamaedorea elegans

Chamaerops humilis

Chimonanthus praecox

CHAMAEDOREA

This large genus of over 100 species includes the parlour palm, which is a tender plant often grown as a house plant in frost-prone areas. Very small plants can be used successfully as temporary additions in bottle gardens, where they thrive in humid conditions.
Cultivation In areas where the temperature does not drop below 15°C (60°F), the tender parlour palm can be grown outside in neutral to acid, well-drained soil in shade. Elsewhere, it is best grown as a house plant, in a peat-based soil mix, and placed in a well-lit spot on a tray of moist gravel to increase humidity around the leaves. Feed every fortnight with a balanced fertilizer and water as necessary during the growing season. Water sparingly in the winter months.
Pruning No routine pruning is necessary, but remove damaged leaves as soon as they are noticed.
Propagation Sow seed in mid-spring.

Chamaedorea elegans (syn. *Neanthe bella*)
Parlour palm
This popular house plant has a suckering habit and produces upright bamboo-like stems and arching, leathery, dark green, divided fronds. Tiny yellow flowers appear on mature plants during the growing season, followed by small black berries. H 2m (6ft) S 1m (3ft).
Aspect: semi-shade to full shade
Hardiness: tender Zone: 10

CHAMAEROPS

A genus of just one species of suckering, half-hardy, bushy, palms that can be grown outside in full sun in mild areas to help create a tropical atmosphere. However, in frost-prone areas, grow in a large pot on the patio and move to a frost-free spot during the winter months. They also make handsome and easy-to-grow house plants.
Cultivation In frost-free areas this half-hardy fan palm can be grown outside in neutral to acid, well-drained soil in full sun. If grown as a house plant, use soil-based soil mix and stand the pot in a well-lit spot. Feed every fortnight with a balanced fertilizer and water as necessary during the growing season. Water sparingly during the winter months.
Pruning No routine pruning is necessary but remove damaged leaves as soon as they are noticed.
Propagation Sow seed in mid-spring. Separate and pot up rooted suckers in late spring.

Chamaerops humilis
Dwarf fan palm
This plant has spiky, glossy, fan-shaped, grey-green leaves that grow up to 1m (3ft) in length and are produced from suckering palm-like stems. On mature specimens of this plant, insignificant yellow flowers are produced in dense spikes throughout the growing season. H 2m (6ft) S 1m (3ft).
Aspect: sun
Hardiness: ✿ Zone: 10

CHIMONANTHUS

A genus of about five species that includes both deciduous and evergreen shrubs. The deciduous shrubs featured here are grown for their waxy-looking, fragrant, yellow flowers that are borne on bare branches from late winter to early spring, when the garden needs them most. They make unassuming plants for the rest of the year and are most effective when planted in sun close to a path or entrance. The winter stems can be cut when in bud, so the superb sweetly scented flowers can be enjoyed inside over the Christmas period.
Cultivation Grow in any well-drained soil that is reasonably fertile in full sun.
Pruning Once established, prune out one stem in three, starting with the oldest, to encourage a continuous supply of young flowering stems. This should be done directly after flowering.
Propagation Take softwood cuttings in mid-summer. Layer lower stems in late summer.

Chimonanthus praecox
Wintersweet
A vigorous deciduous shrub that bears waxy-looking, fragrant, sulphur-yellow flowers, often with a contrastingly tinted throat, on branches from early winter to late winter. H 4m (13ft) S 3m (10ft).
Named varieties: 'Grandiflorus', large, slightly scented, dark yellow flowers, each with a purple-stained throat. H 4m (13ft) S 3m (10ft). var. *luteus* (syn. *C. praecox* 'Concolor'), waxy-looking, fragrant, clear-yellow flowers that open widely on bare stems from mid-winter to early spring. H 4m (13ft) S 3m (10ft).
Aspect: sun
Hardiness: ✿✿✿ Zones: 7–8

CHOISYA

A popular genus of over five species, including several compact, aromatic evergreen shrubs that produce star-like, white, flowers with a scent that is reminiscent of orange blossoms during late spring and again in late summer. The evergreen foliage is attractive all year round and provides the perfect foil for other flowers, too. It makes a good border filler and can be grown as a permanent container plant, and moved into a prominent position, such as the patio, while in flower.
Cultivation In the garden, grow in any well-drained soil that is reasonably fertile in full sun or dappled shade. In containers, grow in a soil-based compost (soil mix) on a sunny patio. Keep well watered. In colder gardens, plant in a sheltered spot, as cold winds can damage the foliage. Also, protect the less hardy yellow-leaved varieties in winter.
Pruning No routine pruning is required. Remove frost-damaged shoots in spring. Rejuvenate by cutting one stem in three to the ground, starting with the oldest.
Propagation Take semi-ripe cuttings in early summer or mid-autumn.

Choisya ternata

Choisya ternata 'Sundance'

Cistus x cyprius

Cistus x pulverulentus 'Sunset'

Named varieties: 'Aztec Pearl', starry, white flowers that open from pink-tinged buds. H 2.5m (8ft) S 2.5m (8ft). 'Goldfingers', a new introduction that forms a compact shrub with bold yellow foliage and sweetly scented white flowers during mid-spring and late spring. H 1.5m (5ft) S 1.5m (5ft). 'Sundance', a compact evergreen shrub with bright yellow, glossy young leaves that mature to yellow-green, especially when grown in deep shade. A bonus of pretty white flowers are sometimes produced during mid-spring and late spring. H 2.5m (8ft) S 2.5m (8ft).

Neither of the yellow-leaved forms are as hardy as the green-leaved varieties, and can also suffer from scorch if positioned in strong sunlight.

Choisya ternata
Mexican orange blossom
This is a compact evergreen shrub that bears masses of fragrant, starry white flowers in succession during mid-spring and late spring, often with a second flush from late summer to early autumn. The bright green, glossy leaves provide the perfect foil for the sweet and spicy-smelling flowers that give off a lovely aroma when lightly crushed.

H 2.5m (8ft) S 2.5m (8ft).
Aspect: sun and semi-shade
Hardiness: ❁❁❁ Zones: 7–8

CISTUS
Rock rose, sun rose
This genus of 20 species includes many compact evergreen shrubs with spectacular papery summer flowers that thrive in well-drained sun-baked sites. They are an ideal choice for a prominent dry border or bank in sun, or can be grown in a large container on the patio.
Cultivation In the garden, grow in any well-drained soil in full sun. In containers, grow in a soil-based compost (soil mix). Water as necessary.
Pruning Trim the shrub as the flowers fade, cutting back new growth by about two-thirds. Remove frost-damaged shoots in spring.
Propagation Take semi-ripe cuttings in early autumn.

Cistus x corbariensis (syn. *C. x hybridus*)
This is a bushy, evergreen shrub with delicate-looking, papery, white flowers that open from bright red buds during early summer and mid-summer, each with a central boss of yellow stamens. The wavy-edged, dark green leaves make it an attractive

foil for other flowers at other times. H 1m (3ft) S 1.5m (5ft).
Aspect: sun
Hardiness: ❁❁ Zone: 9+

Cistus x pulverulentus 'Sunset' (syn. *C. crispus* 'Sunset')
This is a free-flowering variety that is covered in a succession of rose-pink blooms during early summer and mid-summer, each with a distinctive central boss of yellow stamens. The dense and spreading habit of this shrub makes it a useful ground cover plant. It tolerates salt-laden air. H 60cm (24in) S 90cm (36in).
Aspect: sun
Hardiness: ❁❁ Zone: 9+

Cistus 'Silver Pink' syn. *C.* 'Grayswood Pink'
Masses of delicate-looking, papery, silvery-pink flowers are produced on 'Silver Pink'. These gradually fade to white towards the middle of the petals, with each flower having a distinctive central boss of yellow stamens. The flowers are produced in succession throughout early summer and mid-summer on this compact, evergreen shrub that has narrow, dark green leaves, which have a grey underneath. H 75cm (30in) S 90cm (36in).
Aspect: sun
Hardiness: ❁❁ Zone: 9+

Other good cultivars to look out for:

Cistus x aguilarii 'Maculatus', yellow-centred white flowers with burgundy markings at the base of each petal during early summer and mid-summer H 1.2m (4ft) S 1.2m (4ft).

Cistus x argenteus 'Peggy Sammons', pale pinkish-purple, flowers are borne in early summer and mid-summer above grey-green, downy leaves, H 1m (3ft) S 1m (3ft).

Cistus x dansereaui 'Decumbens', white flowers with faint yellow and crimson marks at the base

of each petal are produced during early summer and mid-summer. H 60cm (24in) S 90cm (36in).

Cistus 'Grayswood Pink', pale pink flowers that fade towards the centre are borne in early summer and mid-summer above wavy-edged, grey-green leaves. H 1m (3ft) S 1m (3ft).

Cistus x skanbergii, yellow-centred, pale pink flowers are produced in early summer and mid-summer above wavy-edged, grey-green leaves. H 75cm (30in) S 90cm (36in).

Clerodendrum trichotomum
var. *fargesii*

CLERODENDRUM

A huge genus of over 400 species, including the deciduous shrub featured here, that bears white, star-like late-summer flowers, followed by striking bright blue berries in autumn. It makes a perfect filler for a shrub or mixed border next to an access point, where its unusual berries can be viewed at close quarters.
Cultivation Grow in well-drained, moisture-retentive soil that is reasonably fertile in full sun.
Pruning No routine pruning is required. Remove frost-damaged shoots in spring.
Propagation Take root cuttings in early winter. Remove rooted suckers in spring.

Clerodendrum trichotomum var. fargesii

An upright, deciduous shrub that is covered in striking turquoise-blue berries, surrounded by a contrasting, star-shaped, maroon calyx during mid-autumn and late autumn. The fruit follow pretty, pink-budded, scented, white, star-shaped flowers that are borne from late summer to early autumn. H 6m (20ft) S 6m (20ft).
Aspect: sun
Hardiness: ✿✿✿ Zones: 7–8

CLETHRA

This genus of over 60 species includes the deciduous summer-flowering shrubs featured here. They are useful, upright-growing shrubs for a shady border or for under-planting deciduous trees in a woodland garden with acid soil.
Cultivation Grow in any acidic well-drained, moisture-retentive soil that is reasonably fertile in dappled shade.
Pruning No routine pruning is required. Neglected shrubs can be rejuvenated in spring by cutting out one stem in three back to a side shoot lower down, starting with the oldest.
Propagation Take softwood cuttings from new shoots in mid-summer.

Clethra alnifolia
Sweet pepper bush
A delightful deciduous shrub that bears candle-like spikes of fragrant, bell-shaped white flowers throughout late summer and early autumn above the oval green foliage. H 2.5m (8ft) S 2.5m (8ft). **Named varieties:** 'Paniculata', H 10cm (4in) white flower spikes. H 2.5m (8ft) S 2.5m (8ft). 'Pink Spire', large pink flower-spikes. H 2.5m (8ft) S 2.5m (8ft). 'Rosea', large deep pink flower-spikes. H 2.5m (8ft) S 2.5m (8ft).
Aspect: semi-shade
Hardiness: ✿✿✿ Zones: 7–8

COLUTEA
Bladder senna
A genus of some 25 species, including the deciduous, summer-flowering shrubs featured here, that are loved by children – who take great pleasure in popping the bloated seed-pods that follow.

Clethra arborea

Colutea arborescens

An unusual novelty shrub for a sunny spot.
Cultivation Grow in any well-drained soil that is reasonably fertile in full sun.
Pruning No routine pruning is required. Neglected shrubs can be rejuvenated in spring by cutting out one stem in three back to a side shoot lower down, starting with the oldest.
Propagation Take softwood cuttings from new shoots in mid-summer. Sow seed in late winter or early spring.

Colutea arborescens
A vigorous, rounded, deciduous shrub that bears 12cm- (4in-) long racemes of bright yellow flowers from early summer to early autumn above finely divided pale green foliage. Green seed-pods follow that become bloated and translucent as they mature. H 3m (10ft) S 3m (10ft).
Aspect: sun
Hardiness: ✿✿✿ Zones: 7–8

Colutea x media 'Copper Beauty'
A bushy deciduous shrub with finely divided, grey-green leaves that set off the 10cm- (4in-) long strings of attractive copper-red flowers from early summer to early autumn. Greenish-brown seed-pods (up to 8cm/3in long) follow that become bloated and turn increasingly copper-tinged and translucent as they mature. H 3m (10ft) S 3m (10ft).
Aspect: sun
Hardiness: ✿✿✿ Zones: 7–8

CONVOLVULUS
A huge genus of over 250 species, including the popular compact silver-leaved, evergreen, early summer flowering shrub featured here. A superb shrub for a hot, sunny rockery, bank or border edge with well-drained soil. Can be grown in a pot on the patio.
Cultivation Needs well-drained, reasonably fertile soil in full sun. If grown in containers, use a soil-based compost (soil mix). Water as necessary.
Pruning Trim as the flowers fade, cutting back new growth by about two-thirds. Remove frost-damaged shoots in spring.
Propagation Take softwood cuttings in late spring or early summer, or semi-ripe cuttings in early autumn.

Convolvulus cneorum

Convolvulus cneorum
Clusters of open, white, trumpet-shaped flowers, each with pinkish veins and a pale yellow centre, are produced in succession throughout late spring and early summer and intermittently thereafter. Silvery foliage looks good at other times. H 60cm (24in) S 90cm (36in).
Aspect: sun
Hardiness: ✻✻ Zone: 9+

CORDYLINE
A genus of around 15 species, including these palm-like shrubs that are grown for their delightfully elegant plumes of arching, lance-shaped, evergreen leaves produced in fountain-like clumps at ground level while the plants are young. These useful evergreens make eye-catching focal points, where they add a tropical touch to borders and in containers on the patio.
Cultivation In the garden, grow in any well-drained soil that is reasonably fertile in full sun or dappled shade. In containers, grow in a soil-based compost (soil mix). Water as necessary. Give winter protection in frost-prone areas.
Pruning No routine pruning is required. Remove dying or damaged leaves to tidy its appearance in spring.
Propagation Remove rooted suckers in spring.

Cordyline australis (syn. Dracaena australis)
New Zealand cabbage palm
This elegant plant forms a plume of arching, lance-shaped, evergreen leaves at ground level when young, eventually growing into a palm-like tree. Give winter protection in frost-prone areas. H 10m (33ft) S 4m (13ft).

Cordyline australis 'Red Star'

Named varieties: 'Atropurpurea', broad, strap-shaped leaves flushed with purple from the base. H 10m (33ft) S 4m (13ft). 'Purple Tower', broad, deep-purple, lance-shaped leaves. H 10m (33ft) S 4m (13ft). 'Purpurea Group', broad, plum-purple, lance-shaped leaves. H 10m (33ft) S 4m (13ft). 'Red Star', spiky fountain of bronze-purple, narrow, strap-like leaves. H 6m (20ft) S 7m (23ft). 'Torbay Dazzler', green leaves strikingly edged and striped with cream. H 10m (33ft) S 4m (13ft).
Aspect: sun
Hardiness: ✻ Zone: 10

CORNUS
Dogwood
Some 45 species make up this genus, including many useful garden shrubs offering a variety of features, including early summer flowers, attractive foliage, autumn tints and colourful winter stems. As they are very easy to grow, they offer great garden value – making them an ideal choice for the first-time gardener.
Cultivation Grow flowering dogwoods in any neutral to acid moisture-retentive, well-drained soil that is reasonably fertile in full sun or dappled shade. Most other varieties can be grown in any moist garden soil, but autumn colour and winter stems are best in full sun.
Pruning Flowering dogwoods require no routine pruning. Dogwoods grown for their decorative stems should be cut back to within a few centimetres of ground level in late winter or early spring every other year. Dogwoods with variegated foliage should have one stem in three removed each year, starting with the oldest.
Propagation Layer low shoots on all types of dogwood in mid-spring. Take hardwood cuttings from thicket-forming dogwoods in late autumn.

Cornus alba 'Aurea'
Red-barked dogwood
Superb golden-yellow leaves and stunning red new stems are the main features of this valuable garden shrub. The leaves also provide autumn colour and there is the bonus of small cream-coloured flowers during late spring and early summer, followed by bluish fruits. The leaf coloration is best in full sun. H 3m (10ft) S 3m (10ft).
Aspect: sun to semi-shade
Hardiness: ✻✻✻ Zones: 7–8

Cornus alba 'Kesselringii'
Grown for its dramatic, near-black, purple-brown winter stems and colourful autumn tints, this unusual dogwood looks particularly striking when planted in sun alongside yellow- or red-stemmed varieties, where it will help to transform the winter garden. Clusters of tiny, creamy-white flowers also appear during late spring and early summer. H 3m (10ft) S 3m (10ft).
Aspect: sun to semi-shade
Hardiness: ✻✻✻ Zones: 7–8

Cornus alba 'Sibirica'
Red-barked dogwood
Brilliant red winter stems make this red-barked dogwood ideal for growing alongside water features, where it will provide much-needed winter interest. Its dark green leaves take on reddish hues in autumn before falling to reveal the stem display. Clusters of tiny, creamy-white flowers also appear during late spring and early summer. H 3m (10ft) S 3m (10ft).
Aspect: sun to semi-shade
Hardiness: ✻✻✻ Zones: 7–8

Cornus alba 'Sibirica'

Cornus kousa

Cornus alba 'Spaethii'
Red-barked dogwood
The yellow-edged, bright green leaves on this plant look good all summer, after which they then take on striking autumn leaf tints before falling to reveal bright red stems that add much-needed interest throughout the winter. Clusters of tiny, creamy-white flowers also appear during late spring and early summer. H 3m (10ft) S 3m (10ft).
Aspect: sun to semi-shade
Hardiness: ❀❀❀ Zones: 7–8

Cornus 'Eddie's White Wonder'
Flowering dogwood
Striking white, petal-like bracts surround each insignificant purplish-green flower during late spring. Great value in a small garden, the green leaves of this bushy dogwood also turn brilliant fiery shades in autumn. Grows and flowers best in full sun, although it will tolerate dappled shade. H 6m (20ft) S 5m (16ft).
Aspect: sun to semi-shade
Hardiness: ❀❀❀ Zones: 7–8

Cornus florida
Flowering dogwood
A conical, deciduous shrub that produces insignificant yellow-tipped green flowers during late spring, surrounded by eye-catching white or pink bracts. The puckered green leaves look attractive during the summer and take on reddish-purple hues in autumn. Ideal for gardens with

neutral to acid soil, but unsuitable for gardens with chalky soil. H 6m (20ft) S 8m (26ft).
Named varieties: 'Cherokee Chief', deepest pink bracts, red-purple autumn tints. H 6m (20ft) S 8m (26ft). 'Rainbow', compact shrub with white or pink bracts and yellow-edged green leaves turning red-purple in autumn with bright red margins. H 3m (10ft) S 2.5m (8ft). 'Rubra', dark pink bracts, red-purple autumn tints. H 6m (20ft) S 8m (26ft).
Aspect: sun to semi-shade
Hardiness: ❀❀❀ Zones: 7–8

Cornus kousa var. *chinensis*
Chinese dogwood
The conspicuous, creamy-white flower bracts fade to white before turning red-pink, surrounding insignificant green flowers during early summer, that are followed by strawberry-like fleshy fruit. This conical, deciduous shrub with dark green leaves takes on crimson-purple tints in autumn. The best leaf colour is achieved when grown in neutral to acid soil. H 7m (23ft) S 5m (16ft).
Aspect: sun to semi-shade
Hardiness: ❀❀❀ Zones: 7–8

Cornus sanguinea 'Midwinter Fire'
A relatively new variety, this shrub has glowing red-tipped orange and yellow winter stems that shine out in the garden. Clusters of tiny, creamy-white flowers also appear in early summer against green leaves that take on orange-yellow hues in autumn. Spherical bluish fruits are also produced. H 3m (10ft) S 2.5m (8ft).
Aspect: sun to semi-shade
Hardiness: ❀❀❀ Zones: 7–8

Cornus stolonifera 'Flaviramea'
Rich yellow stems provide winter interest and look striking planted in sun beside red-stemmed varieties. The dark green leaves take on reddish tints in autumn, before falling to reveal the eye-catching winter stems. Clusters of tiny, creamy-white flowers also appear during late spring and early summer. H 75cm (30in) S 150cm (60in).
Aspect: sun to semi-shade
Hardiness: ❀❀❀ Zones: 7–8

CORONILLA
This genus of about 20 species includes the following very long-flowering evergreen shrubs, with pretty, scented, yellow flowers that are borne from late winter until late summer. This shrub is ideal for planting in a container on the patio, where the flowers and foliage can be appreciated at close quarters.
Cultivation Grow in any well-drained soil that is reasonably fertile in full sun. Shelter from cold winds.
Pruning No routine pruning is required. Neglected shrubs can be rejuvenated by removing one stem in three each year in spring, starting with the oldest.
Propagation Take semi-ripe cuttings in mid-summer or late summer.

Coronilla valentia subsp. *glauca* (syn. *C*. 'Glauca')
This is an exceptionally long-flowering, rounded, bushy, evergreen shrub with dense evergreen growth and blue-green leaves. The scented, clear yellow pea-like flowers are produced throughout late winter and early spring and then intermittently all summer until a further flush in late summer and early autumn. H 80cm (33in) S 80cm (33in).
Named varieties: 'Citrina', pale yellow flowers. H 80cm (33in) S 80cm (33in).
Aspect: sun
Hardiness: ❀❀ Zone: 9

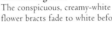
Coronilla valentina subsp. *glauca*

Corylus avellana 'Contorta'

CORYLUS

A genus of over ten species that includes native, deciduous trees and upright shrubs that can be grown as specimens or as an easy-to-grow hedge. Ornamental varieties offer attractive features including colourful spring catkins, good-looking foliage, autumn tints and winter stems. Ideal for growing in a sunny border or in a large permanent container on the patio.
Cultivation In the garden, grow in any well-drained soil that is reasonably fertile in full sun or dappled shade. In containers, grow in a soil-based compost (soil mix). Water as necessary.
Pruning No routine pruning is required for most types. Hazels grown for their colourful foliage should have one stem in three removed each year, starting with the oldest. Do this after flowering in early spring.
Propagation Layer low stems in mid-spring. Remove rooted suckers in early autumn.

Corylus avellana 'Contorta'
Corkscrew hazel, Harry Lauder's walking stick
The amazingly contorted bare stems carry golden catkins throughout late winter and early spring. The unusual stems of this slow-growing shrub are valued by flower arrangers. Will provide year-round interest in a large container. H 5m (16ft) S 5m (16ft).
Aspect: sun or semi-shade
Hardiness: ✿✿✿ Zones: 7–8

Corylus maxima 'Purpurea'
Glossy, dark purple, heart-shaped leaves cover this upright, deciduous shrub, which makes a superb specimen for a sunny garden. Reddish-purple catkins are produced during late winter and early spring and are followed by edible nuts ripening in late summer. This shrub makes a useful border filler. H 6m (20ft) S 5m (16ft).
Aspect: sun
Hardiness: ✿✿✿ Zones: 7–8

COTINUS
Smoke bush
A genus of two species, including the bushy deciduous shrubs featured here. Their airy plumes of flowers create a smoke-like illusion over the shrub during the summer, giving rise to its common name. Brilliant autumn foliage is the main ornamental feature of this plant. Grow in full sun for the most dramatic foliage effects.
Cultivation Grow in any moisture-retentive, well-drained soil that is reasonably fertile in full sun or dappled shade. Grow in full sun for the dramatic foliage effects.
Pruning Cotinus grown for their colourful foliage and smoke-like flowers should have one stem in

Cotinus obovatus

three removed each year, starting with the oldest. Do this in early spring.
Propagation Layer low stems in mid-spring. Remove rooted suckers in early autumn.

Cotinus coggygria 'Flame'
(syn. C. 'Flame')
Smoke bush
The plumes of pale pink flowers that appear on 'Flame' gradually darken during mid-summer and late summer. Later, the foliage spectacularly turns fiery shades of red and orange during the autumn months. H 6m (20ft)

Cotinus coggygria 'Royal Purple'

S 5m (16ft).
Aspect: sun or semi-shade
Hardiness: ✿✿✿ Zones: 7–8

Cotinus coggygria 'Golden Spirit'
A relatively new and compact variety with golden-yellow leaves, that take on eye-catching pink, orange and red coloration in autumn. Plumes of green flowers appear during mid-summer and late summer. H 2m (6ft) S 2m (6ft).
Aspect: sun or semi-shade
Hardiness: ✿✿✿ Zones: 7–8

Cotinus 'Grace'
Smoke bush
The purple-tinged foliage of 'Grace' transforms in mid-summer and late summer when it is covered by airy plumes of pale pink flowers that darken with age. Stunning autumn colour appears as it turns a glowing shade of red. H 6m (20ft) S 5m (16ft).
Aspect: sun or semi-shade
Hardiness: ✿✿✿ Zones: 7–8

Cotinus coggygria 'Royal Purple'
This purple-leaved, bushy, deciduous shrub makes an impressive specimen in any size garden as it responds particularly well to hard pruning each spring. Airy plumes of pale pink flowers that darken with age are produced during mid-summer and late summer. The rich, red-purple leaves then turn brilliant scarlet in autumn. H 6m (20ft) S 5m (16ft).
Aspect: sun or semi-shade
Hardiness: ✿✿✿ Zones: 7–8

DESFONTAINIA

A genus of just one species of densely growing evergreen shrubs with eye-catching, tubular summer flowers. If you can provide the right growing conditions, it makes a useful and unusual border filler in all but the coldest areas, ideally at the base of a sheltered wall or fence.

Cultivation Grow in any moisture-retentive, humus-rich, acid or neutral soil in dappled shade. Provide a sheltered position where it is protected from drying and cold winds.

Pruning No routine pruning is necessary. Any frost-damaged growth should be removed in spring.

Propagation Take semi-ripe cuttings in mid-summer. Remove rooted suckers in early autumn.

Desfontainia spinosa

A bushy evergreen, with holly-like, glossy, dark green leaves. From mid-summer to mid-autumn it bears pendent tubular scarlet flowers with yellow-tipped petals. H 2m (6ft) S 2m (6ft).
Aspect: sun or semi-shade
Hardiness: ✱✱ Zone: 9

DEUTZIA

This genus of about 60 species includes the bushy deciduous shrubs featured here, grown for their early summer flowers that are borne in abundance. Plant in a shrubbery or in a mixed border to provide late spring and early summer colour. A good choice for small gardens.

Cultivation Grow in any moisture-

Deutzia x elegantissima

Diervilla x splendens

retentive, well-drained garden soil that is reasonably fertile and in full sun or dappled shade.

Pruning To encourage good displays year after year, cut back one stem in three to near ground level after flowering, starting with the oldest stems.

Propagation Take hardwood cuttings in mid-autumn.

Deutzia x elegantissima 'Rosealind'

Dark, pink-flushed, white star-like flowers are produced in clusters during late spring and early summer on this compact, rounded shrub. H 1.2m (4ft) S 1.5m (5ft).
Aspect: sun or semi-shade
Hardiness: ✱✱✱ Zones: 7–8

Deutzia gracilis

Fragrant, snow-white, star-like flowers are produced from late spring to early summer on

upright stems clothed in light green leaves. H 1m (3ft) S 1m (3ft).
Aspect: sun or semi-shade
Hardiness: ✱✱✱ Zones: 7–8

Deutzia x hybrida 'Mont Rose'

This elegant, upright shrub bears clusters of star-like, rose-pink flowers with yellow anthers during early summer. H 1.2m (4ft) S 1.2m (4ft).
Aspect: sun or semi-shade
Hardiness: ✱✱✱ Zones: 7–8

DIERVILLA
Bush honeysuckle

A genus of three species that includes the following deciduous shrub with colourful summer flowers and attractive autumn tints – a good choice for a shrubbery or mixed border, or for stabilizing soil on sunny banks.

Cultivation Grow in any well-drained garden soil that is

reasonably fertile and in full sun or dappled shade.

Pruning Maintain a compact shape by cutting back one stem in three to near ground level after flowering, starting with the oldest stems.

Propagation Take semi-ripe cuttings in mid-summer. Remove rooted suckers in early autumn.

Diervilla x splendens

Vibrant sulphur-yellow flowers are produced in clusters at the end of shoots from early summer to late summer on this thicket-forming deciduous shrub. The mid-green leaves take on purple-tints in autumn. H 1m (3ft) S 1.5m (5ft).
Aspect: sun or semi-shade
Hardiness: ✱✱✱ Zones: 7–8

DRIMYS

This is a genus of 30 species that includes the upright, evergreen

Desfontainia spinosa

Drimys winteri

Elaeagnus x ebbingei 'Limelight'

shrub with late spring and early summer flowers featured here. It is ideal for a shrubbery or situated in the dappled shade of a woodland edge.
Cultivation Grow in any moisture-retentive, well-drained garden soil that is reasonably fertile and in full sun or dappled shade. In colder regions, grow in a sheltered position where it is protected from cold winds.
Pruning No routine pruning is necessary. Any frost-damaged growth should be removed in spring.
Propagation Take semi-ripe cuttings in late summer. Layer lower stems in early spring.

Drimys winteri
Winter's bark
This shrub produces delightful jasmine-scented, creamy-white flowers from mid-spring to early summer and lance-shaped, leathery, dark green leaves. H 15m (50ft) S 10m (33ft).
Aspect: sun or semi-shade
Hardiness: ✿✿ Zone: 9

ELAEAGNUS
A genus of about 45 species, including the following brightly coloured variegated evergreens, that provide permanent interest

throughout the year. They make ideal border fillers, where they will help give lacklustre displays an uplift. They are all easy to grow and tolerate cold winds and salt-laden air – making them ideal for providing shelter and screens in coastal gardens. Their tolerance of dry soil and urban pollution means they are widely used by landscapers in towns and cities. Their handsome foliage is also popular with flower arrangers.
Cultivation They will grow in well-drained garden soil that is reasonably fertile and in full sun or dappled shade. However, leaf coloration will be best in full sun.
Pruning No routine pruning is necessary. Neglected plants can be rejuvenated by cutting back one stem in three to near ground level after flowering, starting with the oldest stems. Trim hedges in early summer and early autumn. Remove any reverted plain green shoots as soon as they are noticed.
Propagation Take hardwood cuttings during late winter.

Elaeagnus x ebbingei 'Gilt Edge'
The lustrous, golden-edged, dark green leaves make this a noticeable shrub in winter. Insignificant slightly scented white flowers

appear in mid-autumn. H 4m (13ft) S 4m (13ft).
Aspect: sun or semi-shade
Hardiness: ✿✿✿ Zones: 7–8

Elaeagnus x ebbingei 'Limelight'
Silvery when they emerge, the attractive lime-green and yellow-splashed dark green, leathery leaves are loved by flower arrangers. Insignificant, slightly scented, creamy-white flowers are also produced in mid-autumn. This really tough evergreen will tolerate dry soil too. H 3m (10ft) S 3m (10ft).
Aspect: sun or semi-shade
Hardiness: ✿✿✿ Zones: 7–8

Elaeagnus pungens 'Maculata'
Leathery dark green leaves are boldly marked with bright yellow in the centre and have a slightly frosted shine. Insignificant, slightly scented white flowers are also produced in mid-autumn, followed by brown fruit that ripen to red. H 4m (13ft) S 5m (16ft).
Aspect: sun or semi-shade
Hardiness: ✿✿✿ Zones: 7–8

ENKIANTHUS
This comprises a genus of about ten species, including the deciduous shrubs featured here, that offer early summer flowers and good autumn leaf tints. They are ideal for dappled shade, such as in a woodland-edge planting scheme. A useful and unusual border addition that is easy to

grow if you can provide the right growing conditions.
Cultivation Grow in any well-drained neutral to acid soil in full sun or dappled shade. In colder areas, shelter from winds. Add plenty of organic matter (but not alkaline mushroom compost/ soil mix) to the soil before planting.
Pruning No routine pruning is necessary. Any frost-damaged growth should be removed in spring.
Propagation Sow seed in early winter. Layer suitable stems in early autumn.

Enkianthus campanulatus
Spreading deciduous shrub that bears clusters of bell-shaped, pink-edged, pale yellow flowers during late spring and early summer. The toothed, matt-green leaves provide an attractive backdrop and take on vivid shades of orange and red in autumn. H 5m (16ft) S 5m (16ft).
Aspect: sun or semi-shade
Hardiness: ✿✿✿ Zones: 7–8

Enkianthus cernuus f. rubens
A bushy, deciduous shrub that is covered in pretty clusters of bell-shaped, red flowers during late spring and early summer. The leaves emerge bright green and turn plum-purple in summer, then take on blood-red hues in autumn. Protect in cold gardens. H 2.5m (8ft) S 2.5m (8ft).
Aspect: sun or semi-shade
Hardiness: ✿✿ Zone: 9

Enkianthus chinensis

ERICA

A huge genus of over 700 species of hardy evergreen shrubs with colourful winter flowers, some varieties of which offer autumn and winter foliage tints as well. There are literally thousands of named varieties. All winter-flowering heathers make excellent ground cover plants for open, sunny areas with acid soil. Some are tolerant of neutral or even slightly alkaline soil, as well as dappled shade. Many make useful permanent container plants.
Cultivation In the garden, grow in any well-drained, but moisture-retentive, acid soil in full sun. Add plenty of organic matter (but not alkaline mushroom compost/soil mix) before planting. In pots, grow in ericaceous compost on a sunny patio. Keep watered.
Pruning Trim flowering stems as they fade. Prune those grown for their colourful foliage in spring.
Propagation Take semi-ripe cuttings in mid-summer or layer side shoots in early spring.

Erica carnea 'Ann Sparkes'
Winter heath
Deep pink clusters of urn-shaped flowers that mature to blood-red as they age are produced from mid-winter to mid-spring. The burnished-gold foliage is bronze-tipped in spring. Tolerates slightly alkaline soils and dappled shade. H 25cm (10in) S 45cm (18in).
Aspect: sun or semi-shade
Hardiness: ❀❀❀ Zones: 7–8

Erica carnea 'Challenger'
Winter heath
Masses of urn-shaped flowers provide a splash of magenta from mid-winter to mid-spring above a mound of dark green foliage. Tolerates slightly alkaline soils and dappled shade. H 15cm (6in) S 45cm (18in).
Aspect: sun or semi-shade
Hardiness: ❀❀❀ Zones: 7–8

Erica carnea 'December Red'
Winter heath
Lilac-pink, urn-shaped flowers are produced in clusters from mid-winter to mid-spring above a mound of dark green foliage. Tolerates slightly alkaline soils and dappled shade. H 15cm (6in)

S 45cm (18in).
Aspect: sun or semi-shade
Hardiness: ❀❀❀ Zones: 7–8

Erica carnea 'Foxhollow'
Winter heath
Urn-shaped lilac flowers appear from mid-winter to mid-spring above mounds of yellow foliage that is bronze-tipped in spring, darkening to orange in winter. Tolerates slightly alkaline soils and dappled shade. H 15cm (6in) S 45cm (18in).
Aspect: sun or semi-shade
Hardiness: ❀❀❀ Zones: 7–8

Erica carnea 'King George'
Winter heath
Clusters of dark pink, urn-shaped flowers that darken as they mature are produced from early winter to early spring. Tolerates slightly alkaline soils and dappled shade. H 15cm (6in) S 25cm (10in).
Aspect: sun or semi-shade
Hardiness: ❀❀❀ Zones: 7–8

Erica carnea 'Myretoun Ruby'
Winter heath
Large, urn-shaped, ruby-red flowers that mature to crimson are produced from mid-winter to late spring above a mound of dark green foliage. Tolerates slightly alkaline soils and dappled shade. H 15cm (6in) S 45cm (18in).
Aspect: sun or semi-shade
Hardiness: ❀❀❀ Zones: 7–8

Erica carnea 'Pink Spangles'
Winter heath
Clusters of urn-shaped shell-pink flowers are produced from mid-

Erica x veitchii 'Exeter'

winter to mid-spring above a mound of dark green foliage. Tolerates slightly alkaline soils and dappled shade. H 15cm (6in) S 45cm (18in).
Aspect: sun or semi-shade
Hardiness: ❀❀❀ Zones: 7–8

Erica carnea 'Springwood White'
Winter heath
Long spikes of urn-shaped white flowers are produced from mid-winter to mid-spring above a mound of dark green foliage. Tolerates slightly alkaline soils and dappled shade. H 15cm (6in) S 45cm (18in).
Aspect: sun or semi-shade
Hardiness: ❀❀❀ Zones: 7–8

Erica cinerea f. *alba* 'Pink Ice'
Bell heather
Mini rosy-pink, bell-shaped flowers are produced in masses

from early summer to early autumn above a mound of dark green foliage that is bronze-tinted in spring and again during winter. H 20cm (8in) S 35cm (14in).
Aspect: sun
Hardiness: ❀❀❀ Zones: 7–8

Erica x darleyensis 'Darley Dale'
Clusters of urn-shaped, shell-pink flowers that darken with age are produced from mid-winter to mid-spring above a mound of green foliage that is cream-tipped in spring. H 15cm (6in) S 55cm (22in).
Aspect: sun
Hardiness: ❀❀❀ Zones: 7–8

Erica x darleyensis 'Furzey'
Urn-shaped, lilac-pink flowers are produced in clusters from early winter to late spring above a mound of lance-shaped green leaves that are pink-tipped in spring. H 35cm (14in) S 60cm (24in).
Aspect: sun
Hardiness: ❀❀❀ Zones: 7–8

ESCALLONIA

This genus of over 50 species includes several useful bushy evergreen shrubs with pretty summer flowers that shine out against a backdrop of glossy, dark green leaves. They make excellent border fillers but can be used to make an informal flowering hedge. They tolerate salt-laden air and so are ideal for providing shelter and screens in mild coastal gardens.
Cultivation Grow in well-drained garden soil that is reasonably

Erica x darleyensis 'Darley Dale'

Escallonia

Eucryphia x nymansensis 'Nymansay'

fertile and in full sun. Choose a sheltered position for the less-hardy varieties.
Pruning Cut back wayward shoots in spring to maintain a balanced shape. Trim flowered shoots after flowering to keep shrub compact. Trim hedges after flowering, if necessary, to keep in shape.
Propagation Take softwood cuttings in late spring or semi-ripe cuttings during mid-summer or late summer.

Escallonia 'Apple Blossom'
Masses of pretty, pale pink flowers are produced from early summer to late summer over a compact mound of glossy, dark green foliage. Good for growing as an informal, flowering hedge, but not on exposed sites. H 2.5m (8ft) S 2.5m (8ft).
Aspect: sun
Hardiness: ✿✿ Zones: 9

Escallonia 'Donard Seedling'
An open form of escallonia that produces arching shoots covered in blossom-like, pink-tinted white flowers from early summer to late summer. Very hardy, it is ideal for growing as an informal, flowering hedge even in cold areas. H 2.5m (8ft) S 2.5m (8ft).
Aspect: sun
Hardiness: ✿✿✿ Zones: 7–8

Escallonia 'Iveyi'
A vigorous, upright, evergreen shrub that is covered in clusters of fragrant, white flowers from mid-summer to early autumn. The glossy, dark green leaves

become bronze-tinted in winter. H 3m (10ft) S 3m (10ft).
Aspect: sun
Hardiness: ✿✿✿ Zones: 7–8

Escallonia rubra 'Crimson Spire'
Masses of tubular flowers provide a splash of pale crimson from early summer to late summer against a backdrop of glossy, dark green foliage. Good for growing as an informal, flowering hedge. H 2.5m (8ft) S 2.5m (8ft).
Aspect: sun
Hardiness: ✿✿ Zone: 9

EUCRYPHIA
A genus of about five species, including the following evergreen shrubs, grown for their late summer flowers. Rated among the most attractive summer-flowering shrubs, these shrubs are an ideal choice for planting in a sheltered woodland garden with acid soil, where there is plenty of room to spread, but they are borderline hardy in colder areas.
Cultivation Grow in any well-drained but moisture-retentive, acid to neutral soil in dappled shade. Add plenty of organic matter (but not alkaline mushroom soil mix) to the soil before planting to ensure that it gets a good start. Make sure the planting site is sheltered from cold winds.
Pruning No routine pruning is necessary. Any frost-damaged growth should be removed in spring.
Propagation Take semi-ripe cuttings in mid-summer or late summer.

Eucryphia x intermedia 'Rostrevor'
A large, evergreen, upright shrub that is covered in splendid white-scented, cup-shaped flowers up to 5cm (2in) across throughout late summer and early autumn.
H 10m (33ft) S 3m (10ft).
Aspect: semi-shade
Hardiness: ✿✿✿ Zones: 7–8

Eucryphia x nymansensis 'Nymansay'
Very large, upright-growing, evergreen shrub with toothed, leathery foliage that is smothered in large, showy, white cup-shaped flowers throughout late summer and early autumn. H 15m (50ft) S 5m (16ft).
Aspect: semi-shade
Hardiness: ✿✿✿ Zones: 7–8

EUONYMUS
Spindle tree
This comprises a large genus of about 175 species that includes the useful and varied garden shrubs featured here. The evergreen varieties provide striking variegated foliage and make excellent ground cover and mid-border fillers anywhere in the garden, as well as attractive low hedges in mild areas. Some varieties will also make good wall shrubs, where they will produce aerial roots that are self-supporting. Deciduous euonymus

provide intense autumn colour and attractive berries.
Cultivation Grow in any well-drained soil that is reasonably fertile, in full sun or dappled shade. Make sure the planting site for evergreens is sheltered from cold winds.
Pruning No routine pruning is necessary. Any damaged growth should be removed in spring. Remove any plain green reverted shoots from variegated varieties. Rejuvenate neglected plants by cutting back one stem in three to near ground level after flowering, starting with the oldest stems. Evergreen hedges can be trimmed lightly in mid-spring to maintain a neat shape.
Propagation Take semi-ripe cuttings mid-summer or late summer or hardwood cuttings in mid-winter.

Euonymus europaeus 'Red Cascade'
The dark green leaves of this deciduous European native transform themselves into wonderfully vivid fiery shades during the autumn. Insignificant flowers produced during late spring and early summer are followed by eye-catching rosy-pink berries that last into the winter. Although it will grow in dappled shade, plant in full sun for the best

Euonymus europaeus 'Red Cascade'

Euonymus alatus

Euonymus fortunei 'Emerald 'n' Gold'

autumn colours. H 3m (10ft) S 2.5m (8ft).
Aspect: sun or semi-shade
Hardiness: ❀❀❀ Zones: 7–8

Euonymus fortunei 'Emerald Gaiety'

The white-edged, bright evergreen foliage on this compact, bushy shrub provides useful winter interest when there is little else happening in the garden. Insignificant clusters of tiny green flowers are produced during late spring and early summer. 'Emerald Gaiety' makes a useful ground cover and low hedging plant and does well in sun or shade. It is a good plant for training against a wall or fence. H 1m (3ft) S 1.5m (5ft).
Aspect: sun or shade
Hardiness: ❀❀❀ Zones: 7–8

Euonymus fortunei 'Emerald 'n' Gold'

A bushy, variegated evergreen with glossy, yellow-edged, bright green leaves that become pink-tinged in winter. Insignificant clusters of tiny green flowers are produced during late spring and early summer. It is a useful ground cover and low hedging plant in sun or light shade. H 60cm (24in) S 90cm (36in).
Aspect: sun or semi-shade
Hardiness: ❀❀❀ Zones: 7–8

Euonymus fortunei 'Silver Queen'

A low-growing, compact, busy evergreen with dark green leaves that have creamy-yellow or creamy-white margins that are pink-tinged in winter. Clusters of insignificant, tiny green flowers

appear in late spring and early summer, followed by orange fruits. A good choice for training against a wall or fence in sun or light shade. H 3m (10ft) S 2m (6ft).
Aspect: sun or semi-shade
Hardiness: ❀❀❀ Zones: 7–8

Euonymus fortunei 'Sunspot'

A compact, bushy, evergreen shrub with glossy foliage splashed with gold and held on bright yellow stems. Excellent for winter colour. H 1m (3ft) S 1.5m (5ft).
Aspect: sun or semi-shade
Hardiness: ❀❀❀ Zones: 7–8

EXOCHORDA
Pearl bush

A genus of four species, including the graceful, deciduous shrub featured here, that is smothered with pretty blooms during late spring. Its lax habit makes it an ideal choice for a mixed border, but all look good covering banks or growing as a wall shrub.
Cultivation Grow in any moisture-retentive, well-drained soil that is reasonably fertile in full sun or dappled shade. Shelter evergreens from cold winds.
Pruning Cut back one stem in three to near ground level after flowering, starting with the oldest stems, to keep flowering profuse.
Propagation Take softwood cuttings in mid-spring.

Exochorda x macrantha 'The Bride'

Elegant arching branches are covered in brilliant white flowers during mid-spring and late spring.

The delicate, bluish-green foliage makes a good foil for adjacent flowering plants at other times and then takes on yellow and orange shades in autumn. H 2m (6ft) S 3m (10ft).
Aspect: sun or semi-shade
Hardiness: ❀❀❀ Zones: 7–8

X FATSHEDERA

This bi-generic cross between a bushy evergreen shrub (*Fatsia*) and ivy (*Hedera*) is grown mainly for its handsome foliage. Can be grown as a shrub, trained up a wall or fence or left to sprawl as deep ground cover under deciduous trees. It is an excellent choice for town or coastal gardens since it can tolerate shade, urban pollution and salt-laden winds.
Cultivation Grow in any moisture-retentive well-drained garden soil that is reasonably fertile and in full sun or dappled shade. Grow at the base of a sunny wall in colder areas.
Pruning No routine pruning is necessary. Remove wayward or crossing shoots if necessary during early spring.
Propagation Take semi-ripe cuttings in mid-summer.

x fatshedera lizei

An open, branching shrub with glossy, evergreen, ivy-like leaves that are leathery to the touch. A bonus of creamy-white flowers are sometimes produced during in mid-autumn and late autumn. H 1.2m (4ft) S 3m (10ft).
Named varieties: 'Variegata', frost-hardy form with white-edged

Exochorda x macrantha 'The Bride'

leaves. H 1.2m (4ft) S 3m
(10ft).
Aspect: sun or semi-shade
Hardiness: ❀❀❀ Zones: 7–8

FATSIA

A genus of two species, including
the popular evergreen shrub
featured here. They make excellent
focal points when positioned in a
sheltered area of the garden, where
they will help to create a tropical
atmosphere. They can also be
grown as a permanent specimen in
a large container. This shrub is an
excellent choice for town or coastal
gardens as it can tolerate shade,
urban pollution and salt-laden
winds.

Cultivation In the garden, grow
in any moisture-retentive, well-
drained soil that is reasonably
fertile in full sun or dappled
shade where it is sheltered from
cold winds. If planted in a
container, grow in a soil-based
compost (soil mix). Feed every
fortnight throughout the growing
season and water as necessary.
Pruning No routine pruning is
required. Keep plants compact by
cutting back one stem in three to
near ground level in mid-spring,
starting with the oldest stems.
Propagation Can be air layered in
mid-spring. Take softwood
cuttings in early summer.

Fatsia japonica
A tropical-looking shrub with
large, glossy, leathery, palmate
leaves that help to reflect light
into lacklustre corners. A bonus
of creamy-white flowers is
produced in ball-shaped flower-

heads in early autumn and mid-
autumn, followed by rounded
black fruit. H 4m (13ft) S 4m
(13ft). Named varieties:
'Variegata', half-hardy variegated
form with bright green leaves that
are cream-splashed at the margins.
Ideal for brightening up dark
corners. H 4m (13ft) S 4m
(13ft).
Aspect: sun or semi-shade
Hardiness: ❀❀❀ Zones: 7–8

FORSYTHIA

A genus of over five species,
including the following popular
and spring-flowering shrubs that
can be used as back-of-the-border
fillers, focal points or trimmed as
a deciduous flowering hedge.
They can even be trained into wall
shrubs, arches and standards.
Cultivation Grow in any moisture-
retentive, well-drained soil that is
reasonably fertile in full sun or
dappled shade.
Pruning Keep plants compact and
flowering well by cutting back one
stem in three to near ground level
during early spring, starting with
the oldest stems. Prune hedges
and other ornamental forms
lightly after flowering in mid-
spring.
Propagation Take softwood
cuttings in early summer or
hardwood cuttings in late
autumn.

Forsythia 'Beatrix Farrand'
Masses of 3cm- (1¼in-) wide
orange-yellow blooms are
produced on arching, bare stems
during early spring and mid-
spring. Sharply toothed leaves

Forsythia

provide a plain green backdrop
during the growing season. Very
good for training against a wall.
H 2m (6ft) S 2m (6ft).
Aspect: sun or semi-shade
Hardiness: ❀❀❀ Zones: 7–8

Forsythia x intermedia 'Lynwood'
Masses of delicate, golden-yellow
flowers are produced on bare
stems during mid-spring and late
spring. A dense crop of lobed,
mid-green leaves follows. H 3m
(10ft) S 2m (6ft).
Aspect: sun or semi-shade
Hardiness: ❀❀❀ Zones: 7–8

*Forsythia x intermedia 'Spring
Glory'*
Pale yellow flowers smother the
branches of this deciduous shrub
during early spring and mid-
spring before the lance-shaped
leaves emerge. An excellent choice
for growing as a flowering hedge.
H 2m (6ft) S 3m (10ft).
Aspect: sun or semi-shade
Hardiness: ❀❀❀ Zones: 7–8

*Forsythia x intermedia
'Week End'*
Masses of rich yellow flowers are
produced on bare stems during
early spring and mid-spring as the
leaf buds break. H 3m (10ft) S
3m (10ft).
Aspect: sun or semi-shade
Hardiness: ❀❀❀ Zones: 7–8

FOTHERGILLA

A genus of just two species,
including the deciduous shrubs
featured here, grown for their
brilliant autumn colour. A bonus

of sweetly scented flowers are
borne from mid-spring before the
leaves emerge. They make good
border fillers and seasonal
specimens where suitable growing
conditions can be provided. A
good choice for a woodland-edge
planting on acid soil.
Cultivation Grow in any moisture-
retentive but well-drained acid
soil in full sun or partial shade.
Add plenty of organic matter (but
not alkaline mushroom compost/
soil mix) to the soil before
planting. Flowering and foliage
displays are best in full sun.
Pruning No routine pruning is
required.
Propagation Layer low branches
in early autumn.

Fothergilla gardenii
Witch alder
Upright deciduous shrub with
coarsely toothed green leaves that
turn brilliant crimson in autumn.
Sweetly scented clusters of white
flowers are produced on bare
stems during mid-spring and late
spring. H 1m (3ft) S 1m (3ft).
Aspect: sun or semi-shade
Hardiness: ❀❀❀ Zones: 7–8

Fothergilla major (syn.
Fothergilla monticola)
Glossy, dark green leaves turn
fiery shades of orange, yellow and
red in autumn. Clusters of
sweetly scented white flowers are
produced on bare stems during
mid-spring and late spring.
H 2.5m (8ft) S 2m (6ft).
Aspect: sun or semi-shade
Hardiness: ❀❀❀ Zones: 7–8

Fatsia japonica

Fothergilla 'Huntsman'

Fremontodendron 'California Glory'

Fuchsia

Garrya elliptica

FREMONTODENDRON

A genus of just two species, including the long-flowering evergreen shrub featured here that is ideal for training against a sunny wall in mild areas but can also be grown as a free-standing shrub at the back of a sheltered border. It is mainly grown for its spectacular, waxy-looking flowers and handsome foliage.

Cultivation Grow in any well-drained neutral to alkaline soil in full sun that is sheltered from cold winds.

Pruning No routine pruning is required. Remove frost damaged and awkwardly positions stems in spring.

Propagation Sow seed in early spring.

Fremontodendron 'California Glory'

Eye-catching, saucer-shaped, butter-yellow and waxy-looking flowers are produced in succession from late spring to mid-autumn against a backdrop of leathery, lobed dark green leaves. H 6m (20ft) S 4m (13ft).
Aspect: sun
Hardiness: ✿✿ Zone: 9

FUCHSIA

A large genus of over 100 species, including the hardy types featured here that are grown for their superb summer flowers. In mild areas they can be treated as deciduous shrubs, making useful fillers in mixed borders and shrubberies, or even an unusual informal flowering hedge.

Cultivation Grow in any well-drained soil in full sun or dappled shade protected from cold winds. In colder areas, protect crowns with an insulating layer of leaves or similar material over the winter months.

Pruning In frost-free areas no routine pruning is required. They are more or less evergreen and grown with a permanent woody framework to make good border fillers or an informal long-flowering hedge. Remove any dead or damaged wood each spring. Hedges can be kept in shape by tipping back the new shoots in early spring or mid-spring to maintain dense growth. In colder areas, hardy fuchsias are treated more like herbaceous plants – the top cut back in early spring before new growth starts.

Propagation Take softwood cuttings from mid-spring to early autumn.

Fuchsia 'Mrs Popple'

Scarlet and purple single pendant flowers are produced from early summer to mid-autumn against a foil of dark green leaves. Borderline hardy. H 1.2m (4ft) S 1.2m (4ft).
Aspect: sun or semi-shade
Hardiness: ✿✿✿ Zones: 7–8

Fuchsia 'Pumila'

Scarlet and violet-blue single flowers are produced in succession from early summer to mid-autumn on this dwarf shrub. Borderline hardy. H 50cm (20in) S 50cm (20in).

Aspect: sun or semi-shade
Hardiness: ✿✿✿ Zones: 7–8

Fuchsia 'Riccartonii'

Red and dark purple single flowers are produced in succession from early summer to mid-autumn over bronze-tinted dark green leaves. Borderline hardy, it makes an excellent hedge in frost-free areas. H 3m (10ft) S 2m (6ft).
Aspect: sun or semi-shade
Hardiness: ✿✿✿ Zones: 7–8

GARRYA

This genus of over 10 species includes the tough, upright-growing, evergreen shrubs featured here, grown for their late-winter catkin-like flower tassels. They make an excellent choice for growing against a south- or west-facing wall or fence where they will provide valuable winter interest as well as an attractive foil for other plants throughout the year. This shrub makes a useful plant for town and coastal gardens as they tolerate both pollution and salt-laden air.

Cultivation Grow in well-drained , moderately fertile soil in full sun or dappled shade. In colder areas, protect from icy winds.

Pruning Keep plants in shape by cutting back one stem in three to near ground level in mid-spring, starting with the oldest stems.

Propagation Take semi-ripe cuttings in mid-summer, or hardwood cuttings in early autumn.

Garrya elliptica

A useful wall shrub with leathery, lustrous, wavy-edged evergreen leaves, that is decorated with elegant grey-green catkins tassels from early winter to late winter. H 4m (13ft) S 4m (13ft).
Named varieties: 'James Roof', dramatic silvery catkins up to 20cm long. H 4m (12ft) S 4m (13ft).
Aspect: sun or semi-shade
Hardiness: ✿✿✿ Zones: 7–8

GAULTHERIA

This is a large genus of 170 species, including the low-growing evergreen shrubs that are featured here The plants are mainly grown for their red berries and attractive winter tints. To ensure fruit production, it will be necessary to grow both male and female plants.

Cultivation Grow in a moisture-retentive, well-drained neutral to acid soil in full sun or dappled shade that is moderately fertile.

Pruning No routine pruning is required. Remove any dead or damaged stems each mid-spring.

Propagation Take semi-ripe cuttings in mid-summer or layer shoots in mid-spring.

Gaultheria mucronata 'Mulberry Wine'

Urn-shaped, pinkish-white flowers are produced during late spring and early summer, followed by aromatic, magenta fruit in early autumn that darken to purple. H 1.2m (4ft) S 1.2m (4ft).
Aspect: sun or semi-shade
Hardiness: ✿✿✿ Zones: 7–8

Gaultheria procumbens

Gaultheria mucronata 'Wintertime'

Aromatic, snow-white fruit in early autumn follow pink-flushed, urn-shaped white flowers that were produced during late spring and early summer. H 1.2m (4ft) S 1.2m (4ft).
Aspect: sun or semi-shade
Hardiness: ❈❈❈ Zones: 7–8

Gaultheria procumbens

Urn-shaped flowers in shades of white and pink are produced during late spring and early summer, followed by aromatic scarlet fruit in early autumn. The green leaves take on red and purple tints in winter. They are useful ground cover plants between acid-loving trees and shrubs. H 15cm (6in) S 1m (3ft).
Aspect: sun or semi-shade
Hardiness: ❈❈❈ Zones: 7–8

GENISTA

A genus of over 90 species, including the late-spring and early summer flowering spiny deciduous shrubs. They make excellent border specimens for providing a seasonal splash of colour and can be used to make informal flowering hedges in mild areas. Lower-growing forms also make useful ground cover on sunny banks or can be used to soften the edges of raised beds and rockeries.
Cultivation Grow in a well-drained poor soil in full sun.
Pruning No routine pruning is required. Keep plants bushy by

pinching out shoot tips after flowering.
Propagation Sow seeds in early autumn. Take semi-ripe cuttings in mid-summer.

Genista hispanica
Spanish gorse

Golden-yellow flowers produced in clusters on spiny stems in late spring and early summer stand out against the mound of green leaves. Its prickles make it an excellent impenetrable hedging plant in mild areas. Borderline hardy. H 75cm (30in) S 1.5m (5ft).
Aspect: sun
Hardiness: ❈❈❈ Zones: 7–8

Genista lydia

The prickly, arching, grey-green leaves of this spreading shrub are festooned in golden-yellow flowers throughout late spring and early summer. H 60cm (24in) S 1m (3ft).
Aspect: sun
Hardiness: ❈❈❈ Zones: 7–8

Genista pilosa 'Vancouver Gold'

A spreading, mound-forming shrub that is covered in masses of golden-yellow flowers produced during late spring and early summer. H 45cm (18in) S 1m (3ft).
Aspect: sun
Hardiness: ❈❈❈ Zones: 7–8

Genista tinctoria 'Royal Gold'
Dyer's greenwood

An extremely long-flowering, upright-growing deciduous shrub that bears golden-yellow flowers

Grevillea 'Robyn Gordon'

intermittently from late spring to late summer. H 1m (3ft) S 1m (3ft).
Aspect: sun
Hardiness: ❈❈❈ Zones: 7–8

GREVILLEA

A large genus of over 250 species, including the evergreen shrubs featured here, that are grown for their exotic-looking early summer flowers. If you have the right growing conditions, they make useful and unusual border fillers.
Cultivation In the garden, grow in any well-drained neutral to acid soil that is moderately fertile in full sun. Provide protection in frost-prone areas. Use ericaceous compost if grown in pots. Feed fortnightly in the growing season.
Pruning No routine pruning is required. Remove any dead or damaged stems each mid-spring.
Propagation Take semi-ripe cuttings in mid-summer.

Grevillea juniperina f. sulphurea

A rounded evergreen shrub with upright, branching stems that carry spiky yellow flowers from late spring to mid-summer. Although the plant is frost hardy, but it will need a sheltered site and winter protection in colder gardens. H 1m (3ft) S 1.8m (6ft).
Aspect: sun
Hardiness: ❈❈ Zone: 9

Grevillea 'Robyn Gordon'

This is a spreading evergreen shrub with upright branches that bear dark pink petal-less flowers produced intermittently all year round, but mainly during early summer. In frost-free areas, grow in a sunny, sheltered spot. Elsewhere, grow in a pot and move it inside during the winter. H 1m (3ft) S 1.8m (6ft).
Aspect: sun
Hardiness: ❈ Zones: 7–8

Genista lydia

HAMAMELIS
Witch hazel

This genus of about five species, including the hardy deciduous shrubs featured here, are grown for their fragrant, spidery winter flowers that look spectacular in the garden when illuminated by the low winter sun. Ideal for a sunny shrub border or woodland-edge planting.

Cultivation Grow in a moisture-retentive, well-drained, neutral to acid soil that is reasonably fertile in full sun or dappled shade.

Pruning No routine pruning is necessary. Neglected plants can have wayward branches removed to balance the overall shape of the canopy after flowering in early spring.

Propagation Difficult to propagate. Sow seeds when ripe in mid-autumn; graft named varieties in late winter.

Hamamelis x intermedia 'Arnold Promise'

This vase-shaped deciduous shrub bears clusters of large, sweetly scented, spidery golden flowers from early winter to late winter. The green leaves turn into brilliant autumnal colours in shades of rich yellow. H 4m (13ft) S 4m (13ft).
Aspect: sun or semi-shade
Hardiness: ❁❁❁ Zones: 7–8

Hamamelis x intermedia 'Diane'

Clusters of sweetly scented, spidery, dark copper-red flowers are produced on bare stems from early winter to late winter. The

Hamamelis mollis 'Pallida'

green leaves turn fiery shades of orange, red and yellow in autumn. H 4m (13ft) S 4m (13ft).
Aspect: sun or semi-shade
Hardiness: ❁❁❁ Zones: 7–8

Hamamelis x intermedia 'Jelena'

Large, fragrant, coppery-red or orange flowers are produced in clusters on bare stems from early winter to mid-winter. The green leaves transform into attractive autumnal colours with shades of rich orange and red. H 4m (13ft) S 4m (13ft).
Aspect: sun or semi-shade
Hardiness: ❁❁❁ Zones: 7–8

Hamamelis x intermedia 'Moonlight'

Clusters of sweetly scented, spidery, pale yellow flowers are produced on bare stems from early winter to late winter. Green leaves turn yellow in autumn.

H 4m (13ft) S 4m (13ft).
Aspect: sun or semi-shade
Hardiness: ❁❁❁ Zones: 7–8

Hamamelis x intermedia 'Pallida' (syn. H. mollis 'Pallida')

Bare branches from early winter to late winter carry clusters of large, sweetly scented, sulphur-yellow flowers. The green leaves transform into autumn colours with shades of rich orange and red. H 4m (13ft) S 4m (13ft).
Aspect: sun or semi-shade
Hardiness: ❁❁❁ Zones: 7–8

Hamamelis mollis

Clusters of sweetly scented, spidery, golden flowers are produced on bare stems from early winter to late winter. The slightly hairy mid-green leaves turn bright yellow in autumn. H 4m (13ft) S 4m (13ft).
Aspect: sun or semi-shade
Hardiness: ❁❁❁ Zones: 7–8

HEBE

A genus of around 100 species, including the evergreen shrubs featured here, that are grown for their colourful flowers and attractive foliage. Most are long flowering and make good filler shrubs for a border in sun or dappled shade. They are tolerant of pollution and salt-laden air, and so make a good choice for town and coastal gardens. Some also make excellent low hedges or edging in milder areas.

Cultivation Grow in a moisture-retentive, well-drained neutral to

slightly alkaline soil that is poor to reasonably fertile in full sun or dappled shade, but sheltered from cold winds and freezing temperatures. Borderline hardy, they need winter protection in colder areas.

Pruning No routine pruning is required. Straggly shoots on larger varieties can be pruned right back in mid-spring. Remove all-green reverted shoots from variegated varieties as soon as they are noticed. Trim hedges lightly after flowering to keep the plants dense and compact.

Propagation Take softwood cuttings in late spring or semi-ripe cuttings in early autumn.

Hebe cupressoides 'Boughton Dome'

An unusual hebe that looks more like a conifer, with its grey-green, scale-like evergreen leaves. Slow growing and hardy, it is an ideal choice for troughs and rock gardens. Small blue flowers in late spring are seldom produced.
H 30cm (12in) S 60cm (24in).
Aspect: sun or semi-shade
Hardiness: ❁❁❁ Zones: 7–8

Hebe 'Great Orme'

Slender spikes of bright pink flowers that fade to white are produced from mid-summer to mid-autumn above a mound of lustrous, evergreen leaves on this rounded shrub. Useful foil and gap filler. H 1.2m (4ft) S 1.2m (4ft).
Aspect: sun or semi-shade
Hardiness: ❁❁ Zones: 7–8

Hebe 'Marjorie'

A compact, rounded, evergreen shrub that bears long spikes of mauve flowers that gradually fade to white from mid-summer to early autumn. A useful foil and gap filler and for flower arranging. H 1.2m (4ft) S 1.5m (5ft).
Aspect: sun or semi-shade
Hardiness: ❁❁ Zones: 9

Hebe 'Midsummer Beauty'

The bright evergreen leaves emerge purple-tinged on this rounded shrub that produces dark lilac flower-spikes that fade to white from mid-summer to early

Hebe 'Great Orme'

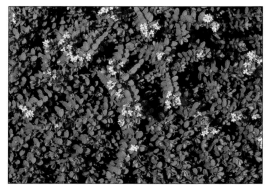

Hebe pinguifolia 'Pagei'

Helianthemum 'Ben Fhada'
A low-growing, spreading shrub that is covered in golden-yellow, cup-shaped flowers with orange centres from late spring to mid-summer. H 30cm (12in) S 30cm (12in).
Aspect: sun
Hardiness: ❈❈❈ Zone: 7–8

Helianthemum 'Ben Heckla'
Cup-shaped, brick-red flowers with orange centres are produced *en masse* from late spring to mid-summer above a spreading mound of grey-green leaves. H 30cm (12in) S 30cm (12in).
Aspect: sun
Hardiness: ❈❈❈ Zones: 7–8

Helianthemum 'Wisley Pink'

autumn on purplish-brown stems. H 2m (6ft) S 1.5m (5ft).
Aspect: sun or semi-shade
Hardiness: ❈❈ Zone: 9

Hebe ochracea 'James Stirling'
The golden conifer-like foliage of this compact evergreen adds colour to the winter garden. Clusters of white flowers on arching stems are produced in early summer. H 45cm (18in) S 60cm (24in).
Aspect: sun or semi-shade
Hardiness: ❈❈❈ Zones: 7–8

Hebe pinguifolia 'Pagei'
A low-growing, compact but spreading evergreen that bears masses of snow-white flowers on purple stems throughout late spring and early summer above fleshy blue-green leaves. Good for edging beds and borders. H 30cm (12in) S 90cm (36in).
Aspect: sun or semi-shade
Hardiness: ❈❈❈ Zones: 7–8

Hebe rakaiensis
A neat, rounded shrub that bears clusters of large white flowers during early summer and mid-summer above glossy evergreen leaves. Its neat habit makes it a good choice for Japanese-style gardens. H 1m (3ft) S 1.2m (4ft).
Aspect: sun or semi-shade
Hardiness: ❈❈❈ Zones: 7–8

Hebe 'Red Edge'
A low-growing, spreading evergreen that bears lilac-blue flowers that fade to white

throughout early summer and mid-summer. The grey-green leaves of young plants have attractive red margins and veining. Good for edging beds and borders. H 45cm (18in) S 60cm (24in).
Aspect: sun or semi-shade
Hardiness: ❈❈ Zone: 9

Hebe 'Rosie'
Its compact mound of evergreen foliage is decorated with pink flower-spikes from late spring to early autumn. H 60cm (24in) S 60cm (24in).
Aspect: sun or semi-shade
Hardiness: ❈❈ Zone: 9

HELIANTHEMUM
Rock rose, sun rose
A genus of over 100 species that includes the short-lived, spreading, evergreen shrubs featured here, grown for their early summer flowers. These low-growing shrubs are ideal for edging a sunny border and can be used in pots and for cascading over the edge of a raised bed. However, they tend to lose vigour as they age so are best replaced when they reach this stage.
Cultivation Grow in a well-drained neutral to slightly alkaline soil that is reasonably fertile in full sun.
Pruning Cut back hard after flowering to encourage a fresh mound of foliage and a second flush of flowers in late summer.
Propagation Take semi-ripe cuttings in early summer or mid-summer.

Helianthemum 'Ben Hope'
A spreading shrub that bears bright red flowers with orange centres in succession from late spring to mid-summer over downy, silvery-green leaves. H 30cm (12in) S 30cm (12in).
Aspect: sun
Hardiness: ❈❈❈ Zones: 7–8

Helianthemum 'Chocolate Blotch'
Cup-shaped, pale orange flowers with chocolate-brown centres appear in succession from late spring to mid-summer above a spreading mound of grey-green leaves. H 30cm (12in) S 30cm (12in).
Aspect: sun
Hardiness: ❈❈❈ Zones: 7–8

Helianthemum 'Henfield Brilliant'
Bright-red, cup-shaped flowers are

produced from late spring to mid-summer above a spreading mound of grey-green leaves. H 30cm (12in) S 30cm (12in).
Aspect: sun
Hardiness: ❈❈❈ Zones: 7–8

Helianthemum 'Wisley Pink'
Clear rose flowers are produced from late spring to mid-summer above a spreading mound of grey-green leaves. H 30cm (12in) S 45cm (18in).
Aspect: sun
Hardiness: ❈❈❈ Zones: 7–8

Helianthemum 'Wisley Primrose'
Primrose-yellow flowers with golden-yellow centres are produced from late spring to mid-summer above a spreading mound of grey-green leaves. H 30cm (12in) S 45cm (18in).
Aspect: sun
Hardiness: ❈❈❈ Zones: 7–8

Helianthemum

Hibiscus rosa-sinensis 'The President'

HIBISCUS

This large genus of over 200 species includes the exotic-looking shrubs featured here, grown for their eyecatching, colourful, trumpet-shaped, late-summer flowers. Useful for creating a tropical feel to a sunny corner or patio.

Cultivation In the garden, grow in a moisture-retentive, well-drained neutral to slightly alkaline soil that is reasonably fertile in full sun. In containers, use a soil-based compost (soil mix), water regularly and feed monthly during the growing season. Water as necessary during winter months.
Pruning No routine pruning is necessary. Remove any frost-damaged growth during spring.
Propagation Take semi-ripe cuttings in mid-summer.

Hibiscus rosa-sinensis 'The President'
Chinese hibiscus
Huge, red, ruffled-edged flowers with darker eyes across (up to 18cm/7in), are produced from mid-summer to early autumn. It is tender, so grow in a heated greenhouse or conservatory in cold areas (minimum temperature 10°C/ 50°F). H 3m (10ft) S 2m (6ft).
Aspect: sun
Hardiness: tender Zones: 9–10

Hibiscus syriacus 'Blue Bird'
(syn. *H. syriacus* 'Oiseau Bleu')
Violet-blue, trumpet-shaped flowers with a maroon eye (up to 8cm/3in across) are produced in succession from late summer to mid-autumn against lobed, dark

green leaves. H 3m (10ft) S 2m (6ft).
Aspect: sun
Hardiness: ✿✿✿ Zones: 7–8

Hibiscus syriacus 'Woodbridge'
Large, deep pink, trumpet-shaped flowers with a maroon eye (up to 10cm/4in across) are produced in succession from late summer to mid-autumn against lobed, dark green leaves. H 3m (10ft) S 2m (6ft).
Aspect: sun
Hardiness: ✿✿✿ Zones: 7–8

HYDRANGEA

A genus of about 80 species, including the summer-flowering deciduous shrubs featured here, that are also grown for their autumn tints and winter seed-heads. Hydrangeas make useful border fillers where their late-summer displays can be appreciated.

Cultivation Grow in a moisture-retentive, well-drained reasonably fertile soil in full sun or dappled shade. Add plenty of organic matter to the soil before planting and mulch annually so that plants do not run short of moisture during the summer months. On shallow, chalky soils, some varieties show signs of chlorosis.
Pruning No pruning is necessary. Remove dead flower-heads in early spring. Remove any frost-damaged growth in spring.
Propagation Take softwood cuttings of deciduous varieties in early summer or mid-summer or hardwood cuttings in late autumn. Take semi-ripe cuttings of evergreen varieties in late summer.

Hydrangea arborescens 'Annabelle' **Sevenbark**
Large heads of creamy-white flowers are produced from mid-summer to early autumn. Pointed, dark green leaves. H 2.5m (8ft) S 2.5m (8ft).
Aspect: sun or semi-shade
Hardiness: ✿✿✿ Zones: 7–8

Hydrangea macrophylla 'Blue Wave'
From mid-summer to late summer flattened heads of dark blue to mauve flowers (lilac-pink

on chalky soils) are produced above a mound of coarsely toothed, lustrous, dark green leaves on this lacecap hydrangea. H 2m (6ft) S 2.5m (8ft).
Aspect: sun or semi-shade
Hardiness: ✿✿✿ Zones: 7–8

Hydrangea macrophylla 'Mariesii'
A rounded, lacecap hydrangea with coarsely toothed, glossy, dark green leaves that is covered in flattened heads of pale-blue flowers (rose-pink on chalky soils) from mid-summer to late summer. H 1.2m (4ft) S 1.2m (4ft).
Aspect: sun or semi-shade
Hardiness: ✿✿✿ Zones: 7–8

Hydrangea macrophylla 'Veitchii'
This is a lacecap hydrangea that bears large, somewhat flattened, heads of blue, pink and white flowers that darken to red with age from mid-summer to late summer. It is an ideal plant for a shady site. H 1.2m (4ft) S 1.2m (4ft).
Aspect: sun or semi-shade
Hardiness: ✿✿✿ Zones: 7–8

Hydrangea paniculata 'Floribunda'
This upright shrub has toothed, dark green leaves with white flower-heads that become pinkish in late summer and early autumn H 4m (13ft) S 2.5m (8ft).
Aspect: sun or semi-shade
Hardiness: ✿✿✿ Zones: 7–8

Hydrangea paniculata 'Tardiva'
A later bloomer, the 23cm- (9in-) white-coloured panicles begin to turn blush pink in autumn as the leaves begin to turn in mid-autumn. The dark green foliage is hairy to the touch. This can grow into a big plant if not pruned to remain contained. H 4m (13ft) S 2.5m (8ft).
Aspect: semi-shade
Hardiness: ✿✿✿ Zones: 7–8

Hydrangea quercifolia
White flowers that fade to pink are produced in conical clusters from mid-summer to early autumn. The foliage turns shades of bronze-purple in autumn. H 2m (6ft) S 2.5m (8ft).
Named varieties: 'Snow Queen', brilliant white conical flower clusters that fade to pink with age. H 2m (6ft) S 2m (6ft).
Aspect: sun or semi-shade
Hardiness: ✿✿✿ Zones: 7–8

Hydrangea serrata 'Bluebird' **(syn. *H.* 'Acuminata')**
A lacecap hydrangea that bears flattened heads of blue flowers (they appear as pink when grown on alkaline soil) from early summer to early autumn. It makes a compact mound of pointed green leaves that dramatically turn shades of red in autumn. Surprisingly resistant to drought. H 1.2m (4ft) S 1.2m (4ft).
Aspect: sun or semi-shade
Hardiness: ✿✿✿ Zones: 7–8

Hydrangea arborescens 'Annabelle'

Hydrangea paniculata 'Tardiva'

Hypericum 'Hidcote'

Hydrangea villosa (syn. H. aspera Villosa Group)

Flattened heads of dark blue flowers are produced throughout late summer and early autumn against lance-shaped dark-green leaves on this upright shrub. H 3m (10ft) S 3m (10ft).
Aspect: sun or semi-shade
Hardiness: ❀❀❀ Zones: 7–8

HYPERICUM
St John's wort

This huge genus of more than 400 species contains the long-flowering shrubs featured here. Tough and easy to grow, they are ideal for covering dry banks and shady corners where little else will grow. In fertile soil they can be invasive.
Cultivation Grow in a well-drained soil that is reasonably fertile in full sun or dappled shade.
Pruning Keep plants in good shape by cutting back one stem in three to near ground level in mid-spring, starting with the oldest stems. Cut *Hypericum calycinum* right back to ground level each spring.
Propagation Take semi-ripe cuttings in early summer or mid-summer.

Hypericum 'Hidcote'

A semi-evergreen bushy shrub with pointed leaves that are decorated by large, cup-shaped, golden-yellow flowers produced in succession from mid-summer to early autumn. H 1.2m (4ft) S 1.5m (5ft).
Aspect: sun or semi-shade
Hardiness: ❀❀❀ Zone: 7–8

Hypericum calycinum
Rose of Sharon

A dwarf, vigorously spreading evergreen shrub with lance-shaped leaves that is covered in saucer-shaped bright yellow flowers, which are produced in succession from early summer to early autumn. Can be invasive, but makes excellent ground cover in shade. H 1.2m (4ft) S 3m (10ft).
Aspect: sun to shade
Hardiness: ❀❀❀ Zones: 7–8

Hypericum x moserianum 'Tricolor' (syn. H. 'Variegatum')

An attractive flowering shrub with green-and-white variegated foliage and distinct red margins. Grow only in shady areas as strong sunlight can scorch the foliage. Cup-shaped yellow flowers are produced from early summer to early autumn. H 30cm (12in) S 60cm (24in).
Aspect: semi-shade
Hardiness: ❀❀❀ Zones: 7–9

ILEX
Holly

This huge genus of over 400 species, including the large shrubs featured here, are grown for their handsome, evergreen foliage and colourful berries that appear in the winter, and greatly help in keeping the wildlife fed. These shrubs are very useful for using as specimens as they take well to being trimmed to form dense, slow-growing hedges or more eyecatching topiary.

Cultivation Grow in a moisture-retentive, well-drained soil that is reasonably fertile in full sun or dappled shade. Grow variegated varieties in sun for the best leaf coloration. Make sure you get a female variety if you want berries.
Pruning No routine pruning is necessary. All-green shoots on variegated varieties should be removed as soon as they are noticed. Trim hedges and topiary in late spring.
Propagation Take semi-ripe cuttings in late summer or early autumn.

Ilex x altaclerensis 'Golden King' (female form)

This compact evergreen carries a small crop of red autumn berries that stand out from the brilliant, yellow-edged, glossy, grey-green, spiny leaves. Good for hedging. H 6m (20ft) S 5m (16ft).
Aspect: sun or semi-shade
Hardiness: ❀❀❀ Zones: 7–8

Ilex aquifolium 'Argentea Marginata' (syn. I. aquifolium 'Argentea Variegata') (female form)

Thick and spiny, glossy, silver-edged, dark green leaves emerge pink-tinged. Brilliant red berries are produced *en masse* in autumn and last well into winter. This holly is a useful shrub for urban or coastal gardens as it copes well with pollution and salt-laden air. Good for hedging. H 14m (46ft) S 5m (16ft).
Aspect: sun or semi-shade
Hardiness: ❀❀❀ Zones 6–10

Ilex aquifolium 'Ferox Argentea' (male form)

A slow-growing upright shrub with cream-edged, leathery, dark green leaves that are covered with spines. No berries. H 8m (26ft) S 4m (13ft).
Aspect: sun or semi-shade
Hardiness: ❀❀❀ Zones: 7–8

Ilex aquifolium 'Golden Queen' (syn. I. aquifolium 'Aurea Regina') (male form)

A fruitless male variety of common English holly with spiny-edged dark green leaves that are decoratively splashed with gold. H 10m (33ft) S 6m (20ft).
Aspect: sun or semi-shade
Hardiness: ❀❀❀ Zones: 7–8

Ilex aquifolium 'J.C. van Tol' (female form)

The lustrous, dark green leaves on dark purple stems are almost prickle-free. Masses of bright red berries are produced from autumn and into winter. Good for hedging. H 6m (20ft) S 4m (13ft).
Aspect: sun or semi-shade
Hardiness: ❀❀❀ Zones: 7–8

Ilex aquifolium 'Silver Queen' (syn. I. aquifolium 'Silver King') (male form)

This slow-growing male variety of holly carries cream-edged, spiny, dark green leaves that emerge pink-tinged on purple stems. It does not produce berries. Good for a large pot. H 10m (33ft) S 4m (13ft).
Aspect: sun or semi-shade
Hardiness: ❀❀❀ Zones: 7–8

Ilex 'J. C. van Tol'

Indigofera amblyantha

Itea ilicifolia

INDIGOFERA

A huge genus of over 700 species, including the exotic deciduous shrubs featured here, valued for their sprays of pink, pea-like late-summer flowers. Excellent choice for growing as a wall shrub. It is very late coming into leaf and so is ideal for under-planting with spring-flowering bulbs and bedding or pairing it with an early flowering climber.

Cultivation Grow in a moisture-retentive, well-drained soil that is reasonably fertile in full sun.

Pruning No routine pruning is necessary. Frost-damaged growth should be removed in spring. If grown as a wall shrub, prune back new growth from the established framework by about two-thirds in mid-spring to late spring.

Propagation Take softwood cuttings in mid-spring or semi-ripe cuttings in mid-summer.

Indigofera amblyantha

Delicate-looking deciduous shrub with light green leaflets. Slender, arching flower-spikes of pea-like, shrimp-pink flowers are produced from mid-summer to early autumn. H 2m (6ft) S 2.5m (8ft).
Aspect: sun
Hardiness: ✿✿✿ Zones: 7–8

Indigofera heterantha (syn. I. gerardiana)

A spreading shrub with delicate-looking light green leaflets that provide a foil for the dense flower-spikes of pea-like,

purplish-pink flowers from early summer to early autumn. H 2.5m (8ft) S 2.5m (8ft).
Aspect: sun
Hardiness: ✿✿✿ Zones: 7–8

ITEA

A genus of some 10 species grown for its handsome foliage and dramatic catkin-like late-summer flowers. It is a useful shrub for growing against sheltered walls and fences. It can also be grown in a large, permanent container, but you will need to wrap up both the top-growth and the container during the winter in colder gardens.

Cultivation Grow in a moisture-retentive, well-drained soil that is reasonably fertile in full sun, but sheltered from cold winds.

Pruning No routine pruning is necessary. Any frost-damaged growth should be removed in spring.

Propagation Take semi-ripe cuttings in mid-summer.

Itea ilicifolia

This shrub has lustrous, dark green, holly-like leaves that provide the perfect backdrop for the 30cm- (12in-) long catkins of vanilla-scented, greenish-white flowers borne throughout late summer and early autumn. Although the shrub is frost hardy, it will require siting where it will get the protection of a sunny wall or fence in colder areas. H 5m (16ft) S 3m (10ft).
Aspect: sun
Hardiness: ✿✿ Zone: 9

JASMINUM
Jasmine

A large genus of over 200 species, including the useful wall shrubs featured here, grown for their fragrant yellow flowers. An excellent choice for providing winter colour near to a well-used entrance or path. It can be allowed to sprawl over banks, or be trained up walls and fences where space is limited.

Cultivation Grow in a well-drained soil that is reasonably fertile in full sun or dappled shade.

Pruning Keep established plants in good shape by cutting back one stem in three to near ground level in mid-spring, starting with the oldest stems.

Propagation Take semi-ripe cuttings in mid-summer. Layer suitable stems in early autumn.

Jasminum humile 'Revolutum' (syn. J. reevesii)

A semi-evergreen bushy, spreading shrub with bright green leaves that is exceptionally long-flowering, producing its pretty yellow fragrant flowers in succession from late spring to early autumn. H 2.5m (8ft)

S 3m (10ft).
Aspect: sun or semi-shade
Hardiness: ✿✿ Zone: 9

Jasminum nudiflorum
Winter jasmine

A popular deciduous shrub with bright green arching shoots that are decorated by scented yellow trumpet flowers from late autumn to late winter before the dark green leaves emerge in spring. H 3m (10ft) S 3m (10ft).
Aspect: sun or semi-shade
Hardiness: ✿✿✿ Zones: 7–8

JUSTICIA

A huge genus of over 400 species, including the tender evergreen shrub featured here, they are grown for their exotic-looking, late-summer flowers. This is an ideal, flamboyant border shrub in mild gardens or can be grown as a conservatory or greenhouse exotic in colder areas.

Cultivation In the garden, grow in a moisture-retentive, well-drained garden soil that is reasonably fertile in dappled shade, but protected from cold winds. In containers, grow in a soil-based compost (soil mix). Feed every

Jasminum nudiflorum

Justicia carnea

month throughout the growing season and water as necessary. Move to a warm spot undercover when the temperature falls below 7°C (45°F) and water sparingly during the winter.
Pruning No routine pruning is required. Pinch out the growing tips of shoots to keep the shrub compact.
Propagation Take softwood cuttings in late spring or semi-ripe cuttings in mid-summer.

Justicia carnea (syn. *Jacobinia carnea*, *Justicia pohliana*)
Flamingo plant
A stiffly branching evergreen shrub with leathery green leaves and flamboyant conical clusters of tubular, lipped, rose-pink flowers from mid-summer to early autumn. H 2m (6ft) S 1m (3ft).
Aspect: semi-shade
Hardiness: tender Zone: 10+

KALMIA

This genus contains around five species, including the evergreen shrubs featured here, grown for their bright pink early summer flowers. An excellent seasonal focal point and border filler if you can provide the right growing conditions. Elsewhere, they can be grown in larger, permanent containers.
Cultivation In the garden, grow in a moisture-retentive, well-drained acid soil in sun or dappled shade. In containers, grow in ericaceous compost (soil mix). Feed monthly during the growing season and water as and when necessary.

Pruning No routine pruning is required. Neglected shrubs can be smartened up and reduced in size by cutting back one stem in three to near ground level in mid-spring, starting with the oldest stems first.
Propagation Take softwood cuttings in late spring or semi-ripe cuttings in mid-summer. Suitable shoots can be layered in mid-spring.

Kalmia angustifolia f. rubra
This mound-forming, evergreen shrub has dark green leaves and is covered in clusters of dark rosy-red, saucer-shaped flowers that appear throughout early summer. H 60cm (24in) S 150cm (60in).
Aspect: sun or semi-shade
Hardiness: ✳✳✳ Zones: 7–8

Kalmia latifolia 'Ostbo Red'
Clusters of bright red buds open to reveal pale-pink saucer-shaped flowers from late spring to mid-summer on this mound-forming evergreen shrub with dark green leaves. H 3m (10ft) S 3m (10ft).
Aspect: sun or semi-shade
Hardiness: ✳✳✳ Zones: 7–8

KERRIA

A genus of just one species of deciduous suckering shrubs that bear golden-yellow late-spring flowers. Easy to grow, it is an ideal choice for the first-time gardener and is ideal for filling gaps at the back of a border.
Cultivation Grow in well-drained

Kalmia latifolia

soil that is reasonably fertile in sun or dappled shade.
Pruning You can encourage a continuous supply of flowering shoots by cutting back one stem in three to near ground level in early summer, starting with the oldest stems. Remove any all-green reverted shoots on variegated varieties as soon as they are noticed.
Propagation Take hardwood cuttings in late autumn. Rooted suckers can be separated in mid-spring.

Kerria japonica 'Golden Guinea'
Masses of large, single, golden-yellow flowers are produced in succession on graceful arching stems during early spring and mid-spring on this upright shrub. H 2m (6ft) S 2.5m (8ft).
Aspect: sun or semi-shade
Hardiness: ✳✳✳ Zones: 7–8

Kerria japonica 'Picta' (syn. *K. japonica* 'Variegata')
The sharply toothed cream-and-green variegated foliage on this compact and less invasive shrub is a good choice for the smaller garden. Single golden yellow flowers are produced during early spring and mid-spring. H 1m (3ft) S 1.5m (5ft).
Aspect: sun or semi-shade
Hardiness: ✳✳✳ Zones: 7–8

Kerria japonica 'Pleniflora'
Pompon-like, double, golden-yellow early spring flowers are produced in succession during

Kerria japonica 'Golden Guinea'

Kolkwitzia amabilis 'Pink Cloud'

early spring and mid-spring on graceful arching stems with sharply toothed green leaves. Good wall shrub. H 3m (10ft) S 3m (10ft).
Aspect: sun or semi-shade
Hardiness: ✳✳✳ Zones: 7–8

KOLKWITZIA

A genus of just one species of deciduous suckering shrubs that bear masses of bell-shaped pink early summer flowers. It is an undemanding shrub that provides a useful splash of late spring colour when planted in a sunny border. It can also be used as a filler shrub in a mixed border or planted to grow up against walls and fences.
Cultivation Grow in any well-drained soil that is reasonably fertile in sun.
Pruning Encourage a continuous supply of flowering shoots by cutting back one stem in three to near ground level in early summer, starting with the oldest stems first.
Propagation Take semi-ripe cuttings in late summer. Rooted suckers can be separated in mid-spring.

Kolkwitzia amabilis '**Pink Cloud**'
Masses of dark pink flowers are produced on arching stems during late spring and early summer. They appear against a backdrop of pointed dark green leaves that turn yellow in autumn. H 4m (13ft) S 3m (10ft).
Aspect: sun
Hardiness: ✳✳✳ Zones: 7–8

Lantana camara

LANTANA

This genus of about 150 species includes the long-flowering evergreen shrub featured here that is loved by butterflies and other beneficial insects. Ideal for growing as a specimen or in a sunny border, or in a large container in a heated conservatory or greenhouse in cold areas.
Cultivation In the garden, grow in any moisture-retentive, well-drained garden soil that is reasonably fertile and in full sun. In containers, grow in a soil-based compost (soil mix). Feed every month throughout the growing season and water as necessary. Move to a warm spot under cover when the temperature falls below 10°C (50°F) and water sparingly during the winter.
Pruning No routine pruning is necessary. Any damaged growth should be removed in spring. In the conservatory or greenhouse, prune back new growth on established plants to 10cm (4in) of the permanent framework during late winter.
Propagation Take semi-ripe cuttings in mid-summer.

Lantana camara
The attractively wrinkled dark green leaves of this tender evergreen shrub provide the perfect foil for clusters of vibrant flowers borne from late spring to late autumn in different colours ranging from white to pink. H 2m (6ft) S 2m (6ft).
Named varieties: 'Fabiola', pink and yellow flowers. H 2m (6ft)

S 2m (6ft). 'Goldmine' (syn. 'Mine d'Or'), bright yellow flowers. H 2m (6ft) S 2m (6ft). 'Radiation', red and orange flowers. H 2m (6ft) S 2m (6ft). 'Snow White', pure white flowers. H 2m (6ft) S 2m (6ft).
Aspect: sun
Hardiness: tender Zone: 10

LAVANDULA
Lavender
A genus of over 20 species, including the popular long-flowering, mostly fragrant and nectar-rich evergreen shrubs with aromatic foliage featured here. Lavender makes a useful specimen plant on the patio or in pots. The more compact varieties also make excellent low hedges. In the border, plant in groups of three or five for impact, although larger varieties can be used as single specimens. The flowers can also be used to make pot pouris.
Cultivation In the garden, grow in any well-drained garden soil that is reasonably fertile and in full sun. In colder regions, grow less hardy varieties in a sheltered position, protected from cold winds and excessive wet. In containers, grow in a soil-based compost (soil mix). Feed monthly throughout the growing season and water as necessary.
Pruning Trim off any flowering stems as they fade. Encourage bushy growth by trimming lightly before the new growth appears in the spring. Be careful not to cut back into old wood. Trim hedges lightly during early spring or mid-

spring to maintain shape.
Propagation Take semi-ripe cuttings in early autumn.

Lavandula angustifolia
Very fragrant purple flowers are produced in dense spikes from mid-summer to early autumn above a mound of grey-green aromatic foliage. Excellent for hedging and pot pourri. H 1m (3ft) S 1.2m (4ft).
Named varieties: 'Hidcote', dark violet flowers. H 60cm (24in) S 75cm (30in). 'Hidcote Pink', pale pink flowers. H 60cm (24in) S 75cm (30in). 'Lady', mauve-blue flowers. H 25cm (10in) S 25cm (10in). 'Loddon Pink', soft pink flowers. H 45cm (18in) S 60cm (24in). 'Munstead', purplish-blue flowers. H 45cm (18in) S 60cm (24in). 'Nana Alba', white flowers. H 30cm (12in) S 30cm (12in). 'Rosea', rose-pink flowers. H 75cm (30in) S 75cm (30in). 'Royal Purple', bluish-purple flowers. H 75cm (30in) S 75cm (30in).
Aspect: sun
Hardiness: ✳✳✳ Zones: 7–8

Lavandula 'Fathead'
French lavender
A recent introduction with very broad, almost rounded, midnight-purple flower-heads from late spring to mid-summer each topped by plum-purple wing-like bracts. Borderline hardy.
H 40cm (16in) S 40cm (16in).
Aspect: sun
Hardiness: ✳✳✳ Zones: 7–8

Lavandula stoechas

Lavandula 'Helmsdale'
French lavender
Plump spikes of fragrant dark purple flowers topped by purple wing-like bracts are produced from late spring to mid-summer above a compact mound of grey-green aromatic foliage. Borderline hardy. H 60cm (24in) S 60cm (24in).
Aspect: sun
Hardiness: ✳✳✳ Zones: 7–8

Lavandula x intermedia 'Grappenhall'
Slightly fragrant purplish-blue flowers appear on slender spikes from mid-summer to late summer above large grey-green, aromatic leaves. It is only frost hardy, so it is best grown in a container and moved indoors in cold areas.
H 1m (3ft) S 1.5m (5ft).
Aspect: sun
Hardiness: ✳✳ Zones: 9

Lavandula x intermedia 'Grosso'
Dense spikes of fragrant, deep violet flowers on slender stems are produced *en masse* from mid-summer to early autumn above a mound of grey-green aromatic foliage. H 30cm (12in) S 40cm (16in).
Aspect: sun
Hardiness: ✳✳✳

Lavandula stoechas 'Kew Red'
French lavender
A recent introduction with plump, fragrant, cerise-pink flower-heads that are borne from early summer to late summer, topped by pale pink wing-like bracts. Borderline

Lavandula angustifolia

hardy. H 60cm (24in) S 60cm (24in).
Aspect: sun
Hardiness: ✿✿✿ Zones: 7–8

Lavandula stoechas 'Papillon'
French lavender
Tufted spikes of lavender-purple flowers, with long, wing-like bracts, are produced during early summer and mid-summer above a mound of grey-green aromatic foliage. Borderline hardy. H 60cm (24in) S 60cm (24in).
Aspect: sun
Hardiness: ✿✿✿ Zones: 7–8

Lavandula stoechas 'Rocky Road'
French lavender
A new variety that bears goblet-shaped purple flower-spikes topped by large, pale-violet, wing-like bracts from mid-summer to late summer above a mound of grey-green aromatic foliage. Borderline hardy.
H 50cm (20in) S 50cm (20in).
Aspect: sun
Hardiness: ✿✿✿ Zones: 7–8

Lavandula stoechas 'Snowman'
French lavender
Slender spikes of white flowers, topped by snow-white wing-like bracts throughout early summer and mid-summer above a mound of grey-green aromatic foliage. Only frost hardy, so best grown in a pot and moved indoors in cold areas. H 60cm (24in) S 60cm (24in).
Aspect: sun
Hardiness: ✿✿ Zones: 7–8

LAVATERA
A genus of about 25 species, including the fast-growing, deciduous summer-flowering shrubs featured here, grown for their speed of growth and eye-catching, hibiscus-like, trumpet-shaped flowers. Quick to establish and flowering well, they are ideal for new borders. They also make useful gap fillers.
Cultivation Grow in any well-drained garden soil (preferably sandy) that is reasonably fertile and in full sun. In colder regions, protect from cold winds.
Pruning For best flowering, cut back all stems to within a few centimetres of ground level in mid-spring. Remove reverted shoots with the wrong colour flowers.
Propagation Take semi-ripe cuttings in mid-summer. Take hardwood cuttings in late autumn.

Lavatera x clementii 'Barnsley'
Large white blooms, each with a red eye, are produced from early summer to early autumn. The blooms gracefully age to pale pink. H 2m (6ft) S 2m (6ft).
Aspect: sun
Hardiness: ✿✿✿ Zones: 7–8

Lavatera x clementii 'Burgundy Wine'
A succession of dark pink flowers that are attractively veined are produced from early summer to early autumn on this compact variety with dark foliage.
H 1.5m (5ft) S 1.5m (5ft).
Aspect: sun
Hardiness: ✿✿✿ Zones: 7–8

Lavatera x clementii 'Kew Rose'
A succession of attractively veined, frilly, dark pink blooms appear from early summer to early autumn. H 2m (6ft) S 2m (6ft).
Aspect: sun
Hardiness: ✿✿✿ Zones: 7–8

Lavatera olbia 'Rosea' (syn. *L. x clementii* 'Rosea')
A succession of large dark pink blooms are produced from early summer to early autumn on this vigorous-growing variety. H 2m (6ft) S 2m (6ft).
Aspect: sun
Hardiness: ✿✿✿ Zones: 7–8

Lavatera

LEPTOSPERMUM
A genus of about 80 species, including the slightly tender, early summer flowering shrub featured here. It makes a good back-of-the-border seasonal focal point.
Cultivation In the garden, grow in any well-drained garden soil that is reasonably fertile and in full sun or dappled shade. In colder regions, grow in pots of soil-based mix. Feed monthly and water as necessary during the growing season. Before frosts, move under cover, stop feeding and water sparingly in winter.
Pruning No routine pruning is required.
Propagation Take semi-ripe cuttings in mid-summer.

Leptospermum scoparium 'Red Damask'
A compact shrub with arching stems and narrow, pointed, aromatic, green leaves. During late spring and early summer it is covered in masses of double, dark red flowers. H 3m (10ft) S 3m (10ft).
Aspect: sun or semi-shade
Hardiness: ✿ Zone: 10

LEUCOTHOE
A genus of about 50 species, including the versatile evergreen shrub featured here, that are grown for their eye-catching foliage and clusters of pretty, urn-shaped spring flowers. They are ideal for a shady shrub or mixed border that offers suitable growing conditions. It can also be used as a deep

Leptospermum

Leucothoe fontanesiana 'Rainbow'

groundcover plant between deciduous trees in a woodland-edge planting.
Cultivation Grow in any moisture-retentive, well-drained acid soil in deep or dappled shade. Add plenty of organic matter (but not alkaline mushroom compost/soil mix) to the soil before planting.
Pruning To get the best foliage displays and maintain a compact shape, cut back one stem in three to near ground level during mid-spring, starting with the oldest stems first.
Propagation Layer low branches in early spring or take semi-ripe cuttings in late summer.

Leucothoe fontanesiana 'Rainbow'
A spectacular shrub with glossy, lance-shaped, dark green variegated foliage splashed with cream and pink. A bonus of white, urn-shaped flowers are produced in clusters during mid-spring and late spring.
H 1.5m (5ft) S 2m (6ft).
Aspect: semi-shade or deep shade
Hardiness: ✿✿✿ Zones: 7–8

Leucothoe fontanesiana 'Scarletta'
Although first emerging red-purple, the dark evergreen foliage turns bronze during the winter. A bonus of white, urn-shaped flowers are produced in clusters during early spring and mid-spring. H 150cm (60in) S 40cm (16in).
Aspect: semi-shade or deep shade
Hardiness: ✿✿✿

Leycesteria formosa

Ligustrum lucidum 'Tricolor'

LEYCESTERIA

A genus of about five species, including the fast-growing and suckering deciduous shrub featured here, that is grown for its unusual pendent, Chinese-lantern-shaped bracts, tipped with summer flowers, followed by autumn berries. A useful shrub for extending the season of interest in the garden and for filling a space at the back of a border.

Cultivation Grow in any well-drained garden soil that is reasonably fertile and site in full sun or dappled shade. In colder regions, these shrubs need to be protected from cold winds. In addition, you will need to cover its roots with a deep insulating mulch, which should be applied during the autumn.

Pruning For best flowering performance, cut back one stem in three to near ground level during mid-spring, starting with the oldest stems.

Propagation Take softwood cuttings in early summer or take hardwood cuttings in late autumn.

Leycesteria formosa
Himalayan honeysuckle
Long-lasting clusters of pendent, wine-coloured bracts, tipped with white flowers, are produced in succession from mid-summer to early autumn, followed by eye-catching purple berries. Borderline hardy. H 2m (6ft) S 2m (6ft).
Aspect: sun or semi-shade
Hardiness: ✽✽✽ Zones: 7–8

LIGUSTRUM
Privet

This genus of about 50 species includes the deciduous and evergreen shrubs featured here, grown for their foliage and dense growing habit. These shrubs are very useful back-of-the-border fillers and make very popular hedging plants.

Cultivation Grow in any well-drained garden soil that is reasonably fertile and in full sun or dappled shade. However, for best foliage coloration, grow in full sun.

Pruning No routine pruning is necessary. Clip occasionally to maintain the plant's shape or to keep it compact. Neglected or overgrown plants can be rejuvenated by cutting back all the stems to within 10cm (4in) of ground level. All-green reverted shoots on variegated varieties should be removed completely when they are noticed. Trim hedges into shape in late spring and early autumn.

Propagation Take semi-ripe cuttings in mid-summer or take hardwood cuttings in late autumn.

Ligustrum japonicam 'Rotundifolium'
A compact and slow-growing evergreen with glossy, dark green, leathery leaves. Insignificant white flowers are produced in mid-summer and late summer. H 1.5m (5ft) S 1m (3ft).
Aspect: sun or semi-shade
Hardiness: ✽✽✽ Zones: 7–8

Ligustrum lucidum 'Excelsum Superbum'
A variegated evergreen with cream-edged, bright green leaves. Insignificant white flowers are produced in late summer and early autumn. H 10m (33ft) S 10m (33ft).
Aspect: sun or semi-shade
Hardiness: ✽✽✽ Zones: 7–8

Ligustrum lucidum 'Tricolor'
A variegated evergreen with white-edged, grey-green leaves that emerge pink-tinged. Insignificant white flowers are produced in late summer and early autumn.
H 10m (33ft) S 10m (33ft).
Aspect: sun or semi-shade
Hardiness: ✽✽✽ Zones: 7–8

Ligustrum ovalifolium
The glossy, dark green, evergreen foliage of the oval leaf privet makes an excellent hedge in urban areas as it is particularly pollution-tolerant. Insignificant white flowers are produced in mid-summer and late summer, followed by shiny black berries. H 4m (13ft) S 4m (13ft).
Aspect: sun or semi-shade
Hardiness: ✽✽✽ Zones: 7–8

Ligustrum ovalifolium 'Aureum' (syn. *L. ovalifolium* 'Aureomarginatum')
Golden privet
The yellow-margined, broad green leaves are retained all winter in all but the coldest of gardens. Makes a useful hedge in urban areas as it is particularly pollution-tolerant. Insignificant white flowers are produced in mid-summer and late summer, followed by shiny black berries. H 4m (13ft) S 4m (13ft).
Aspect: sun or semi-shade
Hardiness: ✽✽✽ Zones: 7–8

LONICERA
A varied genus of over 180 species, including the deciduous and evergreen shrubs featured here, grown for either its fragrant winter flowers or colourful evergreen leaves. Plant winter-flowering varieties with fragrant blooms next to much-used paths and sheltered entrances, where they will be appreciated most. Evergreen types make excellent border fillers or edging plants and can be trimmed into low hedges.

Cultivation Grow in any well-drained garden soil that is

Lonicera nitida 'Baggesen's Gold'

reasonably fertile and in full sun or dappled shade. For best foliage coloration, grow in full sun.
Pruning Flowering shrubby honeysuckles require no routine pruning. Neglected specimens can be rejuvenated by cutting back one stem in three to near ground level after flowering, starting with the oldest stems. Small-leaved, evergreen varieties need to be trimmed in mid-spring to maintain a compact shape.
Propagation Take semi-ripe cuttings in mid-summer or take hardwood cuttings in late autumn.

Lonicera fragrantissima
A bushy, semi-evergreen shrub that bears scented, creamy-white flowers on naked stems during mild spells in mid-winter and early spring. Plant next to an entrance or path to appreciate its fragrant winter flowers. H 2m (6ft) S 3m (10ft).
Aspect: sun or semi-shade
Hardiness: ❋❋❋ Zones: 7–8

Lonicera nitida 'Baggesen's Gold'
Arching shoots are covered in masses of tiny golden leaves on this fast-growing, bushy evergreen. Insignificant, creamy-white flowers are produced in mid-spring. Ideal for trimming into a low hedge or garden topiary. H 1.5m (5ft) S 1.5m (5ft).
Aspect: sun or semi-shade
Hardiness: ❋❋❋ Zones: 7–8

Lonicera pileata
A low-growing, spreading, dense, evergreen shrub with glossy, dark green leaves. It also makes an excellent ground cover plant in urban areas as it is very pollution-tolerant. Insignificant, creamy-white flowers are produced in late spring followed by purple berries. H 60cm (24in) S 250cm (96in).
Aspect: sun or semi-shade
Hardiness: ❋❋❋ Zones: 7–8

Lonicera x purpusii 'Winter Beauty'
The bare branches of this shrubby honeysuckle carry clusters of highly fragrant, creamy-white flowers from early winter to early spring. Plant next to an entrance or path to appreciate its fragrant winter flowers. H 2m (6ft) S 2.5m (8ft).
Aspect: sun or semi-shade
Hardiness: ❋❋❋ Zones: 7–8

MAGNOLIA
A genus of about 125 species, including the spectacular early-flowering deciduous shrubs featured here, many of which are compact enough for the smallest of gardens. Although they are grown for their flamboyant floral displays in spring, many varieties look good at other times – offering handsome foliage, autumn tints and attractive winter buds. Grow as seasonal focal points anywhere in the garden, even in large, permanent containers.
Cultivation In the garden, grow in well-drained garden neutral to acid soil that doesn't dry out in summer and is reasonably fertile. Star magnolias can tolerate slightly alkaline soils. All will grow in sun or partial shade where they are sheltered from cold winds. In containers, grow in a soil-based mix. Feed every fortnight throughout the growing season and water as necessary.
Pruning No routine pruning necessary.
Propagation Layer low-growing shoots in mid-spring.

Magnolia 'Heaven Scent'
An upright, deciduous magnolia that bears scented, goblet-shaped, pale pink flowers with white inside from mid-spring to early

Magnolia stellata

summer. This later flowering variety avoids most frosts. H 10m (33ft) S 10m (33ft).
Aspect: sun or semi-shade
Hardiness: ❋❋❋ Zones: 7–8

Magnolia x loebneri 'Leonard Messel'
A large, deciduous shrub with mid-green leaves that bears deep pink buds that open during mid-spring to reveal pale pink, star-shaped flowers. H 8m (26ft) S 8m (26ft).
Aspect: sun or semi-shade
Hardiness: ❋❋❋ Zones: 7–8

Magnolia x soulangeana
A spreading deciduous shrub that has large dark green leaves bearing white to rose-pink flowers on branches during mid-spring and late spring as the leaves start to emerge. H 6m (20ft) S 6m (20ft).

Named varieties: 'Alba' (syn. *M. x soulangeana* 'Alba Superba'), large, fragrant, white flowers that are pink-flushed at the base. H 6m (20ft) S 6m (20ft). 'Lennei', dark pinkish-purple, goblet-shaped flowers. H 6m (20ft) S 6m (20ft).
Aspect: sun or semi-shade
Hardiness: ❋❋❋ Zones: 7–8

Magnolia stellata
Star magnolia
Silky buds open on bare branches during early spring and mid-spring to reveal lightly scented, white, star-shaped flowers. A compact, bushy, deciduous shrub that is ideal for small gardens. H 3m (10ft) S 3m (10ft).
Named varieties: 'Rosea', rose-pink star-shaped flowers. H 3m (10ft) S 4m (13ft). 'Royal Star', pink-flushed buds open into white, star-shaped flowers. H 3m (10ft) S 4m (13ft). 'Waterlily', white, waterlily-like flowers. H 3m (10ft) S 4m (13ft).
Aspect: sun or semi-shade
Hardiness: ❋❋❋ Zones: 7–8

Magnolia 'Susan'
A bushy, upright shrub, 'Susan' produces beautiful dark red flowering buds that open from mid-spring to early summer to reveal slim, goblet-shaped, fragrant, purple blooms with slightly twisted petals. It makes a glorious deciduous magnolia for a small garden with acidic soil. H 4m (13ft) S 3m (10ft).
Aspect: sun or semi-shade
Hardiness: ❋❋❋ Zones: 7–8

Magnolia 'Susan'

Mahonia aquifolium 'Apollo'

MAHONIA

This genus of about 70 species includes the winter-flowering evergreen shrubs featured here. They make useful architectural specimens and border fillers to provide winter interest or can be pruned to form ground cover.
Cultivation Grow in any moisture-retentive, well-drained garden soil that is reasonably fertile. Position shrub in full sun or dappled shade.
Pruning No routine pruning is required for this shrub. However, straggly plants can be renovated by pruning back hard in mid-spring. Plants grown for ground cover should be cut back hard in mid-spring.
Propagation Take semi-ripe cuttings in late summer.

Mahonia aquifolium 'Apollo'

A compact shrub that bears masses of large, fragrant, yellow flowers on densely packed spikes from late winter to mid-spring. The holly-like leaves are tinged red in winter. A good ground cover plant between deciduous trees in a woodland-edge planting. H 1m (3ft) S 1m (3ft).
Aspect: sun or semi-shade
Hardiness: ❈❈❈ Zones: 7–8

Mahonia japonica Bealei Group

Handsome whorls of blue-green, holly-like leaves provide year-round interest topped by upright sprays of fragrant, pale yellow flowers from early winter to early spring. H 2m (6ft) S 3m (10ft).
Aspect: sun or semi-shade
Hardiness: ❈❈❈ Zones: 7–8

Mahonia x *media* 'Buckland'

Long, arching, fragrant sprays of bright yellow flowers are produced from early winter to mid-spring above handsome evergreen holly-like leaves. H 5m (16ft) S 4m (13ft).
Aspect: sun or semi-shade
Hardiness: ❈❈❈ Zones: 7–8

Mahonia x *media* 'Charity'

Upright spreading sprays of fragrant lemon-yellow flowers are produced from late autumn to early spring, above whorls of dark green holly-like foliage. H 5m (15ft) S 4m (12ft).
Aspect: sun or semi-shade
Hardiness: ❈❈❈ Zones: 7–8

Mahonia x *media* 'Lionel Fortescue'

Dense cluster of scented bright yellow flowers are produced from late autumn to early spring on upright spikes above dark green, holly-like leaves. H 5m (16ft) S 4m (13ft).
Aspect: sun or semi-shade
Hardiness: ❈❈❈ Zones: 7–8

MYRTUS
Myrtle

A genus of just two species, including the common myrtle featured here, that are grown for their sweetly scented summer flowers and aromatic, glossy, evergreen foliage. It is a useful plant for a mixed or shrub border, but it can also make an unusual, informal flowering hedge.
Cultivation Grow in any moisture-retentive, well-drained garden soil that is reasonably fertile and in full sun. Grow against a warm, sunny wall in colder areas. Mulch in spring and insulate from cold, drying winds in winter.
Pruning No routine pruning is required. Any frost-damaged growth should be removed in spring.
Propagation Take semi-ripe cuttings in late summer.

Myrtus communis

A handsome upright and bushy evergreen shrub with very aromatic leaves. It bears fragrant, cup-shaped white flowers, each with prominent fluffy tufts of stamens in the centre, during

mid-summer and late summer, followed by purple-black berries. H 3m (10ft) S 3m (10ft).
Named varieties: subsp *tarentina* (syn. *M.* 'Jenny Reitenbach', *M.* 'Microphylla', *M.* 'Nana'), a compact variety with smaller leaves and flowers, followed by white berries. H 1.5m (5ft) S 1.5m (5ft).
Aspect: sun
Hardiness: ❈❈ Zones: 7–8

NANDINA

A genus of just one species of evergreen shrubs, grown for their handsome foliage and long-lasting autumn tints and berries. This bamboo lookalike is an excellent choice for winter interest.
Cultivation Grow in any moisture-retentive, well-drained garden soil that is reasonably fertile and in full sun, but sheltered from cold winds. Grow against a warm, sunny wall in colder areas.
Pruning No routine pruning is required. Neglected specimens can be rejuvenated by cutting back one stem in three to near ground level in mid-spring, starting with the oldest stems.
Propagation Divide the clump in early spring as you would a perennial, or take semi-ripe cuttings in mid-summer.

Nandina domestica 'Fire Power'
Heavenly bamboo

The handsome, bamboo-like leaves of this compact evergreen

Myrtus communis

Mahonia x *media* 'Charity'

Nandina domestica 'Fire Power'

take on fiery shades of orange and red in autumn. Clusters of tiny starry flowers are produced in mid-summer, followed by arching sprays of long-lasting bright red fruit. H 45cm (18in) S 60cm (24in).
Aspect: sun
Hardiness: ✿✿ Zones: 7–8

NERIUM
Oleander
A genus of just two species of tender evergreen flowering shrubs, grown for their colourful late summer blooms. In warm regions they make wonderful freestanding specimens, are valuable border fillers and can be grown as an informal flowering hedge. However, elsewhere they are best grown as wall shrubs where there are no winter frosts. In colder regions they can be planted in containers on the patio and moved undercover when the temperature threatens to fall below 5°C (41°F).
Cultivation Grow in any moisture-retentive, well-drained, reasonably fertile soil in full sun. Shelter from cold winds. In frost-prone areas, grow in pots and protect. Use a soil-based compost (soil mix), feed monthly and water as necessary. Stop feeding and water sparingly in winter.
Pruning Cut back flowering shoots by half as the flowers fade. Cut back non-flowering shoots to 10cm (4in) of the framework.
Propagation Air layer in mid-spring or take semi-ripe cuttings in mid-summer.

Nerium oleander
Rose bay
A spreading evergreen shrub with slender grey-green leaves that bears clusters of pink, red or white tubular flowers from early summer to mid-autumn. H 3m (10ft) S 2m (6ft).
Aspect: sun
Hardiness: tender Zones: 10+

OLEARIA
Daisy bush
This genus of about 130 species includes the evergreen summer-flowering shrubs featured here. All of those mentioned make useful border fillers and good hedges or windbreaks for coastal gardens, as they can tolerate strong winds and salt-laden air.
Cultivation These shrubs can be grown in any reasonably well-drained garden soil in full sun, but they need sheltering from cold winds.
Pruning No routine pruning is necessary. Cut back any dead shoots in mid-spring.
Propagation Take semi-ripe cuttings in mid-summer.

Olearia x haastii
During mid-summer and late summer masses of yellow-centred daisy-like flowers smother the branches of this dense, compact evergreen with glossy dark green leaves. H 2m (6ft) S 3m (10ft).
Aspect: sun
Hardiness: ✿✿✿ Zones: 7–8

Nerium oleander

Olearia ilicifolia
Mountain holly
A spreading bushy shrub with leathery, holly-like, grey-green leaves, that is covered in scented daisy-like white flowers during early summer. Borderline hardy. H 3m (10ft) S 3m (10ft).
Aspect: sun
Hardiness: ✿✿✿ Zones: 7–8

Olearia macrodonta
A vigorous upright shrub with holly-like glossy dark green leaves that are silvery underneath. During mid-summer and late summer the branches are smothered in masses of red-centred, daisy-like white flowers. Borderline hardy. H 6m (20ft) S 5m (16ft).
Aspect: sun
Hardiness: ✿✿✿ Zones: 7–8

OSMANTHUS
(syn. x Osmarea)
This genus of over 15 species, including the featured evergreen summer-flowering shrubs here, are grown for their highly scented, jasmine-like blooms. Plant them next to an entrance or path so that you can appreciate their early summer fragrance. Alternatively, smaller-growing osmanthus can be grown in a permanent container on the patio. They can even be grown as informal flowering hedges and trained as topiary.
Cultivation In the garden, grow in any well-drained garden soil that

Olearia x haastii

Osmanthus heterophyllus 'Tricolor'

is reasonably fertile and in full sun or dappled shade, sheltered from cold winds. When grown in containers, use a soil-based compost (soil mix), feed monthly and water as necessary during the growing season. Stop feeding and water sparingly in winter.
Pruning No routine pruning necessary.
Propagation Take semi-ripe cuttings in mid-summer or layer suitable shoots in mid-spring.

Osmanthus delavayi (syn. Siphonosmanthus delavayi)
A rounded evergreen with lustrous, dark grey-green, sharply toothed leaves covered in masses of scented white jasmine-like flowers during mid-spring and late spring. Good for hedging. H 6m (20ft) S 4m (13ft).
Aspect: sun or semi-shade
Hardiness: ✿✿✿ Zones: 7–8

Osmanthus heterophyllus 'Tricolor' (syn. O. heterophyllus 'Goshiki'
An attractive evergreen with glossy, dark green, holly-like leaves that are a mottled creamy-yellow and pink as they emerge. From mid-summer to early autumn it bears a succession of delicate and fragrant white flowers. Plant in the shelter of a sunny wall in cold areas. Because of its small and compact shape, this shrub makes an excellent container plant. H 1.5m (5ft) S 1m (3ft).
Aspect: sun or semi-shade
Hardiness: ✿✿ Zones: 8–9

Pachysandra terminalis

Paeonia delavayi

PACHYSANDRA

A genus of about five species, including the low-growing, evergreen sub-shrub featured here, grown for their handsome foliage and pretty early summer flowers. It is a useful ground cover plant between shrubs and trees as well as the difficult areas by hedges.
Cultivation Grow in any well-drained garden soil that is reasonably fertile in dappled shade to deep shade.
Pruning No routine pruning is necessary. Rejuvenate neglected plants by cutting back to about 5cm (2in) off the ground in early spring.
Propagation Divide clumps as you would a perennial. Take softwood cuttings in early summer.

Pachysandra terminalis
The handsome, coarsely toothed, glossy dark green leaves of this spreading, evergreen sub-shrub are the perfect foil for the clusters of tiny white flowers produced during late spring and early summer. H 20cm (8in) S indefinite.
Aspect: semi-shade or deep shade
Hardiness: ✳✳✳ Zones: 7–8

PAEONIA
Peony
This genus contains over 30 species, including the woody-stemmed tree peonies featured here, grown for their showy late-spring flowers and attractive foliage. They make a spectacular seasonal focal point in a mixed border or shrubbery.

Cultivation Grow in any moisture-retentive, well-drained garden soil that is reasonably fertile in full sun or dappled shade, but shelter from cold winds and morning sun.
Pruning No routine pruning is necessary. Overgrown plants can be rejuvenated by cutting back one stem in three to near ground level during mid-spring, starting with the oldest stems.
Propagation Take semi-ripe cuttings in mid-summer. Air layer or layer suitable stems in early spring.

Paeonia delavayi
An upright shrub that bears single, cup-shaped, blood-red flowers from mid-spring to early summer above dark green leaves that emerge red-tinged in spring. H 2m (6ft) S 1.2m (4ft).
Aspect: sun or semi-shade
Hardiness: ✳✳✳ Zones: 7–8

Paeonia lutea var. ludlowii (syn P. delavayi var. ludlowii)
The large, bright yellow flowers of this upright tree peony are produced during mid-spring and late spring against lush apple-green foliage that emerges bronze-tinted in spring. H 2.5m (8ft) S 2.5m (8ft).
Aspect: sun or semi-shade
Hardiness: ✳✳✳ Zones: 7–8

Paeonia suffruticosa 'Duchess of Kent'
Tulip-shaped buds open to reveal deep rose-pink, semi-double, cup-shaped flowers. This plant flowers well from a young age.

H 2.2m (7ft) S 2.2m (7ft).
Aspect: sun or semi-shade
Hardiness: ✳✳✳ Zones: 7–8

Paeonia suffruticosa 'Duchess of Marlborough'
This shrub has huge, double, pale pink flowers with crinkle-edged petals that fade to silvery-white at the margins. H 2.2m (7ft) S 2.2m (7ft).
Aspect: sun or semi-shade
Hardiness: ✳✳✳ Zones: 7–8

Paeonia suffruticosa 'Mrs William Kelway'
This shrub has double white flowers with crinkle-edged petals and contrasting yellow anthers in the centre. H 2.2m (7ft) S 2.2m (7ft).
Aspect: sun or semi-shade
Hardiness: ✳✳✳ Zones: 7–8

Paeonia suffruticosa 'Reine Elisabeth'
An upright tree peony with dark green foliage tinged with blue underneath. Bears double, salmon-pink, frilly-edged blooms. H 2.2m (7ft) S 2.2m (7ft).
Aspect: sun or semi-shade
Hardiness: ✳✳✳ Zones: 7–8

PARROTIA
A genus of just one species of deciduous shrub that eventually develops a clear trunk to form a small tree. They are mainly grown for their dramatic, fiery autumn tints, but their handsome foliage, peeling bark and early spring

Parrotia persica

flowers make them year-round specimens for mixed borders, shrubberies or as a seasonal focal point.
Cultivation Grow in a moisture-retentive, well-drained acid soil in sun or dappled shade. Add plenty of organic matter (but not alkaline mushroom compost/soil mix) to the soil before planting. Although it will grow in neutral and even slightly alkaline soils, the autumn colour will not be as good.
Pruning No routine pruning is necessary. Remove damaged or misplaced branches in early spring.
Propagation Sow seed in early autumn or layer a suitable low branch during early autumn.

Parrotia persica
Persian ironwood
Attractive glossy green leaves transform in autumn as they take on fiery autumn tints in shades of amber, crimson, purple and gold. Established plants will produce curious, spidery-looking red flowers on bare stems during late autumn and early winter that complement the attractive peeling bark. H 8m (26ft) S 10m (33ft).
Named varieties: 'Pendula', weeping and compact so suitable for small gardens. H 1.5m (5ft) S 3m (10ft).
Aspect: sun or semi-shade
Hardiness: ✳✳✳ Zones: 7–8

PHILADELPHUS
Mock orange
A genus of about 40 species, including the deciduous shrubs featured here, grown for their orange blossom-scented early summer flowers and attractive foliage. They are also a good choice for town and coastal gardens as they tolerate urban pollution and salt-laden air.
Cultivation Grow in any well-drained garden soil that is reasonably fertile and in full sun or dappled shade.
Pruning For the best flowering, cut out one in three of the stems that have flowered – cutting back to a younger side branch – starting with the oldest stems. The young shoots that did not flower this year will flower next year.

Philadelphus 'Belle Etoile'

Propagation Take semi-ripe cuttings in early summer or take hardwood cuttings in late autumn.

Philadelphus 'Beauclerk'
A stiffly arching deciduous shrub that bears scented, cup-shaped, single white flowers that are flushed pink in the centre during early summer and mid-summer. H 2.5m (8ft) S 2.5m (8ft).
Aspect: sun or semi-shade
Hardiness: ❀❀❀ Zones: 7–8

Philadelphus 'Belle Etoile'
Very fragrant, single, cup-shaped white flowers with contrasting pinky-purple centres are carried throughout early summer and mid-summer on arching branches. H 1.2m (4ft) S 2.5m (8ft).
Aspect: sun or semi-shade
Hardiness: ❀❀❀ Zones: 7–8

Philadelphus coronarius 'Aureus'
Single, fragrant, creamy-white, cup-shaped flowers are carried throughout early summer on upright stems with golden-yellow leaves that become greenish-yellow in summer. Grow in dappled shade. H 2.5m (8ft) S 1.5m (5ft).
Aspect: semi-shade
Hardiness: ❀❀❀ Zones: 7–8

Philadelphus coronarius 'Variegatus'
Pure white, fragrant, cup-shaped flowers are carried throughout early summer on upright stems with white-edged, apple-green variegated foliage.

H 2.5m (8ft) S 2m (6ft).
Aspect: sun or semi-shade
Hardiness: ❀❀❀ Zones: 7–8

Philadelphus x lemoinei 'Lemoinei'
The arching branches of this upright mock orange are covered by masses of very fragrant clusters of single, cup-shaped white flowers throughout early summer and mid-summer. H 1.5m (5ft) S 1.5m (5ft).
Aspect: sun or semi-shade
Hardiness: ❀❀❀ Zones: 7–8

Philadelphus 'Manteau d'Hermine'
Elegantly arching shoots are festooned with very fragrant, double, creamy-white flowers throughout early summer and mid-summer on this compact, bushy, deciduous shrub. An ideal choice for a small garden. H 75cm (30in) S 150cm (60in).
Aspect: sun or semi-shade
Hardiness: ❀❀❀ Zones: 7–8

Philadelphus microphyllus
Single, white, fragrant, flowers are carried in clusters throughout early summer and mid-summer against a backdrop of glossy green leaves on this compact plant. H 1m (3ft) S 1m (3ft).
Aspect: sun or semi-shade
Hardiness: ❀❀❀ Zones: 7–8

Philadelphus 'Virginal'
Fully double, white, fragrant flowers festoon upright branches

throughout early summer and mid-summer on this vigorous mock orange. Its dark green leaves go yellow in autumn. H 3m (10ft) S 2.5m (8ft).
Aspect: sun or semi-shade
Hardiness: ❀❀❀

PHLOMIS
A genus of about 100 species, grown for their unusual tiered summer flowers on upright stems and woolly grey foliage.
Cultivation Grow in any well-drained garden soil that is reasonably fertile and in full sun. Grow in the protection of a sunny wall in colder areas.
Pruning In spring, cut back the previous year's growth to about 10cm (4in) of the ground as new shoots emerge from the base.
Propagation Take softwood cuttings in early summer, or semi-ripe cuttings in early autumn.

Phlomis fruticosa
A spreading evergreen shrub, with sage-like, aromatic, grey-green leaves that throws up vertical spikes that carry whorls of hooded, golden-yellow flowers in tiers throughout early summer and mid-summer. Borderline hardy. H 1m (3ft) S 1.5m (5ft).
Aspect: sun
Hardiness: ❀❀❀ Zones: 7–8

Phlomis italica
Upright spikes carry whorls of hooded lilac-pink flowers during early summer and mid-summer

above this compact evergreen shrub with silvery-grey woolly leaves. H 30cm (12in) S 60cm (24in).
Aspect: sun
Hardiness: ❀❀ Zone: 9

PHOENIX
A genus of over 15 species, including the tender miniature date palm featured here, grown for their handsome foliage. Ideal border plant in milder areas or for an exotic touch to the patio.
Cultivation Grow in a reasonably fertile, moisture-retentive, well-drained soil in full sun. In pots, use a soil-based mix, water regularly and feed monthly in the growing season. Water sparingly in winter. Needs a warm spot if the temperature falls below 10°C (50°F) and water sparingly.
Pruning No routine pruning is necessary.
Propagation Sow seed in mid-spring.

Phoenix roebelenii
Miniature date palm
This stemless palm has narrow, dark green leaflets that are grey-green when young. Mature plants carry clusters of cream flowers in early summer and mid-summer, followed by edible black fruit. Move to a heated greenhouse or conservatory in cold areas (min 10°C/50°F) over winter. H 2m (6ft) S 2.5m (8ft).
Aspect: sun
Hardiness: tender Zones: 10+

Philadelphus 'Manteau d'Hermine'

Phlomis italica

Phoenix roebelenii

Photinia x fraseri 'Birmingham'

PHOTINIA

A genus of about 60 species grown for their colourful new shoots in spring. It is useful for adding much-needed colour to mixed borders and shrubberies early in the year and for providing an attractive foil at other times.
Cultivation Grow in any moisture-retentive, well-drained soil that is reasonably fertile and in full sun. Train against a sheltered, sunny wall in colder areas.
Pruning No routine pruning is necessary. Cut back straggly plants by about one-third to rejuvenate them and encourage more foliage.
Propagation Take semi-ripe cuttings in mid-summer.

Photinia x fraseri 'Birmingham'
Eye-catching purple-red young foliage is the main feature of this handsome evergreen shrub.

Photinia x fraseri 'Red Robin'

Clusters of insignificant white flowers are carried in mid-spring and late spring, followed by red berries. H 5m (16ft) S 5m (16ft).
Aspect: sun
Hardiness: ✿✿ Zone: 9

Photinia x fraseri 'Red Robin'
A compact evergreen shrub with brilliant red glossy young foliage and clusters of insignificant white flowers carried in mid-spring and late spring, followed by red berries. H 5m (16ft) S 5m (16ft).
Aspect: sun
Hardiness: ✿✿ Zone: 9

PHYGELIUS

A genus of just two species, grown for their elegant summer flowers. A good choice for adding late colour in borders.
Cultivation Grow in any reasonably fertile, moisture-retentive, well-drained soil in full sun. Shelter from cold winds and apply a mulch in autumn.
Pruning No routine pruning is necessary. Deadhead for the best flowering displays. In cold areas, cut back to near ground level in early spring.
Propagation Take softwood cuttings in late spring.

Phygelius aequalis 'Yellow Trumpet'
An upright, suckering evergreen shrub that bears clusters of pale creamy-yellow tubular flowers on slender stems from early summer to late summer.

Phygelius x rectus 'Moonraker'

H 90cm (36in) S 90cm (36in).
Aspect: sun
Hardiness: ✿✿ Zone: 9

Phygelius x rectus
Tubular pale red flowers are produced in loose open sprays on the slender stems of this upright, suckering evergreen shrub from early summer to late summer on this shrub. H 1.2m (4ft) S 1.5m (5ft).
Named varieties: 'African Queen', red and orange flowers, H 1m (3ft) S 1.2m (4ft). 'Devil's Tears', red flowers, H 1m (3ft) S 1.2m (4ft). 'Moonraker', cream-coloured flowers, H 1m (3ft) S 1.2m (4ft). 'Pink Elf', pink flowers, H 75cm (30in) S 90cm (36in). 'Salmon Leap', pale orange flowers, H 1.2m (4ft) S 1.5m (5ft).
Aspect: sun
Hardiness: ✿✿ Zone: 9

PIERIS

A genus of over five species, including the evergreen shrubs featured here, grown for their fragrant clusters of lily-of-the-valley-like spring flowers and colourful new foliage. They make excellent border fillers, while some compact varieties are also suitable for growing in large containers.
Cultivation In the garden, grow in any well-drained acid soil in dappled shade, but in colder areas shelter from cold winds. Add plenty of organic matter (but not alkaline mushroom compost/soil mix) to the soil before planting. In containers, grow in ericaceous soil mix and keep well watered.
Pruning No routine pruning is necessary. Remove any frost-damaged stems in early summer.
Propagation Take semi-ripe cuttings in late summer, or layer low branches in mid-autumn.

Pieris formosa var. forrestii 'Wakehurst'
An upright, evergreen shrub that bears pendent clusters of fragrant, white, urn-shaped flowers during mid-spring and late spring when the glossy, brilliant red young foliage emerges. H 5m (16ft) S 4m (13ft).
Aspect: semi-shade
Hardiness: ✿✿✿ Zones: 7–8

Pieris 'Forest Flame'
The fiery red new foliage of this upright evergreen turns pink and cream before maturing to dark green. Clusters of white, urn-

Pieris 'Forest Flame'

shaped flowers festoon the shrub during mid-spring and late spring. H 4m (13ft) S 2m (6ft).
Aspect: semi-shade
Hardiness: ✽✽✽ Zones: 7–8

Pieris japonica 'Purity'
Clusters of white, urn-shaped flowers are borne in abundance during mid-spring and late spring and stand out against the lustrous young, pale green foliage that darkens with age on this compact evergreen. H 1m (3ft) S 1m (3ft).
Aspect: semi-shade
Hardiness: ✽✽✽ Zones: 7–8

Pieris japonica 'Valley Valentine'
An early and long-flowering compact variety that produces dark pink flowers from early spring until late spring against lustrous dark green leaves. H 4m (13ft) S 3m (10ft).
Aspect: semi-shade
Hardiness: ✽✽✽ Zones: 7–8

Pieris japonica 'Variegata'
New foliage is flushed pink, maturing to green with white margins on this variegated variety. Clusters of white, bell-shaped flowers are produced throughout mid-spring and late spring. H 80cm (32in) S 80cm (32in).
Aspect: semi-shade
Hardiness: ✽✽✽ Zones: 7–8

PITTOSPORUM
A genus of around 200 species, including the handsome, bushy evergreens featured here. They make good border fillers or specimens with year-round interest and can be trimmed into an attractive hedge in mild areas.
Cultivation Grow in reasonably fertile, moisture-retentive, well-drained soil in full sun or dappled shade. Grow against a sheltered, sunny wall in colder areas.
Pruning No routine pruning is necessary. Shrubs can be clipped to keep them compact during mid-spring. Trim hedges in mid-spring and early summer.
Propagation Take semi-ripe cuttings in mid-autumn.

Pittosporum 'Garnettii'
Half-hardy variegated evergreen with pink-spotted grey-green

leaves that have creamy-white, wavy edges. Purple, bell-shaped flowers are borne in late spring and early summer. H 4m (13ft) S 3m (10ft).
Aspect: sun or semi-shade
Hardiness: ✽ Zone: 10

Pittosporum tenuifolium 'Silver Queen'
This is a large, ornamental shrub that has handsome, white-variegated, wavy-edged, grey-green leaves that appear on contrasting near-black young stems. Honey-scented dark purple flowers are sometimes produced during late spring and early summer. H 4m (13ft) S 2m (6ft).
Aspect: sun or semi-shade
Hardiness: ✽✽ Zones: 9

Pittosporum tenuifolium 'Tom Thumb'
As its names suggests, this is a compact, rounded evergreen with wavy-edged, purple-bronze leaves and near-black young stems. Honey-scented dark purple flowers are sometimes produced during late spring and early summer. H 90cm (36in) S 60cm (24in).
Aspect: sun or semi-shade
Hardiness: ✽✽ Zone: 9

Pittosporum tenuifolium 'Variegatum'
A large bushy evergreen with creamy-white, variegated, wavy-edged, grey-green leaves on near-black young stems. It makes an attractive, variegated windbreak or hedge in mild coastal areas.

H 4m (13ft) S 2m (6ft).
Aspect: sun or semi-shade
Hardiness: ✽✽ Zone: 9

POTENTILLA
Cinquefoil
A large genus of over 500 species, including the summer-flowering, deciduous shrubs featured here. Smaller, compact varieties are useful for adding summer-long colour in confined spaces and all can be grown on poor soils. Ideal for rock gardens, sunny banks or the sunny base of hedges.
Cultivation Grow in any well-drained soil in full sun.
Pruning For good flowering, trim new growth by one-third each mid-spring. Rejuvenate neglected plants by cutting the plant back to ground level in mid-spring.
Propagation Take semi-ripe cuttings in early autumn.

Potentilla fruticosa 'Abbotswood'
Compact, bushy, deciduous shrub with blue-green foliage that bears masses of brilliant white flowers from late spring to mid-autumn. H 75cm (30in) S 120cm (48in).
Aspect: sun
Hardiness: ✽✽✽ Zones: 7–8

Potentilla fruticosa 'Goldfinger'
Large, bright yellow flowers are produced in abundance from late spring to mid-autumn against a backdrop of small, dark green leaves on this mound-forming deciduous shrub. H 1m (3ft) S 1.5m (5ft).
Aspect: sun
Hardiness: ✽✽✽ Zones: 7–8

Potentilla fruticosa 'Primrose Beauty'
Primrose-yellow flowers resembling wild roses appear from late spring to mid-autumn above a compact mound of deciduous grey-green leaves. Pest- and disease-free, it tolerates partial shade but flowers best in full sun. H 1m (3ft) S 1.5m (5ft).
Aspect: sun
Hardiness: ✽✽✽ Zones: 7–8

Potentilla fruticosa 'Red Ace'
Vermilion-red flowers each with a yellow centre and undersides are borne en masse from late spring to mid-autumn and stand out against the dark green leaves. H 1m (3ft) S 1.5m (5ft).
Aspect: sun
Hardiness: ✽✽✽ Zones: 7–8

Potentilla fruticosa 'Royal Flush'
Masses of rich pink flowers, each with a yellow centre that fades to white with age, cover this compact, deciduous shrub from late spring to mid-autumn. H 45cm (18in) S 75cm (30in).
Aspect: sun
Hardiness: ✽✽✽ Zones: 7–8

Potentilla fruticosa 'Sunset'
The unusual, burnt-orange flowers that appear on this shrub are produced in succession from late spring to mid-autumn and appear above a mound of dark green deciduous foliage. H 1m (3ft) S 1m (3ft).
Aspect: sun
Hardiness: ✽✽✽ Zones: 7–8

Pittosporum tenuifolium 'Variegatum'

Potentilla fruticosa 'Abbotswood'

Prostanthera cuneata

Prunus 'Hirtipes'

PROSTANTHERA
Mint bush

A genus of some 50 species, including the bushy evergreen shrub featured here, grown for their eye-catching summer flowers. It is a useful front-of-the-border filler and for adding continuity to the garden display.
Cultivation Grow in any moisture-retentive, well-drained soil that is reasonably fertile and in full sun. Grow against a sheltered, sunny wall in colder areas.
Pruning No routine pruning is necessary. Deadhead to keep neat and help prolong flowering. Trim lightly after flowering to keep compact.
Propagation Take semi-ripe cuttings in mid-summer.

Prostanthera cuneata
Alpine mint bush
Tubular white flowers with distinctive purple and yellow flecks in the throat are produced in clusters from early summer to late summer on this small, bushy, evergreen shrub. H 1m (3ft) S 1m (3ft).
Aspect: sun
Hardiness: ✿✿ Zone: 9

PRUNUS
A large and varied genus of over 200 species, including the bushy evergreen shrubs featured here, grown for their handsome foliage and spring flowers, as well as deciduous shrubs grown for their spring blossom. Plant spring-flowering varieties as seasonal focal points where they will be

appreciated most; evergreen types make excellent border fillers, ground cover and hedges, depending on the variety.
Cultivation Grow in any moisture-retentive, well-drained soil that is reasonably fertile and in full sun, dappled shade, even deep shade.
Pruning No routine pruning is necessary. Formal evergreen hedges and screens can be trimmed during early spring and late summer. Neglected or straggly evergreen shrubs can be cut back hard into old wood during early spring. Deciduous shrubs can be kept compact and flowering well by cutting back one stem in three during early summer, starting with the oldest.
Propagation Take semi-ripe cuttings in early autumn.

Prunus laurocerasus 'Otto Luyken'
A compact, bushy, evergreen shrub with narrow, pointed, dark green leaves. Candle-like spikes of small white flowers appear during mid-spring, followed by cherry-red berries. Good ground cover. H 1m (3ft) S 1.5m (5ft).
Aspect: sun, semi-shade to deep shade
Hardiness: ✿✿✿ Zones: 7–8

Prunus laurocerasus 'Rotundifolia'
A large, dense and bushy evergreen shrub with big, glossy, dark green leaves. Candle-like spikes of small white flowers are produced during mid-spring, followed by cherry-red berries. Good hedging plant.

H 5m (16ft) S 4m (13ft).
Aspect: sun, semi-shade to deep shade
Hardiness: ✿✿✿ Zones: 7–8

Prunus laurocerasus 'Zabeliana'
A low-growing, spreading, evergreen shrub with very narrow, pointed, dark green leaves. Candle-like spikes of small white flowers are produced during mid-spring, followed by cherry-red berries. Good ground cover. H 1m (3ft) S 2.5m (8ft).
Aspect: sun, semi-shade to deep shade
Hardiness: ✿✿✿ Zones: 7–8

Prunus lusitanica
Portugal laurel
A large, dense, evergreen shrub with dark green leaves that have red stalks. Candle-like spikes of small white flowers are produced during mid-spring, followed by red berries that mature to purple. Good hedging plant and can tolerate chalky soils. H 20m (70ft) S 20m (70ft).
Aspect: sun, semi-shade to deep shade
Hardiness: ✿✿✿ Zones: 7–8

Prunus tenella 'Fire Hill'
Dwarf Russian almond
An upright-growing, compact and bushy deciduous shrub with narrow, glossy, dark green leaves. The bare stems are smothered with bright pink blossom-like flowers during early spring and mid-spring as the leaves emerge, followed by velvety fruits. H 1.5m (5ft) S 1.5m (5ft).
Aspect: sun or semi-shade
Hardiness: ✿✿✿ Zones: 7–8

Prunus triloba
Flowering almond
Peach-pink, blossom-like flowers are borne on the bare stems of this dense, twiggy, deciduous shrub during early spring and mid-spring as the leaves emerge, followed by red berries. H 3m (10ft) S 3m (10ft).
Aspect: sun or semi-shade
Hardiness: ✿✿✿ Zones: 7–8

PYRACANTHA
A genus of over five species, including the spreading, spiny evergreen shrubs featured here,

grown for their intruder-resistant properties, spring flowers and colourful autumn fruit that are loved by birds. They can be used as freestanding shrubs or hedges or be trained against a wall or fence. They make useful town garden plants, as they are very tolerant of urban pollution.
Cultivation Grow in any well-drained soil that is reasonably fertile in full sun or dappled shade, sheltered from cold winds. Grow less hardy varieties against a sunny wall in colder areas.
Pruning No routine pruning is necessary. Hedges and screens can be trimmed between late spring and mid-summer to keep in shape. Wall-trained specimens should be trimmed back at this time in summer. Cut back all the new shoots after they have flowered, to expose the developing berries.
Propagation Take semi-ripe cuttings in early autumn.

Pyracantha 'Golden Charmer'
A vigorous and bushy shrub that produces masses of small white flowers on arching branches during early summer, followed by clusters of dark orange berries that are resistant to disease. H 3m (10ft) S 3m (10ft).
Aspect: sun or semi-shade
Hardiness: ✿✿✿ Zones: 7–8

Pyracantha 'Mohave'
Masses of small white flowers are produced in clusters during early summer, followed by clusters of long-lasting bright red berries on this vigorous, bushy shrub. H 4m (13ft) S 5m (16ft).

Pyracantha 'Saphyr Orange'

Aspect: sun or semi-shade
Hardiness: ❀❀ Zone: 9

Pyracantha 'Orange Glow'

Clusters of small white flowers
are produced in late spring against
lustrous, dark green leaves,
followed by brilliant orange
berries that last well into winter
on this open, spreading shrub.
H 3m (10ft) S 3m (10ft).
Aspect: sun or semi-shade
Hardiness: ❀❀❀ Zones: 7–8

Pyracantha 'Saphyr Orange'

This vigorous, evergreen shrub is
a recent introduction that bears
sprays of small white flowers
during early summer, followed by
clusters of disease-resistant,
orange berries that last well into
winter against a backdrop of
glossy, dark green leaves.
Pyracantha 'Saphyr Rouge' is
similar but bears carmine-red
berries that mature to orange.
H 4m (13ft) S 3m (10ft).
Aspect: sun or semi-shade
Hardiness: ❀❀❀ Zones: 7–8

Pyracantha 'Soleil d'Or'

Large clusters of long-lasting,
disease-resistant, golden-yellow
berries follow masses of white
flowers produced in early summer
on red-tinged spiny shoots of this
upright evergreen shrub. H 3m
(10ft) S 2.5m (8ft).
Aspect: sun or semi-shade
Hardiness: ❀❀❀ Zones: 7–8

RHAMNUS

A genus of around 125 species,
including the variegated evergreen

shrub featured here, grown for
their handsome foliage. It makes
an attractive freestanding shrub or
hedge, but in cold areas it is best
trained against a large sunny wall
or fence. It also makes an
excellent permanent container
shrub that provides year-round
interest.
Cultivation In the garden, grow in
any garden soil that is reasonably
fertile and in full sun. In colder
regions, grow in a sheltered
position, protected from cold
winds. In containers, use a soil-
based mix, feed monthly and
water as necessary.
Pruning No routine pruning is
necessary.
Propagation Take semi-ripe
cuttings in mid-summer.

Rhamnus alaternus 'Argenteovariegata' (syn. R. alaternus 'Variegata')

A variegated evergreen shrub,
grown for its white-edged grey-
green leaves. Small, insignificant
mustard-coloured flowers are
produced in late spring and early
summer, followed by red fruits
that ripen to black. H 5m (16ft)
S 4m (13ft).
Aspect: sun
Hardiness: ❀❀ Zones: 7–8

RHAPIS

A genus of over ten species of
multi-stemmed palms, including
the miniature fan palm featured
here, that will add a tropical touch
to mild gardens or can be grown
as a house plant in colder regions.
Cultivation Grow in a well-drained

soil that is reasonably fertile in
dappled shade. In containers, use
a soil-based compost (soil mix),
water regularly and feed monthly
during the growing season. Move
to a warm spot undercover when
the temperature falls below 10°C
(50°F) and water sparingly
throughout the winter.
Pruning No routine pruning is
necessary.
Propagation Sow seed or divide
large clumps in mid-spring.

Rhapis excelsa (syn. R. flabelliformis) Miniature fan palm

A tender dwarf palm that forms a
clump of bamboo-like stems with
large, deeply lobed, matt green,
palm-like leaves. Insignificant
cream flowers are produced in
early summer and mid-summer.
H 1.5m (5ft) S 5m (16ft).
Aspect: semi-shade
Hardiness: tender Zones: 10+

RHODODENDRON (including azalea)

A huge genus of nearly 1,000
species, including the medium-
sized and dwarf forms of
evergreen azaleas and
rhododendrons and the deciduous
azaleas featured here, all grown
for their spectacular flowering
displays. Use according to their
size: all make wonderful seasonal
focal points, with smaller varieties
best suited at the front or middle
of borders, while bigger forms
with larger, eye-catching flowers
can be best accommodated
towards the back of the scheme.
Compact varieties also make
excellent permanent container
plants.
Cultivation Shallow-plant in any
well-drained acid soil in dappled
shade, but in colder areas provide
shelter and plant where it gets
afternoon sun. Some varieties are
best grown in full sun. Add plenty
of organic matter to the soil
before planting. In containers,
grow in ericaceous soil mix and
keep well watered. Wherever the
shrub is planted, bear in mind
that the flowers are susceptible to
damage by a frost that is followed
by rapid thaw, so avoid
positioning in east-facing areas
that get early morning spring sun.

Pruning Deadhead after flowering.
Prune straggly branches of
established plants to maintain the
overall shape during late winter or
early spring.
Propagation Layer low branches in
early spring or take semi-ripe
cuttings in late summer.

EVERGREEN RHODODENDRONS

Rhododendron 'Blue Diamond'

Violet-blue funnel-shaped flowers
that age to lavender-blue are
borne during mid-spring and early
spring. It has small, aromatic,
dark, evergreen leaves. Best in full
sun. H 1.5m (5ft) S 1.5m (5ft).
Aspect: sun
Hardiness: ❀❀❀ Zones: 7–8

Rhododendron 'Blue Peter'

Frilly edged, lavender-blue flowers
with purple markings are
produced in clusters throughout
early summer. Large, dark,
evergreen leaves. H 3m (10ft)
S 3m (10ft).
Aspect: semi-shade
Hardiness: ❀❀❀ Zones: 7–8

Rhododendron 'Cilpinense'

Clusters of pale pink, funnel-
shaped flowers are produced in
profusion during early spring on
this compact evergreen
rhododendron, which has small,
dark leaves. H 1.1m (3½ft)
S 1.1m (3½ft).
Aspect: sun or semi-shade
Hardiness: ❀❀❀ Zones: 7–8

Rhododendron 'Cunningham's White'

Trusses of white, funnel-shaped
flowers with brown or purple
markings are produced
throughout late spring. Compact
evergreen with dark green leaves.
H 2.2m (7ft) S 2.2m (7ft).
Aspect: semi-shade
Hardiness: ❀❀❀ Zones: 7–8

Rhododendron 'Dopey'

Masses of long-lasting, glossy,
red, bell-shaped flowers, spotted
dark-brown inside, are produced
throughout late spring on this
compact evergreen rhododendron.
H 2m (6ft) S 2m (6ft).
Aspect: semi-shade
Hardiness: ❀❀❀ Zones: 7–8

Rhamnus alaternus 'Argenteovariegata'

Rhapis excelsa

Rhododrendron 'Dopey'

Rhododendron 'Grumpy'
Funnel-shaped, pink-flushed, cream flowers are produced in flat-topped trusses during mid-spring and late spring. The glossy, dark green leaves are woolly underneath. H 1.2m (4ft) S 1m (3ft).
Aspect: semi-shade
Hardiness: ✽✽✽ Zones: 7–8

Rhododendron 'Lord Roberts'
Dark crimson, funnel-shaped flowers with black markings are produced in clusters during early summer. Compact evergreen with dark green leaves. H 1.5m (5ft) S 1.5m (5ft).
Aspect: semi-shade
Hardiness: ✽✽✽ Zones: 7–8

Rhododendron 'Pink Drift'
Funnel-shaped, rose-lavender flowers are produced *en masse* throughout mid-spring and late spring on this very compact, dwarf evergreen rhododendron, which has small, pale green leaves. Good choice for small gardens. H 50cm (20in) S 50cm (20in).
Aspect: semi-shade
Hardiness: ✽✽✽ Zones: 7–8

Rhododendron 'Pink Pearl'
White-edged, soft-pink, funnel-shaped flowers that age to white are produced during mid-spring and late spring. Large, pale, evergreen leaves. H 4m (13ft) S 4m (13ft).
Aspect: sun
Hardiness: ✽✽✽ Zones: 7–8

Rhododendron 'Purple Splendor'
Frilly edged, funnel-shaped, deep purple flowers, each with a blackish-purple throat, are produced during late spring and early summer on this late-flowering variety. H 3m (10ft) S 3m (10ft).
Aspect: semi-shade
Hardiness: ✽✽✽ Zones: 7–8

Rhododendron 'Sapphire'
Masses of small, pale blue, funnel-shaped flowers are produced *en masse* during mid-spring and late spring on this compact evergreen, which has small, dark leaves. H 50cm (20in) S 50cm (20in).
Aspect: semi-shade
Hardiness: ✽✽✽ Zones: 7–8

Rhododendron 'Scarlet Wonder'
Wavy-margined, ruby-red, funnel-shaped flowers are produced *en masse* throughout mid-spring on this compact evergreen, which has small, dark leaves. H 2m (6ft) S 2m (6ft).
Aspect: semi-shade
Hardiness: ✽✽✽ Zones: 7–8

DECIDUOUS AZALEAS
Rhododendron luteum
Sweetly scented, the yellow, funnel-shaped blooms appear throughout late spring and early summer on this vigorous-growing deciduous azalea. Mid-green leaves turn fiery shades in autumn.
H 4m (13ft) S 4m (13ft).

Aspect: sun or semi-shade
Hardiness: ✽✽✽ Zones: 7–8

Rhododendron 'Debutante'
Pink, funnel-shaped flowers with orange markings are produced en masse throughout late spring. Mid-green leaves turn fiery shades in autumn. H 2m (6ft) S 2m (6ft).
Aspect: semi-shade
Hardiness: ✽✽✽ Zones: 7–8

Rhododendron 'Gibraltar'
Frilly, bright orange, funnel-shaped flowers appear in late spring on this deciduous azalea. A useful pot specimen on the patio. H 1.5m (5ft) S 1.5m (5ft).
Aspect: sun or semi-shade
Hardiness: ✽✽✽ Zones: 7–8

Rhododendron 'Glowing Embers'
Flaming reddish-orange, funnel-shaped flowers are produced in conical clusters during mid-spring and late spring. H 2m (6ft) S 2m (6ft).
Aspect: semi-shade
Hardiness: ✽✽✽ Zones: 7–8

Rhododendron 'Homebush'
Pretty pink, semi-double, funnel-shaped flowers are borne throughout late spring. A good pink variety for small gardens. H 1.5m (5ft) S 1.5m (5ft).
Aspect: semi-shade
Hardiness: ✽✽✽ Zones: 7–8

Rhododendron 'Klondyke'
Coppery-red flower buds open to reveal flaming red-flushed, golden-orange, funnel-shaped

flowers throughout late spring. The mid-green leaves turn fiery shades in autumn. H 2m (6ft) S 2m (6ft).
Aspect: semi-shade
Hardiness: ✽✽✽ Zones: 7–8

Rhododendron 'Koster's Brilliant Red'
Vivid, orange-red, funnel-shaped flowers are produced during mid-spring and late spring on this early-flowering variety. Mid-green leaves turn fiery shades in autumn. H 2m (6ft) S 2m (6ft).
Aspect: semi-shade
Hardiness: ✽✽✽ Zones: 7–8

Rhododendron 'Persil'
Large clusters of orange-flushed, white funnel-shaped flowers are borne throughout April (mid-spring) on this bushy, deciduous azalea. The mid-green leaves turn fiery shades in autumn.
H 2m (6ft) S 2m (6ft).
Aspect: semi-shade
Hardiness: ✽✽✽ Zones: 7–8

EVERGREEN AZALEAS
Rhododendron 'Blue Danube'
Clusters of small, funnel-shaped, violet-blue flowers are produced *en masse* during late spring and early summer on this compact evergreen azalea. Very hardy.
H 80cm (32in) S 100cm (36in).
Aspect: semi-shade
Hardiness: ✽✽✽ Zones: 7–8

Rhododendron 'Geisha Red'
Masses of small, funnel-shaped, pillar-box-red flowers are produced during late spring and

Rhododendron 'Persil'

Rhododendron luteum

early summer on this compact evergreen azalea. It makes a useful container specimen on the patio. H 60cm (24in) S 100cm (36in).
Aspect: semi-shade
Hardiness: ✹✹✹

Rhododendron 'Gumpo White'
Wavy-edged, funnel-shaped, white flowers are produced *en masse* throughout early summer on this dwarf, evergreen azalea. It makes a useful container specimen on the patio. H 1m (3ft) S 1m (3ft).
Aspect: semi-shade
Hardiness: ✹✹✹ Zones: 7–8

Rhododendron 'Mother's Day'
Small, funnel-shaped, semi-double, rose-red flowers are produced in profusion during late

spring and early summer.
H 80cm (32in) S 100cm (36in).
Aspect: semi-shade
Hardiness: ✹✹✹ Zones: 7–8

RHUS
A large genus of over 200 species, including the upright, suckering shrub featured here, grown for their handsome foliage that turns fiery shades in autumn. They make spectacular specimen plants for a sunny shrub or mixed border, providing an ever-changing year-round point of interest.
Cultivation Grow in a moisture-retentive, well-drained garden soil that is reasonably fertile and in full sun or dappled shade. Grow in full sun for the best autumn tints. Remove suckers by digging

a hole to expose their point of origin and ripping them from the root. Do not prune off as this will just exacerbate the problem.
Pruning No routine pruning is necessary. Neglected plants can be cut back hard in mid-spring.
Propagation Take semi-ripe cuttings in mid-summer.

Rhus typhina
Stag's horn sumach
The velvet-covered red winter shoots gave rise to the common name, but it is the finely cut dark green foliage, which turns fiery shades of orange-red in autumn, that is the highlight. Mustard flowers on conical spikes appear in early summer and mid-summer, followed by dark red autumn fruits on female shrubs that make a useful food source for birds in winter. Prone to throwing up suckers, so avoid planting next to a lawn or driveway, or restrict its spread with a sucker-proof barrier.
Named varieties: 'Dissecta' (syn. *R. typhina* 'Laciniata'), has more finely cut leaves and rarely produces suckers. H 2m (6ft) S 3m (10ft).
Aspect: sun or semi-shade
Hardiness: ✹✹✹ Zones: 7–8

RIBES
Flowering currants
A genus of some 150 species, including the deciduous, quick-growing shrubs here, are grown for their spring flowers and autumn fruit. Useful shrubs for filling gaps and for providing quick results in new gardens.

Cultivation Grow in any reasonably fertile, well-drained soil in full sun or dappled shade.
Pruning Encourage better flowering by pruning annually, cutting out one stem in three after flowering in late spring.
Propagation Take hardwood cuttings in mid autumn.

Ribes sanguineum 'Brocklebankii'
A compact and upright deciduous shrub, with aromatic, golden-yellow leaves, that carries clusters of pink flowers during mid-spring, followed by blue-black fruit in autumn. Hot midday sun can scorch the foliage. H 1.2m (4ft) S 1.2m (4ft).
Aspect: semi-shade
Hardiness: ✹✹✹ Zones: 7–8

Ribes sanguineum 'King Edward VII'
Clusters of dark red flowers in mid-spring are followed by blue-black fruit during the autumn on this upright deciduous shrub with aromatic dark green leaves. H 2m (6ft) S 2m (6ft).
Aspect: sun
Hardiness: ✹✹✹ Zones: 7–8

Ribes sanguineum 'Pulborough Scarlet'
Clusters of white-centred red flowers appear in mid-spring, followed by blue-black fruit in autumn, on this vigorous shrub with dark green leaves. H 3m (10ft) S 2.5m (18ft).
Aspect: sun
Hardiness: ✹✹✹ Zones: 7–8

Rhododendron 'Pink Pearl'

Rhus typhina

Ribes sanguineum

Rosa 'Alec's Red'

ROSA
Rose

A large genus of over 150 species that includes the varied collection of popular, deciduous, summer-flowering shrubs featured here. Grow roses in traditional blocks to provide a stunning display, or use single specimens in between other shrubs and flowers for a summer-long splash of colour. Combine different varieties to get a succession of flowers and hips.
Cultivation Grow in any garden soil that is reasonably fertile and in full sun. They prefer the soil to remain moist in summer, so incorporate plenty of organic matter before planting. Avoid siting new rose plants in soil that has recently been used for growing other roses.
Pruning To keep neat, open and healthy, prune annually by cutting back the previous season's growth to within 10–15cm (4–6in) of a permanent twiggy framework before new growth starts in late winter or early spring. Traditionally, this was carried out using secateurs (pruners), but recent trials have shown rough pruning with a hedge trimmer to be equally effective. The sizes for individual varieties given here assume regular pruning. Ground-cover roses should have unwanted stems cut back to an outward-facing bud. In containers, use a soil-based compost (soil mix), water regularly and feed monthly during the growing season. Water as necessary during the winter months.

Propagation Take hardwood cuttings in mid-autumn.
Aspect: sun
Hardiness: ❁❁❁ Zones: 7–8

LARGE-FLOWERED BUSH ROSE
Includes the long-flowering hybrid tea roses with large, shapely blooms on long stems and attractive foliage that make them ideal for cutting.

Rosa 'Alec's Red'
Large, double, sweetly fragrant, crimson flowers are borne in succession from mid-summer to early autumn. Glossy, mid-green leaves. H 100cm (36in) S 60cm (24in).

Rosa 'Alexander'
Double, slightly fragrant, vermilion-red flowers with scalloped petals are produced from mid-summer to early autumn. Lustrous, dark green leaves. H 200cm (72in) S 80cm (32in).

Rosa 'Blessings'
Double, slightly fragrant, coral-pink flowers are borne in succession from mid-summer to early autumn. Glossy, dark green leaves. H 110cm (42in) S 75cm (30in).

Rosa 'Congratulations'
Double, slightly fragrant, rose-pink flowers on long stems are borne from mid-summer to early autumn. Glossy, mid-green leaves. H 1.5m (5ft) S 1m (3ft).

Rosa 'Fragrant Cloud'
Strongly fragrant, double, deep-scarlet flowers are produced from mid-summer to early autumn. Lustrous, dark green leaves. H 75cm (30in) S 60cm (24in).

Rosa 'Ice Cream'
Large, fragrant, ivory-white flowers are borne in succession from mid-summer to early autumn. Lustrous, bronze-tinted, dark green leaves. H 100cm (36in) S 70cm (28in).

Rosa 'Ingrid Bergman'
Fragrant, double, deep red flowers are borne from mid-summer to

Rosa 'Ingrid Bergman'

early autumn. Lustrous, dark green leaves. H 80cm (32in) S 65cm (26in).

Rosa 'Just Joey'
Fragrant, double, coppery-red flowers with wavy-margined petals are borne from mid-summer to early autumn. Matt, dark-green leaves. H 75cm (30in) S 70cm (28in).

Rosa 'Loving Memory'
Double, slightly scented, dark red flowers are borne in succession from mid-summer to early autumn. Matt, dark-green leaves. H 110cm (42in) S 75cm (30in).

Rosa 'Peace'
Double, pink-flushed, deep yellow, slightly fragrant flowers are borne from mid-summer to early autumn. Glossy, dark green leaves. H 1.2m (4ft) S 1m (3ft).

Rosa 'Just Joey'

Rosa 'Peace'

Rosa 'Polar Star'
Large, double, white flowers are borne in succession from mid-summer to early autumn. Matt, dark green leaves. H 100cm (36in) S 70cm (28in).

Rosa 'Remember Me'
Large, fragrant, double, coppery-orange, flushed-yellow flowers are borne from mid-summer to early autumn. Glossy, dark green leaves. H 100cm (36in) S 60cm (24in).

Rosa 'Royal William'
Double, deep-crimson flowers with a spicy fragrance are borne from mid-summer to early autumn. Matt, dark green leaves. H 100cm (36in) S 75cm (30in).

Rosa 'Ruby Wedding'
Slightly fragrant, double, ruby-red flowers are borne in succession from mid-summer to early autumn. Glossy, dark green leaves. H 75cm (30in) S 70cm (28in).

Rosa 'Silver Jubilee'
Fragrant, double, rose-pink flowers flushed salmon-pink are borne from mid-summer to early autumn. Matt, dark green leaves. H 100cm (36in) S 60cm (24in).

CLUSTER-FLOWERED BUSH ROSE
Including floribunda roses, which produce masses of flowers throughout the summer and autumn. They tend to be hardier and more disease-resistant than large-flowered varieties.

Rosa 'Amber Queen'
Fragrant, double, amber-yellow
flowers are borne in succession
from mid-summer to early
autumn. Glossy, leathery, dark
green leaves emerge reddish-green.
H 50cm (20in) S 60cm (24in).

Rosa 'Arthur Bell'
Large, semi-double, very fragrant,
golden-yellow flowers are borne
from mid-summer to early
autumn. Glossy, mid-green leaves.
H 100cm (36in) S 60cm (24in).

Rosa 'Chinatown'
Fragrant, double, pink-edged
yellow flowers are produced by
'Chinatown' from mid-summer
to early autumn. Glossy, dark
green leaves. H 1.2m (4ft)
S 1m (3ft).

Rosa 'Golden Wedding'
Double, slightly fragrant, golden-
yellow flowers are produced from
mid-summer to early autumn.
Glossy, dark green leaves. H 75cm
(30in) S 60cm (24in).

Rosa 'Iceberg'
Double, slightly fragrant, white
flowers are produced from mid-
summer to early autumn. Glossy,
mid-green leaves. H 80cm (32in)
S 65cm (26in).

Rosa 'Many Happy Returns'
Cup-shaped, fragrant, semi-
double, pale pink flowers are
borne in succession from mid-
summer to early autumn. Glossy,
mid-green leaves. H 75cm (30in)
S 75cm (30in).

Rosa 'Mountbatten'

Rosa 'Masquerade'
Lightly fragrant, semi-double,
yellow flowers that age to salmon-
pink and red are borne from mid-
summer to early autumn. Glossy,
dark green leaves. H 80cm (32in)
S 60cm (24in).

Rosa 'Mountbatten'
Large, fragrant, double, golden-
yellow flowers are produced from
mid-summer to early autumn.
Glossy, mid-green leaves.
H 120cm (48in) S 75cm (30in).

Rosa 'Queen Elizabeth'
Double, slightly fragrant, pale
pink flowers are produced in
succession and appear from mid-
summer to early autumn. Glossy,
dark-green leaves. H 2.2m (7ft)
S 1m (3ft).

Rosa 'Ruby Anniversary'
Double, slightly scented, ruby-red
flowers are produced in
succession from mid-summer to
early autumn. Glossy, mid-green
leaves. H 60cm (24in) S 45cm
(18in).

Rosa 'Southampton'
Large, double, slightly scented,
red-flushed apricot flowers with
ruffled petals from mid-summer
to early autumn. Glossy, dark
green leaves. H 100cm (36in)
S 70cm (28in).

Rosa 'The Times Rose'
Double, slightly fragrant,
dark crimson flowers are
produced in succession from
mid-summer to early autumn.

Glossy, purplish-tinged green
leaves. H 60cm (24in) S 75cm
(30in).

SHRUB ROSE
A varied collection of roses that
grow in bushy, informal plants
with spectacular displays of
flowers. Many are sweetly scented
and some have hips. All are useful
for growing in a mixed border
with other shrubs. Many old
varieties and species roses bloom
only in early summer but most
modern varieties repeat bloom.

Rosa 'Ballerina'
Slightly scented, white-centred,
pale pink flowers are produced
from mid-summer to early
autumn. Mid-green leaves.
H 1.5m (5ft) S 1.2m (48in).

**Rosa 'Blanche Double de
Coubert'**
Large semi-double, very fragrant,
white flowers are borne from mid-
summer to early autumn, followed
by red rose-hips. H 1.5m (5ft)
S 1.2m (48in).

Rosa 'Bonica'
Small semi-double, slightly
fragrant, rose-pink flowers are
borne from mid-summer to early
autumn. Glossy, dark green leaves.
H 85cm (34in) S 110cm (42in).

Rosa 'Boule de Neige'
Pink-tinged buds open to produce
fragrant, double, white flowers
from mid-summer to early
autumn. Matt, dark green foliage.
H 1.5m (5ft) S 1.2m (4ft).

Rosa 'Buff Beauty'
Double, fragrant, pale apricot-
yellow flowers are borne from
mid-summer to early autumn.
Purple-tinged, dark green leaves.
H 1.2m (4ft) S 1.2m (4ft).

Rosa 'Cardinal de Richelieu'
Fragrant, double, deep purple
flowers are borne in clusters
during early summer and
mid-summer. Lustrous, dark
green leaves. H 1m (3ft)
S 1.2m (4ft).

Rosa 'Charles de Mills'
Double, fragrant, magenta-pink
flowers are produced in a single
flush during mid-summer.
Mid-green leaves. H 1m (3ft)
S 1.2m (4ft).

Rosa 'Cornelia'
Very fragrant, double, apricot-
pink flowers are produced from
early summer to early autumn.
Matt, dark green leaves. H 1.5m
(5ft) S 1.5m (5ft).

Rosa 'Fantin-Latour'
Slightly fragrant, double, pale
pink flowers are produced
throughout early summer and
mid-summer. Glossy, dark green
leaves. H 1.5m (5ft) S 1.2m
(4ft).

Rosa 'Felicia'
Sweetly fragrant, double, apricot-
yellow flowers that are flushed
with pale pink from early summer
to early autumn. Matt, mid-green
leaves. H 1.5m (5ft) S 2.2m
(7ft).

Rosa 'Arthur Bell'

Rosa 'Iceberg'

Rosa 'Felicia'

Rosa 'Fru Dagmar Hastrup'
Clove-scented, single, light-pink
flowers are produced in
succession from mid-summer to
early autumn, followed by dark
red autumn hips. Matt, dark green
leaves. H 1m (3ft) S 1.2m (4ft).

Rosa glauca
Clusters of single, cerise-pink
flowers with pale-pink centres are
produced during early summer
and mid-summer on almost
thornless stems, followed by
spherical red rosehips.
H 2m (6ft) S 1.5m (5ft).

Rosa 'Graham Thomas'
Double, fragrant, yellow flowers
are produced in succession from
mid-summer to early autumn.
Matt, bright green leaves.
H 1.5m (5ft) S 1.2m (4ft).

Rosa 'Heritage'
Cup-shaped, fragrant, double, pale
pink flowers that age to white are
produced from mid-summer to
early autumn. Matt, dark green
leaves. H 1.2m (4ft)
S 1.2m (4ft).

Rosa 'L.D. Braithwaite'
Large, double, fragrant, bright-
crimson flowers are produced
in succession from mid-summer
to early autumn. Matt, grey-
green leaves. H 1m (3ft)
S 1.2m (4ft).

Rosa 'Louise Odier'
Fragrant, double, mauve-tinged
pink flowers are borne from mid-

summer to early autumn. Matt,
pale green leaves. H 2m (6ft)
S 1.2m (4ft)

Rosa 'Mary Rose'
Cup-shaped, double, fragrant,
rose-pink flowers are borne in
succession from mid-summer to
early autumn. Matt, mid-green
leaves. H 1.2m (4ft) S 1m (3ft).

Rosa 'Madame Pierre Oger'
Very fragrant, double, pale silvery-
pink flowers are produced in
succession from mid-summer to
early autumn. Matt, pale green
leaves. H 2m (6ft) S 1.2m (4ft).

Rosa moyesii 'Geranium'
Scented, single, cream-centred,
bright red flowers are produced
during late spring and early
summer. Matt, dark-green leaves.
H 2.5m (8ft) S 1.5m (5ft).

Rosa 'Penelope'
Semi-double, fragrant, pale
creamy-pink flowers are produced
from early summer to early
autumn. Matt, dark green, bronze-
tinged leaves. H 1m (3ft)
S 1m (3ft).

Rosa 'Queen of Denmark'
Double, very fragrant, deep to
light pink flowers in a single flush
appear in mid-summer. Matt,
grey-green foliage. H 1.5 (5ft)
S 1.2m (4ft).

Rosa 'Rose de Rescht'
Double, mauve-red flowers that
age to magenta-pink are produced

in a single flush in mid-summer.
Matt, mid-green leaves. H 90cm
(32in) S 75cm (30in).

Rosa 'Roseraie de l'Haÿ'
Strongly fragrant, double, red-
purple flowers are borne in
succession from mid-summer
to early autumn. H 2.2m (7ft)
S 2m (6ft).

Rosa rugosa 'Rubra'
Fragrant, single, yellow-centred,
purple-red flowers are produced in
succession from mid-summer to
early autumn, followed by
attractive red or orange-red
rosehips. H 2.5m (8ft)
S 2.5m (8ft).

Rosa 'Sharifa Asma'
Rose-pink, fragrant, double
flowers are borne from mid-
summer to early autumn. Matt,
mid-green leaves. H 100cm
(36in) S 75cm (30in).

Rosa 'William Lobb'
Fragrant, semi-double, purple-
magenta flowers that age to
lavender are produced during early
summer and mid-summer. Matt,
dark green leaves. H 2m (6ft)
S 2m (6ft).

Rosa 'Winchester Cathedral'
Double, cup-shaped, white flowers
are produced in succession from
mid-summer to early autumn.
Matt, mid-green leaves.
H 1.2m (4ft) S 1.2m (4ft).

Rosa xanthina 'Canary Bird'
Musk-scented, single, yellow
flowers are produced in a single
flush during late spring. Matt,
fern-like, grey-green leaves.
H 3m (10ft) S 4m (13ft).

PATIO ROSE
These are compact floribunda
roses that produce masses of
flowers throughout the summer
and autumn months and can be
used at the front of the border
or in containers.

Rosa 'Golden Anniversary'
Large, semi-double, fragrant,
apricot-pink flowers are produced
from mid-summer to early
autumn. Glossy, mid-green leaves.
H 45cm (18in) S 45cm (18in).

Rosa 'Happy Anniversary'
Sweetly fragrant, deep-pink
flowers appear in succession from
mid-summer to early autumn.
Glossy, dark green leaves.
H 80cm (32in) S 75cm (30in).

Rosa 'Happy Birthday'
Double, creamy-white flowers are
produced in succession from mid-
summer to early autumn and
Glossy, mid-green leaves.
H 45cm (18in) S 45cm (18in).

Rosa 'Pearl Anniversary'
Semi-double, pearl-pink flowers
are produced in succession from
mid-summer to early autumn.
Glossy, mid-green leaves.
H 60cm (24in) S 60cm (24in).

Rosa 'Queen Mother'
Cup-shaped, semi-double, pink
flowers appear in succession from
mid-summer to early autumn.
Glossy, mid-green leaves.
H 40cm (16in) S 60cm (24in).

Rosa 'Sweet Dream'
Fragrant, cup-shaped, double,
peach-apricot flowers are
produced in succession from mid-
summer to early autumn. Glossy,
dark-green leaves. H 40cm (16in)
S 35cm (14in).

GROUND-COVER ROSE
These are low-growing and
spreading roses that produce
masses of small blooms and offer
good disease resistance. As this
category name suggests, they are
very useful for covering the
ground and also preventing weeds.

Rosa 'Kent'
Slightly fragrant, semi-double,
white flowers appear from mid-
summer to early autumn, followed
by small red hips. H 45cm (18in)
S 100cm (36in).

Rosa 'Oxfordshire'
Slightly fragrant, semi-double,
pale pink flowers are produced in
succession from mid-summer to
early autumn. H 60cm (24in)
S 150cm (60in).

Rosa 'Suffolk'
Single, slightly fragrant, golden-
centred, deep-scarlet flowers
are borne in succession from

Rosa 'Queen Mother'

mid-summer to early autumn, followed by orange-red rosehips. H 45cm (18in) S 100cm (36in).

Rosa 'Surrey'
The cup-shaped, fragrant, double rose-pink flowers of 'Surrey' are produced in succession from mid-summer to early autumn. Matt, dark green leaves. H 80cm (32in) S 120cm (48in).

Rosa 'Sussex'
The slightly fragrant, double, apricot flowers of 'Sussex' are borne in succession from mid-summer to early autumn. The flowers are borne above, mid-green leaves. H 60cm (24in) S 100cm (36in).

ROSMARINIUS
Rosemary
A small genus of just two species, grown for their early summer flowers and aromatic foliage. Widely used in culinary dishes. Good for a sunny border or can be trimmed into a dense hedge.
Cultivation Grow in any well-drained garden soil that is poor or reasonably fertile and in full sun. In colder areas, choose a sunny spot that is sheltered from cold winds or grow in a pot. Use a soil-based mix. Feed monthly during the growing season and water as necessary.
Pruning To keep neat and bushy, cut back the previous year's growth to within 10cm (4in) of the main framework or the

ground during mid-spring. Trim hedges after flowering.
Propagation Take semi-ripe cuttings in mid-summer or late summer.

Rosmarinus officinalis
Common rosemary
An evergreen culinary herb that forms a dense and rounded bush bearing purple-blue flowers during late spring and early summer along the stems of evergreen, strongly aromatic, dark green leaves. Good choice for growing as a hedge. H 1.5m (5ft) S 1.5m (5ft).
Named varieties: 'Miss Jessopp's Upright', vigorous, upright-growing rosemary, purple-blue flowers. H 2m (6ft) S 2m (6ft). 'Majorca Pink', compact, pale pink flowers. H 1m (3ft) S 1m (3ft). 'Severn Sea', arching stems carry bright blue flowers. H 1m (3ft) S 1.5m (5ft).
Aspect: sun
Hardiness: ✽✽ Zone: 9

RUBUS
A genus of about 250 species, including the tough, thicket-forming deciduous shrubs here, grown for their summer flowers and striking winter stems.
Cultivation Grow in any well-drained, reasonably fertile soil in full sun or dappled shade. Site those grown for winter stems where they will catch winter sun.

Pruning For the best flowering and stems cut back one in three stems near to ground level during early spring. Rejuvenate neglected plants by cutting back stems to near ground level in early spring.
Propagation Layer shoots or dig up rooted suckers in mid-spring.

Rubus biflorus
A prickly-stemmed, deciduous shrub with a brilliant white bloom when young. Small white flowers appear during late summer and early autumn, followed by yellow fruits. H 3m (10ft) S 3m (10ft).
Aspect: sun
Hardiness: ✽✽✽ Zones: 7–8

Rubus cockburnianus
Thicket-forming deciduous shrub with prickly purple stems that have a brilliant white bloom when young. Insignificant purple flowers are produced during late summer and early autumn, followed by black, inedible fruits. H 2.5m (8ft) S 2.5m (8ft).
Aspect: sun
Hardiness: ✽✽✽ Zones: 7–8

Rubus odoratus
Flowering raspberry
Fragrant, rose-pink, cup-shaped flowers appear from early summer to early autumn on this vigorous thicket-forming, deciduous shrub. H 2.5m (8ft) S 2.5m (8ft).
Aspect: sun or semi-shade
Hardiness: ✽✽✽ Zones: 7–8

Rosa 'Sussex'

Rosmarinus officinalis

Rubus odoratus

Ruta

RUTA
Rue

A genus of over five species that includes the evergreen shrub featured here, grown for their summer flowers and feathery aromatic foliage. An ideal choice for a sunny mixed border or can be trimmed to make a low hedge.
Cultivation Grow in any reasonably fertile, well-drained garden soil in full sun or dappled shade. Wear gloves and long sleeves when working with rue, as contact with the leaves can cause painful skin blistering in sunlight.
Pruning To keep plants neat and compact, cut back hard during mid-spring. Trim hedges after flowering.
Propagation Sow seed in early spring. Take semi-ripe cuttings in late summer.

Ruta graveolens 'Jackman's Blue'
This compact, rounded form has aromatic, steel-blue feathery leaves and tiny, mustard-coloured flowers from early summer to late summer. H 60cm (24in) S 75cm (30in).
Aspect: sun or semi-shade
Hardiness: ✱✱✱ Zones: 7–8

SALIX
Willow

This is a large and varied genus of some 300 species, including the low-growing deciduous shrubs featured here. They are grown for their silvery catkins and colourful bark. Compact and slow-growing varieties make excellent specimen plants for a small, sunny garden.

Willow trees to grow as shrubs

A few willow trees can be kept to shrub-like proportions by annual pruning. Cut all stems to near-ground level in early spring every year.

Salix alba 'Chermesina'
Bright red winter stems.
H 3m (10ft) S 3m (10ft).

Salix alba subsp. *vitellina* 'Britzensis'

Fiery orange-red winter stems. H 3m (10ft) S 3m (10ft).

Salix daphnoides
Violet-purple young stems with a white bloom. H 3m (10ft) S 3m (10ft).

Salix irrorata
Purple young stems with a white bloom. H 3m (10ft) S 3m (10ft).

Cultivation Grow in any moisture-retentive, well-drained garden soil in full sun.
Pruning No routine pruning is necessary other than removing wayward or damaged stems in early spring.
Propagation Take hardwood cuttings in late winter.

Salix hastata 'Wehrhahnii'
A neat, slow-growing shrub with dark purple shoots and bright green leaves that turn yellow in autumn. Large, silvery catkins appear in early spring on bare stems before the leaves emerge. H 1m (3ft) S 1m (3ft).
Aspect: sun
Hardiness: ✱✱✱ Zones: 7–8

Salix lanata
Woolly willow
This compact, slow-growing and bushy shrub produces stumpy shoots that are white and woolly

when young. Small yellow catkins are borne in mid-spring as the leaves emerge. H 1m (3ft) S 1.5m (5ft).
Aspect: sun
Hardiness: ✱✱✱ Zones: 7–8

SALVIA
Sage

This huge genus of around 900 species, includes the evergreen sub-shrubs featured here, are grown for their handsome aromatic foliage and widely used in culinary dishes. Grow in a mixed or herb border or in a container on a sunny patio.
Cultivation In the garden, grow in a moisture-retentive, well-drained soil that is reasonably fertile and in full sun or dappled shade. In pots, grow in any fresh general-purpose compost (soil mix).
Pruning To keep plants neat and compact, cut back hard to near ground level during mid-spring.

Salix vitellina 'Britzensis'

Salvia officinalis

Replace neglected plants.
Propagation Sow seed in early spring. Take semi-ripe cuttings in early autumn.

Salvia officinalis
Common sage
An evergreen culinary herb with grey-green aromatic foliage that carries spikes of lilac-blue flowers borne from late spring to mid-summer. H 80cm (32in) S 100cm (36in).
Named varieties: 'Icterina', variegated form with yellow-edged green leaves, mauve-blue flowers. H 80cm (32in) S 100cm (36in). 'Purpurascens', bright purple young leaves age to grey-green, mauve-blue flowers. H 80cm (32in) S 100cm (36in). 'Tricolor', grey-green leaves, splashed with cream and reddish-purple, mauve-blue flowers. H 80cm (32in) S 100cm (36in).
Aspect: sun or semi-shade
Hardiness: ✱✱✱ Zones: 7–8

SAMBUCUS
Elder

A genus of about 25 species grown for their handsome foliage and summer flowers. Useful back-of-the-border plants. They are ideal for filling gaps.
Cultivation Grow in a moisture-retentive, well-drained garden soil that is reasonably fertile in full sun or dappled shade.
Pruning To get the best foliage displays, cut back hard to near ground level during early spring each year. For flowers and berries, cut back one stem in three during the dormant season, starting with the oldest.
Propagation Take hardwood cuttings in late winter.

Sambucus nigra 'Black Beauty'
A new variety with near-black, darkest burgundy foliage that contrasts with the flat heads of lemon-scented pale-pink flowers during early summer, followed by purple-black berries in autumn. H 3m (10ft) S 3m (10ft).
Aspect: sun or semi-shade
Hardiness: ✱✱✱ Zones: 7–8

Sambucus nigra 'Black Lace'
An exciting recent introduction with near-black, finely cut foliage

Sambucus racemosa 'Plumosa Aurea'

that provides a foil for the flat heads of pale-pink flowers that open from cream-coloured buds during late spring and early summer. Good choice for small gardens. H 3m (10ft) S 2m (6ft).
Aspect: sun or semi-shade
Hardiness: ❋❋❋ Zones: 7–8

Sambucus racemosa 'Plumosa Aurea'
Emerging bronze-tinted, the deeply cut, almost feathery, foliage turns golden yellow as it matures. Arching shoots bear conical clusters of creamy-yellow flowers during mid-spring. Grow in dappled shade to avoid scorching the delicate foliage. H 3m (10ft) S 3m (10ft).
Aspect: sun or semi-shade
Hardiness: ❋❋❋ Zones: 7–8

Sambucus racemosa 'Sutherland Gold'
The deeply cut, almost feathery, foliage emerges bronze-tinted before turning golden yellow with age. Conical clusters of creamy-yellow flowers during mid-spring are followed by glossy red fruits. H 3m (10ft) S 3m (10ft).
Aspect: sun or semi-shade
Hardiness: ❋❋❋ Zones: 7–8

SANTOLINA
A genus of nearly 20 species, including the compact evergreen shrubs featured here, grown for their grey, aromatic foliage and button-like summer flowers. Ideal for a hot spot, such as sunny banks and gravel gardens, or edging sunny borders. They can even make an attractive low, informal flowering hedge or garden divider.
Cultivation Grow in any well-drained garden soil that is poor to reasonably fertile and in full sun, but sheltered from cold winds.
Pruning To keep plants neat and compact, cut back to 5cm (2in) off ground level during mid-spring before new growth emerges. Neglected plants can be rejuvenated by cutting back hard into old wood during mid-spring

Santolina pinnata

to encourage new growth from lower down. Deadhead edging plants and hedges to keep neat all summer.
Propagation Take semi-ripe cuttings in early autumn.

Santolina chamaecyparissus var. *nana*
Cotton lavender
Feathery, greyish-white, aromatic leaves set off the masses of tiny, lemon-yellow button-like flowers throughout mid-summer and late summer on this dense and rounded evergreen shrub. H 30cm (12in) S 45cm (18in).
Aspect: sun
Hardiness: ❋❋ Zones: 7–8

Santolina chamaecyparissus 'Lambrook Silver'
Cotton lavender
The silvery mound of finely dissected woolly leaves that this shrub produces is the perfect foil for the tiny lemon-yellow and button-like flowers that are borne during mid-summer and late summer. H 30cm (12in) S 45cm (18in).
Aspect: sun
Hardiness: ❋❋ Zone: 9

SARCOCOCCA
Sweet box
A genus of around 15 species, including the dense-growing, evergreen shrubs featured here, grown for their neat habit and sweet vanilla-scented winter flowers. An ideal choice for a dark, shady corner where nothing else will grow. Well suited to

Santolina chamaecyparissus var. *nana*

Sarcococca confusa

urban gardens as it is pollution tolerant.
Cultivation Grow in a moisture-retentive, well-drained garden soil that is reasonably fertile and in dappled or deep shade.
Pruning No routine pruning is necessary. Remove any damaged growth in mid-spring.
Propagation Take hardwood cuttings in mid-autumn.

Sarcococca confusa
A dense, evergreen shrub with glossy, dark green leaves that bears clusters of sweetly scented white flowers from early winter to early spring. H 2m (6ft) S 1m (3ft).
Aspect: semi-shade to deep shade
Hardiness: ❋❋❋ Zones: 6–9

Sarcococca hookeriana var. *digyna*
A thicket-forming shrub with slender, pointed, dark green leaves and small creamy-white or pink-tinged flowers that are produced in clusters from early winter to early spring. H 1.5m (5ft) S 2m (6ft).
Aspect: semi-shade to deep shade
Hardiness: ❋❋❋ 6–9

Sarcococca hookeriana var. *humilis* (syn. *S. humilis*)
Compact, clump-forming evergreen shrub with slender dark green leaves and small, creamy-white or pink-tinged flowers produced in clusters from early winter to early spring. H 60cm (24in) S 100cm (36in).
Aspect: semi-shade to deep shade
Hardiness: ❋❋❋ 6–9

Skimmia japonica 'Rubella'

SKIMMIA

A small genus of just four species, including the compact evergreen shrubs featured here, grown for their fragrant flowers, neat foliage and long-lasting colourful autumn berries. They make useful border fillers in shade. Compact forms make excellent winter pots.
Cultivation Grow in a moisture-retentive, well-drained garden soil that is reasonably fertile and in dappled or deep shade. In containers, grow in any fresh general-purpose soil mix. To be sure of berries, grow both male and female forms.
Pruning No routine pruning is necessary. Remove any damaged growth in mid-spring.
Propagation Take semi-ripe cuttings in early autumn.

Skimmia japonica 'Rubella' (male form)
A compact shrub with handsome, red-margined, dark green leaves

and dense clusters of deep red flower-buds in autumn that do not open until early spring to reveal fragrant white flowers. H 1.5m (5ft) S 1.5m (5ft).
Aspect: semi-shade to deep shade
Hardiness: ❈❈❈ Zones: 7–8

Skimmia japonica subsp. reevesiana (hermaphrodite form)
A large, spreading, evergreen shrub with narrow, tapered, dark green leaves and clusters of white flowers during mid-spring and late spring, followed by bright red berries. H 7m (23ft) S 1m (3ft).
Named varieties: 'Robert Fortune', dark-edged, pale green leaves, white flowers, followed by bright red berries. H 7m (23ft) S 1m (3ft).
Aspect: semi-shade to deep shade
Hardiness: ❈❈❈ Zones: 7–8

Skimmia x confusa 'Kew Green' (male form)
Dome-shaped, compact, evergreen

shrub with aromatic, pointed, leaves that set off the dense clusters of sweetly scented, cream-coloured flowers produced during mid-spring and late spring. H 3m (10ft) S 1.5m (5ft).
Aspect: semi-shade to deep shade
Hardiness: ❈❈❈ Zones: 7–8

SOPHORA

A genus of about 50 species, including the evergreen shrubs featured here, grown for their clusters of bell-shaped flowers that hang from zigzag shoots covered in symmetrical leaves that are tiny, oval, dark green leaflets. Good seasonal specimens for a sunny border, or can be trained against a wall or fence.
Cultivation Grow in any well-drained garden soil in full sun. Grow against a sunny wall in colder areas.
Pruning No routine pruning is necessary. Remove any wayward or damaged growth in mid-spring.
Propagation Sow seed in early spring.

Sophora microphylla (syn. Edwardia microphylla)
Open, spreading, frost-hardy evergreen shrub that carries pendent clusters of pea-shaped yellow flowers from arching branches during mid-spring and late spring. H 8m (26ft) S 8m (26ft).
Named varieties: 'Sun King', a recent fully hardy introduction that forms a more compact, but still open, bushy shrub with drooping clusters of bell-shaped

yellow flowers during early spring and mid-spring. H 3m (10ft) S 3m (10ft).
Aspect: sun
Hardiness: ❈❈ or ❈❈❈
Zones: 7–9

SPARTIUM
Spanish broom
A genus of just one species of deciduous shrubs grown for their long-lasting and fragrant golden summer flowers. Good border filler or back-of-the-border shrub for a sunny spot. Pollution- and salt-tolerant, they are therefore well-suited for growing in town and coastal gardens.
Cultivation Grow in any well-drained, reasonably fertile, garden soil in full sun. Grow by a sunny wall in colder areas.
Pruning Prevent it going woody at the base and encourage flowering by trimming new growth lightly directly after flowering.
Propagation Sow seed in early spring.

Spartium junceum
A slender shrub with dark green shoots that carries masses of pea-like flowers in succession from early summer to late summer, followed by dark brown seed-pods. H 3m (10ft) S 3m (10ft).
Aspect: sun
Hardiness: ❈❈ Zone: 9

SPIRAEA
A genus of about 80 species, including the easy-to-grow, deciduous, summer-flowering shrubs featured here, some of

Sophora microphylla

Spartium junceum

which are grown mainly for their eye-catching foliage. A useful border filler in sun or can be grown as an informal low hedge.
Cultivation Grow in a moisture-retentive, well-drained, reasonably fertile soil in full sun.
Pruning Varieties that flower on the previous season's growth need no routine pruning. Otherwise, cut out one stem in three during early spring, starting with the oldest. Informal hedges should be trimmed after flowering. Remove all-green reverted shoots on variegated varieties as soon as they appear.
Propagation Take semi-ripe cuttings in mid-summer, or hardwood cuttings in late autumn.

Spiraea 'Arguta'
Bridal wreath
Beautiful arching sprays of tiny, saucer-shaped, white flowers dominate this dense, rounded shrub during mid-spring and late spring. H 2.5m (8ft) S 2.5m (8ft).
Aspect: sun
Hardiness: ✿✿✿ Zones 7–8

Spiraea japonica 'Anthony Waterer'
Emerging bronze-tinted, the sharply toothed foliage matures to

dark green with pink and cream margins. Flat heads of rose-pink flowers appear from mid-summer to late summer. Good informal hedge. H 1.5m (5ft) S 1.5m (5ft).
Aspect: sun
Hardiness: ✿✿✿ Zones 7–8

Spiraea japonica 'Goldflame'
Bronze-red emerging foliage turns bright yellow and then ages to luminous green on this compact shrub. Dark pink flowers are borne in clusters during mid-summer and late summer. Good informal hedge. H 75cm (30in) S 75cm (30in).
Aspect: sun
Hardiness: ✿✿✿ Zones: 7–8

Spiraea japonica 'Golden Princess'
The foliage emerges bronze-red on this clump-forming shrub before turning bright yellow then red in autumn. Purplish-pink flowers are produced in clusters during mid-summer and late summer. H 2m (6ft) S 1.5m (5ft).
Aspect: sun
Hardiness: ✿✿✿ Zones: 7–8

Spiraea nipponica 'Snowmound' (syn. *S. nipponica* var. *tosaensis*)
The rounded, dark green leaves of

Stephanandra incisa 'Crispa'

this spreading deciduous shrub make the perfect backdrop for the arching sprays of cup-shaped white flowers that are produced throughout early summer and mid-summer. H 2.5m (8ft) S 2.5m (8ft).
Aspect: sun
Hardiness: ✿✿✿ Zones: 7–8

Spiraea prunifolia (syn. *S. prunifolia* 'Plena')
Finely toothed, bright green leaves that are silvery beneath, cover this deciduous shrub, which has arching stems that are wreathed in double white flowers throughout early spring and mid-spring. H 2m (6ft) S 2m (6ft).
Aspect: sun
Hardiness: ✿✿✿ Zones: 7–8

Spiraea thunbergii
From mid-spring to early summer, arching sprays of tiny, saucer-shaped, white flowers cover this dense and bushy deciduous shrub. The pale green leaves turn yellow in autumn. H 1.5m (5ft) S 2m (6ft).
Aspect: sun
Hardiness: ✿✿✿ Zones: 7–8

STEPHANANDRA
This is a small genus comprising just four species, including the deciduous early summer-flowering shrubs featured here. These plants make useful front-of-the-border fillers when planted in sun or

dappled shade. They can also be used for edging or ground cover.
Cultivation Grow in a moisture-retentive, well-drained garden soil that is reasonably fertile in full sun or dappled shade.
Pruning Prune out one stem in three during early spring, starting with the oldest.
Propagation Take semi-ripe cuttings in mid-summer or hardwood cuttings in late autumn.

Stephanandra incisa 'Crispa'
The deeply lobed and wavy-edged leaves cover this thicket-forming, low-growing shrub and turn orange-yellow in autumn before they fall to reveal rich brown stems. This shrub makes a good edging and ground cover plant. H 60cm (24in) S 3m (10ft).
Aspect: sun or semi-shade
Hardiness: ✿✿✿ Zones: 7–8

Stephanandra tanakae
This is a thicket-forming, bushy shrub that has striking bright orange-brown stems that are revealed during the winter. The arching shoots are covered in toothed green leaves at other times before turning shades of yellow and orange in autumn. Bears greenish-yellow flowers throughout the summer. H 3m (10ft) S 3m (10ft).
Aspect: sun or semi-shade
Hardiness: ✿✿✿ Zones: 7–8

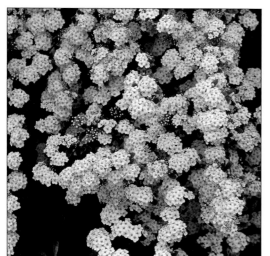

Spiraea 'Arguta'

Symphoricarpos x doorenbosii 'Mother of Pearl'

SYMPHORICARPOS
Snowberry

A genus of over 15 species, including the deciduous thicket-forming shrubs featured here, grown mainly for their handsome foliage or long-lasting, marble-sized, autumn berries. Useful border fillers in sun or dappled shade. They make attractive informal low hedges.
Cultivation Grow in any reasonably fertile, well-drained soil in full sun or dappled shade.
Pruning For brightly coloured foliage displays, prune out one stem in three during early spring, starting with the oldest. Informal hedges can be trimmed every couple of months during the summer to keep neat.
Propagation Take semi-ripe cuttings in early summer or hardwood cuttings in late autumn.

Symphoricarpos x chenaultii 'Hancock'
Low-growing and spreading snowberry that has green leaves that turn orange-red in autumn. Small bell-shaped flowers are produced in late summer, followed by conspicuous dark pink berries. H 3m (10ft) S 3m (10ft).
Aspect: sun or semi-shade
Hardiness: ❀❀❀ Zones: 7–8

Symphoricarpos x doorenbosii 'Mother of Pearl'
A thicket-forming shrub with dark green leaves and arching stems that carry small, bell-shaped flowers during mid-summer, followed by conspicuous pearl-like pink-flushed white berries from early autumn. The best fruiting variety. H 2m (6ft) S indefinite.
Aspect: sun or semi-shade
Hardiness: ❀❀❀ Zones: 7–8

Symphoricarpos orbiculatus 'Albovariegatus'
A compact, thicket-forming shrub with variegated white and green leaves on a dense and busy shrub. Few berries are produced. H 2m (6ft) S 2m (6ft).
Aspect: sun or semi-shade
Hardiness: ❀❀❀ Zones: 7–8

SYRINGA
Lilac

A genus of about 20 species including the large, spreading deciduous shrubs featured here, grown for their highly fragrant spring flowers. They make useful seasonal specimens and can be trained into attractive multi-stemmed trees.
Cultivation Grow in a moisture-retentive, well-drained neutral to alkaline soil that is reasonably fertile and in full sun.
Pruning After flowering, cut back the fading flowering shoots to the first leaves below the flower cluster. In the dormant season thin out overcrowded branches and rejuvenate neglected shrubs by cutting the whole shrub back to within 1m (3ft) of the ground. Create a multi-stemmed tree by selecting three, four or five of the strongest stems, removing all others and cutting off side branches in successive seasons to raise the height of the canopy. All major pruning should be carried out during the dormant season (early winter to early spring).
Propagation Bud named varieties during mid-summer.

Syringa meyeri var. spontanea 'Palibin'
Fragrant, purple-pink flowers are produced in dense clusters throughout late spring and early summer on this slow-growing Korean lilac. Ideal for small gardens. H 2m (10ft) S 1.5m (5ft).
Aspect: sun
Hardiness: ❀❀❀ Zones: 7–8

Syringa pubescens subsp. microphylla 'Superba'
The oval green leaves provide a backdrop for the rose-pink fragrant flowers that are borne in dense clusters during mid-spring and late spring and intermittently thereafter until mid-autumn. H 6m (20ft) S 6m (20ft).
Aspect: sun
Hardiness: ❀❀❀ Zones: 7–8

Syringa vulgaris 'Charles Joly'
A spreading shrub with heart-shaped, dark green leaves and dense, cone-shaped clusters of double, dark purple flowers in late spring and early summer.
H 7m (23ft) S 7m (23ft).
Aspect: sun
Hardiness: ❀❀❀ Zones: 7–8

Syringa vulgaris 'Katherine Havemeyer'
Dense, cone-shaped clusters of purple buds open during late spring and early summer to reveal strongly scented, double, lavender-purple flowers above heart-shaped leaves. H 7m (23ft) S 7m (23ft).
Aspect: sun
Hardiness: ❀❀❀ Zones: 7–8

Syringa vulgaris 'Madame Lemoine'
This elegant white lilac produces dense, cone-shaped clusters of very fragrant, double, white flowers during late spring and early summer above heart-shaped, apple-green leaves. H 7m (23ft) S 7m (23ft).
Aspect: sun
Hardiness: ❀❀❀ Zones: 7–8

Syringa protolaciniata

Syringa x josiflexa

Syringa vulgaris 'Michel Buchner'
A spreading shrub with heart-shaped, dark green leaves and large, cone-shaped clusters of fragrant, double, rose-mauve flowers with white centres during late spring and early summer. H 7m (23ft) S 7m (23ft).
Aspect: sun
Hardiness: ❀❀❀ Zones: 7–8

TAMARIX
Tamarisk

A genus of over 50 species, including the deciduous shrubs featured here, grown for their feathery, late-summer flowerheads. A good back-of-the-border shrub that makes an excellent windbreak in mild coastal gardens.
Cultivation Grow in any well-drained garden soil in full sun, but sheltered from cold winds.
Pruning To keep in shape, prune flowering stems in early spring, removing half to two-thirds of the previous year's growth.
Propagation Take hardwood cuttings in mid-autumn.

Tamarix ramosissima (syn. T. pentandra)
A vigorous shrub with graceful, arching, red-brown stems that carry airy, plume-like, pale pink flowers in dense clusters during late summer and early autumn. H 5m (16ft) S 5m (16ft).
Named varieties: 'Pink Cascade',

Tamarix 'Rubra'

plumes of tiny, rich pink flowers.
H 5m (16ft) S 5m (16ft).
Aspect: sun
Hardiness: ✿✿✿ Zones: 7–8

Tamarix 'Rubra'
A vigorous shrub with graceful,
arching stems that carry airy,
plume-like, purple-pink flowers in
dense clusters during late summer
and early autumn. H 5m (16ft)
S 5m (16ft).
Aspect: sun
Hardiness: ✿✿✿ Zones: 7–8

TIBOUCHINA
A large genus of over 350 species,
including the spreading tender
evergreen shrub featured here,
grown for its exotic summer

Tibouchina semi-decandra

flowers. An attractive border filler
in warm gardens. Grow in a
container in cooler areas.
Cultivation Grow in a moisture-
retentive, well-drained garden soil
in full sun. In containers, grow in
a soil-based compost (soil mix).
Feed every month throughout the
growing season and water as
necessary. Move to a warm spot
undercover when the temperature
falls below 5°C (41°F) and water
sparingly throughout the winter.
Pruning No routine pruning is
necessary.
Propagation Take softwood
cuttings in mid-spring or semi-
ripe cuttings in mid-summer.

Tibouchina urvilleana
(syn. *Pleroma macrantha*.
T. semidecandra)
Brazilian spider flower
A tall, spreading shrub with
velvety, dark green leaves that are
distinctively veined. Large saucer-
shaped rich purple flowers with a
satin finish are borne from mid-
summer to late autumn. H 4m
(12ft) S 5m (16ft).
Aspect: sun
Hardiness: tender Zones: 10+

VIBURNUM
A varied genus of over 150
species, including the deciduous
and evergreen shrubs featured
here, grown for their clusters of
winter or spring flowers or eye-

catching autumn berries. Most are
good border fillers, with many
coping well with a partly shady
shrub border or woodland-edge
planting scheme. The winter-
flowering deciduous varieties and
fruiting evergreen forms are
useful for adding interest during
the coldest months.
Cultivation Grow in a moisture-
retentive, well-drained garden soil
that is reasonably fertile and in
full sun or dappled shade.
Pruning Evergreen varieties require
no routine pruning. Damaged or
misplaced shoots can be removed
in late spring. If required,
deciduous varieties can be thinned
by removing one stem in three,
starting with the oldest. Prune
winter-flowering varieties during
mid-spring and summer-flowering
varieties in early summer.
Propagation Layer deciduous
shrubs in mid-spring. Take
hardwood cuttings in mid-autumn
or semi-ripe cuttings of evergreen
varieties in early autumn.

EVERGREEN VIBURNUMS
Viburnum davidii
A compact, evergreen shrub with
prominently veined, dark green
leaves that bears small flat heads
of white flowers during late
spring followed by eyecatching
metallic, turquoise-blue berries.
H 1.5m (5ft) S 1.5m (5ft).
Aspect: sun or semi-shade
Hardiness: ✿✿✿ Zones: 7–8

Viburnum x burkwoodii
Clusters of pink buds open on
this lovely viburnum during mid-

Viburnum tinus 'Eve Price'

spring and late spring to expose
deliciously fragrant white flowers
that are followed by red fruit.
H 2.5m (8ft) S 2.5m (8ft).
Aspect: sun or semi-shade
Hardiness: ✿✿✿ Zones: 7–8

Viburnum 'Eskimo'
This is a compact, semi-evergreen
viburnum that produces lovely
round clusters of pink-tinged,
cream buds that open during mid-
spring and late spring to show off
its white tubular flowers against
glossy, dark green leaves.
H 1.5m (5ft) S 1.5m (5ft).
Aspect: sun or semi-shade
Hardiness: ✿✿✿ Zones: 7–8

Viburnum rhytidophyllum
This is a spreading, evergreen
viburnum that bears flat clusters
of cream-coloured flowers
throughout late spring. They are
produced at the ends of arching
shoots of wavy-edged, dark green
leaves. Red berries follow in
autumn. H 3m (10ft)
S 4m (12ft).
Aspect: sun or semi-shade
Hardiness: ✿✿✿ Zones: 7–8

Viburnum tinus 'Eve Price'
Small flatheads of carmine-pink
buds reveal pinkish-white flowers
from early winter to mid-spring
and are followed by dark blue-
black berries. H 3m (10ft)
S 3m (10ft).
Aspect: sun or semi-shade
Hardiness: ✿✿✿ Zones: 7–8

Viburnum tinus 'French White'
This viburnum produces flat
heads of rosy-red buds open in
succession from early winter to
mid-spring to reveal white flowers
that are followed by dark blue-
black berries. H 3m (10ft)
S 3m (10ft).
Aspect: sun or semi-shade
Hardiness: ✿✿✿ Zones: 7–8

Viburnum tinus 'Gwenllian'
Masses of dark pink buds open in
succession on this shrub from
early winter to mid-spring to
reveal pink-flushed white flowers,
that are followed by a profusion
of dark, blue-black berries.
H 3m (10ft) S 3m (10ft).
Aspect: sun or semi-shade
Hardiness: ✿✿✿ Zones: 7–8

Viburnum opulus 'Roseum'

Viburnum plicatum 'Mariesii'

DECIDUOUS VIBURNUMS
Viburnum x bodnantense 'Dawn'
An upright deciduous shrub that carries dense clusters of fragrant dark pink flowers on bare stems from late autumn to early spring. H 3m (10ft) S 2m (6ft).
Aspect: sun or semi-shade
Hardiness: ✿✿✿ Zones: 7–8

Viburnum x bodnantense 'Charles Lamont'
Strongly scented, bright pink flowers are carried in dense clusters on bare stems from late autumn to early spring on this upright deciduous shrub. H 3m (10ft) S 2m (6ft).
Aspect: sun or semi-shade
Hardiness: ✿✿✿ Zones: 7–8

Viburnum x carlcephalum
Rounded clusters of pink buds open during mid-spring and late spring to reveal fragrant white flowers against heart-shaped, dark-green leaves, that turn red in autumn. H 3m (10ft) S 3m (10ft).
Aspect: sun or semi-shade
Hardiness: ✿✿✿ Zones: 7–8

Viburnum carlesii
Dense clusters of pink buds open throughout mid-spring and late spring into fragrant white or pink-flushed white flowers. The dark green leaves take on red-purple tints in autumn.
H 2m (6ft) S 2m (6ft).
Aspect: sun or semi-shade
Hardiness: ✿✿✿ Zones: 7–8

Viburnum x juddii
Pink buds in rounded clusters open during mid-spring and late spring to reveal fragrant pink-tinted white flowers. The oval, dark green leaves take on red-purple tints in autumn.
H 1.2m (4ft) S 1.5m (5ft).
Aspect: sun or semi-shade
Hardiness: ✿✿✿ Zones: 7–8

Viburnum opulus 'Roseum' (syn. *V.* 'Sterile') Snowball tree
Rounded, snowball-like clusters of white flowers are produced during late spring and early summer against a backdrop of dark green leaves that become purple-tinted in autumn. H 4m (12ft) S 4m (13ft).
Aspect: sun or semi-shade
Hardiness: ✿✿✿ Zones: 7–8

Viburnum plicatum 'Mariesii' Japanese snowball bush
Tiered branches carry white, lacecap-like flowers throughout late spring over toothed, prominently veined, dark-green leaves that turn red-purple in autumn. H 3m (10ft) S 4m (13ft).
Aspect: sun or semi-shade
Hardiness: ✿✿✿ Zones: 7–8

Viburnum plicatum 'Pink Beauty'
Horizontal, tiered branches of this deciduous shrub show off the white, lacecap-like flowers in late spring that age to pink. The toothed, prominently veined, dark green leaves turn red-purple in autumn. H 3m (10ft) S 4m (13ft).
Aspect: sun or semi-shade
Hardiness: ✿✿✿ Zones: 7–8

VINCA
Periwinkle
This genus of seven species includes the low-growing sub-shrubs featured here, grown for their colourful spring flowers and their weed-smothering carpet of attractive foliage. It makes excellent ground cover in sun or shade as well as a useful addition to winter containers.
Cultivation Grow in a moisture-retentive, well-drained soil that is reasonably fertile and in full sun or dappled shade. Grow in sun for better flowering displays. In containers, grow in any fresh general-purpose compost (soil mix).
Pruning No routine pruning is necessary, other than to keep it within bounds. Neglected plants can be rejuvenated by cutting all stems back to near ground level during late winter.
Propagation Lift and divide clumps as for perennials or separate and pot-up rooted layers.

Vinca major Greater periwinkle
This is a fast-growing, sprawling, evergreen sub-shrub with large, violet-blue flowers that are

Viburnum carlesii

Vinca minor 'Aureovariegata'

Vinca major

produced in succession from mid-spring to early autumn above dark green leaves. This shrub makes excellent ground cover between deciduous trees and shrubs. H 45cm (18in) S indefinite.
Aspect: sun or semi-shade
Hardiness: ❁❁❁ Zones: 7–8

Vinca minor
Lesser periwinkle
This is a less invasive version of the periwinkle, which has evergreen, lance-shaped, dark green leaves and pale blue flowers borne from mid-spring to early autumn. Good ground cover choice for small areas or for softening the edges of raised beds and containers. H 20cm (8in) S indefinite.
Named varieties: 'Aureovariegata', variegated form with deep purple flowers. H 20cm (18in) S indefinite. 'Gertrude Jekyll', white flowers. H 20cm (8in) S indefinite.
Aspect: sun or semi-shade
Hardiness: ❁❁❁ Zones: 7–8

Vinca minor 'Illumination'
This is a recent introduction that has glossy golden, green-edged leaves on sprawling stems. Light blue flowers are carried in succession from mid-spring to early autumn. Ideal for use in containers or even for trailing over the edge of a hanging basket. H 15m (50ft) S 1m (3ft).
Aspect: sun or semi-shade
Hardiness: ❁❁❁ Zones: 7–8

WEIGELA
A genus of over 10 species, including the summer-flowering deciduous shrubs featured here. These plants can be used all around the garden filling gaps and boosting early summer displays.
Cultivation Grow in any well-drained garden soil that is reasonably fertile and in full sun or dappled shade.
Pruning To keep established shrubs flowering well, cut back one stem in three to near ground level after flowering, starting with the oldest stems.
Propagation Take semi-ripe cuttings in mid-summer or hardwood cuttings in mid-autumn.

Weigela 'Bristol Ruby'
An upright-growing shrub with dark green leaves that is covered in clusters of purple buds. These open into bell-shaped, ruby-red flowers throughout late spring and early summer. H 2.5m (8ft) S 2m (6ft).
Aspect: sun or semi-shade
Hardiness: ❁❁❁ Zones: 7–8

Weigela florida 'Foliis Purpureis'
A deciduous shrub with bronze-green leaves that carries clusters of funnel-shaped, deep pink flowers on arching stems during late spring and early summer. H 1m (3ft) S 5m (16ft).
Aspect: sun or semi-shade
Hardiness: ❁❁❁ Zones: 7–8

Weigela 'Florida Variegata'
Clusters of pale pink funnel-shaped flowers are borne on arching stems throughout late spring and early summer against a

Weigela 'Apple Blossom'

Weigela 'Candida'

backdrop of greyish-green leaves that are edged with white. H 2.5m (8ft) S 2.5m (8ft).
Aspect: sun or semi-shade
Hardiness: ❁❁❁ Zones: 7–8

YUCCA
This genus of about 40 species includes the spiky, evergreen shrubs with sword-shaped leaves featured here. Ideal focal points in a mixed border in sun or shade and provide architectural interest throughout the year.
Cultivation Grow in any well-drained, reasonably fertile soil in full sun or dappled shade. Mulch with gravel to protect the crown.
Pruning Pruning is unnecessary. Remove dead or damaged leaves in mid-spring.
Propagation Separate young offshoots during mid-spring.

Yucca filamentosa
Adam's needle
Spiky clumps of stiff, dark green, sword-shaped leaves provide year-round interest, with the bonus of towering spikes of white, bell-shaped flowers during mid-summer and late summer. H 75cm (30in) S 150cm (60in).
Aspect: sun or semi-shade
Hardiness: ❁❁❁ Zones: 7–8

Yucca flaccida 'Ivory'
Impressive clumps of dark, blue-green, sword-shaped leaves look good all year round, with tall spikes of green-tinged, creamy-white flowers produced in mid-summer and late summer. H 1.5m (5ft) S 1.5m (5ft).
Aspect: sun or semi-shade
Hardiness: ❁❁❁ Zones: 7–8

Yucca flaccida 'Golden Sword'
Clumps of spiky, yellow-striped, sword-shaped, blue-green leaves with green-tinged, creamy-white flowers appearing in mid-summer and late summer. H 55cm (22in) S 150cm (60in).
Aspect: sun or semi-shade
Hardiness: ❁❁❁ Zones: 7–8

Yucca gloriosa 'Variegata'
Spiky clumps of stiff yellow-edged, sword-shaped, dark green leaves are joined by white bell-shaped flowers on vertical spikes from late summer to early autumn. H 2m (6ft) S 2m (6ft).
Aspect: sun or semi-shade
Hardiness: ❁❁❁ Zones: 7–8

Yucca filamentosa

A directory of climbers

This section provides a highly illustrated listing of popular climbers that are available. It demonstrates very clearly just how versatile these plants can be – providing every conceivable colour of bloom, growth achievements and types of foliage. Bearing these factors in mind will enable you to create wonderful effects in any style or size of garden. Increasingly, plants are becoming known by their Latin (botanical) names, so these are given throughout, together with their English (common) names.

The hardiness zones given in the text refer only to the selected main plants featured and not to the whole genus. The height and spread given for each of the plants is an indication only. The dimensions will vary, depending on the growing conditions and the vigour of the individual plants – as well as your ability to care for them. The spread is particularly difficult to predict, as many plants go on increasing their width throughout their lives.

This magnificent climber, *Clematis montana* var. *rubens* 'Elizabeth', tumbles over a wall in full bloom to display its magnificent flowers. It is a prime example of how climbers can enhance any structure in the garden.

Actinidia kolomikta

ACTINIDIA

A genus of about 40 species, including the deciduous, twining climber featured here, which is grown for its seemingly paint-dipped foliage. Useful for adding interest to sunny walls and fences and will quickly cover trellis and arbours. Fast growing, it is an ideal choice for a quick cover-up, too, with a single plant able to smother about two standard fence panels in five years.

Cultivation Grow in any well-drained garden soil that is reasonably fertile and in full sun, but sheltered from strong winds.
Pruning No routine pruning is necessary. Thin out over-crowded stems in late winter. For a quick cover-up, train stems 20cm (8in) apart across the screen and tie in new shoots as necessary. When the screen is complete, cut back new growth to within 15cm (6in) of the established framework of stems in late winter. Neglected plants can be rejuvenated by cutting the oldest stems back to a younger side shoot lower down in late winter.
Propagation Take semi-ripe nodal cuttings in mid-summer.

Actinidia kolomikta
Kolomikta vine
A deciduous climber with dark green, heart-shaped leaves that are splashed pink and white as if the

tips had been dipped in paint. Clusters of fragrant white flowers are produced in early summer. H 5m (16ft) S 4m (13ft).
Aspect: sun
Hardiness: ❉❉❉ Zone: Min. 7

AKEBIA
Chocolate vine
A genus of around five species, including the semi-evergreen vigorous twining climber featured here, grown for its fragrant chocolate-coloured spring flowers. Good for growing up screens and walls next to an entrance, where its fragrance can be appreciated. It is fairly fast-growing, with a single plant covering one standard fence panel in five years.

Akebia quinata

Cultivation Grow in a moisture-retentive, well-drained garden soil that is reasonably fertile and in full sun or dappled shade.
Pruning No routine pruning is necessary. Encourage dense growth and keep tidy by trimming in mid-spring. Neglected plants can be rejuvenated by cutting back the oldest stems to a younger side shoot lower down in late winter.
Propagation Take semi-ripe nodal cuttings in late summer or layer suitable stems in mid-autumn.

Akebia quinata
Pendent clusters of maroon-chocolate flowers that have a sweet and spicy fragrance are produced from early to late spring. The lobed dark green foliage becomes purple-tinged in winter. In long, warm summers, large, sausage-shaped fruit can form. H 10m (33ft) S 10m (33ft).
Aspect: sun or semi-shade
Hardiness: ❉❉❉ Zone: Min. 7

AMPELOPSIS
A genus of about 25 species, including the deciduous self-clinging climbers featured here, grown for their unusual flowers, fruit and autumn tints. They make useful and unusual climbers for south- east- and west-facing supports. If grown over a pergola or other similar open support, they can be trained to create an attractive, hanging curtain-effect of foliage.

Cultivation Grow in a moisture-retentive, well-drained garden soil

that is reasonably fertile and in full sun or dappled shade. Grow in full sun for best fruit production.
Pruning No routine pruning is necessary. Thin out over-crowded stems in late winter. For a curtain effect, cut back all new growth to within a couple of buds from the main horizontal framework overhead in late winter.
Propagation Take softwood cuttings in mid-summer.

Ampelopsis aconitifolia (syn. *Vitis aconitifolia*)
This luxuriant vine will cloak any garden structure effortlessly, creating a highly textured curtain of attractively lush foliage. This is a vigorous climber, with palmate dark green leaves, that carries insignificant green flowers during early and mid-summer, followed by showy bunches of orange-red berries. H 12m (40ft) S 10m (33ft).
Aspect: sun or semi-shade
Hardiness: ❉❉❉ Zone: Min. 7

Ampelopsis glandulosa var. *brevipedunculata* (syn *A. brevipedunculata*)
This plant produces miniature birds' egg-like speckled fruit that change from cream to pink to clear blue as they ripen on this vigorous climber. The fruit follow insignificant green flowers produced during early and mid-summer. H 5m (16ft) S 6m (20ft).
Aspect: sun or semi-shade
Hardiness: ❉❉❉ Zone: Min. 7

Ampelopsis brevipedunculata elegans

Aristolochia littoralis

Ampelopsis megalophylla

A vigorous twining climber with deeply cut foliage that bears insignificant green flowers during early summer, followed by unusual black fruit. H 10m (33ft) S 10m (33ft).
Aspect: sun or semi-shade
Hardiness: ✸✸✸ Zone: Min. 7

ARISTOLOCHIA
Dutchman's pipe

A very large genus of over 300 species, including the tender twining deciduous and evergreen climbers featured here, grown for their intriguing, pipe-shaped summer flowers. In warm gardens they will quickly cover supports with a cloak of handsome foliage to disguise eyesores. Elsewhere, they make an exotic choice for a frost-free conservatory.
Cultivation In the garden, grow in any well-drained garden soil that is reasonably fertile in full sun or dappled shade, but protected from cold winds. In containers, grow in a soil-based compost (soil mix). Feed every month throughout the growing season and water as necessary. Tender plants should be moved to a warm spot undercover when the temperature falls below 7°C (45°F) and watered sparingly during winter.
Pruning No routine pruning is necessary. Cut back wayward stems after flowering.
Propagation Take softwood cuttings in early spring for tender species indoors and in mid-summer for hardy species outside.

Berberidopsis corallina

Aristolochia littoralis
(syn. *A. elegans*)

A tender climber with evergreen kidney-shaped, pale green leaves. During early summer and mid-summer it bears unusual rounded purple flowers, spotted with white. H 10m (33ft) S 10m (33ft).
Aspect: sun or semi-shade
Hardiness: tender Zones: 10–12

Aristolochia macrophylla
(syn. *A. durior*, *A. sipho*)

A robust, twining, deciduous climber, with dark green, heart-shaped leaves, that bears unusual rounded, green flowers, spotted with yellow, purple and brown, during early summer. H 10m (33ft) S 10m (33ft).
Aspect: sun or semi-shade
Hardiness: ✸✸ Zones: Min. 7

BERBERIDOPSIS

A genus of just one species of evergreen climbers, grown for their eye-catching pendent summer flowers. Useful for adding colour to shady structures.
Cultivation Grow in a moisture-retentive, well-drained neutral to acid soil that is fertile and in dappled shade, but protected from cold winds. In colder regions, apply an insulating mulch in autumn to protect the crown.
Pruning No routine pruning is necessary. Cut back wayward stems in mid-spring.
Propagation Take semi-ripe cuttings in late summer.

Berberidopsis corallina
Coral plant

A twining climber with spiny-edged, dark green, heart-shaped leaves that are lighter beneath.

Strings of dark red flowers hang from shoot tips from early to late summer. 5m (16ft) S 6m (20ft).
Aspect: semi-shade
Hardiness: ✸✸ Zones: Min. 7

BILLARDIERA

This comprises a genus of over five species, including the evergreen climber featured here, which are grown mainly for their colourful fruit. This plant makes an unusual climber for screens and fences and will grow over many different structures, such as fences, arbours, trellis or walls.
Cultivation Grow in a moisture-retentive, well-drained neutral to acid soil that is reasonably fertile and in full sun or dappled shade, but protected from cold winds.
Pruning No routine pruning is necessary.
Propagation Take semi-ripe cuttings in late summer or layer suitable stems in mid-spring.

Billardiera longiflora
Climbing blueberry

This is a twining climber, with lance-shaped, dark green leaves, that bears pale green flowers during early and mid-summer, followed by plum-shaped, violet-purple, red, white or pink fruit. H 2.5m (8ft) S 1m (3ft). The purple colour of the fruit gives it its blueberry common name.
Aspect: sun or semi-shade
Hardiness: ✸✸ Zones: Min. 7

Billardiera longifolia

Bougainvillea

BOUGAINVILLEA

This genus of about 15 species, including the evergreen climbers featured here, is grown for their long-lasting displays of colourful petal-like bracts. All produce stiff thorny stems. It can be grown in gardens where the weather is mild and will quickly cover a large wall. Alternatively, it can be allowed to scramble over the ground. Elsewhere, grow in containers on the patio and give winter protection – they are a good choice for a large, cool conservatory that is frost-free.
Cultivation In the garden, grow in any well-drained soil that is reasonably fertile in full sun. If growing in containers, use a soil-based compost (soil mix). Feed every month throughout the growing season and water as necessary. Move to a cool but frost-free undercover spot when the temperature falls below 3°C (37°F) and water sparingly throughout the winter.
Pruning No routine pruning is necessary, other than to keep it in within bounds.
Propagation Take softwood cuttings in early spring or semi-ripe cuttings stems in early summer.

Bougainvillea glabra

This is a vigorous evergreen climber with lustrous, dark green leaves, which bears spectacularly attractive sprays of delicate-looking white, pink and red floral bracts from early summer to mid-autumn. It is borderline half-hardy. H 6m (20ft) S 3m (10ft). Named varieties: 'Snow White', sprays of brilliant white floral bracts. H 6m (20ft) S 3m (10ft). 'Variegata' (syn. B. 'Sanderiana'), cream-edged grey-green leaves and sprays of purple floral bracts. H 6m (20ft) S 3m (10ft).
Aspect: sun
Hardiness: ✿ (borderline)
Zone: Min. 5

Bougainvillea 'Miss Manila' (syn. B. 'Tango')

Spectacular displays of sugar-pink floral bracts are produced in sprays from early summer to mid-autumn against the rounded, lustrous green leaves on this vigorous climber. Borderline half-hardy. H 10m (33ft) S 10m (33ft).
Aspect: sun
Hardiness: ✿ (borderline)
Zone: Min. 5

Bougainvillea 'Raspberry Ice' (syn. B. 'Tropical Rainbow')

Luminescent, cerise-pink, flowering bracts shine out from early summer to mid-autumn on this vigorous-growing bougainvillea. The eye-catching cream-splashed dark green leaves provide year-round interest. Borderline half-hardy. H 10m (33ft) S 10m (33ft).
Aspect: sun
Hardiness: ✿ (borderline)
Zone: Min. 5

Bougainvillea 'Scarlett O'Hara' (syn. B. 'Hawaiian Scarlet')

This vigorous evergreen climber produces sprays of red floral bracts from early summer to mid-autumn against lustrous dark green leaves. Borderline half-hardy. H 10m (33ft) S 10m (33ft).
Aspect: sun
Hardiness: ✿ (borderline)
Zone: Min. 5

CAMPSIS
Trumpet vine

A genus of just two species, including the vigorous deciduous climber featured here, grown for its startling, trumpet-shaped, late-summer flowers. It is an ideal choice as a scrambling plant over a sunny wall or fence, with a single plant covering about two standard fence panels in five years. The tendrils of this vigorous climber can damage old masonry, so make sure the pointing is sound before planting.
Cultivation Grow in a moisture-retentive, well-drained soil that is reasonably fertile in full sun, but sheltered from cold winds. In colder areas, grow by a sunny wall.
Pruning Keep this fast-growing climber within bounds by cutting new growth back hard to within a couple of buds from the main framework during late winter.
Propagation Take semi-ripe nodal cuttings in mid-summer or hardwood cuttings in mid-autumn.

Campsis grandiflora (syn. Bignonia grandiflora, C. chinensis, Tecoma grandiflora)
Chinese trumpet vine

Reddish-orange, funnel-shaped

Campsis radicans

flowers appear in succession from late summer to early autumn on this vigorous climber, which has dark green leaves. H 10m (33ft) S 10m (33ft).
Aspect: sun
Hardiness: ❀❀ Zone: Min. 7

Campis radicans 'Flamenco'
Eye-catching trumpet-shaped, yellow flowers appear in succession from late summer to early autumn and stand out against the dark green leaves of this vigorous climber. H 10m (33ft) S 10m (33ft).
Aspect: sun
Hardiness: ❀❀ Zone: Min. 7

Campsis x tagliabuana 'Madame Galen'
This is a vigorous climber that bears trumpet-shaped, salmon-red flowers throughout late summer and early autumn highlighted against its dark green leaves. H 10m (33ft) S 10m (33ft).
Aspect: sun
Hardiness: ❀❀

CELASTRUS
Staff vine
A genus of about 30 species, including the vigorous deciduous climber featured here, which is

grown for its bead-like yellow berries. It provides quick cover for eyesores such as an old stump or dilapidated shed, but it also makes an attractive climber for walls and fences — one plant covers about three standard fence panels in five years. The twining stems can be constricting, so avoid planting through young trees and shrubs.
Cultivation Grow in any well-drained soil that is reasonably fertile in full sun or dappled shade.
Pruning No routine pruning is necessary. Thin out over-crowded stems in late winter.
Propagation Take semi-ripe nodal cuttings in mid-summer.

Celastrus orbiculatus (syn. C. articulatus)
Oriental bittersweet
This is a vigorous, deciduous climber with scalloped green leaves that turn yellow in autumn. Clusters of insignificant green flowers in mid-summer are followed by yellow berries that split to reveal their contrasting red seeds. H 14m (46ft) S 6m (20ft).
Aspect: sun or semi-shade
Hardiness: ❀❀❀ Zone: Min. 7

Cissus rhombifolia

CISSUS
This large genus of over 350 species includes the tender evergreen climbers featured here. They are mainly grown as house plants because of their handsome foliage. Outside in warm areas, a single plant will quickly cover several standard fence panels or can be left to scramble over the ground and up banks. Elsewhere, they are an ideal choice for a shady but warm conservatory and, as they are very pollution tolerant, they make a good choice for smoke-filled rooms, too.
Cultivation In the garden, grow in a moisture-retentive, well-drained garden soil in full sun or dappled shade. In containers, grow in a soil-based compost (soil mix). Feed every month throughout the growing season and water as necessary. Move to a warm spot undercover when the temperature falls below 5°C (41°F) and water sparingly throughout the winter.
Pruning No routine pruning is necessary. Thin out overcrowded

stems in late winter.
Propagation Take semi-ripe cuttings in mid-summer.

Cissus antarctica
Kangaroo vine
This is a woody, tendril climber with toothed, polished green, leathery leaves, which bears insignificant green flowers from early summer to late summer, followed by black fruit. H 5m (16ft) S 3m (10ft).
Aspect: sun or semi-shade
Hardiness: tender Zones: 10–12

Cissus rhombifolia (syn. Rhoicissus rhombifolia)
Grape ivy
This is a coarsely toothed, woody, tendril climber, with attractive trifoliate evergreen leaves, which bears insignificant green flowers from early summer to late summer, followed by blue-black fruit. H 3m (10ft) S 2m (6ft).
Aspect: sun or semi-shade
Hardiness: tender Zones: 10–12

Celastrus orbiculatus

Clematis alpina

CLEMATIS
Old man's beard

This is a large and varied genus of over 200 species that includes the deciduous and evergreen climbers featured here, mainly grown for their spectacular flowers. Clematis makes a coverall climber that can be used on all types of structures, established trees and shrubs, as well as scrambling across the ground. Vigorous varieties are ideal for covering eyesores and will cloak up to three standard fence panels within five years. Combine different varieties to give a succession of colour throughout the year.

Cultivation Grow in a moisture-retentive, well-drained garden soil that is reasonably fertile and in full sun or dappled shade, with their roots shaded from hot sun.

Pruning Clematis can be divided into three groups: those that produce all their flowers on old wood (Pruning Group 1); those that produce blooms on both old wood and new growth (Group 2); and those that flower on new growth only (Group 3). Pruning Group 1 requires no routine pruning other than the removal of dead, damaged or diseased stems. Pruning Group 2 should be thinned to avoid congestion by pruning back unwanted stems to a pair of plump buds lower down or at their point of origin. Pruning Group 3 should have all stems cut back to the lowest pair of buds during February (late winter). For further information, *see* Pruning Clematis, page 122.

Propagation Take double-leaf bud cuttings in June (early summer).

SPRING-FLOWERING CLEMATIS
Clematis alpina
Alpine clematis

Small, bell-shaped, lavender-blue flowers with creamy-white centres are produced during mid- and late spring, followed by fluffy seed heads. Pruning Group 1.
H 3m (10ft) S 1.5m (5ft).
Aspect: semi-shade
Hardiness: ❀❀❀ Zones: 4–11

Clematis alpina 'Frances Rivis'

Nodding, bell-shaped, blue flowers are borne in profusion during mid- and late spring, followed by fluffy seed-heads. Pruning Group 1.
H 3m (10ft) S 1.5m (5ft).
Aspect: semi-shade
Hardiness: ❀❀❀ Zones: 4–11

Clematis alpina 'Frankie'

Double, nodding, bell-shaped, blue flowers are produced during mid- and late spring, followed by fluffy seed-heads. Pruning Group 1.
H 3m (10ft) S 1.5m (5ft).
Aspect: sun or semi-shade
Hardiness: ❀❀❀ Zones: 4–9

Clematis armandii 'Apple Blossom'

Almond-scented, pale pink flowers are produced during early and mid-spring against leathery evergreen leaves that are bronze-tinted when young. Pruning Group 1.
H 5m (16ft) S 3m (10ft).
Aspect: sun or semi-shade
Hardiness: ❀❀❀ Zones: 8–11

Clematis 'Early Sensation'

Masses of small, green-centred, white, bowl-shaped flowers are produced in a single flush during mid- and late spring. Pruning Group 1. H 4m (13ft) S 2m (6ft).
Aspect: sun
Hardiness: ❀❀❀ Zones: 8–11

Clematis macropetala 'Markham's Pink'

Semi-double, clear pink flowers with creamy-yellow centres are produced throughout mid- and late spring, followed by silvery seed-heads. Pruning Group 1.
H 3m (10ft) S 1.5m (5ft).
Aspect: sun or partial shade
Hardiness: ❀❀❀ Zones: 4–9

EARLY SUMMER-FLOWERING CLEMATIS
Clematis 'Barbara Jackman'

Large, pale purple flowers with a distinctive red stripe are produced during late spring and early summer and again in early autumn. Pruning Group 2.
H 3m (10ft) S 1m (3ft).
Aspect: sun or partial shade
Hardiness: ❀❀❀ Zones: 4–11

Clematis 'Bees' Jubilee'

A compact variety that bears large dark pink flowers with darker pink bars during late spring and early summer and again in early autumn. Pruning Group 2.
H 2.5m (8ft) S 1m (3ft).
Aspect: sun or partial shade (zones 4–9); partial shade (zones 10–11)
Hardiness: ❀❀❀ Zones: 4–11

Clematis 'Mrs Cholmondeley'

Clematis 'Belle of Woking'

Large, double, silvery-mauve flowers with creamy-white centres are produced during late spring and early summer and again in early autumn. Pruning Group 2. H 2.5m (8ft) S 1m (3ft).
Aspect: partial shade
Hardiness: ❀❀❀ Zones: 4–11

Clematis 'Doctor Ruppel'

A compact variety that bears large, dark pink flowers with darker bars in succession during late spring and early summer and then again in early autumn. Pruning Group 2. H 2.5m (8ft) S 1m (3ft).
Aspect: sun or partial shade (zones 4–9); partial shade (zones 10–11)
Hardiness: ❀❀❀ Zones: 4–11

Clematis armandii 'Apple Blossom'

Clematis 'Lasurstern'

Clematis 'Duchess of Edinburgh'

Yellow-centred, double white flowers are produced in succession during late spring and early summer with a second flush occasionally produced during early autumn. Pruning Group 2. H 4m (13ft) S 2m (6ft). Aspect: partial shade
Hardiness: ✤✤✤ Zones: 4–11

Clematis 'Fireworks'

Large purple flowers with red bars and crimped petals are borne in succession during late spring and early summer and then again in early autumn. Pruning Group 2. H 4m (13ft) S 2m (6ft). Aspect: sun or partial shade
Hardiness: ✤✤✤ Zones: 4–11

Clematis 'Gillian Blades'

Large, mauve-flushed, white flowers that age to white with golden-yellow centres are produced in succession through late spring and early summer, with a second flush produced in early autumn. Pruning Group 2. H 2.5m (8ft) S 1m (3ft). Aspect: sun or partial shade
Hardiness: ✤✤✤ Zones: 4–11

Clematis 'Lasurstern'

Large, cream-centred, purple-blue flowers with wavy-edged petals that fade in full sun are borne throughout late spring and early summer and again in early autumn. Pruning Group 2. H 2.5m (8ft) S 1m (3ft). Aspect: sun or partial shade
Hardiness: ✤✤✤ Zones: 4–11

Clematis 'Miss Bateman'

Green-striped white flowers that age to white with chocolate centres are produced during late spring and early summer, with a second flush in late summer. Pruning Group 2. H 2.5m (8ft) S 1m (3ft).
Aspect: Sun or partial shade
Hardiness: ✤✤✤ Zones: 4–11

Clematis montana var. rubens 'Elizabeth'

Masses of fragrant, pale pink flowers with golden-yellow centres are produced during late spring and early summer, against purple-flushed, green foliage on this vigorous clematis. Pruning Group 1. H 7m (23ft) S 3m (10ft).
Aspect: sun or partial shade
Hardiness: ✤✤✤ Zones: 4–11

Clematis montana var. rubens 'Pink Perfection'

A vigorous variety of clematis that bears fragrant pink flowers that appear during late spring and early summer against a backdrop of purple-flushed foliage. Pruning Group 1. H 7m (23ft) S 3m (10ft).
Aspect: sun or partial shade
Hardiness: ✤✤✤ Zones: 4–11

Clematis 'Mrs Cholmondeley'

Chocolate-centred, lavender-blue flowers with darker veins appear in succession from late spring to early autumn. Pruning Group 2. H 3m (10ft) S 1m (3ft).
Aspect: sun or partial shade
Hardiness: ✤✤✤ Zones: 4–11

Clematis 'The President'

Clematis 'Multi Blue'

Large, double, pale-centred, dark blue flowers appear in late spring, early summer, late summer and early autumn. Pruning Group 2. H 4m (13ft) S 2m (6ft). Aspect: sun or partial shade
Hardiness: ✤✤✤ Zones: 4–11

Clematis 'Nelly Moser'

One of the most commonly found clematis in gardens,

Clematis montana var. rubens 'Elizabeth'

chocolate-centred pink flowers with darker stripes fading in full sun appear in late spring and early summer with a second flush in early autumn. Pruning Group 2. H 4m (13ft) S 2m (6ft). Aspect: partial shade
Hardiness: ✤✤✤ Zones: 4–11

Clematis 'The President'

Large, red-centred, purple flowers with pointed petals that are silvery underneath appear from early summer to early autumn. Foliage on 'The President' is bronze-tinted when young. Pruning Group 2. H 3m (10ft) S 1m (3ft). Aspect: Sun or partial shade
Hardiness: ✤✤✤ Zones: 4–11

Clematis 'Vyvyan Pennell'

Double, golden-centred, mauve, violet and purple flowers appear in late spring and early summer and again in early autumn. This clematis is fully hardy. Pruning Group 2. H 3m (10ft) S 1m (3ft). Aspect: sun or partial shade
Hardiness: ✤✤✤ Zones: 4–11

Clematis 'Bill MacKenzie'

Clematis florida var. sieboldiana

LATE SUMMER-FLOWERING CLEMATIS

Clematis 'Alba Luxurians'
Bell-shaped, green-tipped, white flowers with purple centres are produced from mid-summer to early autumn against grey-green leaves. Wind and wilt tolerant. Pruning Group 3. H 4m (13ft) S 1.5m (5ft).
Aspect: sun or partial shade
Hardiness: ❀❀❀ Zones: 4–11

Clematis 'Betty Corning'
Nodding, bell-shaped and fragrant creamy-white flowers edged and flushed with lilac-blue, are produced in succession from mid-summer to early autumn. This variety is wind and wilt-tolerant. Pruning Group 3. H 2m (6ft) S 1m (3ft).
Aspect: sun or partial shade
Hardiness: ❀❀❀ Zones: 4–11

Clematis 'Bill MacKenzie'
Butter-yellow, bell-shaped flowers are produced in succession from mid-summer to early autumn against ferny mid-green leaves, followed by large, fluffy seed-heads. Pruning Group 3. H 7m (23ft) S 3m (10ft).
Aspect: sun or partial shade
Hardiness: ❀❀❀ Zones: 4–11

Clematis 'Comtesse de Bouchaud'
A popular variety that bears masses of large, yellow-centred, mauve-pink flowers in succession from mid-summer to early autumn. Pruning Group 3. H 3m (10ft) S 1m (3ft).
Hardiness: ❀❀❀ Zones: 4–11

Clematis 'Ernest Markham'
Large, cream-centred, purple-red flowers are produced in succession from mid-summer to mid-autumn. Pruning Group 3. H 4m (13ft) S 1m (3ft).
Aspect: sun
Hardiness: ❀❀❀ Zones: 4–11

Clematis 'Etoile Violette'
A vigorous clematis that produces masses of yellow-centred, dark purple flowers in succession from mid-summer to early autumn. Wind and wilt resistant. Pruning Group 3. H 5m (16ft) S 1.5m (5ft).
Aspect: sun or partial shade
Hardiness: ❀❀❀ Zones: 4–11

Clematis flammula
Fragrant, starry white flowers are produced en masse from mid-

summer to mid-autumn on this vigorous clematis, followed by shimmering seed-heads. Pruning Group 3. H 6m (20ft) S 1m (3ft).
Aspect: sun or partial shade
Hardiness: ❀❀❀ Zones: 4–9

Clematis florida var. sieboldiana
This is an unusual passion flower-like plant that produces creamy-white flowers with dark purple centres that appear in succession from early summer to early autumn, followed by shimmering seed-heads. Pruning Group 2. H 2.5m (8ft) S 1m (3ft).
Aspect: sun or partial shade
Hardiness: ❀❀❀ Zones: 4–11

Clematis 'General Sikorski'
Easy-to-grow clematis with large, yellow-centred, purple-blue flowers produced in succession from early summer to early autumn. Fully hardy. Pruning Group 2. H 3m (10ft) S 1m (3ft).
Aspect: sun or partial shade
Hardiness: ❀❀❀ Zones: 4–11

Clematis 'Gipsy Queen'
Red-centred, bright purple flowers are produced in succession from mid-summer to early autumn. Pruning Group 3. H 3m (10ft) S 1m (3ft).
Aspect: sun or partial shade
Hardiness: ❀❀❀ Zones: 4–11

Clematis 'Hagley Hybrid'
Cup-shaped, mauve-pink flowers with red centres that fade in the sun are produced in succession

from mid-summer to early autumn. Pruning Group 3. H 2m (6ft) S 1m (3ft).
Aspect: sun or partial shade
Hardiness: ❀❀❀ Zones: 4–11

Clematis 'Henryi'
Attractive large white flowers with chocolate centres are produced in succession from mid-summer to early autumn. Pruning Group 2. H 3m (10ft) S 1m (3ft).
Aspect: sun or partial shade
Hardiness: ❀❀❀ Zones: 4–11

Clematis 'Huldine'
Attractive and large, cup-shaped, yellow-centred, silvery-white flowers with pale lilac undersides appear from mid-summer to early autumn. Pruning Group 3. H 5m (16ft) S 2m (6ft).
Aspect: sun
Hardiness: ❀❀❀ Zones: 4–11

Clematis 'Comtesse de Bouchaud'

Clematis 'Jackmanii'

Clematis 'Marie Boisselot'

Clematis 'Rouge Cardinal'

Clematis viticella 'Purpurea Plena Elegans'

Clematis 'Jackmanii'
Large, green-centred, purple flowers are produced in succession from mid-summer to early autumn. Pruning Group 3. H 3m (10ft) S 1m (3ft). Aspect: sun or partial shade Hardiness: ❀❀❀ Zones: 4–11

Clematis 'Jackmanii Superba'
Red-flushed, dark purple flowers with cream-coloured centres are produced in succession from mid-summer to early autumn. Ideal for a north-facing site. Pruning Group 3. H 3m (10ft) S 1m (3ft). Aspect: sun or partial shade Hardiness: ❀❀❀ Zones: 4–11

Clematis 'Marie Boisselot'
Large white flowers with golden centres and overlapping petals are produced in succession from early summer to early autumn. Pruning Group 2. H 3m (10ft) S 1m (3ft). Aspect: sun or partial shade Hardiness: ❀❀❀ Zones: 4–11

Clematis 'Niobe'
Golden-centred, dark ruby-red flowers are produced in succession from mid-summer to early autumn. Pruning Group 3.

H 3m (10ft) S 1m (3ft). Aspect: sun or partial shade Hardiness: ❀❀❀ Zones: 4–11

Clematis 'Perle d'Azur'
Yellow-centred, lilac-blue flowers of medium size, that are pink-tinged at the base, are produced in succession from mid-summer to early autumn. Pruning Group 3. H 3m (10ft) S 1m (3ft). Aspect: sun or partial shade Hardiness: ❀❀❀ Zones: 4–9

Clematis 'Perle d'Azur'

Clematis 'Polish Spirit'
Red-centred and rich purple saucer-shaped flowers are produced in succession from mid-summer to early autumn on this vigorous variety. Pruning Group 3. H 5m (16ft) S 2m (6ft). Aspect: sun or partial shade Hardiness: ❀❀❀ Zones: 4–11

Clematis 'Prince Charles'
Pale mauve-blue flowers with green centres are produced in succession from mid-summer to early autumn. Pruning Group 3. H 2.5m (8ft) S 1.5m (5ft). Aspect: sun or partial shade Hardiness: ❀❀❀ Zones: 4–11

Clematis 'Princess Diana'
Clear pink, cream-centred, tulip-like flowers are produced in succession from late summer to mid-autumn. Pruning Group 3.

Clematis tangutica

H 2.5m (8ft) S 1m (3ft). Aspect: sun Hardiness: ❀❀❀ Zones: 4–11

Clematis 'Rouge Cardinal'
Rich velvet-crimson flowers appear during mid-summer to early autumn. Pruning Group 3. H 3m (10ft) S 1m (3ft). Aspect: sun or partial shade Hardiness: ❀❀❀ Zones: 4–9

WINTER-FLOWERING CLEMATIS
Clematis cirrhosa 'Jingle Bells'
From early to late winter the large, creamy-coloured, bell-shaped flowers stand out against the dark evergreen leaves. Pruning Group 1. H 3m (10ft) S 1.5m (5ft). Aspect: sun Hardiness: ❀❀❀ Zones: 7–9

Clematis cirrhosa var. *balearica*
Fragrant, creamy-white, bell-shaped and waxy-looking flowers blotched with maroon inside are produced from early to late winter against glossy bronze-tinted leaves. Pruning Group 1. H 3m (10ft) S 1.5m (5ft). Aspect: sun Hardiness: ❀❀❀ Zones 7–9

Clematis cirrhosa 'Wisley Cream'
Bronze-tinted leaves in winter set off the small, creamy, bell-shaped, waxy-looking flowers borne from early to late winter. Frost hardy. Pruning Group 1. H 3m (10ft) S 1.5m (5ft). Aspect: sun Hardiness: ❀❀❀ Zones 7–9

Clerodendrum thomsoniae

Clianthus puniceus 'Roseus'

CLERODENDRUM

This large genus of over 400 species includes the tender, twining, evergreen climber featured here, which is grown for its clusters of bell-shaped summer flowers. In warm gardens it can reach 3m (10ft) or more and can also be trained to make an attractive standard. Elsewhere, it makes an ideal plant for adding an exotic touch to a heated conservatory.

Cultivation In the garden, grow in any well-drained, moisture-retentive soil that is reasonably fertile. Site in full sun, but protected from wind. If grown in containers, use a soil-based compost (soil mix). Feed every month throughout the growing season and water as necessary. Move to a warm spot undercover when the temperature falls below 10°C (50°) and water sparingly throughout the winter.

Pruning No routine pruning is necessary. Cut back wayward stems, shortening shoots by about two-thirds of their length, in mid-spring.

Propagation Take softwood cuttings in mid-spring.

Clerodendrum thomsoniae
Glory bower

This is a woody-stemmed, evergreen, twining climber that during early summer to early autumn bears clusters of bi-coloured flowers made up of a white lantern-shaped calyx and a crimson star-shaped corolla, against large green leaves.

H 4m (13ft) S 2m (6ft).
Aspect: sun
Hardiness: tender Zones: 10–12

CLIANTHUS

This comprises a genus of just two species, including the evergreen climber featured here, which are grown for their unusual lobster-claw or beak-like flowers that appear in early summer. It makes an interesting choice for sunny and sheltered screens and fences or can be left unsupported to form a sprawling shrub.

Cultivation Grow in any well-drained soil that is reasonably fertile in full sun, but protected from wind. In very cold areas, grow in a cool conservatory.

Pruning No routine pruning is necessary. Cut back wayward stems and thin congested growth during early summer.

Propagation Sow seeds in early spring or take semi-ripe cuttings in early summer.

Clianthus puniceus
Lobster claw, Parrot's bill

This is a sprawling evergreen climber, with dark green leaves, which bears dramatic and unusual lobster-claw-like scarlet flowers in clusters during late spring and early summer. If not left to sprawl, it requires tying into its support. H 4m (13ft) S 2m (6ft).
Named varieties: 'Albus', white flowers. H 4m (13ft) S 2m (6ft).
Aspect: sun
Hardiness: ❋❋ Zone: Min. 6

COBAEA

This genus of about 20 species includes the evergreen tendril climber featured here, grown for its spectacular fragrant summer flowers. In warm gardens, it is a good choice for covering a sheltered sunny wall or fence. Elsewhere, grow in a container and move undercover during the winter months, or use it as a permanent addition to a large heated greenhouse or conservatory.

Cultivation In the garden, grow in any well-drained, moisture-retentive soil that is reasonably fertile in full sun, but protected from wind. In containers, grow in a soil-based compost. Feed every month throughout the growing season and water as necessary.

Move to a warm spot under cover when the temperature falls below 5°C (41°F) and water sparingly throughout the winter.

Pruning No routine pruning is necessary. Cut back wayward stems and thin congested growth during early autumn.

Propagation Sow seeds in early spring.

Cobaea scandens
Cathedral bell, cup-and-saucer plant

This is a vigorous tendril climber that bears huge, scented, bell-shaped, creamy-green flowers that age to dark purple from early summer to early autumn, against a backdrop of dark green leaves.
H 20m (70ft) S 3.5m (12ft).
Aspect: sun
Hardiness: tender Zones: 10–12

ECCREMOCARPUS
Chilean glory flower

A genus of some five species, including the vigorous evergreen climber featured here, grown for its succession of unusual and colourful summer flowers. It makes a perfect choice for a fence or screen next to a sunny patio.

Cultivation Grow in any well-drained soil that is reasonably fertile in full sun, but protected from cold wind. Plant out after the last frost in colder areas.

Pruning No routine pruning is necessary. In colder areas, treat as

Cobaea scandens

Eccremocarpus scaber

Hedera canariensis 'Gloire de Marengo'

Hedera colchica 'Dentata Variegata'

a perennial and cut frost-damaged top-growth back during mid-spring.
Propagation Sow seeds in February (late winter).

Eccremocarpus scaber
A quick-growing, evergreen, tendril climber that produces a profusion of red, pink, orange or yellow flowers in succession from early summer to mid-autumn on slender stems. It requires tying into a support to get it started. H 5m (16ft) S 5m (16ft).
Aspect: sun
Hardiness: ❀❀ Zone: Min. 7

FALLOPIA
A genus of over five species, including the very vigorous deciduous climber featured here, it is grown for its rapid speed of growth and clouds of late-summer flowers. It makes a useful plant for covering up eyesores and for quick garden makeovers. However, a word of caution is necessary with this climber: a

single plant will smother an area equivalent to about 10 standard fence panels in five years.
Cultivation Grow in a moisture-retentive, well-drained soil that is poor to reasonably fertile in full sun or dappled shade.
Pruning No routine pruning is necessary. Cut back wayward or congested stems in mid-spring.

Fallopia baldschuanica

Propagation Take semi-ripe cuttings in early summer.

Fallopia baldschuanica (syn. Bilderdykia baldschuanica, Polygonum baldschuanicum) Russian vine, mile-a-minute
Very fast growing and vigorous, this is a woody, deciduous climber that is covered in clouds of tiny, funnel-shaped, white flowers with pink tinges throughout late summer and early autumn.
H 12m (40ft) S 4m (13ft).
Aspect: sun or semi-shade
Hardiness: ❀❀❀ Zone: Min. 7

HEDERA
This genus of about 10 species includes many popular, self-clinging, evergreen climbers, some of which are featured here. They are grown for their easy-going nature and handsome foliage. Many of these plants are excellent on shady north-facing walls and fences, while others thrive in full sun. A single plant covers one standard fence panel in five years. Some can provide weed-smothering groundcover and a few also make year-round house plants.
Cultivation Although these plants are very tolerant of a wide range of conditions, they grow best in a moisture-retentive, well-drained neutral to alkaline soil that is reasonably fertile. Variegated ivies prefer dappled shade and shelter from cold winds; green-leaved varieties can cope with anything from full sun to deep shade.

Pruning No routine pruning is necessary. Remove frost-damaged growth and all-green reverted stems from variegated varieties in mid-spring.
Propagation Take semi-ripe nodal cuttings in early summer.

Hedera canariensis 'Gloire de Marengo'
Huge, three-lobed, silvery-green glossy leaves, edged with creamy-white, cover this vigorous evergreen climber. Use indoors or outside in sheltered, dappled shade. H 4m (13ft) S 5m (16ft).
Aspect: semi-shade
Hardiness: ❀❀ Zone: Min. 7

Hedera colchica 'Dentata Variegata'
A variegated evergreen ivy with huge, heart-shaped, cream-edged, mottled grey-green leaves. It is useful climber for brightening up semi-shade or for growing as weed-smothering groundcover.
H 5m (16ft) S 5m (16ft).
Aspect: semi-shade
Hardiness: ❀❀❀ Zone: Min. 5

Hedera colchica 'Sulphur Heart' (syn. H. colchica 'Paddy's Pride')
A fast-growing, self-clinging, variegated, evergreen ivy with heart-shaped green leaves splashed with creamy yellow. It is useful for brightening up semi-shade or for growing as weed-smothering groundcover. H 5m (16ft) S 5m (16ft).
Aspect: semi-shade
Hardiness: ❀❀❀ Zone: Min. 5

Hedera helix 'Goldchild'

Hedera helix 'Buttercup'
This is a sun-loving, vigorous, self-clinging, evergreen ivy with lobed bright yellow leaves that turn pale green in shade. Insignificant pale green flowers are borne in mid- to late autumn, followed by spherical black fruit. H 2m (6ft) S 2.5m (8ft).
Aspect: sun
Hardiness: ✱✱✱ Zone: Min. 7

Hedera helix 'Glacier'
Ideal for use as groundcover, this variegated evergreen climber has triangular and lobed grey-green leaves with silver and cream splashes. Pale green flowers appear in mid- to late autumn. H 2m (6ft) S 2m (6ft).
Aspect: semi-shade
Hardiness: ✱✱✱ Zone: Min. 7

Hedera helix 'Goldheart' (syn. *H. helix* 'Jubilaum Goldhertz', *H. helix* 'Jubilee Goldheart', *H. helix* 'Oro di Bogliasco')
Vigorous once established, this fast-growing, variegated, evergreen climber has glossy, three-lobed, dark green leaves splashed with yellow. Insignificant pale green flowers are borne in mid- to late autumn. H 8m (26ft) S 5m (16ft).
Aspect: semi-shade
Hardiness: ✱✱✱ Zone: Min. 7

Hedera helix 'Green Ripple'
A vigorous evergreen climber with large, glossy, bright green leaves that are five-lobed and sharply pointed with distinctive veining. They turn copper-bronze over

winter. Insignificant pale green flowers are borne in mid-autumn and late autumn. H 2m (6ft) S 2m (6ft).
Aspect: semi-shade
Hardiness: ✱✱✱ Zone: Min. 7

Hedera helix 'Ivalace' (syn. *H. helix* 'Mini Green')
Suitable for use indoors and outside, this adaptable ivy has glossy, five-lobed, wavy-edged, dark green leaves. Insignificant pale green flowers are borne in mid- to late autumn.
H 1m (3ft) S 1.2m (4ft).
Aspect: semi-shade
Hardiness: ✱✱✱ Zone: Min. 7

Hedera helix 'Parsley Crested' (syn. *H. helix* 'Cristata')
The glossy dark green and wavy-edged leaves on this vigorous, self-clinging evergreen climber are ideal for covering a wall or fence in shade. Insignificant pale green flowers are borne in mid- to late autumn. H 2m (6ft) S 1.2m (4ft).
Aspect: semi-shade to deep shade
Hardiness: ✱✱✱ Zone: Min. 7

HIBBERTIA
A genus of around 120 species, including the twining evergreen featured here, grown for their bright yellow flowers. They make useful groundcover in warm gardens, where they also look good trained over arches and pergolas. They are also tolerant of salt-laden air, and so make a good choice for mild coastal gardens. Elsewhere, grow in a container

and move under cover during the cold winter months.
Cultivation In the garden, grow in any well-drained, moisture-retentive soil that is reasonably fertile in dappled shade, but protected from wind. In containers, grow in a soil-based compost (soil mix). Feed every month throughout the growing season and water as necessary. Move to a warm spot under cover when the temperature falls below 5°C (41°F) and water sparingly during the winter.
Pruning No routine pruning is necessary. Cut back wayward stems and thin congested growth during early autumn after flowering.
Propagation Sow seeds in early spring.

Hibbertia scandens (syn. *H. volubilis*)
This is a vigorous, twining evergreen with lustrous, leathery, green leaves that are distinctively veined and notched. The climber has red hairy stems and the leaves are also covered in paler hairs underneath. Saucer-shaped, bright yellow flowers are borne from early summer to late summer.
H 3m (10ft) S 2m (6ft).
Aspect: semi-shade
Hardiness: tender Zones: 10–12

HOYA
This genus of over 200 species includes the epiphytic climber featured here, which is grown for its waxy-looking clusters of night-scented summer flowers and

handsome foliage. It is best grown in a container as this promotes flowering. It makes a good choice for a sunny conservatory, greenhouse or porch.
Cultivation Grow in a soil-based compost. Feed every month throughout the growing season and water as necessary. Move to a warm spot under cover when the temperature falls below 5°C (41°F) and water sparingly during the winter.
Pruning No routine pruning is necessary. Pinch out growing tips to promote bushy growth.
Propagation Sow seeds in early spring.

Hoya carnosa
Wax plant
A vigorous evergreen climber with leathery dark green oval leaves that climbs using clinging aerial roots. Large, dense clusters of waxy-looking star-shaped and night-scented white flowers that are pink-flushed, each with a crimson eye, are produced from late spring to early autumn.
H 6m (20ft) S 2m (6ft).
Aspect: sun
Hardiness: tender Zones: 10-12

HUMULUS
Hop
This comprises a genus of just two species, including the vigorous deciduous climber featured here, which is grown for its yellow foliage. It is ideal for growing over sturdy arches and pergolas, or for allowing it to scramble through coloured trellis.

Hibbertia scandens

Hoya carnosa

Humulus lupulus 'Aureus'

Cultivation Grow in any well-drained, moisture-retentive soil that is reasonably fertile in full sun or dappled shade. Choose a sunny site to achieve the best leaf coloration.
Pruning Treat this climber as a perennial in colder areas, cutting back all stems to near ground level in early spring.
Propagation Take leaf-bud cuttings in early summer.

Humulus lupulus 'Aureus'
Golden hop
This climber has striking, bright yellow, deeply lobed leaves that mature to yellow-green on twining stems. Tie these into the support in spring. Green flowering cones are produced in early autumn. H 6m (20ft) S 6m (20ft).
Aspect: sun to semi-shade
Hardiness: ❋❋❋ Zone: Min. 7

HYDRANGEA
A genus of about 80 species, including the deciduous climber featured here, that is grown for its summer flowers and handsome foliage. They are useful for covering large north-facing walls, although they take a few years to get established.
Cultivation Grow in a moisture-retentive, well-drained and reasonably fertile soil in full sun or dappled shade. Before planting, add plenty of organic matter to the soil.
Pruning No routine pruning is necessary. Cut back wayward stems in late winter.

Propagation Take softwood basal cuttings in mid-spring or layer suitable shoots in mid-spring.

Hydrangea anomala subsp. petiolaris (syn. H. petiolaris)
Climbing hydrangea
Huge flat heads of creamy lace-cap flowers stand out against a backdrop of dark green leaves from late spring to mid-summer on this woody, deciduous climber. The leaves turn butter-yellow in autumn before falling to reveal flaking brown bark. H 1.5m (5ft) S 3m (10ft).
Aspect: sun to shade
Hardiness: ❋❋❋ Zone: Min. 7

JASMINUM
This comprises a genus of over 200 species, including the deciduous and evergreen climbers featured here, which are grown for their sweetly scented summer flowers. It is a good choice for sheltered structures near entrances, paths and patios, covering a standard fence panel in about five years. Others make excellent fragrant house plants.
Cultivation In the garden, grow in any well-drained soil that is reasonably fertile in full sun or dappled shade. Choose a sunny site for the best leaf coloration. In containers, grow in a soil-based compost (soil mix). Feed every month throughout the growing season and water as necessary.
Pruning No routine pruning is necessary. Overcrowded shoots on *Jasminum officinale* can be thinned after flowering.

Hydrangea anomala subsp. *petiolaris*

Propagation Take semi-ripe basal cuttings in mid-summer.

Jasminum beesianum
Fragrant pinkish-red flowers are produced in small clusters throughout early and mid-summer against strap-shaped, dark green leaves on this twining and woody evergreen climber. This plant requires the shelter of a sunny south- or west-facing wall or fence. H 5m (16ft) S 5m (16ft).
Aspect: sun
Hardiness: ❋❋ Zone: Min. 7

Jasminum officinale
Common jasmine
A succession of fabulously fragrant white flowers cover this vigorous semi-evergreen, twining climber from early summer to early autumn. H 12m (40ft) S 3m (10ft).
Aspect: sun to semi-shade
Hardiness: ❋❋❋ Zone: Min. 7

Jasminum officinale 'Devon Cream'
A new and very compact variety of common jasmine, this woody and twining deciduous climber bears large, fragrant, creamy-white flowers from mid-summer to early autumn. Give it the shelter of a sunny south- or west-facing wall or fence. H 2m (6ft) S 1m (3ft).
Aspect: sun
Hardiness: ❋❋ Zone: Min. 7

Jasminum officinale 'Fiona Sunrise'
This is a recent introduction that has eyecatching golden foliage and a succession of fragrant white flowers from early summer to early autumn. It is a compact variety that does best in the shelter of a sunny south- or west-facing wall or fence. H 3m (10ft) S 2m (6ft).
Aspect: sun
Hardiness: ❋❋ Zone: Min. 7

Jasminum polyanthum
This vigorous and twining evergreen climber is a very popular house plant. It produces fabulously fragrant white flowers that open from pink buds throughout mid-spring and early summer when grown outside. When grown inside, it will fill the house with scent from late autumn to mid-spring. H 3m (10ft) S 2m (6ft).
Aspect: sun to semi-shade
Hardiness: ❋ Zone: 10+

Jasminum x stephanense
Scented pale pink flowers are produced in clusters throughout early and mid-summer on this vigorous and twining deciduous climber. Give it the shelter of a sunny south- or west-facing wall or fence. H 5m (16ft) S 5m (16ft).
Aspect: sun
Hardiness: ❋❋ Zone: Min. 7

Jasminum officinale 'Fiona Sunrise'

LAPAGERIA

This is a genus of just one species of twining evergreen climber, grown for its exotic and colourful waxy-looking summer flowers. It is ideal for growing against a sheltered sunny wall or fence or on a post in a sheltered garden.
Cultivation In the garden, grow in a moisture-retentive, well-drained neutral to acid soil that is reasonably fertile. Site in dappled shade, but sheltered from cold winds. In containers, grow in an ericaceous compost (soil mix). Feed every month in the growing season and water as necessary.
Pruning No routine pruning is necessary. Wayward shoots can be thinned after flowering.
Propagation Sow seeds or layer suitable stems in mid-spring.

Lapageria rosea
Chilean bellflower
Exotic, elongated, bell-shaped, pink to crimson flowers are produced singly or in small clusters from leaf joints on this twining evergreen climber from mid-summer to mid-autumn. The leathery, lustrous, dark green leaves look good at other times. Borderline frost hardy. H 5m (16ft) S 3m (10ft).
Aspect: semi-shade
Hardiness: ❁❁ (borderline)
Zone: Min. 8

LONICERA
Honeysuckle

A genus of over 180 species, including the deciduous and evergreen twining climbers

Lapageria rosea

featured here, grown for their spidery, often highly fragrant, summer flowers. A coverall climber, it is ideal for east- and west-facing screens and fences or for training through established shrubs and trees. A single specimen will cover a standard fence panel in about five years.
Cultivation Grow in a moisture-retentive, well-drained soil that is reasonably fertile in full sun or dappled shade. Add plenty of organic matter to the soil before planting time.
Pruning Honeysuckles that flower on the current year's growth do not need regular pruning; those that flower on the previous season's growth should have old growth that has flowered cut back to a newer shoot produced lower down on the stem. All neglected honeysuckles can be rejuvenated by removing one in three stems, starting with the oldest.
Propagation Take leaf-bud cuttings in early summer or mid-summer, layer suitable shoots in late summer or take hardwood cuttings in mid-autumn.

Lonicera x americana
Very large, fragrant, yellow, tubular flowers that are purple-flushed are produced in succession from early summer to early autumn against a backdrop of oval dark green leaves.
H 7m (23ft) S 2m (6ft).
Aspect: sun to semi-shade
Hardiness: ❁❁❁ Zone: Min. 7

Lonicera x brownii 'Dropmore Scarlet'
Long, trumpet-shaped, bright scarlet flowers are produced in succession from mid-summer to early autumn against handsome blue-green foliage, occasionally followed by red berries. H 4m (13ft) S 2m (6ft).
Aspect: sun to semi-shade
Hardiness: ❁❁❁ Zone: Min. 7

Lonicera x heckrottii 'Gold Flame'
A vigorous twining climber that bears very fragrant, orange-yellow tubular flowers that are pink-flushed in succession from early to late summer, occasionally followed by red berries.

Lonicera x brownii 'Dropmore Scarlet'

H 500cm (180in) S 50cm (20in).
Aspect: sun to semi-shade
Hardiness: ❁❁❁ Zone: Min. 7

Lonicera henryi
Scarlet trumpet honeysuckle
Reddish-purple tubular flowers, each with a yellow throat, are produced throughout early and mid-summer against lustrous, dark green leaves on this vigorous evergreen variety. H 10m (33ft) S 1m (3ft).
Aspect: sun to semi-shade
Hardiness: ❁❁❁ (borderline)
Zone: Min. 7

Lonicera japonica 'Halliana'
Fabulously fragrant, tubular, white flowers that age to yellow are borne in succession from mid-spring to late summer, appearing against handsome dark green leaves on this vigorous evergreen variety. H 10m (33ft) S 2m (6ft).
Aspect: sun to semi-shade
Hardiness: ❁❁❁ Zone: Min. 7

Lonicera japonica 'Hall's Prolific'
Tubular white and sweetly fragrant flowers that age to yellow are borne in succession from mid-spring to late summer on this free-flowering vigorous variety

that has dark green foliage.
H 4m (13ft) S 3m (10ft).
Aspect: sun to semi-shade
Hardiness: ❁❁❁ Zone: Min. 7

Lonicera japonica var. repens
Very fragrant, tubular, reddish-purple flowers that age to yellow and are white-flushed are borne from mid-spring to late summer on this long-flowering and vigorous variety that has purple-tinged foliage. H 10m (33ft) S 5m (16ft).
Aspect: sun to semi-shade
Hardiness: ❁❁❁ Zone: Min. 7

Lonicera periclymenum 'Graham Thomas'

Mandevilla splendens

Lonicera periclymenum 'Belgica'
Early Dutch honeysuckle
Very fragrant, tubular, reddish-purple flowers that are yellow-lipped are produced *en masse* during late spring and early summer on this twining vigorous climber. H 7m (23ft) S 1m (3ft).
Aspect: sun to semi-shade
Hardiness: ❋❋❋ Zone: Min. 7

Lonicera periclymenum 'Graham Thomas'
Large, tubular and sweetly fragrant white flowers that age to yellow are produced from mid-summer to early autumn against a backdrop of oval green leaves on this vigorous deciduous climber. H 7m (23ft) S 1m (3ft).
Aspect: sun to semi-shade
Hardiness: ❋❋❋ Zone: Min. 7

Lonicera periclymenum 'Harlequin'
This is an unusual variegated honeysuckle that is covered in fragrant and tubular reddish-purple and yellow-lipped flowers from early summer to late summer on this twining vigorous climber. H 7m (23ft) S 1m (3ft).
Aspect: sun to semi-shade
Hardiness: ❋❋❋ Zone: Min. 7

Lonicera periclymenum 'Serotina'
Late Dutch honeysuckle
Superbly fragrant and tubular

creamy-white flowers that are purple-streaked are produced from mid-summer to mid-autumn on this vigorous, late-flowering, deciduous cultivar. It is a good climber to have growing in dappled shade. H 7m (23ft) S 1m (3ft).
Aspect: semi-shade
Hardiness: ❋❋❋ Zone: Min. 7

Lonicera x tellmanniana
Striking-looking, bright orange, tubular flowers open from red-tinged buds from late spring to mid-summer against a backdrop of large, dark green leaves. H 5m (16ft) S 2m (6ft).
Aspect: sun to semi-shade
Hardiness: ❋❋❋ Zone: Min. 7

MANDEVILLA
This genus of about 120 species includes the twining and woody climbers featured here, which are grown for their exotic summer flowers. It is an ideal patio plant in warm gardens as it responds well to being grown in pots, but it can be grown at the back of sheltered borders and used to cover trellis and fences. In cooler areas it can be grown as a houseplant and will add colour to a heated conservatory in colder areas.
Cultivation In the garden, grow in a moisture-retentive, well-drained soil that is reasonably fertile in

full sun, but sheltered from cool winds. If grown in containers, grow in a soil-based compost (soil mix). Feed every month throughout the growing season and water as necessary. Move to a warm spot undercover when the temperature falls below 10°C (50°F) and water sparingly in winter.
Pruning Cut back side shoots on established plants to 3 buds of the woody framework after it has flowered.
Propagation Sow seeds in mid-spring or take softwood cuttings in late spring.

Mandevilla x amabilis 'Alice du Pont' (syn. M. x amoena 'Alice du Pont')
Fragrant pink, tubular flowers are produced throughout mid- to late summer against a backdrop of wavy-edged green leaves on this twining and woody climber.
H 7m (23ft) S 2m (6ft).
Aspect: sun
Hardiness: tender Zones: 10–12

Mandevilla boliviensis (syn. Dipladenia boliviensis)
White tubular flowers with a yellow eye are carried throughout mid- to late summer against a backdrop of glossy, narrow, green foliage on this twining, woody climber. H 4m (13ft) S 2m (6ft).
Aspect: sun
Hardiness: tender Zones: 10–12

Mandevilla splendens (syn. Dipladenia splendens)
Showy, rose-pink, tubular flowers

are borne in succession from mid- to late summer on this twining climber, which has hairy stems and glossy green leaves.
H 5m (16ft) S 2m (6ft).
Aspect: sun
Hardiness: tender Zones: 10–12

MONSTERA
This genus of over 20 species, including the tender evergreen climber featured here, are grown for their handsomely cut, lustrous foliage. It is grown outside in tropical areas but in colder climates it makes an attractive and easy-to-please house plant.
Cultivation Grow in a fresh general-purpose compost (soil mix). Feed every month during the growing season and water as necessary. If kept outside, move to a warm spot undercover when the temperature falls below 15°C (60°F). Water sparingly in winter.
Pruning No routine pruning is necessary.
Propagation Air layer in early autumn.

Monstera deliciosa
Swiss cheese plant
Large, deeply notched and sometimes perforated, glossy, dark green, leathery leaves are displayed on arching stems that splay outwards from a vigorous climbing stem supported in part by aerial roots. Mature plants may flower, producing creamy, arum-like spathes from late spring to late summer. H 10m (33ft) S 2m (6ft).
Aspect: semi-shade
Hardiness: tender Zones: 10–12

Monstera deliciosa

Parthenocissus quinquefolia

Passiflora caerulea

PARTHENOCISSUS

Comprising a genus of about ten species, including the vigorous deciduous tendril climbers featured here, they are grown for their handsome foliage and fiery autumn tints. It makes a cover-all climber that is excellent for camouflaging ugly buildings and other eyesores. A single specimen will cloak about two standard fence panels in five years.
Cultivation Grow in any well-drained soil that is reasonably fertile in full sun, dappled shade or full shade.
Pruning No routine pruning is necessary. Keep plants in check by pruning out unwanted stems in late winter.
Propagation Take semi-ripe stem cuttings in late summer; alternatively, take hardwood cuttings in late autumn.

Parthenocissus henryana (syn. Vitis henryana)
Chinese Virginia creeper
The handsome, deeply divided dark green leaves with distinctive white and pink veins turn fiery shades in autumn. It is less vigorous than other varieties. H 10m (33ft) S 5m (16ft).
Aspect: sun, semi-shade to deep shade
Hardiness: ❀❀❀ (borderline) Zone: Min. 7

Parthenocissus quinquefolia (syn. Vitis quinquefolia)
Virginia creeper
The deeply divided, slightly

puckered, green leaves transform in autumn as they take on brilliant shades of crimson and purple on this vigorous deciduous climber. H 15m (50ft) S 5m (16ft).
Aspect: sun, semi-shade to deep shade
Hardiness: ❀❀❀ Zone: Min. 7

Parthenocissus tricuspidata 'Robusta'
A very vigorous deciduous climber with large, dark green leaves that are deeply lobed, turning brilliant crimson and purple in autumn. H 20m (70ft) S 10m (33ft).
Aspect: sun, semi-shade to deep shade
Hardiness: ❀❀❀ Zone: Min. 7

Parthenocissus tricuspidata 'Veitchii' (syn. Ampelopsis veitchii)
Lustrous, deeply lobed, dark green leaves transform in autumn into a spectacular cloak of red and purple on this very vigorous variety. H 20m (70ft) S 10m (33ft).
Aspect: sun, semi-shade to deep shade
Hardiness: ❀❀❀ Zone: Min. 7

PASSIFLORA
Passion flower
This large genus of over 400 species includes the evergreen tendril climbers featured here, which are grown mainly for their distinctive and tropical-looking

summer flowers. They are a very good choice for growing up a pergola, arch or open screen, as this allows the flowers and fruit to hang down attractively.
Cultivation In the garden, grow in a moisture-retentive, well-drained soil that is reasonably fertile in full sun or dappled shade, sheltered from cold winds. In containers, grow in a soil-based compost (soil mix). Feed every month in the growing season and water as necessary. Protect from severe frost in cold areas.
Pruning Thin overcrowded plants in early spring. In cold areas, treat as a perennial and cut back all stems to near ground level in mid-autumn then protect the

Parthenocissus tricuspidata

Passiflora 'Amethyst'

Passiflora caerulea 'Constance Elliot'

Philodendron scandens

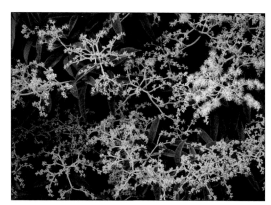

Pileostegia virburnoides

crown with an insulating mulch.
Propagation Take semi-ripe nodal
cuttings in mid-summer.

Passiflora 'Amethyst'
Large, showy purple flowers, each
with a ruff of spiky filaments and
darker eye, are produced in
succession from mid-summer to
early autumn, followed by egg-
shaped yellow-orange fruit.
H 10m (30ft) S 2m (6ft).
Aspect: sun or semi-shade
Hardiness: ❀❀ Zone: 8–9

Passiflora caerulea
Blue passion flower
Exotic, waxy-looking white
flowers, each with a purple, blue
and white ruff of spiky filaments
at the centre, are produced from
mid-summer to early autumn.
Egg-shaped, yellow-orange fruit
follow. H 10m (33ft) S 1m (3ft).
Aspect: sun or semi-shade
Hardiness: ❀❀ Zone: Min. 7

Passiflora caerulea
'Constance Elliot'
A succession of fragrant, waxy-
looking white flowers, each with a
bluish-white ruff of spiky
filaments, are borne from mid-
summer to early autumn, followed
by egg-shaped yellow-orange fruit.
H 10m (33ft) S 2m (6ft).
Aspect: sun or semi-shade
Hardiness: ❀❀ Zone: Min. 7

PHILODENDRON
A large genus of over 500 species,
including the fast-growing, tender,
evergreen climber featured here,

grown for its handsome foliage. It
makes an attractive house plant.
In tropical areas they can be
grown up posts and over sturdy
supports, such as arches.
Cultivation Grow in a fresh,
general-purpose potting compost
(soil mix). Feed every month
throughout the growing season
and water as necessary. Move to a
warm spot undercover when the
temperature falls below 15°C
(60°F) and water sparingly
during the winter.
Pruning No routine pruning is
necessary. Pinch out shoot tips to
encourage bushy growth.
Propagation Take tip cuttings in
late spring or early summer or air
layer in mid-spring.

Philodendron scandens
Heart leaf, sweetheart plant
Slender stems of heart-shaped,
glossy green leaves are sometimes
flushed with purple underneath.
It is able to tolerate low light and
some degree of neglect – and
so this makes it an ideal first-
timer's house plant. H 3m (13ft)
S 2m (6ft).
Aspect: semi-shade
Hardiness: tender Zone: 10+

PILEOSTEGIA
A small genus of just four species,
including the evergreen climber
featured here, which is grown for
its handsome foliage and star-
shaped late-summer flowers. It is
ideal for covering shady walls and
fences, as well as growing through
a well-established tree.

Cultivation Grow in any well-
drained soil that is reasonably
fertile in full sun or dappled
shade. Shelter from cold winds.
Pruning No routine pruning is
necessary. Overgrown plants can
have their stems thinned and
shortened after flowering in
early autumn.
Propagation Take tip cuttings in
mid-spring.

Pileostegia viburnoides (syn. Schizophragma viburnoides)
Star-shaped, creamy-white flowers
are produced in generous clusters
throughout late summer and early
autumn against a backdrop of
glossy, dark green and leathery
leaves. H 6m (20ft) S 2m (6ft).
Aspect: sun or semi-shade
Hardiness: ❀❀ Zone: Min. 7

PLUMBAGO
This genus contains at least ten
species, including the evergreen
climber featured here, grown for
its summer and autumn flowers.
Ideal for a frost-free, sheltered
and protected spot. In warmer
areas, it can be grown as ground
cover, through shrubs or as an
informal hedge.
Cultivation Grow in any well-
drained soil that is reasonably
fertile in full sun but sheltered
from cold winds. In frost-prone
areas, grow in a container using a
soil-based compost (soil mix).
Feed every month in the growing
season and water as necessary.
Protect in winter by moving it to
a frost-free area.

Pruning Cut back after flowering,
removing around two-thirds of
the new growth.
Propagation Sow seeds in early
spring or take semi-ripe cuttings
in mid-summer.

Plumbago auriculata (syn. P. capensis)
Cape leadwort
An extremely long-flowering
climber that bears sky-blue
flowers in trusses from early
summer to late autumn against
matt, apple-green leaves.
H 6m (20ft) S 3m (10ft).
Aspect: sun
Hardiness: ❀ Zone: 9+

Plumbago auriculata var. alba

Solanum crispum 'Glasnevin'

SOLANUM

This comprises a huge genus of over 1400 species, including the evergreen climbers featured here, that are grown for their abundant clusters of summer flowers. They are ideal for a sheltered spot where they will cover all types of garden structures. A single specimen will cover an area the size of a standard fence panel in five years.
Cultivation Grow in a moisture-retentive, well-drained neutral to slightly alkaline soil that is reasonably fertile. Grow in full sun, but protected from cold winds. In frost-prone areas, grow half-hardy solanums in containers using a soil-based compost (soil mix). Feed every month during the growing season and water as necessary. Move to a frost-free conservatory or greenhouse in winter.
Pruning Thin out established plants and cut out any frost-damaged shoots in mid-spring. Neglected climbers can be cut back hard to 15cm (6in) of ground level in mid-spring.
Propagation Take basal cuttings in early summer.

Solanum crispum 'Glasnevin'
(syn. *S. C.* 'Autumnale')
Chilean potato tree
A vigorous climber with dark green leaves that bears fragrant, pale purple flowers from early summer to early autumn, followed by creamy-white fruit.
H 6m (20ft) S 4m (13ft).
Aspect: sun
Hardiness: ❄❄ Zone: Min. 7

Solanum jasminoides 'Album'
Glossy, dark green leaves provide the perfect foil for the clusters of jasmine-scented flowers borne from early summer to early autumn. Each star-shaped white bloom has a yellow eye and is followed by round, purple-black berries. H 6m (20ft)
S 6m (20ft).
Aspect: sun
Hardiness: ❄ Zone: Min 9

SOLLYA

A small genus of just three species, grown for its pendent flowers that appear in summer. It can be grown in a sheltered spot in mild gardens, but it will need tying into its support. It is best grown as a conservatory climber in other conditions.
Cultivation Grow in a moisture-retentive, well-drained neutral to slightly alkaline soil that is

Sollya heterophylla

reasonably fertile in full sun, but protected from midday sun scorch and cold winds. In frost-prone areas, grow in a container using a soil-based compost (soil mix). Feed every month throughout the growing season and water as necessary. Protect in winter by moving it to a frost-free conservatory or greenhouse.
Pruning Thin established plants and cut out any frost-damaged shoots in mid-spring. Neglected climbers can be cut back hard to 15cm (6in) of ground level in mid-spring.
Propagation Take softwood cuttings in mid-spring.

Sollya heterophylla
(syn. *S. fusiformis*)
Bluebell creeper
From early summer to early autumn, sky blue, bell-shaped flowers hang from this twining climber, which is clothed in lance-shaped, dark green leaves, followed by edible blue berries. Borderline half hardy. H 2m (6ft) S 2m (6ft).
Aspect: sun
Hardiness: ❄ Zone: Min. 5

STEPHANOTIS

This genus of about 10 species includes the long-flowering evergreen climber featured here, grown for its fragrant clusters of waxy-looking flowers. Grow on a sunny wall in warm gardens or, in colder areas, in a heated greenhouse or conservatory.
Cultivation In the garden, grow in a moisture-retentive, well-drained

Stephanotis floribunda

garden soil in full sun but protected from midday sun scorch and cold winds. In containers, grow in a soil-based compost (soil mix). Feed every month throughout the growing season and water as necessary. Move to a warm spot undercover when below 15°C (60°F) and water sparingly in the winter.
Pruning Cut back damaged or weak stems. Lateral shoots on congested plants can be shortened to within 15cm (6in) of the main framework in late winter.
Propagation Take softwood cuttings in mid-spring.

Stephanotis floribunda
(syn. *S. jasminoides*)
Bridal wreath, Madagascar jasmine
Small cluster of fragrant, waxy-looking, creamy-white flowers are borne from late spring to mid-autumn on this twining evergreen climber that has glossy, leathery, dark green leaves. H 3m (10ft) S 2m (6ft).
Aspect: sun
Hardiness: tender Zones: 10–12

TRACHELOSPERMUM

This genus of about 20 species includes the woody evergreen climbers featured here, grown for their fragrant clusters of summer flowers. Grow against a sheltered, structure or through a well-established tree in a sunny spot or allow it to scramble over the soil as groundcover.
Cultivation Grow in any well-drained soil that is reasonably fertile in full sun or dappled shade that is sheltered from cold winds. In very cold areas, grow in a container using a soil-based compost (soil mix). Feed every month throughout the growing season and water as necessary. Protect against cold in winter.
Pruning No routine pruning is necessary. Wayward shoots can be removed in mid-spring.
Propagation Take semi-ripe cuttings in mid-summer.

Trachelospermum asiaticum
Asian jasmine
Jasmine-scented, creamy-white, tubular flowers are produced in clusters throughout mid- and late

Trachelospermum jasminoides

summer and are set off by this twining climber's dark evergreen leaves. H 6m (20ft) S 3m (10ft). Aspect: sun or semi-shade Hardiness: ❊❊ Zone: Min. 7

Trachelospermum jasminoides
Star jasmine

Clusters of jasmine-scented, white, tubular flowers are borne in mid- and late summer on this twining evergreen climber, which has glossy, dark green leaves. H 9m (28ft) S 3m (10ft). Aspect: sun or semi-shade Hardiness: ❊❊ Zone: Min. 7

VITIS
Vine

This genus contains about 65 species, including the deciduous tendril climbers featured here, which are grown mainly for their handsome foliage. This takes on fabulously coloured autumn tints. Vitis are reliable cover-all climbers for walls and fences, but they can also be used to scramble through established trees and hedges, as well as covering the ground in a carpet of foliage. They are very fast-growing and so make an ideal choice if you are looking for a quick cover-up – a single plant will be able to smother about two standard fence panels in five years.
Cultivation Grow in any well-drained neutral to alkaline soil that is reasonably fertile, in full sun or dappled shade. Add plenty of organic matter to the soil before planting.

Pruning No routine pruning is necessary. Keep plants in check by pruning out unwanted stems in early summer.
Propagation Layer suitable shoots in late spring, take semi-ripe cuttings in mid-summer or take take hardwood cuttings in late autumn.

Vitis 'Brant'

This is a vigorous, deciduous, ornamental grape vine with serrated, lobed, apple-green leaves that turn rust-red between the main veins in autumn. Large bunches of edible blue-black grapes are also produced. H 7m (23ft) S 5m (16ft). Aspect: sun or semi-shade Hardiness: ❊❊❊ Zone: Min. 7

Vitis coignetiae
Crimson glory vine

Huge, heart-shaped and lobed, dark green leaves turn fiery shades of red in autumn, accompanied by bunches of small, blue-black, inedible grapes. H 15m (50ft) S 5m (16ft). Aspect: sun or semi-shade Hardiness: ❊❊❊ Zone: Min. 7

Vitis vinifera 'Purpurea'

This is a deciduous tendril climber with lobed, pale green young leaves that mature to claret red, becoming plum purple in autumn, accompanied by bunches of small purple inedible grapes. H 7m (22ft) S 3m (10ft). Aspect: sun or semi-shade Hardiness: ❊❊❊ Zone: Min. 7

Vitis vinifera 'Purpurea'

Wisteria sinensis

WISTERIA

A genus of about ten species, including the twining deciduous climbers featured here, wisterias are grown for their enormous pendent clusters of beautiful early summer flowers. They are ideal for growing up sun-drenched walls and sturdy structures, such as pergolas and arches, where their cascading flowers can be seen at their best.
Cultivation Grow in a moisture-retentive, well-drained soil that is reasonably fertile in full sun or dappled shade. Add plenty of organic matter to the soil before planting time.
Pruning Prune in two stages: cut back all new whippy growth to four or six leaves during late summer. Later, after leaf fall, cut these stumps back to just two or three buds of the main structural framework.
Propagation Take semi-ripe basal cuttings in late summer, or layer suitable shoots in late spring.

Wisteria floribunda
Japanese wisteria

Scented violet-blue to white pea-like flowers hang down in elegant pendent clusters during early summer, followed by felty green pods. The airy, grey-green leaves on this vigorous climber turn yellow in autumn. It is slow to get established and may take several

years to start flowering. H 9m (28ft) S 5m (16ft). Named varieties: 'Alba' (syn. *W.* 'Shiro-Noda'), white flowers. H 9m (28ft) S 5m (16ft). 'Macrobotry' (syn. *W.* 'Kyushaku', *W. multijuga*, *W.* 'Naga Noda'), mauve flowers. H 9m (28ft) S 5m (16ft). 'Royal Purple' (syn. *W.* 'Black Dragon', *W.* 'Kokuryu'), violet-purple flowers. H 9m (28ft) S 5m (16ft). Aspect: sun or semi-shade Hardiness: ❊❊❊ Zone: Min. 7

Wisteria x formosa

Fragrant violet-blue and pea-like flowers with white and yellow markings are borne in pendent clusters during late spring and early summer. H 9m (28ft) S 5m (16ft). Aspect: sun or semi-shade Hardiness: ❊❊❊ Zone: Min. 7

Wisteria sinensis (syn. *W. chinensis*)
Chinese wisteria

Clusters of fragrant, mauve, pea-like flowers hang down in pendent clusters during late spring and early summer, often followed by felty green pods. H 9m (28ft) S 5m (16ft). Named varieties: 'Alba', white flowers. H 9m (28ft) S 5m (16ft). Aspect: sun or semi-shade Hardiness: ❊❊❊ Zone: Min. 7

Calendar of care

Most of the essential tasks in ornamental gardens are seasonal and so have to be carried out at a certain time of the year. With many shrubs and climbers the most important job is pruning, which has to be carried out at the right stage of growth to prevent flowering production or loss in the following season. On the following pages you will find a comprehensive guide to what to prune and when.

There is also a quick-reference checklist to all the other seasonal tasks, including propagating, planting, feeding, watering, weeding and protecting, so that you can be sure to complete all necessary tasks at the right time of the year. If you are short of time, prioritize your gardening workload to make sure that the most critical tasks are carried out first.

It should be remembered that the beginning and end of the seasons varies from year to year as well as with your local climate, so the exact timing should depend on how your plants are growing at the time. For example, a spring-flowering plant in a sheltered garden in a relatively warm country can flower up to four weeks earlier than the same plant growing in a more exposed spot elsewhere.

Note: In the pruning calendars for shrubs and climbers featured on the following pages, plants featured in more than one month can be pruned at any time in this period.

The gardener's tasks continue throughout the year, making sure that each season yeilds the best show of flowers and foliage, providing a rich reward for all the work that it entails.

Seasonal jobs checklist: spring and summer

Spring is when the garden starts to come alive again. But there are also a few other tasks awaiting your attention, which are listed here.

Things to do in spring
- Check plants for winter damage
- Firm in any new plants loosened by winter frosts
- Water all new additions
- Trim winter-flowering heathers
- Plant new shrubs and climbers

- Plant evergreen and deciduous hedging
- Keep control of weeds
- Complete rose pruning
- Complete renovation of overgrown shrubs and climbers
- Check supports of all climbers
- Apply a general fertilizer to established plants
- Propagate by layering
- Sow seeds collected last summer and given cold treatment over winter

- Take leaf-bud cuttings
- Take softwood cuttings
- Separate rooted layers from parent plants and pot up or plant out
- Watch out for pests and disease
- Tie in new stems of climbers as they grow
- Prune early flowering shrubs
- Prune grey-leaved shrubs
- Prune evergreens
- Trim formal edging shrubs
- Start clipping hedges

What to prune in spring

Early spring shrubs
Artemesia
Buddleja davidii
Colutea
Convolvulus cneorum
Cotinus
Daphne (after flowering)
Forsythia (after flowering)
Fothergilla (after flowering)
Griselinia
Hamamellis (after flowering)
Hebe cupressoides
Hebe pinguifolia
Hebe rakaiensis
Hydrangea arborescens
Hydrangea paniculata
Hypericum calycinum
Lavatera
Mahonia (after flowering)
Rhus
Ribes sanguineum (after flowering)
Rosa
Skimmia (after flowering)
Spiraea japonica
Symphoricarpos
Viburnum farreri (after flowering)
Viburnum opulus (after flowering)
Vinca

Early spring climbers
Cissus
Clematis (Group 3)
Cobaea
Eccremocarpus
Hedera
Humulus
Jasminum nudiflorum (after flowering)
Lonicera

Mid-spring shrubs
Abutilon megapotamicum
Aucuba (fruiting)
Callicarpa
Calluna
Camellia (after flowering)
Caryopteris
Ceanothus 'Autumnal Blue'
Ceanothus 'Burkwoodii'
Ceratostigma
Cistus
Clerodendrum bungei
Corylopsis (after flowering)
Cotoneaster frigidus 'Cornubia'
Cotoneaster x watereri
Erica (after flowering)
Euonymus japonicus
Euphorbia pulcherrima (after flowering)
Exochorda (after flowering)
Fatsia
Forsythia (after flowering)
Hebe macrantha
Hebe salicifolia
Hebe speciosa
Helichrysum
Hydrangea macrophylla
Hydrangea serrata
Hypericum 'Hidcote'
Kerria (after flowering)
Lavandula
Leycesteria
Ligustrum
Lonicera fragrantissima (after flowering)
Lonicera x purpusii (after flowering)
Olearia
Osmanthus (after flowering)
Perovskia
Phygelius

Pieris (after flowering)
Pittosporum
Potentilla
Pyracantha

Mid-spring climbers
Cissus
Passiflora
Solanum

Late spring shrubs
Abelia
Akebia quinata
Chaenomeles (after flowering)
Choisya (after flowering)
Helichrysum petiolare
Hibiscus
Ribes speciosum (after flowering)

Late spring climbers
Berberidopsis
Cissus
Clematis (group 1, after flowering)

Prune cistus plants, including the Cistus x skanbergii shown here, after flowering.

What to prune in summer

Early summer shrubs
Berberis darwinii (after flowering)
Berberis linearifolia (after flowering)
Berberis x stenophylla (after flowering)
Cornus kousa var. *chinensis*
Cornus mas
Cornus officinalis
Cytisus x praecox (after flowering)
Deutzia (after flowering)
Helichrysum petiolare
Hippophae
Magnolia liliiflora
Magnolia x soulangeana
Magnolia stellata
Rosmarinus (after flowering)
Spiraea 'Arguta' (after flowering)
Syringa (after flowering)

Mid-summer climbers
Clematis (group 1, after flowering)

Mid-summer shrubs
Buxus
Carpenteria
Ceanothus arboreus 'Trewithen Blue'
(after flowering)
Ceanothus 'Concha' (after flowering)
Ceanothus impressus (after flowering)
Ceanothus thyrsiflorus (after flowering)
Cytisus battandieri (after flowering)
Escallonia 'Apple Blossom' (after
flowering)

Euphorbia characias (after flowering)
Euphorbia myrsinites (after flowering)
Fremontodendron (after flowering)
Helianthemum (after flowering)
Helichrysum petiolare
Kolkwitzia (after flowering)
Laurus
Lonicera nitida
Paeonia (after flowering)
Philadelphus microphyllus (after flowering)
Rhododendron luteum (after flowering)
Rubus cockburnianus (after flowering)
Sophora
Tamarix (after flowering)
Tinus (after flowering)
Viburnum plicatum (after flowering)
Weigela (after flowering)

Mid-summer climbers
Wisteria

Late summer shrubs
Buddleja alternifolia (after flowering)
Buxus
Callistemon (after flowering)
Elaeagnus x ebbinge,
Elaeagnus glabra
Elaeagnus macrophylla
Elaeagnus pungens 'Maculata'
x *Fatshedera*
Genista hispanica (after flowering)
Grevillea (after flowering)

Helianthemum (after flowering)
Laurus
Nerium
Philadelphus 'Belle Etoile' (after flowering)
Philadelphus coronarius (after flowering)
Philadelphus delavayi (after flowering)
Philadelphus 'Virginal' (after flowering)
Pyracantha
Thymus

Late summer climbers
Billardiera (after fruiting),
Clerodendrum (after flowering)
Clianthus (after flowering)
Hydrangea (after flowering)
Jasminum polyanthum (after flowering)

Prune Clematis Group 1 plants in late spring,
like this *Clematis armandii* shown here.

Summer is when you can really enjoy the fruits of your labours and revel in the splendour of your garden. It is also a time of plant maintenance, so that you can keep your garden looking its very best and allowing your shrubs and climbers to dazzle.

Trim hedges like *Osmanthus het*. 'Tricolor' shown here. Cut out any reverted leaves on varigated types when you see them.

Things to do in summer
- Water all new additions
- Take semi-ripe cuttings
- Move out tender plants to a sheltered position outdoors
- Prune early clematis
- Prune climbers and wall shrubs after flowering
- Prune early summer-flowering shrubs after flowering
- Clear ground for autumn planting
- Spray against rose diseases
- Pot up rooted cuttings taken in the spring
- Deadhead large-flowered shrubs after flowering
- Remove suckers from roses
- Trim conifer hedges
- Train climbing and rambler roses
- Trim lavender after flowering
- Harvest lavender for drying
- Maintain control over pest and disease outbreaks
- Summer prune wisteria
- Keep weeds under control
- Cut out any reverted shoots on variegated shrubs and climbers
- Prune rambler roses after flowering

Seasonal jobs checklist: autumn and winter

Early autumn, if it is kind, can provide an Indian summer in the garden, prolonging the flowering times of your shrubs and climbers. Gradually, glorious leaf shades appear on the plants, providing a spectacular last display before dropping in mid- to late autumn.

What to do in autumn
- Take hardwood cuttings
- Pot on semi-ripe cuttings taken in summer
- Prune late-flowering shrubs
- Part-prune tall shrubs to prevent wind rock
- Plant new shrubs, climbers and hedges
- Trim vigorous hedges
- Keep weeds under control
- Tie in whippy shoots on climbers
- Collect seed and berries for propagation
- Protect borderline hardy shrubs and climbers
- Bring tender plants under cover before the first frosts
- Propagate from suitable stems by layering
- Clear away diseased leaves from roses

Autumn is the time for pruning in the garden. Vigorously growing hedges can take quite a bold cutting back at this time of year.

- Take root cuttings
- Plant deciduous shrubs and climbers
- Protect container-grown hardy shrubs and climbers, if necessary
- Take root cuttings
- Dig over vacant ground when soil conditions allow
- Move awkwardly placed shrubs and climbers or those that you wish to relocate elsewhere in the garden
- Check tree ties and stakes and replace if necessary
- Take measures to make sure nothing can be damaged on windy nights
- Plant shrubs, roses and hedging plants that are sold with bare roots

What to prune in autumn

EARLY AUTUMN
Shrubs
Abelia (after flowering)
Buxus
Lonicera nitida
Nerium

Climbers
Jasminum officinale (after flowering)
Lathyrus latifolius (after flowering)
Lonicera periclymenum
Lonicera x americana
Lonicera x brownii
Lonicera x tellmanniana
Passiflora (after flowering)
Rosa (climbing, after flowering)

MID-AUTUMN
Shrubs
Santolina (after flowering)

Climbers
Parthenocissus

LATE AUTUMN
Shrubs
Amelanchier
Aucuba (non-fruiting)

Climbers
Parthenocissus

Autumn produces spectacular colour displays, as shown by Calluna vulgaris 'Wickwar Flame'.

Winter is usually a dormant time in the garden, although there is still much to do. The main aim in winter is to protect plants from the ravages of wind, frost and snowfalls. However, it is also a time for the pruning and propagation of certain shrubs and climbers.

What to do in winter

- Clear heavy falls of snow off hedges and evergreens, if necessary
- Take hardwood cuttings from roses
- Prune climbing roses
- If it's a mild winter, continue to cut the lawn, as long as it is still growing, but raise the height of the mower blades
- Prevent container-grown plants from freezing by wrapping them with bubble wrap or taking them under shelter
- Remove algae and moss patches on the patio and paving by scrubbing with a broom or blasting with a pressure washer
- Feed indoor plants occasionally
- Order seed catalogues and look on the internet to plan what you're going to grow in the spring
- Winter prune wisteria
- Carry out all winter pruning jobs
- Protect berried holly branches to preserve fruit for winter decoration
- Protect new additions with windbreak netting
- Renovate overgrown shrubs and climbers
- Prune tall-growing bush roses by about a half to help prevent wind-rock damaging roots, and shorten all the branches on standard roses for the same reason
- Plant bare-rooted rose bushes
- Water plants sparingly
- Be on the watch for any pests on overwintering plants and destroy them

What to prune in winter

EARLY WINTER
Shrubs
Amelanchier
Aucuba (non-fruiting)
Berberis thunbergii
Berberis x ottawensis
Salix caprea 'Kilmarnock'
Sambucus

Climbers
Ampelopsis
Parthenocissus
Vitis
Wisteria

MID-WINTER
Shrubs
Aucuba (non-fruiting)
Cotoneaster horizontalis
Salix caprea 'Kilmarnock'
Sambucus

Climbers
Actinidia
Ampelopsis
Bougainvillea
Campsis
Celastrus
Mandevilla
Vitis
Wisteria

LATE WINTER
Shrubs
Aucuba (non-fruiting)
Buddleja globosa
Chimonanthus (after flowering)
Cornus alba
Cornus sanguinea
Cornus stolonifera
Corylus
Cotoneaster dammeri
Cotoneaster microphyllus
Euonymus europaeus
Euonymus alatus
Garrya ellipticus (after flowering)
Rosa (bush)
Sambucus

Climbers
Actinidia
Bougainvillea
Campsis
Clematis (Group 2 & Group 3)
Hedera
Humulus
Jasminum nudiflorum (after flowering)
Lonicera japonica
Lonicera henryi
Rubus

Keep the heat in the greenhouse by covering the glass panes with bubble wrap. This will help to insulate it and retain heat. Use a foil covering under the wrap on the north-facing side.

TREES

What are trees?

Trees are one of the oldest living forms of plant life. They also live longer than any other organism on the planet. In California, USA, there are Bristlecone pines that are known to be over 4,500 years old and in the UK there are yew trees of similar age.

Colonization by trees

Trees are amazing organisms that have evolved over millennia to colonize a wide and diverse range of habitats around the world. They inhabit many natural and urban landscapes, and have adapted to survive in almost any circumstances.

This astonishing diversity can be seen in the range of trees that grow in our gardens.

Trees cover almost a third of the earth's dry land and there are estimated to be more than 80,000 different species, ranging from small Arctic willows that are only a few inches high, to the lofty giant coast redwoods, which can grow to an amazing 113m (368ft).

The role of trees

Trees have always played an integral part in human development by providing food, shelter, shade, medicines, timber and fuel, among

This beautiful *Nyssa sylvatica* (tupelo), like all trees, plays a vital role in the ecology of the earth.

other things. They also serve to feed and shelter all kinds of wildlife and increase its diversity.

Forests of trees help to regulate water flow and can reduce the effects of flooding and soil erosion. They also influence weather patterns by increasing humidity and generating rainfall. But more than that, trees are essential to animal life – they process vast amounts of carbon dioxide from the atmosphere by absorbing it through their leaves and then emit life-giving oxygen, which we breathe in.

However, despite their wonderful benefits, humans are putting the future of trees at risk. Over ten per cent of the world's trees are now endangered. More than 8,750 species are threatened with extinction – and some are literally down to their last one or two specimens.

What defines a tree is an open question. The laburnum on the right is always classified as a tree, while the virburnum on the left is designated a shrub, but here they both serve as trees.

Longevity

Trees are very long lived compared to shrubs or other plants. The longevity of different types of tree varies tremendously; a short-lived tree like a cherry tree may last between 50 and 100 years, while a long-lived tree such as an oak may live between 100 and 700 years – or even longer.

Definition of a tree

For most purposes, a tree may be defined as a large, woody plant with a trunk that persists above ground all year. The main feaure distinguishing it from a shrub is that the trunk, clear of branches, is normally a significant proportion of the total height of the tree. Trees also differ from shrubs in that they have secondary branches that are supported on the single main stem or trunk.

Some definitions give a minimum size for a mature specimen, but heights and spreads vary widely and there are many exceptions to any rule on this – a large shrub can be much bigger than a small tree.

Tree or shrub?

Distinguishing between a tree and a shrub might seem a straightforward task, but the differences between the two are often subtle. We expect a tree to be tall, with branches and leaves held high above a clear trunk, while a shrub is supposed to be smaller, with a multitude of branches originating from close to the ground. However, as with most things in nature, plants can be difficult to categorize and sometimes a tree can be grown as a shrub – and vice versa. This is due to climate, altitude, exposure, soil, rainfall, shade, health and vigour – as well as interventional pruning to deliberately make a tree a shrub, or a shrub a tree.

The mighty coast redwood (*Sequoia sempervirens*) can live up to 2,000 years, and is the tallest tree in the world, reaching up to 113m (368ft) in height and 7m (23ft) in diameter at the base.

Because of the great diversity of their habitats, some tree families contain massive specimens, while closely related species can be much smaller, resembling shrubs in both their growth and habit, but which are still called trees.

Definition of a shrub

A shrub (or bush) is usually described as being smaller than a tree, but the main feature is that the 'trunk' forms only a small proportion of the overall height, and above the point where it branches there is no longer a central, vertical trunk that is significantly thicker than the other branches.

Many shrubs have several branches originating from, or close to, soil level. Although some shrubs can achieve tree-like proportions, there are few that produce a clear trunk.

Like trees, shrubs produce a framework of branches. Many types are small and low-growing, whereas

The berries of tree fruits are often brightly coloured, since this seems to attract birds, which play an integral role in seed dispersal.

Whether grown as a tree or to shrub-like proportions, *Acer palmatum* 'Osakazuki' will brighten up any garden, particularly during the autumn when its leaves turn a rich, vibrant red.

the only way that trees can be kept to these proportions is through regular pruning or bonsai.

Sometimes there is a choice; you can grow a particular plant as either a tree or a shrub. Some maples, for example, can be small or large, depending on how they are trained, pruned and planted. When potted up in containers, their root development is restrained, and this limits the tree's ultimate height. This versatility means that anyone can potentially grow a tree – whether in the biggest garden or on the smallest patio.

In the face of such diversity, it is easy to understand why trees hold so many 'world records', such as the oldest, tallest and widest specimens, as shown in the box on the opposite page.

Tree facts

• The oldest living tree is the ancient bristlecone pine (*Pinus longaeva*), which is thought to be 4,733 years old. Bristlecone pines grow very slowly due to the extreme conditions found in the White Mountains, near the Sierra Nevada, California, USA, where they grow in the remains of what was once an ancient forest some 3,000m (10,000ft) above sea level. At this altitude the trees are battered by wind and rain and baked by the drying sun, conditions that have 'pruned' them into strange shapes and forced them to slow down their growth.

• The world's tallest living tree is the Stratosphere Giant, a coast redwood (*Sequoia sempervirens*), which was 112.6m (369ft 4.8in) tall in 2002 when it was last measured. It was discovered in 2000, growing in the Rockefeller Forest at the Humboldt Redwoods State Park, California, USA.

• The tallest tree ever measured was an Australian eucalyptus (*Eucalyptus regnans*), which was found to be a staggering 132.6m (435ft) tall when measured in 1872, although other reports estimate that it may have measured over 150m (500ft). The Dyerville Giant, another coast redwood, was estimated to be 1,600 years old when it fell over in 1991. It measured 113.4m (372ft) in height, excluding the 1.5m (5ft) of buried trunk. Like many other monumental redwoods, it grew in the Humboldt Redwoods State Park.

• The biggest living tree is the famous General Sherman, a Wellingtonia (*Sequoiadendron giganteum*) growing in the Sequoia National Park in the Sierra Nevada, California. It is the largest living tree by volume in the world. The volume was estimated in 1975 and calculated to be approximately 1,486.6m³ (52.500 cubic feet).

• The heaviest-ever tree record belongs to another coast redwood, which blew over in 1905 and had a total trunk volume of 2,549m³ (90,000 cubic feet) and a mass of 3,300 tonnes (3,248 tons).

• The widest-spreading tree is the great bayan (*Ficus benghalensis*) growing in the Indian Botanical Garden in Calcutta, India. It covers a vast 1.2ha (3 acres). Its

The widest-spreading tree in the world is a *Ficus benghalensis* (bayan).

branches are supported by 1,775 stilt or supporting roots. This massive tree has a circumference of 412m (1,350ft) and was planted in 1787.

• The earliest surviving species of tree that is still grown in gardens today is the maidenhair tree (*Ginkgo biloba*) of Zhejiang, China, which first appeared 160 million years ago during the Jurassic era, when it colonized several continents.

• Some types of ornamental cherry trees can live between 50 and 100 years, whereas a long-lived tree, such as a *Quercus* (oak), may live between 100 and 700 years – or even more.

• Britain is thought to have the largest population of 'ancient' trees compared with the rest of Europe.

• Some trees produce life-saving medicines. For example, Taxol (a drug used to treat cancer patients) can be produced from yew leaves, and aspirin was originally created from research into white willow bark, which is a natural source of salicin and other salicylates – compounds similar in structure to aspirin.

• Broad-leaved trees change colour in the autumn because the green chlorophyll in the leaf breaks down and is reabsorbed by the tree prior to leaf shed.

• Trees have adapted numerous methods to pollinate their flowers. Pollination can be as simple as wind dispersal, or pollination by insects or even bats.

Ginkgo biloba (maidenhair tree) is the earliest surviving species of tree still grown today.

The importance of trees

Trees are one of the most complex and successful forms of plant life on earth. They have been around for 370 million years.

With their myriad shades of green and stunning flowers, foliage, fruit and bark, trees make our gardens, countryside and urban areas more colourful and spiritually uplifting. They increase wildlife diversity and create a more pleasant living and working environment, while at the same time providing shade in summer and shelter in winter.

Trees inhabit many natural landscapes, ranging from the cold, snow-capped mountainous regions to the hot, arid deserts, and from the salt and wind of coastal areas to the choking pollution of crowded cities. In almost every terrain and every climate, you will find trees that not only have adapted to their climate and habitat but are thriving.

Trees provide an ever-changing backdrop to our lives. Through the different seasons, they provide a beauty that is breathtaking.

The benefits of trees

Trees add immense beauty to our gardens: their fruit, foliage and flowers offer a dazzling array of colours and textures, while their forms soften the harsh lines of buildings and screen unsightly views. However, their value is practical as well as aesthetic.

Cleaning the air

Trees play a vital role in the environment, releasing oxygen into the atmosphere through the process of photosynthesis, as well as cleaning our air by filtering out pollutants. In addition to this, they can be used to provide security, privacy and shade in our gardens.

Air pollution is usually worse in towns and cities than in rural areas. Fortunately for us, garden and street trees are able to absorb many of the pollutants from the atmosphere, and heavier pollutants and dust particles sometimes adhere to the surfaces of leaves rather than being breathed in by us, until they are washed away by rainwater and into the nearest drain.

Improving soil

Tree roots help to bind the soil together, preventing soil erosion, by keeping it stable while allowing rainwater to drain into the soil. As they decompose, fallen leaves are dragged into the soil by worms and other soil-dwelling organisms, further improving the structure and moisture-retaining capacity of the soil, which helps to minimize run-off, which, in turn, reduces flooding.

Shade and shelter

In hot climates, trees can be grown to shade houses from direct sunlight, which experts have estimated can

Microclimate

Trees affect a garden's microclimate by slowing air movements and increasing humidity. This occurs because water is constantly evaporating from the surface of leaves during the growing season. Trees can also lower temperatures produced from the heating effect of concrete and brick buildings by providing shade. This creates a more acceptable climate for other plants as well as for us.

reduce the cost of air-conditioning by as much as 30 per cent. Similarly, planting trees to provide shelter from cold prevailing winds can also help to reduce winter heating bills.

Trees make effective shelter belts by protecting areas from damaging wind streams. The most effective shelter planting is an even mixture

Power stations constantly pollute the atmosphere, but if the surrounding countryside is planted with trees, they will help to filter out pollutants.

Trees support all kinds of life, from birds and insects to fungi and lichens.

Trees can provide a windbreak and muffle unpleasant sounds such as road traffic. They are also invaluable in absorbing pollution.

of deciduous and evergreen species. This slows down the wind, rather than deflecting it up and over the windbreak, which would force the deflected air back behind the windbreak in a more turbulent way.

Noise absorbers

Trees planted in dense blocks can be used to reduce the level of traffic noise by providing a barrier that deadens the sound. Conversely, trees can be quite noisy themselves. The quaking aspen (*Populus tremuloides*) is often planted so that the continual rustling of its leaves competes with and helps to block out unwanted background noise.

Wildlife benefits

A major benefit of trees is their value to wildlife. Whenever we plant a new tree we will attract birds, animals and insects into our garden. In addition, because trees create shade and shelter for other plants, our garden environment becomes

much more diverse and is able to develop into a more sustainable habitat, where beneficial insects can flourish and help to retain a natural balance between pests and diseases and their natural predators and prey.

Trees are also the natural habitat of birds and a wide variety of wild animals, which use the trees as a permanent or temporary home, or as a convenient shelter from bad weather or predators.

Trees provide protection and shade for other plants and are the natural habitat of a wide variety of wildlife, including birds and insects, which assist with pollination and seed dispersal.

The structure of trees

Trees truly are marvels of nature. They are woody, perennial plants that have clearly defined trunks, which hold the branches and leaves towards the light to gain sustenance. Each part of a tree's structure is designed to give the tree the best chance of growing and thriving.

Wood

As trees grow, they produce a large, woody framework of roots, trunk and branches, which enables them to survive and thrive in many different climates and soil types.

The wood consists of a series of compartments or layers that grow each year. As these compartments grow, the tree increases in girth and height. The trunk and other woody parts of a tree (the branches and large anchoring roots) are made up of a number of distinct zones.

The woody trunk provides the structural strength of the tree, while a tough, waterproof bark protects the delicate tissues that transport water and nutrients to the leaves and simple sugars to all parts of the tree. These sugars are the energy that feeds the tree, and they are produced in the leaves.

Bark

The material that grows on the outside of the branches and trunk is called bark. It is a corky layer of dead cells and it prevents the tree from becoming too hot or too cold, protects it from moisture and allows the cells inside to breathe. The bark also protects the tree from boring insects, fungi and bacteria.

Most bark is waterproof, so the trunk beneath will not rot, but bark has to be able to breathe. It does this by way of tiny openings, called lenticels. These are the dark oval marks you can see on the trunk.

Each year, as the trunk and branches increase in girth, the bark splits and regrows. The ways in which the bark does this gives each species its individual bark pattern.

Some bark splits and falls in small, angular flakes, as is seen on *Pinus* spp. (pine), while the bark of *Eucalyptus* falls in long strips, and *Betula* (birch) shreds in papery strips. This enables bark to be

constantly replaced by fresh tissue. In the case of *Platanus* x *hispanica*, it enables the tree to survive in a heavily polluted atmosphere, since the contaminated layer of bark is regularly shed – thus earning the tree the name of London plane, as it is widely planted in that city's streets.

Some trees have light, smooth bark. The thin, whitish bark of *Betula pendula* (silver birch) stops the trunk

THE STRUCTURE OF A TREE

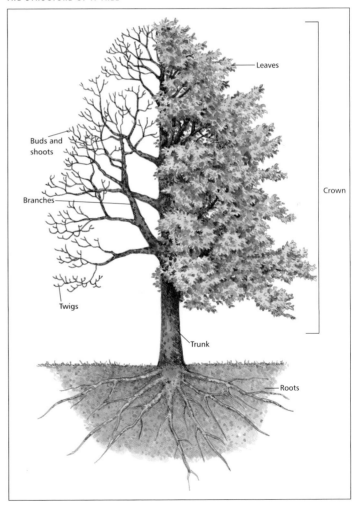

Leaves

Buds and shoots

Branches

Twigs

Crown

Trunk

Roots

from overheating in summer and in winter, when reflection from lying snow can cause air temperatures to rise quickly and split frozen wood.

The trunks of many palm trees are covered with a matted layer of the fibrous remains of the leaf stalks, and this acts as insulation during hot weather. Some trees, such as the *Sequoiadendron giganteum* (sierra redwood), have exceptionally thick bark, which is an adaptation that allows them to survive forest fires following lightning strikes.

Sapwood and heartwood

The sapwood consists of the outer annual growth rings in a tree's trunk, through which water and nutrients are carried from the roots upward to the branches, stems and leaves.

The heartwood is found at the centre of the trunk. It consists of old cells that have a high wood (lignin) content. This is a hardening material found in the cell walls of woody tissues and is the substance that gives trees their strength.

Although these cells are old, they are not dead; their growth has slowed, and they no longer breathe or require energy to continue to function. This heartwood acts like a skeleton, providing the framework on which the rest of the tree grows.

Calocedrus decurrens (incense cedar) has strongly corrugated bark.

The beauty of bark

Betula utilis var. *jacquemontii* 'Snow Queen'

Eucalyptus (gum tree)

Bark splits and regrows each year as the tree increases in girth. It may shred in shallow, paper-like sheets, in long strips, as on a eucalyptus, or in big flakes, as on some pine trees. The ways in which the bark splits and regrows give each species its individual bark pattern.

Many species are well known for their highly ornamental bark, including *Acer capillipes*, *A. davidii*, *A. grosseri* var. *hersii* and *A. pensylvanicum* (snakebark maples), *Betula* spp. (birch), *Eucalyptus* spp. (gum tree), *Prunus serrula* (Tibetan cherry), *Stewartia* spp., *Pinus* spp. (pine) and *Platanus* spp. (plane).

Some trees, such as *Acer griseum* (paperbark maple) and *Prunus serrula* (Tibetan cherry), have highly polished, mahogany-coloured bark, which shreds and hangs from the branches in winter. Any tree with shredding bark may be used as a focal point in the garden, and every effort should be made to position it so that it is backlit by the winter sun.

Trees with stark white bark, such as *Betula utilis* var. *jacquemontii* (Himalayan birch), can also be used to create a focal point in the garden, where the eerie, ghost-like stems will illuminate even the darkest of corners.

Cambium layer

Immediately beneath the bark and at the tips of roots and shoots is the cambium layer, which is the growth tissue of a tree. As it grows, the trunk, branches and the stems of a tree increase in size.

The cambium layer is made up of two types of living cell: phloem and xylem. The soft phloem cells transport nutrients and energy from the leaves to the rest of the plant and the woody (lignified) xylem cells transport water and support the tree.

The phloem and xylem cells divide and increase in number throughout the growing season, and this division process produces the annual rings we see in a tree trunk and which we use to age a tree when it is cut down.

In temperate climates the rings are produced from spring until autumn. However, in tropical climates, which have no distinct seasons, the rings are produced throughout the year. If the cambium layer is damaged sufficiently deeply to cut off the phloem and xylem cells, the tree cannot transport water and nutrients and may die.

Root system

Trees have an extensive root system that is made up of branch-like, woody structures designed to anchor the tree into the soil, while a network of much finer roots absorbs the nutrients and water. The farther they are away from the trunk, the finer roots become.

Growing from these fine roots are millions of tiny hairs, which absorb moisture and nutrients from the soil. These nutrients include minerals, which are essential for the tree's growth. The roots also store food, such as starch produced by the leaves, for later use.

The rings in a tree trunk are produced by the division of phloem and xylem cells.

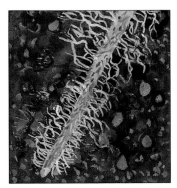

Root hairs have a lifespan of a few weeks and are constantly replaced.

Contrary to popular belief, most tree roots do not penetrate very deeply into the soil; the roots of even the tallest tree seldom reach down more than 3m (10ft). However, the roots spread quite wide just under the surface of the soil. As the top layers of the soil are usually rich in the organic material, minerals and moisture required to nourish the tree, they have no need to go much deeper, but every need to spread out.

Leaves

There are a huge number of different types of leaf, which come in a vast array of shapes, sizes, colours and textures. As well as being attractive, leaves play a vital role. They generate food so that the tree can live, grow and thrive. They do this using a process called photosynthesis, whereby the leaves absorb carbon dioxide and emit oxygen during the daytime.

Leaves contain a green pigment called chlorophyll that absorbs light energy from the sun. This energy is used to combine the carbon dioxide in the atmosphere with water taken up from the soil, creating glucose and oxygen.

The oxygen is released back into the atmosphere, but the glucose is used to provide energy and can be transformed into either starch or cellulose for storage or to form the cell walls of the tree.

Phloem cells in the cambium layer under the bark transport the sugary products of photosynthesis from the leaf to all other parts of the tree. This energy can either be stored for later use, used to produce flowers or seeds, or employed to heal any wounds the tree may receive.

How to date a tree

Some trees can live hundreds of years. Dating when they were planted is possible by reading the ring growth the tree produces. Each year the new cells that are produced under the bark create a new ring of tissue, visible in a cross section of the tree. The growth occurs at the outside of the trunk, just under the bark.

Each ring has light and dark sections. The light tissue is less dense and is made up of cells produced in the spring when the tree is growing at its fastest rate. The dark part of the ring is composed of cells laid down in the summer when the rate of growth has slowed. These rings are known as growth rings, with each light and dark ring pair representing a year of growth.

By counting the growth rings, it is possible to work out the age of the tree. The rings can be read either by taking a cross section of the trunk, if the tree is dead, or with just a core section taken from the trunk.

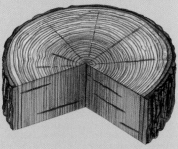

Photosynthesis

The sugars that the tree uses to grow are produced by a process called photosynthesis, which involves nutrients, water, carbon dioxide and sunlight. Oxygen is a by-product of photosynthesis. The leaves of a tree are able to absorb and harness the power of sunlight, like a solar cell.

The cells that absorb sunlight (chloroplasts) are green and give the leaves their colour. All woody parts of a tree are able to store simple sugars, which the tree will use as an energy supply in winter or at times when growth is difficult, such as during a drought or an infestation of insects. Trees can also absorb carbon monoxide and help to filter and purify our environment.

Flowers

Considered by many to be the most delightful part, flowers herald a change in the seasons and reaffirm the cycle of life. Indeed, giving life is their function, as they are the reproductive part of the tree.

The range of flowers on trees is as remarkable as the different leaf forms. Most trees flower in spring or summer, although some temperate trees, such as *Parrotia persica* (Persian ironwood), reap the benefits of winter flowering. Many tropical trees bear decorative blooms throughout the year, as there is little change in conditions from season to season.

Flowers can vary in shape and size – from the cup-and-saucer pink and white flowers of *Magnolia campbellii*, which may be 30cm (12in) across, to the clusters of dainty flowers borne by spring-flowering cherries, such as *Prunus* 'Amanogawa' (ornamental cherry).

Most wind-pollinated trees evolved in areas where there was a shortage of insects, and so they are quite common in northern temperate zones of the world. Most conifers, for example, are wind pollinated.

Pollination by insects is much more common, however. Flowers that produce copious amounts of nectar

Flowers of *Prunus sargentii* are a pretty shade of pink to attract pollinators.

attract insects, such as bees, but they need to get the attention of the insects first, and many trees are often highly scented for just this reason, with their aroma lingering for days.

Other trees bear flowers that open up to produce their intoxicating scent for only a day. Some trees flower at night so that their blooms may be pollinated by night-flying moths or bats.

DIFFERENT LEAF SHAPES

Metasequoia glyptostroboides (dawn redwood) has spirally arranged fern-like foliage (needles).

Liquidambar stryaciflua 'Palo Alto' has maple-like (palmate) leaves that are alternate along the stem.

Carya ovata has leaves that are made up of five long, pointed leaflets. These are arranged along slender stems (rachis).

Male and female

Individual male sex cells are referred to as pollen. Individual female sex cells are contained in specialized cells, called ovules, which are normally located in flower parts. Fertilization is the name given to the fusing of pollen and ovule nuclei, leading to the formation of a seed.

Reproduction

Some trees, such as cherries, have male and female organs within the same flower and so can self-pollinate in order to reproduce. Others, such as hazels, have separate male and female flowers on the same tree.

Another group of trees only produce flowers of one sex, and therefore require another tree of the opposite sex to be somewhere in the vicinity in order to be pollinated.

Trees in the latter two groups cannot go out and search for a mate so they rely on a go-between to transport the pollen, either from the male to the female part of the tree or from a male tree to another tree of the opposite 'sex'. This can be achieved by wind, water or an animal.

This need to attract a vast array of potential pollinators has caused many trees to produce magnificent-looking and highly specialized flowers to act as a lure. Flowers that are pollinated by birds and butterflies tend to be tubular in shape in order to keep the nectar out of reach of other pollinators. As the birds bend in to collect the nectar, the pollen brushes on to them and is later transferred to another flower.

Seeds

Once the flowers have been pollinated, they develop into fruits of some kind, with the ultimate aim of dispersing seeds to begin a new generation of trees; each seed contains all that is necessary to start the creation of a new tree.

Dispersal occurs by different means. Some seeds, such as those of the maple, have 'wings' to aid dispersal by the wind. Nuts, for example, are buried by animals such as squirrels, which sometimes fail to return for them, thus leaving a 'planted seed'. Berries with small seeds are eaten by birds, which then excrete the seeds in their droppings. These fruits are usually brightly coloured, to attract birds, and contain nutritious flesh as well as the seeds.

Fruit

The production of fruit is often associated with autumn in temperate regions. This is because the warm weather of the growing season provides the best conditions for the development of fruits and seeds. In tropical countries, however, due to more favourable weather conditions fruit production can take place throughout the year.

The flowers of *Catalpa bignonioides* are trumpet-shaped. Pollinators collect the nectar and transfer pollen to other trees.

Conifers, such as *Juniperus chinensis* (Chinese juniper), bear their seeds in cones, which vary greatly in size and shape.

The seeds of the Seville orange (*Citrus aurantium*) are contained in the fleshy fruit.

Rowans produce brightly coloured berries that attract animals, which disperse the seeds.

Indian horse chestnut buds open to reveal down covered leaves.

Tree fruits range from the cones borne by coniferous species to drupes (stones enclosed in a soft, fleshy case), like mangoes and plums. There are also fleshy fruits such as oranges, small nuts, pea-like pods, spiky chestnuts, acorns and two-winged maple seeds. Many fruits are highly decorative and are a welcome addition when there is little else of interest in the garden.

Buds

A tree bud consists of next year's leaves, stems and often flowers, which are folded and twisted tightly together in a waterproof covering of modified leaves. These are known as bud scales. Sometimes extra protection is provided by a coating of hair, wax, resin or gum on the outside. Inside the bud is everything the tree will need to resume growing once the days lengthen and the temperature increases in spring.

As spring arrives, the buds begin to open and the leaves gradually emerge. Common factors such as warmth and light trigger off this process, but each species has its own particular triggers depending on its life cycle, which is affected by factors such as the length of the growing season in its geographical area.

Cones

Trees that bear their fruit in cones – usually brown, woody structures with scales – are called conifers. The reproductive organs are the male and female cones. The male cone produces the pollen, while the seed develops in the female cone, which is often larger in size.

The entire proces of reaching maturity, fertilization and seed ripening can take a number of years.

The structure of seed

A seed consists of a protective shell and a food-storage facility that allows the germinating seed to start growing and, eventually, develop into a seedling. Inside every ripe tree seed are the beginnings of a root, shoot and one or two specialized leaves, known as cotyledons (palms are monocots). If a seed manages to be fertilized, it will either germinate immediately or wait until conditions are right for it to commence growth.

The first thing to emerge from the seed is the root. Whichever way the seed is lying, the root will instinctively grow downwards into the soil. Once established, the two cotyledons emerge and begin the process of photosynthesis. Shortly afterwards, true leaves appear from a bud between the cotyledons and the tree begins to grow.

Cupressus abramsiana, like all conifers, bears its seeds in hard, protective cones.

Different types of tree

Trees fall into several distinctive categories, each of which has its own particular defining characteristics. These categories are: deciduous trees, evergreen trees, coniferous trees and palms. Each of these categories can be further divided into flowering trees and fruiting trees.

Deciduous trees

Trees that lose their leaves in autumn in response to lower light levels and falling temperatures are called deciduous trees. At this time of the year the green pigment in the leaves breaks down and the other coloured pigments in the leaves are revealed, producing a range of colours.

Even in tropical climates where the seasons are less defined and temperature and light levels are steady, the leaves of some trees turn attractive colours just before they fall. This is not, however, a response to low temperatures, but the result of the tree drawing back any useful minerals that remain in the leaf.

The leaves of the yellow birch, *Betula alleghaniensis*, turn yellow in autumn.

Quercus coccinea (scarlet oak), is a deciduous species native to North America.

Juglans ailanthifolia is a type of walnut, which is grown for its prized timber, spring catkins, autumn colour and fruits.

Popular deciduous trees

Acer spp. (maple)
Aesculus spp. (horse chestnut)
Alnus spp. (alder)
Betula spp. (birch)
Carpinus spp. (hornbeam)
Carya spp. (hickory)
Castanea spp. (sweet chestnut)
Catalpa bignonioides (bean trees)
Cornus (dogwood)
Corylus spp. (hazel)
Crataegus monogyna (common hawthorn)
Davidia (handkerchief tree, dove tree, ghost tree)
Diospyros virginiana (American persimmon, possumwood)
Fagus spp. (beech)
Fraxinus spp. (ash)
Ginkgo biloba (maidenhair fern)
Jacaranda mimosifolia (jacaranda)
Juglans spp. (walnut)
Koelreuteria spp. (gold pride of India)
Laburnum spp. (golden rain)
Larix spp. (larch)
Liquidambar spp. (sweetgum)
Liriodendron spp. (tulip tree)
Maackia spp.
Magnolia spp.
Malus spp. (crab apple)
M. domestica (common apple)

Metasequoia (dawn redwood)
Morus spp. (mulberry)
Nyssa spp. (blackgum)
Oxydendron (sorrel tree, sourwood)
Parrotia spp. (Persian ironwood)
Paulownia spp. (coffin tree)
Platanus spp. (plane)
Plumeria spp. (frangipani, temple tree, pagoda tree)
Populus spp. (poplar, aspen, cottonwood)
Prunus 'Accolade'
P. cerasifera (cherry plum, myrobalan)
P. 'Ichiyo'
P. sargentii (Sargent cherry)
P. 'Taihaku' (Great white cherry)
Pseudolarix amabilis (golden larch)
Pterocarya spp. (wing nut)
Punica granatum (pomegranate)
Pyrus spp. (pear)
Quercus spp. (oak)
Robinia spp. (acacia)
Salix spp. (willow, osier, sallow)
Sassafras spp.
Sorbus (mountain ash/rowan)
Staphylea spp. (bladdernut)
Taxodium distichum (swamp cypress)
Tilia spp. (lime, linden)
Ulmus spp. (elm)
Zelkova spp.

Cryptomeria japonica 'Lobbii' is a beautiful cultivar of Japanese cedar.

Ficus benjamina, or weeping fig, has long, glossy dark green leaves and a weeping habit.

Popular evergreen trees

Acacia spp. (wattle)
Agathis spp.
Arbutus spp. (strawberry tree)
Banksia spp.
Calliandra spp.
  (powder puff tree)
Callistemon spp. (bottlebrush)
Calophyllum spp.
  (Alexandrian laurel)
Eucalyptus spp (gum tree)
Eucryphia spp.
Ficus spp. (fig)
Grevillea spp. (spider flower)
Ilex spp. (holly)
Lithocarpus spp. (tan oak)
Luma spp.
Magnolia delavayi
Magnolia grandiflora
  (Bull bay)
Maytenus spp. (mayten)
Michella (banana tree)
Metrosideros spp. (rata)
Pittosporum spp.
Protea spp.
Psidium spp. (guava)
Schefflera spp. (umbrella tree)
Tabebuia (trumpet tree)
Thuja spp. (arborvitae)
Tsuga spp. (hemlock)

Evergreen trees

Both tropical and temperate evergreen trees retain their leaves for longer than a year and then shed them gradually, so that they always have leaves. The advantage for the tree of retaining its leaves is that it has a longer growing period.

Among evergreen trees, some species such as wattles, have very narrow leaves, which lose very little water during the hot summer months. In periods of extreme drought, however, they will lose all their leaves in order to conserve even more moisture.

Other species, such as *Magnolia grandiflora* (Bull bay), have glossy leaves that reflect sunlight and hairy undersides that help to reduce transpiration.

In tropical regions, most trees are evergreen because there is little to distinguish one season from the next, so the tree has less need to drop its leaves in one go. In cooler, temperate zones, where there is a marked difference between winter and summer temperatures and where freezing occurs, most evergreen trees are conifers, although some broadleaf evergreen trees can also be found. The term broadleaf distinguishes these trees from conifers, which have needle-like leaves. Broadleaf evergreen trees bear true flowers, rather than cones.

Arbutus unedo 'Elfin King' has a distinctively shaped strawberry-like fruit, which makes it a very popular evergreen tree for a small garden.

Malus 'Red Jade' is named for the colour of its fruit, but the flowers are also highly decorative.

Bauhinia x blakeana produces highly fragrant, brightly coloured flowers.

pollinate their flowers. Some trees, like *Betula* spp. (birch), *Corylus* spp. (hazel), *Fagus* spp. (beech) and *Quercus* spp. (oak), are wind pollinated and, like conifers, bear insignificant flowers. Others have evolved to bear extremely decorative (and often scented) flowers, which attract insect pollinators.

Many fruit trees, including apples, pears, apricots, cherries and plums, as well as date and coconut palms, fall into this category, producing a wonderful display of stunning flowers every year.

Flowering trees

The vast majority of trees produce seeds that are encased in a protective shell or in a fruit, and these trees are termed angiosperms ('angio' being the Greek word for 'vessel'). This group of trees includes both deciduous and evergreen species that grow in both tropical and temperate climates.

Infinitely versatile, flowering trees have adapted to meet the challenges of a variety of different habitats by developing ingenious methods to

Trees that are wind pollinated produce insignificant flowers. However, the ornamental cherries shown here rely on insects for cross-pollination and so produce fragrant, showy flowers.

Popular flowering trees

Aesculus spp. (horse chestnut/buckeye)
Albizia spp. (silk tree)
Aleurites spp. (candlenut)
Banksia spp. (banksia)
Brownea spp. (flame tree)
Calliandra spp. (powder puff tree)
Callistemon spp. (bottlebrush)
Cassia spp. (shower tree)
Catalpa spp. (bean tree)
Cercis spp. (Judas tree/redbud)
Citrus spp. (citrus)
Cladrastis spp. (yellow wood)
Cornus spp. (dogwood)
Crataegus spp. (hawthorns/haws)
Davidia involucrata (handkerchief tree)
Embothrium coccineum
   (Chilean fire bush)
Eucryphia spp.
Grevillea spp. (spider flower)
Halesia spp. (snowdrop tree)
Jacaranda spp. (jacaranda)
Koelreuteria spp. (golden rain tree)
Laburnum spp. (golden rain)
Lagerstroemia spp. (Crape myrtle)
Magnolia spp. and cvs. (magnolia)
Malus spp. and cvs. (crab apples)
Metrosideros spp. (rata)
Oxydendron arboreum (sorrel tree)
Paulownia spp. (empress tree)
Plumeria spp. (frangipani)
Portlandia grandiflora (tree lily)
Protea spp. (protea)
Prunus spp. and cvs (cherry)
Pyrus spp. and cvs (pear)
Tecoma spp. (yellow elder)

Citrus limon is a popular choice for growing under glass in a cool temperate climate.

Plum and cherry trees require moisture-retentive but free-draining soil.

Conference pears have a distinctive elongated shape, and are delicious raw or cooked.

Fruit trees

Both tropical and temperate fruit trees exist, and they may be deciduous or evergreen. Many species, such as *Malus domestica* (apple), have been hybridized for commercial reasons to produce forms bearing larger, tastier fruits, with improved disease resistance, and higher yield.

When choosing fruit trees for your garden, you must remember that, although some fruit trees are self-fertilizing and will produce a good crop on their own, most species will require a pollination partner, which must be a different variety of the same fruit species that flowers at about the same time and is compatible in other respects.

While temperate fruits, such as apples, peaches, pears and plums, can be grown relatively easily in tropical climates. Most tender tropical fruits are very difficult to grow in temperate climates unless they are given a lot of shelter or grown under glass. For many people, however, the rewards of producing exotic fruit make it worth the effort.

Crab apples, such as *Malus* 'Butterball', can be used as pollinators for domestic apples, and have the added benefit of being beautiful garden trees.

Popular fruit trees

Artocarpus altilis (breadfruit)
Carica papaya (papaya)
Citrus sinensis (sweet orange)
Eriobotrya japonica (loquat)
Litchi chinensis (lychee)
Malus domestica (apple)
Mangifera indica (mango)
Morus spp. (mulberry)
Olea europaea (olive)
Persea americana (avocado pear)
Prunus armeniaca (apricot)
P. avium (sweet cherry)
P. cerasus (sour cherry)
P. domestica (plum)
P. italica (greengage)
P. persica (peach)
Psidium guajava (common guava)
Punica granatum (pomegranate)
Pyrus communis (common pear)

Choosing trees for different climates

Trees are found all over the world except at the very highest altitudes and areas where the ground is frozen hard and covered by snow and ice all year round. The geographical extent of habitats in which trees can survive is a result of climatic conditions and they are classified according to their ability to thrive in certain areas.

Tropical trees

For obvious reasons, tropical trees are so called because they come from the tropics, a region of the world around the equator that is bounded by the Tropic of Cancer in the north and the Tropic of Capricorn in the southern hemisphere.

A tropical climate is classified as one that is warm and humid, and where the average temperature stays above 18°C (64.4°F) throughout the year. This means that in these regions the temperatures are relatively stable, and they are also frost-free. As such, these regions do not have seasonal variations like those found in temperate zones.

Generally in the tropics the soils tend to be relatively poor, as a lot of the nutrients are washed out by the constant rain showers and downpours. However, tropical plants – many of which have beautiful flowers and foliage and are quite quick to grow and mature – can also be grown in subtropical zones, where temperatures may fall lower in the winter months than those of the tropics, but still remain frost-free.

In addition, climate change is increasing the range of tropical and subtropical trees that can be grown

Ailanthus altissima (tree of heaven) is very adaptable and will grow on poor soil.

in temperate zones, where gardeners have always experimented with microclimates, with the result that the use of these trees is becoming more widespread.

The bottlebrush tree, *Callistemon citrinus* 'Splendens', is very drought-resistant, making it an ideal tree for subtropical, tropical and protected microclimates in warm temperate regions.

Tropical or temperate?

The tropics are defined as a geographic region, the centre of which is on the equator, and which is limited in latitude by the two tropics: the Tropic of Cancer in the northern hemisphere and the Tropic of Capricorn in the southern hemisphere. The tropics include all the parts of the Earth where the sun reaches an altitude of 90°, or a point directly overhead, at least once during the solar year.

In the temperate zones, which are north of the Tropic of Cancer and south of the Tropic of Capricorn, the sun never reaches an altitude of 90° or directly overhead.

A tropical climate is defined as a non-arid climate in which yearly mean temperatures are above 18°C (64.4°F). At latitudes higher and lower than subtropical, the climate is called temperate, with annual mean temperatures less than 20°C (68°F) and the warmest month achieving averages over 10°C (50°F).

Aesculus x *carnea* is a temperate tree that bears beautiful pink flowers in late spring.

Temperate *Cornus kousa* bears flowers in the summer and strawberry-like fruits in the autumn.

Acer saccharum (sugar maple) provides vivid autumn colour in temperate regions.

Temperate trees

Trees that can survive in a climate with four distinct seasons – spring, summer, autumn and winter – are known as temperate trees. In northerly latitudes winters are cold, with temperatures below freezing.

With such low temperatures, plants have had to adapt to survive; many trees lose all their leaves during the autumn and conserve energy by hibernating during winter (these are termed deciduous). Others retain their leaves to make the maximum use of the low light in winter; these include broad-leaved evergreens and the conifers.

In northern Europe, cold, long winters are the norm. Trees grown in this area need to be able to withstand low temperatures, while they await the arrival of spring.

Acacia dealbata (mimosa) is a subtropical evergreen tree that is frost-hardy.

Microclimate factors

The word microclimate is often used to refer to the prevailing conditions in a relatively small area, such as a woodland or forest, or even a garden.

Local effects

Microclimates are the conditions created by the effect of buildings, hedges and fences, as well as other trees and shrubs. The ways in which such factors affect the general climate in a geographical area sometimes allow us to grow plants that may not be naturally suited to the location.

Built-up areas often become what are known as 'urban heat islands', which is when a city or large town becomes warmer than the surrounding countryside. This phenomenon occurs because the hard surfaces of buildings and roads absorb heat during the day and release it at night and in the early morning, generating higher ambient temperatures in the vicinity.

Buildings can also slow down or divert winds, which can cause temperatures to rise. The heat generated by vehicles and given off from central-heating and air-conditioning systems also helps to increase the overall temperature in cities to a few degrees above that of the surrounding countryside.

A lack of trees and other vegetation in cities gives rise to far greater heat absorption than in less developed areas. In wooded areas, trees absorb heat during the day and, as they cool, their leaves release water vapour, which in turn cools the air. This process is called transpiration and it continues throughout the day as long as the trees have an adequate supply of water around their roots.

Walls that face the sun

On a small scale, we can create microclimates in our own gardens. For centuries, gardeners have used walls to protect tender plants. Walls that face the sun will absorb heat during the day and reflect it back into the surroundings in the evening. This extra warmth will allow wood to ripen sufficiently before the onset of winter, so that the tree behaves as if it is hardier than if it was grown in the open garden.

A tree-lined garden greatly reduces the movement of air within it, which allows for a higher relative humidity, as the air is loaded with evaporated water droplets produced through transpiration. Wind speeds also tend to be reduced by the filtering effect of the leaves and the various layers provided by shrubs and intermediate and top canopy trees.

Fences are often erected in gardens to screen a practical corner from view, or to provide support for a climber. In addition to these functions, fences will affect the microclimates in the garden by providing shelter from the wind and shade from the sun.

In a cool climate, the heat stored by a wall will improve the flowering and fruiting performance of a plum fan trained against it.

The temperature of the canopy of a dense forest will be different from the forest floor.

In tropical areas, a range of exotic trees and plants can flourish. Although cooler countries may covet such greenery, local microclimate factors make it impossible for these plants to thrive there.

Local temperature

The treetops of a high, dense forest can form an almost unbroken surface. During the day the treetops absorb sunlight, which results in high temperatures at the top of the canopy and lower temperatures below this level because of the natural shading effect of the trees.

Similarly, the garden floor is generally cooler than the canopy and surrounding countryside. The difference in daytime temperature in summer can be as much as 5°C (8–9°F). At night, the heat is trapped below the canopy so the air stays warmer longer.

Summer heat

It is now becoming widely recognized that summer temperatures are an important factor in a plant's survival, and a system of heat zones has been devised based on the number of days in a particular area when the temperature reaches at least 30°C (86°F). In much of North America the heat zones correspond to the hardiness zones, mainly because of geographical factors.

In North America, heat zones can be used to indicate areas where a plant might be at risk from prolonged high temperatures. In northern Europe, however, they can be used to indicate where a plant would not have sufficient warmth in summer to ripen the wood so that it could survive winter.

Most of the British Isles has a US hardiness zone rating of 8 or 9 but a heat zone rating of only 1 or 2. This is just one of the reasons why woody trees and palms that are widely grown and thrive in the southern states of the USA do not do well in Europe, unless they are grown in very protected and artificial environments, such as palm houses or conservatories.

As with all life, water is essential to a tree's survival. Climate change in recent years has meant that some trees are being adversely affected by drought and are therefore at risk.

Tree shapes

When choosing a tree, it is vital to consider what shape it will be – not only when it is young, but when it is fully grown. There are several recognized shapes, but remember that trees are living things, and distinctions between the types are often blurred – some trees might be described as either vase-shaped or globular, for example.

Function of the tree

The first consideration when selecting a tree is to decide what you want to achieve. For example, if you wanted to hide a telephone or utility pole, you could choose from among the numerous columnar, conical, pyramidal or narrow-growing deciduous and coniferous trees as well as some tropical palms.

Once established, the tree would occupy less space than a spreading species, but its habit of growth would provide interest while not having a huge impact on the surrounding planting, apart from competing for light and water. However, if you wanted to block out a house or other large view, a broadly spreading tree would be a more appropriate choice.

Columnar trees

As the name suggests, these trees have a tall, cylindrical, narrow habit with upswept and slightly twisted branches. This growth trait gives them strength as the branches are tightly packed to the trunk.

Columnar trees (also called fastigiate trees) have a clear, dominant central leader and narrow, acutely positioned branches. They are often distinguished by being the same width all the way up, almost to the top, which sometimes spreads slightly or ends in a narrow point.

Plant columnar trees where little canopy spread is required and where a variation in tree line is required to contrast with broadly spreading trees and shrubs. Columnar conifers are often grown to create focal points in Mediterranean-style garden landscapes because they are similar in outline to *Cupressus sempervirens* (Italian cypress).

They can be planted in groups to great effect, and they form unusual-looking avenues where space is limited. They can also be used to frame views and when used as lawn specimens they add formality.

A broadly spreading tree, such as these horse chestnuts, would be ideal for blocking out an unsightly view or for creating a sense of privacy.

This *Acer rubrum* 'Columnare' is a good example of a columnar tree.

Trees with a columnar habit

Acer campestre 'Elsrijk' (field maple)
A. davidii 'Serpentine' (David's maple)
A. platanoides 'Erectum'
  (Norway maple)
A. rubrum 'Columnare' (red maple)
A. saccharum subsp. *nigrum*
  'Monumental' (sugar maple)
A. saccharum subsp. *nigrum*
  'Newton Sentry' (sugar maple)
Betula pendula 'Obelisk' (silver birch)
Calocedrus decurrens (incense cedar)
Carpinus betulus 'Frans Fontäne'
  (hornbeam)
Chamaecyparis lawsoniana cvs.
  (Lawson's cypress)
Corylus colurna (Turkish hazel)
Crataegus monogyna 'Stricta'
  (hawthorn)
x *Cupressocyparis leylandii* cvs.
  (Leyland cypress)
Cupressus sempervirens
  (Italian cypress)

Eucryphia spp.
Fagus sylvatica 'Dawyck'
  (Dawyck beech)
Ginkgo biloba 'Fastigiata'
  (maidenhair tree)
Juniperus chinensis (Chinese juniper)
Koelreuteria paniculata 'Fastigiata'
  (golden rain tree)
Liquidambar styraciflua 'Slender
  Silhouette' (sweet gum)
Liriodendron tulipifera 'Fastigiata'
  (tulip tree)
Pinus sylvestris Fastigiata Group
  (Scots pine)
Populus nigra 'Italica' (Lombardy poplar)
Pyrus calleryiana (Callery pear)
Robinia pseudoacacia 'Pyramidalis'
  (false acacia)
Taxodium distichum var. *imbricaria*
  'Nutans' (pond cypress)
Taxus baccata 'Fastigiata' (Irish yew)
Tilia platyphyllos 'Fastigiata' (lime)

Cedrus deodara 'Golden Horizon' is a good example of a naturally conical tree.

Conical and pyramidal trees

These trees look rather like upside down ice-cream cones. They have a less tight habit of growth than columnar or fastigiate trees. Many conifers are naturally conical in shape, as are several broadleaf trees.

The main difference between a conical and a columnar tree is that the spread of the lower branches of a conical tree is wider than that of a columnar tree – 2m (6ft) or more across – and can be as much as one-quarter of the tree's height.

Conical trees can be extremely useful for framing views. They are often used to great effect in avenues and can also provide an attractive contrast when they are planted in combination with a group of broad spreading deciduous species.

Many trees that appear columnar or conical when young can widen in spread as they age as the lower branches increase in length and begin to sag under their own weight.

Thuja plicata (arborvitae) has a typical conical habit, and can also be used for hedging.

A pyramidal tree will have a wider spread than both columnar and conical trees – it can be as much as half its height. These trees have a strong central leader. The lower branches are sometimes raised so that other plants can grow underneath, although this can sometimes make the overall shape look somewhat stunted.

Pyramidal trees can be used effectively as specimen trees in lawns and included in mixed plantings to diversify the planting and produce a range of canopy shapes. They also make interesting avenues and can be grown in groups to create a more formal design.

Vase-shaped trees

Small, vase-shaped trees are preferred in some locations and are especially useful in smaller gardens where a spreading tree is required but where lower-canopy space is limited.

Because of their shape, these trees cast greater shade than columnar, conical or pyramidal trees. On the

Tilia platyphyllos (broad-leaved lime) is typical of a broad-spreading pyramidal tree.

This *Taxodium distichum* (bald cypress) is a good example of a narrow, pyramidal tree.

Trees with a conical or pyramidal habit

Abies spp. (fir)
Acer campestre 'Queen Elizabeth'
  (field maple)
A. x *freemanii* cvs. (Freeman's maple)
A. saccharum cvs. (red maple)
Agathis spp. (kauri pine)
Araucaria spp. (monkey puzzle)
Cedrus atlantica (Atlantic cedar)
C. deodara (deodar cedar)
Chamaecyparis spp. (false cypress)
Cornus nuttallii (Pacific dogwood)
x *Cupressocyparis leylandii* cvs.
  (Leyland cypress)
Cupressus spp. (cypress)
Ilex x *altaclarensis* cvs. (Highclere holly)
I. aquifolium cvs. (English holly)
I. latifolia
Larix spp. (larch)
Laurus nobilis (bay)

Magnolia grandiflora cvs.
  (bull bay magnolia)
Oxydendron arboreum (sorrel tree)
Picea spp. (spruce)
Pinus spp. (pine)
Pseudolarix amabilis (golden larch)
Quercus acutissima (sawtooth oak)
Sequoia sempervirens (coast redwood)
Sequoiadendron giganteum
  (sierra redwood)
Taxodium distichum (swamp cypress)
Thuja spp. (arborvitae)
Thujopsis dolabrata (hiba)
Tilia cordata 'Corinthian'
  (small-leaved lime)
T. platyphyllos (broad-leaved lime)
T. platyphyllos 'Princess Street'
  (broad-leaved lime)
T. tomentosa (European white lime)

The multiple branches of *Zelkova carpinifolia* sweep upwards in a classic vase shape.

Acer 'White Tigress' has a defined vase shape.

plus side, however, they have an attractive, interesting shape, even when small, and cast less shade than a round-headed or weeping tree.

Vase-shaped trees differ from columnar, conical and pyramidal trees in that they lack a central leader. Their multiple branches originate from the trunk and point upwards. The numerous upswept branches are tightly placed and form a canopy with a flat top.

Because of the distinctive branch structure of vase-shaped trees, many of the internal branches can be safely removed to allow views through the tree. They can also be successfully and attractively pruned to allow for electricity or overhead services wires.

Small lower understorey, medium-sized upper understorey and upper-canopy vase-shaped trees are available and can be used in mixed canopy plantings. They are also invaluable as understorey trees in woodland gardens. When they are used in avenues they produce effective 'cathedral' avenues that are clear near the base and arched together higher up, resembling a cathedral arch.

Vase-shaped trees are useful for blocking out unattractive views but they are often less impressive when used as specimens in lawns. This is because their twisted branches can look rather unsightly in winter. However, careful pruning when they are young can help to alleviate this and improve their overall appearance.

Trees with a vase-shaped habit

Acer davidii (David's maple)
A. palmatum (Japanese maple)
A. rubrum (red maple)
A. saccharum (sugar maple)
Cercis siliquastrum (Judas tree)
Cladrastis lutea (yellow wood)
Koelreuteria paniculata (golden rain tree)
Lagerstroemia fauriei
Magnolia x *soulangeana* (Chinese magnolia)
Malus spp. and cvs. (crab apple)
Parrotia persica (Persian ironwood)
Prunus 'Kanzan' (ornamental cherry)
P. sargentii (Sargent cherry)
Pterocarya stenoptera (wing nut)
Quercus frainetto (Hungarian oak)
Sassafras albidum
Ulmus parvifolia (Chinese elm)
Zelkova serrata 'Green Vase'

Round-headed trees

Of the tree shapes available, this is probably the type most often seen. Round-headed trees are as wide as they are tall and have a symmetrical crown that looks round in silhouette.

These trees cast considerable shade, and can occupy the space that would be taken by several columnar, conical, pyramidal or vase-shaped trees of similar height, though their water and nutrient requirements will be less than those of a group of narrower trees.

Round-headed trees are best used as upper-canopy trees when maximum spread and shade are required. They make good lawn specimens if there is sufficient space for their canopy to develop and enough space surrounding them so that they do not dominate the landscape. Ideally, the nearest tree to them should not be closer than half the height of the larger tree when it is mature.

Round-headed trees can also be used where just a single tree is needed, especially where maximum shade is essential. They are used in avenues or allées only where there is room for their spread, otherwise the avenue may feel very narrow and claustrophobic.

This *Crataegus coccinea* (scarlet haw) is a good example of a typical round-headed tree, and can be used to block out an unsightly view.

Trees with a round-headed habit

Acacia spp. (mimosa/wattle)
Acer campestre (field maple)
A. davidii (David's maple)
A. griseum (paperbark maple)
A. japonica (full-moon maple)
A. platanoides (Norway maple)
A. rufinerve (red-vein maple)
Aesculus spp. (horse chestnut)
Ailanthus altissima (tree of heaven)
Albizia julibrissin (silk tree)
Arbutus unedo (strawberry tree)
Artocarpus altilis (breadfruit)
Betula ermanii (Erman's birch)
Brownea macrophylla
  (Panama flame tree)
Calophyllum inophyllum
  (Alexandrian laurel)
Carpinus spp. (hornbeam)
Castanea spp. (sweet chestnut)
Catalpa spp. (bean tree)
Citrus aurantium (Seville orange)
C. x paradisi (grapefruit)
Cornus florida cvs. (flowering dogwood)
C. kousa cvs. (kousa dogwood)
Crataegus spp. and cvs.
  (hawthorn/may)
Davidia involucrata (handkerchief tree)
Dillenia indica (chulta)
Diospyros spp. (persimmon)
Fagus spp. (beech)
Fraxinus spp. (ash)
Gleditsia spp. (locust)
Grevillea robusta (silky oak)
Juglans spp. (walnut)
Koelreuteria paniculata
  (golden rain tree)
Laburnum spp. (golden rain)
Liquidambar styraciflua (sweet gum)
Liriodendron tulipifera (tulip tree)
Lithocarpus spp. (tan oak)
Magnolia stellata (star magnolia)
Malus spp. and cvs. (crab apple)
Morus spp. (mulberry)
Nyssa spp. (tupelo)
Platanus spp. (plane)
Plumeria spp. (frangipani)
Prunus spp. and cvs. (cherry)
Psidium spp. (guava)
Quercus spp. (oak)
Robinia spp. (locust/false acacia)
Sophora japonica
  (Japanese pagoda tree)
Tilia spp. (lime)

Globular trees

Trees with a globular habit are similar to round-headed trees but they are slightly wider than they are tall. Unlike round-headed trees, the overall shape, not just the canopy, is round. Globular trees are broadly spreading and cast more shade than round-headed trees. They are widely used as upper-storey and upper understorey trees where wide shapes are desired. Their spreading canopy makes them unsuitable for use as lawn specimens or in avenues and allées, but they can be used in groups as landscape trees in parkland.

Liquidambar styraciflua 'Variegata' is a widely grown globular tree.

Sorbus aria 'Lutescens' is a deciduous globular tree from Europe.

Trees with a globular habit

Acer macrophyllum (Oregon maple)
A. platanoides (Norway maple)
A. pseudoplatanus (sycamore)
A. sterculiaceum (Himalayan maple)
Aesculus x *carnea* (red horse chestnut)
A. indica (Indian horse chestnut)
A. turbinata
  (Japanese horse chestnut)
Amelanchier spp. (Juneberry)
Brachychiton acerifolius (flame tree)
Carpinus betulus (hornbeam)
Cercidiphyllum spp. (katsura)
Cercis spp. (Judas tree/redbud)
Cornus mas (Cornelian cherry)
C. officinalis (dogwood)
Cotinus spp. (smoke tree)
Eriobotrya japonica (loquat)
Ficus spp. (fig)
Liquidambar styraciflua (sweet gum)
Ligustrum lucidum (Japanese privet)
Magnolia x *soulangeana*
Myrtus communis (myrtle)
Parrotia persica
  (Persian ironwood)
Quercus cerris (Turkey oak)
Q. ilex (holm oak)
Q. robur (common oak)
Q. suber (cork oak)
Sorbus aria (whitebeam)
S. megalocarpa
S. thibetica
Taxus baccata (yew)

Ficus benghalensis (banyan) is a fast-growing, globular tree that is widely used in the tropics for avenue or street planting.

Weeping trees

Often giving a rather shaggy appearance, weeping trees have long branches that hang downwards. Most weeping trees are cultivars – the form is less common among wild species.

Because the stems and foliage often touch the ground, it is difficult to grow other plants below weeping trees. For this reason, they are best used as focal points in the garden or as lawn specimens, where their beautiful habit and foliage can be fully appreciated. They also provide a wonderful opportunity for children to enjoy having a secret hiding place under the branches.

Trees with a weeping habit

Ailanthus altissima 'Pendula'
  (tree of heaven)
Alnus incana 'Pendula'
  (weeping grey alder)
Betula nigra 'Cascade Falls'
  (weeping river birch)
B. pendula 'Youngii'
  (Young's weeping birch)
Cassia fistulosa (golden shower tree)
Cedrus deodara (deodar cedar)
Cercidiphyllum japonicum f. *pendulum*
  (weeping katsura)
Cercis canadensis var. *texensis* 'Traveller'
  (weeping eastern redbud)
Chamaecyparis lawsoniana 'Intertexta'
  (Lawson's cypress)
Cupressus cashmeriana
  (Kashmir cypress)

Eucalyptus coccifera
  (Tasmanian snow gum)
Fagus sylvatica 'Pendula'
  (weeping common beech)
Ficus benjamina (weeping fig)
Fraxinus excelsior 'Pendula' (weeping ash)
Juniperus recurva
  (Himalayan weeping juniper)
Larix decidua 'Pendula' (weeping larch)
Malus 'Royal Beauty' (weeping crab apple)
Morus alba 'Pendula' (weeping mulberry)
Nyssa sylvatica 'Autumn Cascade'
  (weeping tupelo)
Pinus strobus 'Pendula' (weeping white pine)
Robinia x *margaretta* 'Pink Cascade'
Salix babylonica (weeping willow)
Tilia tomentosa 'Petiolaris'
  (weeping silver lime)

Although many conifers are grown for their conical habit, a number, such as this *Chamaecyparis nootkansensis* 'Pendula', have beautiful weeping branches.

The foliage of *Picea breweriana* (Brewer's spruce) hangs like curtains from its weeping branches.

Prostrate trees

Trees that do not grow upright are known as prostrate trees. They lie along the ground and can be used to create focal points in the garden. They are useful for planting over banks where their strange shapes provide ground cover. Prostrate trees can also be trained up a framework, rather like a wall-shrub.

Horizontally branched trees

The branches on horizontally branched trees grow at an angle of 90 degrees to the trunk and give a layered appearance. *Cedrus libani* (cedar of Lebanon) and *Cornus controversa* (table dogwood) are good examples. Their winter silhouette is distinctive and can be dramatically enhanced by pruning to encourage the layered effect. Horizontally branched trees are best used as focal points or specimen trees in lawns, but they can be included in mixed planting if there is space for them to grow unimpeded by other trees.

Low-branched and feathered trees

Many shade-tolerant trees do not shed their lower branches with age, often retaining them down to the ground. Although many nurseries prune the lower branches off to create a clear trunk (standard trees), some will not, and these are sold as feathered trees.

Feathered trees usually have a less contrived shape than standard trees and are best used as lawn specimens and in avenues and allées where, in order to create a tunnelled effect, trees reaching down or close to the ground are required. Many coniferous trees look more natural when they are grown this way, although the denseness of the lower branches means that nothing can be grown beneath them.

Cornus controversa 'Variegata' (pagoda dogwood) has horizontal branches, shown here in full bloom.

This *Araucaria araucana* has been feathered at the nursery so that it retains its lower branches. Here it is used to good effect as a focal point specimen in a lawn.

Choosing trees

Trees are among the longest-living organisms on our planet – which can make it a bit daunting when choosing one for your garden. Deciding what you need in terms of size, shape, colour and seasonal interest, as well as taking into account soil and climate conditions, only adds to the difficulties.

The answer is to do your homework, which is not as arduous as it sounds. Visiting a nearby arboretum or park is usually helpful, as you will see full-grown trees that are suited to the local conditions, and they should be labelled with their names. Looking at your neighbours' gardens will also give you an idea of what is likely to do well in your own. To further ensure the trees you choose are suitable, check out their requirements and potential size in a reference book such as this, or on the internet.

Once armed with this information, you can go to your local garden centre or nursery to further whittle down your selection, based on availability and price.

With so many different types of tree to choose from, you may well find that you are spoilt for choice when you visit a nursery. It is important that you take the shape, colour and ultimate size of the tree into account to ensure you buy the right one for your garden.

Researching trees

Buying a tree for your garden requires careful planning. Most of us have space for only a limited number, and many of the trees we might like to grow will simply be too large for the average garden. However, there will still be an enormous range of possibilities. When making your choice, remember that, all being well, any tree you plant will be an important feature in your garden for many years to come.

Arboreta

The most common form of tree collection where you can start your research is an arboretum, which is a botanical collection of trees grown mainly for their scientific and educational value. Arboreta, like botanical gardens, originally were — and still are to some extent — used to help sort out the problems with tree names and the classification of trees.

Many universities and botanic gardens throughout the world have specialized tree collections within their grounds or even a separate arboretum. These tree collections are invaluable when looking at the growth, habit and form of specific trees, but until relatively recently were not a great deal of help when looking at the aesthetics of trees in the landscape.

However, to increase the interest in rather obscure tree collections there has been considerable new landscaping in order to display trees in numerous innovative ways. These include trees that are grouped by their countries of origin; trees with special adaptations, such as tolerance of heavy or waterlogged soils or urban environments; trees with exceptional autumn colour, flowers and habit; and rare trees.

Any of these themes can be implemented in the garden environment, but most need careful

Not only are arboreta invaluable resources for scientists, but they are also popular attractions for those with a more general interest in trees.

planning as the most attractive trees often do not make the most attractive landscape unless carefully arranged.

An arboretum is, strictly, a collection of trees, although many also include other woody plants, such as shrubs and climbers. A pinetum is an arboretum specializing in coniferous plants. Botanic gardens contain plants other than trees.

Botanic gardens

A botanic garden is a collection of plants amassed by a particular institution for the purposes of research and public education. Each may specialize in a different group of trees, but will also include a number of commonly grown and some more unusual plants. These can be organized in numerous ways, such as by plant family, geography, type of ornamental features (tree shape, season of interest, flower, fruit or foliage) and so on.

Botanic gardens give an opportunity to compare different trees that may be growing near each other. They also have expert staff who can advise you on your choice.

Learning about trees

Both botanic gardens and arboreta have the advantage that the plants are labelled with their botanic and common name. Both organizations usually maintain records, including information on when each tree was planted so that you can tell how tall and wide it has grown in a given period. They also often produce leaflets and handouts, have

Sources of information

Nurseries and some larger garden centres are good places to start when researching trees, although they may only stock a limited range of small trees. However, they are likely to stock books and pamphlets, and you may be able to speak to an expert with local knowledge of the best trees to grow in your area.

A vast amount of data is available on the internet, including images, comprehensive details about the tree and its ideal growing conditions. Reading through professionally run websites allows you to view the trees that interest you and compare them with others.

regular guided walks and may have web-based plant records that you can consult from home.

Parks and other public spaces are good places to begin learning to recognize different trees, although these trees are rarely labelled, so you need to know what you are looking for before you see them.

Tree collections should remain the main goal of those who wish to collect trees simply for their individual beauty – and who have sufficient space to amass a sizeable tree collection. The rest of us have to rely on visits to gardens, parks and woodland to appreciate trees in profusion.

Take a visit to your local park to see what sort of tree you want. If you have trouble identifying an unnamed tree, the park authorities will help you.

Choosing the right tree

Selecting a new tree is not something that should be undertaken lightly. It is not like shopping for a refrigerator or kettle because your new purchase is alive and will require care and attention for many years to come.

Factors to consider

Before you choose a tree, you need to consider many different factors so that you can draw up a shortlist of potential candidates. Whether you are adding a single specimen or turning your entire garden over to trees, the first step is to assess the conditions in your garden. Aim to build up a comprehensive overview of your existing garden before you even think about choosing a tree.

Once you have answered these questions, there are then other, less practical and more aesthetic considerations. Trees have so many qualities – shape and habit of growth, leaf colour and form, flowers, fruit and bark – that it can be difficult to know which attribute is most important.

Before you decide what species of tree you are going to buy, it is a good idea to ask yourself some simple questions, making a note of the answers so that you can easily find the best tree for your garden.

The importance of scale

Before you base your decision about a new tree for your garden on a particular species' aesthetic attributes, consider its ultimate size, which is not just its height but also its spread. Many trees have broadly spreading crowns, which cast dense shade under which little else will grow. In a small garden in particular, height and spread must be your first considerations.

Knowing the height and spread of a tree will help you make the right choice. A tree should blend in to the scale of your existing plants and with the wider garden landscape.

All plants grow more quickly in a climate where their growth is not affected by late spring frosts, where

Robinia pseudoacacia 'Frisia' is a beautiful tree that is suitable for small-to-medium gardens.

Important questions to ask yourself

What is my soil like? Is it:
- Acidic?
- Alkaline?
- Neutral?
- Free-draining?
- Waterlogged?

Why do I want to plant a tree?
- For shape?
- To screen an object?
- To reduce noise?
- To absorb pollution?
- For a windbreak?
- For decorative effect (fruit, flower, foliage or bark)?
- For protection or privacy?
- As a focal point?
- As a habitat for wildlife?

What shape of tree do I want?
- Broadly spreading?
- Upright?
- Conical?
- One for producing a special effect by pruning (coppicing, pollarding)?
- Deciduous or evergreen or with exotic foliage, like a palm?

What size of tree do I want?
- How much space do I have?
- How big are my existing plants and trees?

What are my location and site like?
- What type of climate do I have?
- Is the site protected or in a frost pocket?
- Is the garden exposed to wind?
- What is the surrounding tree cover like and do I want to blend a new tree in with existing trees?
- How do we use the garden and how will we use it in the future?
- How far will it be from the house and other buildings?
- How far will it be from services (electricity and utility cables, drains and paths)

How much money am I prepared to spend, both buying and caring for the tree?

How much time do I want to spend caring for the tree?

there is adequate rainfall throughout the growing season and where they are growing in fertile, moisture-retentive soil. In such conditions a tree could be expected to attain its maximum height and spread when its reaches maturity.

In contrast, the same tree might grow only half as tall if it was grown in a nutrient-poor, free-draining soil, with below average rainfall in a location where it was not fully hardy and the new growth was killed by frost in spring.

The heights and spreads given for different species featured in the Directory section are only a guide and are given on the assumption that the tree is growing in the optimum conditions. If possible, visit a park or arboretum to view examples of the trees that interest you before you buy.

Another factor to consider is the space available. If a tree is grown as a lawn specimen it does not have to compete with nearby trees for light and nutrients, and it would be more likely to develop a balanced crown. However, when the same species is grown in a group, it will have to compete with its neighbours so may not grow as wide.

Morus alba 'Pendula' (weeping mulberry) is a popular ornamental tree with a low-growing, weeping habit that is ideal for a small space.

Small garden trees

If the space in your garden is limited, you may find that only a small, slow-growing species can be comfortably accommodated. Most trees look best when allowed to grow freely and retain their natural shape, but you might choose a species that will respond well to annual pruning or pollarding to restrict its size. In very small gardens, it might be best to consider a large shrub instead of a tree.

Small garden trees can also be used as understorey trees, where there are already larger trees forming an upper canopy. You might have a tall top canopy from a number of established trees and existing shrub cover at a lower level. An intermediate tree canopy will introduce a more diverse range of plants, providing an additional flowering layer or autumn colour theme. It will also provide shade and a more balanced planting scheme.

Trees for small gardens

Abies koreana (Korean fir)
Acacia dealbata (mimosa)
Acer japonicum (full-moon maple)
A. palmatum (Japanese maple)
Arbutus unedo (strawberry tree)
Banksia spp.
Bauhinia spp. (mountain ebony)
Betula pendula 'Youngii'
  (Young's weeping birch)
Bismarckia nobilis (noble palm)
Calliandra spp. (powder puff tree)
Callistemon spp. (bottlebrush)
Calophyllum inophyllum (Alexandrian laurel)

Caryota spp. (fishtail palm)
Cercis canadensis (eastern redbud)
C. siliquastrum (Judas tree)
Citrus spp.
Cladrastis spp.
Cornus florida (flowering dogwood)
Crataegus spp. (hawthorn, most)
Erythrina spp. (coral tree)
Grevillea spp. (spider flower)
Ilex spp. (holly, most)
Koelreuteria paniculata
  (golden rain tree)
Lagerstroemia spp.

Livistona chinensis (Chinese fan palm)
Magnolia spp.
Malus spp. and cvs. (crab apple, most)
Oxydendrum arboreum (sorrel tree)
Plumeria spp. (frangipani)
Prunus spp. (ornamental cherry, most)
Psidium spp. (guava)
Sabal palmetto (cabbage palmetto)
Schefflera elegantissima (false aralia)
Sorbus spp. (mountain ash, most)
Stewartia spp. (most)
Tecoma stans (yellow elder)
Trachycarpus fortunei (Chusan palm)

Medium-sized garden trees

This group includes species of garden trees that grow between 15 and 30m (50–100ft) tall. Trees that are at the upper end of the medium-size height range can be included to provide the top canopy, whereas the lower growing species can be used as intermediate or lower-canopy trees to create a succession of height, interest and habitat.

Trees for medium-sized gardens

Acacia spp. (mimosa/wattle)
Acer platanoides (Norway maple)
Aesculus flava (yellow buckeye)
Albizia spp. (silk tree)
Betula ermanii (Erman's birch)
Carpinus betulus (common hornbeam)
Catalpa bignonioides (Indian bean tree)
Cercidiphyllum japonicum (katsura tree)
Clusia major (autograph tree)
Corylus colurna (Turkish hazel)

Davidia involucrata (handkerchief tree)
Fraxinus spp. (ash, many)
Ginkgo biloba (maidenhair tree)
Gleditsia spp. (many)
Liquidambar styraciflua (sweet gum)
Magnolia obovata (Japanese big-leaf magnolia)
Metrosideros spp. (rata)
Phoenix spp. (date palm)
Tabebuia spp.

Beware the tree you choose. This *Pinus sylvestris* (Scots pine) is extremely tall when fully grown.

Large and parkland trees

Trees that grow to 30m (100ft) or more are suitable only for the largest of gardens. They often form the backbone of parkland planting and can be used individually or in small groups in extensive landscapes. Sometimes a group of three or five will be used to create the impression of a single specimen when viewed from a distance.

Many of these trees are extremely long-lived, exceeding 150 years of age, so their positioning requires the utmost care. In large urban gardens, such trees would form the upper canopy, with medium-sized trees forming the intermediate canopy and small trees the lower canopy.

While few gardeners have the space for full-grown specimens, some choose to plant them anyway, to enjoy them while they are small and then transplant them to a more suitable location.

Trees that grow quickly

When they are grown in ideal conditions some trees can, in just a few years, reach a significant height, bringing a degree of maturity to even a young garden. This ability to establish and grow quickly also makes this group of trees valuable as nurse trees, which are grown to protect and provide shelter for the 'real' garden trees while they establish. Nurse trees are generally removed once they have completed their work as they will quickly compete for light, water and nutrients with the trees that they are protecting.

Fast-growing trees can also be used to provide windbreaks and shelter-belts. They are also effective at creating quick shade and can, therefore, be used as upper-storey, shade trees.

Trees for large gardens

Abies grandis (giant fir)
Aesculus hippocastanum (horse chestnut)
Agathis australis (kauri pine)
Araucaria araucana (monkey puzzle)
Carya spp. (hickory, most)
Cedrus libani (cedar of Lebanon)
Cinnamomum spp. (camphor tree)
Eucalyptus spp. (gum tree, many)
Ficus benghalensis (banyan)
F. elastica (India rubber tree)

Jacaranda mimosifolia
Liriodendron tulipifera (tulip tree)
Pinus sylvestris (Scots pine)
Platanus x hispanica (London plane)
Quercus spp. (oak)
Roystonea regia (Cuban royal palm)
Sequoia sempervirens (coast redwood)
Sequoiadendron giganteum (sierra redwood)
Tilia x europaea (common lime)

Fast-growing trees

Abies spp. (silver fir)
Aesculus spp. (horse chestnut)
Aleurites moluccana (candlenut)
Alnus spp. (alder)
Betula spp. (birch)
Calocedrus decurrens
  (incense cedar)
Calodendron capense
  (Cape chestnut)
Calophyllum inophyllum
  (Alexandrian laurel)
Catalpa bignonioides
  (Indian bean tree)
Cedrus atlantica Glauca Group
Chamaecyparis lawsoniana
  (Lawson's cypress)
x *Cupressocyparis leylandii*
  (Leyland cypress)
Eucalyptus spp. (gum tree)
Fagus spp. (beech)
Jacaranda mimosifolia
Liquidambar styraciflua (sweet gum)
Metasequoia glyptostroboides
  (dawn redwood)
Olea europaea (European olive)
Paulownia tomentosa (empress tree)
Pinus palustris (pitch pine)
Platanus spp. (plane)
Populus spp. (poplar)
Pterocarya stenoptera (wing nut)
Quercus spp. (oak)
Robinia pseudoacacia 'Frisia'
Salix spp. (willows)
Sassafras albidum
Sequoiadendron giganteum
  (sierra redwood)
Thuja plicata (western red cedar)
Tilia spp. (lime)

Nurse trees

Nurse species provide shade and protection so choicer trees can develop below their rapidly growing crowns. It is their speed of growth rather than their ultimate height that is the important factor. They often do well in less than favourable conditions. Nurse species should be removed once the main trees have developed and no longer require protection.

Acer platanoides is a fast-growing tree that will thrive in nutrient-poor soil. It provides quick shade and is a good nurse tree.

Shape and habit

One of the first considerations is the shape of a tree, which must fit into the overall garden landscape (see Tree shapes, pages 286–93). Fastigiate, columnar and upright-growing trees, such as *Taxus baccata* 'Fastigiata', are excellent for hiding narrow objects, such as telephone or utility poles. Trees like *Quercus robur* f. *fastigiata* or *Cupressus sempervirens* Stricta Group can produce a tropical feel if they are planted with yuccas and palms.

Pendulous or weeping trees bring a graceful silhouette to a landscape. Round-headed trees bring massive green outlines and their trunks create interesting architectural patterns that change during the day as the sun gives way to shade.

Evergreen conifers with a conical shape conjure images of snow-covered mountains. Such trees require a fairly large garden so they do not quickly grow out of scale and become too dominant.

Palms can often be difficult to accommodate in traditional temperate landscapes, as their bold foliage and distinctive outlines have a tropical feel, reminiscent of sunny, sandy beaches on deserted tropical islands; a tropicana landscape that would not suit every garden.

Aesthetic considerations

Wherever possible, especially in a small garden, the aim should be to choose a tree that offers as much year-round interest as possible.

For example, *Trachycarpus fortunei* (Chusan palm) has amazing architectural foliage compared to many evergreens. In spring the palm produces large panicles of bright yellow flowers, followed by clusters of blue-black fruits. As the main stem matures it becomes covered with a matted, fibrous material. In a mild climate this would be an ideal candidate if you are looking for a small, ornamental tree for year-round interest.

Eriobotrya japonica (loquat) will grow massive ovate leaves if it is coppiced.

Trees with architectural foliage

Acer x *conspicuum* 'Elephant's Ear'	*Catalpa bignonioides* (Indian bean tree)	*M. grandiflora* (bull bay magnolia)
A. macrophyllum (Oregon maple)	*C. bignonioides* 'Aurea'	*Paulownia* spp.
A. pensylvanicum (striped maple)	*C. bignonioides* 'Variegata'	*Phoenix* spp.
A. sterculiaceum (Himalayan maple)	*Chamaerops humilis* (dwarf fan palm)	*Pinus coulteri* (big cone pine)
Aesculus hippocastanum (horse chestnut)	*Cryptomeria japonica* 'Lobbii'	*P. palustris* (pitch pine)
Artocarpus altilis (breadfruit)	*Dillenia indica* (chulta)	*P. patula* (Mexican weeping pine)
Bismarckia nobilis (noble palm)	*Eriobotrya japonica* (loquat)	*Pterocarya stenoptera* (wing nut)
Butia capitata (pindo palm)	*Ficus* spp. (fig)	*Roystonea* spp. (royal palm)
Caryota spp. (fishtail palm)	*Licuala* spp. (palas)	*Sabal* spp. (palmetto)
	Livistona spp. (fountain palm)	*Schefflera* spp.
	Magnolia delavayi	*Trachycarpus* spp.

Architectural foliage

As well as beautiful flowers or edible fruits, unusual and architectural foliage should be a consideration when you are selecting a new tree. This type of foliage increases the level of contrast in the garden and, if the tree is carefully positioned, can create a dramatic and breathtaking impression. Architectural foliage is most commonly a characteristic of trees used for lawn specimens or as focal points in the garden.

These trees are distinguished by large leaves, which are attractive in their own right. Most palms fall into this category, and they also associate well with other large-leaved plants to create a lush, exotic effect even in a temperate climate.

Some trees, such as *Paulownia tomentosa* (empress tree) and *Catalpa bignonioides* (Indian bean tree), can be coppiced to a small framework of branches. This hard pruning encourages the growth of large leaves, creating an architectural tree.

No tree is more distinctive in the landscape than the palms, with their large architectural leaves held high above their bare stems. They are widely used as upper-canopy trees in a tropical landscape.

Attracting wildlife

Garden trees and shrubs that provide food and cover are sought out by many birds and mammals, both resident and migratory. A mixture of deciduous and evergreen material provides valuable cover for many animals, especially if dense conifers are incorporated into the planting.

Evergreen species often attract winter songbirds and provide valuable shelter for game birds, and their food can be supplemented by bird feeders placed in or near the trees. Conifers and thorny bushes and trees are used by summer visitors and residents alike as safe nesting and roosting sites.

Trees and shrubs that provide food in the form of seeds, nuts and fruit are highly desirable, and those that last into the winter and possibly into the following spring are preferred. Included in this group are *Malus* species and cultivars (crab apple) and *Sorbus* species (mountain ash).

Trees that fruit in spring, summer and early autumn include *Morus* spp. (mulberry), *Prunus* spp. (cherry) and *Cornus* (dogwood). Conifers that

Many trees provide invaluable shelter and food for different species of birds and other wildlife during the cold months of winter.

hold their seeds in semi-loose cones will attract seed-eaters and also provide winter nesting sites.

Trees such as *Quercus* (oak), *Juglans* (walnut), *Carya* (hickory), *Corylus* (hazel) and *Fagus* (beech), which produce hard winter nuts (masts), attract large seed-eating birds and small mammals.

Standing dead wood in trees, including snags and trees with dead tops or limbs, will attract many different species of animal, so don't always be in a hurry to tidy up dead wood. These trees furnish cavity nest sites for many songbirds, squirrels or bats, as well as providing insect larvae for woodpeckers.

Trees to encourage wildlife

Aesculus hippocastanum (horse chestnut)
Betula alleghaniensis (yellow birch)
B. lenta (cherry birch)
B. nigra (black birch)
B. pendula (silver birch)
Bismarckia nobilis (noble palm)
Butia capitata (pindo palm)
Carpinus betulus (common hornbeam)
C. caroliniana (American hornbeam)
Carya illinoinensis (pecan)
Caryota spp. (fishtail palm)
Castanea dentata
   (American sweet chestnut)
C. sativa (sweet chestnut)
Catalpa bignonioides (Indian bean tree)

Chamaerops humilis (dwarf fan palm)
Corylus colurna (Turkish hazel)
C. jacquemontii
Crataegus spp. (hawthorn)
Dillenia indica (chulta)
Eucalyptus spp. (gum tree)
Fagus (American beech)
F. orientalis (oriental beech)
F. sylvatica (common beech)
Ficus spp. (fig)
Juglans regia (common walnut)
Licuala spp. (palas)
Livistona spp. (fountain palm)
Magnolia spp. and cvs.
Malus spp. and cvs. (crab apple)

Morus spp. (mulberry)
Olea europaea (European olive)
Phoenix spp. (date palm)
Plumeria spp. (frangipani)
Psidium guajava (common guava)
Punica granatum (pomegranate)
Pyrus spp. (pear)
Quercus spp. (oak)
Roystonea spp. (royal palm)
Sabal spp. (palmetto)
Sassafras albidum
Sorbus spp. (mountain ash)
Syzygium spp. (wild rose)
Tilia spp. (lime)
Trachycarpus spp.

Eucalyptus dalrympleana (mountain gum) is grown for its attractive silver-blue leaves, clusters of flowers and mottled bark.

The leaves of *Eucalyptus cordata* (silver gum) are leathery and silver-blue so they reflect the sunlight.

Silver and blue foliage

The highest proportion of trees with silver and blue foliage is conifers. The brightness of the blue or silvery shoots is often more noticeable on new growth in spring and early summer. The colour is also enhanced in full sunlight, so these trees are best planted in open positions where they will receive as much direct sun as possible. They are often grown as lawn specimens.

Trees with silver and blue foliage

Abies concolor 'Candicans'	*Fitzroya cupressoides*
Acacia dealbata (silver wattle)	(Patagonian cypress)
Aleurites moluccana (candlenut)	*Livistona* spp. (fountain palm)
Bismarckia nobilis (noble palm)	*Phoenix* spp.
Butia capitata (pindo palm)	*Picea pungens* (Colorado spruce)
Cedrus atlantica Glauca Group	*P. pungens* 'Hoopsii'
C. deodara (deodar)	*P. pungens* 'Koster'
C. deodara 'Shalimar'	*Pinus sylvestris* (Scots pine)
C. libani (cedar of Lebanon)	*P. densiflora* (Japanese red pine)
Chamaecyparis lawsoniana spp.	*P. strobus* (Eastern white pine)
Chamaerops humilis var. *argentea*	*Pyrus salicifolia* 'Pendula'
(dwarf fan palm)	(willow-leaved pear)
x *Cupressocyparis leylandii*	*Roystonea* spp. (royal palm)
'Naylor's Blue'	*Sabal* spp. (palmetto)
x *C. leylandii* 'Silver Dust'	*Sequoiadendron giganteum* 'Glaucum'
Cupressus sempervirens	*Trachycarpus* spp.
Stricta Group	*Tsuga mertensiana* (mountain hemlock)
Eucalyptus spp. (gum tree)	*Washingtonia* spp.

Variegated foliage

Tree flowers tend to last only a couple of weeks, but variegated foliage lasts much longer and can provide year-round interest. The leaves of this type of tree can be green, edged with white or yellow; mottled green with white or green; or white and yellow. They tend to be slower growing than trees with all-green foliage, which makes them suitable for small gardens.

You should use trees with variegated foliage in moderation to avoid a messy, confused appearance. They are best positioned where they offer a dramatic contrast against a background of plain green or purple-leaved trees. Some variegated foliage can be susceptible to sun scorch and requires light, dappled shade for best results.

One of the main drawbacks of trees with variegated foliage is that they are susceptible to reversion, which happens when a stem grows

The leaves of *Ilex x altaclerensis* 'Golden King' have green centres and bright gold margins.

The variegated leaves of *Ilex aquifolium* 'Golden Queen' have strong golden-yellow edges, making it a desirable small garden tree.

with plain green leaves that contain more chlorophyll than the variegated leaves. Because chlorophyll controls the food-making activity in plants, all-green leaves are stronger and grow more quickly than the stems with variegated leaves, and they soon outgrow the variegated portion of the tree.

Any all-green shoots on a variegated plant should be pruned out. As a rule, evergreen trees with variegated foliage are more tolerant of sunlight than deciduous trees with variegated foliage, which may be more prone to scorch in spring when the new leaves appear. Once fully formed, the risk is reduced.

The new leaves of *Liquidambar styraciflua* 'Variegata' are edged with cream in spring, before becoming flushed with pink in the summer.

Trees with variegated foliage

Acer campestre 'Carnival'
A. negundo 'Flamingo'
A. negundo 'Variegata'
A. platanoides 'Drummondii'
A. pseudoplatanus 'Simon-Louis-Frères'
A. rufinerve 'Hatsuyuki'
A. 'Silver Cardinal'
Bauhinia spp. (mountain ebony)
Castanea sativa 'Albomarginata'
Catalpa bignonioides 'Variegata'
Citrus limon 'Variegata'
Cornus controversa 'Variegata'
C. florida 'Rainbow'
Erythrina spp. (coral tree)
Ficus benjamina 'Variegata'
Ficus elastica cvs.
Ginkgo biloba Variegata Group
Ilex aquifolium cvs.
I. x altaclerensis cvs.
Liquidambar styraciflua 'Variegata'
Liriodendron tulipifera 'Aureomarginatum'
L. tulipifera 'Mediopictum'
Melia azedarach 'Jade Snowflake'

Trees for seasonal interest

All trees produce flowers, but we tend to value most those that provide colourful, spectacular or unusual blossom or fruits that last for a long time.

Spring and summer flowers

Most deciduous garden trees flower in spring and summer in response to increasing temperatures and light levels. The variety in size, shape, colour and scent of the flowers of garden trees is quite remarkable, and with careful planning it is possible to have a succession of blooms from early spring to late summer.

In temperate areas, late spring frosts sometimes damage flower buds or the flowers themselves, so take care when siting early-flowering trees – early morning sun will increase any frost damage.

Trees for spring flowers

Acacia dealbata (mimosa)
A. baileyana
Acer pycnanthum
 (Japanese red maple)
Aesculus 'Dallimorei'
A. hippocastanum (horse chestnut)
A. turbinata (Japanese horse chestnut)
Aesculus x carnea (red horse chestnut)
Bauhinia spp. (mountain ebony)
Calliandra spp. (powder puff tree)
Callistemon spp. (bottlebrush)
Calophyllum inophyllum
 (Alexandrian laurel)
Cassia spp. (shower tree)
Cercis canadensis (eastern redbud)
C. canadensis var. *texensis*
C. siliquastrum (Judas tree)
Clusia major (autograph tree)
Cornus florida (flowering dogwood)
C. nuttallii (Pacific dogwood)
Davidia involucrata
 (handkerchief tree)

Dillenia indica (chulta)
Erythrina spp. (coral tree)
Eucalyptus spp. (gum tree)
Grevillea spp. (spider flower)
Halesia spp. (snowdrop tree)
Jacaranda mimosifolia
Laburnum x watereri 'Vossii'
Magnolia spp. and cvs.
Malus spp. and cvs. (crab apple)
Melia azedarach (bead tree)
Michelia doltsopa 'Silver Cloud'
Paulownia spp.
Prunus spp. (ornamental cherry)
Pyrus calleryana 'Bradford'
P. calleryana 'Chanticleer'
Sorbus spp. (mountain ash)
Staphylea holocarpa 'Rosea'
Stewartia spp.
Styrax spp. (snowbell)
Tabebuia spp.
Trachycarpus fortunei
 (Chusan palm)

Japanese flowering cherries, with their delicate pink and white single or double flowers, are among the most breathtaking of spring-flowering trees.

The early spring flowers of deciduous trees are more visible because there are no leaves to hide the flowers. Blooms can vary in size from the huge blooms of *Magnolia campbellii* (Campbell's magnolia), which can grow to 30cm (12in) across, to the clusters of dainty flowers of the *Prunus* cultivars (Japanese flowering cherries).

Conifers are wind pollinated and have no need for decorative flowers to attract pollinating insects, but many palm trees do have large clusters of flowers. Among the most attractive are those produced by *Trachycarpus fortunei* (Chusan palm) and its close relatives, which produce panicles, 60cm (24in) or longer, of hundreds of small yellow flowers.

Among the flowering evergreens are the forms of *Eucalyptus* spp. (gum tree), which feature small clusters of creamy-white, pink and occasionally red flowers.

The stunning array of trees that flower during the spring heralds the arrival of the new season in temperate zones. Spring is the most colourful of the seasons.

The giant blooms of *Magnolia campbellii* are a welcome sight in spring, and their true beauty is best revealed when they are viewed against a clear blue sky.

Crataegus laevigata 'Punicea', like many hawthorns, has stunning flowers.

Trees for summer flowers

Aesculus indica (Indian horse chestnut)	C. *kentukea* 'Perkins Pink'
Banksia spp.	C. *sinensis* (Chinese yellow wood)
Barringtonia asiatica	Cornus 'Porlock'
Brownea macrophylla (Panama flame tree)	C. *kousa* (kousa dogwood)
Calliandra spp. (powder puff tree)	C. Stellar hybrids
Callistemon spp. (bottlebrush)	*Crataegus* spp.
Calodendrum capense (Cape chestnut)	*Eucalyptus* spp. (gum tree)
Catalpa bignonioides (Indian bean tree)	*Lagerstroemia* spp.
	Magnolia grandiflora (bull bay magnolia)
Catalpa fargesii (Chinese bean tree)	M. *obovata* (Japanese big-leaf magnolia)
C. *fargesii* f. *duclouxii*	*Metrosideros* spp. (rata)
C. *ovata* (yellow catalpa)	*Robinia* x *margaretta* 'Pink Cascade'
C. x *erubescens* 'J.C. Teas' (syn. 'Hybrida')	*Robinia* x *slavinii* 'Hillieri'
Citrus spp.	*Stewartia* spp.
Cladrastis kentukea (yellow wood)	*Tabebuia* spp.

Autumn colour

One of the most dramatic sights in our gardens, autumn colour occurs as the cool, lush foliage of summer gives way to autumnal tints that herald the arrival of winter.

Some species begin to change colour earlier than others, so that the period extends from summer to late autumn. For example, *Liquidambar styraciflua* (sweet gum) can begin to adopt its autumn hues in midsummer and still be producing stunning burgundy, red and yellow shades in mid-autumn, giving almost five months of interest.

The range and intensity of autumn colour can vary from year to year according to the amount of rainfall and what the summer temperatures were. They can also be affected by how quickly temperatures fall in early autumn, when the green pigment in the leaves (chlorophyll) breaks down to reveal the other pigments.

If a tree is under stress – if it is short of water or planted in nutrient-poor soil, for example – it will produce good autumn colour but the leaves will fall off quickly. If summer has been kind, with adequate rain, the pigments will break down slowly and the autumn colour will last much longer.

Another major influence on the autumn colour that a tree produces is soil pH. Many trees produce better autumn colour when they are grown in acidic soils than they do in alkaline soils, even if they can thrive in soils with a high pH.

Of the major species of tree that are planted for autumn colour, most will produce their best hues when they are grown in neutral to acidic soil. *Acer rubrum* (red maple), for example, will grow in slightly alkaline soil, but the autumn colour will be much more impressive when it is sited in acidic soil.

Acer japonicum (full moon maple) is a good small garden tree with vibrant autumn colour.

However, there are exceptions to the rule. *Parrota persica* (Persian ironwood) will produce vibrant autumn colour in alkaline soils.

The colourful autumn leaves brighten up the dullest day and provide a beautiful flourish before the trees shed their leaves and lie dormant until spring.

The white trunk of *Betula papyrifera* (paper birch) contrasts with the fiery autumn tints.

Taxodium distichum (swamp cypress) produces rich brown autumn tints as its fern-like green foliage changes in autumn. In winter, its silhouette is one of the most distinctive of all trees.

In larger gardens, trees with bold autumn tints can be planted to replicate the colours that are seen in natural woodlands. The aim should be to plant trees so that various tints are mixed together. In a small garden, however, combining autumn colours should be approached with caution, although the careful planting of shrubs and perennial grasses will enhance and complement the effect of the trees.

Trees for autumn colour

Acer buergerianum (trident maple)
A. campestre (field maple)
A. capillipes (snakebark maple)
A. cappadocicum (Cappadocian maple)
A. davidii (David's maple)
A. davidii 'Ernest Wilson'
A. davidii 'George Forrest'
A. davidii 'Madeline Spitta'
A. x freemanii 'Armstrong' (Freeman's maple)
A. x freemanii 'Autumn Blaze'
A. x freemanii 'Celebration'
A. x freemanii 'Morgan'
A. griseum (paperbark maple)
A. grosseri var. *hersii* (Hers's maple)
A. japonicum 'Aconitifolium' (full moon maple)
A. japonicum 'Vitifolium'
A. palmatum (Japanese maple)
A. platanoides 'Palmatifidum'
A. pycnanthum (Japanese red maple)
A. rubrum (red maple)
A. rubrum 'October Glory'

A. rubrum 'Schlesingeri'
A. rufinerve (red-vein maple)
A. saccharinum (silver maple)
A. saccharum (sugar maple)
A. sterculiaceum (Himalayan maple)
A. triflorum (three-flowered maple)
Carpinus betulus (common hornbeam)
C. caroliniana (American hornbeam)
Carya cordiformis (bitternut)
C. illinoinensis (pecan)
C. ovata (shagbark hickory)
Castanea dentata (American sweet chestnut)
C. sativa (sweet chestnut)
Cercidiphyllum japonicum (katsura tree)
Cladrastis kentukea (yellow wood)
Cornus florida (flowering dogwood)
C. 'Eddie's White Wonder'
Cotinus spp. (smoke tree)
Crataegus spp. (hawthorn)
Fagus grandifolia (American beech)
F. orientalis (oriental beech)
F. sylvatica (common beech)
Fraxinus americana 'Autumn Purple'

F. angustifolia 'Raywood' (claret ash)
F. ornus (manna ash)
Ginkgo biloba spp.
Koelreuteria paniculata (golden rain tree)
Lagerstroemia spp.
Liquidambar spp. (sweet gum)
Liriodendron spp. (tulip tree)
Malus spp. and cvs. (crab apple)
Metasequoia glyptostroboides (dawn redwood)
Nyssa sylvatica (tupelo)
Parrotia persica (Persian ironwood)
Prunus sargentii (Sargent cherry)
Pseudolarix amabilis (golden larch)
Pyrus calleryana 'Bradford'
P. calleryana 'Chanticleer'
Quercus spp. (oak, some)
Sassafras albidum
Stewartia spp.
Taxodium distichum (swamp cypress)
T. distichum var. *imbricatum* 'Nutans'
Ulmus spp. (elm)
Zelkova spp.

Buying trees

Once you have decided upon a tree, you need to ensure that the one you buy is strong, healthy and the right size. There are two main outlets for purchasing trees – a nursery or a garden centre. However, the internet is fast becoming an outlet for more exotic trees.

Tree nurseries

When buying a tree, specialized tree nurseries are a good option, as the staff should be able to give you up-to-date information on the best trees for your garden. Some nurseries open only at limited times, so check before you visit.

Many nurseries specialize in different growing techniques and offer large, container-grown plants for people who want an instant effect. Others sell only bare-root or rootballed plants in winter and spring. If you can, visit more than one nursery so you can compare the plants that are available. The smaller nurseries usually offer modest quantities of a limited number of tree species – and then only to personal callers. Others have a mail-order service, but only send out plants at limited times of the year.

Garden centres

General plant nurseries and garden centres usually carry a wide range of container-grown trees throughout

Specialist nurseries carry a wide range of trees and shrubs. Many have a mail-order service, which can be invaluable if the nursery is not easy for you to reach.

the year and at certain times in winter. Also, a few of the larger outlets stock bare-root and rootballed specimens. The most commonly grown trees will usually be available at these outlets, and from time to time you might find some slightly more unusual trees.

Large DIY stores are offering an increasingly wide range of trees, although these are mostly container-grown specimens. Although they are often inexpensive, unfortunately,

they are frequently poorly cared for, so look at potential 'bargains' carefully before you commit yourself.

Internet and mail order

Mail order and the internet offer much wider selections of trees than those available from a single supplier and many of the larger nurseries now also offer online searching and purchase. The disadvantages are that you do not see the plants before they arrive; there is always a risk that the tree may be damaged in transit; and with a bare-rooted specimen you must be ready to plant the tree as soon as it is delivered, which may not always be convenient.

What to buy

Trees are available in different sizes and forms. Large trees provide instant effect, but small ones establish much more easily and may even overtake a larger (and more

Bare-rooted trees are sold with their roots exposed after most of the soil has been removed and their roots trimmed. These trees need to be planted immediately after purchase.

expensive) specimen planted at the same time. If you want to plant at any time during the year (except when the ground is frozen or waterlogged), container-grown trees are the best option. If you wish to plant in winter, bare-rooted or rootballed (balled and burlapped) plants are worth considering.

Container-grown trees

Trees that are grown in plastic pots, wooden boxes or some other type of container should have been regularly potted on so that their root systems were able to develop freely. Container-grown plants are not usually affected by transplanting as they have well-established root systems, which are only slightly disrupted during planting.

Container-grown trees can be planted at any time of the year, except when the ground is frozen or waterlogged. Periods of drought are also best avoided unless you are prepared to undertake the necessary watering. If they have to be kept for a while before you have time to plant, store them in a shady, sheltered place and water regularly.

Container-grown trees tend to be more expensive than bare-root or rootballed trees, and the restriction on the size of the pot required for a large tree is a major disadvantage.

Rootballed trees

You can buy deciduous trees more than 4m (12ft) high, palms over 1.5m (5ft) and many evergreens, including conifers, in this form, and they are usually less expensive than container-grown trees. The plants are grown in nursery beds and are lifted in winter. The whole root system is wrapped in netting, hessian (burlap) or a similar material. When you are moving a rootballed plant,

you should carry it by holding the rootball. Before planting, make sure that all the wrapping material around the rootball has been removed.

Although a rootballed plant can be stored for a while before planting, if necessary, it is best planted as soon after purchase as possible because the root system will have been disturbed when it was taken from the nursery bed.

If the plant has to be stored for any period of time, place it in a shady position, water the rootball if it looks dry and apply a mulch, such as composted bark, to prevent it from drying out. Rootballed trees should be planted between midwinter and early spring.

Bare-root trees

As their name suggests, bare-root trees have no soil around the roots when they are sold, which is during the trees' dormant period in winter. The only trees that can be sold as

bare-rooted specimens are deciduous trees that are dormant and leafless when lifted.

Bare-rooted trees are the cheapest and most portable of all the types of tree available for purchase, but the range of varieties is usually more limited. They are grown in a nursery bed, and each year they are undercut, which involves pruning the main roots to encourage the tree to develop a vigorous, branching root system.

When the tree is ready for sale, it is lifted and the roots are again trimmed. At this time, all or most of the soil is removed from around the roots, so the tree should be planted as soon after purchase as possible.

If the plant has to be stored the root system should be covered with damp compost (soil mix) or bark chippings or it should be heeled in (quickly and roughly planted) in another part of the garden until you are ready to plant it properly in the site you have chosen.

Bare-rooted plants need planting immediately after you buy them so that the roots do not dry out or become damaged.

After being lifted at the nursery, rootballed trees are sold with their root system wrapped in netting or hessian (burlap).

Choosing a healthy tree

Once you have decided on the type of tree you want, you need to make sure you acquire a healthy specimen. As well as the obvious benefits, there is always a risk of introducing pests and diseases into your garden with a new tree, especially if it is in a container.

Buying trees

Specialist nurseries offer the widest choice of trees for sale, but you should visit nurseries or garden centres to see if the plants look well cared for, as well as asking other gardeners which suppliers they recommend.

When you are selecting a garden tree, there are three areas to which you should pay particular attention: the root system, the trunk and the branches and leaves.

Roots

A well-developed and healthy root system is essential if a tree is to become successfully established in your garden, so when you are selecting a new tree the first task is to check the roots. Avoid plants with roots that emerge from the soil at peculiar angles or that seem to be strangling or cutting across the trunk. This is especially important if the tree is container-grown or rootballed.

If a container-grown tree has been allowed to grow for too long in a pot that is too small, it will be pot-bound and the roots will be tightly wound around the sides of the pot. When you plant the tree, the roots won't grow out into the surrounding soil, causing the tree to be unstable, nor will the roots extend into the soil in search of nutrients.

Another indication that a tree is pot-bound is if there are roots protruding through the drainage holes. Even worse, the tree may have rooted itself into the ground beneath the pot. Avoid plants where you can see that large roots have been cut off close to the drainage holes.

Misshapen plastic pots, distorted by the roots exerting pressure on the sides as they have developed, are another sign of neglect. Avoid container-grown plants with weeds on the surface of the soil, as this suggests that the plants have been neglected. Weeds not only compete for nutrients but can also be hosts for pests and diseases.

Sometimes roots grow too close to the trunk and circle the base of a tree at or just below the surface. As the trunk increases in girth, so does the root, and as both grow they exert pressure on each other, sometimes causing the trunk to grow abnormally or, even worse, to fail at this point. This is known as girdling.

Trunks

There should be a clear taper along the trunk, with a distinct flail or flare at the base where it meets the ground. Trees naturally develop reaction or reinforced timber at points where they move or bear extra weight.

When a trunk constantly sways in the wind, the movement is transferred down the trunk to the point where it cannot move – that is, where it joins the root system. This pressure is distributed along the lower one-third of the trunk, preventing it from cracking or breaking. This point is reinforced with additional wood fibre, which is why it is thicker.

When you are selecting a tree, check the trunk for defects, such as linear cracks, which may lead to

Although container-grown trees are more expensive, they are easier to handle as they can be planted when you are ready.

This *Acer griseum* has a sound trunk and straight growth. These are qualities that you should look for when buying a tree.

structural damage or even trunk failure. There should be no damaged or dead sections of bark, caused during lifting, transplanting or growing, because they can lead to stem or trunk rot which will affect the structural integrity of the trunk.

Branches and leaves

The last areas to inspect are the branches and leaves. The branches should be well spaced along the trunk, and there should be no damaged, dead or crossing branches. Smaller branches may cross within the crown, but any larger ones should have been removed by the nursery to allow the crown to develop with an open and balanced array of branches.

Check to see how recently removed branches have been pruned – cuts that have been made too close to the trunk may allow a disease to penetrate the tree's natural defences, causing serious problems. Look at the bark on the branches to check that there are no splits and cracks.

Make sure that the leaves and shoots are completely free from pests and diseases. Check, too, that the leaves are the appropriate colour for the tree. They should not be too yellow or otherwise discoloured, nor should there be patches of yellow between the veins,

This stunning *Acer japonicum* 'Vitifolium' is a good example of healthy tree, with well-spaced branches, a straight trunk, and good leaf colour.

Check for healthy leaves before you buy your tree. This *Eucryphia glutinosa* has rich, natural-coloured and pest-free leaves.

as this is a symptom of nutrient deficiency. If you are specifically buying a tree for an unusual leaf colour or variegation, make sure that all the leaves are coloured and show no signs of reversion.

Finally, look at the extension growth of the stem, which is a good indicator of the level and consistency of a tree's vegetative growth from year to year. Each tree produces new shoots, which will grow throughout the summer until autumn, when the growth is stopped by falling

temperatures and lower light levels. When new growth begins the following year, a scar appears, indicating the end of the previous year's growth and the beginning of the current year's growth.

If a tree has been well cared for at the nursery and consistently had sufficient nutrients, water and sunlight, the extension or vegetative growth should be similar from year to year. If the tree has been subjected to any setbacks during a year, the vegetative growth will be shorter.

Tree gardening techniques

Trees can be used in myriad ways in the garden, not only to create attractive landscapes, but also to produce fruit, block out noise, frame a view or provide a focal point. Whatever the purpose of the tree, it is crucial that you fully understand how to nurture and care for garden trees. This understanding must start from the ground itself – with a knowledge of how to prepare the earth and provide a nutrient bed in which to plant the young tree – and work up to pruning and training, so that you can manipulate the habit of your trees.

If things go wrong, however, you may also need to know how to transplant a tree and re-establish it in a new location.

The careful choosing, nurturing and siting of trees can produce the most stunning effects in the garden.

Different soils

There are are several different types of soil, which are distinguished by the basic particles they contain, such as sand, clay, silt and composted organic material. In addition, the soil is colonized by earthworms and other soil-dwelling organisms that help break down nutrients and make them available to plants. This, too, alters the nature of the soil.

Sandy soils

Free-draining sandy soils tend to warm up quickly in spring, so plants get away to an early start. However, they also cool down quickly in winter. The proportion of sand compared to other particles determines just how freely the soil drains, and these soils can also vary according to the proportion of silica or quartz particles they contain.

Sandy soils may be either acidic or alkaline. Soils that were once part of the seabed may, for example, contain a high proportion of shells, which are made up of calcium, and so they will be alkaline. A sandy soil that has evolved over time and has

been exposed to high rainfall, cool temperatures and slowly decomposing conifer needles will be acidic.

Because it is free-draining, nutrients are quickly washed through this type of soil. It can be worked at any time of the year, but it requires close attention in spring and summer, when it can dry out quickly.

Digging in plenty of organic matter will improve its ability to retain both moisture and nutrients. Mulching with organic material, such as garden compost, bark chippings, rotted manure, mushroom compost or leaf mould, will help to conserve moisture in the soil and reduce the chance of weeds germinating and competing for nutrients. More importantly, it will also add valuable nutrients to the soil. For this reason, it is essential to mulch free-draining soils annually.

Sandy loams

A soil that is described as 'sandy loam' is one of the best types to have. The soil consists of a blend of sand, clay and silt particles, with the

sand being present in the highest proportion. These soils are not only free-draining and moisture-retentive but also rich in nutrients.

They are easy to work at any time of the year and warm up quickly in spring but cool at a more even rate in autumn. They tend to be less hungry than sandy soils and require less frequent irrigation and the addition of less organic matter.

Clay soils

Although they are the most difficult to cultivate, once clay soils are successfully worked they are among the most fertile because clay particles are able to attract and hold nutrients in a form that makes them readily available to plants.

Clay particles bond together tightly, so when this type of soil is wet it can be difficult to dig. Moreover, the surface of the soil may compact and cause puddling. As it dries, large cracks can appear in the soil, while the surface forms an impermeable layer from which water simply runs into the cracks and is quickly carried away.

Testing soil

sandy

silty or loamy sand

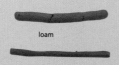

loam

clay loam

clay

Finding out what type of soil you have is easy and does not require any specialist equipment. This test is ultimately a matter of judgement and will only give you a relative picture of the sort of soil you have. However, it is surprisingly accurate. Simply take a small amount of soil – about a teaspoonful will do – in the palm of your hand. Moisten

with a little water (not too much but enough to make it just workable). Once moistened, try to form the soil into one of the shapes shown above.

1 Begin by forming a ball. If it stays together, then proceed to the next shape. If it does not form a ball, then you have a sandy soil.

2 If you can flatten the ball without it breaking up, then you have a silty sand or a loamy sand.
3 If you can roll the flattened ball into a thick sausage shape, then you have a loam.
4 A soil that can be rolled into a thin 'sausage' is a clay loam.
5 If you can bend the soil into a ring shape, then you have a clay soil.

Clay soils retain water, which makes them slow to warm up in spring but slow to cool down in autumn and winter. Adding large quantities of horticultural sand will improve the drainage, although if puddling persists it might be necessary to investigate underlying problems and even install a drainage system.

When a new tree is planted into poorly drained clay soil it can be set slightly proud of the surrounding level to allow it to establish before its roots grow into the wider soil. Remember that planting proud will make the roots dry out more easily in periods of drought.

Digging over clay soils in autumn allows winter frosts to weather the particles and this helps to unbind the clay. Organic matter can be more easily incorporated in spring, when the soil is more workable. You can also add it as a mulch, allowing earthworms to take it down into the soil. Adding garden lime in autumn or spring can help to unbind the particles and open up the soil, although adding large quantities of lime will raise the pH if it is applied annually and over many years. Garden lime is highly soluble and will cause nutrient deficiencies in lime-hating plants.

Peaty soils

Depending on how they were formed, peaty soils can be highly acidic or neutral. Upland peat is formed by the decay of mosses and other plant material over a long period to form a dense layer of acidic organic matter.

Lowland or marsh peat results when flooded areas of marsh slowly decompose over a long period of time. Areas of natural peat are often exposed and have high annual rainfall, even flooding for part of the year.

PREPARING THE GROUND FOR PLANTING TREES

1 Organic material such as well-rotted garden compost or farmyard manure is high in nutrients. Fork in when the soil is dug. For heavy soils this is best done in the autumn.

2 If the soil has already been dug, the organic material can be lightly forked in or left on the surface. The worms will complete the task of working it into the soil.

Trees that occur naturally on peat soils are able to deal with the high quantities of some nutrients, like iron, as well as deficiencies of other minerals. Peat soils, found in most gardens, develop in areas that were once coniferous forests and that have high annual rainfall. Over thousands of years, the needles from the coniferous trees decomposed to form a peaty layer on the soil surface. This layer, which can be quite deep, is rich in humus and is moisture-retentive – ideal conditions for trees.

Peat soils are often slow to warm up in spring but cool down quickly in autumn, while the drainage will depend on the nature of the subsoil. A much wider range of plants can be grown in peaty soils than in chalk.

Chalk soils

Often free-draining, open and quite shallow, chalk, or calcareous, soils are one of the most difficult types to cultivate. Because the chalk keeps the soil open, they are, like sandy soils, hungry. The clay or silt particles they contain can cause them to bind during wet weather, but although the surface of the soil may compact when it is wet, it seldom cracks when dry.

The shallow nature of chalk soil will inhibit the depth to which the root system of trees can spread, so the roots of trees in chalk soil may be much shallower and less extensive than those growing in deeper soil. This may cause young trees to become unstable in strong winds, and they will often be prone to drought.

Chalk soils have a high pH, which will limit the range of plants that can be grown because lime will lock up other nutrients and cause poor growth and yellowing of the leaves. Such soils require an annual application of bulky, well-rotted farm manure, deep mulching and occasional irrigation.

Understanding soil

Of all the factors that influence the way garden trees grow, the most important is the soil. Its make-up and pH (acidity or alkalinity) may result in not just poor growth but even the death of a newly planted tree – but get it right and your tree will thrive.

Reducing soil acidity

The acidity of your soil can be reduced by adding lime some weeks before planting. First, check the soil with a soil-testing kit to see how much lime is required.

Soil-testing kits of various degrees of sophistication are widely available, such as this electronic meter, which tests the pH level.

Topsoil

Most gardeners are concerned with the top layer of soil – the topsoil. This is a comparatively shallow zone that contains oxygen, nutrients and moisture in forms that the tree roots can use. This area can vary greatly in depth, although 25–30cm (10–12in) is normal.

However, in shallow soils over chalk or rock and in tropical forests, the layer may be as little as 10cm (4in) deep, whereas at the base of valleys, in river basins and in areas that have been cultivated for a long time, topsoils can be much deeper – as much as 1–2m (3–6ft) deep or more.

Subsoil

The layer of soil below the topsoil is known as subsoil, which can vary greatly in character. It can be very stony or formed of chalk or clay and the composition will influence the way the topsoil drains.

Subsoil can be easily identified because it is a different colour from the topsoil. It is deficient in the beneficial oxygen, humus and micro-organisms that are found in topsoil, although it can be cultivated into a workable medium that will eventually become topsoil.

If the subsoil is of reasonable quality, tree roots will grow into it for improved anchorage. Some new housing complexes are developed on sites where the existing topsoil has been removed, leaving only the subsoil.

On completing the buildings, the contractors often return a shallow layer of topsoil and then turf the gardens. In such areas the soil will require considerable work to improve its aeration and humus content.

Soil pH

Perhaps the most important aspect of soil is its pH. This is the measure of a soil's acidity or alkalinity, and it will determine the plants you can grow in your garden.

A soil's pH is measured on a scale from 1 to 14. Soils with a pH below 7 are acidic (ericaceous); soils with a pH above 7 are alkaline. Plants that have adapted to growing on acidic soil are known as calcifuges and plants that have adapted to soil with a high pH (alkaline) are calcicoles, which means they are acid-hating or lime-loving plants.

The availability or otherwise of minerals in the soil affects a plant's growth. On soils with a pH below 4.5, nutrients such as aluminium, iron and manganese are so readily

THE STRUCTURE OF THE SOIL

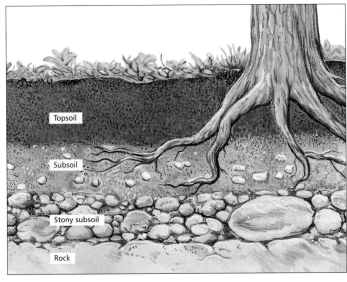

Topsoil

Subsoil

Stony subsoil

Rock

available that they become toxic to certain plants. However, other mineral elements, including nitrogen, phosphorus, potassium, calcium and magnesium, are locked up and plants suffer from mineral deficiencies.

In low pH soils the activity and effectiveness of fungi and bacteria, which normally help break down organic matter, are greatly reduced, as is the activity of earthworms. When the pH is above 7, deficiencies of manganese and iron are likely to occur, while lime is freely available.

The best pH for most trees is between 5.5 and 7.5, when essential nutrients are readily available and earthworms and other beneficial organisms can survive.

Planting an acid-loving tree in chalky soil quickly causes its leaves to turn yellow, stunts its growth, and the tree might eventually die, because the green pigment in the leaves begins to die and the tree cannot function.

Soil-testing kits

Cheap and reliable soil-testing kits are available from garden retailers that will indicate the nutrient balance in your soil and its pH level. For this to be of value you must test a representative sample of soil.

The most reliable way of doing this is to lay four canes on the soil surface in a large W shape, then use a trowel to dig a small hole, 15cm (6in) deep, at each point of the W, making a total of five holes. Scoop out some soil from each hole and place it in a garden sieve (strainer) over a bucket. Mix the soil from the different holes before testing.

Make sure you do not test the soil where a compost heap has been, or where you have added a fertilizer, since this will not give you a true result for the garden as a whole.

TESTING YOUR SOIL FOR ITS NUTRIENT VALUES

1 Collect a soil sample from 10cm (4in) below the surface. Take several different samples and mix together for a representative test.

2 Follow the instructions on the kit. Usually, you mix 1 part soil with 5 parts distilled water. Shake well and then allow the water to settle.

3 Using the pipette provided with the kit, draw off some of the liquid from the top of the jar.

4 Having drawn off about 5cm (2in) of the solution, transfer the sample to the test chamber in the plastic container.

5 Select a colour-coded capsule (one for each nutrient). Put in the chamber, replace the cap and shake well. The result will appear.

6 After a few minutes, you can compare the colour of the liquid with the shade panel shown on the side of the container.

Beneficial soil organisms for trees

In recent years we have become more aware that many of our garden trees grow in a stressful environment where they do not have the benefit of the soil-borne fungi and bacteria that are found in their natural ecosystems. Without these elements, which help trees absorb nutrients, it is harder for them to flourish.

Fighting deficiencies

To combat this deficit in the somewhat sterile conditions of our garden soils, where little nutrient recycling takes place, mycorrhizal fungi or biostimulants can be incorporated into a tree planting pit or applied to an ailing mature tree. This will dramatically increase nutrient and water uptake and improve the overall well-being of the tree.

It is often recommended that one or the other system is adopted, but they can complement each other.

Today many such products are available from a variety of outlets, making them widely available to the amateur gardener, so check on the packaging to find out which one is suitable for your tree.

Mycorrhizal fungi

Widespread in natural habitats such as forests and woodlands, mycorrhizal fungi have a symbiotic relationship with the root systems of trees. They colonize the roots and greatly increase the area that the trees' roots are able to cover, and so assist with and increase the uptake of water and nutrients.

Various different species of mycorrhizal fungi exist and certain trees have developed particular relationships with specific fungi: some are only found on conifers; others are only found on deciduous trees; and some groups are specifically associated with certain habitats, or a certain tree species.

However, recent studies have proved that the percentage of mycorrhizal fungi found in garden borders, lawns and in urban settings is considerably less than the quantity that is found in a native meadow, woodland or forest. This is mainly because there is far less nutrient recycling in gardens due to our constant urge to clean dead and dying material away, rather than let it break down naturally.

Mycorrhizal fungi groups

Mycorrhizal fungi can be broken down into two specific groups. One colonizes the outside of tree roots and is called ectomycorrhizae, and is generally associated with the roots of conifers and hardwoods, such as *Fagus*, *Betula* and *Quercus*.

The second grows into the cells of the root system and is called endomycorrhizae. These are often found on hardwood trees, fruit and nut trees and shrubs. However, due to the relationships between different types of trees, most mycorrhizal fungi mixes contain both types with a broad spectrum mix, as those fungi unable to colonize will perish.

Benefits to trees

Mycorrhizal fungi can improve the overall health of trees, and so make them more drought- and disease-resistant, which in turn can make them more adaptable to a wide range of garden habitats.

The benefits of mycorrhizal treatments can increase the total surface area of root systems by as much as 700 per cent. Due to the increase in volume, they can occupy more than a hundred times more soil than a non-mycorrhizal-inoculated tree root system. They can grow through the soil up to 6m (20ft), radiating away from a host tree, and help the tree to become more resistant to many root diseases caused by soil-borne fungi and pests.

These safe and simple to use inoculants are now widely available from garden centres and over the internet. They can be added to a planting pit and lightly forked in to the soil. However, conditions must be right for their colonization: the soil must be moist and warm enough and the fungi should be in direct contact with the roots.

Bay boletus are found only under conifers.

The brown birch bolete thrives under birches.

In a woodland setting there is a constant supply of organic matter being broken down by a wide range of organisms. This organic matter in turn provides nutrients for the plants and trees that grow there, enabling them to flourish and proliferate in great numbers.

Biostimulants

The term biostimulant is used to describe various natural products that can be applied in a similar manner to a fertilizer, and that will have a positive effect on the vigour or health of a tree. Biostimulants are enzymes and essential elements that occur naturally in the soil. They can also be added to the soil to increase the number of friendly soil-borne bacteria and fungi.

During periods when trees are under stress, vital elements are used to protect the tree. However, if they become deficient in the soil or the root system has insufficient energy to absorb them, the tree's health may decline and allow disease to spread.

When this occurs, the tree or its roots will not produce enough vitamins, amino acids or hormones to recover from such stress. However, adding biostimulants can help the tree recover by enhancing food production and increasing the efficiency of the leaves to trap sunlight, so increasing the production of simple sugars. They also increase antioxidants, nutrient availability and the water-holding capacity of the soil.

Another major benefit of biostimulants is that they can increase the quantity of humus in the soil. Humus is made up of decomposed organic matter that builds up in the soil over time, and which improves moisture and nutrient retention.

Biostimulants also increase the availability of two important micronutrients, phosphate and potash, while stabilizing nutrient uptake in high pH or very salty soils. Also, because biostimulants increase the efficiency of nutrient uptake, less fertilizer is needed.

A variety of mycorrhizal fungi and biostimulant products is available and these can be applied directly into the soil during planting, or watered in, or in the case of biostimulants applied as a soil drench or foliar feed.

Biostimulants can be watered in to the soil.

Planting a tree

After choosing and buying a tree that is suitable for your garden, the next important step is to plant it so that it becomes successfully established. Of all the causes of death associated with newly planted trees, the most common is planting too deeply, which suffocates the trunk and causes it to rot. However, if you observe a few simple guidelines, tree planting is relatively easy.

Digging the hole

A common mistake is to assume that a tree will require a deep, wide hole, filled with organic matter, growth regulators and improved soil. However, although soil improvers may be needed in a few situations, they are not usually necessary because it is far better to allow the tree to acclimatize to the soil in which it will spend the rest of its life rather than having to mollycoddle it for the rest of your life.

If possible, prepare the hole six to eight weeks before planting to allow the soil to settle, which will stop the tree from settling deeply. If the hole can be dug in autumn, when the soil is usually drier and more workable,

so much the better because it will make the planting process easier and will reduce the risk of smearing the sides of the hole in heavy clay or silt soils. It will also minimize the risk of compacting the soil by standing on it or moving equipment around when it is wet.

If the tree is to be grown as a lawn specimen, then cut the turf to leave a square or circle of exposed soil between one and a half and two times the diameter of the container or rootball. For all other planting, dig a hole that is slightly deeper than the root system of the tree, and three times wider than the container or the rootball. If you are unsure of the size of the tree dig a square hole 1.2m x 1.2m (4ft x 4ft) and 30cm (12in) deep. Remove any perennial weeds and large stones and fork over the base. Fill the hole again and allow the area to settle.

When you have your tree, dig a hole slightly wider than the container or rootball and lightly fork the bottom. It is essential that the tree is planted so that it is the same level as it was originally, no matter how it was supplied. Lay a piece of

Placing mulch at the base of the newly planted tree will not only help to preserve the moisture in the soil but also help to prevent weed seeds from germinating.

timber or a cane across the hole so that you can check that it lines up with the nursery mark or dark stain at the base of the trunk, just above the point where the roots flare out from the trunk. If this mark is not clear, plant the tree slightly proud.

PREPARATION PRIOR TO PLANTING

1 Prepare a circular or square area wider than the tree's rootball you are intending to plant.

2 After digging through the area, break any large lumps of soil with a folk, and remove any weeds.

3 Ensure that the hole is deep and wide enough to accomodate the tree's roots.

4 Add grit or sand on heavy soils, or organic matter on light soils. Allow to settle prior to planting.

HOW TO PLANT

1 Remove the tree from its wrapping or pot and place in the centre of the hole.

2 Begin to backfill around the tree with the excavated soil, using a spade.

3 Insert a stake to one side of the main stem, taking care not to damage the roots.

4 Tie the stem loosely to the cane with soft string or rubber tree ties.

5 Firm the tree in well with your hands or feet, without over compacting the soil.

6 Water the tree well after planting to help it to become established.

7 Mulch with straw to conserve moisture in the soil.

How to plant the tree

If the tree is in a container, remove the pot and use your fingers or a hand fork to carefully prise away some of the roots. Remove the sacking (burlap) from rootballed plants just before planting and tease out some of the roots. If you notice any damaged roots on a bare-rooted tree cut them away.

Set the tree in the hole and check the depth again, adding or removing soil if necessary. You can add biostimulants or mycorrhizal fungi to improve the uptake of nutrients and water (see pages 324–5).

Begin to refill the hole, making sure that the soil is worked well between the roots. This is especially important for bare-rooted trees. Use your fingers or the heel of your shoe to make sure that there is maximum contact around the base of the tree and around the edge of the root zones, but be careful not to overcompact the soil. Refill in layers, firming as you go, until the tree is planted.

Water well and stake (see pages 332–5). To ensure that the tree gets off to the best possible start install a mulch mat and mulch around the tree (see pages 338–9).

Planting trees in containers

Some species can be successfully grown in containers. This allows us to grow trees that are unsuitable for our gardens' soil, that are not hardy and need protection, or that we want to move around to create flexibility in our gardens' design.

The advantage of pots

Using a container is one way of growing trees in locations where there is not a sufficient depth of soil for them to thrive, as with roof gardens. It is also possible to position trees in containers close to house walls without risking damaging the foundations.

Species that do not suit the type of soil in the wider garden can be grown in pots filled with acidic (ericaceous) or alkaline compost (soil mix), and it is also possible to choose comparatively tender species that would not survive outdoors in winter but that, when grown in a container, can be moved to the shelter of a greenhouse or conservatory during the coldest weather.

As long as they have been container-grown from the start, many tree species can be successfully grown in containers, where they can be kept smaller and more compact than similar species grown in the garden. Ideal species include palms, *Acer japonicum* and *A. palmatum* (Japanese maple), *Taxus* (yew), *Ilex* (holly) and many types of fruit tree, including apples, pears, oranges, loquats and olives.

In most cases, growing a tree in a container will restrict its ultimate size, but eventually, over time, many species will become too large and top-heavy, and it may be necessary to install an anchor system to secure the tree or its container to the ground to keep them stable.

Trees that are grown in containers have the same requirements as those that are grown in the open garden, but pruning, fertilizing and watering are even more important. Whenever you choose a container, you should remember that the weight and size of the tree and its container may make repotting the tree or replacing all the compost difficult or, in some cases, impossible.

Position is less of an issue with trees in containers because the tree can be moved, although the weight

Japanese maples are widely grown in containers because their graceful habit, attractive foliage, and ease of pruning make them easy to cultivate.

of the tree and a soil-filled container may mean that special equipment or extra help is necessary.

Types of container

A tree requires the largest possible container to accommodate the rootball and soil. Trees above 3m (10ft) in height can become unstable, and evergreens, including conifers and palms, are most likely to be blown over because they retain

PLANTING A TREE IN A POT

1 Layer the pot with broken crocks or stones to help drainage and top with a layer of grit or vermiculite.

2 Begin to fill the pot with compost (soil mix). Add compost until the container is about a third full.

3 Remove the tree from the pot and gently tease out the roots, using a garden fork or your fingers.

their foliage throughout the year. Broad-based containers, such as half-tubs, tend to be more stable than narrow-based containers shaped like traditional plant pots.

Terracotta pots are widely available in a multitude of sizes and styles and at a wide range of prices, although larger, frost-resistant pots are expensive. They are available in traditional shapes, sometimes ornately patterned, or as straight-sided square or rectangular pots, which are more stable. Terracotta is attractive and suits most gardens.

When filled with moist soil terracotta pots are heavy, and they will break easily if blown over or if the tree roots exert too much pressure on the sides. Water evaporates more quickly from terracotta, so it is important to water regularly, sometimes every day, in sunny or windy weather. In areas with hard water, terracotta eventually becomes discoloured by lime scale.

Plastic containers have the advantages of being cheap and available in a range of colours, styles and sizes. They are lighter than terracotta pots and are a better choice if you want to move the tree around.

Plastic containers are less likely than terracotta ones to be damaged if they fall over. Water does not evaporate through plastic, but because the material is thinner the roots within the container are more susceptible to changes in temperature, and the rootball may suffer not only from cold in winter but from overheating in summer.

Inexpensive plastic fades in strong sun, so the pots may not look as attractive, and they may become brittle, causing problems if you try to move the tree. Even expensive plastics will become discoloured in time.

Wooden and metal containers are available, and both materials are more stable and robust than terracotta and plastic and less likely to split or fall over. However, even treated wood will rot over time, and for this reason wooden tubs often have liners, and metal containers may rust.

The weight of both types means that they are difficult to move, and they are best kept for trees in permanent positions. It is essential that there are drainage holes in the base of the container, no matter what it is made from.

Aftercare

Every year in early spring remove the top 5–10cm (2–4in) of compost (taking care not to damage surface roots), replace it with fresh compost and water thoroughly. You should then add a slow-release fertilizer to the fresh compost to help replenish any lost or deficient nutrients.

A tree that has been in the same container for several years will become pot-bound and the roots will occupy most of the available space. When this happens the roots quickly take up water, and the tree is more prone to drying out and needs regular and thorough watering.

In hot weather it may be necessary to water several times a day to get sufficient water into the root zone. If possible, use collected rainwater, especially for ericaceous species, rather than domestic water. No matter how carefully you choose the species and containers, trees will eventually outgrow the volume of compost that can be held by their pots.

Root pruning, a technique used in bonsai, and completely replacing the compost both help to control a tree's size and keep it growing well. Root pruning should be done in late winter or early spring, and it involves trimming back individual roots with secateurs (hand pruners). Shake the old compost from the existing roots before you return the plant to its container so that you can replace all the old compost with fresh compost.

The amount of water applied to the container will cause nutrients to leach from the compost. Although nutrients are easy to add in the form of slow-release, pellet fertilizers, the tree may not be able to absorb them. To improve its uptake, you can add a biostimulant or a mycorrhizal fungi to the compost every two or three years (see pages 324–5).

4 Place in the centre of the pot and fill with compost to about 2.5cm (1in) from the top to allow for watering.

5 Water in well and, if you like, top-dress with grit to help retain moisture and make the pot look smart.

Planting conifers and palms

Conifers, palms and evergreen trees require more aftercare than deciduous trees planted while dormant, as their foliage will lose water, which they will be unable to replenish until their roots grow out into the soil. For this reason they require additional watering and protection from the sun and wind.

When to plant conifers

Mid-spring, when the soil is moist and warm, is the best time to plant conifers. This allows the plants to establish before winter. However, container-grown conifers can also be planted at other times of year (particularly early autumn), provided they are kept well watered in summer and protected from winds in winter.

If conditions are not immediately suitable for planting when the conifers arrive, plant them in a trench in a sheltered spot (known as heeling in) until conditions improve. Do not take container-grown plants out of their pots until you can plant them properly, or you will risk drying out their delicate roots.

How to plant conifers

Conifers should be planted in the same way as other trees and shrubs, but after planting protect them from cold and drying winds by erecting a windbreak.

To do this, insert three stout stakes firmly into the ground, then wrap a windbreak sheet, hessian, or layers of horticultural fleece around the outside of the posts. Tie securely to the stakes and peg down at the bottom to secure. Once the conifer is well established this protection can be removed. Tall trees may also need staking so that they are not blown over by the wind.

Aftercare

Do not feed conifers unless they are showing signs of starvation (unnatural yellowing foliage). If they are given too much food, conifers will grow more quickly, producing lush, often uncharacteristic, growth that does not look attractive and is prone to damage caused by drying and cold winds.

During the winter, some conifers are susceptible to damage caused by the weight of accumulated snow. This can cause the plant either to be pulled out of shape or have limbs broken. You can prevent damage by tying up susceptible plants before winter or routinely knock heavy falls of snow from exposed plants before damage is caused.

HOW TO PLANT A CONIFER

1 Place the conifer in the prepared hole and check the planting depth. The soil mark should be at the same level as the surrounding soil.

2 When the plant is in position, untie the wrapper and slide it out of the hole. Avoid disturbing the ball of soil around the roots.

3 Replace the soil around the plant and firm down to eliminate big pockets of air. Water and occasionally spray the foliage on sunny days.

4 It is worth mulching the ground after planting. It will conserve moisture, and some mulches, such as chipped bark, look attractive.

Pest control

Once established, conifers will largely look after themselves. Mites and aphids can be problems on pines and spruces respectively, causing the needles to drop and producing unsightly bare stems. Aphids are easy to control with insecticidal sprays, but mites are more persistent (you may wish to get in a professional to treat an affected specimen). Mites are particularly active during warm, dry years when conifers are under stress. You can help prevent outbreaks by watering conifers during a drought and spraying the foliage occasionally to increase air humidity. Do this in the evening to avoid scorching the foliage on a sunny day.

When to plant palms

In temperate climates palms are best planted from late spring to late summer so that they are established before winter. However, in more tropical climates palms are best planted during the wet or rainy season and when the soil temperature is above 18°C (65°F).

How to plant palms

Regardless of how the palm tree is bought, initial aftercare is essential for its successful survival and quick establishment. A critical factor for ball and burlapped palms is the ratio between the prepared rootball and the length of the stem. Although some palms can thrive with a shallow rootball, it is often better to buy a palm with a large rootball as this will improve its chances of survival.

When planting the palm tree the principles are the same as planting any other containerized or ball and burlapped tree, although it is important to remember that palms generally prefer well-drained soils.

If water does not drain through the bottom of the planting pit, then plenty of organic material and/or horticultural grit or sand should be dug into the soil. It is critical that palms are not planted any deeper than the depth to which they were originally grown.

Large ball and burlapped palms will require support for the first year until the root system fully establishes. Since traditional techniques can be difficult to master, the triple staking and rubber guy wire system can be used instead (see pages 334–5), although there is also a specialized system that utilizes a metal collar and tensioning wires to provide support. Smaller palm trees require little or no support.

All palms have very large leaves which lose lots of water. To reduce evaporation, the leaves can be tied closely together, or the foliage can be sprayed with water to help cool them during hot weather.

Aftercare

Newly planted palms will require daily watering for the first six weeks after planting, and it is a good idea to spray the leaves with water when watering the rootball to help counteract moisture loss via the leaves while the roots are becoming established.

Although overheating may be less of a problem for container- or pot-grown palms, large ball and burlapped palms, which will have had their crown of leaves reduced by over half to protect the heart of the palm's crown, may suffer. In some species that are difficult to establish, like the sabal palm, the leaves may be removed altogether and will only re-grow as the palm tree establishes.

Generally palms do not require any soil improvement. Although the use of mycorrhizal fungi or soil biostimulants has been shown to increase the rate of establishment, fertilizer should only be added the season after they establish.

Once the root system is established a general NPK 15-5-10 fertilizer can be applied during the growing season. Do not add it too early in the spring, however, as a high-nitrogen feed applied during cool weather will cause the plant to produce soft green growth rather than growing upwards, which may result in stunted growth.

Bad weather damage

The occurrence and extent of winter damage in palms depends on the lowest temperature and the duration of cold. Cold damage appears first in the foliage, and causes the leaves to turn brown and die. However, as long as the root system and crown of the palm survive then the damage may only be superficial. If the root system freezes the palm will not recover. The roots will often tolerate temperatures several degrees cooler than the foliage, so even if the foliage dies there is still a chance that the palm will re-sprout when the temperature rises in spring.

Staking trees

The trunk of a healthy, well-grown tree will exhibit an obvious thickening towards the base. If trees are staked for too long or have been grown too close together, or are simply young, they do not have this reinforcement wood, so they are easily blown over, even during moderate winds. Sometimes, the trunks crack or eventually break. To avoid this, staking is necessary, as it allows the root system to anchor the tree into the surrounding soil.

Types of stake
There are numerous types of stake: they can be round or square in shape, and made from hardwood, softwood, recycled plastics or concrete. As the purpose of the stake

is to hold the trunk while the roots colonize the surrounding soil, the stake material is largely irrelevant, although one that will rot and fail over time should be preferred to one that will not. All tree stakes should be removed once the root system has established. The best stakes are made from wood, and most, both hard and softwood, are treated (tanalized) with preservative to prevent them from rotting.

Types of tree tie
There is a huge range of tree ties available. The most effective ties are those made from a material that has a certain amount of elasticity and can be adjusted. If you are using a single, low, straight stake, an angled stake or the T-bar method, it is important that a rubber cushion or spacer is used to protect the tree from rubbing against the stake.

Most ties have an integral spacer that can be adjusted. Some use a buckle, others lock on themselves and some use Velcro. Whichever tie you use, check it regularly so that it does not rub against or constrict the developing trunk.

When to stake trees
It is often necessary to stake recently planted trees so that they are supported during early growth. However, the staking should be done in such a way that the tree can still move. The stake should be left in place for no more than three growing seasons. If a tree cannot support its own weight after this time it should be pruned hard and a new leader trained. Alternatively, it should be pruned so that it develops into a multi-stemmed tree.

A newly planted tree is staked to allow the root system to anchor and grow into the soil, while allowing the

Flexible tree ties allow the trunk of the tree to grow, without harming the tree. The buckle mechanism should always go around the stake, otherwise it will damage the bark. This picture shows a tie being incorrectly fitted.

Some fruit trees require more secure staking when they are trained into a specific shape.

trunk and branches to sway so that reaction timber forms naturally in the trunk. However, if the roots move so that they are no longer in touch with the soil, the tree will fail to establish and diseases may invade the root system.

The larger the tree that has been planted, the more substantial the stake should be. A tree that is less than 1m (3ft) tall and that has been planted in a protected site where there is little wind movement will not need a stake. However, a larger tree needs a stake because it will have a small rootball compared to its branch area, which would act like a sail in the wind, and even a small tree may need staking in a very windy site.

Different staking methods

The appropriate way of staking will depend on the type of tree you plant and how it has been grown. Some trees are going to need considerably more support than others, especially if they are planted in exposed sites, such as seaside, mountainous and hilly regions or in wind funnel areas of towns and cities.

In all cases, the stake should be positioned so that the prevailing wind blows the tree away from the stake, not towards it, as this would cause the stake to rub against the trunk and cause damage. Use the following guidelines for choosing a system:

Container-grown trees These trees need either a stake angled at 45°, a T-bar or a three-stake system (see page 334). Specimens over 3m (10ft) tall need an underground or above-ground guying system. Container-grown conifers, evergreens and palms are best with a T-bar.

Bare-rooted trees These trees require a straight, single stake driven in before planting; a stake set at an angle of 45 degrees; or a T-bar or three-stake system. With any of these systems the stake should be no higher than 50cm (20in).

Rootballed trees These need a stake angled at 45 degrees or a T-bar or three-stake system. Specimens over 3m (10ft) tall need an underground or above-ground guying system. The T-bar system should be used for rootballed conifers, evergreens and palms. Use an angled stake whenever you need to protect the rootball.

Multi-stemmed trees These trees require a modified T-bar or three-stake system in order to secure the stems.

Trees planted on a slope Trees planted in this position need an angled stake.

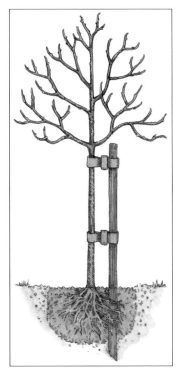

Single stake method shown for a larger bare-rooted tree.

Angled stake method shown for a larger containerized tree.

Single staking

A low single stake is driven vertically into the ground and fixed to the tree with a tree tie. The overall height of the stake should not exceed 50cm (20in) above ground when it is fully driven in. This method is only suitable for bare-rooted trees because the stake can be inserted without causing any damage to the roots.

The stake should be placed with the tree in the planting hole first to find the best position. The tree is then removed so that the stake can be driven in. Once secure, the tree is planted before being tied to the stake.

This is one of the most widely used staking techniques and it can be adapted for use on a variety of different sized trees. Larger trees will require taller stakes, which should be reduced in height or removed once the tree has established.

Angled staking

Suitable for vulnerable container-grown or rootballed trees, angled staking is when a stake is driven into the ground away from the base of a planted tree at an angle of 45 degrees. This technique prevents damage to the root system. About 50cm (20in) of the stake should be above ground. The tree is then securely attached to the stake with a flexible tree tie.

For larger container or rootballed trees a longer angled stake can be used, but should be removed as soon as the tree has established.

Three-stake system shown for a large tree.

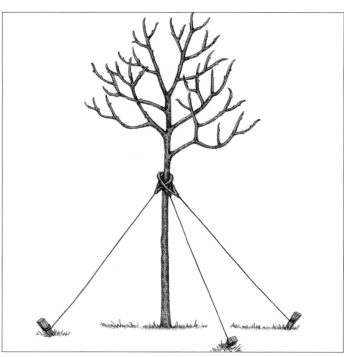

Wire guying can be used to support large rootballed or container-grown trees.

T-bar and three-stake system

These methods are becoming increasingly popular, and can be adapted for use in a wide range of situations. They should be used for medium to large trees, whether they are bare-root, container-grown or rootballed plants.

In the T-bar system, two posts are driven vertically into the ground on either side of the planting pit so that about 50cm (20in) of each stake is above ground. A treated wooden horizontal bar is then nailed to the upright bars so that the tree blows away from the cross-bar. The tree is held with a rubberized tie with a spacer to make sure that the trunk does not rub against the cross-bar.

In the three-stake system, three posts are driven into the ground to the same depth as in the T-bar

method. However, instead of using a wooden cross piece, three wires or ropes are used, and these are passed through a protective sleeve as they pass around the tree trunk and are fixed to the stakes so the tree can still sway in the wind. Once the tree has established the system should be removed.

Wire guying

This is an expensive method of supporting a tree because it requires specialized equipment. It is mainly used for large rootballed or container-grown standard trees and conifers, but it is not suitable for palms.

After the tree has been planted, three or four bullet-shaped anchors are driven into the ground around the tree. Attached to each anchor is a stainless steel cable. The movement

of the cables as they are brought under tension locks the anchors into the ground. Each cable runs through a plastic or rubber sleeve, placed around the trunk of the tree and usually positioned above a branch to stop it from slipping down the trunk. Although the cables support the tree higher up the trunk, they allow it to sway in strong winds.

It is usual to install the cables so that the protective collars do not form a constricting circle around the same area of the trunk. They are usually arranged at various heights from about 1.8m (6ft) up. The cables can be adjusted as the tree grows, and the system usually remains in place for three or four years. When the cables are removed, the ground anchors can be carefully dug out or left in the ground.

Staking with bamboo canes

This method is suitable for small container-grown trees, which require a minimum amount of staking and may need support for only a year. A bamboo can be pushed into the ground at an angle of 45 degrees away from the rootball. The cane is then cut off, leaving about 50cm (20in) above ground. A tree tie attached to the cane and the tree holds it firmly. A spacer may be needed to prevent the cane from rubbing against the trunk and the tie should be checked and loosened from time to time so that it does not become too tight.

Triple stakes and rubber guy wires

An alternative to the wire guying system, this method is less expensive and requires no specialist equipment. It is suitable for palms, conifers and medium-sized standard or feathered trees, whether they are sold as bare-rooted, rootballed or container-grown plants.

Three wooden posts are driven into the ground at equal intervals around the edge of the planting hole after the tree has been planted. The posts should be vertical with 50–75cm (20–30in) remaining above ground. A long, flexible rubber tree tie is attached to one of the wooden stakes, wound around the trunk and attached to the same stake, usually by nailing or stapling. This process is repeated on the other two stakes. The flexibility of the ties allows the tree to sway.

Underground guying

This method is used only on large container-grown or rootballed trees and palms in locations where an above-ground guying system is impracticable – if someone might walk into the cables, for example – or where appearance is important. It requires specialized installation and is invisible when in place. It uses similar ground anchors and cables to the above-ground wire guying method, but instead of being attached to the trunk, the cables are attached to a special collar that fits around the tree's root plate. This allows the trunk to sway freely.

Below-ground staking of palms

Palms have relatively small rootballs and are often transplanted or sold as mature specimens. Their fibrous trunks make it is impossible to use a traditional guying system so the below-ground method is used instead. An adjustable, padded steel collar is fitted around the trunk and is then attached to traditional guy wires, installed with the same equipment as for above-ground guying.

Bamboo canes are suitable for staking small, container-grown trees that don't require very strong support.

If you have reduced the number of leaders on a tree, use a stake to encourage the remaining one to grow vertically.

If you are inserting a stake when the tree has already been planted, put it at an angle to avoid damaging the roots.

Watering newly planted trees

Effective and timely watering is the most important factor for the survival of a newly planted tree. Tree roots, especially the microscopic root hairs that absorb moisture from the soil, are easily damaged during planting, no matter how careful you are. For the tree to establish there must be sufficient water both in the tree's rootball and in the surrounding soil so that new roots can grow and proliferate out from the tree.

Misting

In dry and windy conditions newly planted trees will require daily watering, which should be undertaken either in the early morning or in the late afternoon to early evening.

To help cool down the foliage of trees, the leaves can be sprayed throughout the day with a fine mist of water. As the water evaporates from the surface of the leaves it will help cool them down and thus reduce the level of transpiration between the roots and the leaves, conserving water.

Rainwater collected from roofs and stored in water butts does not contain the chemicals that are found in domestic water, and has the added advantage of being free.

Waterlogged ground is a sure sign of poor drainage, in which case you should only water the tree little and often, ensuring that the water drains completely between applications.

Following planting, apply plenty of water to allow the soil to settle around the roots.

Avoid misting trees in strong sun as the droplets can act like tiny magnifying glasses and burn the foliage. In such conditions drape some shade netting over the tree, and water the soil more regularly.

How much water?

Overwatering, which causes as many new plants to die as underwatering does, is likely to be a problem on ground that is naturally slow to drain, such as clay or compacted soils. In these conditions water little but often, making sure each time that the water has drained away completely. Too much water around the roots will restrict oxygen levels and cause the roots to die.

Water should be applied at the following rate: 2.5cm water per litre of container-grown tree (3.7in per gallon). This means that a 10-litre (2.6-gallon) container-grown tree will require 25cm (10in) of water every day during a dry period.

On poorly drained soils this quantity can be reduced by half, and the total volume of water is best given in two applications, one in the morning and one in late afternoon. If the soil remains wet and soggy between each of the waterings then you are overwatering.

Water drains more easily on light, sandy soils, so you may find you have to apply more water if the tree is planted in this type of soil.

However, you should carefully monitor the water given to rootballed trees planted in sandy soils. This is because they might have been lifted from clay soil, so the water will not drain easily from the rootball into the surrounding sandy soil.

As your tree establishes, water it less frequently so that the tree can be slowly weaned off its reliance on regular artificial watering.

Signs of thirst

Evergreen trees and container-grown deciduous trees that are planted out of their dormant season usually require much more aftercare than other trees. This is because they can quickly succumb to drought.

Touching the foliage throughout the day, especially in late morning, will help you determine if the tree is stressed. If the foliage feels warmer than the ambient air temperature then you should lightly water the tree and mist the foliage to cool the leaves.

If the leaves feel noticeably cooler than the air temperature, there is sufficient water available to the roots

Young trees will require daily watering in windy or dry conditions, but you should take care not to overwater, which restricts the amount of oxygen that can reach the roots of the tree.

Sunken irrigation systems are available and allow water directly into the root zone.

for it to be drawn up into the trunk, through the branches, and to the leaves. Once it reaches the leaves it evaporates from their surface and keeps them cool.

If there is insufficient water available to the roots the leaves will overheat and, if unnoticed, they can curl and die.

Watering methods

There are a number of useful devices widely available that will make watering less of a chore during hot or windy weather.

Porous plastic pipes can be installed around the outside of the rootball before planting. These have a reservoir that protrudes above

ground so that it can be easily filled to allow water to seep through the pipes into the ground. This type of system minimizes surface evaporation and places the water directly in the soil around the roots.

Another system uses a high-density polythene irrigation bag, which is placed on the surface of the soil and wrapped around the base of the trunk. The bag is then filled with water, which seeps through small holes at the base and into the root zone.

This reduces surface evaporation from the soil, and it can be removed when it is no longer needed, unlike the buried pipes, which cannot be retrieved once installed.

Understanding mulching

After planting a new tree, it is important to minimize the competition for light, water and nutrients from other plants, especially weeds. One of the best ways of keeping the ground clear is to apply a mulch. A mulch is placed on the surface of exposed soil to reduce evaporation, inhibit the germination of annual weeds and, when the mulch consists of a natural material, provide nutrients as it decomposes.

Types of mulch

The most often-used of the natural mulches is composted bark, which is derived from wood waste from the forestry industry, when the material is passed through a chipping machine to break it into small nuggets. The material is graded and composted before being sold. The chips can vary in size and quality because of the different types of tree from which they are derived.

Another popular mulching material is garden compost, made by composting household and

In nature, the natural woodland floor provides suffcent quantities of mulch in the form of well-rotted leaves and other organic material.

garden waste; a similar material is sometimes available also through municipal recycling centres. Other useful materials are coir, shredded newspaper, sawdust, spent hops, farmyard manure and grass clippings, all of which should be thoroughly composted before use. Farmyard manure is particularly good for adding fertility to soil, and garden compost also contains a good range of nutrients.

Artificial mulches and mulch mats are made from woven materials, such as polypropylene or other plastics. Woven plastic mats are permeable to air and water, but some types of black plastic matting are not, which means that rain cannot reach the soil. Artificial mulch mats, which may break down or degrade slowly, are unattractive and are often used in conjunction with natural mulches, which are laid on top.

Even if they do biodegrade, artificial mulches, unlike natural mulches, do not supply any nutrients. Their main advantages are that they are long-lasting and are effective at inhibiting the growth of both annual and perennial weeds.

Several natural mulches have been bonded together to form mulch mats that will break down over about two years. Commonly used materials include flax, hemp, sisal and coir fibre. Like other mulch mats, they should be held down with some other material, and they are widely used with organic mulches.

The benefits of mulches

Applying a mulch, whether natural or artificial, has several advantages for newly planted and established trees. Mulches help to keep moisture in the soil by reducing evaporation from its surface, thereby reducing the need for watering.

Overmulching

A mulch that is deeper than 10cm (4in) can create excessive moisture around the root zone and force oxygen out of the soil, and this will stress the tree and increase its susceptibility to root-borne diseases. Piling a mulch against the trunk can cause temperatures to rise as the mulch breaks down, and this may damage the bark, leading to insect infestation or disease. A deep mulch can also be a wonderful habitat for harmful rodents, which eat the bark of new trees.

Mulches that are not properly composted or those containing material that is high in nitrogen, such as grass clippings, can have an effect on the soil's pH or take nitrogen from the soil as they decompose. The continued use of such mulches can lead to nutrient deficiencies.

A mulch 5–10cm (2–4in) thick will also reduce the germination and growth of annual weeds and grasses.

Mulches can be used to protect the roots of less hardy trees by acting as an insulating layer on the surface of the soil and reducing the level of frost penetration into the soil. They can also protect the surface of the soil from high temperatures during summer.

Natural mulches gradually introduce organic matter into the soil, thus improving the water-retaining capacity of light soils, while improving the drainage and aeration on heavier soils. In addition, the beneficial soil fungus and bacteria that invade the mulch to break it down can produce a physical mat of fungi roots (hyphae) that can inhibit the growth of disease-spreading fungi in the area of the root zone. Natural mulches also create the kind of area that would be found around the tree in a forest or woodland, thereby

MULCHING A TREE

1 Grass and other plants growing close to a young or newly planted tree will make it harder for the tree to establish.

2 Tie a loose line around the base of the tree and, using an edging iron, mark out a circle around the tree.

3 Using a garden spade or turfing iron, carefully remove the grass from the circular area around the tree.

4 Carefully remove any perennial weeds and, if the soil is dry, water the area surrounding the tree well.

5 An artificial mulch mat could be used, or simply spread a mulch of bark chips out to the damp line.

6 Make sure that the mulch is not too deep or banked up against the stem, or it may damage the bark.

encouraging natural nutrient recycling. As the mulch decomposes, it encourages mycorrhizal and other nutrient activity, which in turn help the tree's health and vigour.

Mulching around trees helps to reduce the risk of the trunk being damaged by lawnmowers and strimmers. An artificial mulch around an established tree can help to maintain its health by reducing compaction of the root zone, which it does by providing a cushion to protect it from foot or vehicle traffic.

Mulches can give a newly planted tree an attractive and properly planted appearance, keeping down weeds at a time when it is important that nothing competes with the tree for moisture and nutrients.

Applying a mulch

After planting the tree, remove any annual or perennial weeds, including grass. If using a mulch mat, apply this first. Then apply a 5–10cm (2–4in) layer of organic or natural mulch. If the tree prefers acidic soil, mulch

with composted pine bark or needles, which will not raise the soil pH or hinder the tree's take-up of nutrients.

If a mulch needs to be reapplied, remove the top layer of the old mulch and place new mulch on top. Check that the final mulch is not too deep and do not pile mulch against the tree trunk as it will prevent air getting to the bark. Instead, rake it back so that it forms a doughnut around the trunk and spreads beyond the edge of the branches or beyond the drip line.

Moving trees

It is of course best to begin by planting a tree or shrub in its final position, but even in the best planned garden mistakes can happen. Moving established plants, even small ones, is hard work and needs careful forethought. However, with a few helpers and good preparation, many plants can be moved successfully.

When to move trees

The best time for transplanting most established trees is during the dormant season (late autumn to early–mid-spring), as long as the soil is not waterlogged – in which case digging could damage the soil structure – or frozen, which would make digging impossible. Spring planting gives a full season's growth before the winter; an autumn move allows the plant to develop a good root system before spring. Evergreens, including conifers, are best moved in mid-spring when the soil is moist and warm enough to encourage rapid root growth.

What size rootball?

The rootball diameter and depth will depend on the size of the plant you are trying to move. The diameter

In gardens where space is limited or where there is close planting, established pruning is required to control the size of a tree and so prevent it from smothering other plants. If, however, the tree does start to outgrow its space, it may need to be moved.

Root pruning

The chances of successfully moving trees can be improved by pruning the roots in advance, a technique known as root pruning. It should be done up to a year before the move.

To root prune, simply dig a vertical trench around the tree, along the line where you plan to dig it up, and sever any roots you find, then refill the trench with soil. The tree will produce more fibrous roots in the soil nearer to the trunk, and these will form part of the rootball, increasing the tree's chances of survival after the move.

should be about the same as the spread of the branches and about one-third the height of a tree. The depth of the rootball depends on the type of soil in your garden. The lighter the soil the more penetrating the roots and so the deeper the rootball will have to be. For example, a 30cm (12in) deep rootball on clay soil may need to be twice that depth on a light, sandy soil. Bear in mind that rootballs with soil attached can literally weigh a ton if you are moving a small tree. Make sure you have sufficient help before you start.

Making moves

Before you start, decide on the new position of the tree and prepare the planting hole, which should be about twice as wide and slightly deeper than the rootball. Fork over the

bottom of the hole, incorporating a bucketful of grit on heavy soils to improve drainage.

Use a spade to cut a slit-trench around the tree being moved to mark out the size of the rootball and to sever any roots near to the surface. Then cut a second slit-trench about 30cm (12in) further out and dig out the soil in between to form a trench around the specimen. Make this trench as deep as the rootball.

Undercut the rootball from the trench by inserting the spade at an angle of about 45 degrees all the way round. Small rootballs should then be completely undercut and can be wrapped. Larger rootballs may need further excavation to expose any vertical roots under the middle of the rootball.

HOW TO MOVE A SMALL TREE

1 Before moving a tree, make sure that the planting site has been prepared and the hole excavated. Water the plant well the day before moving it.

2 Dig a trench around the tree, leaving a large rootball (the size depends on the size of the tree). Carefully sever any lateral roots that you encounter to release the rootball.

3 Dig under the tree, cutting through any vertical taproots that hold it in place.

4 Rock the tree to one side and insert sacking or strong plastic sheeting as far under the tree as you can get it. Push several folds of material under the rootball. Ask someone to help if you are finding it difficult to do on your own.

5 Rock the tree in the opposite direction and pull the sacking or plastic sheeting through towards you, so that it is completely under the rootball of the tree. Depending on the size of the tree, you may be able to lift the rootball slightly to make this easier.

6 Pull the sacking round the rootball and tie it firmly at the neck of the plant with some string. The tree is now ready to move. If it is a small plant, one person may be able to lift it out of the hole and transfer it to its new site on their own.

7 If, as is likely, the plant plus the soil is quite heavy, it is best moved by two people. Tie a length of wood or metal to the sacking. With one person on each end, lift the tree out of the hole.

8 Lower the transplanted tree into the prepared planting hole. Unwrap and remove the sheeting from the rootball. Make sure that the plant is in the right position, refill the hole, and water well.

Move the tree by pulling on the polythene sheeting, not the trunk. Use a short plank (board) or pair of planks as a ramp out of the hole and then drag it to its new position or get a gang of helpers to lift it. It may be easiest to fix a pole to help carry the tree.

Replant the tree immediately in the prepared hole and water and mulch well. Stake, using one of the techniques described previously, if necessary. Spray the foliage of evergreens after planting and every few days for the first month to help prevent wilting. It is also worth putting up a windbreak around conifers. Keep all transplants well watered throughout their first growing season.

After the rootball has been freed, carefully rock it back and slip a sheet of folded heavy-duty polythene or hessian (burlap) under one side, then rock it over the other way and then pull the folded polythene through. Tie the corners of the sheeting over the top of the rootball around the main stem to form a neat package, so that the soil is held firmly. Use rope or strong string to reinforce the rootball on all sides.

Problems with mature trees

Planting the right tree in the right location and carefully nurturing it can greatly reduce the risk of stress, which is an undesirable state that can lead to the tree being attacked by diseases or pests.

Most trees are completely trouble-free for many years. If you have correctly planted a healthy sapling into well-cultivated soil in an appropriate site, the tree is likely to outlive you without suffering any serious problems. However, if you have acquired a house with a mature tree in the garden you might encounter a few difficulties.

Fighting disease

Trees are highly complex plants that have evolved over millions of years, and they have developed mechanisms to protect themselves against the organisms that cause decay. Their ability to fight off disease depends on the current health of the tree and its inherited resistance.

Trees survive following injury or infection by 'walling off' or compartmentalizing the damaged area to limit the spread of disease to as small a part of their wood as possible. This process of erecting a series of chemical barriers around the area restricts the spread of infection that has entered via a wound to a tree's bark, which might have been caused by careless pruning, a lawnmower or strimmer, the weather or animals.

Some aggressive diseases affect a tree's tissues without a wound, but this is rare and only those trees that are already under stress are likely to be infected.

If the tree is healthy and its boundary-setting processes are good, the decay organism will be halted and the infection will remain localized. If the tree is in poor health and the decay organism is aggressive, the tree's walls may be unable to prevent the decay from spreading,

and this may also lead to other, secondary infections, although the decay cannot spread into new stems and branches.

Some trees are able to wall off infection rapidly and effectively. Many trees, in fact, cope perfectly well while having hundreds of infections safely walled off inside their trunks and branches. Those trees that do not respond quickly and effectively often lose an entire branch or may even die. The ability of individual trees to ward off infections is largely hereditary, although the overall health of the tree is also a major factor.

Cavities

A well-established tree can survive for many years with a hollow section in its trunk if the outer layer of sapwood is healthy and continues to transport nutrients from the roots to the branches and leaves. It will be able to survive strong prevailing winds, although if it becomes exposed to wind from the opposite direction – if a shelter-belt is removed, for example – the trunk may twist, causing it to collapse.

Tree defence systems

The natural defence system is known as CODIT (compartmentalization of decay in trees) and has two stages. The first occurs in the tree's living tissue, the vascular bundle, which runs the length of the tree, from the roots to the tips of the branches and the leaves. A tree will resist the spread of an infection by creating barriers above and below the site of the infection and to both sides.

The second stage creates a barrier between the existing wood and the wood that has not yet grown. This is why hollow trees continue to grow and survive.

It was once usual to gouge out the decayed area and fill the cavity with bricks and mortar, but modern practice is to leave the cavity untouched. You should not drill a hole through the cavity to release trapped water because this hole will allow decay from the cavity to spread to the healthy tissue behind it.

The best option is to leave the cavity alone but to check it every year, seeking the advice of a tree expert if necessary, and to improve the vigour of the tree by fertilizing the soil, mulching and, if circumstances dictate, hiring a tree surgeon to inject compressed air in conjunction with mycorrhizal inoculation or biostimulants (see pages 324–5).

Bracing

This is a way of supporting the weight of a branch that might have a natural weakness, such as a codominant stem (see page 358).

Flexible steel support cables were once used to prevent the collapse of branches weakened by decay or narrow forks or to support large, heavy branches. Such cables were often fixed into the living tissue of

This ancient *Quercus robur* (English oak) has managed to survive for centuries, despite having a large cavity in its trunk.

Extreme temperatures as well as some fungal diseases can often cause tree bark to split.

the tree with eye-bolts. Today, however, non-invasive proprietary systems wrap a sling around the trunk and incorporate elastic shock absorbers that allow the trunks being held to sway.

This type of bracing is expensive and should be considered only for prized trees that cannot be treated in some other way.

Pests and diseases

Insect pests and diseases usually affect trees that are already under stress, such as that caused by drought, nutrient deficiency, overpruning or damage to the root system. It is important, therefore, to ensure that your trees are fed regularly and pruned appropriately, if necessary, and that the ground around the base of the trunk is kept clear of weeds and grass.

Dead branches at the uppermost canopy indicate there are problems in the root zone.

Successfully tackling a pest or disease depends on identifying the problem in the first instance. If a tree in your garden is clearly not thriving, inspect it carefully for anything unusual.

Symptoms that will suggest that something is amiss include strangely coloured foliage, curled leaves or leaves changing colour early in the year. Liquid oozing from the bark, bark flaking or falling off, swellings or sunken areas on branches or the trunk and any signs of decaying wood should all be investigated immediately.

The organisms causing holes in the bark or leaves can usually be fairly easily identified. Among the culprits are mushrooms and toadstools, which are the fruiting bodies of fungi that have caused or will cause decay and should be identified and dealt with immediately.

Dealing with pests and diseases

The secret to healthy garden trees is understanding their growth habits and providing them with the best possible conditions to allow them to thrive. Carrying out a programme for monitoring and caring for their needs throughout their life is also essential. The aim is to promote a healthy tree, which is more likely to be able to resist disease.

Inspecting trees

Tree inspections are usually carried out by professional tree care specialists, but it would be wise to learn from them and monitor the condition of your trees annually – or more often if you prefer.

A professional tree care specialist may recommend that you mulch around trees in order to conserve moisture in the soil, helping to keep the soil healthy.

Using a hoe to remove weeds from around young trees or shrubs is the surest way of catching them all. It is best carried out in hot weather so that any weeds hoed up die quickly.

Nutrient deficiencies

Nitrogen deficiency is common on free-draining soils. A deficiency can manifest itself in a number of ways, but it often appears as off-colour or slightly yellowish leaves or leaves that are smaller than they should be. Apply a high-nitrogen fertilizer (either chemical, such as sulphate of ammonia, or organic, such as dried blood or rotted manure) during late spring and summer.

Phosphorus deficiency is uncommon in gardens, but can occur in acid soils or areas of high rainfall. Growth will be slowed and young foliage dull or yellowish. A fertilizer containing superphosphate, or bonemeal as an organic alternative, will help.

Potassium deficiency is most common in free-draining soils, or those containing a lot of chalk or peat. It causes discoloured leaves, poor growth and reduced flowering and fruiting. Sulphate of potash or wood ash should be applied.

Trace elements are also important for plant health. Applying liquid seaweed extract, either watered in or sprayed on the leaves, ensures a good supply.

Tree inspections should evaluate a number of different things, but special attention should be paid to the condition of new leaves and buds, leaf size and colour, twig growth, the percentage and regularity of dead wood within the crown, as well as spotting any visual warning signs (cavities or poorly attached branches, for example).

If, after an inspection, you think that something is not right, a second opinion may be required. If the inspection is undertaken by a tree care specialist they may recommend a future maintenance programme of preventative care.

This programme may include recommendations concerning the mulching, weed control, irrigation, improving drainage, and fertilizing of the tree. These simple maintenance tasks may be linked to more specialized work such as crown pruning, bracing, tree root aeration and mycorrhizal treatments, or pest and disease control.

Diseases

A plant disease can be defined as an organism (pathogen) or a substance that interferes with and disrupts the normal cycle of growth and in doing so causes visible signs of damage. In addition to diseases there are also disorders such as wind and frost damage or nutrient deficiencies, and these will also limit tree growth and overall health.

Plant diseases can be divided into two very broad groups: those caused by fungi, bacteria and viral pathogens that invade and break down the structure of a tree; and those that are caused by some of the insects and animals that rely on trees for food and shelter.

Tree diseases caused by pathogens generally become more widespread within the tree as it gets older. They can often go unnoticed for many years and eventually cause serious damage. They can also move from tree to tree. It is essential, therefore, to carry out regular inspections.

Mildew

This condition can affect a wide variety of trees and can be separated out into three main categories: downy mildew, powdery mildew and grey mould. Downy mildew is associated with humid weather and shows itself as a fluffy white bloom (fungal hyphae) on the underside of the leaf.

Increasing air movement through the canopy of the tree can reduce the humidity and limit the spread of mildew, as can removing any infected leaves as they appear. Controlling the disease using a fungicide should be a last resort.

Powdery mildew is associated with dry soil and stagnant air. It shows itself as a fluffy, white bloom that usually grows on the upper surface of the leaf, but occasionally on both surfaces. Spraying the foliage can reduce the spread, as will fungicidal treatment.

Grey mould is caused by a number of fungal diseases that produce a grey, fuzzy growth on the leaves, which quickly shrivel and die. Control it in a similar way to downy mildew.

Canker

This is caused by a variety of fungi and bacteria, which infect healthy tissue and cause a circular area of the tissue to die and produce a roughly circular wound that harbours the spores, which will re-infect other areas of the tree. Such infected areas may ooze a watery substance, a thick gum or small pustules. Generally, canker infections seldom heal and remain like a weeping sore allowing re-infection to occur.

There are various cankers that are specific to a wide range of trees. They are commonly found on

Aesculus spp. (horse chestnut); *Castanea sativa* (sweet chestnut); *Cupressus* spp. (cypress); *Ficus* spp. (fig); *Laburnum* spp. (golden rain); *Larix* spp. (larch); *Picea* spp. (spruce); *Pinus* spp. (pine); *Populus* spp. (poplar); *Prunus* spp. (cherry); *Prunus domestica* spp. (plum); *Pseudotsuga menziesii* (Douglas fir); *Quercus* spp. (oak) and *Tilia* spp. (lime).

Many cankers are difficult to control, although removal of the infected tissue or spraying with a fungicide may help to slow the spread of the disease.

Coral spot

The fungus *Nectria cinnabarina*, which causes coral spot, is often found on dead or dying branches, and can also affect weakened or badly pruned branches. The disease cannot penetrate through unbroken bark; it must gain entry via a wound. The disease spreads quickly and produces the typical salmon-pink pustules that erupt through the infected bark.

Limiting infection involves good hygiene, and removing dead wood from the garden. Infected material

should be removed back to healthy tissue and the tree regularly sprayed with a fungicide.

Fireblight

This is a serious disease caused by *Erwinia amylovora* and it affects members of the rose family (*Rosaceae*), including *Sorbus*, *Crataegus*, *Malus* and *Pyrus*.

Infection starts in spring when the disease enters flowers or wounds and quickly spreads through the trunk and branches. Infected branches subsequently die, and always have distinctive dried and shrivelled leaves attached and resemble branches burnt by fire. Part of or the entire tree may be affected, and quick removal of infected branches is recommended.

In areas where fireblight is prevalent it is wise not to grow *Malus* spp. (apple), *Prunus domestica* spp. (plum), *Sorbus* spp. (mountain ash) or *Crataegus* spp. (hawthorn), since these are particularly susceptible. Quick identification and removal of infected material is the only successful method of control.

Coral spot affects broad-leaved shrubs and trees. It causes shoots to die back and produces pink to coral red pustules.

The greyish-white spores of powdery mildew cover the underside of the leaves, making it look like a coating of powder.

Silver leaf

Chondrostereum purpureum is a very common disease of plums and cherries but also affects other members of the rose family including almonds, apricots, apples, pears and hawthorns.

It causes leaves to develop a silvery sheen. Although the leaves are the first sign of the disease they do not spread the disease; instead purplish pustules develop along the bark and increase the infection.

Although many leaves may die, often trees will recover, especially if any dead or dying branches are quickly removed back to healthy tissue. Any regular pruning should be undertaken during summer when the disease is less prevalent.

Anthracnose

This is a common disease in flowering dogwoods, willows, American plane trees, palms, figs, hornbeam, birch, redbud, oak, ash and maples, and it is caused by the fungus *Discula*.

Symptoms vary, but they generally involve leaf spots that develop very small, round silver pustules which spread, causing leaves to die or curl, leading to tip die-back or stem lesions. Quick removal of infected material may slow the spread of the disease through the tree and spraying with a broad spectrum fungicide throughout late spring and early summer helps prevent it occurring.

Honey fungus

A wood-rotting disease caused by *Armillaria*, honey fungus infects stumps and dead wood and can then spread to any stressed or wounded trees in the vicinity via black, threadlike rhizomorphs, commonly called bootlaces. The disease can spread quickly up the trunk and causes a wet ooze to develop.

Susceptible trees include privet, sycamore, magnolia, snowdrop trees, maples, birch and walnut. Removal of infected material is essential to limit the spread. Fungal treatments in the form of root drenches may

The fruiting bodies of honey fungus are apparent as they emerge in autumn.

help, and artificial root barriers may limit the growth of the rhizomorphs, as will mulching around the canopy of garden trees.

Dutch elm disease

The disease is spread by the elm bark beetle that feeds on stressed trees during the spring, then tunnels into the bark, and infects the tree with Dutch elm fungus, *Ceratocytstis ulmi*. The disease spreads quickly through the tree's branch and trunk section and causes the new shoots and stems to bend over into a crook shape.

Although there is no successful control method there are a number of disease-resistant forms of the elm tree.

Sudden oak death

A disease that was first identified in California, sudden oak death has killed large populations of oaks.

The disease is caused by *Phytophthora ramorum* and *Phytophthora kernoviae* and it has a very wide range of hosts, including *Abies* spp.

The brown area in the centre of this plane leaf indicates anthracnose.

Silver leaf has stained this cherry wood a mid-brown colour.

Grey mould can cause dead and discoloured patches on leaves and fruit.

(silver fir); *Acer* spp. (maple); *Aesculus* spp. (horse chestnut); *Arbutus* spp. (strawberry tree); *Castanea* (sweet chestnut); *Chaemaecyparis* spp. (false cypress); *Fagus* spp. (beech); *Fraxinus* spp. (ash); *Magnolia* spp.; *Northofagus* spp. (southern beech); *Salix* spp. (willow); *Sequoia* spp. (coast redwood) and *Taxus* spp. (yew).

The disease can induce a range of symptoms but dark lesions on leaves, tip die-back and inverted 'V' shaped rot pattern up the trunk with dark brown-black blotches are common.

Diseased material must be removed completely and destroyed safely, and constant monitoring of nearby plants is essential. There is currently no fungicide effective against this disease.

Grey mould

The fungus that causes grey mould (*Botrytis cinerea*) is the most damaging pest of ornamental container plants as well as conifer seedlings in container tree nurseries.

It attacks most species of container seedlings but certain species are particularly susceptible, such as the redwood and giant sequoia, western larch, some pines, Douglas fir, Scots pine, blue spruce, mountain hemlock, noble fir and Alaska-cedar.

This disease can be identified by grey, cottony mycelia and spore masses on the surface of affected shoot tissue. These spore-producing structures show a fuzzy appearance. As the disease progresses, infected shoot tissue becomes watersoaked and brown lesions often develop. The fungus may spread to the main stem, where cankers eventually girdle and kill the shoot.

Phytophthora root rot

This is caused by the fungus *Phytophthora*, which is most problematic in wet or waterlogged soils. The disease produces motile spores that can move through soil water and affect the roots of trees.

The infected roots then die, causing an unexplained death of the crown of the tree. Like sudden oak death a 'V' shaped decay pattern develops with yellow-brown ooze, and the bark dries during summer and can provide an entry point for other diseases.

Removal of infected material and improved drainage to limit the spread of the disease are the best forms of action.

This dead tree may have been killed by sudden oak death, a disease that affects a wide range of trees, and for which there is, as yet, no cure.

Wind damage

This type of damage affects the leaves of a tree, causing them to turn brown and dry up along the edges or curl up and fall off prematurely. The damage is usually noticeably restricted to one side of the tree, and is common in early spring, during summer (especially during periods of drought) and during winter on conifers. Many trees are especially prone during early spring as the emerging leaves are easily damaged. This problem is common in Japanese maples, coffin and bean trees.

Frost damage

This is similar to wind damage, although it is often widespread across the entire canopy of the tree and causes die-back of some younger shoots. It causes the entire leaf to shrivel, often turning black and dying, with the leaves remaining attached.

Any tree can be damaged, but walnuts, bean trees, redbuds, magnolia, golden rain tree and southern beech are susceptible. Avoid planting these in frost pockets and wrap small trees in horticultural fleece in winter.

The flowers of spring-flowering magnolias may be turned brown by frost.

Crown gall and witches' broom

A common occurrence in many trees, crown gall looks unsightly, but will seldom cause any long-term harm.

The disease is caused by the bacterium *Agrobacterium tumefaciens*, which causes the bark to rupture and new growth to swell and burst from the stem. It tends to be more problematic on poor-draining soils where the bacteria can gain easier access to the tree. Infected areas should be pruned back rigorously to healthy wood and any clippings must be destroyed.

Ladybirds (ladybugs) help to keep garden pests in check.

Witches' broom, a similar disease to crown gall, is caused by the fungus *Tuphrina*, or by microscopic mites. The effect is similar and causes irregular growth of hundreds of new shoots that originate from one point along the stem, making it look like the end of a broom.

Animals that cause harm

Many insects, mammals and birds can cause injury and damage to trees by eating or burrowing into the leaves, feeding on the tree sap and creating an entry point for other pathogens such as fungal spores to enter. They also burrow into the bark and affect the structure of the tree.

Most insect problems are not life-threatening to the tree unless the insect can rapidly multiply its numbers and cause serious problems by repeatedly defoliating the tree.

Control of insect pests is based on the understanding of their life cycle and how to disrupt their breeding patterns so that their numbers never escalate out of control. This can be achieved by integrated pest management which utilizes physical control such as removing infected material quickly, or washing off or hand removing the pest, as well as encouraging or introducing natural

Trees sometimes show unusual growth patterns in response to environmental conditions. Here, the growth of a tree has been affected by the wind.

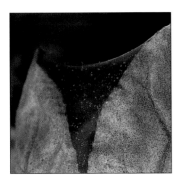

Spider mites produce a very fine webbing on the surface of leaves.

predators to limit their numbers, and if all this fails then the last resort, the use of pesticides.

Aphids

These small green, brown or black insects suck sap from buds and the underside of leaves, especially new growth, and cause them to shrivel. They also excrete sticky honeydew, which can encourage sooty mould.

Removing the infected leaves can help control the spread, along with using biological controls such as the parasitic wasps *Aphiduis* and *Aphidoletes* that lay their eggs into adult aphids. Encouraging other predators such as hoverflies and ladybirds can also help. Spraying with insecticidal soap or using an insecticide should be done before the winged adults appear and colonize other trees.

Scale insects

These tiny insects have semi-hard or hard shells that resemble oyster shells. The females can initially fly, then form their shell and stay in one place to feed. They are often found clustered along young branches and on new leaves. Removal is difficult due to their shell, but spraying with insecticidal soap, horticultural oil, or a systemic pesticide will help.

Red spider mites

These tiny, red or brownish, spider-like pests feed on the underside or surface of the leaf and spin a very fine web that covers its surface. Tiny yellow dots appear on the leaf, and when the number of mites increases the leaf can turn brown and shrivel up. *Phytoseiulus*, a predatory mite, is used as a biological control, or you can spray with insecticidal soap or an insecticide.

Caterpillars

These small creatures come in many shapes and sizes and they can affect our garden trees primarily by chewing the leaves or shoots.

Of the many species that cause significant damage, one of the most serious is the Gypsy Moth which has devastated deciduous oak forest along the eastern seaboard of the USA. The female adult moth is a silvery white with occasional brown and black, bark-like markings; the males are brown in colour.

The voracious caterpillars are hairy and black-bodied with blue spots near the head and red spots on the lower body. They feed on oak, hemlock, maple, apple, alder, black gum, fir, pine, walnut and bean tree.

Trees can be defoliated during summer and, if defoliated twice, can die. Most conifers die after being defoliated once. A biological control is *Bacillus thuringiensis*, a bacterium that grows inside and kills the caterpillars. Predatory beetles are also used. During large outbreaks aerial spraying with an insecticide can be effective. In a garden setting insecticide can be used.

A wide variety of other caterpillars also feed on leaves and cause damage by chewing the edges of the leaves or by removing the middle or just part of the leaf. Other caterpillars

stay in colonies, or build a spider-like web to protect themselves, while others curl over the leaves and seal the opening with silk to protect themselves from predators.

Effective control can involve the use female pheromone traps to trap male butterflies and moths. Useful biological controls include *Bacillus thuringiensis* and nematodes, and you can also spray the caterpillars with insecticide when they first appear. Hand removing the eggs before they hatch will also control infestations.

Leaf miners

Commonplace on birch, elm, alder, hawthorn, oak, locust, strawberry trees and maples, these pests will also affect a variety of other trees. Leaf miners are the juvenile offspring of either sawflies, or beetles that lay their eggs in between the layers of a leaf. The larva then tunnels inside the leaf, devouring the soft tissue. The leaves become discoloured and distorted and may fall early, but usually after the larvae have hatched.

Caterpillars can cause visible damage to leaves of trees as they feed.

Hand removal of affected leaves can control the disease, as can spraying with a systemic pesticide. Sticky traps can also be used against the adults.

Leaf-eating beetles

Like caterpillars, a wide variety of adult beetles and their larvae feed on trees. Flea beetles are very small, metallic black beetles that can hop. They eat out uneven shaped notches from the leaves and can even defoliate trees.

Fuller rose beetles devour the young shoots and leaves of maples, persimmon, palms, peach, oaks and pears. In doing so the rusty brown beetles are evident along with their numerous droppings.

Japanese beetles are widespread and will feed on the foliage and shoots of Japanese maples, birch, elm, willow, American sycamore, dogwoods and hollies. The adults are quite large with metallic green heads and coppery-red wing cases. The damage appears as numerous small holes in the leaf that are surrounded by a brown edge.

The vine weevil and other weevils cause distinctive notched damage along the leaf edges as they feed during the evening. Pheromone traps are fairly effective, as are sticky traps to catch the mobile males, and systemic insecticides will provide some control.

Leaf-cutting ants

Like leaf-eating beetles, leaf-cutting ants can defoliate trees, in some extreme cases completely stripping them of leaves in just a few hours. Affected trees are usually within sight of the nest, and you may be able to see the ants themselves carrying the leaves. There may also be a trail of leaf fragments along the foraging path.

Leaf-cutting ants are difficult to control, since they feed on fungus that grows on the leaves, rather than the leaves themselves, so they do not respond to insecticides that are applied to the leaves.

Acephate dusts and insecticide granules are among the more effective controls available, and should be applied directly to the

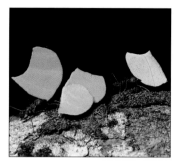

Leaf-cutting ants can potentially strip a tree of leaves in just a few hours.

nest openings, according to the manufacturer's instructions. These treatments may not be totally effective, however, and several applications may be required.

Bark boring beetles

The ambrosia beetle or shothole borer is found boring into the trunk of young maples, hazels, dogwoods, sassafras and hornbeam. The adult beetles are flat, 3mm (1/8in) long with a distinct flat head, and they bore into the trunk of trees and produce an effect as if the trunk has been shot with a shotgun.

Leaf diseases

The diseases that can affect leaves are very varied and can include leaf blotches, tar spots, leaf blisters, peach leaf curl and a number already covered, like anthracnose. Most leaf diseases are caused by fungi, viruses or mites and they are seldom severe enough to cause the tree any lasting damage although their effects can look unsightly. If infected leaves fall prematurely they are best disposed of safely and not composted.

Improving the vigour of a tree by keeping a close eye on its growing environment will help to limit the disease as spraying is expensive and will not resolve the current infection.

Keep a look out for the early signs that a pest, disease or disorder may be present. Small-scale scarring or discoloured leaves could be an indicator.

Birch borers cause serious damage to the bark of birch trees in the USA, as this bronzy coloured beetle lays its eggs under the bark, which hatch into larvae that consume the bark as they grow. The beetle seeks out stressed trees, especially those suffering from the heat of summer. Pheromone traps can be used against adults, and planting non-susceptible species is advised.

Grubs and larvae

Chafer grubs are semicircular, whitish, and have copper-coloured legs and head. The eggs hatch in the soil and develop into grubs which then feed on the roots of trees. Although this is never fatal, it can restrict the growth of young trees. A bacterial biological control will effectively deal with chafer grubs.

The grubs of the adult weevil can also cause a problem to tree roots, especially on young trees. The grubs are whitish in colour, with a copper head with black mandibles, but without visible legs, unlike the chafer grubs. The larvae can be controlled by bacteria or nematodes.

Deer can cause serious problems for trees. Not only do they consume large amounts of foliage, but they can also damage the bark.

Bark boring birds

Sapsuckers and woodpeckers cause some superficial damage to trees as they bore into the trunk in search of insect grubs. They will bore into a variety of trees including maple, birch, conifers, magnolia, apples, willow, palms, grevilleas and locust.

Occasionally trees may be killed if birds ring-bark the trunk and they can also open up wounds to other decay organisms. Control involves the use of a bird scarer, protecting the bark of susceptible trees, or planting trees not commonly affected.

Mammals

Deer, rabbits and squirrels can cause quite serious damage especially to young trees, by eating the bark, shoots or foliage. Evidence of their work can be seen by the level of damage to the trees, their footprints or droppings.

Fencing or protecting young trees is the best line of defence, along with live traps, scarers or scented deterrents to keep them away from garden trees.

Squirrels cause extensive damage by stripping bark from the trunk and branches of trees.

Rabbits can be problematic as they will feed on young trees and ring-bark older trees.

Pruning trees

Some gardeners dislike the idea of pruning, or feel there is so much mystique attached to it that they prefer not to undertake it at all. This, however, may not be in the tree's best interests.

Fortunately, established trees rarely need pruning unless they have dead, diseased or damaged branches or have outgrown their allotted space. It is not the same for young trees, which may greatly benefit from formative pruning. Pruning when they are young allows them to develop a strong leader and a good framework of branches in the canopy, all of which leads to a healthy, robust tree with a beautiful, well-proportioned shape.

Although pruning on mature trees is usually carried out for cosmetic reasons, when it comes to productive trees, such as those that bear fruit, there are also other good reasons for it, since these trees need annual pruning if they are to continue to crop reliably.

The careful choosing, siting and pruning of trees produces the most stunning effects in the garden – whether grandly formal, as shown here, or otherwise.

Tools and equipment

These can be divided into four groups. There are those that perform the cuts, such as saws, secateurs (pruners) and knives; those that are used for clearing up, such as rakes, forks and shredders; safety equipment; and finally the means to gain access to taller plants, such as ladders and towers. They can further be divided into manual tools and powered ones, such as hedge trimmers and chainsaws.

Wear safety gloves to protect your hands when pruning. Use a proper pruning saw to cut thicker branches. Avoid using carpenters' tools as they are not suitable for pruning.

Be extra careful when working at heights. Use a wide-based stepladder for extra stability. If this is not possible, ensure that someone holds the ladder at the base to keep it steady.

Cutting equipment

The most essential tool is a good pair of secateurs. These should be kept sharp. Poor-quality ones, with blades that move apart when you cut, or blunt ones will tear the wood as it passes through. They may also crush and bruise the wood. To a skilled user, a sharp knife can replace secateurs in certain instances.

Long-arm pruners are secateurs on an extension arm that can reach into tall shrubs or trees but are operated from ground-level. For wood thicker than 1cm (½in) a pair of long-handled pruners can be used, and for anything more than 2.5cm (1in) thick you should use a saw.

Saws come in a variety of shapes and sizes. Small folding saws are the most useful for the small-garden owner. These are usually very sharp and remain so for some years. Instead of sharpening, as one used to do, it is usual to buy a new one when it begins to blunt.

Bow saws and even chainsaws may be necessary in larger gardens. Some of the folding saws can be attached to extension arms so that higher branches can be removed without the need for ladders.

Shears are useful for hand-clipping hedges or shearing over certain shrubs such as lavender or ground cover. They are generally used for topiary where curves and trickier corners are concerned. You can also use sheep-shearing shears, but these are not the easiest things to use and scissors are easier for really intricate pieces.

Power tools

In small gardens it may be unnecessary to use power tools, but in a larger one they can be a boon. The crucial thing about such tools is to use them sensibly. Make certain that you know how to operate them and that you are well protected. If you are uncertain about your abilities, have any work that entails their use done by professionals.

Chainsaws are probably the most dangerous tool and should be used only if you have taken a course on their use. It is also very important that power tools are kept in good condition. They should be serviced professionally at least once a year. The settings and running of the engine should be checked and the cutters sharpened. Do this in advance of when you will next need them.

You can get power secateurs but these are very expensive and really useful only if you have a very large orchard and have a lot of fruit pruning or a vast amount of roses to keep in shape.

Clearing up

Most tools needed for this, such as rakes, brooms, forks, wheelbarrows and carrying sheets, should be available as part of the general garden toolkit. Another piece of power equipment of general use to the pruner is the shredder, which will reduce all the waste to small pieces suitable for composting or mulching. Electrically powered equipment is cheaper but generally less powerful and less manoeuvrable; petrol-driven machines tend to be heavier but are more mobile and therefore more suitable for larger gardens.

You also need to exercise discretion if you opt to burn prunings. Bonfires should be lit at dusk and must be supervised at all times. Check with your local council to see if there are any legal restrictions on bonfires in your area.

PRUNING EQUIPMENT

Most gardeners can prune the majority of their plants with just a pruning saw and a pair of secateurs (pruners), but the larger the garden and the more varied the jobs, the larger the collection of tools you will need. It is well worth investing, for example, in a long-arm chainsaw or hedge trimmer if you have tall hedges or trees that need tackling.

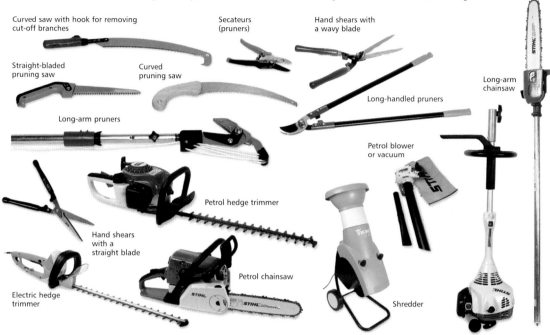

Curved saw with hook for removing cut-off branches

Straight-bladed pruning saw

Curved pruning saw

Secateurs (pruners)

Hand shears with a wavy blade

Long-arm chainsaw

Long-handled pruners

Long-arm pruners

Petrol blower or vacuum

Petrol hedge trimmer

Hand shears with a straight blade

Electric hedge trimmer

Petrol chainsaw

Shredder

Safety

Observing safety precautions is very important if accidents are to be avoided. The operator should always be fully protected, with ear protectors, goggles, hard hats, gloves and boots with steel toecaps all being very important. A hard hat that also includes a face shield and ear protectors is a very good idea.

Providing bystanders with safety equipment should not prove necessary, as they should be kept well out of harm's way at all times. When you are wearing ear protectors, someone may approach you undetected, so always keep a sharp eye out. If your hat takes a heavy knock from a branch, replace it, as the impact may have impaired its strength.

SAFETY EQUIPMENT

Safety gloves

Ear protectors

Visor and ear protectors

Hard hat

Eye protectors

Safety boots

To be an effective gardener, you need to garden safely. Always wear protective clothing to avoid serious injuries to your head, limbs, eyes, ears, hands and feet.

An introduction to pruning

Many people feel that, far from nurturing the tree, they are harming it by severing limbs and removing fruit before it has had time to ripen. In fact, the opposite is the case. Pruning can create well-proportioned, healthy trees and removing unripe fruit improves the size and quality of the remainder.

General principles

Nursery-grown trees are occasionally furnished with lower branches almost to the ground. Although these make the tree appear well-proportioned and attractive, and such trees can make good lawn specimens when young, they are seldom appropriate as garden trees because we usually want to grow something else below them. Nursery-grown standards should have clear trunks. Those used as a garden or shade tree will need to have about 2.4m (8ft) clearance on their trunks.

Street trees must be pruned so that they have at least 5m (16ft) clearance for pedestrians or traffic. On the other hand, a tree planted as a lawn specimen, focal point, grown to obscure an eyesore or act as a windbreak may have branches sweeping almost to the ground, and would be termed feathered.

The lateral branches contribute to the development of a sturdy, well-tapered trunk so it is important to leave some of these lateral branches in place, even though they may be pruned later. Removing the branches too early would restrict the trunk's development.

The spacing of branches, both around and up the trunk, should be encouraged from the start. Branches selected as permanent framework or scaffold branches must be evenly spaced along the trunk and should grow out spirally to produce a well-balanced crown.

It is important to prevent two main branches from originating from the same side of the trunk or almost directly on top of each other. These can be easily removed from a young tree, but if they have been allowed to develop they are best left alone, because removing large branches creates wounds that heal slowly and may make the tree more susceptible to disease.

In general, never remove more than one-quarter of the total leaf area of a tree during pruning. Overpruning can lead to the production of thin shoots from the wounds, known as epicormic or adventitious shoots. These have to be cut away before they develop or they will leave unsightly scars when they are eventually removed.

When to prune

The timing of pruning is a matter of much debate. In the past it was considered a winter job, often because there were fewer demands on the gardener's time than in spring and summer.

However, summer pruning has become more popular as it is now recognized that a tree can heal itself more quickly when it is actively

An attractive group of silver birches, *Betula pendula*, that might have benefited from a little more attention with initial training so that they grew more upright.

Unusual trees, such as this weeping cherry, need special attention or they will lose the quality that makes them such an attractive feature in the garden. Regular, careful thinning should achieve this.

growing and has more energy to protect itself. Another advantage of summer pruning is that you can see how much canopy cover has been removed.

Some trees, such as *Betula* (birch), *Acer* (maple) and *Juglans* (walnut), produce heavy sap flows in late winter and early spring as they begin to re-grow after the winter dormancy, so these are best pruned when the tree is in full leaf.

Trees belonging to *Rosaceae* (the rose family), such as apples, pears, plums and cherries (including ornamental forms), can be affected by a disease called silver leaf (see page 346), which infects wounds in late summer, so these trees are best pruned in early summer.

How to prune

The position of pruning cuts is crucial. On established trees where there is dead wood, a branch should be removed just beyond the branch collar, which is a swelling of the bark around the base of the branch where it joins the tree. The branch collar is

part of the trunk and not part of the branch, and it must remain intact. To achieve this, draw an imaginary line parallel to the trunk from the end of the branch bark ridge through the branch. This is where the branch would naturally heal if it

were removed. If the tree were growing in the wild and the branch died back, it would be at this point that the tree would sever its connection with the branch.

When we prune a tree, we should aim to follow these natural lines. Do not cut into or otherwise damage this area. Cutting too close to the trunk will breach the tree's natural defences and allow disease to spread.

When you are pruning larger branches, remove some of the weight of the branch before you make the final cut (see page 358). If you are training a branch or trying to change its direction it has to be cut back to a lateral branch or bud.

This may cause masses of new shoots to develop, which will, in turn, have to be reduced in number, but the process is essential if you want to redirect a young branch to train it in a different direction. Pruning early in the tree's life will result in small wounds that will heal fairly quickly.

The beauty of this *Pinus densiflora* (Japanese red pine) is shown to its best advantage as a neatly pruned and well-positioned lawn specimen.

Natural target pruning

This type of pruning involves locating the position of the branch collar. However, before removing the whole branch, it is important to remove part of it first, so that its weight does not cause the bark and branch tissue to tear past the pruning cut if the branch falls to the ground.

A fairly small branch can be simply cut to remove about three-quarters of its length in one or two goes. Branches thicker than about 2.5cm (1in) across should be tackled more carefully.

Begin by making a small cut on the underside of the branch. About 5cm (2in) away from the undercut (which is closer to the trunk) on the upper side of the branch, cut through from the top to remove the branch. Next, locate the branch bark ridge and imagine a point just in front of it. The next target is the lower point where the branch collar joins the branch, which will feel like a bulge just before the branch starts.

Imagine a line between the two: this is where the final cut is made. If either target is not obvious, cut 2.5cm (1in) beyond the branch bark ridge.

Codominant stems

Upright, columnar or fastigiate trees naturally have branches that grow at tight angles to the trunk. If two branches grow from the same point and are left to develop (become codominant), as the tree grows, bark becomes trapped in the angle between them.

So that a single dominant leader develops in the centre of the tree, other branches that might compete with the leader should be removed. Some species that develop a round-headed shape usually have a strong leader and should be allowed to develop naturally. However, some species develop double leaders, known as codominant stems, which can lead to structural weaknesses, so one of these stems should be removed while the tree is young.

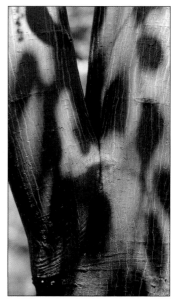

Codominant stems occur when two or more main stems (leaders) of about the same diameter grow from the same location on the main trunk of the tree. As the tree grows older, the stems remain similar in size without any single one becoming dominant, which can lead to structural weakness.

REMOVING A LARGE TREE BRANCH

1 Make a cut about 20–25cm (8–10in) out from where the final cut will be on the underside of the branch. Cut about a third of the way into the branch.

2 Make a cut about 10cm (4in) nearer the position of the final cut, cutting until the branch snaps. The initial undercut prevents the wood splitting or bark from stripping.

3 Position the saw for the last cut to avoid damaging the swollen area at the base of the branch. The cut will heal in a couple of seasons. No wound painting is necessary.

Codominant stems or branches originate from the same point on a tree and are usually about the same thickness. Although some codominant stems are naturally quite strong, others are not. When the bark of the trunk or the branch turns upwards, the trunk will have a strong union.

However, if the bark of the trunk turns inwards, the union will be weak. The closeness of the angle is not necessarily an indication of weakness, although in general the tighter the angle between the two branches, the weaker the union is likely to be.

If the union fails, the bark and underlying tissue will often tear along the entire length of the trunk unnoticed, because the downward-pointing bark hides the start of a large structural crack.

Before you remove a codominant stem, cut back the branch to remove the weight. Then make a 45 degree cut from the top of the branch bark ridge to the base of the codominant

HOW TO TRAIN A STANDARD BIRCH TREE

1 Most birch trees develop a natural shape without any intervention, so there is not much pruning required.

2 However, if there are any unwanted branches, as at the bottom of this particular tree, then they should be cleanly removed.

branch. Some trees might suffer additional die-back because the tree cannot compartmentalize in the same

way as it can with a normal branch, but wound tissue will develop under the cut and seal the wound.

Newly planted trees

The only pruning that should be carried out on a newly planted tree should be limited to correcting any urgent problems while the tree is still relatively young.

Dead, diseased or damaged branches should be removed, although if you have bought the tree from a reputable supplier this should not be necessary. Otherwise, formative pruning should be left until the subsequent years.

The temptation to reduce the crown to compensate for root loss should be avoided, because trees need their canopy and leaves to photosynthesize and the woody stems and branches are used to store energy, which the tree needs to grow.

This branch has been pruned too close to the branch collar. This may result in a disease being able to penetrate the tree's natural defences and cause serious problems.

Early removal of branches along the main trunk while a tree is young will result in a clear stem that will show little evidence of puning as the tree ages.

Establishing a sound structure

A good structure of main framework
branches is essential and should be
encouraged by formative pruning
while the tree is young. The goal
of formative pruning is to establish
a strong, clear trunk with sturdy,
well-spaced branches and a balanced
crown. The structural strength of
the branches depends on their
relative size, the angles at which
the branches grow and the spacing
between the limbs.

Some species, such as *Quercus robur*
(common oak), are comparatively
easy to train so that they have a
good crown and branch structure.
Other trees, however, including
fastigiate forms, such as *Populus nigra*
'Italica' (Lombardy poplar), have a
dense, upswept crown with many
tightly angled branches. Attempting
to create a well-balanced, open crown
on such a tree would be pointless.
With such columnar trees, formative
pruning should focus on removing
dead, crossing and structurally weak
branches while maintaining the tree's
natural shape and habit.

Good formative pruning has resulted in a well-cleared trunk, which shows off the distinctive silvery
bark for which this beautiful birch is valued.

PRUNING A MULTI-STEMMED TREE

YEAR ONE Cut through the trunk of a
suitable feathered tree at the height at
which you want the multiple stems to start.

YEAR TWO After a year, select the most
suitable stems in order to create a balanced
tree and remove the rest.

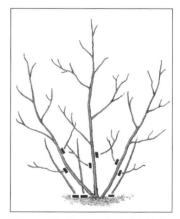

YEAR THREE Continue to train the individual
main stems by removing any dead wood or
branches that cross or rub against each other.

Pterocarya stenoptera grows as a suckering tree in the wild, a habit it retains in our gardens, but will still require some pruning.

Pruning multi-stemmed trees

Some trees naturally form multiple trunks and tend to look rather like overgrown shrubs. In fact, they are often regarded by gardeners as shrubs, rather than trees. The number of trunks can vary from just two or three stems to what amounts to a thicket.

The initial formative pruning required to create a multi-stemmed tree is relatively simple. If you have a young, single-stemmed tree, you just have to be bold and cut through the main stem just above ground level, or at whatever height you want the division of the multiple trunks to begin.

Once new growth appears from the base, select the required number (three or more) of shoots and remove all of the others. These remaining shoots will form the basis of your tree, so select the strongest growing ones to make a balanced tree. Continue to train these as you

would a tree with a single stem, removing diseased, dead and weak or crossing growth.

Not all trees will shoot from the base after such drastic action, but a surprising number will. You should be selective, as not all trees look very good with multiple stems, although those with highly ornamental bark usually do look attractive.

The best species for training by this method are: *Acer griseum* (paperbark maple); *Acer* x *conspicuum*; *Acer* 'White Tigress'; *Albizia* spp. (silk tree); *Betula* spp. (birch); *Embothrium coccineum* (Chilean fire bush); *Halesia* spp. (snowdrop tree); *Jacaranda mimosifolia*; *Lagerstroemia* spp.; *Platanus* spp. (plane); *Salix* spp. (willow); and *Stewartia* spp.

Multi-stemmed trees, such as this *Acer palmatum* (Japanese maple), grow less tall than single-trunked trees, and their bushy shape can make them an attractive feature.

Maintenance pruning

After the initial training, most trees need only a check-up once or twice a year. In many cases no work will actually be necessary, but if problems do arise, you need to know how to deal with them in good time.

The three Ds

A healthy tree is a far safer one – as well as a prettier one – so it is vital that you perform an annual survey of all the trees you have in your garden. This involves the three Ds – checking for diseased, damaged and dead wood. Any that is found should be cut out cleanly. It is a good idea to check at the end of the growing season, in autumn, and

again after the winter as strong winds and frost may have damaged the trees.

Fallen branches should have the snags cut off and any tears should be cleaned up with a sharp knife to remove loose wood. Any heavy branches that are to be removed should be cut off in sections to prevent splitting and tearing caused by the whole weight of a branch being removed in one go. There is no need to dress wounds, even those left by the removal of large branches.

Most trees at some point produce branches that cross others, creating congestion and often wounds where the bark of one rubs against that of another in the wind. Any such

Using secateurs is a quick method of removing suckers, but you must ensure that they are cut out where they are attached to the tree or they will simply grow back.

In gardens where space is limited or where there is close planting, regular pruning is required to control the size of a tree so that it can fill its alloted space and allow other plants to flourish around and below it.

DEALING WITH EPICORMIC SHOOTS

Any dead or dying branches should be clearly cut back to their point of origin, or a point where no damage is visible.

1 Some trees – lime (*Tilia*) in particular – produce what are known as water shoots or epicormic shoots on their trunks.

2 The best way of dealing with them is to rub them out with your fingers as soon as you see them.

crossing wood should be removed. If you are creating a branch-headed standard, then it is also a good idea to thin the timber in the centre of the tree so that air and light can circulate.

From time to time, it is likely that a tree will throw out some wayward growth: an odd stem will suddenly shoot off into space, spoiling the shape of the tree. These should be removed at some point within the shape of the tree. Similarly, if the tree is a variety with variegation or non-standard foliage, it may throw out reverted stems, with leaves that are plain green, and these stems should be removed.

Epicormic shoots and suckers
Some trees produce water (epicormic) shoots. These are shoots that appear around wounds where, for example, a branch has been removed or where a lawnmower has damaged the bark at the base of the trunk. Rub these epicormic shoots out at their base.

If the tree has been grafted, any shoots that appear from below the graft union should be removed, even

if they look as though they are in the ideal place, as these will be different from the rest of the tree.

Similarly, suckers often appear from below ground. These may come from a grafted rootstock or just as a natural suckering habit. Unless you want to develop a multi-stemmed tree, these should be removed right back to their point of origin. It may even be necessary to carefully dig back below soil level in order to get rid of them.

Controlling size
There is nothing more magnificent than a tree that has been allowed to grow to its full size. You have only to visit an arboretum to see how majestic they look. However, this is often not always possible in the average garden due to various considerations, but predominantly those of space and shadow.

In many cases, controlling the size of a tree is simply a question of removing a few side branches, but in other cases, it may mean reducing the height of the whole tree. One way of doing this is a technique

known as 'drop-crotching', a form of thinning used to reduce the size of large trees, which involves the removal of a main branch (or leader) by cutting it back to a large lateral branch. The original outline of the tree is kept the same but it is much reduced in size.

This should only be done once the tree has reached its full size but when the branches are still young, so that the shaping will not be too unsightly. On a large tree it might be best to leave this job to a professional arborist, who may undertake the reduction over two or more years.

Crown raising or lifting
Raising the crown of a tree is undertaken to allow clearance below the lower branches to allow other plants to grow beneath them, to enhance or expose a view, to allow more of the trunk to be seen, to allow vehicle or pedestrian access or to clear branches away from utilities.

The distance from top to bottom of the canopy should be at least twice the length of clear trunk that remains after pruning. For example, a 10m (33ft) tall tree should have branches on the top 7m (23ft), which would mean that the maximum height to which the crown should be raised would be 3m (10ft).

Crown raising or lifting can involve the total removal of a branch to lift the canopy. Sometimes it is done more subtly by removing some of the lateral growth, lightening the weight, which will naturally lift the branch. A mixture of branch lifting and removal is usually required. The process can be undertaken in summer or winter.

Crown thinning

Mainly used on broadly spreading established trees, crown thinning allows greater light to penetrate through the canopy, which is particularly useful if you want the light to be directed towards any shrubs or perennial plants growing beneath the tree.

The aim is to lighten the interior of the branch structure by removing smaller branches, but to avoid overpruning by never removing more than one-quarter of the total crown area. Overpruning will cause stress and lead to the excessive growth of epicormic shoots, which is the way a tree forces dormant buds to grow in order to increase its leaf area.

To avoid stressing the tree, crown thinning should be carried out over several years. During the process, any codominant stems with weak connections should be removed, allowing dominance to return to the remaining stem. Structural problems, such as weak-growing, diseased or rubbing branches, can be rectified at the same time, and all pruning should be to a branch collar or ridge.

Crown thinning is best undertaken when the tree is in full leaf in mid- to late-summer, when the tree will heal quickly. It is seldom carried out on conifers, unless a tree has lost its main leader, when it is important to remove dominance from the other branches by training a new leader.

Crown reduction

When a tree is losing vigour because of old age and the canopy is beginning to die back, the dead ends of branches

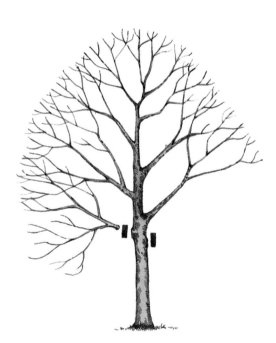

CROWN RAISING More light can be obtained below a tree by removing some of the lower branches so that the light from above is able to shine through and down the canopy.

CROWN THINNING An alternative method is to thin out some of the branches from the crown area so that dappled light is able to filter its way down through the canopy of the tree.

can be seen projecting above the leafy canopy, which is sometimes known as stag heading. In such cases, or if a tree has simply grown too large, crown reduction may be necessary.

Crown reduction is also called 'drop-crotching' because the branches are pruned back to a fork in the branch – a crotch – further back down the stem so that its overall length is reduced. The end result should look natural, and the canopy a pleasing shape but smaller in height and spread.

Crown reduction is a long process and requires considerable skill. As with other methods of pruning established trees, the total area of removed foliage and branches should not exceed one-quarter of the total area of the canopy. Crown reduction is best carried out in summer, although on old trees it is often done in winter as it is easier to see the outline of the branches.

Topping

This is a method of reducing the overall height of a tree by about one-quarter. It is mostly used to clear branches away from power lines, but it can be carried out in the garden to keep a tree smaller.

It is an aggressive type of pruning that severely stresses the tree and causes epicormic growth, so it should only be done when absolutely necessary. The multitude of pruning cuts and the fact that a lot of foliage is removed often make the tree susceptible to disease.

Topping is considerably more damaging than pollarding because it is conducted less frequently, and problems occur as the epicormic branches develop, since they are not connected as securely as naturally formed branches.

The delightful weeping habit of a weeping willow has been delicately pruned here to provide a view and frame the seat that has been positioned around the trunk.

Ageing trees

Trees are capable of outliving humans by centuries. Indeed, some English yews are estimated to be as much as 4,000 years old, their presence spanning many ages of time and history. The potential lifespan of a tree varies greatly. With oaks, it can be several hundred years, while in the case of birches, 30 years is about the average age.

However, there are a few drawbacks associated with trees of a great age. One is the development of 'stag's head', a problem seen in various trees, particularly oaks. Some of the branches die, leaving them bare and stripped of bark – supposedly resembling antlers.

In some cases, this makes the tree look attractively aged, while in others it will simply look diseased and unsightly. Although the tree is usually very healthy, these branches can be removed to return the tree to its normal appearance.

Another problem is that the branches may start to sag and fall away. A similar and more frequent occurrence is when the trunks of multi-stemmed trees start to fall apart. These susceptible branches can be braced if the tree is an important one. This is best left to the professionals, as an inadequately braced tree may fall at a later date, damaging the tree and possibly injuring passers-by.

Felling small trees

Trees unfortunately need to be felled from time to time, whether because they are growing in the wrong place – such as too near a building – or because they are dying. For large, well-established trees it is usually best left to the experts, but some amateur gardeners will be able to cope with felling small trees.

Assessing the task

Generally, felling trees is a job for the expert. Even if the way is clear in the garden, it is still a skilled job to get the tree to drop exactly where required, and if it is growing among other trees or shrubs, or stands near fences or buildings, it may need to be taken down branch by branch, which involves quite a lot of clambering around in the tree.

Apart from the skills this requires, there is also the question of equipment. Not many gardeners have chainsaws capable of dealing with a tree and, although you can hire them, they are tools that have to be handled with caution and expertise.

Professional tree surgeons specialize in doing this type of work and they should know precisely how to get the tree down without damaging the property or themselves. There is also the question of what you will do with the wood afterwards, whereas tree surgeons will dispose of it for you. If they shred the wood and leaves, you could ask them to leave it for you to turn into compost or to use as a mulch.

What can you tackle?

If you feel sufficiently confident, you may be able to tackle a small tree, especially a multi-stemmed one that is not too tall or heavy, yourself. Before cutting, ensure that the ground is clear and that you have an exit plan for a quick getaway if things should go wrong. It is important that you establish the lean of the tree to ensure that it falls where you want it to. Trees are large, heavy objects, especially when horizontal, so take care that you have enough space.

For a clear fell, cut a notch on the side in the direction you want the tree to fall and then cut through from the other side level with this notch. The tree will start to topple in the right direction just before the trunk is cut through. Once it is down, dig up the remaining stump. This is a tough job.

Employing professional arborists

Always ensure that you are employing people who have been properly trained and belong to a professional association. It is also important to check that they are fully insured. Avoid using anyone who knocks on your door to offer to chop trees down as such people are rarely skilled enough to do the job properly and, if anything goes wrong, you could be faced with a very large compensation bill.

One tree has fallen into another and it will be a difficult job, involving climbing into the tree canopy, to get it down safely.

FELLING A SMALL TREE

1 Small trees, such as this birch, that are situated in a clear space may well be within the capabilities of most gardeners, but do not tackle the job if you have any doubts at all.

2 Start by making a sloping cut at 45 degrees on the side of the tree that is facing the direction in which you want it to fall. Saw into the tree by between a quarter and one-third.

3 Follow this initial cut with a horizontal cut just below it, so that the two cuts eventually meet, cutting out a wedge in the side of the trunk.

4 Remove the wedge from the trunk. This should ensure that when the tree is cut through, it will fall on the side where you have cut the wedge.

5 Start sawing on the other side of the tree opposite the horizontal cut. As the saw nears the removed wedge of wood, the tree will begin to fall forward.

6 Step back quickly as the tree falls, just in case it springs back as it hits the ground. Remove the remaining stump or cut it flush to the ground and leave it there to rot.

Renovation pruning

If you take over an old garden when you buy a new house, you may well find that any older trees or those that have been neglected for many years will require renovation pruning.

When to renovate?

Trees take a long time to grow to maturity and will leave a large gap if removed. If at all possible, it is best to try and bring them back to their former glory.

There may also be preservation orders on the trees, so it might be illegal to remove or prune them without permission. It could even be illegal to carry out major renovation work without permission, so it is always best to check with local authorities before you begin work on an old tree.

Pruning steps

Your aim with neglected trees is to turn back the clock and perform all the tasks that should have been carried out in previous years. The best time to rejuvenate is in the late autumn or early winter.

Tree renovation times

Mid- to late winter (before growth starts)
Acer spp. (maple)
Aesculus spp. (horse chestnut)
Betula spp. (birch)
Conifers
Juglans spp. (walnut)
Salix spp. (willow)

Any season, apart from spring
Carpinus (hornbeam)
Fagus spp. (beech)
Quercus spp. (oak)
Tilia spp. (lime)

Early summer
Cornus spp. (dogwood)
Ornamental plums and cherries

RENOVATING AN OVERGROWN TREE

1 Some trees, such as this contorted hazel, can become overgrown and need to be carefully renovated to bring back their shape and interest.

2 Start the renovation by removing all the dead and damaged wood. This will allow you to see what remains much more clearly.

3 Thin out some of the branches in order to remove the congestion, especially towards the middle of the tree. Remove old and weak growths first.

4 The dead stub reveals how poor pruning can cause die-back, as the previous cut was made too high. Cut back tightly, as shown here.

Start, as always, by removing any dead, diseased and damaged wood. This should remove quite a bit of material and allow you to begin to see the structure of a tree.

Next, remove any water or epicormic shoots along with any weak growths, especially those that have developed in the centre of the tree. Where branches cross over or rub, cut them out. The tree should now begin to show its true shape.

Step back and examine the tree closely to determine whether there is any overcrowding and whether any other branches require removal.

Overgrown trees, like this *Malus* (crab apple), will inevitably contain a lot of dead or damaged wood. This should be one of the first things to be removed during renovation pruning as it will allow you to assess the extent to which further pruning is required.

Any crossed and rubbing branches should also be carefully removed during renovation pruning. Use a proper pruning saw to cut thicker branches and wear gloves and suitable clothing.

Also, check if the previous owner has merely pruned the outside of the tree, removing the new extension growth on the tips of the branches, so that it has thickened up around the perimeter, looking rather hedge-like. You will have to reduce and thin this growth drastically to bring the tree back to something resembling a normal appearance.

Not all trees like to be pruned hard all in one go. In some cases, it can kill them. It is usually better to prune them over a number of years, taking out just a bit at a time. This means that the tree will look untidy over this period, but it should benefit by your patience.

Aftercare

Renovation is a drastic treatment for any tree, so ensure that it is fed and kept well watered during any dry spells the following summer so that it can recover properly. Mulching will help to preserve the moisure in the soil around the tree roots, where it is most needed.

Over time, weeping trees can develop a congested habit, as shown by the crown of this tree. Thinning out and formative pruning should be carried out in winter.

Pollarding and coppicing

The traditional techniques of pollarding and coppicing have been of value, both economically and aesthetically, for many centuries. While less common now as a means of harvesting wood, both are still used to control the size and shape of trees.

Landscaping and conservation

Today, pollarding and coppicing have largely dropped out of use as a rural industry, and in the countryside are mainly done for landscaping and conservation reasons. However, in urban areas, trees often require pollarding to prevent them from outgrowing their allotted space, casting shade and obstructing utility wires, cables and street lighting.

Pollards that have not been cut for many years will have top-heavy crowns and re-pollarding them should only be done by experts. Unfortunately, a pollarded tree looks rather ugly in a garden, but the work may be necessary in order to avoid the possibility of bad weather or structural weakness causing branches to fall.

Pollarding

This technique involves cutting back the heads of main branches, or cutting off all the branches to leave only the main stem. This results in a profusion of new shoots being produced at the ends of the framework branches, or from the top of the trunks, the following year. Every three to four years these shoots are removed back to exactly the same points.

Pollarding has been undertaken for many centuries to manipulate the shape and height of trees, and it is a successful way of controlling a tree's height and spread, because the tree becomes accustomed to having its foliage removed regularly.

The technique was also often practised in order to produce repeated crops of small-sized wood growing out of reach of hungry deer and livestock. The wood produced could be used in a number of ways – oaks and sweet chestnuts were popular choices for contstruction and firewood – and the shoots and foliage were cut for additional animal fodder.

Willows are often pollarded not only to keep them contained, but also to show off their vibrant, beautiful and colourful young stems.

This tree has been regularly pollarded; the branches are rising from the top of the trunk.

POLLARDING A TREE

1 Remove all the branches, using either a pair of strong long-handled pruners or a saw. At this stage, it doesn't matter if some of the stubs are a bit long.

2 Tidy up the pruned cuts by sawing through the base of each of the branches. The new shoots will eventually appear around the edge of these cuts.

Pollarding prolongs a tree's life and, if carried out regularly, pollarded trees can survive for centuries.

Coppicing

This is the ancient art of cutting back all the main shoots of a multi-stemmed tree almost to ground level to promote vigorous regrowth and provide a sustainable supply of timber. These then regenerate and another set of main shoots develops, only for these to be removed as well.

Trees and shrubs that are cut down this way can produce shoots that grow over 30cm (12in) in a week, and a coppiced tree may live many times longer than if the tree had not been coppiced.

For example, willow is often coppiced annually, to produce thin, flexible stems that are used for weaving – in the past these were in great demand for making baskets and fencing, and these skills are still practised. To obtain large, strong poles, *Castanea sativa* (sweet chestnut) can be coppiced on a 14-year cycle.

Many broad-leaved trees, particularly *Corylus* (hazel), can be cut right down to the stump. In the case of hazel, the poles are harvested approximately every eight years.

For the gardener, it can be an interesting experience growing the poles, which have many uses in the garden, depending on the size at which they are cut. Other trees, such as *Catalpa* (bean tree) and *Paulownia* (coffin tree), can be coppiced annually to produce large, lustrous leaves.

How to coppice

Grow the tree as a multi-stemmed form. Once the stems have reached the required size, cut them off near to the base with a saw, between late winter and early spring. The cuts should be slightly sloped to allow rainwater to run off.

In subsequent years, new shoots will appear and the cycle of growth and coppicing can be repeated. Prune out the weakest shoots to ensure only the strongest grow, and to allow equal spacing between the shoots.

Hazel can be coppiced back to a low framework of branches. This will promote the growth of many straight stems, which can be cut regularly.

Pruning conifers

Conifers are very popular trees, forming an architectural backbone to the garden that varies little from season to season. They are also relatively easy to grow, require little attention once they have been planted and their foliage appears in myriad colours.

Different treatment

Unfortunately, many gardeners do not realize that conifers must be treated differently to their deciduous relatives. As a result, it is not unusual to see a row of dead coniferous trees in a garden where the owner has decided that the trees have grown too large and so has lopped off half of each tree – only to discover that the foliage does not grow back.

Cutting into old wood

Most conifers are reluctant to put out new shoots from old wood, so only cut back into the new growth. Cutting back into the older wood creates a bald patch, and removing too much can kill the tree.

If you want to control the height, either ensure that the tree you buy will reach only to the height you want, or be prepared to clip in once or twice a year, removing only some of the new growth.

How to prune

Most conifers produce resinous sap that bleeds freely from the stems if they are cut while the tree is in active growth. For this reason, pruning is best carried out from autumn to midwinter.

If you need to limit the size of the tree, clip it lightly every year, keeping the natural shape as far as possible. This can be quite effective, but it takes some skill to achieve a really natural look. As always, any dead, dying or diseased wood should be cut out, preferably as far back as possible. You should also remove any

TRAINING A YOUNG CONIFER

Most conifers are better left to grow unchecked, but you can alter their shape successfully if you begin when they are young and avoid cutting into old wood.

YEAR ONE To create a bare trunk, remove the bottom branches, as well as any crossing or dead branches.

SUBSEQUENT YEARS Continue to remove any crossing or dead branches, as well as any new growth low down on the trunk.

Young conifers rarely need any training, and will form a pleasing shape if they are allowed to grow naturally.

odd growths that stick out beyond the shape required. Do not leave these for too long, or they may grow too vigorously and leave a hole where you removed them.

Similarly, on variegated forms, there may be some reversion to plain green leaves and this needs to be removed or it will gradually outgrow the variegation.

Conifers that have a strong vertical habit display a characteristic known as central leader dominance. A single stem, ending in a terminal bud, grows upwards and thickens to form a solid trunk. Sometimes, as a result of damage, two leaders form. It is essential to remove one or the tree will not develop its characteristic shape and the fork of the trunk will be a weak point that is prone to further damage.

Pruning conifers

Most conifers will stand a little light pruning as long as you restrict yourself to the new growth. In general, this will apply only if you are cutting the tree to a shape, as in topiary, or creating a hedge. If done every year, this will help to restrict the size. However, once a conifer has reached maturity, there is little that can be done to reduce its size, except for the following examples:

Cephalotaxus	Sequoia
Cryptomeria	Taxus
Cunninghamia	Torreya

These will tolerate being cut back into old wood. One of the most common garden conifers, the Lawson cypress (Chamaecyparis lawsoniana), will not break from old wood, so do not attempt to prune it except for a light trim to retain its size and shape. Young conifers can have their side shoots pinched out to produce bushier growth and a denser branching habit.

PRUNING TECHNIQUES FOR CONIFERS

1 If you need to prune a conifer, cut the shoots well back into the tree, so they don't show.

2 Dead wood spoils the appearance of the conifer, so remove it and wait for new growth to fill in the gaps.

3 Conifers do not need much pruning, but new growth can be clipped back to restrict the size of the tree. Do not cut into old wood.

4 If you shear the conifer, you will cut some of its leaves in half. Instead, pinch out the growing tips to restrict growth.

Tying in

As tight-growing trees get old and large, snow and sometimes wind can pull a branch out of place so that it sticks out sideways. This is a problem for shaped trees that have several main stems or near-vertical branches. If removed, these will leave a large gap that is unlikely to be refilled with new shoots. The only solution is to pull them back into position and tie them in place.

If large branches are involved, you may need professional help. If the tree is distorted badly, it may be advisable to start again with a new tree. A conifer in such a poor state is very difficult to renovate and can look very ugly if left as it is. It is also common practice to wire hoops around the branches to encourage a more conical shape. These are periodically removed and replaced if the wire starts to damage the branches.

Pruning palms

Palm trees require little pruning
except for the cosmetic removal
of old leaves when they die.
Additional cosmetic work can be
undertaken to remove the fibrous
material that builds up on trunks.

Smart palms

In an attempt to make your palm
tree look smart at all times, you
could be in danger of over-pruning,
which could weaken or even kill it.
Just like other trees, palms need
an adequate number of fronds to
process enough energy to develop
and flower. As this cycle goes on, the
older fronds die off naturally. At this
point they can be safely removed
from the tree to tidy it up.

Many people mistakenly believe
that palms should be pruned in
order to reduce the danger of
damage by strong winds. In fact, the
flexible leaves and trunks, and low
wind-resistance, of palms make them
nearly storm-proof. Despite this, in
many coastal areas it is common
practice to remove all but the top
tier of leaves each year just before
the hurricane season – the technique
is known as hurricane pruning.
Though unneccessary, the practice
does not seriously harm the trees as
long as enough green leaves are left
each time it is carried out.

Buta capitata (Pindo or jelly palm) is grown for its architectural arching branches. Like most
palms, it requires little pruning apart from the removal of spent flower trusses and dead leaves.

Pruning palms

The older, dying fronds should be
pruned off close to the base of the
stem, but care should be taken to
ensure that the main trunk and crown
are not damaged. A short section of
the leaf stalk should be left intact
and allowed to fall naturally or
removed the following year.

Removal of dead leaves can be
undertaken at any time of the year,
although it is best done during late
spring, once the palm tree is actively

growing, so that any wounds can
heal quickly. In warmer climates,
where the risk of cross-infection
from diseases spreading from
pruning cuts is higher, equipment
should be sterilized when moving
from tree to tree. A good-quality
household disinfectant can be used
to clean any pruning equipment.

However, leaving the dead leaves
presents no health risk to the palm
as in their natural habitats the dead
fronds would remain attached and

develop into dead 'skirts' that may
extend down the trunk of the palm
and can provide useful habitats for
insects and birds. However, this is
often considered unsightly and an
uncluttered stem with the dead
leaves removed is the usual option.

Green leaves can be removed, but
care should be taken not to rip or
tear off the leaves as this will scar
the trunk and increase the risk of
infection. If you do need to remove
a green frond, don't remove those

Palm pest problems

There are a number of caterpillars, bark boring beetles and weevils that affect palm trees and most of these cause physical damage to the leaves or stems which can make them look unsightly, but will seldom kill the palm tree.

However, there are also a number of soil-borne organisms, such as bud rot, which kills the crown of the palm, and fusarium wilt, which causes yellowing and eventual death of the fronds, and once infected there is no real cure.

Ganoderma butt root is a disease that rots the base of palms, causes the stem to die, makes the palm structurally unsound, and rots out the trunk. Finally, lethal yellowing disease causes the palm fronds to turn yellow and droop, beginning on the lower leaves and spreading throughout the crown of the palm, and causes all the fronds to die.

Treatment is expensive as the disease is not fully understood although it is believed it is caused by a bacterium-like organism and spread by insects. Infected trees should be removed and destroyed to stop the spread.

only be superficial. However, if the root system freezes, the palm will not recover.

The roots will often tolerate temperatures several degrees cooler than the leaves, so even if the foliage dies there is still a chance that the palm will re-sprout when the temperatures warm in spring. Any damaged foliage should be trimmed before the emergence of new leaves in spring.

In subtropical and tropical climates, many of the problems associated with palms are caused by compacted nutrient-deficient soils that place the palm under stress and make it less likely to be able to ward off pests and diseases. For this reason, you should make every effort to provide the correct soil conditions for your particular palm. Soil aeration and foliar feeding may overcome short-term problems.

growing horizontally or upward. Remove only the downward-growing ones, as these would naturally be shed in the future.

Aftercare for palms

Although palms are relatively trouble-free landscape plants, they may succumb to a number of ailments. In cooler climates, winter damage on palms depends on the lowest temperature and the duration of cold. Cold damage appears first in the foliage and causes the leaves to turn brown and die. Although the foliage may die completely, as long as the root system and crown of the palm survives then the damage may

Bismarckia nobilis is a stunning tropical palm, and the ones shown here are excellent specimens, with clear trunks and balanced heads of leaves.

Pruning fruit trees

All fruit trees require pruning to ensure that they continue to produce fruit. Some require twice yearly pruning while others need considerably less.

Training and pruning cordons

Cordons have a single stem trained at an angle of 45 degrees. After planting at the correct angle, tie a bamboo cane behind the main stem and to the top wire. Prune side shoots to just above the third bud.

In the first summer, tie extension growth to the cane and prune back any new shoots from the main stem to above the third bud. Prune new shoots produced from the stubs of the side shoots produced the previous year to their first leaf.

Each winter afterwards, cut back the main stem's new growth to within 15cm (6in). Once the tree reaches the top of its support, cut any extension growth to the first bud.

The pole-grown apples above have been grown as vertical cordons. The bottoms of the trunks have been protected against rabbit attack with wire guards.

Each summer, prune new shoots produced from the stubs that were cut back the previous year to the first leaf.

Training and pruning fan trees

Fan-trained trees have up to ten equally spaced ribs radiating from the main stem. It is a good way of training fruit trees because it produces

These pears have been grown in a cordon against a trellis, which is a method suitable for small gardens. Cordons provide height, rather than the spread achieved with a fan.

a large number of fruit-bearing stems. Use five to seven parallel wires, about 30cm (12in) apart. Pull them taut and held 10–15cm (4–6in) away from the wall. The bottom wire should be about 45cm (18in) above ground-level. For a free-standing fan, the posts must be solidly set in the ground, 2–2.5m (6–8ft) apart.

PRUNING AN ESTABLISHED APPLE CORDON

1 Established cordon apples against a fence. They take up very little space and enable the gardener to grow several different varieties.

2 In the winter, prune back any new side shoots to one or two buds.

3 New growth on existing side shoots should also be cut back to one or two buds in the winter.

4 In summer, cut back the main leader once it has reached the top support. Do this every summer, cutting back to one or two buds.

5 In summer, you should also cut back any new shoots to two or three leaves.

6 Any new shoots on existing side shoots should be cut back to one leaf.

Buy a feathered tree that has two strong shoots just below the proposed position of the bottom wire. Cut off the leader just above the upper of these two. Tie the laterals to canes, then attach these to the wires at an angle of 40 degrees. Shorten the shoots to about 45cm (18in) to a bud on the underside. This will stimulate the production of side shoots later that year. Tie these in to new canes as they develop.

The top bud will produce a new leader for each of the main arms. Tie this in along the cane in the same direction. Cut out any unwanted shoots, keeping both sides balanced. Remove new growth from the main trunk. Cut back the tips of laterals on either side of the main stems.

Remove any growth that projects from the fan. Over the next three years, allow the fan to develop so that it branches more towards the periphery and covers the space evenly.

Training and pruning espaliers

Espalier trees have three or four horizontal tiers of branches trained along the supporting wires. Follow the method described for pruning fans, except that the main stem should be pruned back to just above the horizontal wire, and the side shoots should be trained along canes held at 45 degrees in their first year, then lowered to the horizontal wire in their second.

Each summer, all unwanted new shoots should be pruned to the first leaf and suitably placed new shoots should be tied in to the next pair of canes. Once the tree covers the support, cut back the extension growth of the main stem to one bud above the top wire and treat each branch following the technique described for a cordon.

TRAINING AN APPLE FAN

Fans, like most decorative forms of apple, need a lot of care and attention in order to prevent them from becoming overgrown and out of hand. An apple trained in this way will need attention both in the summer and in the winter.

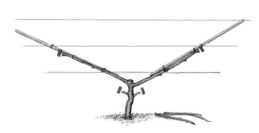

YEAR ONE, WINTER Start with a feathered tree which is planted in winter. Cut off the leader just below the bottom wire and tie in two laterals to canes attached to the wires at 40 degrees. Cut these back to about 45cm (18in). Shorten any other remaining laterals to a couple of buds.

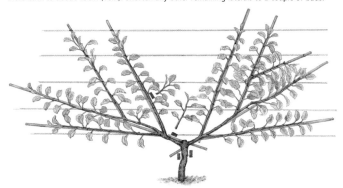

YEAR ONE, SUMMER In the following summer tie in the side shoots that develop on the laterals to form an even spread of branches, but remove any that crowd the space. Now remove any side shoots that you cut back in the winter from the main trunk.

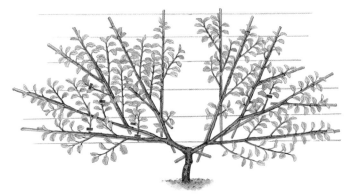

SUBSEQUENT YEARS, SUMMER Continue to tie in the developing side shoots so that a fan-like framework of branches is developed. Cut out their tips so that they continue to branch. Cut back any unwanted shoots to two or three leaves to create fruiting spurs.

Apple trees

As a general rule, apple trees are pruned to encourage new shoots that bear fruit and remove any surplus wood. However, if the tree is left unpruned, its growth will become congested. This in turn causes poorer fruit production because less light is able to enter the canopy, preventing the tree from bearing as many flowers as it should and stopping the fruit from ripening.

Pruning is usually carried out once the tree has become dormant during late autumn and winter. The aim is to achieve an open shape with a good framework of about five main branches. This will allow light into the canopy. In order to do this you will need to remove any weak, damaged, dead or diseased wood, and epicormic shoots.

What is the difference between espalier and cordon trees?

Cordons are single-stemmed trees that are planted at an angle of 45 degrees and supported by wirework. Any side branches are pruned away. Cordons crop earlier than most other forms and take up less space, allowing more varieties to grow.

Growing fruit trees as espaliers is a technique of training trees by pruning them to create formal, two-dimensional patterns with the branches of the tree. The technique was popular many centuries ago and was used to decorate walls. When trees are grown as an espalier against a sunny wall, they receive almost as much sunlight as a regular tree, despite being smaller. The wall will reflect the sunlight, as well as providing shelter and storing warmth from the sun. These factors allow espalier-grown fruit trees to succeed in cooler climates. They also allow the fruit to ripen more quickly.

With older trees, fruit quality and yield diminishes significantly so some quite heavy pruning will need to be carried out in order to increase the tree's productivity and get it back into shape.

If the tree has become too large for its space and casts too much shadow over the garden, you should cut back the top portion to the lateral branches.

Spur- and tip-bearers

Having achieved a sound, basic framework that allows adequate light to reach the canopy, attention now needs to be given to the rest of the tree. The method used depends on whether the tree is spur-bearing or tip-bearing.

Spur-bearing trees, which are the most common type of apple tree, bear most of their fruit on older wood. Tip-bearing trees, on the other hand, produce most of their fruit buds at the tips of slender young shoots that have grown during the previous summer.

For spur-bearing apple trees, remove any overly vigorous and unwanted wood, as well as any branches that are crossing or rubbing. The leaders of all the previous season's growth can then be reduced by about a quarter to one-third. If any of the spurs are overcrowded, remove the older and less productive wood.

For tip-bearing apple trees, you can either leave the young wood unpruned or just cut the tip back to the first strong bud. Take out the older shoots back to a young shoots to ensure renewal and continued fruiting. Having done this, carefully take out any crossing and rubbing branches, along with any branches that are too vigorous or that are misplaced.

Plums are ready for picking when they are slightly soft to the touch. You can usually tell by their colour, too. Once they are ripe they should be easy to remove from the tree.

Thinning the crop

Though it seems wasteful, it is necessary to reduce the fruit to one apple per cluster. This will actually result in a better crop, since it is seed production, rather than the juicy flesh, that takes most of the tree's energy – the fewer the fruits, the larger they will be. They will also receive better exposure to the sun This also applies to pear trees.

Pear trees

Generally, pear trees are more upright than apple trees, but the pruning techniques are very similar. It is usual to prune pear trees during the winter.

Once the tree is established, the tree will not grow in a particularly vigorous way, so pruning is restricted to just thinning the spurs. However, you should remove any over-vigorous and unwanted wood, along with any branches that cross or rub against each other.

If the leaders are over-long, reduce them by about a quarter to one-third of the previous season's growth. Check the spurs: any that are overcrowded should have their older and less productive wood removed.

Plum and cherry trees

Once the basic shape of the tree has been established, cherry and plum trees need little pruning apart from the removal of dead, diseased or congested growth as well as any weak or crossing wood.

Plum trees should be pruned during the summer in order to prevent them from getting silver leaf disease and canker. Sour cherries are produced on one-year-old wood and should be pruned after the fruit has been harvested. Cut back about one-third of the fruiting stems to the first new shoot lower down the stem.

Plum and sweet cherry trees produce most of their fruit at the base of one-year-old and older shoots. This means that they are not suitable for training as cordons or espaliers but can be trained as fans, bushes or pyramids.

After formative pruning of a fan-trained tree has established the framework, you need to ensure that there is a constant supply of new growth. In summer, cut back all shoots that have fruited to a new shoot lower down. Tie this in to the supporting cane and prune out any unwanted growth to maintain the shape.

Harvesting fruit and storing gluts

Pick the fruit as soon as it is ripe. You can pick plums when they are slightly under-ripe and store them in the refrigerator for a couple of weeks. Sweet cherries do not continue to mature after picking so do not harvest them until they are ready. Ripe fruit is best eaten straight away, although it will last a few days if kept somewhere cool. Gluts of fruit can be made into jams and preserves. Plums and sweet cherries can be frozen after they have been split to remove the stone (pit).

TRAINING A PLUM DWARF PYRAMID

Some varieties of plum lend themselves to being grown on a dwarfing stock and can be grown as dwarf pyramids. Check that you buy a suitable variety. These are particularly useful in a small garden where just a small quantity of plums is required.

Because of their small size it may be possible to grow several varieties of plum as pyramids in a small area.

YEAR ONE, WINTER Plant a feathered tree in winter. In early spring, cut out its leader at about 1.5m (5ft) from the ground. Cut out all the side shoots below about 45cm (18in) and then reduce all remaining laterals by about half.

YEAR ONE, SUMMER The following midsummer you will need to cut back the new growth on the main branches to about 20cm (8in) to an outward-facing bud. You should also cut back all the sub-laterals to around 15cm (6in).

YEAR TWO, SPRING In the second spring cut back the new growth made by the leader by about two-thirds. No other pruning is required at this time of the year.

ESTABLISHED PRUNING, SUMMER The tree may be mature by the third or fourth spring. Once mature, cut back any vigorous growth to a few leaves in summer, and remove any dead, diseased or damaged wood and thin out any congested areas by taking out older wood.

Propagating trees

Most gardeners with an average-sized plot will have room for only a small number of trees, and will usually prefer to buy ready-grown trees rather than wait for them to grow from seeds or cuttings. Some people also choose to propagate trees simply because they find the process fascinating and rewarding in itself, though many varieties require specialist equipment.

Seed propagation is the easiest method of growing new trees, as long as you remember some basic rules and are prepared to accept that the seedling trees may not be identical to the parent tree, and might even be hybrids. Many tree seeds also require special treatment to help them overcome dormancy.

Propagating trees by asexual (or vegetative) 'cloning' methods such as cuttings, grafting or layering is the only sure way to guarantee that the offspring will be identical to their parents, as they will be clones. However, the more sophisticated the method, the more sophisticated the equipment and facilities required, and the more skill needed by the propagator.

Saving seeds is by far the easiest method of propagation as it requires little specialist equipment.

Propagating from seed

Growing trees from seeds at home is similar to growing any other garden plants. However, if you collect the seed yourself, the resulting plant may vary from the tree from which the seed came. Alternatively, you can buy seed, which is more likely to come true to type and match the parent tree. However, some commercial seed may have been collected from wild plants and will not necessarily come true, as many trees hybridize in the wild.

Collecting seed

For trees that will be grown outdoors it is sensible to obtain seed only from species that will grow in your garden. It would be pointless, for example, to collect tree seed in Hawaii and expect it to grow outside in Canada. Seed collected in the south of a temperate country might grow in the north, but the tree might come into leaf so early that it will be killed by spring frosts.

Collect seed from trees that are healthy and have the qualities you want, such as good leaf colour, attractive habit, hardiness and disease resistance. Many countries

Fleshy fruit would normally be eaten by birds and animals and digested, so you need to ensure that you reproduce similar conditions for them to germinate.

Tamarind pods grow up to 18cm (7in) long and contain a soft, edible pulp.

do not permit the importation of unlicensed plant material, so check before you collect seeds abroad, or you may lose them at customs.

Most seed should be collected when it is ripe. Some seed, such as *Acer*, has a natural inhibitor to prevent it from germinating too soon, so collect it before it is fully ripe. If you are collecting from conifers spread out the unopened cones on a sheet of paper in a well-ventilated, warm room until the scales open. Shake the cones to release the seed. Some pines, such as *Pinus coulteri* (big-cone pine), require high temperatures to release the seeds, and should be placed near a fire to open.

The seeds contained within fleshy fruits, such as those of *Sorbus* (mountain ash) and *Crataegus* (hawthorn), are released by mashing the fruit to a pulp, then floating the remains in water to separate the seeds from the pulp. These seeds often require a period of fermentation to mimic the passage through a bird's

digestive system before they will germinate, so keep them in warm water for a few days.

Dry fruit, such as that from *Betula* (birch), *Catalpa* (bean tree) and *Stewartia*, can be spread thinly on a sheet of paper in a warm, well-ventilated room. The fruit will split and the seeds can be collected.

Seed dormancy

Without a proper period of dormancy, seeds might germinate in the middle of winter and the young plants would be killed by cold. The length and type of dormancy varies from species to species. Ripened seed of *Ulmus* spp. (elm), *Populus* spp. (poplar) and *Pinus sylvestris* (Scots pine) shows little dormancy and germinates easily. The seed of *Acer* spp. (maple), *Fraxinus* spp. (ash), *Liquidambar* and *Sorbus* (mountain ash) requires a cold period (similar in duration and temperature to winter) followed by a period of warmth (to imitate spring) to germinate.

EXTRACTING SEED FROM FLESHY BERRIES

1 Cut a spray of ripe berries from the tree (shown here are rowan berries) and squash individual fruits to release the seed.

2 Wash the seed in lukewarm water, rubbing it gently, and leave in a warm place to soak for a few days.

3 Dry the seed on an absorbent paper towel. The seed is then ready for sowing in pots or seed trays.

Seed dormancy

When tree seed does not readily germinate following ripening, it is probably waiting for the right treatment to 'break' its dormancy. Dormancy is the mechanism that prevents seed from germinating until the conditions are right for the young tree to grow successfully.

The dormancy of many species can be overcome by sowing the seed in containers, placing them outside and letting nature run its course. Seed bought in spring should be placed in some compost (soil mix) in a plastic bag and stored in a refrigerator for six weeks, before being moved to a warm place, such as an airing cupboard. The seed can then be sown into a container and allowed to germinate.

Sow seed thinly on the surface of a container filled with a suitable growing medium such as seed compost (soil mix). Do not cover fine seed. Larger seed should be covered by about 2.5cm (1in) of sieved compost. Carefully label the containers before placing them in a greenhouse or cold frame or on a sunny window ledge.

After the seed has germinated and when two true leaves have grown (palms are monocots and have just one true leaf), the seedlings can be carefully transplanted to larger containers and grown on.

SOWING SEED

1 Prepare pots or seed trays of seed compost (soil mix). Water the compost well and allow the water to drain. The compost should be moist but not sodden. Lightly place the seed on the surface.

2 Gently press the seed into the compost. The seed should be covered to its own depth with compost. Very fine seeds should be surface sown.

3 Lightly topdress the container with grit and place in a cold frame or in a cool, sheltered spot outdoors.

Propagating from cuttings

Trees are generally more difficult than shrubs to grow from cuttings because the wood is older and less likely to root without special facilities and equipment. Despite this, there are some species that can be propagated successfully from stem tip, softwood and hardwood cuttings.

Stem tip cuttings

Propagation by cutting, a vegetative process, differs from growing from seed because the cuttings will produce plants that are identical to the parent plants. Some species of tree, such as *Quercus* spp. (oak), are difficult to root from cuttings, but conifers, *Ilex* spp. (holly) and *Catalpa* spp. (bean tree) are generally easier, as are some maples.

Stem tip cuttings are the most widely used method of propagation. Softwood cuttings of deciduous trees should be collected in early summer and will require moist,

humid conditions, such as those found in a propagator, to prevent them from wilting before they root. Conifers are propagated from more ripened wood, so take material for cuttings in late autumn.

Taking softwood cuttings

Cut a terminal tip about 15cm (6in) long, cutting just below a leaf node, and remove the lower leaves so that there are leaves on the top two-thirds of the cutting. Remove any flowerbuds or seedpods.

Fill a container with a suitable rooting medium, such as equal quantities of peat and sand, peat and perlite, or coir and perlite. Dip the base of the cutting in a hormone rooting compound, shaking off the excess, use a stick or dibber to make a hole in the compost (soil mix) and insert the cutting so that it stands up. Make sure that the leaves do not touch the compost. Cut large leaves in half to reduce water loss.

Laurus nobilis (bay) is suitable for propagation by stem tip cutting, which should be taken from the parent tree in spring.

Rooting hormones

You can increase your chances of success with most stem cuttings, particularly those that are reluctant to root, by using a rooting hormone. When applied to the cut surface at the base of the cutting, the hormone encourages root formation and increases the speed of rooting. Rooting hormones are usually formulated as powders, but you may also come across liquids and gels.

To avoid contaminating the hormone, tip a small amount into a saucer. Dip the cutting's cut end into the hormone, shaking off excess if you use powder, and insert into the compost (soil mix). After treating the batch of cuttings, discard any powder that is left over in the saucer. Rooting hormone deteriorates rapidly, so buy fresh stock every year to make sure of its effectiveness.

Holly are easier to root from semi-ripe stem cuttings than many other species of tree.

TAKING TIP CUTTINGS OF EVERGREEN AND DECIDUOUS TREES

1 Take cuttings from the tree you want to propagate, just above a leaf joint. *Laurus nobilis* (bay) is shown here.

2 Trim each cutting at the base below a leaf joint. The cutting should be about 10–15cm (4–6in) long.

3 Remove the lower leaves to expose a clear length of stem.

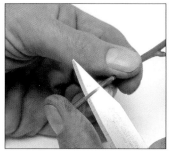

4 On evergreen trees, to accelerate rooting, pare away a sliver of bark 2.5cm (1in) long at the base of the cutting. Dip in rooting hormone.

5 Insert the cutting into a pot of compost (soil mix) using a dibber to make the hole. Label clearly.

6 Firm in the cutting and water well. Place in a cold frame or in a sheltered outdoor spot, ensuring that the cutting is kept humid.

Keep the cuttings moist at all times by covering the container with a polythene bag or placing it in a propagator and misting. Spraying with a fungicide will reduce the risk of mould. Any dead leaves should be removed quickly.

Check the cuttings periodically for signs of roots growing out of the bottom of the container, but remove them only when fibrous feeder roots are evident, potting them on into a proprietary potting compost. Don't forget to label the pots.

When you come to plant the cuttings outside, remember that they have been kept in a very humid environment and so will require careful acclimatization.

Trees such as this alder can be propagated from seed, soft tip cutting, hardwood cutting or from suckers.

Propagating from hardwood cuttings

At the end of the growing season, after the leaves have fallen off the trees and the current year's growth has fully ripened, hardwood cuttings can be taken. Unlike other methods, hardwood cuttings require no special facilities.

When to take cuttings

Many deciduous trees are easily propagated from hardwood cuttings, which are taken when the tree is fully dormant and showing no obvious signs of active growth. The wood for hardwood cuttings is firm and does not bend easily. Trees propagated this way include *Cornus* (dogwood), *Salix* (willow) and *Populus* (poplar). Most will root successfully in the open ground.

Rooting occurs when the cut surface successfully undergoes a period of callusing over the winter. This then enables the roots to appear in the spring. By altering the planting depth of the cuttings, you can control whether a single-stemmed or multi-stemmed tree is produced.

Propagating from tree suckers

Some trees naturally produce numerous shoots that form thickets, which are called suckers. These can be separated from the parent tree by severing the roots around the sucker. Keep the plant roots moist until you are ready to plant them up. This should be done following the usual planting procedures.

Trees that produce suckers suitable for propagation include: *Populus tremula* (aspen); *Alnus* (alder); *Cornus sanguinea* (dogwood); *Ligustrum lucidum* (glossy privet); *Populus canescens* (grey poplar); *Pyrus communis* (wild pear); and *Ulmus* spp. (elms).

Types of cuttings

The three types of hardwood cuttings are straight, mallet and heel. A straight cutting is the technique most commonly used. Mallet and heel cuttings are used for plants that might otherwise be more difficult to root, such as some deciduous conifers like *Larix* spp. (larch).

For the heel cutting, a small section of older wood is included at the base of the cutting. This is because the plant produces more hormones at this point, so including it as part of the cutting means that the propagation is more likely to be successful.

For the mallet cutting, an entire section of older stem wood is included with the cutting.

How to take cuttings

To take the cuttings, cut lengths of the current season's growth, from a healthy, disease-free tree. Each stem will probably yield two or three cuttings, making this a very economical method of propagation.

Remove any flowers and flower buds when preparing cuttings so the cutting's energy can be directed towards producing new roots rather than flowers.

Hardwood cuttings will take up to a year to root. If a heavy frost lifts them, gently firm them in again, using your feet or hands. Once they have rooted, they can be grown on *in situ* for a further season or two before being transferred to their final positions in the garden.

Cornus (dogwood) is one of the easiest types of tree to propagate by hardwood cutting, and once they have rooted they will establish and grow quite quickly.

TAKING HARDWOOD CUTTINGS

1 Choose stems that are firm and of pencil thickness. The length of the cutting will depend on the plant, but about 15cm (6in) is appropriate for most. Make a cut straight across the stem, just below a node.

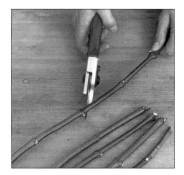

2 Using a pair of secateurs (pruners), make the second cut about 15cm (6in) above the first. Make the cut above a node, but this time at an angle so that you will know which is the top and which the bottom of the cutting.

3 Although a rooting hormone is not essential, it can increase the success rate, especially with plants that are difficult to root. Moisten the bases of the cuttings in water first, then shake off excess water.

4 Dip each cutting into the hormone powder, and tap or shake off any excess. Rooting hormones are also available in liquid and gel forms, in which case you do not need to dip the cuttings in water first.

5 Make a slit trench with a spade, a little shallower than the length of the cuttings. Choose an unobtrusive and fairly sheltered spot in the garden to leave the cuttings undisturbed for a year.

6 Sprinkle some grit or coarse sand in the base of the slit if the ground is poorly drained. This will help to prevent waterlogging around the cuttings. Firm lightly to make sure there are no air pockets.

7 Insert the cuttings 8–10cm (3–4in) apart, upright against the back of the slit, leaving about 2.5–5cm (1–2in) above the ground.

8 Firm the soil around the cuttings, to eliminate any pockets of air that would cause the cuttings to dry out.

9 Water the cuttings and label. Continue to water them in dry weather, especially during the spring and summer months.

Propagating by layering

Layering is one of the easiest of all methods of propagating trees, since it mimics the way some species naturally form roots on low-growing branches that touch the ground.

Simple layering

Depending on the species, simple layering can be carried out in autumn, early winter or spring. It involves burying a still-attached branch in soil so that the tip of the stem emerges above the ground. Roots form on the buried section,

and once this has happened the new plant can be detached from its parent and replanted elsewhere.

The process can be made more successful by nicking the underside of the stem to be buried and either pegging the stem down into a large container or into a hole filled with good-quality soil. Cover the portion of the layer that has been pegged to the soil with more soil and firm lightly before watering thoroughly. Water and weed as necessary during the following year, also checking that rooting is taking place. Water well in

dry periods. The method is suitable for plants that have flexible, low-growing stems, such as *Amelanchier* (juneberry), *Cercis*, *Corylus* (hazel), *Magnolia*, *Parrotia* (Persian ironwood) and *Thuja* (arborvitae).

Air-layering

The straightforward technique of air-layering is more suitable for trees with upright, inflexible stems. A branch is wounded and then surrounded in a moisture-retaining wrapper such as sphagnum moss, which is further surrounded in a

SIMPLE LAYERING

1 Dig over the soil where you want to make the layer, incorporating some well rotted manure or compost.

2 Select a low stem and trim off side shoots. Bend it down until it touches the ground. Make a small slit in the stem at that point.

3 Make a hole 10cm (4in) deep, and lay the stem on it sloping the stem towards the parent plant. Secure in place using a hook.

4 Alternatively, you can secure the stem using a rock, as nature would have done if left to her own devices.

5 Regularly check if the plant has rooted. When it has, cut it off from the parent plant using secateurs. Make a clean cut.

6 You should now have an independent plant with its own root system. Pot up and grow on until it is big enough to be planted out.

HOW TO AIR-LAYER

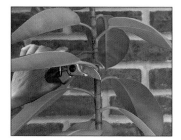

1 Air-layering can be used to propagate plants whose stems cannot easily be lowered to ground level. Using secateurs (pruners), remove a few leaves from the point on the stem where you want to make the layer.

2 Using a sharp knife, carefully make an upward slit in the stem, about 2.5cm (1in) long, below an old leaf joint. Do not cut more than halfway through the stem, otherwise it may break.

3 Cut a piece of plastic that is large enough to wrap around the stem of the plant, making a wide sleeve with space to add a thick layer of moss. Fix the bottom a short distance below the cut with a twist-tie or adhesive tape.

moisture barrier such as black plastic film. Rooting hormone is often applied to encourage the wounded region to grow roots.

A branch that gets sun will root better. Use only upright branches and select an area on the branch that will allow you to cut below the future rootball so the new feeder roots will be at the top of the container to be potted in.

Two methods of injuring the branch can be used. The first method consists of removing a 1–2.5cm (½–1in) ring of bark from the branch by making two circular cuts. After removing the bark, expose the wood to be sure that the cambium layer (the light green area immediately beneath the bark) is removed to prevent bark formation and allow the roots to develop.

With the second method, a long slanting upward cut is made about ½–1cm (¼–½in) through the stem and the incision is kept open by inserting a small chip of wood. This method is used on plants where the bark does not peel off easily. Plants that are commonly air-layered include Japanese maples, figs, magnolias, mangoes, olives, loquats and many conifers.

4 Brush or wipe a small amount of rooting hormone compound (powder or gel) into the wound to speed rooting. Pack a small amount of sphagnum moss into the wound to keep it open. Alternatively, a small piece of wood can be inserted to ensure the cut stays open.

Dusting the wound with a rooting hormone will assist rooting on some hard-to-root trees such as figs. After removing the bark or making the cut, enclose the injured area in a ball of moist sphagnum moss as soon as possible, to avoid contamination. Make sure you squeeze out excess moisture before applying the moss to the cut surface, otherwise the wood might rot.

When sufficient roots have grown from the wound, the stem from the parent plant should be removed below the wounded area. The stem can then be labelled, potted up and grown on.

5 Pack plenty of damp sphagnum moss around the stem to enclose the wound, then cover with the sheet of plastic and secure at the top with another twist-tie or tape. Make sure that the moss is kept moist, and carefully check for roots after a month or so. When well rooted, sever from the parent to pot up.

Japanese maples are difficult to propagate from cuttings, but they can be produced by air-layering.

Propagation by grafting and budding

Some trees are too slow or too difficult to grow and establish when they are propagated from seed or cuttings. In these cases, they are propagated by grafting or budding. Both methods have their limitations and require specialized tools and techniques as well as an understanding of the aftercare needed.

Grafting technique

The technique that involves the uniting of two plants is called grafting. The plant to be propagated is called the scion, and it is grown on the rootstock of a compatible species, which is selected because it is readily available and more vigorous than the scion, or has some other quality, such as size or disease resistance, that the scion lacks. The scion material must be dormant, and the rootstock must be held back but ready for growth if the union is to be successful. The two plants being united must also be related: you cannot graft a *Morus* (mulberry tree) on a *Ficus* (fig tree), but you can graft *Acer platanoides* (Norway maple) on *A. rubrum* (red maple).

Budding technique

A form of grafting that is often used with fruit trees, budding involves inserting a well-developed bud from one tree under the bark of another.

The timing of both techniques is crucial, but they are rewarding methods. They can be carried out only at very specific times when weather conditions and the physiological stage of plant growth are both optimum. The timing depends on the species and the technique used.

Most selected varieties of *Sorbus aucuparia* (mountain ash) are winter grafted on to seedling grown rootstocks of *Sorbus* spp. However, in recent years budding has been more widely used.

Grafted trees are easily recognized by the grafting union near the base of the stem.

PROPAGATION BY BUDDING

1 Select good bud wood that is true to type and free from obvious damage from pests or diseases. If you are doing this in the summer, you must first remove the leaves.

2 Remove the bud from the stem using a very sharp knife. Cut out the bud with a thin shaving of the wood below the bark and leave a 'V' shape at the base.

3 Prepare the stock plant that you are going to graft on to by carefully cutting a notch from its stem that is exactly the same thickness as the bottom end of the chipped bud.

4 Place the bud into the notch, fitting the 'V'-shaped base into the notch at the base of the other cut snugly, with the cut edge of the bud wood in contact with the edge of the other notch.

What are chip- and T-budding?

Chip-budding, the technique shown above, is used to propagate woody plants such as *Sorbus*, *Malus* and *Prunus*, on a rootstock grown from seed or hardwood cuttings.

T-budding is often used for summer budding of apples, crab apples, dogwoods and pears. T-budding can only be carried out when the bark is able to 'slip'. This means that, when cut, the bark lifts off easily or peels off without tearing in one uniform layer from the underlying wood.

The exact time when this condition occurs depends on factors such as soil moisture, temperature and the time of year. A T-shaped cut is made and two flaps of bark are opened. The bud is then placed behind the flaps, trimmed off level with the top of the flaps, and secured with tape as for chip-budding.

5 Secure the graft firmly with grafting tape to ensure that the join does not dry out. The graft will usually take about 4–6 weeks in the summer, but winter grafting can take longer.

Landscaping with trees

Garden landscapes are multi-dimensional areas in which we experience the passing seasons and where we can take time out to enjoy the fragrances, colours, sounds, textures and visual stimulation offered by our garden plants, and especially trees.

Trees not only provide height and width, but they also impart a sense of scale. They are so versatile in their many different forms that they can be used in any style of garden. Whether you choose to create a formal or informal scheme, your viewing pleasure will be greatly enhanced by careful landscaping.

Garden trees also enclose areas, mark boundaries, reduce wind and create a microclimate to protect the plants growing beneath them. Carefully selected trees can significantly enhance the beauty of our gardens, which become an extension of our own homes and personalities.

Trees need to fit in with the overall design of a garden. For instance, an oddly placed palm in an English cottage garden will look ill-at-ease, but it can make a stunning focal point when it is sited among complementary plantings. A little pre-planning will help you to avoid costly errors, and this section shows you how.

In this garden surrounded by natural woodland, the trees blend seamlessly with the background, creating a stunning spectacle.

The art of landscaping

Trees are the structural building blocks of any landscape design, and their position and the function you want them to perform should be foremost when planning a garden.

Design principles

Whether you are embarking on a new garden design, or adding trees to an established garden, it is helpful to begin by considering four factors: simplicity, balance, proportion, and rhythm and line.

Simplicity means using the same or similar tree species consistently throughout a design to create cohesion. The planting should follow a straight or slightly curved line, avoiding complex shapes or patterns.

Using symmetry and asymmetry

When you are using trees as part of a cohesive planting scheme, plant either several specimens of similar species or a number of small groups

Attractive walkways can be achieved by fan-training a tree, such as this *Laburnum*, over a framework.

An avenue of trees in a woodland garden can be used to draw the eye into the distance and create a sense of space.

A willow tunnel forms a stunning corridor.

An arrangement of golden and purple-leaved trees can create contrasting background planting.

of the same species so that each group forms a single shape when seen from a distance.

In formal landscapes, trees are often used to provide a symmetrical balance. The trees may form corridors or avenues around an obvious central focal point or around some other axis, with everything on one side being copied on the other, in a mirror-like effect.

Alternatively, asymmetrical design uses different trees on either side of an imaginary axis so that the design has harmony, fluidity and unity along its axis but is not as obviously rigid and balanced as a symmetrical design.

Proportion, rhythm and line

You should ensure that the trees are in scale not only with each other but also with nearby buildings and other

structures in the garden. The difficulty lies in the fact that a tree might be in proportion to its surroundings when it is 15–20 years old, but that it might grow too large in either height or breadth as it matures further. For this reason, always consider a tree's ultimate height and spread when you are designing a garden.

Achieving rhythm and line requires the use of more formal landscape techniques. They include the repetitive planting needed in a formal avenue to create a line for the eye to follow into the distance, where a view or focal point, such as a piece of sculpture, can be admired.

Rhythm and line can also be invoked by creating a series of garden rooms using trees and hedges as screens, with the openings framing views into the next room.

Planning a design

The first thing you should do when you are planning a design is to draw a scale plan of your garden.

In order to work out where to position a new tree, you can use triangulation, a technique that fixes the position of an object in relation to the things around it. In order to do this, first find two points already fixed on your plan: the corners of the house are often used. Then go outside and measure the distance from each of the two points to the tree.

Convert these measurements to the scale of the plan, then set a pair of compasses (a compass) to each of the scale distances in turn. For each of the distances, place the point of the compasses on the relevant point on the plan and scribe an arc in the approximate position of the tree. The triangulation point is the spot where the second arc intersects the first.

Landscaping with groups

A group planting of trees should be in harmony with its surroundings. To achieve the best effect the trees should be ranked according to their size, with the smallest ones at the front and the tallest at the back. However, care should be taken to avoid regimentation.

Group plantings

Trees are often evaluated in terms of their ultimate height and spread, and although this can vary according to local growing conditions, it is helpful to define trees in terms of their height:

- Upper-canopy or major shade trees higher than 18m (60ft)
- Upper understorey trees 12–18m (40–60ft) high
- Lower understorey or small garden trees 6–12m (20–40ft) high.

In smaller gardens upper understorey trees will take the place of upper-canopy or major shade trees, and shrubs will take the place of lower understorey trees.

If you are designing a garden from scratch the tree selection process should begin with the larger trees that will form the upper canopy. Work down in scale through the upper understorey and lower understorey, to the lower shrub layers. If you are working within an existing framework, begin by evaluating the trees that are already there, starting with the largest.

It is important that you also consider the relationship of the tree with the plants around it and how the new tree will fit within the wider landscape. For example, if the existing planting includes

tropical foliage plants that require lots of sunlight, a dense, broadly spreading tree such as *Acer rubrum* (red maple) would cast too much shade and adversely affect the growth of other plants as it became established. In time it would create so much shade that it would limit the growth of the tropical foliage plants, and its overall appearance would probably be out of keeping with the wider landscape.

A group of *Washingtonia robusta* (thread palm) would be more fitting in this setting. Their bold foliage would provide a strong contrast with other tropical plants and would create less shade than the maple

In a cooler climate *Trachycarpus fortunei* (Chusan palm) would be a hardier option. If a greater level of dappled shade is required, *Jacaranda*

This group of Japanese maples have been carefully selected and positioned. The result is a very attractive group that fits into the surroundings well.

mimosifolia would lightly shade the tropical foliage plants, and its fern-like foliage and attractive flowers would be in perfect harmony with its surroundings. A hardier choice with the same attributes would be *Robinia pseudoacacia* (false acacia).

Gardening in layers

Planting trees in mixed groups increases the amount of diversity in habit, height and spread and foliage and the seasonal variation in flowers, fruit and foliage. It will also help to attract wildlife to the garden in greater numbers and variety. Before deciding on the trees you want to plant, consider the relationships between the different trees and how they will interact.

As a starting point the planting might consist of an upper-canopy tree, a series of upper understorey trees and several different lower understorey trees to create a stepped or layered effect. Planting in this way has other benefits, including creating a microclimate and providing a woodland effect that is attractive to other plants, while also acting as a windbreak.

The upper canopy should consist of trees that are fast-growing and that can tolerate competition for light, nutrients and water. They should be hardy and suitable for your garden.

The upper understorey and lower understorey trees must be shade tolerant and able to compete with the taller, more dominant upper-canopy trees.

To achieve a natural-looking effect do not plant trees in straight lines and remember to space the trees according to their ultimate height and spread. For example, a mature *Acer platanoides* (Norway maple) will grow to an optimum height of 25m

Year-round appeal should be considered when you are planting groups of trees. Here, the birch provides autumn and winter appeal, while the cherry tree is at its stunning best in spring.

(80ft) and spread of 15m (50ft), so a smaller upper understorey tree should not be planted any closer than 7m (23ft) from it trunk.

In general, plant no closer than half the radius of the spread of the tree. In the case of two specimens of *A. platanoides* a distance of 10–15m (33–50ft) would be appropriate and would allow the canopies of the two trees to blend naturally. However, this distance may take a long time to fill in, so additional trees can be planted around the main tree and removed once the main tree is beginning to make an impact. To achieve this, the gardener must be brave and ensure that 'filler' trees or shrubs are removed.

Nurse species

A fast-growing tree that is used to protect a slower growing tree is often referred to as a nurse species. It is important that nurse trees are removed once they are no longer needed, otherwise the group planting will become too dense and the overall natural feeling will be lost. Remember, they are only there to provide protection for the more prized trees.

If a quick effect is required the trees can be planted at a much tighter density and will compete more directly against each other, but if you do this then they will require regular pruning to limit their size if all the trees are to continue to occupy their positions.

Landscaping for avenues

An avenue or allée of trees is a double row of trees of the same or similar species, planted in straight lines to create a formal avenue, or curved lines to follow a drive or pathway. They can be planted along the sides of a path or road to form a screen, to frame a vista or to direct the attention to a distant object, such as a statue or feature in the landscape.

Creating symmetry

Allées, avenues and boulevards (another name for a street lined with trees) have always been popular in landscape design because they allow a formal axis to be developed, thereby creating formal symmetry in the garden landscape.

Allées

Originally introduced as a landscape feature during the Renaissance in Italy, allées were widely planted throughout Europe during the seventeenth and eighteenth centuries as a feature in formal landscape gardens. The word allée derives from the French aller, meaning 'to go', and refers to a walkway or drive bordered by rows of evenly spaced trees of the same species and of a similar age.

Avenues

Although the grandeur and scale of the avenue planting that took place in the landscaped gardens of the past are difficult to re-create in suburban gardens, avenues are still being planted in our cities. On a smaller scale, a short avenue, created from small, fastigiate trees, can be an interesting linking feature in any garden large enough to accommodate it.

One of the most difficult aspects of planting an avenue is determining the spacing between trees and the spacing between the parallel rows. The trees must be allowed sufficient room for their lower branches to develop, and there must be enough space between the rows to make the avenue usable. If the space between the rows is too wide the avenue may not succeed in its purpose of framing or enhancing a view, and if the trees are too close together the avenue will be overcrowded.

For example, an avenue of *Tilia* x *europaea* (common lime), which has a canopy spread of about 15m (50ft), should be planted 10m (33ft) from a path that is about 2m (6ft) wide so that there is 22m (72ft) between the rows.

However, if a tighter, cathedral avenue is required, the trees could be planted so that there is 18–20m (60–65ft) between the rows, which would eventually lead to the avenue being enclosed by the canopies.

If your garden is large enough to accommodate it, a pollarded avenue can be an interesting feature.

Trees suitable for planting in small avenues

Acer buergerianum (trident maple)
A. campestre cvs.
A. griseum (paperbark maple)
A. palmatum (Japanese maple)
Butia capitata (jelly palm)
Carpinus betulus (common hornbeam)
C. betulus 'Frans Fontaine'
C. caroliniana (American hornbeam)
Cornus florida (flowering dogwood)
C. kousa (kousa dogwood)
C. Stellar hybrids
Cupressus sempervirens Stricta Group
Koelreuteria
Laburnum x *watereri* 'Vossii'
Lagerstroemia spp.
Magnolia spp. and cvs.
Malus spp. and cvs. (crab apple)
Olea europaea (European olive)
Paniculata cvs. (golden raintree)
Pinus sylvestris Fastigiata Group
Robinia x *margaretta*
  'Pink Cascade'
R. pseudoacacia 'Frisia'
  (golden false acacia)
R. x *slavinii* 'Hillieri'
Sorbus spp. (mountain ash)
Stewartia spp.
Trachycarpus fortuneii spp.

Trees suitable for planting in large and medium-sized avenues

Acer platanoides (Norway maple)
A. pseudoplatanus (sycamore)
A. pycnanthum (Japanese red maple)
A. rubrum (red maple)
Aesculus hippocastanum (horse chestnut)
A. indica (Indian horse chestnut)
A. turbinata (Japanese horse chestnut)
Agathis australis (kauri pine)
Araucaria araucana (monkey puzzle)
A. bidwillii (bunya-bunya)
A. cunninghamii (Moreton Bay pine)
Bauhinia spp. (mountain ebony)
Brownea macrophylla
  (Panama flame tree)
Calocedrus decurrens (incense cedar)
Calophyllum inophyllum
  (Alexandrian laurel)
Cassia spp. (shower tree)
Castanea sativa (sweet chestnut)
Catalpa bignonioides (Indian bean tree)
Cedrus atlantica Glauca Group
C. deodara (deodar)
Clusia major (autograph tree)
Corylus colurna (Turkish hazel)
Cryptomeria japonica (Japanese cedar)
Cunninghamia lanceolata (Chinese fir)
Davidia involucrata
  (handkerchief tree)
Dillenia indica (chulta)
Elaeocarpus angustifolius
  (blue quandong)
Eucalyptus spp. (gum tree)
Fagus grandifolia (American beech)
F. orientalis (oriental beech)
F. sylvatica (common beech)
F. sylvatica 'Dawyck'
Ficus spp. (fig)
Metasequoia glyptostroboides
  (dawn redwood)
Platanus spp. (plane)
Quercus spp. (oak)
Salix spp. (willow)
Sciadopitys verticillata
  (Japanese umbrella pine)
Sequoiadendron giganteum 'Glaucum'
Tabebuia spp.
Taxodium distichum (swamp cypress)
Tilia spp. (lime)
Ulmus spp. (elm)
Zelkova spp.

Formal avenues of *Tilia* x *europaea* (common lime) have been used throughout history to create majestic avenues and allées, due to its height and shape.

Planting distances

The planting distances between each individual tree forming the avenue will depend on the type of tree species used, and the following table indicates the recommended distance for the most commonly used species for avenue planting:

Acer platanoides (Norway maple)	10m (33ft)
Aesculus hippocastanum (horse chestnut)	10–15m (33–50ft)
Araucaria araucana (monkey puzzle)	10m (33ft)
Castanea sativa (sweet chestnut)	10–15m (33–50ft)
Cedrus deodara (deodar)	10–15m (33–50ft)
Fagus sylvatica (common beech)	10–15m (33–50ft)
Jacaranda mimosifolia	7–10m (23–33ft)
Platanus x *hispanica* (London plane)	10–15m (33–50ft)
Prunus sargentii (Sargent cherry)	7m (23ft)
Quercus petraea (sessile oak)	10–15m (33–50ft)
Quercus robur (common oak)	10–15m (33–50ft)
Tilia cordata (small-leaved lime)	7–10m (23–33ft)
Tilia x *europaea* (common lime)	7–10m (23–33ft)
Tilia platyphyllos (broad-leaved lime)	7–10m (23–33ft)
Ulmus parvifolia (Chinese elm)	15m (50ft)

Landscaping with garden dividers

Trees can be successfully used as hedges, screens and windbreaks to provide shelter, make garden rooms and create microclimates by slowing wind movement.

Barriers

In order for trees to be effective as barriers, the wind must be able to pass through them rather than being deflected over the top, which has the unwanted effect of creating an area of low pressure behind the barrier. This sucks down the wind to create a turbulent area behind the barrier known as an eddy.

The aim when using trees as a barrier is to slow down the strength of the wind over as long a distance as is practicable before it can return to full strength.

A mixed evergreen and deciduous barrier can provide shelter for a distance of about 20 times the height of the barrier on the downwind side, and about three times its height on the upwind side. The wind will sweep around the ends of the belt as well as over the top, leaving a triangular sheltered zone behind the barrier.

The most effective barriers to the wind are those that contain a mixture of evergreen and deciduous trees, creating 40–50 per cent permeability through the barrier.

Screens and windbreaks

Consisting of narrow bands of trees, sometimes just one tree deep, screens and windbreaks are planted to provide shelter from the wind. Careful planting is required on the windward side so that the air is deflected up and over the taller trees, reducing turbulence on the leeward side.

Windbreaks direct wind over and through or around areas that need to be sheltered. This reduction in wind speed has many benefits in the garden, including improved growth, fewer misshapen trees and shrubs, warmer temperatures in winter and shade in summer.

Narrow belts are effective in most gardens, although wider belts will give considerably more protection if garden space can be sacrificed. The trees are planted in staggered rows or randomly spaced, allowing 2.4m (8ft) between trees and 1.8m (6ft) between rows. Where maximum shelter is required from minimum width, plant tall-growing trees on the windward edge, with smaller trees on the leeward side. Mixed planting of conifers and deciduous material will increase the permeability of the windbreak.

The overall height of the barrier is the most important factor, because this will determine the area behind the windbreak that is protected. For example, a permeable barrier 1.8m (6ft) tall will slow down the wind for up to 20m (65ft) before it picks up to full strength again. The taller the windbreak, the greater the zone of protection, but the less permeable the windbreak the shorter the zone.

Diversity of planting within a shelter-belt or screen can dramatically increase the range of wildlife seen in the garden.

Hedges

Garden hedges, unlike windbreaks and screens, are usually planted with a single species, most often evergreens, which gives a more formal appearance than a mixed planting, but is a less effective windbreak.

Hedges can be used in many ways in a garden: they create a barrier that encloses the garden and gives privacy and protection from intruders; they provide a boundary to the garden to divide the property from its neighbours; they protect plants within the garden from the elements by creating a microclimate; they obscure unwanted views and eyesores; and they can be used within a garden to create separate 'rooms'.

Depending on the species chosen, hedges can be left to grow and trimmed annually so they are informal or clipped regularly to create neat, formal boundaries.

A single row of poplars can be used to form an effective windbreak in the garden.

Hedges grown from trees are normally planted in a double staggered row, with rows positioned about 1.8m (6ft) apart and the trees in each row also about 1.8m (6ft) apart. While the plants are establishing it is important to keep the base weed-free so that the hedge is fully furnished down to soil level.

Hedges are generally clipped to produce a flat-topped or rounded hedge with sloping sides. Hedges should be wider at the base so that snow slides off. Formal hedges may require one or two trims a year depending on the species, and evergreen hedges generally require more clipping than deciduous ones.

Deciduous trees such as beech and hornbeams make very attractive hedges that will exhibit more seasonal variation than the more traditional evergreen screen.

Pleached hedges

Often called 'hedges on stilts' or 'aerial hedges', pleached hedges comprise trees that have been trained to form a hedge while leaving clear and visible trunks. The word pleaching is derived from the French word *plessier*, which means to intertwine or knot, and it has been practised since the Middle Ages.

Pleached hedges can be used to create boundaries in the garden, and in some situations a pleached hedge looks more attractive than a hedge that is furnished down to the ground. They are often planted in double rows to form an avenue, when the branches at the top are trained to create a tunnel, and they can also frame views and walkways.

Pleaching a hedge takes several years. Begin by planting a row of flat-headed trees at equal intervals against a framework of posts that are at least 3m (10ft) tall and to which parallel wires are attached along its length, about 30cm (12in) apart, with the first wire 1–1.2m (3–4ft) from the ground. The young lateral branches

are trained along the wires, while sideways growth is allowed to develop to the required depth of the hedge, which is usually less than 1m (3ft).

The hedge section is clipped annually to produce the required hedge effect, and branches on the trunks are gradually cleared to

the desired height to create the stilts effect. Lime trees, such as *Tilia cordata* (small-leaved lime) and *T. x platyphyllos* (broad-leaved lime), are most often planted for this purpose, although *Ulmus* spp. (elm), *Fraxinus* spp. (ash) and *Carpinus* spp. hornbeam) can also used.

Trees suitable for use as hedges or windbreaks

Abies spp. (silver fir)	*Cryptomeria japonica* (Japanese cedar
Acer campestre (field maple)	x *Cupressocyparis leylandii*
Alnus cordata (Italian alder)	(Leyland cypress)
Araucaria araucana (monkey puzzle)	*Dillenia indica* (chulta)
Banksia spp.	*Elaeocarpus angustifolius*
Bauhinia spp. (mountain ebony)	(blue quandong)
Calliandra spp. (powder puff tree)	*Eucalyptus* spp. (gum tree)
Callistemon spp. (bottlebrush)	*Fagus sylvatica* (common beech)
Calocedrus decurrens (incense cedar)	*Ficus* spp. (fig)
Calodendron capense (Cape chestnut)	*Grevillea* spp. (spider flower)
Calophyllum inophyllum	*Pinus sylvestris* Fastigiata Group
(Alexandrian laurel)	*Populus* spp. (poplar)
Carpinus betulus (common hornbeam)	*Sorbus* spp. (mountain ash)
C. betulus 'Frans Fontaine'	*Thuja koraiensis* (Korean arborvitae)
C. caroliniana (American hornbeam)	*Taxus baccata* (yew)
Chamaecyparis lawsoniana	*Thujopsis dolobrata* (hiba)
(Lawson cypress)	*Tilia* spp. (lime)
Clusia major (autograph tree)	*Tsuga canadensis* (eastern hemlock)
Crataegus spp. (hawthorn)	*T. heterophylla* (western hemlock)

Trees as focal points or backdrops

Selecting a tree for a focal point in the lawn or as a specimen elsewhere in the garden is one of the most difficult choices because the tree must be in scale with the overall garden but also attractive enough to provide interest. Choosing a tree for such a position is as subjective as selecting a piece of sculpture for a prominent place in the garden.

Trees as focal points

A tree that is going to be used as a lawn specimen or a focal point needs to be as attractive as possible throughout the year, so ideally it should have at least one of the following attributes:

- Eye-catching habit or shape, such as columnar, conical, pyramidal or weeping (see pages 286–93)
- Attractive foliage, whether deciduous or evergreen, coloured in summer (yellow, purple, blue or variegated) or boldly architectural, such as a palm or the leaves of *Catalpa bignonioides* (Indian bean tree)
- Beautiful flowers, such as a spring-flowering cherry or summer-flowering jacaranda
- Colourful fruits, such as the yellow-orange fruits of *Eriobotrya japonica* (loquat) or the ivory-white berries of *Sorbus cashmeriana* (Kashmir rowan)
- Attractive bark, especially if it flakes like that of *Acer griseum* (paperbark maple) or *Pinus bungeana* (lacebark pine)
- Attractive twigs, which are less obvious in the growing season but can be appreciated in winter; maples are noted for their attractive twigs, including the scarlet ones of *Acer palmatum* 'Sango-kaku' (coral bark maple) or the salmon-pink, orange and yellow branches of *Acer* x *conspicuum* 'Phoenix'.

Scale and position

A lawn tree should look like an extension of the surrounding tree and shrub layers or as if a clearing has been cut through a wooded area.

The most important factors when planting a focal point tree are the size of the tree and the distance from it to the nearest trees or shrubs. It is important to allow enough space for the tree to look comfortable in its landscape.

This distance should be at least half to three-quarters of the height of the tree when it is fully mature, measured from the outer point of the nearest tree canopy to the trunk of the proposed specimen.

It can be helpful to hammer a tree stake into the ground where the proposed tree is to be planted and walk around the garden and house to view it from different locations, moving the stake about until you locate the right spot.

Determining the position of a focal point can be done by viewing the garden from various windows – the kitchen or sitting room, for example – or by identifying a view or part of the garden to which you want to direct the viewer.

Trees as backdrops

A mixed border planting in a small garden performs the same role as a wooded area in a larger garden, and when they are used in this way trees provide shade and protection for the shrubs and herbaceous material beneath them. Trees in borders have a number of functions, including providing a foil or backdrop for the border plants that surround them and providing an additional seasonal interest with their architectural form.

Trees that are grown to provide a backdrop for border plants should have relatively plain foliage that is a uniform colour. Most evergreen

Magnolia stellata is a stunning tree that produces star-shaped white flowers and which makes a fantastic focal point specimen in the garden.

Lawn specimen and focal point trees

Acer griseum (paperbark maple)
A. negundo 'Flamingo'
A. palmatum (Japanese maple)
A. pensylvanicum (striped maple)
A. pseudoplatanus 'Brilliantissimum'
Araucaria araucana (monkey puzzle)
Betula albosinensis var. *septentrionalis*
B. ermanii (Erman's birch)
B. utilis var. *jacquemontii* (Himalayan birch)
Bismarckia nobilis (noble palm)
Butia capitata (pindo palm)
Calliandra spp. (powder puff tree)
Calocedrus decurrens (incense cedar)
Cassia spp. (shower tree)
Castanea sativa 'Albomarginata'

Catalpa bignonioides 'Aurea'
Cercidiphyllum japonicum f. *pendulum*
Cornus kousa
Cupressus sempervirens Stricta Group
Dillenia indica (chulta)
Elaeocarpus angustifolius (blue quandong)
Eucalyptus spp. (gum tree)
Fraxinus excelsior 'Pendula' (weeping ash)
Gleditsia triacanthos 'Sunburst'
Jacaranda mimosifolia
Koelreuteria paniculata 'Fastigiata'
Lagerstroemia spp.
Livistona spp. (fountain palm)
Magnolia spp. and cvs.
Malus spp. and cvs. (crab apple)

Melia azedarach 'Jade Snowflake'
Metasequoia glyptostroboides 'Gold Rush'
Olea europaea (European olive)
Phoenix spp. (date palm)
Robinia pseudoacacia 'Frisia'
Roystonea spp. (royal palm)
Sciadopitys verticillata
  (Japanese umbrella pine)
Stewartia spp.
Tabebuia spp.
Taxodium distichum var.
  imbricatum 'Nutans'
Tilia tomentosa 'Petiolaris'
Trachycarpus spp.
Washingtonia spp.

trees fit these criteria, and their deep or light green foliage is an excellent background for flowering shrubs and herbaceous plants.

Trees that are used to enhance a mixed border should follow the same selection process as trees for focal points. However, the selection of both must also consider the scale of the planting so that the tree doesn't dominate the border. A tree for a mixed border should be at least three times the overall depth of the border. For example, a border 3m (10ft) deep could accommodate a tree about 9m (30ft) tall, depending on its spread and form.

Any tree selection for such a location should provide light dappled shade so that sufficient light can penetrate the canopy.

Embothrium coccineum (Chilean fire bush) makes a spectacular lawn specimen.

The purple foliage of this focal point tree not only gives height and structure to the border, but also provides a contrasting colour for the surrounding herbaceous planting.

Landscaping for woodland

Using trees to create areas of woodland in the garden offers considerable potential for planting a wide range of species that would naturally grow in shady to semi-shaded locations.

Creating a woodland area

Woodland in a garden should be a scaled-down version of natural woodland and as such should create habitats that include deep shade, dappled shade and sunny woodland edge or fringe planting. So that sufficient light can still enter the garden, lower limbs can be removed from the trees to allow shrubs and herbaceous plants to develop beneath and around them.

The most important decision facing the gardener who wants to create a woodland area is whether to use native or exotic trees to create the upper canopy. A woodland planted with native species will create and support higher levels of biodiversity than one composed entirely of exotic species, although its aesthetic value may not be as great. A mixture of both, however, can provide a balance, both being aesthetically pleasing and having the potential to support biodiversity.

Whichever decision is made, the trees chosen should include both deciduous and evergreen species to provide year-round cover for wildlife; trees and shrubs that flower

Woodland areas in gardens are an invaluable source of food and shelter for a wide range of native and migratory animals. Here, a red squirrel buries an acorn in a sunny patch of the woodland floor.

throughout the year (early and late flowers are especially important for bees); and fruit- or berry-bearing trees and shrubs to provide food for native and migratory animals.

Tree densities can vary, but ideally species should be planted at distances that are equal to half their ultimate spread when they are mature. For example, a tree that will eventually has a spread of 10m (33ft) should be planted at a distance of no less than 5m (16ft) from the centre of the neighbouring tree.

Varying the planting distance will help to create a range of habitats, which can most easily be achieved by planting a small grove of trees with different canopy heights or creating areas of coppice or shrub. A more open wooded area will attract a greater diversity of wildlife, although such openness can allow in the elements, making it less suitable for some types of less robust plant.

The same rules apply to planting a group of trees for a woodland as for planting a shelter-belt or windbreak (see page 400).

Many wild flowers, such as daffodils, bluebells, primroses and foxgloves, grow naturally in woodland areas, and provide a stunning display of spring colour in your garden.

Dead and decaying wood piles can provide habitats for small mammals, insects and fungi. As the wood slowly decays, nutrients are released into the soil, which in turn benefit the trees.

To provide maximum wind protection the planting should contain a mixture of deciduous and evergreen trees to provide permeability, which slows down, rather than deflecting, the wind. Denser shrub planting around the edge of the woodland area will offer cover for wildlife and at the same time protect the inner woodland areas from potential wind damage.

Managing woodland gardens

Woodland areas require attention to ensure that enough light enters the area for the trees to flourish, creating dappled shade. The lower branches of upper-canopy trees should be removed in order to allow lower-canopy trees to survive, a process that should be carried out regularly as part of an annual cycle when the lowest whorl of branches is removed. In the short term, nurse trees (see page 397) can be used for shelter while the upper-canopy trees are allowed to mature.

A newly planted woodland garden will need thinning and pruning to prevent the under-storey planting becoming congested and create a good diversity of habitats.

You can coppice some of the trees if you like (see pages 370–1), and if you do not need to use the resultant cut wood, it can be left in piles to rot, which will help to increase biodiversity.

Woodland clearings appear naturally when individual trees die and fall, but you may need to thin the trees further to ensure that enough light penetrates the upper canopy and reaches the woodland floor, in order to encourage a wide range of plants.

Landscaping with conifers

There is a very wide range of conifers available for planting in the garden. These vary in size, shape, colour and form, but all of them can be used to provide the structural backbone of planting schemes.

Versatile conifers

Although most commonly planted to create windbreaks, conifers can also be used for structural planting, to create traditional or unusual looking avenues, as focal points in lawns or mixed borders, and as upper- and lower-canopy trees, where they will display year-round interest, striking silhouettes and in some cases spectacular autumn colour.

The word conifer means 'cone-bearer' and this indicates that the seeds of these trees are protected in a cone or a cone-like structure. There are many different evergreen trees that make up the conifer group, including cypress, cedar, fir, juniper, larch, pine and spruce, as well as western red cedar or thuja, which is normally grown for hedging.

However, there is also a smaller group of conifers that lose their needles-like leaves in autumn. These include the larch, dawn redwood, and the swamp and pond cypress, and it is these varieties that produce the most spectacular autumn hues.

Conifers are highly adaptable trees and their size can range from gigantic, like the Giant Redwood (*Sequoiadendron giganteum*), to a small pin-cushion-sized conifer, such as the Norway spruce (*Picea abies* 'Nana Compacta'), which will grow to just 30cm (12in). In their native habitats, where deciduous trees would fail, conifers may face freezing temperatures, driving winds, swamp-like soils and baking sun. This means that they will tolerate almost any conditions, making them extremely useful garden trees.

Many conifers have distinctive shapes, unusual habits, attractive bark and amazing cones. Their needles range in colour from hues of bronze and gold to blue and green, and some even display variegated needles with gold and green or green and white.

With such a diverse array of conifers to choose from, there is certain to be a species suitable for every location in the garden.

Using conifers

The use of conifers as garden trees is forever going in and out of vogue with gardeners, even though they possess the desirable qualities of providing year-round interest and being relatively maintenance-free.

Conifers were traditionally planted to accompany heaths in heather gardens, used with alpine plants and other dwarf shrubs in rock gardens, or even planted on their own in more specialized botanical collections like pinetums, where their different shapes and forms are shown to their full extent. However, conifers do not need to be restricted to such specialized companion planting, and they can easily be incorporated in more traditional garden settings.

Conifers provide year-round interest, but come into their own during the winter months when they add a splash of colour to a winter garden.

Dwarf conifers

As a result of the growing number of smaller-sized gardens, there is an increasing demand for smaller trees, which has in turn led to an interest dwarf conifers.

Although the definition of what constitutes a 'dwarf' tree varies, they are generally trees that grow to a maximum height of 1.8m (5.9ft) over ten years. There are many dwarf varieties available, including *Chamaecyparis lawsoniana* 'Gnome', *Juniperus communis* 'Compressa' and *Picea abies* 'Little Gem', and they make useful, attractive specimens when they are grown in containers or rockeries.

Dwarf conifers are easy to grow since they naturally maintain neat shapes, so very little pruning or trimming is required. Although they are highly adaptable and will tolerate a wide range of habitats, they will not tolerate competition from more vigorous garden varieties and are easily shaded out by larger conifers, which can quickly and easily outgrow their allotted space.

Conifers in avenues

The different shapes of conifers can provide a distinct outline when they are used in avenues. In traditional situations monkey puzzle (*Araucaria araucana*), deodar cedar (*Cedrus deodara*), larch (*Larix decidua*) or Scots pine (*Pinus sylvestris*) have all been used to great effect.

However, the weeping habit of Nootka cypress (*Chamaecyparis nootkatensis*) or Brewer's spruce (*Picea breweriana*) can be used to introduce a graceful and more unusual look. If space is at a premium then you can create a Mediterranean look by planting an avenue of Italian cypress (*Cupressus sempervirens*) or Chinese juniper (*Juniperus chinensis* 'Aurea').

Conifers develop a range of habits, including upright, conical and spreading. Planted together in the garden they can make a striking group.

Conifers as focal points

As a result of their unique and distinctive shapes, conifers make ideal focal point trees. The use of a deciduous conifer – such as *Metasequoia glyptostroboides* 'Gold Rush', which has striking yellow foliage that turns a pinkish brown in autumn, as well as a distinctive outline and fluted brown bark – as a winter feature in such a location can add a dramatic element to a garden.

Conifers in borders

The bright foliage and interesting shapes of many conifers make them suitable for any border, as long as they do not get shaded out by other plants. Tall, narrow species, such as *Taxus baccata* 'Fastigiata Aureomarginata', are ideal for adding height to a shrub border, while spherical ones, such as *Thuja occidentalis* 'Danica', add shape to a border of dainty perennials.

Landscaping with palms

Except in tropical garden landscapes, palms remain one of the most underused landscape trees. This is probably due to the fact that their form and foliage create a very tropical look, which can appear out of place in gardens in temperate regions.

Using palm trees

Although palms are often difficult to site in temperate landscapes, it is worth persevering as not only do they have bold linear trunks and exotic foliage, but these plants also provide an air of tropical lushness in any garden situation.

Palms can be used in a variety of ways in the landscape. They can provide the shade and upper-canopy produced by a major shade tree; they can be used to create formal avenues; they make excellent lawn specimens and focal points; and they can be used in tropical foliage borders.

Palm trees can thrive in a variety of different habitats, including tropical rainforests, exposed, salt-laden beaches, mangrove swamps, oases of deserts, tropical and temperate mixed forests – and a few species are able to survive occasional freezing temperatures in temperate regions of the world.

In fact, a surprising number of temperate gardens can successfully incorporate palms into the design, and they can establish and grow quite quickly if they are provided with the optimum growing conditions.

Nevertheless, the fact remains that the largest distribution and greatest diversity of palm trees are found throughout tropical zones of the world, and this stunning array provides us with a massive selection of highly desirable landscape trees that are grown for their attractive architectural form, fern-like foliage, distinctive and slender hessian-covered trunks, attractive flowers and interesting, sometimes edible, fruits.

In tropical climates palms are easier to accommodate and can be used to great effect as the dominant tree in the landscape. Careful selection and combining of the palms in the landscape can produce a wide variety of foliage shapes, colour, texture and heights, while providing an evergreen backdrop to show other plants against.

Palms for temperate areas

Although many gardens will simply be too cold for palms, there are some varieties that are hardier than most people realize, and it is worth growing these if you can – their wonderful habit and foliage will introduce an air of tropical lushness to even the dreariest of temperate gardens.

Just like any other landscape tree, palms make ideal focal point plants in the garden, with their bold foliage that can be either feathery, fern-like (pinnate) or fan-shaped (palmate), and their linear growing habit, which provides one of the most distinct silhouettes in the landscape.

Palms are often planted as lawn specimens, either singly or in small groups, with the close-cut lawn

An abundance of palms creates a luxurious, tropical effect as well as providing shade and protection for other plants and wildlife.

In temperate climates, palms and cordylines create stunning landscapes if they are planted with care and thought.

adding to the formality of the arrangement. When positioned as if a piece of sculpture, a specimen palm can be viewed from all sides, dominating the landscape with its bold, architectural foliage and trunk.

Although palm trees can be used as a single specimen, they are best planted in groups, as this style of planting seems more natural, provides more of a focal point and helps to harmonize them with their surroundings. Planting in groups also provides shade and protection for the plants that can flourish below them.

Whether grown singly or in loose groups, one major benefit of palm trees is they do not cast dense shade unless they are planted very tightly together. Many palms have adapted

to become highly shade tolerant and as such make excellent lower-canopy trees, with larger trees above, and providing an attractive feature that casts little shade below.

In many tropical countries, palms are grown in formal avenues or along the sides of roads, where their linear form creates a strong formality with the symmetry of the roadside verges; their stems remain cleanly exposed as any dying leaves can be removed to show off their attractive stems.

Palm trees are very adaptable and are able to survive in soils that are low in nutrients, and in areas with only occasional rainfall. As they are tolerant of salt spray and scorching winds, many palms are found in coastal locations. However, the one thing they do dislike is very compacted soils.

For temperate regions, specialized microclimates are required and only the most hardy of cold-resistant palms will grow.

Palms for tropical and temperate climates

For tropical, subtropical and Mediterranean regions:
Bismarckia nobilis (noble palm)
Caryota mitis (fishtail palm)
Licuala grandis (ruffled fan palm)
Livistonia australis (cabbage palm)
Roystonea regia (regal palm)
Washingtonia filifera
  (thread palm)

For temperate regions:
Butia capitata (jelly palm)
Chamaerops humilis (fan palm)
Phoenix canariensis (date palm)
Trachycarpus fortunei (Chusan palm)

Directory of trees

Whether you want a tree purely for its aesthetic qualities, or for a more practical reason – such as wanting increased privacy, more shade, a barrier to muffle noise or diffuse wind, a boundary marker to your property or in order to encourage wildlife to your garden – there is a tree to meet every requirement. This directory is designed to help you to identify and choose the best trees for your needs.

For each tree, there is a detailed description, including seasonal variations and any interesting or desirable features – such as shape, colour, flowering habits, fruits, leaves and bark – as well as its potential height and spread.

Important information is given regarding the growing requirements of each genus, including the type of soil it prefers (and where it grows naturally in the wild), whether it likes sun or shade, and its hardiness. There is also advice on how to care for each tree, its pruning requirements, and the best ways to propagate it.

With such a massive range of sizes, shapes, heights, and colours, there is an ideal tree for your garden.

ABIES
Silver fir

These evergreen conifers are native to mountainous areas of Europe, North America, Asia and North Africa. There are about 50 species, from which a number of cultivars have been hybridized. They make good specimen trees and can also be used in windbreaks.

Cultivation Grow in fertile, moisture-retentive but well-drained, neutral to acidic soil in full sun. Protect young plants from cold winter winds.

Pruning Firs require very little in the way of regular pruning. However, while young they will benefit from occasional pruning to develop clear leaders while tipping back side shoots to encourage bushy growth.

Propagation Propagation is by seed for the species and it should be collected while the cones are still fresh. Cultivars are propagated by winter indoor grafting on to seedling grown rootstocks.

A. alba
European silver fir, common silver fir

The species is a conical tree with long, slightly drooping branches. The small, needle-like leaves are attached to the branches in Vs. They are dark green above and silvery beneath. The brown, resinous cones are upright with the scales arching slightly backwards, and they fall apart by late autumn. A fast-growing tree, it is occasionally susceptible to damage by frosts in late spring. H 40m (130ft), S 20m (65ft). Aspect Prefers full sun, but is more shade tolerant than most other firs.
Hardiness ✿✿✿ Zones 4–6

A. bracteata
Santa Lucia fir, bristlecone fir

A fast-growing, very beautiful conifer, this has narrow, dark green needles up to 5cm (2in) long, borne almost flat against the stems and with two distinct white bands along the underside. The straw-coloured buds are pointed. The spiky, egg-shaped cones turn brown with age. This is an adaptable but large conifer, which will grow on a wide range of soils. H 35m (115ft), S 6m (20ft).
Aspect Full sun.
Hardiness ✿✿✿ Zone 7

A. concolor
White fir, Colorado white fir

A beautiful, strongly conical conifer, this has blue-green needles, up to 6cm (2½in) long, which lie forwards and upwards along the stem. If branches are left unpruned they will arch and sweep down to the ground. It is a widely planted tree and is adaptable to both heat and cold. H 25–40m (80–130ft), S 5–7m (16–23ft).
Named varieties The cultivar 'Candicans' is an initially narrow-growing form that spreads with age. The foliage is a ghostly pale blue-grey.

Trees in the Lowiana Group (Pacific white fir) are seed-raised forms with short branches that produce a narrow, conical shape. The greenish-grey needles are arranged in V-shaped bands along the stems.
Aspect Full sun.
Hardiness ✿✿✿ Zones 4–7

A. firma
Japanese fir, momi fir

This large, quick-growing conifer will reach its potential height in its natural habitat in Japan, where it grows in fertile, moist soils in areas of high rainfall. However, in most gardens it will be much smaller. It is a beautiful tree with stiff, almost spiky needles and a branching, almost fern-like canopy. H 20–40m (65–130ft), S 6–10m (20–33ft).
Aspect Full sun.
Hardiness ✿✿✿ Zones 6–9

A. nebrodensis
Sicily fir

This reasonably small conifer has a flattish top and beautiful cones. The needles are dark green and arranged in a V shape around the stems. It is one of the most beautiful of garden-sized conifers and will do well in shallow, free-draining soil. H 10m (33ft), S 5m (16ft).
Aspect Full sun.
Hardiness ✿✿✿ Zone 6

A. pinsapo
Spanish fir, hedgehog fir

This distinctive, drought-tolerant fir has clusters of stout, blue-green needles, up to 2cm (¾in) long, arranged in a spiral around each shoot. It does best in free-draining, alkaline soil. H 25m (80ft), S 8m (26ft).
Named varieties The slower growing cultivar 'Aurea' has beautiful gold-coloured needles that turn blue-green in summer. It does not have such a neat habit of growth as the species.
Aspect Full sun to light shade.
Hardiness ✿✿✿ Zone 6

ACACIA
Wattle

This is a very large genus of 1,100 or more species of ornamental deciduous and evergreen trees.

Abies alba

They are native to Australia, southern Africa and Central and South America, and they are tolerant of poor soils and drought.

They are grown for their dense clusters of often scented, bright yellow flowers. Some species have alternate, fern-like leaves; other species bear phyllodes (flattened leaf stalks), which look and function like leaf blades. The dark green phyllodes are narrow, and during droughts they often fall to enable the plant to conserve water, while the stems and branches alone produce the tree's energy.

Some species are hardier than others and can be grown with minimal winter protection in temperate areas; in warmer climates some species may be invasive.

Cultivation Grow in free-draining, neutral to acidic soil in full sun.

Pruning Formative pruning should aim to produce a clear trunk and a balanced crown. Occasional pruning is required to remove any dead, dying, diseased or crossing branches.

Propagation Seed is the easiest method of propagation and should be collected when fresh, soaked in warm water for 24 hours and sown into a free-draining compost

Abies bracteata

in a container greenhouse and kept frost-free until ready to plant out.

A. auriculaeformis
Black wattle

This attractive and quick-growing tree has brownish-silver bark. In winter and early spring it bears dense spikes of yellow flowers. These are followed by dark brown fruits shaped like curled pea pods. H 30m (100ft), S 20m (65ft).
Aspect Full sun.
Hardiness ✿ Zones 10–12.

A. baileyana
Cootamundra wattle

A fast-growing, strongly arching, small evergreen tree, this is grown for its small clusters of scented, golden-yellow flowers that appear in late winter. The attractive, fern-like foliage has a silvery sheen. H and S 8m (26ft).
Named varieties The cultivar 'Purpurea' has stunning purple foliage and yellow flowers.
Aspect Full sun.
Hardiness ✿ Zones 9–11.

A. confusa
False koa

This beautiful small tree has long, pointed, dark green phyllodes. In winter and early spring it bears profuse and dense clusters of bright yellow flowers amid the foliage. H and S 15m (50ft).
Aspect Full sun.
Hardiness ✿ Zones 9–12.

Acacia dealbata

A. dealbata
Mimosa, silver wattle

A widely grown, fast-growing evergreen tree, the mimosa has slender, silver-green foliage. Abundant clusters of fragrant, bright yellow flowers are produced in late winter and early spring. In a favourable climate it will develop into an open-headed tree. H and S 15m (50ft).
Aspect Full sun.
Hardiness ✿ Zones 8–10.

A. longifolia
Sydney golden wattle

This beautiful but invasive tree is one of the most lime-tolerant of the wattles. In early spring abundant clusters of highly scented, bright yellow flowers are borne alongside the long, dark green leaves. H and S 8m (26ft).
Aspect Full sun.
Hardiness ✿ Zones 9–11.

A. melanoxylon
Blackwood wattle

A broadly spreading, evergreen tree, the species has angular stems and blue-green foliage. It bears clusters of small, creamy-yellow flowers in early spring. H 25m (80ft), S 12m (40ft).
Aspect Full sun.
Hardiness ✿ Zones 9–11.

A. pravissima
Oven's wattle

The small, triangular phyllodes of this deciduous species are dark green. It is an open-headed tree with slightly weeping branches, bearing fragrant, bright yellow flowers in late winter. It is one of the hardiest of the wattles, but it will require protection when young in temperate areas. H and S 8m (26ft).
Aspect Full sun.
Hardiness ✿ Zones 8–11.

ACER
Maple

About 150 species of maples grow in temperate regions of the world. They are usually deciduous trees, but a number of evergreen forms exist. They are easily distinguished by their opposite leaves and winged fruits (commonly known as keys). The wings allow the seeds to be widely

Abies pinsapo

distributed by the wind, so they germinate away from the parent tree and do not compete with it.

Many maples have fine flowers but their chief characteristics are their palmate (hand-shaped) leaves (often brilliantly coloured in autumn), bark and elegant habit.
Cultivation Most maples prefer an open, sunny location in fertile, moisture-retentive soil, but this is a large group of trees, and the individual requirements of the species may differ, as noted below.
Pruning Generally, maples require little pruning apart from the removal of dead, diseased, dying or crossing branches, which should be removed during winter or summer. Reverted green shoots of variegated leaf forms should be removed as soon as they appear.
Propagation Some species can be propagated by fresh seed, which germinates readily. Propagate

cultivars by winter indoor grafting or budding. Take softwood cuttings in late summer, allow them to root and do not pot them on until the following summer.

A. buergerianum
Trident maple, three-toothed maple

Native to China and Japan, this species is grown in hot areas instead of A. palmatum, which is less tolerant of high summer temperatures. It is a small to medium-sized tree with red to orange autumn colour. It does best in moist, slightly acidic soil, and grows well in either sun or shade. It is often grown as a multi-stemmed specimen. H and S 15m (50ft), but H up to 30m (100ft) in its natural habitat.
Aspect Full sun or semi-shade.
Hardiness ✿✿✿ Zones 5–9.

Acer x *conspicuum* 'Phoenix'

A. cappadocicum
Cappadocian maple, Caucasian maple

This spreading tree has five- to seven-lobed leaves, up to 10cm (4in) long, which turn yellow in autumn. Native to the Caucasus, the Himalayas and western China, it is an adaptable, quick-growing tree that will tolerate a wide range of soils and habitats, including alkaline soils. H 20m (65ft), S 15m (50ft).

Named varieties 'Aureum' is a slower growing form. The leaves are red when they first emerge but turn yellow and remain long into summer, when they become lime green, finally turning yellow again before they fall. This is best planted in semi-shade because the foliage will scorch in full sun. H 15m (50ft), S 10m (33ft).

'Rubrum' is more vigorous than 'Aureum' but is just as beautiful. The emerging leaves are bronze-red and remain red-tinted long into summer, before turning yellow in autumn. This is one of the most widely grown forms.
Aspect Full sun or semi-shade.
Hardiness ❋❋❋ Zone Min. 6.

A. x conspicuum

The hybrids in this group include crosses between *A. pensylvanicum* and *A. davidii*. They are grown for their spectacular snakebark trunks and beautiful autumn colours. They require neutral to acidic soil and cool summers.
Named varieties 'Elephant's Ear' has large, unlobed leaves, which turn bright yellow in autumn and, once fallen, reveal purplish stems and white-striped bark.

'Phoenix' is perhaps the best of the group; it is a quick-growing tree with stark white stripes up its green trunk. Striking bright red winter shoots are complemented by vibrant yellow autumn colour.

'Silver Cardinal' has attractive variegated foliage.

'Silver Vein' is a small tree similar to *A. pensylvanicum*, but its arching branches are more like *A. davidii*. Its stems are heavily striped and the leaves are glowing butter yellow in autumn. H 10m (33ft), S 5m (16ft).
Aspect Full sun or semi-shade.
Hardiness ❋❋❋ Zone Min. 6.

A. davidii
Père David's maple, snakebark maple

This is one of the most useful of the snakebark maples. It was named after the French missionary Jean-Pierre-Armand David, who discovered this delightful tree in China in 1869. It has glossy, dark green leaves, up to 15cm (6in) long, which turn red, yellow and orange in autumn.

It is a woodland tree, preferring a cool root run in slightly acidic soil and thriving under the shade of other more dominant trees. Occasional spring frost damage may occur, and it is intolerant of high temperatures. H and S 15m (50ft).

Named varieties 'Ernest Wilson' is perhaps the best of the available cultivars. More compact than the species, it has arching branches and pale green leaves, which turn vibrant orange and yellow into autumn. H 8m (26ft), S 10m (33ft).

'George Forrest', another fine selection, is more widely grown than any of the other forms. It has a widely spreading habit and dark green leaves, up to 20cm (8in) long, and red stalks. The autumn colour is less intense than the species and tends to be slightly disappointing.

Acer 'Ginger Bread'

A. campestre
Field maple, hedge maple

The species, native to Europe and North Africa, is a dainty tree with a rounded habit. The dark green, palmate leaves, up to 6cm (2½in) long, are red-purple when they first emerge. When grown in moist, acidic soil, autumn colours can range from dark red or purple through to orange-red; otherwise, the leaves turn butter yellow.

The leaves and corky branches weep a milky sap if broken or cut. It is a highly adaptable tree, which is often found growing in hedgerows on shallow, free-draining, alkaline soils. It can tolerate regular, close clipping and makes an attractive hedge. H and S 15m (50ft).

Named varieties 'Carnival' is a striking Dutch cultivar with leaves broadly edged in white.

'Elsrijk', another Dutch selection, has a narrow habit and makes a good street tree.

'Postelense' is a small, mop-headed tree with leaves that are golden-yellow as they emerge but fade to light green in summer. It is excellent for a small garden.

'Queen Elizabeth' is a widely grown selection with a narrow habit and good autumn colour, but it is susceptible to mildew in cooler climates.

'Streetwise' is a narrow-growing form with red keys and butter yellow autumn colour.
Aspect Full sun or semi-shade.
Hardiness ❋❋❋ Zones 4–8.

The Dutch cultivar 'Karmen' is best grown as a small, multi-stemmed tree and pruned to maintain this habit. Such treatment will encourage deeply striped bark that is flushed with dark purple, which makes this a favourite landscape tree for winter bark. The young leaves are bronze, turning yellow-orange in autumn.

The Dutch cultivar 'Serpentine' has an upright habit and is the best choice for winter stem effects, having purple shoots and wonderful striations on the bark. The leaves, up to 10cm (4in) long, colour well in autumn.
Aspect Full sun or semi-shade.
Hardiness ✳✳✳ Zone Min. 6.

A. x freemanii
Freeman's maple, hybrid red maple
This is a distinctive group of named forms that are hybrids between *A. rubrum* and *A. saccharinum*. First raised in 1933, its characteristics are intermediate between both parents, and it will grow in the same conditions as both. It is a quick-growing, upright tree, which spreads with age. The leaves are dark green, with a deeply cut shape, and produce superb autumn colour.

Widely planted in North America, it is less well known in Europe. A number of heat- and

Acer griseum

cold-tolerant forms have been developed from natural stands where the parent species have hybridized. H 25m (80ft), S 5m (16ft).
Named varieties The first form to be sold, 'Armstrong', has now been superceded by superior forms. 'Autumn Blaze' is a broad, dense, oval-shaped tree with brilliant and long-lasting red and orange autumn colour.

'Celebration' is a more compact form with strongly upright branches and deeply cut leaves that turn golden-red in autumn.

'Morgan' is both vigorous and fast-growing, with an attractive open habit and large, deeply lobed leaves that turn brilliant red-purple, scarlet and orange-yellow in autumn.
Aspect Full sun or semi-shade.
Hardiness ✳✳✳ Zones 4–7.

A. 'Ginger Bread'
This interesting hybrid between *A. griseum* and *A. maximowiczianum* (syn. *A. nikoense*; Nikko maple) was introduced in the USA in 1995 and is becoming more popular. The bark is intermediate between both parents but less fluted than *A. griseum*. It is quicker growing and more heat and cold tolerant than either parent. It has exceptional red autumn colour. H and S 10–15m (33–50ft).
Aspect Full sun or semi-shade.
Hardiness ✳✳✳ Zones 5–7 (poss. 8).

A. griseum
Paperbark maple, Chinese paperbark maple
This medium-sized tree is a delightful year-round garden tree. Native to China, it has cinnamon-coloured, flaking bark and beautiful autumn colour, although this can vary as it is mainly seed propagated. The leaves, up to 10cm (4in) long, are trifoliate (having three leaflets). They are dark green above and silver-blue beneath. It will grow in a range of conditions, including acidic and alkaline soils, as long as they are deep and humus rich. H and S 10–15m (33–50ft).
Aspect Full sun or semi-shade.
Hardiness ✳✳✳ Zones 5–7 (poss. 8).

Acer japonicum 'Vitifolium'

A. grosseri var. hersii
(syn. A. davidii subsp. grosseri, A. grosseri, A. hersii)
Hersii maple
This is perhaps the most beautiful of the snakebark maples. It is a small tree from northern China with stunning marbled bark and shallowly lobed leaves, which colour well in autumn. H 8m (25ft), S 10m (30ft).
Aspect Semi-shade.
Hardiness ✳✳✳ Zone 6.

A. japonicum
Full moon maple, Japanese maple
This species of maple is native to Japan. There are numerous cultivars, all of which will thrive in moist, slightly acidic, free-draining soil. They are best grown

in the shade of other trees where they can be protected from cold winds, especially in spring when the delicate new leaves are emerging. H and S 10m (33ft).
Named varieties Among the cultivars is 'Aconitifolium' (syn. 'Filicifolium', 'Laciniatum'), a superb form with typical lime green, deeply cut foliage, which turn ruby red in autumn. H 5m (16ft), S 6m (20ft).

'Vitifolium' has broadly fan-shaped leaves, with up to 12 lobes, which are up to 8cm (3in) long. They turn yellow and orange-red in autumn.
Aspect Full sun or semi-shade.
Hardiness ✳✳✳ Zones 5–7 (but not heat tolerant in the southern USA).

Acer japonicum 'Aconitifolium'

ÔA. macrophyllum
Oregon maple, big-leaf maple
This spreading tree with coarse leaves is suitable only for large gardens or open parkland. The deeply lobed leaves, up to 25cm (10in) across, are glossy, dark green, and if removed in summer they weep a milky sap. Autumn colours are yellow, orange and orange-brown. H 25m (80ft), S 20m (65ft).
Aspect Full sun or semi-shade.
Hardiness ❋❋❋ Zone 5–7 (poss. 9 in milder regions).

Acer palmatum

A. negundo
Box elder, ash-leaved maple
This is a tough but quick-growing maple, which is heat tolerant, very cold hardy and adaptable to a range of soil conditions. The light green leaves, up to 20cm (8in) long, turn yellow in autumn. It is a small to medium-sized garden tree with attractive, tassel-like, green-yellow flowers. H 20m (65ft), S 10m (33ft).
Named varieties 'Flamingo' is the most widely grown cultivar. The new leaves are edged with salmon-pink, which fades to a white variegation in summer. Intense leaf colour appears on trees that are coppiced every two years.
'Kelly's Gold', which originated in New Zealand, has yellow-green leaves that rarely scorch in the sun.
'Winter Lightning' is a green-leaved form with stunning, vivid yellow-white winter stems. It is best grown as a coppiced tree.
Aspect Full sun or semi-shade.
Hardiness ❋❋❋ Zones 3–9.

A. palmatum
Japanese maple
The trees in this group are probably the most widely planted of the maples, because of their extraordinary range of shape, size and colour. The larger forms will tolerate alkaline soils and are more resistant to wind damage. Nevertheless, they require moist, free-draining soil and protection from cold spring winds. H 15m (50ft), S 10m (33ft).
Named varieties 'Bloodgood' is a widely grown cultivar with deeply cut, dark reddish-purple leaves, which turn crimson in autumn and contrast with the iridescent bright crimson, winged fruits. H and S 5m (16ft).
'Chitoseyama' is a graceful maple with deeply cut, green leaves that turn shades of purple-red in autumn. It eventually becomes a mound-like small tree with strongly arching branches. H 1.8m (6ft), S 3m (10ft).
A. palmatum var. dissectum 'Crimson Queen' has very finely cut, purple leaves that retain their colour long into summer before turning dark scarlet in autumn. H 3m (10ft), S 4m (12ft).
The strongly growing A. palmatum var. dissectum 'Garnet' has deeply cut, purple leaves that turn red-purple in autumn.
A. palmatum var. dissectum 'Inaba-shidare' is a distinctive form with large, finely divided foliage that is purple throughout the growing season and turns crimson in autumn.
'Ōsakazuki' is one of the most widely grown cultivars because of its amazing scarlet autumn colour. The leaves are green in spring and summer. H and S 6m (20ft).

Acer palmatum 'Ōsakazuki'

'Sango-kaku' (syn. 'Senkaki'; coral bark maple) has red young branches, which contrast with the small, butter yellow autumn leaves. It is one of the smallest of the green-leaved forms of A. palmatum. H 6m (20ft), S 5m (16ft).
Aspect Best in semi-shade.
Hardiness ❋❋❋ Zones 5–8.

A. pensylvanicum
Striped maple, moosewood, snakebark maple
This small, shade-loving tree is often grown as a multi-stemmed tree. Another of the snakebark maples, its trunk is pale green with white stripes that are more conspicuous on younger branches. The bright green leaves, up to 20cm (8in) long, turn butter yellow in autumn. H 8m (26ft), S 5m (16ft).
Aspect Best in semi-shade.
Hardiness ❋❋❋ Zones 3–7.

A. platanoides
Norway maple
The species is an adaptable, fast-growing tree, tolerant of atmospheric pollution and poor soils, and often used as a pioneer species. It bleeds if cut in summer, like A. macrophyllum. H 25m (80ft), S 15m (50ft).
Named varieties Among the many cultivars is 'Cleveland', a broadly upright but spreading form with gorgeous yellow autumn colour.

Widely planted as a street tree, 'Crimson King' has dark maroon, palmate leaves that darken to almost purple-red by midsummer. It grows poorly in extreme summer heat and is slightly slower growing than some of the other purple-leaved forms.

'Drummondii' is a wonderful form with light green leaves edged with white. Susceptible to reversion, it needs constant pruning to remove any plain green leaves. H and S 10–12m (33–40ft).

'Erectum' is a strongly growing, upright form, similar in some ways to *A. saccharum* subsp. *nigrum* 'Monumentale'.

'Emerald Lustre' is very quick growing when young and matures into a round-headed tree. The leaves are reddish-green initially, puckered along the edges, but fade to dark green in late summer.

'Palmatifidum' (syn. 'Lorbergii') has deeply lobed, long, pointed leaves that are attractive early in the year and again when they turn yellow-orange in autumn. It is a wide, spreading tree.

'Schwedleri', a parent of many purple-leaved cultivars, is grown for its purple foliage, which is even more stunning if the tree is pollarded and pruned hard every second year.
Aspect Full sun or semi-shade.
Hardiness ❁❁❁ Zones 4–7.

A. pseudoplatanus
Sycamore, plane tree maple, great maple
This large tree, native to Europe and south-western Asia, is tolerant of a wide range of growing conditions and highly tolerant of exposed locations, making it especially useful for seaside planting. H 25–30m (80–100ft), S 15–25m (50–80ft).
Named varieties
'Brilliantissimum' is a delightful small garden tree with salmon-pink leaves in spring, turning pale yellow and finally green. H 6m (20ft), S 8m (26ft).

A. pseudoplatanus f. *erythrocarpum* is a green-leaved form with vivid red winged fruits that develop through late summer and last long into winter.

Introduced from New Zealand, *A. pseudoplatanus* Purpureum Group encompasses all green-leaved forms that have purple undersides, most of which are seedling selections.

The leaves of *A. pseudoplatanus* f. *variegatum* 'Esk Sunset' are pink at first, turning green mottled with pink, white and grey-green as they age. H and S 10m (33ft).
Aspect Full sun or semi-shade.
Hardiness ❁❁❁ Zones 4–7 (but will not perform well in warmer areas of the southern USA).

Acer platanoides

A. pycnanthum
Japanese red maple
Although it is widely planted in its native Japan as a street tree because it is heat tolerant and drought resistant, this medium-sized tree is little grown elsewhere. It bears its blooms in spring. It has bright green foliage, which turns crimson and yellow in autumn. It is best grown in a free-draining, acidic soil. H 15m (50ft), S 10m (33ft).
Aspect Full sun or semi-shade.
Hardiness ❁❁❁ Zone 6.

A. rubrum
Red maple, scarlet maple, swamp maple
A large tree from eastern North America, *A. rubrum* produces scarlet autumn colour when it is grown in neutral to acidic soil. It will grow well in chalk soils, but the autumn colour is often poor. The dark green leaves, up to 10cm (4in) long, have three to five lobes, the central one being longer than the others. Red flowers are produced in spring. H 25m (80ft), S 15m (50ft).
Named varieties Several cultivars have been developed for heat and cold tolerance. 'Armstrong', a fast-growing, upright form, has deeply cut leaves and vivid autumn tints.

'Columnare' is narrow, almost pillar-like and produces fantastic autumn colour. H 25m (80ft), S 3m (10ft).

'October Glory', a widely planted form of US origin, has long-lasting, red autumn colour.

'Red Sunset' produces red-orange colour early in autumn; it has a pyramidal habit, ageing to a round-headed tree.

'Schlesingeri' is usually the first red maple to colour in autumn, showing scarlet mixed with the patchwork of the green leaves that have yet to turn. The colour lasts over a long period in autumn.
Aspect Full sun.
Hardiness ❁❁❁ Zones 3–9.

Acer pseudoplatanus

Acer rubrum 'Columnare'

A. rufinerve
Red-vein maple, grey-budded snakebark maple

This small to medium-sized tree is similar in many respects to *A. pensylvanicum*, although its leaves are smaller, up to 12cm (5in) long, and turn a lovely red and orange-yellow in autumn. It prefers cool, moist, acidic soil. H and S 10m (33ft).

Named varieties 'Erythrocladum' is a slow-growing tree with pale yellow new shoots in summer, which intensify in colour as temperatures fall. They eventually turn red by winter.

'Hatsuyuki' (syn. 'Albolimbatum', 'Albomarginatum') is an interesting form with mottled and variegated leaves, which are splashed with white. It has incredibly vibrant autumn colour.
Aspect Full sun or semi-shade.
Hardiness ✽✽✽ Zones 5–7.

A. saccharinum
(syn. A. dasycarpum)
Silver maple

This large, stately tree has five-lobed leaves, up to 20cm (8in) long, that are pale green above and silver-white beneath, turning bright yellow in autumn. It is a fast-growing, heat-tolerant tree that can adapt to both moist, fertile soils and nutrient-poor, drier soils. H 30m (100ft), S 20m (65ft).
Aspect Full sun.
Hardiness ✽✽✽ Zones 3–9.

A. saccharum
Sugar maple, rock maple

The species, native to eastern North America, is a large ornamental tree that is also cultivated for the production of maple syrup. It is widely grown in North America for its long-lasting autumn colours, which

Acer saccharum

are vivid orange, scarlet, crimson and gold. It does best in fertile, neutral to acidic, free-draining soil. H 30m (100ft), S 20m (65ft).

Named varieties Among the cultivars 'Adirondak' is a strongly growing, upright form with five widely lobed leaves. It has orange autumn colour and shows good drought resistance.

'Arrowhead', a tight growing form with a distinct central leader, has dark green leaves that turn orange in autumn. H 20m (65ft), S 8m (26ft).

'Crescendo' is probably the best form for both heat and drought tolerance. It has dark green leaves, which turn yellow in autumn.

A. saccharum subsp. *nigrum* 'Monumentale' (syn. *A. saccharum* 'Temple's Upright') is often confused with 'Newton Sentry', but it has a strong central leader and beautiful autumn colour. H 20m (65ft), S 5m (16ft).

A. saccharum subsp. *nigrum* 'Newton Sentry' (syn. *A. saccharum* 'Columnare') is a strongly growing, upright form with vivid autumn colour but without a distinct central leader. H 10m (33ft), S 2.4m (8ft).

'Sweet Shadow' has finely cut, dark green foliage, which produces vivid yellow-orange autumn

colour. It is vase-shaped and very cold tolerant.
Aspect Full sun.
Hardiness ✽✽✽ Zones 4–8.

A. sterculiaceum
(syn. A. villosum)
Himalayan maple

The species has large, rather architectural, palmate leaves that are pale green in summer, turning orange in autumn. It looks striking in spring with its large, pendulous flowers. A broadly

Acer x conspicuum 'Silver Cardinal'

Acer 'White Tigress'

Aesculus x carnea

Aesculus indica

Pruning Requires little regular pruning apart from the removal of dead, dying, diseased or crossing branches, which are best removed during summer when the tree is in full leaf.
Propagation Species of horse chestnuts and buckeyes can be produced by seeds, which should be sown as soon as they ripen and fall from the tree. Cultivars are propagated by grafting on to seedling chestnuts or buckeyes and propagated as winter indoor grafts. It can also be successfully chip- or T-budded during summer.

A. x *carnea*
Red horse chestnut

A hybrid between *A. hippocastanum* and *A. pavia*, this slow-growing tree has a compact habit and red flowers. The palmate leaves are dark green and up to 25cm

(10in) long. It is widely used in avenues for street planting. H and S 20m (65ft).
Named varieties Among the cultivars 'Briotii' is grown for its darker red flowers and more compact growth.

'Plantierensis' is a sterile form that bears no fruit, and so is often used in street planting. It has pale pink flowers and is closer in habit and growth to *A. hippocastanum*.
Aspect Full sun.
Hardiness ✲✲✲ Zones 5–7.

A. *hippocastanum*
Horse chestnut

The species, which is native to south-eastern Europe, is ultimately a large, broadly spreading and showy spring-flowering tree. The palmate leaves, up to 30cm (12in) long, are attached to the petiole (leaf stalk) at the base and turn brown and yellow in autumn.

The showy white flowers appear in spring and are borne in large, upright panicles. Each flower has a yellow and red blotch. It will grow in a range of soil types in sun. H and S 30m (100ft).
Named cultivars 'Baumannii' (syn. 'Flore Pleno') is a sterile form with big, double, white flowers.

The slow-growing 'Hampton Court Gold' has yellow leaves in spring that fade to pale yellow-green. The foliage often scorches in strong sunlight, so this cultivar is best grown in light shade.

'Pyramidalis' has a more upright habit and is suitable for smaller gardens where space is restricted.
Aspect Full sun or semi-shade.
Hardiness ✲✲✲ Zones 4–8.

A. *indica*
Indian horse chestnut

This medium to large tree may be distinguished from *A. hippocastanum* by its finer leaves and narrower clusters of flowers. These are borne in late spring and are whitish-pink, blotched yellow and red. The flowers are followed by the typical chestnut seedcases, but these are small and spineless. It does best in moist, deep, fertile soil, which may be alkaline or acidic. H and S 30m (100ft).
Aspect Full sun.
Hardiness ✲✲✲ Zone 7.

spreading tree, it is especially suitable for milder maritime climates, thriving in moist, free-draining soil. H and S 10 (33ft).
Aspect Full sun or semi-shade.
Hardiness ✲✲ Zone 8.

A. 'White Tigress'

Another snakebark maple of uncertain parentage, this may be a hybrid of *A. tegmentosum* and *A. davidii*. It is a graceful, small tree with a multi-stemmed habit and blue-green and white striped bark. The smallish leaves turn golden-yellow in autumn. It requires neutral to acidic soil and cool summer temperatures. H 10m (33ft), S 5m (16ft).
Aspect Full sun or semi-shade.
Hardiness ✲✲✲ Zones 5–7.

AESCULUS
Horse chestnut, buckeye

The 15 species of deciduous trees in this genus are found in woodlands in Europe, North America and eastern Asia. They have opposite leaves and are grown for their flower panicles in late spring to early summer, as well as for their distinctive fruits. They make fine specimens in large gardens.
Cultivation Grow in deep, fertile, moisture-retentive soil in sun or semi-shade.

Aesculus hippocastanum

Aleurites moluccana

A. x neglecta 'Erythroblastos'
Sunrise horse chestnut
This is an ideal chestnut for a
small garden. It is also one of
the showiest because in spring the
emerging leaves are salmon-pink.
The foliage turns pale yellow by
summer, then green. New growth
may be damaged by frosts in late
spring, so it does best if grown
in fertile soil in semi-shade or
sheltered by other trees. H 6m
(20ft), S 3m (10ft).
Aspect Semi-shade.
Hardiness ❀❀❀ Zone 7.

A. turbinata
Japanese horse chestnut
The flowers of this species are
similar to those of *A. hippocastanum*
but often appear a few weeks later.
They are white, stained yellow
with a red spot, and are borne in
cylindrical panicles. The leaves, up
to 40cm (16in) long, are heavily
veined and turn yellow-brown in
autumn. A large tree, widely used

in parkland or avenue planting,
it is easy to grow in any free-
draining soil. H 20m (65ft),
S 12m (40ft).
Aspect Full sun.
Hardiness ❀❀❀ Zones 5–7.

AGATHIS
Kauri pine, dammar pine
The genus contains 13 species
of evergreen, coniferous trees
that are native to the southern
hemisphere. They are large trees
with exposed trunks and upswept
branches. The foliage is dark
green and quite thick, rather
than needle-like. The cones are
extremely large. Kauris are slow-
growing but ultimately large trees,
which can live for more than
1,000 years.
Cultivation Grow in deep, free-
draining, fertile soil in sun or
semi-shade.
Pruning Formative pruning should
aim to encourage a clear trunk
and a balanced crown, while

tipping the lateral branches of
young trees will encourage a
denser crown.
Propagation Seed is the easiest
method of propagation and
should be collected when fresh
and be sown into a container in a
heated glasshouse in a frost-free
and humid environment until
germination occurs. Softwood
cuttings will also root during
summer if the cutting base is
dipped in a rooting hormone and
placed in a glasshouse in a humid
environment until rooting occurs.

A. australis
Kauri pine
A widely planted avenue tree,
these are used extensively where
large evergreen trees are required
in tropical climates. They have
a distinctive outline with a clear
trunk and upright, tufted
branches. Young trees need to
be protected from strong winds.
H 25m (80ft), S 5m (16ft).
Aspect Full sun.
Hardiness ❀ Zones 9–11.

A. robusta
**Queensland kauri, smooth-bark
kauri**
This slow-growing tree tolerates
temperatures below freezing for
very short periods. It is a widely
planted coastal tree, and drought
tolerant, so it is widely planted
in exposed locations. H 50m
(165ft), S 10m (33ft).
Aspect Full sun.
Hardiness ❀ Zones 9–11.

AILANTHUS
The genus contains five species of
deciduous shrubs and spreading
trees, which are native to Australia
and South-east Asia. They are
fast-growing plants and will grow
in poor soils, which is why they
are often used as pioneer trees.
They also tolerate pollution. Male
and female flowers are borne on
separate trees in long racemes, but
it is the female flowers that develop
into long, flat, greenish-red seeds
that persist long into winter.
Cultivation Grow in fertile, deep
and well-drained soil in sun or
semi-shade.
Pruning Formative pruning should
aim to encourage a clear trunk and
a balanced crown, with occasional

pruning to remove dead, dying,
diseased or crossing branches
when the tree is in full leaf.
Propagation Fresh seed germinates
readily if it is sown in a container
in a unheated glasshouse or cold
frame. Alternatively, you can dig
up root suckers in winter and pot
them up.

A. altissima
(syn. A. glandulosa)
Tree of heaven
This broadly columnar tree is
the most widely planted species
in the genus. It grows very
quickly, and often produces root
suckers, which can prove to be
somewhat troublesome.
   Female forms produce masses
of seeds, so it is not surprising
that in some parts of the world
this tree is a weed. Male forms
do not pose this problem, but
the seeds are one of the attractive
features of the tree. This is one
of the most adaptable trees for
difficult locations, especially on
very poor or polluted soils. H
25m (80ft), S 12–15m
(40–50ft).
Named varieties The cultivar
'Pendula' is identical in many
respects to the species in growth
and overall height, except that
it has long foliage, which droops
heavily to produce a graceful
weeping effect.
Aspect Full sun or semi-shade.
Hardiness ❀❀❀ Zones 4–8
(although may not be adaptable
to tropical climates).

Ailanthus altissima

ALBIZIA
Silk tree

The genus contains about 150 species of deciduous trees and shrubs from Asia, South and Central America and Australia. They are grown for their delicate foliage and mimosa-like flowers.
Cultivation Grow in fertile, well-drained soil in full sun or semi-shade.
Pruning Formative pruning should encourage a clear trunk and a balanced crown. Prune occasionally to remove dead, dying, diseased or crossing branches.
Propagation Sow fresh seed in a pot in a humid and frost-free heated glasshouse.

A. julibrissin
(syn. *Acacia julibrissin*)
Silk tree

This tree is well adapted to nutrient-poor, dry soils. Dark green fern-like leaves turn pale yellow in autumn. Clusters of greenish-yellow flowers appear in summer, followed by flat, brown pods in autumn. It can be grown in protected locations in temperate areas. H and S 10m (33ft).
Named varieties *A. julibrissin* f. *rosea* is a widely grown form with pale pink flowers.
Aspect Full sun or semi-shade.
Hardiness ❊❊ Zones 7–10.

ALEURITES

The six species in the genus are evergreen trees that are native to tropical and subtropical areas of China, Indonesia and the western Pacific. They are tender trees that grow well in warm areas but should otherwise be grown under glass.
Cultivation Grow in moisture-retentive but well-drained, neutral to acidic soil. They prefer full sun but will tolerate semi-shade.
Pruning Formative pruning should aim to encourage a clear trunk and a balanced crown.
Propagation Sow fresh seed in a pot in a humid and frost-free heated glasshouse until germination occurs. Root hardwood cuttings by dipping in a rooting hormone. Keep in a humid, frost-free environment.

A. moluccana
Candlenut

This attractive, often multi-stemmed tree from South-east Asia produces maple-like new leaves that are strongly felted and white. These coincide with clusters of small, white flowers. From a distance the tree looks as if it has been touched by frost. This species is more tolerant of alkaline soils than others in the genus, and it is also resistant to drought and salt spray. H 20m (65ft), S 10m (33ft).
Aspect Full sun.
Hardiness (Min. 7°C/45°F) Zone 11.

ALNUS
Alder

The genus contains some 35 species of fast-growing, deciduous trees and shrubs. In spring, male and female catkins are borne on the same plant.
Cultivation Most species prefer damp soil, which does not need to be especially fertile, but individual preferences are noted below.
Pruning Little pruning is required apart from the removal of dead, dying, diseased or crossing branches, or pruning to encourage a clear leader. Many alders respond favourably to coppicing or pollarding. This should be undertaken during winter, with trees being pollarded or coppiced every three years.
Propagation Most alders can easily be grown from seed, as long as it is sown quickly once ripe. Cultivars can be grown from

Alnus cordata

softwood cuttings during summer or from hardwood cuttings during winter. Ornamental forms are also produced from winter indoor grafting or chip- and T-budding during summer.

A. cordata
Italian alder

A fast-growing, conical tree native to Italy and Corsica, this is one of the alders that will tolerate free-draining soil. It has a neat habit and glossy, dark green leaves that grow up to 10cm (4in) long. Yellow catkins appear in late winter and early spring, followed by dark green fruits, which mature to dark brown. It is often grown as a windbreak. H 25–30m (80–100ft), S 10m (33ft).
Aspect Full sun.
Hardiness ❊❊❊ Zones 4–7.

A. glutinosa
Common alder

This species thrives in damp conditions, although when under stress it is susceptible to root rot. The dark green leaves, up to 10cm (4in) long, are sticky in spring. Yellow catkins are borne in late winter to early spring. H 25m (80ft), S 10m (33ft).
Named varieties 'Aurea' has yellow leaves in spring and summer and a more compact habit. H 12m (40ft), S 5m (16ft).
'Imperialis' has deeply cut leaves and is the most decorative of the alders.
'Pyramidalis' is a conical form with a tight habit and strong central leader. H 15m (50ft), S 5m (16ft).
Aspect Full sun.
Hardiness ❊❊❊ Zones 4–7.

Albizia julibrissin

Alnus glutinosa 'Laciniata'

A. incana
Grey alder

The hardiest and most cold-tolerant of the alders, *A. incana*, which is native to Europe, is more compact than either *A. cordata* or *A. glutinosa*. The yellow-brown catkins appear in late winter to early spring, before the leaves, up to 10cm (4in) long, which are dark green above and covered with white hairs beneath. It will grow in free-draining soil. H 20m (65ft), S 10m (33ft).
Named varieties The cultivar 'Pendula' is a small weeping tree. H 10m (33ft), S 6m (20ft).
'Ramulis Coccineis' is a beautiful small tree. In spring the shoots are tinged with pinkish-red and the leaves are yellow. The catkins are orange-yellow. H 10m (33ft), S 5m (16ft).
Aspect Full sun.
Hardiness ✳✳✳ Zones 2–6.

AMELANCHIER
Juneberry, snowy mespilus, shadbush

Most of the 25 deciduous species in the genus are small to medium-sized shrubs, but there are a few small trees, which are grown for their spring to early summer flowers and vibrant autumn colours. If left unpruned they will be shrub-like, but with regular formative pruning a tree-like habit can be achieved.
Cultivation Grow in fertile, moisture-retentive but well-drained, acidic or alkaline soil in full sun or semi-shade.

Pruning Some species are best grown as multi-stemmed trees with the lower sections of the trunks kept clear of branches. However, a few can be easily trained as small garden trees with a single trunk and balanced crown. Occasional pruning is required to remove diseased, damaged or crossing branches.
Propagation Seed germinates if collected fresh and sown in an unheated glasshouse or cold frame until germination occurs. Semi-ripe cutting are taken in late summer, dipped in a rooting hormone, and placed in a humid environment until rooting occurs.

A. × grandiflora

This hybrid of *A. arborea* and *A. laevis* is a shrubby plant with a spreading habit. The young leaves, up to 8cm (3in) long, are bronze, turning green and, in autumn, red and orange. Racemes of white flowers are borne in spring and are followed by black berries. H 8m (26ft), S 10m (33ft).
Named varieties The best cultivar is 'Ballerina' (sometimes classified as a clone of *A. laevis*), which is a beautiful garden tree with masses of small, rose-like, white flowers in early spring, coinciding with the emerging leaves, which are small, pointed and toothed, bronze-green when young and turning red-purple in autumn. H and S 6m (20ft).
Aspect Full sun or semi-shade.
Hardiness ✳✳✳ Zones 4–7.

Araucaria araucana

A. laevis
Allegheny serviceberry

This small tree or, more often, large shrub, will be covered with masses of white flowers, which contrast with the pinkish new foliage. Autumn colour is spectacular: the leaves, up to 6cm (2½in) long, turn yellow, orange and purple-red. H 8–12m (26–40ft), S 8m (26ft).
Aspect Full sun or semi-shade.
Hardiness ✳✳✳ Zones 4–8.

A. lamarckii

In spring this broadly spreading tree, which is naturalized in Europe but of uncertain origin, produces an explosion of tiny white flowers from beneath the bronzy-coppery-red new foliage. In early autumn the leaves produce a range of fiery tints before they fall. H 10m (33ft), S 12m (40ft).
Aspect: Full sun or semi-shade.
Hardiness ✳✳✳ Zones 4–7.

ARAUCARIA

The genus of evergreen, coniferous trees contains about 18 species, which are found in Australia, Oceania and South America. Only one species, *A. araucana*, is hardy and makes a handsome specimen tree.
Cultivation Outdoors, grow in moisture-retentive but well-drained soil. All young plants should be protected from cold winter winds.

Amelanchier lamarckii

Pruning Formative pruning should aim to encourage a clear trunk and a balanced crown, while tipping the lateral branches of young trees will encourage a denser crown. Occasional pruning is required for the removal of dead, dying, diseased or crossing branches.

Propagation Seed is the easiest method of propagation and should be collected when fresh and be sown into a container in a heated glasshouse in a frost-free and humid environment until germination occurs.

A. araucana
(syn. *A. imbricata*)
Monkey puzzle, Chilean pine
This large tree has whorled and spiky foliage and long, rather lax branches. In mild areas all the lower branches remain attached, but elsewhere the lower branches are soon lost and the tree assumes the distinctive umbrella-like shape. It is an adaptable tree that is tolerant of salt spray. It does best in fertile, moisture-retentive but well-drained soil with some protection from cold winds. H 25m (80ft), S 10m (33ft). Aspect: Full sun.
Hardiness ❃❃❃ Zone 8.

A. heterophylla
(syn. *A. excelsa*)
Norfolk Island pine
A distinctive and widely grown conifer in warmer climates, the species is tolerant of salt spray and heat and is often planted in

coastal locations to help stabilize sandy soils. The foliage takes the form of upswept, V-shaped fans, which spiral around the branches while the trunk is left almost bare. Despite their potential size, young plants are popular houseplants in temperate areas. H 60m (200ft), S 30m (100ft). Aspect Full sun to light shade. Hardiness ❃ Zones 9–11.

ARBUTUS
Strawberry tree, Madroño
The genus contains about 14 species of ornamental, small-leaved, evergreen trees, which are grown for their highly polished bark, heather-like flowers and small, hard strawberry-like (but unpalatable) fruits, which ripen in autumn. The bark is particularly attractive in winter. The flowers are quite showy and are produced from late summer to autumn.

Although some species are relatively tender when they are young, once they mature they are all relatively hardy, and all will tolerate coastal planting.
Cultivation Grow in fertile, well-drained soil; *A. andrachne*, *A. x andrachnoides* and *A. unedo* will tolerate alkaline soil, but *A. menziesii* prefers acidic conditions.
Pruning Remove dead, dying, diseased or crossing branches. Lower branches should be removed so their ornamental bark can be seen. Occasionally the crown of *Arbutus unedo* may require thinning. This is best done during late spring or early summer.

Arbutus unedo 'Elfin King'

Propagation Strawberry trees can be propagated by seed, which should be sown into acidic compost. Semi-ripe cuttings can be taken in late summer, dipped in a rooting hormone and then placed in a humid environment to root. *Arbutus* 'Marina' is produced by winter indoor grafting on to *Arbutus unedo* rootstock.

A. andrachne
Grecian strawberry tree
Native to south-eastern Europe, this is a small, round-headed tree with glossy, dark green leaves. Creamy-white flowers are borne on short stalks in late spring and are followed by orange-red fruits. The rough bark is orange-brown but flakes to reveal attractive bright orange underbark. H and S 10m (33ft).
Aspect Full sun or semi-shade.
Hardiness ❃❃ Zone 8.

A. x andrachnoides
This interesting tree is a hybrid between *A. andrachne* and *A. unedo*. It has reddish-brown, flaking bark that peels in long strips. It develops into a small, round-headed tree with glossy, mid-green leaves, up to 10cm (4in) long. The small white flowers are not usually followed by fruit. H and S 10m (33ft).
Aspect Full sun or semi-shade.
Hardiness ❃❃❃ Zone 8.

A. 'Marina'
Although the parentage of this cultivar is unknown, it is probably a hybrid between *A. x andrachnoides* and *A. canariensis* (Canary Island strawberry tree). Its endearing features are its shiny, cinnamon-coloured, flaking bark, the white, pink-flushed autumn flowers and the masses of small strawberry fruits that ripen alongside the flowers. It grows into a small, wide-spreading, round-headed tree. H and S 10m (33ft).
Aspect Full sun or semi-shade.
Hardiness ❃❃❃ Zone 8.

A. unedo
Strawberry tree
This broad-headed tree is also the hardiest and is most tolerant of salt spray. It grows wild in exposed coastal locations throughout Europe and Asia Minor, and it is sometimes known as the Killarney strawberry tree.

In autumn it bears small clusters of white flowers, which ripen alongside the fruit that develop from the previous year's flowers. The large fruit is initially orange, turning orange-red, and sometimes grows up to 2.5cm (1in) across. Its bark is dark brown and does not flake or shed. 'Elfin King' is a compact growing form. H and S 10m (33ft).
Aspect Full sun or semi-shade.
Hardiness ❃❃❃ Zone 6.

Arbutus 'Marina'

Banksia spinulosa

ARTOCARPUS
Breadfruit
This is a genus of about 50 evergreen and deciduous trees found in the tropics. The best-known species, *A. altilis*, is the breadfruit sought by Captain Bligh on the ill-fated voyage from Tahiti on HMS *Bounty*.
Cultivation These trees need tropical conditions: reliably warm weather and plentiful moisture.
Pruning Formative pruning should aim to encourage a clear trunk and a balanced crown, while tipping the lateral branches of young trees will encourage a denser crown. Occasional pruning is required for the removal of dead, dying, diseased or crossing branches.
Propagation Breadfruit can easily be propagated by bending lower branches down and layering them

Artocarpus altilis

in situ or from root cuttings taken during the dormant season and potted up and placed in a frost-free, humid environment until shoots develop.

A. altilis
(syn. A. communis)
Breadfruit
This broadly spreading tree has evergreen leaves resembling those of *Monstera deliciosa* (Swiss cheese plant) but with white veins across the surface of the leaves. The rounded, pear-like, light green fruits ripen in summer. They have a white, fleshy, potato-like centre that must be boiled or baked prior to eating. H and S 20m (65ft).
Aspect Full sun or semi-shade.
Hardiness (Min. 5°C/41°F) Zones 10–11.

BANKSIA
The genus contains about 70 species of highly ornamental evergreen shrubs and small trees, which rank alongside the South African proteas in their beauty. Banksias are native to Australia and New Guinea. They vary in height but are often large, multi-stemmed trees. Like other members of the *Proteaceae* family (including *Protea*, *Grevillea* and *Leucadendron*), banksias are intolerant of phosphate, so take care with fertilizers.
Cultivation In the wild, banksias grow in nutrient-poor, moist to dry, sandy soil. A few can grow in dry, warm temperate areas, but they dislike damp winters.

Pruning Formative pruning should aim to encourage a clear trunk and a balanced crown. Tipping the lateral branches on young trees encourages a dense crown. Occasional pruning is required for the removal of dead, dying, diseased or crossing branches.
Propagation In the wild, fire is required for the 'cones' to open and release the seeds. The easiest way to replicate these conditions and force the seeds to germinate is to place the seeds in a shallow container, cover with boiling water and leave to soak overnight. Alternatively, place the seeds on a baking tin (pan) in the oven at 200°C (400°F) for 10 minutes. Allow them to cool before sowing in an acidic potting medium in a frost-free and humid environment.

B. baxteri
This small tree has light green, angular leaves, up to 17cm (7in) long, which sometimes turn reddish. The large, creamy-yellow, protea-like flowerheads are produced in reasonable numbers in late summer and autumn. It is an unusual tree that is certain to turn heads when in flower. H and S 3m (10ft).
Aspect Full sun.
Hardiness ❀ Zone 9 (will require winter protection).

B. coccinea
Scarlet banksia
The dark green leaves of this small tree are toothed and silver on the underside. Columns, up to 8cm (3in) long, of spiky scarlet flowers are produced throughout spring and summer. This is a tree that requires winter protection. H 5m (16ft), S 3m (10ft).
Aspect Full sun.
Hardiness ❀ Zone 9.

B. integrifolia
Coast banksia
Erect columns of spiky, bright yellow flowers are borne on the tree in summer and autumn. The dark green leaves are notched at the tip and a beautiful silver underneath. It is tolerant of free-draining, sandy, acidic soil. H 7m (23ft), S 3m (10ft).
Aspect Full sun.
Hardiness ❀ Zones 10–11.

B. menziesii
Firewood banksia
An attractive, small tree that flowers over a long period from summer to autumn. It produces spiky columns of reddish flowers that fade to orange, occasionally pinkish and then bronze-brown. The stout foliage is covered with reddish hairs at first, but as the leaves mature they turn dark grey-green. Requires winter protection. H 15m (50ft), S 10m (33ft).
Aspect Full sun.
Hardiness (Min. 3–5°C/37–41°F) Zone 9.

B. serrata
Saw banksia
This banksia has extremely dramatic foliage. The long leaves, which have strongly toothed edges, are reddish-grey at first but turn glossy, dark green. The flowers are yellowish-grey and orange-yellow on the inside, and they are borne in late summer and autumn. It is a relatively fast-growing tree but it requires winter protection.
H 20m (65ft), S 8m (26ft).
Aspect Full sun.
Hardiness ❀ Zone 9.

BAUHINIA
Mountain ebony, orchid ebony
There are between 250 and 300 species of evergreen or deciduous trees and shrubs in the genus, which are grown mainly for their orchid-like flowers. They are not reliably hardy but may be grown in a glasshouse environment.
Cultivation Outside, grow in fertile, moisture-retentive, well-drained alkaline soil in full sun.
Pruning Formative pruning should aim to encourage a clear trunk and a balanced crown, while tipping the lateral branches of young trees will encourage a denser crown. Occasional pruning is required for the removal of dead, dying, diseased or crossing branches.
Propagation Seed is the easiest method of propagation. Collect fresh seed and sow in a pot in a heated glasshouse in a frost-free and humid environment until germination occurs. Softwood tip cuttings can also be rooted during late spring and early summer.

Bauhinia x blakeana

Dip in rooting hormone and place in a frost-free, humid environment until they root.

B. x blakeana
Hong Kong orchid tree
This stunning evergreen hybrid between *B. variegata* and *B. purpurea* originated in China. The round-headed trees are quick-growing but sterile, and so do not bear fruit. The fragrant flowers are maroon-pink and broadly striped with white through the centre. H 12m (40ft), S 10m (33ft). Aspect Full sun. Hardiness (Min. 7°C/45°F) Zones 10–12.

B. purpurea
Fall orchid tree
The narrowly cut petals, which make the flowers appear more ruffled than those of other

species in the genus, are purple-pink streaked with white. H 12m (40ft), S 10m (33ft). Aspect Full sun. Hardiness (Min. 7°C/45°F) Zones 10–12.

B. variegata
Poor man's orchid
The heart-shaped leaves of this wide-spreading, loose-crowned, deciduous tree consist of two lobes and have veins radiating from the stalk to the tip. The large flowers, a bit like a honeysuckle, are dark magenta, streaked with white. They appear over a period from summer to autumn. The pea-like seedpods are bright red. H 12m (40ft), S 10m (33ft). Named varieties *B. variegata* var. *alba* is a stunning form with elegant white flowers. It has a similar habit to the species but is somewhat shy to flower. Aspect Full sun. Hardiness ✱ Zones 10–12.

BETULA
Birch
The 60 or so species of deciduous trees and shrubs in the genus are found throughout the northern hemisphere. Male and female catkins are borne on the same plant in spring. Many species have attractive bark and are planted for their autumn colour and graceful habit of growth. *Cultivation* Grow in deep, moisture-retentive but well-drained soil in full sun or semi-shade.

Betula alleghaniensis

Betula albosinensis var. septentrionalis

Pruning Most birch require little pruning apart from the removal of dead, dying, diseased or crossing branches. Lower branches may be removed so their ornamental bark can be seen. This is best done during late spring or early summer; if undertaken too early in spring the cut surfaces will 'bleed' profusely.
Propagation Birch are most widely propagated by seed or winter indoor grafting. Sow ripe seed in a pot and place in an unheated glasshouse or cold frame until germinated. Most forms with ornamental bark are produced by winter indoor grafting on to *Betula pendula* rootstock. The forms of *Betula nigra* are widely produced by softwood cuttings during summer.

B. albosinensis
Chinese red birch
This graceful and elegant tree has finely toothed leaves, up to 8cm (3in) long, which turn yellow in autumn. It has coppery-pink peeling bark. It will grow well

in most soils, but prefers damp conditions. H 25m (80ft), S 10m (33ft). Named varieties Some consider *B. albosinensis* var. *septentrionalis* as the best form of the species. It has pink and pale grey flaking bark that turns darker in winter. The winter shoots are reddish-brown. The branches weep slightly and produce a beautiful outline in spring and summer. Aspect Full sun or semi-shade. Hardiness ✱✱✱ Zones 5–6.

B. alleghaniensis
(syn. *B. lutea*)
Yellow birch
A fast-growing and ultimately large tree from North America, the species has golden-brown flaking bark. In autumn the leaves turn yellow. The stems smell of wintergreen if the bark is rubbed or the leaves are crushed. It is a shade-tolerant birch that does best in fertile, free-draining soil. H 30m (100ft), S 15m (50ft). Aspect Full sun or semi-shade. Hardiness ✱✱✱ Zone 3.

Betula pendula

B. ermanii
Erman's birch, Russian rock birch, gold birch
This ultimately large and spreading pyramidal tree is grown for its creamy-white bark, which peels in long strips to reveal creamy-pink underbark. The dark green leaves, up to 10cm (4in) long, turn yellow in autumn, and slender, long catkins are borne in spring. It is an excellent year-round tree for fertile, free-draining, neutral to acidic soils. H 25m (80ft), S 20m (65ft).
Named varieties There are several cultivars, including 'Grayswood Hill', which has exceptionally beautiful white bark.
'Hakkoda Orange', which originated in a batch of seed from Japan, has attractive flaking orange bark.
Aspect Full sun or semi-shade.
Hardiness ❋❋❋ Zones 5–6.

B. 'Hergest'
Sometimes sold as a cultivar of *B. albosinensis*, this is a fast-growing form with salmon-pink and whitish flaking bark. H 25m (80ft), S 10m (33ft).
Aspect Full sun or semi-shade.
Hardiness ❋❋❋ Zones 5–6.

B. lenta
Cherry birch, sweet birch
This species is similar in many respects to *B. alleghaniensis*. It is native to the east of the USA, where it is found in fertile woodlands. Young leaves and the

bark smell and taste of wintergreen when crushed or rubbed. The yellow-green leaves, up to 10cm (4in) long, turn yellow in autumn. It grows well on neutral, moisture-retentive, fertile soil. H 25m (80ft), S 12m (40ft).
Aspect Full sun or semi-shade.
Hardiness ❋❋❋ Zone 3.

B. nigra
Black birch, river birch
This species from North America is distinguished from other birches by its purplish-orange shaggy bark, which looks as if sheets of paper have been stuck to the trunk. It is a slender tree with slightly weeping branches, and the glossy leaves, up to 8cm (3in) long, turn yellow in autumn. It is tolerant of wet sites

Betula ermanii 'Grayswood Hill'

but does as well in free-draining soil. H and S 30m (100ft).
Named varieties The cultivar 'Cascade Falls' has a strongly weeping form, similar to, but more graceful than, that of *B. pendula* 'Youngii'; it is probably the best weeping birch currently available.
The most widely planted cultivar, 'Heritage', has whitishpink flaking bark and a good pyramidal habit. It is equally beautiful whether trained as a single-stemmed, upright tree or as a multi-stemmed bushy tree.
'Dura-Heat', a US selection, is more heat-tolerant than 'Heritage' and has glossier leaves and whiter bark.
Aspect Full sun or semi-shade.
Hardiness ❋❋❋ Zones 3–9.

B. papyrifera
Paper birch, canoe birch
This fast-growing, cold-tolerant birch from North America has whitish peeling bark. The dark green leaves, up to 10cm (4in) long, turn orange-yellow in autumn. This tree will not do well in shallow, free-draining, strongly alkaline soil. H 30m (100ft), S 15m (50ft).
Named varieties The cold-tolerant cultivar 'Saint George' is grown for its white bark and dark brown branches.
'Vancouver' has duller, pinkish-brown and white bark and a lovely orange autumn colour.
Aspect Full sun or semi-shade.
Hardiness ❋❋❋ Zones 2–7.

B. pendula
Silver birch
The silver birch, which is native to Europe, is widely grown for its whitish bark, which turns black at the base as the tree matures. It has mid-green leaves, up to 6cm (2in) long, which turn yellow in autumn, and yellow-brown catkins in early spring. The species is more tolerant of drier conditions than many other birches and will do well in shallow, free-draining, alkaline soil. H 30m (100ft), S 10m (33ft).
Named varieties 'Golden Cloud' is a pretty form with vivid yellow leaves that turn yellow-green in summer. H 6m (20ft), S 5m (16ft).

'Obelisk' is an upright form with a strong main leader and twisted, upswept branches.
The graceful 'Purpurea' has purplish bark and leaves; the latter turn yellow in autumn. It is slower growing than many other forms of the silver birch. H 10m (33ft), S 3m (10ft).
'Youngii' (Young's weeping birch) is a small, graceful weeping tree, which requires regular pruning to maintain its attractive shape. H 8ft (26ft), S 5ft (16ft).
Aspect Full sun or semi-shade.
Hardiness ❋❋❋ Zones 2–7.

B. utilis var. jacquemontii
Himalayan birch
The species is usually represented in gardens by this naturally occurring form, which is one of the most widely planted garden trees, grown for its stunning white bark, long, dangling catkins in spring and yellow autumn leaf colour. A broadly conical tree, it is fast-growing when first planted. It does best in fertile, moist, neutral to acidic soil. H 25m (80ft), S 10m (33ft).
Named varieties Among the cultivars of *B. utilis* var. *jacquemontii*, the Dutch selection 'Doorenbos' has whitish bark that peels to reveal an orange underbark.
'Grayswood Ghost' has stunning white bark and very long catkins and is quick to establish.
The quick-growing 'Jermyns' has extremely long catkins, which are up to 15cm (6in) long, and beautiful bark. It is ultimately a tall, broadly spreading birch.
'Silver Shadow' is the smallest birch of this group, has the starkest white bark, and is one of the best for general planting.
B. utilis 'Ramdana River' is an exquisite form with white, pink-tinged bark and glossy green leaves in summer.
Aspect Full sun or semi-shade.
Hardiness ❋❋❋ Zones 5–6.

BISMARCKIA
The bismarckia palm is only found on the island of Madagascar where it flourishes in open grassland and grows quickly. It is one of the most ornamental palms, with beautiful bluish-tinted foliage, and is widely

Bismarckia nobilis

planted. As a landscape palm, it has many uses and can be planted as a specimen or in groups.
Cultivation Although they will grow in poor, dry conditions, these palms will grow more quickly in fertile, free-draining soil. They will not survive temperatures below 15°C (59°F), although those with the most intense blue-coloured leaves are the most hardy.
Pruning Like most palms, little pruning is required apart from the removal of dead leaves and spent flower clusters in early summer.
Propagation Seed should be collected when fresh and sown into a pot in a heated glasshouse in a humid environment at 29°C (84°F) until germination occurs.

B. nobilis
Noble palm
This palm, which is native to Madagascar, has silver-grey, fan-shaped leaves, which can be over 3m (10ft) across. The palmate fans are upright and angled in a different direction above the main trunk. The trunk itself is brown and slightly matted. Female plants

bear clusters of fleshy brown fruits.
H 12m (40ft), S 6m (20ft).
Aspect Full sun.
Hardiness ❊ Zones 9–11.

BRACHYCHITON
Bottletree, kurrajong
There are some 30 species of evergreen and deciduous trees in the genus, native to Australia and Papua New Guinea. They are tender plants, which can be grown as specimens in mild areas but otherwise are grown under glass.
Cultivation Outdoors, grow in fertile, free-draining, neutral to acidic soil in full sun.
Pruning Formative pruning should encourage a clear trunk and a balanced crown. Tipping the lateral branches will encourage a denser crown. Occasional pruning is required to remove dead, diseased or crossing branches.
Propagation Collect seeds when fresh and sow in a pot in a heated glasshouse in a frost-free and humid environment until germination occurs. Semi-ripe cuttings can be taken in late summer. Place in a frost-free, humid environment until rooted.

B. acerifolius
(syn. Sterculia acerifolia)
Flame tree, flame kurrajong
In warm areas this Australian species is a widely grown street tree. In spring, masses of small, bell-shaped, scarlet flowers cover the upswept branches and give the effect of vivid autumn colour. This large tree stores water in its thick trunk during droughts.
H 40m (130ft), S 20m (65ft).
Aspect Full sun.
Hardiness (Min. 10°C/50°F) Zones 9–11.

BROWNEA
The genus of about 25 species of evergreen trees and shrubs is native to tropical South America. These plants are tender and need restrictive pruning if grown under glass in temperate areas.
Cultivation Outdoors, grow in moisture-retentive but well-drained, neutral to acidic soil in semi-shade.
Pruning Formative pruning should aim to encourage a clear trunk and a balanced crown. Tipping the lateral branches of young trees will encourage a denser crown. Occasional pruning is required to remove dead, dying, diseased or crossing branches.
Propagation Sow fresh seed in a heated glasshouse until germination occurs. Semi-ripe cuttings can be rooted in late summer. Dip in a rooting hormone and place in a frost-free, humid environment until they root.

B. macrophylla
Panama flame tree
In summer this tree bears stunning scarlet flowers with stamens pointing in every direction. The new leaves are flushed with pink, turning dark green as they mature. Seeds are borne in long, dark brown pods.
H and S 20m (65ft).
Aspect Light to semi-shade.
Hardiness ❊ Zones 10–12.

BUTIA
Yatay palm, jelly palm
The 12 species come from cool areas of South America, where they develop into tall, straight-stemmed palms. They can be grown as houseplants when they are young. x *Butiagrus nabonnandii* is a hybrid between *B. capitata* and *Syagrus romanzoffiana* (queen palm), and it is one of the hardiest and most tropical-looking of the V-leaved palms. It has the graceful habit of *B. capitata* and the quality of *S. romanzoffiana*.
Cultivation This tree will grow in any free-draining but fertile soil. It thrives in full sun but will tolerate light, dappled shade.
Pruning Jelly palms require little annual pruning apart from the removal of the dead fronds and fruit spikes as and when needed.
Propagation Fresh seed germinates readily if it is planted in loam-based potting compost, in a frost-free humid environment with temperatures around 29°C (84°F).

Brownea grandiceps

Butia capitata

B. capitata
(syn. *Cocos capitata*)
Pindo palm, jelly palm
This slow-growing palm has distinctive, strongly arching, V-shaped, silver-green fronds. Brown, dead leaves hang from the trunk, and are best removed to reveal the wide-based trunk. The leaves can measure up to 3m (10ft) long. In summer it bears panicles of yellow flowers. H 6m (20ft), S 3m (10ft).
Aspect Full sun.
Hardiness (Min. 5–10°C/41–50°F) Zones 8–11.

CALLIANDRA
Powder puff tree
There are over 200 species of evergreen shrubs, trees and perennials in the genus. They are native to tropical and subtropical areas in India, Africa and Central and South America. Although they will withstand temperatures of -3°C (27°F), in temperate areas they are grown as conservatory plants.
Cultivation Outdoors, grow in fertile, well-drained soil in full sun.
Pruning Formative pruning should aim to encourage a clear trunk and a balanced crown. Occasional pruning is required for the removal of dead, dying, diseased or crossing branches.
Propagation Sow fresh seed in a heated glasshouse until germination occurs. Softwood tip cuttings can be rooted during late spring and early summer. Dip in a rooting hormone and place in a frost-free, humid environment until they root.

C. haematocephala
(syn. *C. inaequilatera*)
This small, broadly spreading tree bears pompons of silky, dark rosy-red flowers on short days, mainly in the late autumn and winter. The glossy, dark green leaves, up to 45cm (18in) long, are fern-like. H 6m (20ft), S 4m (12ft).
Aspect Full sun.
Hardiness (Min. 13°C/55°F) Zones 9–12.

C. tweedii
Mexican flame bush
This small tree has whitish-yellow flowers over a long period from winter to late spring. The leaves, up to 15cm (6in) long, are mid-green. It is more tolerant of drought than other species. H 5m (16ft), S 1.8m (6ft).
Aspect Full sun.
Hardiness (Min. 13°C/55°F) Zones 9–12.

CALLISTEMON
Bottlebrush
The 25 species of bottlebrush are native to Australia, where they are found in reliably moist soil. These evergreen trees are recognizable from the spikes of colourful flowers. Although the majority are shrubs, many attain sufficient height to make beautiful landscape trees.
Cultivation Outdoors, grow in moisture-retentive but well-drained, neutral to acidic soil in full sun.
Pruning Formative pruning should aim to encourage a clear trunk and a balanced crown. Tipping the lateral branches of young trees will encourage a denser crown. Remove dead, dying, diseased or crossed branches.
Propagation Sow fresh seed in a heated glasshouse in a frost-free and humid environment until germination occurs. Semi-ripe cuttings can be rooted in late summer. Dip in a rooting hormone and place in a frost-free, humid environment until rooted.

C. citrinus
Crimson bottlebrush
This tree has brown flaking bark and, in spring and summer, dense clusters of scarlet flowers. It is a widely planted species, often best grown as a multi-stemmed small tree. Requires winter protection. H 10m (33ft), S 8m (26ft).
Aspect Full sun.
Hardiness ❋ Zones 8–11.

C. salignus
Willow bottlebrush, white bottlebrush
A small tree with white, papery bark, this bottlebrush has willow-like leaves and masses of bright red flowers, which are borne at the ends of the stems from late spring to midsummer. Although

Callistemon citrinus

Calliandra haematocephala

Calocedrus decurrens

the red-flowering form is most often seen, there are also forms with pink and whitish-green flowers. Requires winter protection. H 15m (50ft), S 5m (16ft). Aspect Full sun. Hardiness ✽ Zones 8–11.

C. viminalis
Weeping bottlebrush
This highly variable species usually has large scarlet flowers in clusters at the end of the stems. However, white, pink and mauve forms have also been introduced. It has a strongly weeping habit and coppery new growth in spring. H and S 8m (26ft). Aspect Full sun. Hardiness ✽ Zones 9–11.

C. viridiflorus
Green bottlebrush
The hardiest of the bottlebrushes, this makes a large shrub or small tree. It has dark green leaves, up to 3cm (1½in) long, and pale yellow-green flowers in mid- to

late summer. New growth is flushed pink. Requires winter protection. H and S 10m (33ft). Aspect Full sun. Hardiness ✽✽ Zones 8–11.

CALOCEDRUS
Incense cedar
The three species of evergreen conifer in the genus come from North America and South-east Asia. They can be grown as specimen trees.
Cultivation Grow in any moisture-retentive but well-drained, fertile soil in sun or semi-shade.
Pruning Formative pruning should aim to produce a clear trunk and a balanced crown. Tipping the lateral branches of young trees will encourage a denser crown. Prune to remove dead, dying, diseased or crossing branches.
Propagation Sow fresh seed in a pot in an unheated glasshouse or cold frame until germination occurs. Semi-ripe and softwood cuttings can be rooted in summer.

C. decurrens
(syn. *Heyderia decurrens*, *Libocedrus decurrens*)
Incense cedar
This beautiful, tightly conical, columnar tree is usually available in the form 'Fastigiata' or 'Columnaris', and plants may not be so named. (The true species will be more open and less columnar in habit.) It produces flat sprays of dense foliage, similar to a cypress, but with a strongly corrugated bark. H 20m (65ft), S 1.8m (6ft).
Aspect Full sun.
Hardiness ✽✽✽ Zone 7.

CALOPHYLLUM
The genus contains over 180 species of evergreen trees and shrubs, but only a few are cultivated.
Cultivation Grow in humus-rich, moisture-retentive soil in full sun.
Pruning Formative pruning should aim to encourage a clear trunk and a balanced crown. Tipping the lateral branches of young trees will encourage a denser crown. Remove dead, dying, diseased or crossing branches.
Propagation Sow fresh seed in a heated glasshouse in a frost-free and humid environment until germination occurs.

C. inophyllum
Alexandrian laurel, Indian laurel, laurelwood
This large tree has leathery, oval leaves, up to 20cm (8in) long. The fragrant, waxy, creamy-white blooms are borne in dense clusters

above the foliage. The flowers, which appear late in the day and fade by the following morning, appear in late spring and summer, followed by blue-green, golf-ball-sized fruits, which ripen o brown. H 35m (115ft), S 20m (65ft). Aspect Full sun to semi-shade. Hardiness (Min. 8°C/46°F) Zones 10–11.

CARPINUS
Hornbeam
The 40 or so species of hornbeam are deciduous trees found in Europe, North America and Asia. They are useful for hedging or as specimen trees, providing good autumn colour, an attractive habit and catkins in spring.
Cultivation Grow in moisture-retentive but well-drained soil in sun or semi-shade (but see species requirements).
Pruning Most hornbeams require little pruning apart from the removal of dead, dying, diseased or crossing branches. The habit of many of the hornbeams is usually slightly untidy and so it is difficult to prune for shape without removing too many branches. Any pruning is best done during early summer and care is needed.
Propagation Sow fresh seed in a container and place outside in an unheated glasshouse or cold frame until germination occurs. Some forms can be grown from softwood cuttings during summer, or grafted on to the common hornbeam during winter.

Carpinus betulus linnaeus

Carya illinoinensis

C. betulus
Common hornbeam
The species is widely planted as a medium-sized to large specimen tree. It has fluted grey bark and leaves similar to *Fagus sylvatica*

(common beech). In spring it bears both male and female catkins on the same tree, followed in autumn by clusters of green fruits that turn yellow-brown as they age. These plants tolerate close pruning and are shade tolerant. They make attractive hedges. H and S 30m (100ft). Named varieties 'Frans Fontaine' has a narrow habit, similar to that of *Cupressus sempervirens* (Italian cypress), rarely exceeding 6m (20ft) across, and it is useful where space is limited.
Aspect Full sun or semi-shade.
Hardiness ✲✲✲ Zones 4–7.

C. caroliniana
American hornbeam
This small, graceful tree has spreading, slightly upturned branches. The blue-green leaves, up to 12cm (5in) long, turn vivid

shades of yellow and orange-red in autumn, especially when the tree is growing in moist, fertile, alkaline soil. H and S 10–12m (33–40ft).
Aspect Full sun or semi-shade.
Hardiness ✲✲✲ Zones 3–9.

CARYA
Hickory
Found in woodland in North America and eastern Asia, the 25 or so species are deciduous trees that are grown for their very attractive foliage. Both male and female produce catkins, which are borne on the same plant in late spring. All the species have alternate, pinnate leaves. They are long-lived trees that require plenty of space for their questing roots. However, they can be slow to establish and do not transplant well so are best planted as container-grown saplings.
Cultivation Grow in deep, fertile, moisture-retentive but well-drained soil in sun or semi-shade.
Pruning Hickories require little pruning apart from the removal of dead, dying, diseased or crossing branches. They do require formative pruning to encourage a nice straight trunk and an even balanced crown. Any pruning is best done during early summer when the tree is in full leaf.
Propagation Hickories are widely grown from seed, which should be sown when fresh and placed in an unheated glasshouse or cold frame to germinate. Seedlings are best planted in their eventual location as they can take a considerable amount of time to establish and do not transplant well. Selected forms can also be grown from softwood cuttings during the summer, or grafted on to seedling hickories during the winter.

C. cordiformis
Bitternut, bitternut hickory, swamp hickory
Like most hickories, this is a large tree with a broadly spreading habit. The mid-green leaves, up to 25cm (10in) long, turn golden-yellow in autumn. H 30m (100ft), S 15m (50ft).
Aspect Full sun or semi-shade.
Hardiness ✲✲✲ Zones 4–9.

Caryota mitis

C. illinoinensis
Pecan
The mid-green, pinnate leaves, up to 50cm (20in) long, of this quick-growing tree have 11–17 leaflets along the main leaf stem and turn yellow in autumn. The nuts, up to 6cm (2½in) long, are edible in warm areas. H 30m (100ft), S 15m (50ft).
Aspect Full sun.
Hardiness ✲✲✲ Zones 5–9.

C. ovata
Shagbark hickory
This broadly conical tree has distinctive grey bark, which forms large, detached curls as the tree matures. The leaves, up to 30cm (12in) long, have five slender leaflets. These are mid-green, turning golden-brown and yellow in autumn. The spent bark is widely used in the production of hickory flakes for barbecues or smoking meat. The small nuts, produced in their thousands in autumn, are edible. S 30m (100ft), S 15m (50ft).
Aspect Full sun or semi-shade.
Hardiness ✲✲✲ Zones 4–8.

CARYOTA
Fishtail palm
These upright palms are native to South-east Asia, India, Australia and the Solomon Islands. In temperate areas small plants are often grown as houseplants, but in tropical zones they make handsome specimen trees.
Cultivation Outdoors, grow in deep, humus-rich, moisture-retentive but well-drained soil. Shelter from the midday sun.

Carya ovata

Castanea sativa

Pruning Fishtail palms require little annual pruning, apart from the cosmetic removal of the dead fronds and fruit spikes during late spring or early summer.
Propagation Fresh seed germinates readily if planted in loam-based potting compost, in a humid glasshouse with temperatures around 29°C (84°F).

C. mitis
Burmese fishtail palm, clustered fishtail palm
This is a densely clumping palm. It is monocarpic: after the flower spikes are produced and the fruits ripen, the top growth dies. However, because it produces suckers, the whole plant does not die. The pinnate leaves consist of small, angular, opposite leaflets with serrated edges. In summer, cream-coloured flowers are borne in panicles, up to 30cm (12in) long. H 6m (20ft), S 4m (12ft).
Aspect Full sun to semi-shade.
Hardiness (Min. 15°C/59°F) Zones 10–11.

CASSIA
Shower tree
This large genus contains over 500 species, comprising evergreen or deciduous trees and shrubs. Many of the species have been reclassified into the genus *Senna*.
Cultivation Outdoors, grow in fertile, deep, moisture-retentive soil in full sun.
Pruning Formative pruning should encourage a clear trunk and a balanced crown. Prune only occasionally to remove dead, dying, diseased or crossing branches.

Propagation Seed is the easiest method of propagation and should be collected when fresh, soaked in water and sown into a pot in a heated glasshouse in a frost-free and humid environment until germination occurs.

C. fistula
Golden shower tree, Indian laburnum, pudding pipe tree
This semi-evergreen, medium-sized tree has a slightly arching habit. The pinnate leaves, up to 60cm (24in) long, consist of 6–16 bright green leaflets. From late spring to early summer it has hanging clusters of golden, pea-like flowers. The flowers are followed by large, brown, cylindrical pods. H 20m (65ft), S 15m (50ft).
Aspect Full sun.
Hardiness (Min. 15°C/59°F) Zones 10–12.

C. javanica
Pink shower tree, rainbow shower tree
In spring, this broadly spreading, deciduous tree with spiny branches and trunk bears long, rigid clusters of rose-pink, fading to whitish pink, flowers. H and S 25m (80ft).
Aspect Full sun.
Hardiness (Min. 16°C/61°F) Zones 10–12.

CASTANEA
Sweet chestnut
The 12 or so species of long-lived deciduous trees in the genus are found in Europe, North America, Asia and northern Africa. They have handsome foliage and sometimes edible nuts. In summer catkins bear fragrant flowers.
Cultivation Grow in deep, fertile, free-draining soil that is on the acid side of neutral.

Pruning Remove dead, dying, diseased or crossing branches. Formative pruning encourages a straight trunk and evenly balanced crown. Remove suckers when they appear, as well as reverted shoots on the variegated leaf forms. Prune during early summer when the tree is in full leaf.
Propagation Fresh seed should be sown in an unheated glasshouse or cold frame until it germinates.

C. dentata
American sweet chestnut
This majestic tree is susceptible to chestnut blight. The long, tapered, toothed leaves, up to 25cm (10in) long, are mid-green, turning golden-brown in autumn. Edible fruits appear in autumn. H 30m (100ft), S 25m (80ft).
Aspect Full sun or semi-shade.
Hardiness ✳✳✳ Zones 4–8.

Castanea dentata

Castanea sativa

Cedrus atlantica

C. sativa
Sweet chestnut, Spanish chestnut
This ornamental tree is widely grown in Europe for its edible fruits and its timber. It is a broadly spreading tree. Mature specimens are easily identified by the spirally patterned bark. The glossy, mid-green leaves, up to 20cm (8in) long, are slender, with distinctive bristles along the margins. In autumn they turn brown. H 30m (100ft), S 25m (80ft).
Named varieties The cultivar 'Albomarginata' (syn. 'Argenteomarginata') has beautiful dark green, white-edged leaves. The spines on the fruits are also variegated white. This form tends to revert and so needs occasional pruning to remove any all-green shoots. It is slightly less vigorous

than the species.
Aspect Full sun or semi-shade.
Hardiness ✿✿✿ Zones 5–8.

CATALPA
The 11 species of deciduous trees in the genus are native to eastern Asia and North America. They are grown for their large leaves and bell-shaped flowers, which are followed by the distinctive hanging fruits. Most catalpas are susceptible to damage from late spring frosts, but they are tolerant of heat and are particularly suitable for courtyards.
Cultivation Grow in fertile, moisture-retentive but well-drained soil in full sun. Protect from strong, cold winds.
Pruning Bean trees require little pruning apart from the removal of dead, dying, diseased or crossing branches. Formative pruning is important when young as it will encourage a straight trunk and an evenly balanced crown. Suckers should be removed from the trunks as they appear, as should any reverted shoots on the variegated leaf forms. Pruning is best done during early summer when the tree is in full leaf.
Propagation The most widely used methods of propagation are softwood cuttings during the summer and hardwood cuttings during the winter. Softwood cuttings should be placed in a humid environment and the leaves should be cut in half to reduce

water loss. Hardwood cuttings can be rooted in the garden where they are to grow.

C. bignonioides
Indian bean tree, southern catalpa
In summer, this tree bears large, white, bell-shaped flowers with yellow and purple markings. These are followed by large, bean-like fruits, which hang down from the branches in autumn and persist long into winter. The mid-green leaves, up to 25cm (10in) long, are heart-shaped and turn yellow in autumn. Leaves and young shoots are prone to frost damage. H and S 15m (50ft).
Named varieties The golden form, 'Aurea', is a fast-growing tree, with vibrant yellow leaves in early summer that fade to pale green in late autumn. It can be grown as a coppiced tree and will produce massive leaves. H and S 10m (33ft).
'Variegata' has beautiful green, yellow and white variegated and mottled leaves, which gradually fade to pale green in summer.
Aspect Full sun or semi-shade.
Hardiness ✿✿✿ Zones 5–9.

C. x erubescens
The hybrid form arising from a cross between C. bignonioides and C. ovata is usually represented in gardens by 'J.C. Teas' (syn. 'Hybrida'). Its flowers are similar to those of C. bignonioides but they are smaller and more numerous.

The young leaves are tinged with purple. 'Purpurea' is grown for its dark purple new leaves, which become dark green by summer, but the shoots remain purple. When it is coppiced, the leaves retain their purple colour longer into summer. H 15m (50ft), S 10–15m (33–50ft).
Aspect Full sun or semi-shade.
Hardiness ✿✿✿ Zones 5–9.

C. ovata
Yellow catalpa
This slow-growing tree produces large panicles of small white flowers, blotched with yellow and red, in midsummer. The pale green leaves, up to 25cm (10in) long, are slightly lobed and turn yellow in autumn. H 15m (50ft), S 10m (33ft).
Aspect Full sun or semi-shade.
Hardiness ✿✿✿ Zones 5–8.

CEDRUS
Cedar
The four species of delightful evergreen conifers in the genus are native to the Mediterranean and Himalayas. These large, imposing trees are best grown as specimen trees in spacious gardens so that their handsome shape can be admired.
Cultivation Grow in any well-drained, fairly fertile soil in a sunny, open position.
Pruning Formative pruning should aim to produce a clear trunk and a balanced crown. Tipping the

Catalpa bignonioides

Cedrus deodara

Cedrus deodara 'Aurea'

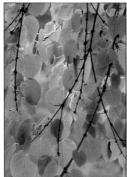

Cercidiphyllum japonicum f. *pendulum*

lateral branches on young trees encourages a denser crown. Prune to remove dead, dying, diseased or crossing branches.
Propagation Sow fresh seed in a pot in an unheated glasshouse or cold frame until germination occurs. Selected forms can be winter grafted on to seedling-raised rootstocks.

C. atlantica
(syn. *C. libani* subsp. *atlantica*)
Atlas cedar
This is an initially fast-growing, upright tree, which spreads as it matures. The green to grey-green needles are arranged in whorls at the tips of small stems, which are arranged along the branches. It is a widely planted conifer in parks and large estates. H 40m (130ft), S 10–20m (33–65ft).
Named varieties Trees in Glauca Group (blue cedar) are beautiful and widely grown selections. They have electric blue foliage, which is silver-white at first, and upswept branches, which give this stately tree its spiky, shaggy appearance.
Aspect Full sun.
Hardiness ❋❋❋ Zone 7.

C. deodara
Deodar, deodar cedar
This is grown for its long, pendulous foliage and conical habit. Although it is often planted in suburban gardens, it is not really suitable for such small spaces as it is ultimately a very large tree indeed. It is reasonably cold hardy and drought tolerant. H 50m (160ft), S 20m (65ft).

Named varieties The slow-growing 'Aurea' (golden deodar) is a beautiful and more compact form with glorious gold-coloured needles in spring that fade to greenish-yellow by summer.
'Cream Puff', also a slow-growing variety, has white-tipped green needles.
'Shalimar' is widely grown in the USA for its superior cold hardiness, attractive blue-green foliage and strongly arching habit.
Aspect Full sun.
Hardiness ❋❋❋ Zones 7–9.

C. libani
Cedar of Lebanon
This is the most easily identifiable cedar, with its straight trunk and majestic layers of branches. Widely cultivated throughout the world, it can be seen in many large, landscaped gardens. In exposed positions it will not achieve its full potential height. H 40m (130ft), 20m (65ft).
Aspect Full sun.
Hardiness ❋❋❋ Zones 5–9.

CERCIDIPHYLLUM
Katsura
This genus of deciduous trees is native to China and Japan, where it is found in woodland. It is grown for its beautiful autumn colour.
Cultivation Grow in deep, fertile, moisture-retentive but well-drained, neutral to acidic soil. New growth may be damaged by late spring frosts, so plant in a sheltered position.

Pruning Katsura trees require little pruning apart from the removal of dead, dying, diseased or crossing branches. Formative pruning is important when young as it will encourage a straight trunk and an even balanced crown.
Propagation The most widely used method of propagation is by taking softwood cuttings during the summer. These should be placed in a humid environment until rooted and then hardened off carefully. Seed is also widely used. The weeping forms are produced by indoor grafting in the winter months and are grafted high up on standard grown rootstocks.

C. japonicum
Katsura tree
This wonderful tree has delicate, heart-shaped leaves, which are tinged with bronze-pink in spring and which turn orange-yellow, occasionally pink, in autumn. As the leaves fall in autumn and rot on the ground, they smell of burnt sugar or cotton candy. Small red flowers appear before the leaves emerge. It generally develops an attractive multi-stemmed habit, but can be trained as a standard with a central leader. H 20–30m (65–100ft), S 15–25m (50–80ft).
Named varieties The slow-growing *C. japonicum* f. *pendulum* (syn. *C. magnificum* f. *pendulum*) has long, weeping branches covered with small, heart-shaped leaves in summer. These are flushed with bronze in spring and turn vivid orange-yellow in autumn. It has a beautiful intricate, weeping silhouette against the winter sky. H and S 10m (33ft).

Cercidiphyllum japonicum f. *pendulum*

Chamaecyparis lawsoniana

C. japonicum f. *pendulum* 'Amazing Grace' is a superior weeping form with orange-yellow autumn colour.

C. japonicum 'Strawberry', a striking, slow-growing, pyramidal form, has blue-green, heart-shaped leaves, which turn gold and rose in autumn.

The leaves of 'Tidal Wave' turn yellow in autumn.
Aspect Full sun or semi-shade.
Hardiness ❋❋❋ Zones 4–8.

CERCIS

The six species of deciduous trees in this genus are native to North America, Asia and southern Europe. They are grown for their spring flowers, which are borne before the leaves appear.
Cultivation Grow in deep, fertile, moisture-retentive but well-drained soil in sun or semi-shade. Established plants do not respond well to being transplanted.
Pruning Redbuds and Judas trees require little pruning apart from removing dead, dying, diseased or crossing branches. Formative

pruning when young encourages an even and well-balanced crown. Redbuds are prone to anthracnose and any diseased branches should be removed back to healthy wood.
Propagation Redbuds are difficult to propagate as the seed coat requires special treatment so that water can penetrate it. To expose the pale seed the end of the hard seed coat can be rubbed away using a fine sandpaper, or a thin sliver of the seed coating can be removed using a sharp knife. Alternatively, cover the seed with boiling water and leave to soak for 12 hours before sowing as normal.

C. canadensis
Eastern redbud, redbud
This shrub or multi-stemmed small tree flowers in late spring. The pea-like flowers, which may be red, purplish, pink or white, are borne on the bare stems before the heart-shaped leaves appear. The young leaves are bronze and turn yellow in autumn. It prefers warmer areas than *C. siliquastrum*. H and S 10m (33ft).

Named varieties 'Forest Pansy' has beautiful purple, heart-shaped leaves in summer and orange and yellow autumn colour. The smallish pink flowers are almost overwhelmed by the intense leaf colour. H and S 10m (33ft).

'Royal White' is the first of the white forms to bloom in spring and has the largest flowers.

'Silver Cloud' has leaves that are mottled with white, silver and green and small pale pink flowers. It needs a semi-shaded position.

The mound-forming *C. canadensis* var. *texensis* 'Traveller' has rose-pink flowers and copper-red new leaves, which turn green in summer. H and S 1.8m (6ft).
Aspect Full sun or semi-shade.
Hardiness ❋❋❋ Zones 3–9.

C. chinensis
Chinese redbud
This large shrub or small, multi-stemmed tree bears dark pink flowers before the glossy, mid-green leaves appear. H 6m (20ft), S 5m (16ft).
Named varieties The Chinese redbud is often represented in gardens by the cultivar 'Avondale',

a dark pink flowering form from New Zealand. It is shrubbier than the species. H and S 3m (10ft).
Aspect Full sun or semi-shade.
Hardiness ❋❋❋ Zones 3–9.

C. siliquastrum
Judas tree
The common name alludes to the fact that this tree, which is native to south-eastern Europe and south-western Asia, is said to have been the tree from which Judas Iscariot hanged himself. It is a small, widely spreading tree, which thrives in poor, free-draining soil, including alkaline soil. The heart-shaped, blue-green leaves follow the dense clusters of dark purple flowers, which are borne in late spring, and small pods follow the flowers. H and S 10m (33ft).
Named varieties *C. siliquastrum* f. *albida* (syn. 'Alba') is grown for its white flowers and attractive pale green leaves.

The excellent 'Bodnant' is grown for its very dark purple flowers, which are produced on even young plants.
Aspect Full sun.
Hardiness ❋❋❋ Zones 7–8.

Chamaecyparis nootkatensis

CHAMAECYPARIS
False cypress, cypress

The seven species in the genus used to be classified as *Cupressus* (cypress), but they differ from the true cypress in that they have rather flattened sprays of foliage. They are evergreen conifers, native to Japan, Taiwan and North America. They make excellent specimen trees and are also often used as hedging, although, as with most other conifers, they will not re-shoot from old wood. The heights indicated here are the likely maximum size of garden-grown plants; in the wild species often grow taller.

Cultivation Grow in fertile, moisture-retentive but well-drained, neutral to slightly acidic soil in full sun. These are not as tolerant of very high temperatures as some other conifers.

Pruning Formative pruning should aim to produce a straight trunk with well-spaced branches and a balanced crown. Tipping back side shoots when young will encourage bushy growth.

Propagation Sow fresh seed in an unheated glasshouse or cold frame until germination occurs. Semi-ripe and softwood cuttings can be rooted during summer and placed in a humid environment until rooting occurs.

C. lawsoniana
Lawson cypress

This fast-growing, conical conifer from North America has bright green foliage in fan-shaped sprays and rather drooping branches. The species has given rise to dozens of cultivars, incredibly varied in size, shape and colour, and these are more often seen than the species. H 40–50m (130–165ft), S 5m (16ft). Named varieties Of the cultivars, 'Alumii' is a reliable and widely grown form that has a tight, narrow habit and blue-green foliage. The colour intensifies in bright sunlight. H 15–25m (50–80ft).

'Ellwood's Pillar' has feathery, bluish leaves in a tight, upright column. H 10–15m (33–50ft).

The more compact 'Fletcheri' often develops into a multi-stemmed small tree with a round

but still columnar habit. It is a pretty tree, with feathery, blue-green foliage. H 5–6m (16–20ft).

'Intertexta', a distinctive tall tree, has semi-pendulous branches clothed in long, weeping, fan-like leaves that produce a shaggy effect from a distance. The foliage is grey-green.

'Pelt's Blue' (syn. 'Van Pelt's Blue') is one of the best blue-leaved varieties currently available. H 4m (12ft), S 1.8m (6ft).

The fastigiate 'Wisselii' has slightly weeping branches of fern-like, blue-green foliage. It is easy to identify in spring when the leaves are covered with masses of tiny, purple-red male cones, which, if knocked, release plumes of bright yellow pollen. H 10m (33ft), S 1.8m (6ft).
Aspect Full sun or semi-shade.
Hardiness ✽✽✽ Zones 5–7.

C. nootkatensis
Nootka cypress

This beautiful, dark green conifer, which originates from the western USA, does best in regions with relatively even temperatures throughout the growing season. It is widely grown for its semi-pendulous habit and brown, flaking bark. The foliage is dark green. It is one of the parents of **x** *Cupressocyparis leylandii* (Leyland cypress). H 30m (100ft), S 8m (28ft).
Named varieties The cultivar 'Pendula' is one of the most beautiful of the hardy weeping conifers. It develops into a mass of widely arching branches, the light catching the angled stems and producing a lovely contrast between pale and dark foliage.
Aspect Full sun or semi-shade.
Hardiness ✽✽✽ Zones 4–7.

C. obtusa
Hinoki cypress

This Japanese conifer has attractive, flaking strips of brownish-red bark. The spray-like green leaves are arranged in flat layers along the stems, producing an arching effect. This is not a particularly drought-tolerant tree, although it will grow in sandy soils. There is an array of different forms, and these vary in height, shape and colour. H 20–30m

Chamaecyparis obtusa

(65–100ft), S 6m (20ft).
Aspect Full sun or semi-shade.
Hardiness ✽✽✽ Zones 5–8.

C. pisifera
Sawara cypress

Native to Japan, this is a fairly broad, attractive garden conifer with reddish bark, which peels in long threads. The bright green needles are flattish and fern-like in shape and have small Xs on the underside. Although the canopy looks rather sparse from a distance, this gives a cloud-

like appearance to the foliage. This is a hardy conifer, with good heat and cold tolerance. It will thrive in any moist, deep, fertile, free-draining soil. H 20–35m (65–115ft), S 5m (16ft).
Named varieties The round-headed cultivar 'Filifera Aurea' has fern-like, bright yellow foliage and long, fine, whippy tips, which give a shaggy, fluffy appearance. H 8–12m (25–40ft).
Aspect Full sun or semi-shade.
Hardiness ✽✽✽ Zones 4–7.

Chamaerops humilis

CHAMAEROPS
Dwarf fan palm, European fan palm

This monotypic genus is native to Mediterranean countries. It is one of only two palms (the other is *Phoenix theophrasti*) native to Europe. It is usually grown as a houseplant or in a conservatory in cooler climes, but in milder areas it can be used as a small specimen tree.
Cultivation Outdoors, grow in fertile, well-drained soil in full sun. This palm is drought tolerant.
Pruning Like most palms, little pruning is required apart from removing dead leaves and spent flower clusters in early summer.
Propagation Seed is the easiest method of propagation. Sow fresh seed in a pot in a heated glasshouse in a humid environment at 29°C (84°F) until it has germinated.

C. humilis
This attractive palm develops a single trunk, although mature plants can sucker, forming clumps up to 6m (20ft) across. The pinnate, fan-shaped, blue-green leaves can get up to 1m (3ft) long, and the stems are armed with forward-pointing, usually black thorns. H 3–4m (10–12ft), S 1.8m (6ft).
Named varieties *C. humilis* var. *argentea* (syn. *C. humilis* var. *cerifera*) is similar to the species in most aspects, but the leaves are narrower and a wonderful silver-green colour, with vicious black thorns. It is slower growing and may be hardier than the species.
The cultivar 'Vulcano' has lovely silver-green leaves and a compact habit. It is ideal for growing in a container.
Aspect Full sun.
Hardiness ✿ Zones 8–11.

CITRUS

The genus, which includes oranges, lemons, limes and grapefruits, contains about 16 species of evergreen, often spiny shrubs and small trees. These plants have been cultivated for many centuries in China, Japan and Europe. They are frost tender, and in cooler climates are often grown in large containers so that they can be given the protection of a greenhouse or conservatory during the winter but moved outside for the summer months.
In Europe in the 1600s and 1700s, large, glass-fronted buildings were constructed to house the ever-increasing range of citrus fruits that were arriving from the East. These were known as orangeries. Some were unheated and were used to protect the plants in winter, while others were heated so that growth could be accelerated to produce earlier crops.
The dimensions given below are for plants growing outdoors all year round. Container-grown plants will be significantly smaller. This tree needs shelter.
Cultivation All species require plenty of light and a minimum winter temperature of 5°C (41°F). During the growing season give container-grown plants a balanced NPK fertilizer that also contains trace elements. Pot on every two to three years, using an ericaceous compost, and top dress in other years. Outdoors, grow in moisture-retentive but well-drained, neutral to acidic soil.

Pruning Formative pruning should aim to encourage a clear trunk and a balanced crown. Tipping the lateral branches on young trees will encourage a denser crown. Long, whippy growth is produced during spring and summer and this should be reduced so that a balanced, round-headed crown is produced. Prune to remove dead, dying, diseased, or crossing branches.
Propagation: Most citrus fruits are produced by T-budding, done during the winter when the seedling rootstock is dormant. Limes, oranges, grapefruits and kumquats are used in tropical climates, whereas the trifoliate Japanese orange (*Poncirus trifoliata*) is more widely used in more temperate locations. Many oranges and limes will come true from seed and can be propagated this way, but require an even temperature of above 25°C (77°F) to germinate.
Aspect: Full sun.
Hardiness (Min. 3–5°C/37–41°F) Zones 8–9.

C. aurantiifolia
Lime
The species is native to tropical Asia, where its fruits are produced for pickling and making juice. This is perhaps the least ornamental tree of this group. It is a dense, spiny plant, with masses of criss-crossing branches, which make it useful as a hedge or screen. The green fruits follow the waxy, white flowers. Limes can

Citrus aurantium

Citrus aurantifolia

be grown from seed because this a true species and not a natural or complex hybrid, like many of the other citrus plants. H 5m (16ft) S 1.8m (6ft).
Aspect Full sun.
Hardiness (Min. 3–5°C/37–41°F) Zones 10–12.

C. aurantium
Seville orange, bitter orange, bigarade
This small tree from South-east Asia is widely grown in Spain for its fruit, which is used in marmalade. Mature trees have oval, mid-green leaves, up to 10cm (4in) long. The scented white flowers are followed by flat-topped, thick-skinned fruits. When grown in containers, plants need restrictive pruning. H 10m (33ft), S 6m (20ft).
Aspect Full sun.
Hardiness (Min. 3–5°C/37–41°F) Zones 8–9.

C. limon
Lemon
This small, spiny, broadly spreading tree has been widely grown around the Mediterranean Sea since about 1200, when it was introduced from Asia. The creamy-white, scented flowers are produced in clusters in late spring and summer, followed by the fruits, which ripen by the autumn. H 7m (23ft), S 3m (10ft).
Named varieties There are several cultivars, providing a range of plant size as well as different fruit sizes and colours. They include 'Imperial', which produces very large fruits, and 'Menton', which is believed to be more tolerant of the cold and bears large fruits.

'Quatre Saisons' is widely grown for the quality and reliability of its fruits. It is also known as the 'Eureka' lemon.
'Variegata' has attractive leaves with yellow edges and silver-grey blotches. The fruits are mottled green and yellow.
'Villa Franca' bears large quantities of medium-sized fruits and is almost thornless.
Aspect Full sun.
Hardiness (Min. 3–5°C/37–41°F) Zones 8–9.

C. medica
Citron
This large, spiny shrub or small tree, which originated in south-west Asia, bears purple-tinged, white flowers and broad, dark green leaves, up to 18cm (7in) long. The large, heavy fruits, up to 30cm (12in) long, resemble knobbly lemons. It is slightly hardier than most types of citrus and will survive short periods below -5°C (23°F). H 5m (16ft), S 3m (10ft).
Named varieties The cultivar 'Ethrog' is the most widely available of the forms of citron. It bears fragrant fruits the same size as lemons.
Aspect Full sun.
Hardiness (Min. 3–5°C/37–41°F) Zones 8–9.

C. 'Meyer'
(syn. *C. limon* 'Meyer', *C. x meyeri* 'Meyer')
Meyer's lemon
This may be a hybrid of *C. limon* and *C. sinensis*. It is a small tree with glossy green leaves. The fragrant white flowers are followed by fruit that looks like a lemon in shape but is the colour of *C. sinensis*. This is one of the hardier of the citrus trees and will withstand short periods of temperatures around -5°C (23°F). H 3m (10ft), S 1.5m (5ft).
Aspect Full sun.
Hardiness (Min. 3–5°C/37–41°F) Zones 8–9.

C. x paradisi
Grapefruit
This is grown commercially in Israel, Turkey, California and Florida, where summer temperatures are sufficiently

high to ripen the fruits. Although the origin of the grapefruit is unknown, it may be a hybrid between *C. maxima* (pummelo) and *C. sinensis*. It is a round-headed tree with sparse, spiny leaves, flowering in spring and summer and fruiting in the autumn. H and S 7m (23ft).
Named varieties Orange-fruiting forms include the white-fleshed 'Golden Special' and 'Oro Blanco' and the seedless 'Marsh'.
Red-fruiting forms include 'Red Blush' and 'Star Ruby'.
Aspect Full sun.
Hardiness (Min. 3–5°C/37–41°F) Zones 8–9.

C. 'Ponderosa'
(syn. *C. limon* 'Ponderosa')
Giant American wonder lemon
This dwarf lemon is ideally suited to being grown in a container, when it will fruit and flower regularly. H and S 3m (10ft).
Aspect Full sun.
Hardiness (Min. 3–5°C/37–41°F) Zones 8–9.

C. reticulata
Clementine, mandarin, satsuma, tangerine
These ornamental, compact trees produce glossy, dark green leaves, up to 4cm (1½in) long, and an abundance of sweetly scented white flowers in short racemes in spring and early summer. The yellow-orange fruits are about 8cm (3in) across and are borne from autumn to spring. The skin or rind of these fruits detaches easily from the flesh within, and they are popular because they are so easy to peel, as well as being juicy and tasty and a good source of vitamin C. Due to their ultimate size, they make excellent specimens for growing in containers. H 4m (12ft), S 1.8m (6ft).
Named varieties Many forms have been developed, including 'Clementine', 'Cleopatra', 'Dancy' and 'Kinnow'.
Aspect Full sun.
Hardiness (Min. 3–5°C/37–41°F) Zones 8–9.

Citrus limon

Citrus limon

Citrus sinensis

C. sinensis
Sweet orange
This may be a natural hybrid between *C. maxima* (pummelo) and *C. reticulata*. It has long been cultivated and is widely grown in frost-free climates where summer temperatures are high enough to ripen the fruits. If it is grown in a climate with insufficient summer sun, the fruits may not turn the usual orange colour, but remain a greenish-yellow, although the flesh inside will be sweet and juicy. These are large, spiny trees, with glossy, dark green leaves and fragrant white flowers. H 12m (40ft), S 4m (12ft).
Named varieties Numerous cultivars have been developed for their flavour, colour and size of fruit. They include 'Shamouti' (syn. 'Jaffa', a popular seedless form), 'Valencia', 'Murcia' and 'Washington'.
   Blood fruit forms include 'Malta', 'Moro' and 'Ruby'.
Aspect Full sun.
Hardiness (Min. 3–5°C/37–41°F) Zones 8–9.

C. x tangelo
Ugli fruit
This hybrid between *C. x paradisi* and *C. sinensis* bears fruit that is considerably larger than an orange but not quite as large as a grapefruit. The dark green leaves are longer and more pointed than those of *C. sinensis*. White flowers are followed by the reddish or yellow fruits. H 5m (16ft), S 1.8m (6ft).
Named varieties This fruit was originally hybridized in the USA and there are numerous forms grown today, including 'Minneola'.
Aspect Full sun.
Hardiness (Min. 3–5°C/37–41°F) Zones 8–9.

C. unshiu
(syn. C. reticulata Satsuma Group)
This Japanese tangerine is grown for its masses of small, deliciously sweet and easy-to-peel fruits. It is a dense small tree, which produces creamy-white, highly scented flowers in spring, followed by the bright orange fruits. H and S 3m (10ft).

Aspect Full sun.
Hardiness (Min. 3–5°C/37–41°F) Zones 8–9.

CLADRASTIS
This small genus contains five species of deciduous trees from China, Japan and North America. They are grown for their early summer flowers, which are borne only on mature wood, and their good autumn colour.
Cultivation Grow in well-drained but moisture-retentive soil in sun. Protect from strong, cold winds.
Pruning Little pruning is necessary, apart from the removal of dead, dying, diseased or crossing branches.
Propagation This is by seed, which should be collected as soon as it falls. The seed coat should be rubbed with sandpaper to allow water to enter the seed and then soaked for 24 hours. Sow into containers, and place in an unheated glasshouse or cold frame until it germinates. Root cuttings can also be taken in early winter. The pink flowering forms are self-fertile and should come true from seed, otherwise they are indoor grafted during the winter.

C. kentukea
(syn. C. lutea)
Yellow wood
In summer this beautiful, medium-sized tree, which is native to the south-east of the USA, bears long, wisteria-like panicles of fragrant white flowers. In autumn the leaves turn a vibrant golden-yellow. H 12–15m (40–50ft), S 10m (33ft).
Named varieties 'Perkins Pink' (syn. 'Rosea') has pale pink-white flowers, with the leaves turning yellow in autumn.
Aspect Full sun or semi-shade.
Hardiness ❋❋❋ Zones 4–8.

C. sinensis
Chinese yellow wood
Although this species is rarely seen in gardens, it is just as beautiful as *C. kentukea*. It flowers in mid- to late summer, producing long panicles of white, pink-tinged blooms. H 10m (33ft), S 15m (50ft).
Aspect Full sun or semi-shade.
Hardiness ❋❋❋ Zones 5–8.

CORNUS
Dogwood, flowering dogwood, American boxwood
Although there are only about 45 species of mostly deciduous trees and shrubs in the genus, many cultivars and hybrids have been developed. They are grown for their attractive habit, for their flowers (sometimes with showy bracts) and for their autumn colour and colourful bark.
Cultivation Most dogwoods tolerate any fairly fertile, moisture-retentive but well-drained soil and are not fussy about the position. Grow flowering forms (such as *C. florida*, *C. nuttallii* and their hybrids) in fertile, well-drained but moisture-retentive, neutral to acidic soil in sun or semi-shade.
Pruning Little pruning is required apart from the removal of dead, dying, diseased or crossing branches. The cornelian dogwood and its relatives are difficult to prune due to their dense branch habit, and so are best left to their own devices.
Propagation Seed should be collected as soon as it falls, and soaked for 24 hours. Sow in containers and place in an unheated glasshouse or cold frame until germination. Softwood and hardwood cuttings are used, as is indoor grafting during the winter.

C. 'Aurora'
This is a Stellar hybrid, one of a series of dogwoods that originated in the USA as controlled crosses between *C. nuttallii*, *C. florida* and *C. kousa*. The hybrids, which have characteristics of all the parents, seem to be resistant to anthracnose, the devastating dogwood disease. They are widely planted in the USA and are becoming more available in Europe. This is a vigorous form with an upright habit and numerous flowers with large, creamy-white bracts. H and S to 6m (20ft).
Aspect Full sun or semi-shade.
Hardiness ❋❋❋ Zones 5–8.

C. 'Celestial'
This is a Stellar hybrid (see *C. 'Aurora'*). It is a vigorous, strongly upright form, similar to *C. kousa*,

with smallish, green-white flowers that mature to white. H and S to 6m (20ft).
Aspect Full sun or semi-shade.
Hardiness ❋❋❋ Zones 5–8.

C. 'Constellation'
This is a Stellar hybrid (see C. 'Aurora'). This develops into a large tree, spreading widely as it ages, with white bracts. It is spectacular to see, both up close and from a distance. H and S to 6m (20ft).
Aspect Full sun or semi-shade.
Hardiness ❋❋❋ Zones 5–8.

C. controversa
Table dogwood
This superbly architectural deciduous tree is native to China and Japan. It is grown for its tiered branches. In summer the branch tips are covered in dense clusters of small, creamy-white flowers, which are followed by small black fruit. The narrowly oval leaves, up to 15cm (6in) long, are glossy, dark green and often turn purple in autumn. H 15–20m (50–65ft), S 15m (50ft).
Named varieties The cultivar 'Black Stem' is a vigorous form, grown for its dark purple stems and crimson autumn foliage.
'Variegata' is a beautiful but slow-growing tree. The leaves are broadly edged with creamy-white, and the stems are reddish.
Aspect Full sun or semi-shade.
Hardiness ❋❋❋ Zones 4–7.

C. 'Eddie's White Wonder'
This spectacular hybrid between C. nuttallii and C. florida is one of the best of the flowering dogwoods. It develops into a large shrub or small tree. In late spring tiny, purplish-green flowers are surrounded by large, creamy-white, overlapping bracts. The leaves turn brilliant orange-red in autumn. It needs acidic soil. H and S 12m (40ft).
Aspect Full sun or semi-shade.
Hardiness ❋❋❋ Zone 6.

C. florida
Flowering dogwood, eastern dogwood
This small flowering tree is native to the east of North America. It is grown for its tight clusters of tiny green flowers, which are surrounded by four beautiful pink or white bracts. These are followed by attractive red berries in autumn, when the leaves turn purple, orange and yellow. It is tolerant of most soil types. H 12m (40ft), S 10m (33ft).
Named varieties Several cultivars with especially large, colourful bracts have been developed. 'Cherokee Chief' has very dark pink bracts and beautiful autumn colour.
'Cloud Nine', which is one of the most cold-hardy forms, has flowers with large, white, overlapping bracts.
'Daybreak' (syn. C. florida 'Cherokee Daybreak') has large white bracts and leaves edged with

Cornus kousa

yellow-green. These become green and slightly pink flushed in summer and vibrant pink and red in autumn.
The compact 'Rainbow' is grown for its yellow-margined leaves, turning dark red and purple with scarlet margins in autumn. H 3m (10ft), S 2.4m (8ft).
Aspect Full sun or semi-shade.
Hardiness ❋❋❋ Zone 5.

C. kousa
Kousa dogwood
This is a small, conical tree. It is grown for its green flowerheads, which are surrounded by four pink or white bracts that are produced over several weeks in summer; its strawberry-like fruits; its purple-red autumn colour; and its flaking bark. H 15m (50ft), S 10m (33ft).
Named varieties There are several excellent cultivars to choose from. 'Blue Shadow' has lovely blue-green leaves, which turn reddish in autumn. The bracts are white, occasionally with a second flush in autumn.

C. kousa var. chinensis is more upright and open and has larger leaves than other species. The bracts, up to 5cm (2in) long, are initially creamy-white, fading to white and then reddish-pink.
C. kousa var. chinensis 'China Girl' is a vigorous form with masses of white bracts, even on young plants.
The more compact C. kousa var. chinensis 'Milky Way' has plenty of white bracts, which are followed by plentiful fruits.
'National' is an upright form with large white bracts and very large fruits.
'Satomi' has salmon-pink bracts and dark red-purple autumn colour.
'Temple Jewel' has gold, light pink and light green young foliage, which turns green with age, and white bracts.
The leaves of the rather shrubby 'Wolf Eyes' are boldly variegated with white and turn brilliant pink and red in autumn. The bracts are white.
Aspect Full sun or semi-shade.
Hardiness ❋❋❋ Zones 5–8.

Cladrastis kentukea

Cornus officinalis

C. mas
Cornelian cherry
The species, which is a large shrub or spreading small tree, is native to central and south-eastern Europe. It is especially attractive in late winter, when clusters of small, bright yellow flowers are borne on the bare stems. The bright red fruits that follow are edible. The paired leaves are dark green with strongly marked veins and turn purple in autumn. 'Golden Glory' is similar to the species but has larger leaves and flowers. H and S 5–8m (16–26ft).
Aspect Full sun.
Hardiness ❈❈❈ Zones 4–7.

C. nuttallii
Pacific dogwood, western dogwood
This is one of the larger dogwoods, developing into a large, majestic, deciduous tree. In late spring

small purple and green flowers appear, and these are surrounded by four to six large white or pink-tinged bracts. In autumn the leaves turn yellow and red. It does best where temperatures do not get too hot in summer and where there are high levels of rainfall. H 25m (80ft), S 15m (50ft).
Named varieties 'Colrigo Giant' is a vigorous form with large, creamy-white bracts, sometimes with a second flush of flowers in autumn. 'North Star', another vigorous form, has large white bracts and purplish leaves, turning purple-red in autumn.
Aspect Full sun.
Hardiness ❈❈ Zones 7–9.

C. officinalis
This vigorous, spreading, deciduous shrub or small tree has a rather open habit. In early spring, before the leaves appear,

it produces clusters of yellow flowers, which are followed by bright red fruits. The dark green leaves turn red-purple in autumn. H and S 5m (16ft).
Aspect Full sun.
Hardiness ❈❈❈ Zones 5–8.

C. 'Porlock'
This small, spreading, semi-evergreen or deciduous tree is a hybrid between *C. capitata* and *C. kousa*. Masses of showy white bracts are produced in summer and slowly turn pinkish-red. These are followed by plentiful strawberry-like fruits. H and S 15m (50ft).
Aspect Full sun to semi-shade.
Hardiness ❈❈❈ Zones 7–8.

C. 'Ruth Ellen'
This is a Stellar hybrid (see *C. 'Aurora'*). It is similar to *C. florida* but is lower-growing and has a spreading habit. It flowers in early spring. H and S to 6m (20ft).
Aspect Full sun to semi-shade.
Hardiness ❈❈❈ Zones 5–8.

C. 'Stellar Pink'
This is a Stellar hybrid (see *C. 'Aurora'*). It is a spreading, shrubby plant with soft pink bracts. H and S to 6m (20ft).
Aspect Full sun to semi-shade.
Hardiness ❈❈❈ Zones 5–8.

CORYLUS
Hazel
These deciduous trees come from northern temperate regions and are grown for their attractive

catkins and edible nuts. The best known is *C. avellana*, of which there are several cultivars.
Cultivation Grow in moisture-retentive but well-drained soil in sun or semi-shade. They do well on chalky soil.
Pruning Little pruning is required apart from the removal of dead, dying, diseased or crossing branches. Formative pruning should be used to encourage the horizontal branch effect of the Turkish filbert, so any shoots growing directly up into the crown should be removed.
Propagation Seed should be collected as soon as it falls and sown into containers in an unheated glasshouse or cold frame until germination occurs. Take softwood cuttings during summer and root in a humid environment. Hardwood cuttings can be taken in winter.

C. colurna
Turkish hazel
This quick-growing, attractive, conical tree has a strong architectural habit and is suitable for use in a large garden. The coarse, dark green leaves, up to 12cm (5in) long, are shallowly lobed and turn yellow in autumn. The trunk and stems sometimes show corky growth. In spring large, pendent catkins are produced and occasionally large, fringed cobnuts also. H 20–25m (65–80ft), S 15m (50ft).
Aspect Full sun or semi-shade.
Hardiness ❈❈❈ Zones 4–7.

COTINUS
Smoke tree
The two species of deciduous trees and shrubs in the genus are found in temperate areas of the northern hemisphere. They are grown for their colourful foliage and plumes of tiny flowers, which give the plants their common name.
Cultivation Grow in fertile, moisture-retentive but well-drained soil in sun or semi-shade. Purple-leaved forms do best in full sun.
Pruning Smoke trees grow very quickly when young and produce very long, whippy shoots that require shortening so that a more tree-like habit can be developed.

Corylus avellana

Cornus 'Porlock'

These shoots should be shortened in late spring or early summer. Little other pruning is normally required, apart from the removal of any dead, dying, diseased or crossing branches.
Propagation Softwood cuttings can be taken during summer, then dipped in a rooting hormone and rooted in a humid environment.

C. 'Flame'
(syn. *C. coggygria* 'Flame')
This hybrid between *C. obovatus* and *C. coggygria* (smoke bush, Venetian sumach) has some of the height of the former and the leaf size of the latter. In summer it produces airy plumes of tiny purple flowers; in autumn the light green leaves, up to 10cm (4in) long, turn vibrant orange and yellow. H and S 6–10m (20–33ft).
Aspect Full sun or semi-shade.
Hardiness ✸✸✸ Zones 4–8.

C. obovatus
(syn. *C. americanus*, *Rhus cotinoides*)
American smoke tree, chittamwood
This little-grown species is a striking tree, which is native to the south-eastern USA. The large leaves, up to 12cm (5in) long, are pinkish-bronze in colour as they emerge in spring and turn vivid orange, purple and red in autumn. In summer, large plumes of pink-grey flowers are borne. It is best grown in a sheltered location. H and S 12m (40ft).
Aspect Full sun or semi-shade.
Hardiness ✸✸✸ Zones 4–8.

CRATAEGUS
Hawthorn
This large genus of some 200 species contains deciduous, semi-evergreen and evergreen trees and shrubs, which may be spiny. They usually have good autumn colour. The pink or white flowers are followed by fleshy fruits.
Cultivation Grow in well-drained soil in sun or semi-shade. They will not tolerate waterlogged soil.
Pruning Fire blight can be a problem, so infected material should be removed and destroyed as soon as it appears.
Propagation Seed is widely used and should be collected in autumn before the birds strip the trees. The flesh should be removed by soaking in water. Once all the pulp is removed, the seed can be sown in an unheated glasshouse or cold frame until it germinates. Cultivars are propagated by winter grafting or summer budding on to seed-raised hawthorn and haw rootstocks.

C. coccinea
(syn. *C. pedicellata*)
This spreading deciduous tree has thorny branches and stems. White flowers, produced in late spring, are followed by bright red, pear-shaped, edible berries. H and S 6m (20ft).
Aspect Full sun or semi-shade.
Hardiness ✸✸✸ Zones 5–7.

C. crus-galli
Cockspur thorn
This is a very hardy, small, round-headed, deciduous tree. The glossy green leaves, up to 10cm (4in) long, are a foil for the masses of white flowers borne in early summer. The bright red fruits that follow in autumn persist into winter. The leaves create a vibrant patchwork of bright orange, yellow and red in autumn. Branches and stems are armoured with large, 8cm- (3in-) long thorns. H 8m (26ft), S 10m (33ft).
Aspect Full sun or semi-shade.
Hardiness ✸✸✸ Zones 4–7.

C. flava
Yellow haw
This deciduous shrub or small tree, which deserves to be more widely grown, has dark green leaves, up to 5cm (2in) long, and white flowers in spring to early summer. These are followed in autumn by yellow-green fruits. H 6–10m (20–33ft), S 8m (26ft).
Aspect Full sun or semi-shade.
Hardiness ✸✸✸ Zones 4–7.

C. laevigata
(syn. *C. oxyacantha*)
Midland hawthorn, maythorn
This rounded, deciduous tree is armed with sharp spines. It has dark green leaves, up to 5cm (2in) long, and white flowers in spring and early summer. The round, orange-red berries follow. H and S 8m (26ft).
Named varieties The widely planted cultivar 'Paul's Scarlet' (syn. 'Coccinea Plena') is one of the showiest and most striking species of hawthorn when it is in

Crataegus laevigata 'Punicea'

flower, bearing red-pink, double flowers in spring. H and S 10m (33ft).
'Rosea Flore Pleno' has double pink flowers. H and S 10m (33ft).
Aspect Full sun or semi-shade.
Hardiness ✸✸✸ Zone 5.

C. x lavallei
This hybrid is grown for its bronze autumn colour and bright orange-red fruits, which ripen late in autumn. H 7m (23ft), S 10m (33ft).
Named varieties The hybrid is usually represented in cultivation by 'Carrierei', which is a strongly growing and very thorny tree. White flowers appear in clusters in early summer to midsummer. The dark green leaves turn red in autumn.
Aspect Full sun or semi-shade.
Hardiness ✸✸✸ Zones 5–7.

C. monogyna
Common hawthorn, may, quickthorn
The deciduous leaves of this rounded, small tree are dark green and glossy. The fragrant white flowers appear in late spring and are followed by red berries. H 10m (33ft), S 8m (26ft).
Named varieties The cultivar 'Stricta' is a narrowly conical small tree, with upswept, slightly twisted branches and white flowers in late spring. In autumn numerous, single-stoned, red berries are produced. H 10m (33ft), S 1.8m (6ft).
Aspect Full sun or semi-shade.
Hardiness ✸✸✸ Zones 4–7.

Cotinus 'Flame'

Crataegus laevigata 'Paul's Scarlet'

C. persimilis 'Prunifolia'
(syn. *C. prunifolia*)
This cultivar is the most widely planted of the hawthorns. It is grown mainly for its tidy, round-headed habit, white flowers, autumn colour and persistent red berries. H 8m (26ft), S 10m (33ft). Aspect Full sun or semi-shade. Hardiness ❀❀❀ Zones 5–7.

CRYPTOMERIA
Japanese cedar
Although the genus contains only a single species of evergreen conifer, many handsome cultivars have been selected.
Cultivation Grow in deep, fertile, moisture-retentive but well-drained soil in sun or semi-shade.

Pruning Formative pruning should aim to produce a clear trunk and a balanced crown, while tipping the lateral branches of young trees encourages a denser crown.
Propagation Seed is the easiest method of propagation and should be collected when it is fresh, sown into a container and placed in an unheated glasshouse or cold frame until germination occurs. Semi-ripe and softwood cuttings can be rooted during summer and should be dipped in a rooting hormone and placed in a humid environment until rooting occurs. Selected forms are winter grafted on to seedling raised rootstocks.

Cunninghamia lanceolata

x *Cupressocyparis leylandii*

C. japonica
Japanese cedar
The species is a beautiful and ultimately large tree. It has dark green, slightly weeping leaves, which are arranged in spirals around the stems. The reddish bark is aromatic and peels in long strips. H 25–30m (80–100ft), S 5–6m (16–20ft).
Named varieties Among the best cultivars is 'Lobbii', a beautiful form, widely grown for its narrower and more upright habit than the species. The leaves are pressed more tightly to the stem and the branches are slightly twisted. Aspect Full sun or semi-shade. Hardiness ❀❀❀ Zones 5–8.

CUNNINGHAMIA
Chinese fir
This genus of evergreen conifers is found in China and Taiwan. They are grown for their dense, dark green foliage.
Cultivation Grow in any deep, moisture-retentive but well-drained soil in sun or semi-shade. They are not suitable for windy sites.
Pruning Occasional pruning is required for the removal of dead, dying, diseased or crossing branches.
Propagation Seed is the easiest method of propagation and should be collected when fresh and sown into a container in an unheated glasshouse or cold frame until germination occurs.

C. lanceolata
(syn. *C. sinensis, C. unicaniculata*)
The species has soft, pointed, slender, yew-like needles, which have two distinct bands on the undersides. The needles are arranged spirally around the stems. The bark is an attractive shade of red-brown. H 20–25m (65–80ft), S 6–10m (20–33ft). Aspect Full sun. Hardiness ❀❀❀ Zones 7–9.

x CUPRESSOCYPARIS
The evergreen conifers in this genus are hybrids between *Chamaecyparis* and *Cupressus*. They are fast-growing and can be grown either as specimens or for hedging.
Cultivation Grow in any moisture-retentive but well-drained soil in sun or semi-shade. They are not suitable for small gardens.
Pruning Formative pruning should aim to produce a straight trunk with well-spaced branches and a balanced crown. Tipping back side shoots when young will encourage bushy growth.
Propagation Semi-ripe cuttings taken during late autumn or early spring root quickly if the base of the cutting is dipped in a rooting hormone and the cuttings placed in a humid environment in a frost-free glass house until they root.

x C. leylandii
Leyland cypress
This hybrid between *Cupressus macrocarpa* and *Chamaecyparis nootkatensis* was first bred in 1870,

Cryptomeria japonica 'Lobbii'

since when numerous hybrids have been developed. It is extremely fast-growing and in the right conditions can put on 1m (3ft) or more in a year. It is a conical tree, with dark green leaves and dark brown cones. H up to 35m (115ft), S to 5m (16ft).
Named varieties 'Castlewellan' (syn. 'Galway Gold') is a widely grown form (it is popular for hedging) with golden-yellow young foliage, which turns bronze-yellow with age. H 20–25m (65–80ft).

'Emerald Isle' is a columnar form with green foliage in flattish sprays, creating a more open habit.

'Gold Rider' is the best of the yellow-foliaged forms, with flatter foliage and semi-lax branches.

One of the first hybrids, the fast-growing, narrow 'Leighton Green' has green, flattish foliage and plenty of cones.

'Naylor's Blue' has grey-green foliage, which turns slowly blue-green in winter. The branches are loose and twisted, and the foliage is not as stiff as on other forms.
Aspect Full sun or semi-shade.
Hardiness ✳✳✳ Zones 6–10.

CUPRESSUS
Cypress
The genus contains 20–24 species of evergreen conifers, which are found throughout the

northern hemisphere. They are mostly upright, columnar trees, and they can be used for hedging as long as they are not cut back to the old wood.
Cultivation Grow in any well-drained soil in sun. Do not plant in exposed sites.
Pruning Formative pruning should aim to produce a straight trunk with well-spaced branches and a balanced crown. Tipping back side shoots when young will encourage bushy growth.
Propagation Sow fresh seed into a container in an unheated glass house or cold frame until germination occurs. Semi-ripe and softwood cutting can be rooted during summer and should be dipped in a rooting hormone and placed in a humid environment until rooting occurs. Selected forms are winter grafted on to seedling raised rootstocks.

C. cashmeriana
(syn. *C. torulosa* 'Cashmeriana')
Kashmir cypress, weeping cypress
This beautiful, slender conifer, probably from the Himalayas, is best grown in mild areas. Its blue-green, fern-like foliage is borne on long, slender, pendulous branches. H 20–30m (65–100ft), S 10m (33ft).
Aspect Full sun.
Hardiness ✳ Zone 9.

Davidia involucrata

C. macrocarpa
Monterey cypress
This is a broadly conical conifer, which develops a broader crown as it ages. It has tiny, fern-like, dark green leaves that are pressed tight to the stem. It is widely planted in coastal locations because it is tolerant of salt spray and dry, sandy soils, but young plants are susceptible to damage from late spring frosts. H 25–30m (80–100ft), S 10–12m (33–40ft).
Aspect Full sun.
Hardiness ✳✳✳ Zones 7–9.

C. sempervirens
Italian cypress
The species, which is a widely grown tree in Mediterranean areas, is distinguished by its narrow, column-like habit. A fast-growing conifer, to 50m (165ft) tall in the wild, it tends to be smaller in gardens. It has dense dark green or grey-green foliage. Although young leaves can be damaged by cold winds in spring, these trees are remarkably tolerant of salt spray. H 20m (65ft), S 3m (10ft).
Named varieties A number of forms have been selected for their narrow habit or coloured foliage, usually yellow-tinted, green or blue-green. Trees in the Stricta Group (syn. 'Pyramidalis', *C. sempervirens* var. *sempervirens*) are marginally variable forms, with a pencil-like habit and green foliage.

'Green Pencil' is another tight conical form.
Aspect Full sun.
Hardiness ✳✳✳ Zones 7–9.

DAVIDIA
Handkerchief tree, dove tree, ghost tree
The single species in the genus is a deciduous tree that is native to China. It is usually grown as a specimen tree for the showy white bracts that surround the flowerheads in spring, and which turn green as they age.
Cultivation Grow in fertile, moisture-retentive but well-drained soil in sun or semi-shade. Protect from strong winds. Young growth is susceptible to frost damage in spring.
Pruning Little pruning is required apart from the removal of dead, dying, diseased or crossing branches. Formative pruning should aim to produce a clear straight trunk and a balanced crown.
Propagation Seed should be collected in late summer once it has fallen, then the flesh should be removed and the seed can be sown into deep pots in a warm environment for three months, followed by three months in an unheated glasshouse or cold frame until germination occurs. Softwood cuttings can be taken in summer, then dipped in a rooting hormone and placed in a warm environment. Do not pot on the cuttings until the following spring.

Cupressus arizonica var. 'Glabra'

Cupressus macrocarpa

D. involucrata

This is one of the most delightful and unusual medium-sized trees when it is in flower. In late spring the small, purplish flowers are surrounded by two large, white bracts: one up to about 8cm (3in) long and the other up to about 15cm (6in) long. The leaves, up to 15cm (6in) long, are soft green and covered with silvery hairs underneath. In autumn the foliage turns yellow-brown and occasionally fiery red and orange. H 15–20m (50–65ft), S 10–15m (33–50ft).

Named varieties *D. involucrata* var. *vilmoriniana* is almost identical to the species, but there are no hairs on the underside of the leaves, which are yellow-green above and dark green below.
Aspect Full sun or semi-shade.
Hardiness ❄❄❄ Zones 6–7.

DILLENIA

There are about 60 species of evergreen shrubs and trees in the genus. They are grown for their large leaves, flowers and edible fruits. In temperate areas these potentially large trees should be grown in a frost-free conservatory and pruned to restrict their growth.
Cultivation Outdoors, grow in fertile, moisture-retentive but well-drained, neutral to acidic soil in full sun.

Pruning Formative pruning should encourage a clear trunk and balanced crown. Prune occasionally to remove dead, dying, diseased or crossing branches.
Propagation Seed is the easiest method of propagation and should be collected when fresh and sown into a container in a heated glasshouse in a frost-free and humid environment until germination occurs. Semi-ripe cuttings can also be rooted during late summer and should be dipped in rooting hormone and placed in a frost-free, humid environment until they root.

D. indica
Chulta, elephant apple
This beautiful flowering and foliage tree has large, nodding, white flowers, up to 10cm (4in) across, and large, corrugated dark green leaves, up to 30cm (12in) long. The spring flowers are followed by large green and yellow apple-like fruits. H 15–18m (50–60ft), S 10–15m (33–50ft).
Aspect Light shade or full sun.
Hardiness (Min. 15°C/59°F) Zone 11.

DIOSPYROS

This large genus, containing 475 species of slow-growing deciduous and evergreen trees and shrubs, is perhaps best known for the species *D. ebenum* (ebony), but it also includes persimmons. The

Embothrium coccineum

hardy deciduous species are native to temperate Asia and North America, while the tropical and subtropical species, which are often evergreen, are from south-western Asia to China.
Cultivation Grow in fertile soil in full sun.
Pruning Occasional pruning is required for the removal of dead, dying, diseased or crossing branches, as and when needed.
Propagation Seed is the easiest method of propagation and should be collected when fresh, removed from the fruit and sown into a container in a heated glasshouse in a frost-free and humid environment until germination occurs. Summer budding is also used and is grafted on to seedling grown rootstocks.

D. digyna
(syn. D. ebanaster)
Black sapote
This open, lax evergreen tree has glossy green leaves. Unlike many other forms of persimmon, which have brightly coloured fruits, this species has green fruits, which contain a blackish, jelly-like substance and which are widely used as flavouring for milk, fruit juice or alcoholic drinks. Outdoors it is best used as a screen or windbreak. H and S 20m (65ft).
Aspect Full sun.
Hardiness ❄ Zones 10–12.

D. ebenum
Ebony
This slow-growing, tropical evergreen tree is widely grown for its dense black wood. Although it was once native to areas of tropical India, it has been overexploited and is now rare and threatened in the wild. It is a broadly spreading tree, which bears small, velvety, rust-coloured, edible fruits. H and S 30m (100ft).
Aspect Full sun.
Hardiness ❄ Zones 10–12.

D. kaki
Japanese persimmon, Chinese persimmon, kaki
Although this deciduous species will grow in temperate climates, it requires sufficient summer heat to make the fruits that are borne on female plants palatable. The glossy, dark green leaves, up to 20cm (8in) long, turn orange-yellow in autumn. Even in temperate areas, trees will bear the tomato-sized, yellowish-orange fruits, which ripen in late autumn. It is a slow-growing tree with a broadly spreading habit. H 10–12m (33–40ft), S 7–10m (23–33ft).
Aspect Full sun to semi-shade.
Hardiness ❄❄ Zones 7–10.

D. lotus
Date plum
This deciduous species is similar to *D. kaki* but grows more quickly and the glossy, dark green leaves

Diospyros lotus

are not as colourful in autumn. On female plants the tiny, red-tinged green flowers are followed by inedible, yellow to purplish fruits. H 10–25m (33–80ft), S 6–10m (20–33ft).
Aspect Full sun to semi-shade.
Hardiness ❋❋❋ Zones 6–10.

D. virginiana
American persimmon, possumwood
This is both the hardiest and the largest species. It is grown for the durability of its timber, its long, tapering foliage and its small, orange-yellow, berry-like fruits, which are produced on female trees in autumn. Autumn colour ranges from purplish-red to orange-yellow. H 25m (80ft), S 10m (33ft).
Aspect Full sun to semi-shade.
Hardiness ❋❋❋ Zones 4–9.

EMBOTHRIUM
Chilean fire bush
The eight species of evergreen trees and shrubs in the genus, which are native to South America, are related to proteas. They are grown as ornamental trees for their vivid flowers, which are borne in late spring to early summer. They do best in climates that are moist and not too hot.
Cultivation Grow in fertile, moisture-retentive, neutral to acidic soil in sun or semi-shade.

Pruning Multi-stemmed specimens are widely grown, and pruning for these should aim to remove the lower branches and maintain a section of the trunks free of branch growth. Occasional pruning is required for the removal of dead, dying, diseased or crossing branches.
Propagation Seed is the easiest method of propagation and should be collected when fresh and sown into a container in a heated glasshouse in a frost-free and humid environment until germination occurs. Semi-ripe cuttings can also be rooted during late summer and should be dipped in a rooting hormone and placed in a frost-free, humid environment until they root.

E. coccineum
Chilean fire bush, flame flower
This upright, branched tree with an open, but columnar habit is often better grown as a multi-stemmed shrub, when it can be included in a mixed border or grown as a lawn specimen. It bears vivid orange-red, grevillea-like flowers in late spring. The long, slender leaves are evergreen, but tend to be semi-evergreen in colder areas. Plants in the Lanceolatum Group are similar to the species except that it has very long, lance-like leaves. It is hardier than the species and is the least evergreen form.

Dillenia indica

H 9–10m (30–33ft), S 4–5m (12–16ft).
Aspect Full sun to light shade.
Hardiness ❋❋ Zone 8.

ERIOBOTRYA
Loquat
The 30 or so species in the genus are evergreen shrubs and trees from eastern Asia and the Himalayas. In cold areas they can be grown under glass, although in favourable conditions they make attractive specimen trees and can be considered hardy when grown in protected locations.
Cultivation Protect plants from cold winds. Tender species grown under glass may need pruning to keep them under control. Grow in a free-draining fertile soil, in a warm and sunny location.

Although it will grow in temperate climates and take short periods of freezing temperatures, it is more at home in a subtropical climate where it will produce golden-orange fruits the size of large cherries. In cool, temperate climates it is best grown against a sunny wall.
Pruning Minimal pruning is required other than shortening back any over-vigorous shoots by one-third of their overall length, and removing any weak, crossing, diseased or dying shoots.
Propagation Sow seed in a free-draining medium in a humid environment at a temperature of 18°C (64°F). T-budding can be used to grow selected forms, using seedling loquats, quince (*Cydonia oblonga*) and hawthorns (*Crataegus*) as rootstocks.

Eriobotrya japonica

Eucalyptus dalrympleana

E. japonica
Loquat
This beautiful small tree or spreading shrub is grown for its handsome foliage and fruits. The large, dark green leaves, up to 30cm (12in) long, are glossy and strongly veined. From autumn to winter clusters of small, fragrant, white flowers are borne at the tips of branches on felted brown stems. In spring bright yellow, edible fruits, up to 4cm (1½in) across, appear, but these need a hot summer to ripen fully. H and S 8–9m (26–30ft).
Aspect Full sun.
Hardiness ✿✿ Zones 8–9.

EUCALYPTUS
Gum tree
There are more than 500 species of evergreen trees and shrubs in the genus. Most come from Australia, but they are also found throughout South-east Asia and Melanesia. Some forms are hardy. They are grown for their bark, flowers and foliage, which may be aromatic. Juvenile leaves tend to be round and blue-green or grey-green. Adult leaves are often much narrower (to conserve moisture) and less grey. Although they often have large, straight trunks, the trees can also be coppiced, but require this treatment throughout their lives, because tall, slender branches tend to split.
Cultivation Grow in moisture-retentive but well-drained, neutral to acidic soil in full sun. Protect plants from cold winds.
Pruning Formative pruning should aim to encourage a clear trunk and a balanced crown, while tipping the lateral branches of young trees will encourage a denser crown. Occasional pruning is required for the removal of dead, dying, diseased or crossing branches.
Propagation Seed is the main method of propagation and should be collected when fresh and sown into a container in a heated glasshouse in a frost-free and humid environment until germination occurs.

E. coccifera
Mount Wellington peppermint, Tasmanian snow gum
This wide-spreading tree has pendulous branches and clusters of peppermint-scented, creamy-white flowers in summer. The bark shreds in long, silver-grey plates to reveal the yellow bark developing underneath. Juvenile leaves are round and mid-green. Adult leaves are narrow and grey-green, and scented of peppermint. H 18–20m (60–65ft), S 7m (23ft).
Aspect Full sun.
Hardiness ✿✿✿ Zones 9–12.

E. confertifolia
Half-barked gum
The common name of this narrow tree derives from the fact that the upper branches and stems have smooth, ornamental, silver-orange bark, while the lower part of the trunk is covered with thick, corrugated, blackish bark, which protects the tree against flooding and fire. Creamy-white flowers are borne in dense clusters in spring together with the new leaves, which are tinted with purple. Adult leaves are broad and large and grey-green with wavy margins. H 20m (65ft), S 4m (12ft).
Aspect Full sun.
Hardiness ✿ Zones 10–12.

E. cordata
Silver gum
This dense, widely grown tree has willow-like branches and stunning white bark, which is streaked with green and purple. The silver-green leaves are flat and angled. In late winter and early spring clusters of white flowers are borne. It is not a drought-tolerant species. H 20m (65ft), S 4m (12ft).
Aspect Full sun.
Hardiness ✿ Zones 8–11.

Eucryphia x nymansensis 'Nymansay'

E. dalrympleana
Mountain gum, broad-leaved kindling bark
This alkaline-tolerant, fast-growing tree quickly develops a straight trunk with smooth, creamy-white bark, peeling in long strands. The underbark is almost white in spring. The emerging foliage is bronze. Juvenile leaves are ovate and blue-green; mature leaves are lance-shaped and dark green. H 20–25m (65–80ft), 8m (26ft).
Aspect Full sun.
Hardiness ✿✿✿ Zones 8–10.

E. ficifolia
Red-flowering gum
This beautiful, broadly spreading tree bears large clusters of bright red, sometimes pink or white, flowers from summer to autumn. The mid-green leaves have red-tinged margins. The short trunk is covered with rough, dark brown bark. H 15m (50ft), S 5–15m (16–50ft).
Aspect Full sun.
Hardiness ✿ Zones 9–12.

E. gunnii
Cider gum
This popular and highly ornamental tree has copper-brown bark, which shreds in long strips in summer to reveal the pinkish-white underbark. It is a fast-growing tree, with silver-green leaves and clusters of cream-coloured flowers in summer. H 25m (80ft), S 7m (23ft).
Aspect Full sun.
Hardiness ✿✿✿ Zones 8–10.

Eucalyptus cordata

E. johnstonii
Tasmanian yellow gum
The bark of this attractive tree is smooth, with orange, reddish-yellow and green streaks. The glossy leaves are apple-green, and clusters of small, creamy-white flower are borne in summer. This is one of the best gum trees for poorly drained, sandy soil. H 25–30m (80–100ft), S 7–10m (23–33ft).
Aspect Full sun.
Hardiness ✿✿ Zones 8–11.

E. nicholii
Narrow-leaved black peppermint, Nichol's willow-leaved peppermint, pepper gum
This is a slender tree when it is young, but it develops a wider crown as it matures. As the tree ages it also develops flaking, dark brown bark, and the branches tend to weep. The apple-green leaves smell pleasantly of peppermint. It thrives in medium to heavy sandy soils that remain moist throughout the growing season. It will survive short periods of frost. H 15–18m (50–60ft), S 7–12m (23–40ft).
Aspect Full sun.
Hardiness ✿✿ Zones 8–10.

E. parvula
This small tree is said to be one of the hardiest gum trees, and it is the most suitable variety for a cooler climate. It has a short trunk, often becoming multi-stemmed, covered with dark and light grey and green bark. The long, narrow leaves are blue-green.

Eucryphia glutinosa

It is tolerant of a wide range of soils, including alkaline conditions. H 10m (33ft), S 3m (10ft).
Aspect Full sun.
Hardiness ✿✿✿ Zones 7–10.

E. pauciflora
Snow gum, cabbage gum, weeping gum, white sallee
This dense, spreading, often multi-stemmed tree develops a weeping crown as it matures and has grey and silver-white flaking bark. In summer dense clusters of creamy-white flowers are borne in the leaf axils. The mature leaves are long, narrow and blue-green. H 15–20m (50–65ft), S 15m (50ft).
Aspect Full sun.
Hardiness ✿✿✿ Zones 8–10.

EUCRYPHIA
The genus contains five species of small, mostly evergreen garden trees, which are native to Chile and Australia. They bear fragrant, mallow-like, white flowers in late summer to early autumn.
Cultivation Grow in fertile, moisture-retentive but well-drained, acidic soil. *E. cordifolia* and *E. x nymansensis* tolerate alkaline soil. All forms require cool growing conditions.
Pruning Formative pruning should aim to encourage a clear trunk and a balanced crown, while tipping the lateral branches of young trees will encourage a denser crown. Occasional pruning is required for the removal of dead, dying, diseased or crossing branches.
Propagation Seed is the main method of propagation and should be collected when fresh and sown into a container in a heated glasshouse in a frost-free and humid environment until germination occurs. Summer softwood and semi-ripe cutting root easily if the base of the cutting is dipped in a rooting hormone and the cuttings are then placed in a frost-free, humid environment in a glasshouse.

E. cordifolia
Ulmo, roble de Chile
In late summer this upright, conical, evergreen tree bears clusters of saucer-shaped, white

Eucalyptus gunnii

flowers. The oblong leaves, up to 8cm (3in) long, have wavy edges and are dark green above and greyish below. H 15m (50ft), S 8m (25ft).
Aspect Full sun to light shade.
Hardiness ✿✿ Zone 9.

E. glutinosa
This popular, compact deciduous or semi-evergreen tree has a fairly narrowly columnar habit. The glossy green leaves, up to 6cm (2in) long, are narrower than those of *E. cordifolia* and are heavily toothed; they turn orange-red in autumn. Clusters of scented white, sometimes double, flowers are borne in mid- to late summer. H 10m (33ft), S 3–6m (10–20ft).
Aspect Full sun to semi-shade.
Hardiness ✿✿✿ Zone 8.

E. x intermedia
This broadly columnar, fast-growing, evergreen tree is a hybrid between *E. glutinosa* and *E. lucida*. It has pale green leaves and white flowers. H and S 10m (33ft).
Named varieties The cultivar 'Rostrevor' bears many clusters of beautiful, fragrant white flowers from late summer to autumn.
Aspect Full sun to semi-shade.
Hardiness ✿✿✿ Zone 8.

E. x nymansensis 'Nymansay'
This evergreen hybrid between *E. cordifolia* and *E. glutinosa* is grown for its narrowly columnar habit and mass of flowers. It is a fast-growing tree, producing fragrant white flowers in late summer. H 15m (50ft), S 5m (16ft).
Aspect Full sun to semi-shade.
Hardiness ✿✿✿ Zone 7.

Fagus sylvatica 'Dawyck Purple'

FAGUS
Beech

The ten species of deciduous trees in the genus are found in temperate areas throughout the northern hemisphere. They are grown for their elegant habit and their autumn colour.
Cultivation Grow in moisture-retentive but well-drained soil in sun or semi-shade. Purple-leaved forms give best colour in full sun; yellow-leaved forms should be planted in semi-shade.
Pruning Early formative pruning should produce a clear, straight trunk and a balanced crown. Remove dead, dying, diseased or crossing branches.
Propagation Collect and sow seed in autumn. Put in an unheated glasshouse or cold frame until germination occurs. Winter grafting of ornamental European beech cultivars on to seed-raised European beech is the most effective way of propagating different forms.

F. grandifolia
American beech
A majestic, spreading tree, this specimen will require space around it as it is likely to grow as wide as it is tall. The attractive dark green leaves, up to 15cm (6in) long, are oval and toothed and turn golden-bronze in autumn. H and S 15–20m (50–65ft).
Aspect Full sun or semi-shade.
Hardiness ❋❋❋ Zones 4–9.

F. orientalis
Oriental beech
A fast-growing species native to south-east Europe as well as south-west Asia. The dark green leaves, up to 17cm (7in) long, are toothed and have wavy margins; they turn yellow-brown in autumn. A good alternative to *F. sylvatica* in poor, fast-draining soil. H 30m (100ft), S 15–20m (50–65ft).
Aspect Full sun or semi-shade.
Hardiness ❋❋❋ Zones 5–7.

F. sylvatica
Common beech, European beech
This noble, fast-growing, spreading tree, is grown for its stunning orange, yellow and brown autumn colour. The leaves, up to 10cm (4in) long, have wavy margins and are pale green at first but turn glossy, dark green by midsummer. Less tolerant of dry soil conditions and high summer temperatures than *F. grandiflora* or *F. orientalis*. H 25–30m (80–100ft), S 15m (50ft).
Named varieties 'Dawyck' has a tight, conical habit and twisted, upswept branches that widen with age.
'Dawyck Gold', which is a much slower growing form, has vibrant yellow new leaves that fade to yellow-green in summer.
'Dawyck Purple' is a narrow, upright form with purple-black foliage and lovely autumn colour.
'Pendula' (syn. *F. sylvatica* f. *pendula*; weeping beech) will form a circle of new plants if the outer branches are allowed to layer themselves. H 15m (50ft), S 30m (100ft).
'Riversii' is a beautiful, wide-spreading copper beech that has dark purple leaves and good autumn colour.
Aspect Full sun or semi-shade.
Hardiness ❋❋❋ Zones 4–7.

FICUS
Fig
This large genus, which contains about 800 species of mostly evergreens, is found throughout the world in tropical and subtropical areas, where they are grown as shade trees and for their edible fruits. Many tender species are grown as houseplants

Ficus benjamina

in temperate areas, but the deciduous species *F. carica* (common fig) is hardy in sheltered temperate areas. The species below are tender and should be grown under glass in all but the warmest areas.
Cultivation Grow in fertile, moisture-retentive but well-drained soil sited in sun or semi-shade.
Pruning Prune occasionally to remove dead, dying, diseased or crossing branches.
Propagation Seed should be collected when fresh and sown into a pot in a heated glasshouse in a frost-free and humid environment until germination occurs. Semi-ripe cuttings can be rooted during late summer and placed in a frost-free, humid environment until they root. Low branches can also be layered into the soil.

F. benghalensis
Banyan, Indian fig
This evergreen species develops into a large, spreading tree with strongly horizontal branches, which are supported by prop roots growing from the branches. The prop roots layer and send up new shoots. The glossy green leaves, up to 25cm (10in) long, have distinct veins and are flushed bronze-pink in spring. H 30m (100ft), S 60m (200ft).
Aspect Light shade to full sun.
Hardiness (Min. 15°C/59°F) Zone 10–12.

F. benjamina
Weeping fig
This evergreen species has a beautiful weeping habit. The narrow leaves, up to 12cm (5in) long, are glossy and dark green. These trees develop extensive root systems and do best in deep, fertile soils and humid climates. They are widely grown in the tropics and also in protected environments, such as shopping malls. Although eventually large, trees can be easily pruned. In tropical areas they make dense hedges. H and S 30–50m (100–165ft).
Named varieties There are several cultivars, including 'Exotica', 'Golden King' (with yellow variegated leaves) and 'Starlight' (with white-edged leaves).
The widely available 'Variegata', which has glossy, dark green leaves attractively edged in white, is a popular houseplant.
Aspect Deep shade to full sun.
Hardiness (Min. 15°C/59°F) Zone 10–12.

F. elastica
India rubber tree
This is one of the most widely grown species of fig tree and found in numerous homes as a pot plant. It is now extinct in its natural habitat of India, Burma, Malaysia and Java. It is potentially a large tree with big, thick, copper-flushed leaves, which turn glossy, dark green with age. Like *F. benjamina*, it is easy to prune and shape. H and S 60m (200ft).

Ficus benghalensis

Named varieties 'Decora' has leaves with creamy-white midribs and flushed with red beneath.

The leaves of 'Doescheri' are variegated with grey-green, pale yellow and white and have pink stalks and midribs.

The large leaves of 'Robusta' are mottled with pink, cream and light green. 'Rubra' has dark copper-flushed new growth. 'Variegata' has cream-edged leaves. **Aspect** Light shade to full sun. **Hardiness** (Min. 15°C/59°F) Zone 10–12.

F. lyrata
Fiddle-leaf fig
This spreading evergreen tree has large, leathery, highly corrugated and twisted leaves. It is a drought-tolerant and slow-growing fig, and fruits freely. In the garden: H and S 12m (40ft); in the wild: H and S 30m (100ft). **Aspect** light shade to full sun. **Hardiness** (Min. 15°C/59°F) Zone 10–12.

F. macrophylla
Moreton Bay fig, Australian banyan
This large, dense, evergreen tree has a short trunk and aerial roots, some of which are prop roots for the wide-spreading branches. The leaves, up to 25cm (10in) long, are mid-green above and rusty red below. Masses of purple-green figs are borne on mature trees. H and S 55m (180ft). **Aspect** Light shade to full sun. **Hardiness** (Min. 7–10°C/45–50°F) Zones 10–12.

Fortunella japonica

FITZROYA
Patagonian cypress
The single species in the genus is an evergreen conifer. It is native to Chile and southern Argentina. **Cultivation** Grow in fertile, moisture-retentive but well-drained soil in full sun. Shelter plants from cold winds. **Pruning** Formative pruning should aim to produce a clear trunk and a balanced crown, while tipping the lateral branches of young trees will encourage a denser crown. Occasional pruning is required for the removal of dead, dying, diseased or crossing branches. **Propagation** Seed is the easiest method of propagation and should be collected when fresh and sown into a container in an unheated glasshouse or cold frame until germination occurs. Semi-ripe and softwood cutting can be rooted during summer and should be dipped in a rooting hormone and placed in a humid environment until rooting occurs. Selected forms are winter grafted on to seedling raised rootstocks.

F. cupressoides (syn. F. patagonia)
Patagonian cypress, Alerce
This majestic, weeping conifer is highly prized for its timber and has been over-cropped as a result of this in Chile and Argentina. In the wild it can live up to 3,400 years, and in gardens it is grown for its dark green cypress-like foliage that hangs from long arching branches, and will develop into a broad columnar tree. Cones are small and brownish in colour

Fitzroya cupressoides

Ficus lyrata

and the bark develops with age into a rich reddish brown and shreds in long strips. Best grown in areas where annual rainfall is high, and in free-draining, humus-rich, moisture-retentive soils. H 50m (165ft), S 20m (65ft). **Aspect** Light shade to full sun. **Hardiness** ✻✻✻ Zone 8.

FORTUNELLA
Kumquat
The genus of five evergreen shrubs and small trees is native to woodlands from southern China to Malaysia. They are spiny plants, grown for their white flowers and edible, yellow fruits. Unlike other citrus fruits, the entire fruit of the kumquat can be eaten, including the rind and pips. **Cultivation** Grow in fertile, moisture-retentive soil in full sun. Kumquats are suitable for growing in containers. **Pruning** Long, whippy growth is produced during spring and summer and this should be

reduced so that a balanced, round-headed crown is produced. Occasional pruning is required for the removal of dead, dying, diseased or crossing branches. **Propagation** Most citrus fruits are produced by budding and this can be done during the winter when the seedling rootstock is dormant. Kumquats will come true from seed and can be propagated this way, but require an even temperature of above 25°C (77°F) to germinate.

F. japonica
(syn. Citrus japonica, C. madurensis)
Round kumquat
This dense, bushy tree has spines in the leaf axils, glossy green leaves, up to 10cm (4in) long, and fragrant flowers. The small, slightly oval fruits are yellowish-orange, ripening to orange. H 4–5m (12–16ft), S 1.5m (5ft). **Aspect** Full sun or semi-shade. **Hardiness** (Min. 7°C/45°F) Zones 9–11.

Fraxinus americana

FRAXINUS
Ash
The 65 species of usually deciduous and fast-growing trees in the genus are native to woodlands in the northern hemisphere. They are grown as specimen trees and for their attractive leaves.
Cultivation Grow in moisture-retentive but well-drained, neutral to alkaline soil in sun.
Pruning Little pruning is required apart from the removal of dead, dying, diseased or crossing branches. Early formative pruning should produce a clear straight trunk and a balanced crown.
Propagation Seed should be collected fresh and have three months warm treatment followed by three months in an unheated glasshouse or cold frame until germination occurs. Summer budding on to seedling-grown ash is used for propagation.

F. americana
White ash
The species, which is native to eastern North America, is a fast-growing tree with dark green, pinnate leaves, up to 35cm (14in) long and with 5–9 leaflets. In autumn the leaves turn yellow or purple. H 25–30m (80–100ft), S 15m (50ft).
Named varieties The cultivar 'Autumn Purple' is a smaller, conical tree with dark green leaves that turn red-purple in autumn. H 18m (60ft), S 12m (40ft).
Aspect Full sun or semi-shade.
Hardiness ❋❋❋ Zones 4–9.

F. angustifolia
Narrow-leaved ash
This spreading tree, from northern Africa and south-west Europe, has glossy, dark green leaves, up to 25cm (10in) long, with 13 leaflets. These turn yellow-gold in autumn. H 25m (80ft), S 12m (40ft).
Named varieties The species is not often grown in gardens but is usually represented by the form 'Raywood' (claret ash), which is an upright, fast-growing tree with glossy, dark green leaves that turn dark red-purple in autumn. H 20m (65ft).
Aspect Full sun or semi-shade.
Hardiness ❋❋❋ Zone 5.

F. excelsior
Common ash, European ash
This is a very large, broadly columnar tree, which may be identified by its black winter buds. The dark green leaves, up to 30cm (12in) long, have 9 to 13 leaflets and turn yellow in autumn. Winged fruits (keys) hang in clusters from the stems in winter and fall in spring. H 30–40m (100–130ft), S 20m (70ft).
Named varieties There are several fine cultivars. 'Jaspidea' has stunning yellow new shoots, yellow-green stems in winter and good yellow autumn colour. 'Pendula' (weeping ash) is a weeping form, often grafted on a straight trunk and producing an umbrella-like shape. It is one of the most widely planted weeping trees. 'Westhof's Glorie' has a narrow conical habit, which broadens with age, and is often used as a street tree in Europe.
Aspect Full sun or semi-shade.
Hardiness ❋❋❋ Zones 5–7.

F. ornus
Manna ash, flowering ash
One of the most attractive ashes for general planting, this beautiful, medium-sized, round-headed tree from southern Europe and south-western Asia bears showy clusters of small, scented, creamy-white flowers in early summer. The dark green leaves, which are up to 20cm (8in) long, have 5–9 leaflets and turn purple-red in autumn. H 20m (65ft),
S 15m (50ft).
Aspect Full sun or semi-shade.
Hardiness ❋❋❋ Zones 5–6.

GINKGO
Maidenhair tree
This extraordinary tree is sadly now extinct in the wild. It is an ancient tree, and 200 million years ago the species was widespread across the world. The only species in the genus, it is a deciduous conifer. Male and female trees exist, and it is the female that produces the fruit that is harvested for its nut. Female fruits also have a strong, pungent aroma, so the male form is more widely grown as a garden or street tree, and it is widely planted in towns, streets and gardens because it is tolerant of pollution. It is also relatively disease-free.
Cultivation Grow in well-drained soil in full sun.
Pruning Occasional pruning only is required for the removal of dead, dying, diseased or crossing branches.
Propagation Seed is the easiest method of propagation and should be collected when fresh and sown into a container in an unheated glasshouse or cold frame until germination occurs. Semi-ripe and softwood cutting can be rooted during summer and should be dipped in a rooting hormone and placed in a humid environment until rooting occurs. Selected forms are winter grafted on to seedling-raised rootstocks.

Ginkgo biloba

G. biloba

It is an upright, conical tree with upswept branches. The unusual two-lobed leaves are green with linear veins, and they turn golden-yellow in autumn. H 30–40m (100–130ft), S 8–15m (26–50ft).

Named varieties Numerous cultivars have been developed for their habit or for their autumn colour. 'Autumn Gold', one of the most widely distributed male forms, has a semi-upright but broadly conical shape and fantastic autumn colour. The male 'Fastigiata' is a tight, upright column with twisted branches and good autumn colour. 'Princeton Sentry', a male form, is widely grown in the USA as a street tree; the autumn colour is excellent. The fast-growing male 'Saratoga' is a more compact but still conical tree with good autumn colour. 'Tremonia' is a widely planted European form that originated in Germany. It has beautiful autumn colour, twisted branches and a narrow habit.
Aspect Full sun or semi-shade.
Hardiness ❁❁❁ Zones 6–10.

GLEDITSIA

The genus contains 12–14 species of deciduous, rather spiny trees, which are native to North and South America and Asia. They are grown for their attractive pinnate leaves and for the large seedpods that follow the insignificant flowers.
Cultivation Grow in fertile, well-drained soil in full sun.
Pruning Early formative pruning should aim to produce a clear straight trunk and a balanced crown; little pruning is required apart from the removal of dead, dying, diseased or crossing branches as and when needed.
Propagation Seed is widely used. It should be collected fresh and have three months warm treatment followed by three months in an unheated glasshouse or cold frame until germination occurs. Summer budding on to seedling-grown trees and winter grafting is used to propagate the different forms. Trees can also be propagated by softwood cuttings taken during summer, dipped into a rooting

Gleditsia triacanthos

hormone, and placed in a humid environment until rooted, and then hardened off and potted on.

G. sinensis
Chinese honey locust

A graceful, medium-sized tree, this is armed with numerous thorns on the stems and branches, but it has delicate, light green foliage. When it is grown in free-draining, fertile soil it will bear whitish, pea-like flowers in summer, followed by bean-like pods in autumn. H 20m (65ft), S 15m (50ft).
Aspect Full sun.
Hardiness ❁❁❁ Zone 5.

G. triacanthos
Honey locust

This widely grown tree from North America has a spreading habit and spiny branches and trunk. The glossy, dark green leaves, up to 25cm (10in) long, turn yellow in autumn, when the seedpods, which can be up to 45cm (18in) long, are borne. H 30m (100ft), S 20m (65ft).
Named varieties 'Rubylace' is an unusual, beautiful tree, with an almost weeping habit. The foliage is purple-red as it emerges and remains purple-green through the summer. It never produces seedpods. H and S 8–10m (26–33ft).

The fast-growing 'Shademaster' is a stunning, semi-weeping tree with green foliage, persisting long

into autumn before turning pale yellow. It is almost thornless, and therefore is one of the most widely planted of this group. H and S 10m (33ft).

The broadly conical and thornless 'Sunburst' has golden-yellow young leaves that fade to pale lemon yellow in summer. H 12m (40ft), S 10m (33ft).
Aspect Full sun.
Hardiness ❁❁❁ Zones 4–9.

GREVILLEA
Spider flower

The 250 species of evergreen trees and shrubs in the genus are mostly native to Australia, with a few coming from South-east Asia.
Cultivation Outdoors, grow in fertile, neutral to acidic soil in full sun.
Pruning Occasional pruning only is required for the removal of dead, dying, diseased or crossing branches.
Propagation Seed is the easiest method of propagation and should be collected when fresh and sown into a container in a heated glasshouse in a frost-free and humid environment until germination occurs. Softwood

cuttings can also be rooted during early summer and should be dipped in a rooting hormone and placed in a frost-free, humid environment until they root.

G. banksii

This is a widely branching large shrub or small tree with deeply cut, fern-like leaves, up to 25cm (10in) long. In late winter and spring dense clusters of pale pink or dark red flowerheads are produced at the tips of the stems. With regular pruning to maintain its shape, this is a beautiful small flowering tree for moist, acidic soil. H 10m (33ft), S 5m (16ft).
Aspect Full sun.
Hardiness ❁ Zones 8–11.

G. robusta
Silky oak

A large, fast-growing, flowering and foliage tree, this has deeply cut, fern-like leaves, up to 30cm (12in) long, and one-sided, radially arranged clusters of spidery, bright yellow flowerheads in spring. H 30m (100ft), S 20m (65ft).
Aspect Full sun.
Hardiness (Min. 5°C/41°F) Zones 8–11

Gleditsia sinensis

HALESIA
Snowdrop tree, silver bell
The five species of attractive deciduous shrubs or small trees in the genus are native to south-eastern USA and eastern China. They have attractive bell-shaped flowers, which are followed by winged fruits.
Cultivation Grow in fertile, moisture-retentive but well-drained, neutral to acidic soil in sun or semi-shade.
Pruning Early formative pruning should aim to produce a clear straight trunk and a balanced crown; little pruning is required apart from the removal of dead, dying, diseased, or crossing branches as and when needed.
Propagation Trees can be propagated by softwood cuttings taken during summer, which are dipped into a rooting hormone, and placed in a humid environment until rooted, and then hardened off and potted on. Cuttings are best potted on the following spring, as they establish more quickly.

H. carolina
(syn. *H. tetraptera*)
In spring, before the leaves emerge, masses of pendent, bell-shaped, pink-tinged, white flowers are borne along the branches. They are followed by green fruits with four wings. The mid-green leaves, up to 15cm (6in) long,

turn yellow in autumn. H and S 10–20m (33–65ft).
Aspect Semi-shade to full sun.
Hardiness ❀❀❀ Zones 4–9.

H. monticola
Mountain snowdrop tree
The mid-green leaves, up to 20cm (8in) long, of this fast-growing, conical tree turn yellow in autumn. Bell-shaped white flowers are borne in spring, before the leaves, and are followed by four-winged, green fruits, which are sometimes up to 5cm (2in) long. H 12m (40ft), S 8m (26ft).
Named varieties *H. monticola* var. *vestita* has even larger flowers, which are sometimes tinged with pink. *H. monticola* var. *vestita* f. *rosea* has large, pale pink flowers.
Aspect Semi-shade to full sun.
Hardiness ❀❀❀ Zones 5–8.

ILEX
Holly
The genus contains about 400 species of both evergreen and deciduous trees and shrubs. They are found in temperate, tropical and subtropical areas and can vary immensely in their height and spread, habit, shape, leaf shape and colour and even the colour of the berries. Female trees bear fruit, and most hollies require that both male and female trees are present to produce berries. Although there are some self-fertile forms, these are not common.

Halesia monticola

Cultivation Grow in fertile, moisture-retentive but well-drained soil in sun or semi-shade.
Pruning Early formative pruning should aim to produce a dense conical habit and will involve tipping back side shoots and branches to create a dense crown. A single leader should be produced along with a clear straight trunk and a balanced crown; little pruning is required apart from the removal of dead, dying, diseased or crossing branches as and when needed.
Propagation Trees can be propagated by softwood or semi-ripe cuttings taken from early to late summer, dipped into a rooting hormone, and placed in a humid environment until rooted, and then hardened off and potted on. Seed can also be used, and should be collected when fresh, soaked to remove the pulp, and then grown in an unheated glasshouse or cold frame until it germinates.

I. x altaclerensis
Highclere holly
This hybrid between *I. aquifolium* and *I. perado* forms a large evergreen shrub or small tree. These plants are more heat-tolerant than *I. aquifolium* and have a greater resistance to pollution. The glossy, dark green leaves, up to 12cm (5in) long, are larger than, but not as spiky as, those of *I. aquifolium*. Female forms produce berries, but require a male holly nearby to pollinate the flowers. H to 20m (65ft), S 12–15m (40–50ft).

Named varieties There are many cultivars. The popular, strongly growing female form 'Belgica' has narrow, pale green leaves and an abundance of orange-red fruits in autumn. Its conical habit makes it a popular choice as a focal point.
'Belgica Aurea' (syn. 'Silver Sentinel') is one of the best variegated hollies. It is a female fruiting form, with the attributes of 'Belgica', but it has narrow, yellow-margined leaves. H 12m (40ft), S 5m (16ft).
The pyramidal female form 'Camelliifolia' is widely grown for its glossy, camellia-like, dark green leaves, red berries and purple stems. H 14m (46ft).
'Golden King' is another female form with red berries, but it has a much wider and flatter leaf than 'Belgica Aurea', and mature trees are slightly more open in habit. H 6m (20ft).
The male form 'Hodginsii' does not bear berries, but it is widely planted as a pollinator for this group and for *I. aquifolium*. H 14m (46ft), S 10m (33ft).
'Lawsoniana' is a delightful, open-growing, female form. The broad leaves have a distinct yellow blotch in the centre of the leaf, and the foliage colour contrasts well with the red-brown fruits. H 6m (20ft).
Aspect Full sun to semi-shade.
Hardiness ❀❀ Zone 7.

I. aquifolium
English holly, common holly
This species is widely planted in cool temperate climates where it develops into a broadly columnar

Ilex aquifolium 'Amber'

Ilex aquifolium 'Golden Queen'

Jacaranda mimosifolia

'Pyramidalis Fructu Luteo' is a wonderful conical holly, which makes a fine specimen tree when fully grown. It is widely planted for its habit, glossy green leaves with distinct yellow margins and plentiful bright red berries. H 6m (20ft), S 4m (12ft).
Aspect Full sun to semi-shade.
Hardiness ❀❀ Zone 7.

I. x *koehneana*
This hybrid between *I. aquifolium* and *I. latifolia* is a narrow evergreen shrub. It has large, spiny, glossy green leaves and red berries. H 7m (23ft), S 5m (16ft).
Aspect Full sun.
Hardiness ❀❀❀ Zone 7.

I. latifolia
This pyramidal evergreen species is sometimes known as the magnolia leaf holly as it bears very long, tapering, glossy green, almost spineless leaves, nearly 30cm (12in) long. Female trees produce berries in autumn and these ripen in winter, starting greenish-red and ripening to salmon-pink. This species enjoys high summer temperatures, when the wood can ripen fully before winter, and in more maritime climates it may suffer occasional frost damage. H 7–20m (23–65ft), S 5–10m (16–33ft).
Aspect Full sun.
Hardiness ❀❀ Zone 7.

I. opaca
American holly
This columnar evergreen species is a useful understorey tree, which does much better in a continental climate where the summers are hot and the winters are cold. The spiny leaves are dull green and can grow up to 12cm (5in) long. They are a good contrast with the bright red berries, borne in clusters on female plants. This species needs acidic soil. H 10–15m (33–65ft), S 7–8m (23–26ft).
Aspect Full sun or semi-shade.
Hardiness ❀❀❀ Zone 5.

JACARANDA
There are about 45 species of evergreen and deciduous trees in the genus, and they are found in tropical and subtropical

tree with dark green stems and a dense crown of spiny, evergreen foliage. The glossy, dark green leaves, up to 10cm (4in) long, are spiny. It is not tolerant of high summer temperatures, and specimens grown in poor, free-draining soils are prone to leaf fall during late summer. H 20–25m (65–80ft), S 8–10m (26–33ft).
Named varieties The female form 'Amber' has spiny green leaves. Bright orange-yellow berries are borne in dense clusters at the tips of the stems. H to 6m (20ft), S 2.4m (8ft).
'Argentea Marginata' (syn. 'Argentea Variegata') is a beautiful female form with pinkish new leaves, which develop a crisp creamy-white variegation and sharp spines. These leaves are a wonderful foil for the bright red berries. H 15m (50ft), S 4m (12ft).
The female 'Bacciflava' (syn. 'Fructu Luteo') is the best of the yellow-berried hollies. H 15m (50ft), S 1m (12ft).
'Golden Milkmaid' is one of the most beautiful variegated hollies. The spiny leaves have a striking golden blotch in the centre.
Despite the name, 'Golden Queen' (syn. 'Aurea Regina') is a male form with spiny, grey-green leaves that are edged with yellow. H 10m (33ft), S 6m (20ft).
The widely planted female form 'Madame Briot' has attractive purple shoots and spiny, dark green leaves that are mottled and edged with golden-yellow. H 10m (33ft), S 5m (16ft).

America. They have attractive foliage, and mature plants bear bell-shaped flowers. In temperate areas they make good foliage plants for conservatories, although they can get tall and leggy.
Cultivation Outdoors, grow in fertile, moisture-retentive but well-drained soil in full sun.
Pruning Formative pruning should aim to encourage a clear trunk and a balanced crown, while tipping the lateral branches of young trees will encourage a denser crown.
Propagation Seed is the easiest method of propagation and should be collected when fresh and be sown into a container in a heated glasshouse in a frost-free and humid environment until germination occurs. Softwood

cuttings can be rooted during early summer and should be dipped in a rooting hormone and placed in a frost-free, humid environment such as a greenhouse until they root. Low branches can also be layered into the soil.

J. mimosifolia
(syn. *J. acutifolia*, *J. ovalifolia*)
This deciduous Argentinian species is widely planted wherever it will grow. As the light green, fern-like leaves emerge in spring, many large panicles of bluish-purple flowers are produced. It will not thrive in climates with high winter rainfall. H 15m (50ft), S 10–15m (33–50ft).
Aspect Full sun.
Hardiness (Min. 5–7°C/41–45°F) Zones 9–11.

Ilex x *koehneana* 'Chestnut Leaf'

Juglans ailanthifolia

Juniperus chinensis

J. recurva
Himalayan weeping juniper, drooping juniper
This broadly conical tree has slender, scale-like, blue-green leaves borne on pendulous branches. The reddish bark peels in long flakes. It will flourish in sheltered locations with moist, free-draining but fertile soil. H 10–15m (33–50ft), S 5m (16ft). Named varieties *J. recurva* var. *coxii* (coffin juniper) has more open foliage than the species and long, weeping stems of blue-green foliage. Aspect Full sun.
Hardiness ✿✿✿ Zone 7.

JUGLANS
Walnut
The 15 or so species of deciduous trees in the genus are native to North and South America and an area stretching from south-eastern Europe to South-east Asia. They are grown for their decorative habit, attractive foliage, spring catkins, autumn fruits and distinctively patterned timber.
Cultivation Grow in deep, fertile, well-drained soil in full sun. Plant in a sheltered position.
Pruning Early formative pruning should aim to produce a clear straight trunk and a balanced crown. Subsequently, little pruning is required apart from the removal of dead, dying, diseased or crossing branches.
Propagation Collect seed when fresh, remove the fleshy pulp, crack the hard nut case, and then grow in an unheated glasshouse or cold frame until it germinates. Winter grafting is used to produce the coloured leaved form, which is grafted on to the common walnut.

J. ailanthifolia
Japanese walnut
This deciduous tree is native to Japan and Sakhalin, and due to its bold foliage it makes a good ornamental specimen for large gardens. It has yellow-green pinnate leaves, up to 16cm (6¼in) long, and produces yellow-green catkins in spring. The nuts have a pleasant flavour and an oily texture. H and S 10m (50ft).
Aspect Full sun.
Hardiness ✿✿✿ Zones 4–9.

J. nigra
Black walnut
This large, slow-growing, often straight-trunked tree is valued for the quality of the timber. A noble parkland tree, it has dark green, pinnate, aromatic leaves, up to 60cm (24in) long, which turn yellow in autumn, and large, edible, oily nuts. H 30m (100ft), S 20 (65ft).
Aspect Full sun.
Hardiness ✿✿✿ Zones 4–7.

J. regia
Common walnut
A widely grown tree in Europe for both its wood and edible nuts, this spreading species has glossy green, pinnate leaves, up to 30cm (12in) long, which are flushed with bronze when they first emerge, fading to green in early summer. H 30m (100ft), S 15–20m (50–65ft).
Named varieties Among the various cultivars the slow-growing 'Purpurea' has dark purple leaves, which fade to a purple-green colour in summer.
Aspect Full sun.
Hardiness ✿✿✿ Zones 4–9.

JUNIPERUS
Juniper
The 60 species of evergreen, coniferous shrubs and trees in this genus are found throughout the northern hemisphere. They exhibit an enormous range of shape, size and colour, and numerous cultivars have been developed, providing plants for ground cover as well as tall specimen trees.

Cultivation Grow in fertile, well-drained soil in sun or semi-shade.
Pruning Formative pruning should aim to produce a balanced crown, while tipping the tips of lateral branches of young trees will encourage a denser crown. Occasional pruning only is required for the removal of dead, dying, diseased, or crossing branches.
Propagation Seed is the easiest method of propagation and should be collected when fresh and sown into a container in an unheated glasshouse or cold frame until germination occurs. Semi-ripe and softwood cutting can be rooted during summer and should be dipped in a rooting hormone and placed in a humid environment until rooting occurs.

J. chinensis
Chinese juniper
This narrowly conical tree is similar in habit and appearance to *Cupressus sempervirens*. The dark brown bark peels in long strips. Trees often have spiky juvenile foliage and soft, scale-like, greenish-blue foliage at the same time. H 20–25m (65–80ft), S 5–6m (16–20ft).
Named varieties 'Aurea' is a slow-growing, narrow conifer with both adult and juvenile foliage. The golden-yellow foliage is susceptible to sun scorch. H 10m (33ft), S up to 5m (16ft).
'Obelisk' is a tightly conical tree with blue-green foliage. H 2.4m (8ft), S 60cm (2ft).
Aspect Full sun or semi-shade.
Hardiness ✿✿✿ Zones 6–10.

Juniperus chinensis 'Aurea'

Koelreuteria paniculata

KOELREUTERIA

The three species in the genus are deciduous trees from China and Taiwan. They are grown for their lovely flowers, borne in large panicles in late summer, and seedpods. Trees flower best in hot summers, and although they are hardy they are still susceptible to damage from late spring frosts and do best in a sheltered position.
Cultivation Grow in fertile, moisture-retentive but well-drained soil in full sun.
Pruning Early formative pruning should aim to produce a clear trunk and a balanced crown.

Subsequently, little pruning is required apart from the removal of dead, dying, diseased or crossing branches. Branch damage is common and any such damaged material should be removed as soon as possible.
Propagation Seed is the most common form of propagation. It should be collected when fresh, and be given three months warm treatment followed by three months cold treatment and grown on in an unheated glasshouse or cold frame until it germinates. Root cuttings can be taken in early winter. Upright forms are winter grafted on to seedling rootstocks.

K. paniculata
Golden rain tree, pride of India
This is a spreading tree, with pinnate leaves, up to 45cm (18in) long, which are tinged with pink when they first emerge and which turn yellow in autumn. From mid- to late summer panicles of yellow flowers are borne, and these are followed by papery, translucent, yellow seedheads, which turn brown as they age. H and S 10–12m (33–40ft). **Named varieties** The slow-growing 'Fastigiata' has a tight, conical habit.
'Rose Lantern' has rosy-pink fruit cases, which persist long into autumn.
'September' is later flowering than other species. The flowers are followed by yellowish-green seedheads that turn brown.
Aspect Full sun or semi-shade.
Hardiness ❀❀❀ Zones 6–8.

Laburnum anagyroides

LABURNUM
Golden rain
The two species of deciduous tree in the genus, which are native to south-eastern Europe and western Asia, are grown for their racemes of yellow flowers. They are easy-to-grow plants, but all parts are very poisonous.
Cultivation Grow in well-drained soil in full sun.
Pruning Early formative pruning should aim to produce a clear trunk and a balanced crown, followed by minimal pruning in order to remove any dead, dying, diseased or crossing branches. Canker is common in many laburnums so quickly cut back and discard diseased shoots to healthy growth.
Propagation Seed and softwood cuttings are the most common form of propagation. Seed should be collected when it is fresh, then sown in to a humid environment such as a heated greenhouse or conservatory until germination occurs. Softwood cuttings can

be taken in summer, dipped in a rooting hormone and then placed in a humid environment until rooting occurs.

L. alpinum
Scotch laburnum
This delightful tree produces racemes, up to 40cm (16in) long, of yellow flowers in late spring to early summer. These are followed by narrow seedpods. The glossy, dark green leaves have three leaflets, up to 8cm (3in) long. H and S 6–8m (20–26ft).
Aspect Full sun or semi-shade.
Hardiness ❀❀❀ Zones 4–7.

L. anagyroides (syn. L. vulgare)
Common laburnum
In late spring to early summer racemes, up to 30cm (12in) long, of bright yellow, wisteria-like flowers are produced. The grey-green leaves, each with 3 leaflets, have hairy undersides. H 7–8m (23–26ft), S 3–4m (10–12ft).
Aspect Full sun or semi-shade.
Hardiness ❀❀❀ Zones 5–7.

Juniperus x media pfitzeriana

L. x watereri 'Vossii'

This cultivar, developed from a hybrid between *L. alpinum* and *L. anagyroides*, is the most widely planted of the laburnums. It bears racemes, 50–60cm (20–24in) long, of golden-yellow flowers in late spring to early summer. The leaves are dark green. H and S 7–8m (23–26ft).
Aspect Full sun or semi-shade.
Hardiness ✿✿✿ Zones 5–7.

LAGERSTROEMIA

The genus contains more than 50 species of evergreen and deciduous trees and shrubs. Native to tropical and subtropical regions from Asia to Australasia, they are often grown for their beautiful, colourful flowers and do best where summer temperatures are high. In temperate areas with mild winters they require the heat of a south-facing wall to ripen the wood before the first frosts.
Cultivation Outdoors, grow in well-drained soil in full sun.
Pruning Early pruning should aim to produce a clear trunk and a balanced crown. Apart from that little pruning is required apart from the removal of dead, dying, diseased or crossing branches. They are grown as multi- or single-stemmed trees, with the canopy lifted away from their stems.
Propagation Seed and softwood cutting is the most common form of propagation. Seed

should be collected when fresh, and be sown into a container at 10–13°C (50–55°F). Softwood cuttings should be taken during early summer, dipped in a rooting hormone and placed in a humid environment until rooting occurs.

L. fauriei

This beautiful small, often multi-stemmed, deciduous tree is grown for its stunning reddish-brown bark and panicles of fragrant white flowers, which appear in midsummer. In autumn the dark green leaves, up to 10cm (4in) long, turn yellow. The trees have an arching, vase-shaped habit. H and S 8–10m (26–33ft).
Named varieties The vigorous 'Fantasy' bears masses of off-white flowers in summer on strongly arching branches. The light copper-brown bark is very attractive. H 12m (40ft).
  'Sarah's Favorite' has large clusters of dense white flowers and orange-yellow autumn colour.
Aspect Full sun.
Hardiness ✿✿ Zones 7–9.

L. indica

There are numerous selections of this spectacular small to medium-sized autumn-flowering tree, which are grown for their 30cm (12in) long clusters of white, pink, lavender, red or purple coloured flowers. H 4.5–7.5m (15–25ft). S 4.5m (15ft).

Named varieties 'Byers Wonderful White' is an upright growing form with dense clusters of white flowers. H 6m (20ft)
  'Carolina Beauty' is the most commonly grown red flowering variety, but it is susceptible to mildew. H 6m (20ft).
  'Catawba' has good mildew resistance, stunning autumn colour and rich purple flowers. H 4.5m (15ft).
  'Pink velour' is crimson-coloured when in bud but the flowers are lavender. H 4m (12ft).
Aspect Full sun.
Hardiness ✿ Zones 6–9.

L. indica x L. fauriei

A number of hybrids between *L. fauriei* and *L. indica* have been developed with the aim of increasing disease resistance, improving bark colour and intensifying flower colours. H and S 5–6m (16–20ft).
Named varieties 'Acoma' is a broadly spreading small tree, with beautiful white flowers and light silver-grey, brown bark.
  The upright 'Miami' bears pink flowers and has chestnut-brown bark. H 5m (16ft), S 2.4m (8ft).
  'Muskogee' is popular for its pretty lavender-pink flowers. The bark is silver-grey and brown, and in autumn the leaves turn vibrent shades of yellow, red and purple.
  'Tuskegee' has pale brown and silver-grey bark and vivid coral-pink flowers. H and S 5m (16ft).
Aspect Full sun.
Hardiness ✿✿ Zones 7–9.

LARIX
Larch

The 12–14 species in the genus are unusual in being deciduous conifers. They are found throughout the northern hemisphere and are generally fast-growing trees, grown for their graceful habit, autumn colour and timber. The attractive lime-green foliage may be tinted blue-green in early spring. The needles turn bright golden or butter yellow in autumn. In spring bright red female catkin-like flowers are borne along the stems, and the male cones are small, golden-brown and persist for a long time.

Larix kaemferi

Cultivation Grow in deep, well-drained soil in full sun.
Pruning Early formative pruning should aim to produce a clear trunk and a balanced crown. Otherwise little pruning is required apart from the removal of dead, dying, diseased or crossing branches.
Propagation Seed should be collected when fresh, and be sown into a container outside or in an unheated glasshouse or cold frame until germination occurs. Cultivars are produced in winter by being grafted on to seedling-raised larch rootstocks. Hardwood cuttings can also be taken in winter.

L. decidua
European larch

In Europe this species is grown for its timber, and it is also often used as a pioneer species in reforestation projects because it is tolerant of a wide range of soil conditions. They are fast-growing, strongly conical trees, with long, pendulous branches and good yellow autumn colour. H 30–40m (100–130ft), S 6–10m (20–33ft).
Named varieties 'Fastigiata' has a strongly upright habit and short, twisted branches. It is an excellent choice for a focal point or lawn specimen. H 20m (65ft), S 5m (16ft).
  'Pendula' is usually grown as a graft on a clean stem of the species so that the foliage will arch and weep. Although this

Lagerstroemia 'Acoma'

Larix decidua

gives an attractive shape when the tree is young, with age the crown becomes somewhat dense and overcrowded. H and S 10m (33ft). Aspect Full sun. Hardiness ✸✸✸ Zones 3–6.

L. griffithii
Himalayan larch, Sikkim larch
This larch has a pendulous habit, reddish-brown bark, golden autumn colour and soft, green needles in spring and summer. It also has the largest cones of any of the genus – they may reach 10cm (4in) across – and they persist on the branches. This requires a more sheltered site than *L. decidua*. H 20m (65ft), S 10m (33ft).
Aspect Full sun to light shade.
Hardiness ✸✸✸ Zones 6–7.

L. kaempferi
(**syn.** *L. leptolepis*)
Japanese larch
This large, spreading tree has blue-green foliage that turns an attractive golden-yellow in autumn. It is planted for its quick growth and good-quality timber. H 30m (100ft), S 6–10m (20–33ft).
Aspect Full sun.
Hardiness ✸✸✸ Zones 3–6.

L. laricina
Tamarack, American larch
The species has a conical habit with short branches clothed in blue-green foliage, which turns

Laurus nobilis

Licuala grandis

yellow in autumn. It is widely grown in North America for the quality of its timber and its ability (unusual among larches) to tolerate waterlogged soil. Among the hardiest of the larches, it is intolerant of high summer temperatures and is best grown in areas of high annual rainfall in acidic soil. H 25m (80ft), S 10m (33ft).
Aspect Full sun.
Hardiness ✸✸✸ Zones 1–5.

LAURUS
Laurel, bay
The two species of evergreen trees and shrubs in the genus are native to southern Europe, the Azores and the Canary Islands. They are grown for their small flowers and their aromatic leaves.
Cultivation Grow in moisture-retentive but well-drained soil in full sun.
Pruning Early formative pruning should aim to produce a clear trunk and a balanced crown. Bay trees can be grown as multi- or single-stemmed trees, so training should encourage either type.
Propagation Softwood and semi-ripe cuttings can be taken during early and late summer, then be dipped in a rooting hormone and placed in a humid environment such as a greenhouse until rooting occurs. Low branches can be layered during the autumn or spring, then removed and potted on a year later.

L. nobilis
Bay, sweet bay
This is the species that is grown for culinary purposes. The dark green leaves, up to 10cm (4in) long, are highly aromatic. In spring small yellow-green flowers are borne in dense clusters, and these are followed in autumn on female plants by greenish-black berries. This is a useful evergreen for hedging in maritime areas, and it is tolerant of regular clipping. H and S 15m (50ft).
Named varieties 'Aurea' is a slower growing form. In spring the foliage is yellow, fading to greenish-yellow in summer. H 10m (33ft).
Aspect Full sun to semi-shade.
Hardiness ✸✸ Zone 8.

LICUALA
Palas
There are more than 100 species of stemless or shrubby, sometimes suckering, palms in the genus, mostly found in swamps or rainforests of Australasia and South-east Asia.

Cultivation Outdoors, grow in fertile, moisture-retentive but well-drained soil in full sun.
Pruning Little pruning is required apart from the removal of dead leaves and spent flower clusters.
Propagation Sow fresh seed into a container in a humid environment at 29°C (84°F) until germination occurs.

L. grandis
(**syn.** *Pritchardia grandis*)
Ruffled fan palm
The stem of this tropical palm is initially covered with a mat of brown fibres, which falls away as the palm ages, revealing the whitish-green trunk beneath. The large, glossy, semicircular leaves are sometimes divided into three sections, each up to 1m (3ft) across and deeply corrugated with serrated edges. Long spikes of pale green flowers are borne in summer. H and S 3m (10ft).
Aspect Semi-shade when young, full sun when mature.
Hardiness (Min. 15–16°C/ 59–61°F) Zone 11.

Laurus nobilis 'Aurea'

Liquidambar styraciflua 'Variegata'

L. ramsayi
(syn. L. muelleri)

This single-stemmed palm is native to Australia. It has large, corrugated, semicircular, green leaves, up to 1m or more across, which are divided into several sections, some joined together at the tips. Cream-coloured flowers, borne in large spikes in summer, are followed by round red fruits. H 12m (40ft), S to 5m (16ft). Aspect Semi-shade when young, full sun when mature. Hardiness ❋ Zone 11

LIGUSTRUM
Privet

The genus of about 50 evergreen, semi-evergreen and deciduous trees and shrubs is best known for hedging plants, but a number of the species can be grown as focal points or specimen trees, when they display an attractive round-headed shape, bold foliage, attractive flowers and bark.
Cultivation Grow in well-drained soil in sun or semi-shade.

Pruning Early formative pruning should aim to produce a clear trunk and a balanced crown. Tipping the branches of young trees will encourage a denser crown. Occasional pruning only is required for the removal of dead, dying, diseased or crossing branches.
Propagation Seed should be collected when fresh, and be sown into a container in an unheated glasshouse or cold frame until germination occurs. Semi-ripe cuttings are taken during late summer, and are dipped in a rooting hormone, then placed in a humid environment until rooting occurs. The variegated forms are often winter grafted on to seedling privet as they are difficult to root from cuttings.

L. lucidum
Chinese privet

This evergreen is a stunning large shrub or small garden tree, especially if given sufficient space to develop, when it will assume an almost symmetrical shape. The glossy, dark green leaves, up to 8cm (3in) long, taper to a point and are an excellent foil for the masses of fragrant creamy-white flowers that appear in summer. In late summer small blue-black berries follow the flowers. Eventually, it will develop smooth, silver-grey, fluted bark. It can be planted as a lawn specimen in a small garden or grown as a multi-stemmed tree, and it is widely planted as a small street tree in warmer climates. A good choice for urban locations as it seems to be tolerant of atmospheric pollution. H and S 12m (40ft).
Named varieties 'Excelsum Superbum' is a slower growing form, which is one of the most beautiful of all variegated evergreen trees. The leaves have bold yellow margins and silver-white variegation. New foliage is tinged with pink.
Aspect Full sun or semi-shade.
Hardiness ❋❋❋ Zone 7.

LIQUIDAMBAR

The four species of deciduous tree in the genus have maple-like leaves, which colour well in autumn. Trees bear insignificant flowers in spring, and after long, hot summers these are followed by clusters of round fruit. They are grown to their conical habit, which makes them excellent specimen trees.
Cultivation Grow in moisture-retentive but well-drained, neutral to acidic soil in full sun (for best autumn colour) or semi-shade. Protect young plants from cold winter winds.

Pruning Sweet gums are prone to wind damage. Ensure that an even balanced crown is developed by formative pruning and any narrow angled, weakly attached codominant stems are removed.
Propagation Collect seed when fresh and sow in a pot in an unheated glasshouse or a cold frame until germination occurs. Take softwood cuttings in early summer and keep in a humid environment until rooting occurs. Selected forms are grafted on to seed-grown sweet gums and are either indoor grafted in winter or budded in summer.

L. styraciflua
Sweet gum

This widely grown, broadly conical, ornamental tree has large, maple-like leaves and good autumn colour. The three- to seven-lobed leaves, up to 15cm (6in) across, are green in summer, turning shades of red, purple and orange in autumn. Older stems have a corky appearance. H 25m (80ft), S 10–12m (33–40ft).
Named varieties 'Burgundy' is a strongly growing form with purple-tinted foliage which turns dark purple in autumn and persists into winter.

The clone 'Lane Roberts' has foliage that turns purple in late summer before becoming crimson-purple-black in autumn.

'Moonbeam' has pinkish-yellow mottled leaves, which turn green in summer and red, yellow and purple in autumn. H 10m (33ft), S 6m (20ft).

'Palo Alto' has one of the neatest habits of growth, and has scarlet and orange autumn colour.

Ligustrum lucidium

Liriodendron tulipifera

'Slender Silhouette' is an upright form with red and purple autumn colour; it only occasionally produces fruit.

'Stared' is a graceful form with deeply lobed leaves that turn red-orange in autumn.

The beautiful 'Variegata' has new leaves that are edged with cream and are flushed pink in summer before turning yellow and orange in autumn. H 15m (50ft), S 8m (26ft).

The leaves of the popular form 'Worplesdon' turn purple and then orange-yellow in autumn; it occasionally bears fruit.
Aspect Full sun or semi-shade.
Hardiness ❀❀❀ Zones 5–9.

LIRIODENDRON

The two large, fast-growing deciduous trees are often grown as specimen trees, when the leaves take on good autumn colour.
Cultivation Grow in fertile, moisture-retentive but well-drained, slightly acidic soil in full sun or semi-shade.
Pruning The branches are brittle so care should be taken to ensure that an even balanced crown is developed by formative pruning. Remove narrow angled, weakly attached codominant stems.
Propagation Seed, softwood cuttings, grafting and budding are the most common forms of propagation. Collect seeds when fresh, and sow into a container in an unheated glasshouse or cold frame until germination occurs. Take softwood cuttings during early summer, then dip them in a rooting hormone and place in a humid environment until rooting occurs. The selected forms are grafted on seed-grown tulip trees and are either winter indoor grafted or budded during summer.

L. chinense
Chinese tulip tree
Initially upright in habit, this tree becomes more spreading with age. The three-lobed leaves are dark green, turning yellow in autumn. Greenish-yellow, tulip-like flowers, up to 4cm (1½in) long, are produced in summer. H 20–22m (65–72ft), S 10–12m (33–40ft).
Aspect Full sun.
Hardiness ❀❀❀ Zones 6–9.

L. tulipifera
Tulip tree
This ultimately large tree often sheds its lower branches as it ages. The dark green leaves, up to 15cm (6in) long, are shallowly lobed and turn yellow in autumn. In spring numerous, yellow-green tulip-like flowers, up to 6cm (2½in) long, are borne. H 35m (115ft), S 15–20m (50–65ft).
Named varieties
'Aureomarginatum' is a slower growing form. The leaves are broadly edged with bright yellow, which turns yellow-green in summer to leave a lighter shadow around the edge of the leaves, which turn yellow in autumn. H 20m (65ft), S 10m (33ft).

'Fastigiatum' is an erect, columnar form with twisted, upswept branches. H 15–20m (50–65ft), S 4–8m (12–26ft).

The leaves of 'Mediopictum' have a yellow blotch in the centre, and this does not fade in summer.
Aspect Full sun.
Hardiness ❀❀❀ Zones 4–9.

LITHOCARPUS

This is a large genus of about 300 species of evergreen trees and shrubs. They are found mostly in eastern and southern Asia, but one species is native to North America.
Cultivation Grow in fertile, moisture-retentive but well-drained, neutral to acidic soil in sun or semi-shade.
Pruning Early formative pruning should produce a clear trunk and a balanced crown. Tipping the branches of young trees will encourage a denser crown. Occasional pruning is required for the removal of dead, dying, diseased or crossing branches.
Propagation Seed should be collected when fresh, and sown into a container in an unheated glasshouse or cold frame until germination occurs.

L. edulis
This species is a spreading, small tree, with long, tapering leaves, which are glossy, pale green above and dull green beneath. It produces erect clusters of creamy-white flowers in spring, followed in autumn by masses of acorns with an edible nut inside. H and S 10m (33ft).
Aspect Full sun.
Hardiness ❀❀ Zone 7.

L. henryi
This slow-growing, ornamental tree has pale green, lance-shaped leaves, up to 25cm (10in) long, and a rounded habit. Small white flowers are borne in spikes in late summer, followed by clusters of acorns. H and S 10m (33ft).
Aspect Full sun.
Hardiness ❀❀ Zone 7.

LIVISTONA
Fountain palm
The 28 species of palm in the genus are native to Asia and Australasia. They have single, erect, grey stems. As they age they become ringed and marked with the scars from old leaf cases.

Cultivation Outdoors, grow in fertile, moisture-retentive but well-drained soil in sun or semi-shade. These palms will not tolerate winter wet.
Pruning Little pruning is required apart from the removal of dead leaves and spent flower clusters during early summer.
Propagation Seed is the easiest method of propagation. Sow fresh seed into a pot in a heated glasshouse in a humid environment at 29°C (84°F) until germination occurs.

L. australis
Australian fan palm, cabbage palm
The upright trunk becomes silver-grey as it ages. The semicircular leaves, which can be 1.8m (6ft) or more across and which are borne on long stems, have up to 70 linear lobes, each about half the length of the leaves. These droop gracefully. Flower spikes, to 1.8m (6ft) long, are borne in summer and are followed by brownish, red or black fruits. H 25m (80ft), S 5m (16ft).
Aspect Full sun to light shade.
Hardiness (Min. 3–5°C/37–41°F) Zones 9–11.

L. chinensis
Chinese fan palm, Chinese fountain palm
The glossy green leaves of this palm, to 1.8m (6ft) wide, are nearly circular but have longer drooping tips than *L. australis*, and these give an elegant appearance. H 12m (40ft), S 5m (16ft).
Aspect Full sun to light shade.
Hardiness (Min. 3–5°C/37–41°F) Zones 9–11.

Lithocarpus edulis

Maackia amurensis

MAACKIA

There are about eight species of slow-growing, deciduous trees in the genus, and they are native to eastern Asia. They have attractive foliage and flowers and are grown as small specimen trees.

Cultivation Grow in moisture-retentive but well-drained, neutral to acidic soil in full sun.

Pruning Early formative pruning should aim to produce a clear trunk and a balanced crown. Occasional pruning is required for the removal of dead, dying, diseased or crossing branches.

Propagation Seed is the main method of propagation and should be collected when fresh, then be soaked in hot water for 24 hours and sown into a container in an unheated glasshouse or cold frame until germination occurs.

M. amurensis

This attractive tree has dark green, walnut-like foliage and small, erect clusters of bluish-white flowers in late summer. The flowers are followed in autumn by seedpods up to 5cm (2in) long, and the leaves turn pale yellow. H and S 15m (50ft).
Aspect Full sun.
Hardiness ✻✻✻ Zones 4–7.

MAGNOLIA

The 125 species of deciduous and evergreen trees and shrubs in the genus include some of the most

beautiful of all flowering trees. They have been widely hybridized to produce numerous named forms, developed not only for their flower size and colour, including yellow, but also in an attempt to create later flowering forms so that the delicate blooms are not damaged by late spring frosts.

Cultivation Grow in fertile, moisture-retentive but well-drained, acidic soil in sun or semi-shade. *M. delavayi* and *M. grandiflora* will grow in dry alkaline soil. *M. kobus*, *M.* x *loebneri*, *M. sieboldii*, *M. stellata* and *M. wilsonii* will grow in moisture-retentive, alkaline soil. Protect plants from strong winds.

Pruning Magnolias need a lot of formative pruning when young so that a clear stem and even branch work can be developed. Long, whippy branches are often produced and these should be reduced in overall length during summer. Grafted and budded plants sometimes produce root suckers, which should be removed during summer.

Propagation Seed, softwood cuttings, grafting and budding are the most common forms of propagation. Seed should be collected when fresh, the brightly coloured seed coat should be removed and then sown into a container out-of-doors in an unheated glasshouse or cold frame until germination occurs.

Softwood cuttings are taken during early summer, dipped in a rooting hormone and then placed in a humid environment until rooting occurs. Selected forms are grafted on to seed-grown magnolias and are either winter indoor grafted or budded during summer. Evergreen magnolias can be propagated by semi-ripe cuttings during summer, dipped in a rooting hormone and then placed in a humid environment until rooting occurs.

M. 'Albatross'

This fast-growing hybrid of *M. cylindrica* and *M.* x *veitchii* has large white flowers, flushed pink toward the base, borne in mid-spring. It makes a small, upright, deciduous tree. H and S 6m (20ft).
Aspect Full sun to semi-shade.
Hardiness ✻✻ Zone 7.

M. 'Apollo'

This free-flowering, medium-sized, deciduous tree bears dark purple-pink flowers. H and S 6m (20ft).
Aspect Full sun to semi-shade.
Hardiness ✻✻ Zone 7.

M. 'Athene'

This deciduous tree has an upright habit and bears large, white, scented flowers that are tinged with pink at the base. H and S 6m (20ft).
Aspect Full sun to semi-shade.
Hardiness ✻✻ Zone 7

M. 'Atlas'

This quick-growing deciduous tree produces lilac-pink flowers soon after planting. H and S 6m (20ft).
Aspect Full sun to semi-shade.
Hardiness ✻✻ Zone 7.

Magnolia campbellii subsp. *mollicomata* 'Lanarth'

Magnolia grandiflora 'Goliath'

M. 'Butterflies'

This upright tree produces beautiful, canary yellow flowers. H and S 6m (20ft).
Aspect Full sun to semi-shade.
Hardiness ❋❋❋ Zones 4–9.

M. campbellii
Campbell's magnolia

This vigorous deciduous magnolia, sometimes called the Queen of Magnolias, is native to the Himalayas, from eastern Nepal, Sikkim and Bhutan to Assam. It is a variable tree, with elliptic mid-green leaves, up to 25cm (10in) long, and white, red or pale pink flowers with 12–16 tepals, which are borne before the leaves in late winter to early spring.

The flowers are known as cup-and-saucer type because the inner tepals remain upright, while the outer ones flop outwards. The flowers are particularly susceptible to frosts in late winter and early spring. H 15–20m (50–65ft), S 10m (33ft).
Named varieties The Alba Group includes a number of seed-raised forms with pretty white flowers, which are more common in the wild than the pink-flowering form that was first introduced .

M. campbellii subsp. *mollicomata* 'Lanarth' is a hardier and more compact form that produces masses of lilac-purple flowers in late winter and early spring.

M. campbellii (Raffilli Group) 'Charles Raffill' is a fast-growing, tree-like magnolia with dark pink flowers that open purple-pink.
Aspect Full sun to semi-shade.
Hardiness ❋❋❋ Zones 7–9.

M. 'Elizabeth'

This stunning deciduous form produces bright yellow, scented flowers, up to 15cm (6in) across, on bare branches in spring. The dark green leaves, up to 20cm (8in) long, are tinged with bronze when they emerge. H 10m (33ft), S 6m (20ft).
Aspect Full sun to semi-shade.
Hardiness ❋❋❋ Zones 5–9.

M. 'Galaxy'

This small, fast-growing deciduous tree bears large, fragrant, purple-pink flowers, up to 20cm (8in) across, just before the leaves appear in spring. H 12m (40ft), S 8m (26ft).
Aspect Full sun to semi-shade.
Hardiness ❋❋❋ Zone 7.

M. 'Gold Star'

Attractive, star-shaped, ivory-white to pale yellow flowers are produced on this pyramidal deciduous tree, which is a hybrid of *M. acuminata* var. *subcordata* 'Miss Honeybee' and *M. stellata* 'Rubra'. It has red-tinged young growth. H and S 10m (33ft).
Aspect Full sun to semi-shade.
Hardiness ❋❋❋ Zones 5–9.

M. grandiflora
Bull bay

This exceptional tree, which exhibits great heat tolerance, is one of the most imposing of the evergreen magnolias – indeed, of all flowering trees. It is native to the southern USA, from North Carolina to central Florida and into Texas and Arkansas. It has glossy, dark green leaves, up to 20cm (8in) long, and from late summer to early autumn it bears creamy-white, cup-shaped flowers, which may be up to 25cm (10in) across. In cooler areas it is often grown against walls so that it can benefit from the warmth in winter and the shelter from cold, drying winds. H 25m (80ft), S 10m (33ft).
Named varieties 'Alta' is a strongly growing, upright form. The dark green leaves have brown undersides. Glossy, creamy-white flowers are produced in summer and then occasionally in autumn. H 10m (33ft).

The widely grown 'Bracken's Brown Beauty' is a dense tree. It has glossy, dark green leaves with russet brown undersides and produces masses of flowers.

The fast-growing 'Claudia Wannamaker' is a fine form with dark green leaves with rusty-brown undersides, and it flowers from an early age.

'Goliath', a rather bushy form, is grown for its scented, creamy-white flowers, up to 30cm (12in) across, and large pale green leaves. 'Hasse' is a small-leaved form, with masses of flowers and a strongly pright habit. H 14m (46ft), S 4m (12ft).
Aspect Full sun to semi-shade.
Hardiness ❋❋ Zones 7–9.

Magnolia stellata

M. 'Ivory Chalice'
This hybrid produces masses of
pale yellow flowers throughout
spring, with the main flush
appearing just before the leaves.
H and S 6m (20ft).
Aspect Full sun to semi-shade.
Hardiness ❁❁❁ Zones 5–9.

M. kobus
This small, generally round-
headed but rather variable,
deciduous tree is found in forests
throughout Japan. The mid-green
leaves, up to 20cm (8in) long,
smell of aniseed if crushed. It has
creamy-white flowers, sometimes
tinged purple at the base, in mid-
spring. H 12m (40ft), S 10m
(33ft).
Aspect Full sun to semi-shade.
Hardiness ❁❁❁ Zones 4–8.

M. x loebneri
Loebner's magnolia
This hybrid between M. kobus
and M. stellata is a fast-growing,
broadly spreading deciduous tree.
The mid-green leaves are about
12cm (5in) long, and star-shaped
white flowers, flushed pink-purple
inside and out, are borne in mid-
spring. H 10m (33ft), S 7m
(23ft).
Named varieties The popular
cultivar 'Leonard Messel' is widely
planted for its frost-resistant,
pink-tinged white flowers. H 8m
(26ft), S 6m (20ft).

'Neil McEacharn' is an early-
flowering form with pink-tinged
buds that open creamy-white.
'Raspberry Fun', a form with
darker pink flowers, originated in
Korea from seed collected from
'Leonard Messel'.
'White Stardust' is a vigorous
form, flowering early in spring
with masses of white flowers and
good dark green foliage.
Aspect Full sun to semi-shade.
Hardiness ❁❁❁ Zones 3–7.

M. 'Lois'
This is one of the best and most
reliable of the yellow-flowered
magnolias for cooler climates
where it reliably produces
primrose yellow flowers, which are
borne just before the leaves
emerge. H and S 6m (20ft).
Aspect Full sun to semi-shade.
Hardiness ❁❁❁ Zones 5–9.

M. obovata
(syn. M. hypoleuca)
Japanese big-leaf magnolia
This strongly growing, deciduous
species, which is native to Japan,
has large, mid-green leaves, up to
40cm (16in) long, and creamy-
white, highly scented flowers in
late spring to early summer. It is a
hardy species but must have acidic
soil. H 15m (50ft), S 10m
(33ft).
Aspect Full sun to semi-shade.
Hardiness ❁❁❁ Zones 5–7.

M. x soulangeana
Chinese magnolia, saucer magnolia
This variable, deciduous hybrid
between M. denudata and M. liliiflora
is one of the most widely planted
of the hybrid magnolias thanks to
its tolerance of a wide range of
soils and atmospheric pollution.
It is a spreading small tree or
multi-stemmed large shrub, with
dark green leaves and goblet-
shaped flowers, which may be
white, deep pink or purple-pink
and are borne in mid- to late
spring. H and S 6m (10ft).
Named varieties Several lovely
cultivars have been developed.
'Alba' (syn. 'Alba Superba') is a
dense, erect small tree with
scented white flowers.
The upright 'Alexandrina', one
of the most widely planted forms,
has masses of large saucer-shaped,

white flowers, which are flushed
purple at the base and have a
lovely scent.
The larger and later flowering
'Brozzonii' has large white
flowers, up to 25cm (10in)
across and flushed with purple
at the base. H 8m (26ft).
Aspect Full sun to semi-shade.
Hardiness ❁❁❁ Zones 4–9.

M. stellata
Star magnolia
This is perhaps the best-known
and possibly the most widely
planted species, with its compact
habit and lovely, star-shaped
flowers. It is a slow-growing,
deciduous plant, eventually
making a dense shrub or,
sometimes, a small tree. The dark
green leaves are up to 20cm (8in)
long, and the flowers, which range
in colour from white to rose pink
and purple, are borne in mid- to
late spring, just as the leaves are
emerging. It does best in
moisture-retentive soil in a sunny
position. Protect the flower buds
from cold, drying winds. H 3m
(10ft), S 4m (12ft).
Named varieties Among the many
cultivars 'Centennial' is an upright,
conical form with numerous, 28-
to 32-tepalled white flowers up to
14cm (5½in) across.
'Rosea' is a vigorous form,
occasionally suckering, but
quickly forming a small tree that

Malus 'John Downie'

produces masses of white flowers,
delicately tinged with pink and
striped with pink on the outside.
Aspect Full sun to semi-shade.
Hardiness ❁❁❁ Zones 4–9.

M. x veitchii
This deciduous hybrid between M.
campbellii and M. denudata is a large,
upright magnolia. It has obovate
leaves, up to 30cm (12in) long,
which are tinged with purple when
they first emerge. The pink to
white flowers are borne in mid-
spring, before the leaves. H 30m
(100ft), S 10m (33ft).
Named varieties In late spring,
before the leaves appear, the

Magnolia x loebneri 'Merrill'

Malus 'Butterball'

Malus 'Evereste'

Malus 'Striped Beauty'

hardier cultivar 'Peter Veitch' has goblet-shaped, white flowers, faintly flushed with purple pink. Aspect Full sun to semi-shade. Hardiness ❋❋ Zone 7.

MALUS
Apple, crab apple

This genus of about 35 deciduous trees and shrubs includes the orchard apple, *Malus sylvestris* var. *domestica*. It also includes a group of ornamental hybrid crab apples, which are grown for their spring flowers and also the good autumn colour that many display. They have been hybridized to tolerate a range of soil conditions and to have good disease resistance.
Cultivation Grow in moisture-retentive but well-drained soil in sun. Purple-leaved forms produce their best colour in sun.
Pruning Early formative pruning should aim to produce a clear trunk and a balanced crown. Tipping the branches of young trees will encourage a denser crown. Crab apples are prone to fireblight, canker and occasionally silver leaf and this should be removed as soon as symptoms occur. Occasional pruning is required to remove dead, dying, diseased or crossing branches.
Propagation Seed is used to propagate the species while cultivars are budded on to seed-grown rootstocks. Seed should be collected when fresh, and be sown into a container in an

unheated glasshouse or cold frame until germination occurs. Budding is undertaken during summer.

M. 'American Beauty'
This vigorous US form has exceptionally large, double, red flowers, up to 4cm (1½in) across, and bronze-red foliage that turns bronze-green. It does not produce fruit. H and S 8m (26ft). Aspect Full sun. Hardiness ❋❋❋ Zones 4–7.

M. 'Butterball'
In spring this small, spreading tree produces pink-tinged buds, which open to white flowers. The orange-yellow fruits, to 2.5cm (1in) across, persist long into winter. H and S 8m (26ft). Aspect Full sun. Hardiness ❋❋❋ Zones 4–7.

M. 'Callaway'
Popular in the USA because of its disease resistance, this small tree bears single, scented, white flowers in spring, which open from pink buds, and large reddish-maroon fruits on pendulous branches. H and S 8m (26ft). Aspect Full sun. Hardiness ❋❋❋ Zones 4–7.

M. 'Evereste'
This small, conical tree has dark green leaves, which are sometimes lobed. In late spring, white flowers open from red buds, followed by large, orange-yellow,

red-flushed fruits. Unlike some other crab apples, it retains a good shape as it matures. H and S 7m (23ft). Aspect Full sun. Hardiness ❋❋❋ Zones 4–7.

M. floribunda
Japanese crab apple
This graceful, broadly spreading tree has lobed, dark green leaves. In mid-spring the tree is covered with crimson buds, from which open white or pale pink flowers. In autumn small yellow fruits hang from the branches in clusters. It is usually the first crab apple to flower in spring.

H and S 5m (16ft). Aspect Full sun. Hardiness ❋❋❋ Zones 4–7.

M. hupehensis
Rather larger than the average crab apple, this vigorous species develops into a spreading tree. In early summer the dark green leaves are almost completely hidden by the white flowers, and these are followed in autumn by small, cherry-like, dark red fruits. H and S 12m (40ft). Aspect Full sun. Hardiness ❋❋❋ Zones 4–7.

M. 'John Downie'
Initially erect but developing into a broadly conical tree, this has attractive bright green leaves. In spring small, starry, white flowers open from pink buds. These are followed by orange and red fruits, which are borne in long-stalked clusters. H 10m (33ft), S 6m (20ft). Aspect Full sun. Hardiness ❋❋❋ Zones 4–7.

M. 'Red Sentinel'
This self-fertile tree is best known for its clusters of attractive red crab apples which persist well into the winter. The blossom is white with pink tinges, and is scented. It makes an attractive specimen tree for a small to medium-sized garden.

Malus pumila

Malus 'Red Sentinel'

It is also attractive to wildlife.
H and S 8m (26ft).
Aspect Full sun or partial shade.
Hardiness ❋❋❋ Zones 4–7.

M. transitoria

This wide-spreading, semi-weeping tree has small, bright green leaves, which turn yellow in autumn. In spring white flowers open from pink buds, and in autumn there are masses of small, cherry-like, golden-yellow fruits, which are hidden among the stunning orange-yellow autumn colour but are revealed again once the leaves fall. H 8m (26ft), S 10m (33ft). Aspect Full sun. Hardiness ❋❋❋ Zones 5–7.

MALUS SYLVESTRIS VAR. DOMESTICA
Common apple

This is a huge range of trees that produce edible apples. They are usually upright, spreading and covered in white, cup-shaped flowers in mid- and late spring, followed by apples in autumn.
Cultivation Apples fruit best if they are grown in full sun, with some shelter from wind to allow pollination by bees. Soil conditions can vary, but a free-draining, fertile soil is best.
Pruning Remove any dead, diseased or damaged branches during winter. Thin out spurs that are over-congested along the stems leaving the strongest to encourage large healthy fruit.
Propagation Propagate either by chip- or T-budding in summer or whip-and-tongue grafting on to certified rootstock in early spring to control the ultimate size.

M. s. var. d. 'American Golden Russet' (syn. 'Sheep Snout')

This is a widely grown Irish dessert and culinary apple that was exported to America, and became known as the 'American Golden Russet'. It is not self-fertile and so requires a pollinator. It produces large, yellow-russet fruits that are sharp and crisp to taste and shaped like a sheep's nose. Widely grown on MM.106. rootstock where it will grow to 5m tall and wide (18ft **x** 18ft).
Aspect Full sun.
Hardiness ❋❋❋ Zones 5–8.

M. s. var. d. 'Braeburn'

Bred in New Zealand, this is now widely grown for its medium to large apples that have a sweet and crisp flavour and a yellow-green skin with reddish stripes. Often grafted onto a M.26. rootstock where it will grow 4m wide and tall (12ft **x** 12ft).
Aspect Full sun.
Hardiness ❋❋❋ Zones 5–9.

M. s. var. d. 'Bramley Seedling'

This classic and widely grown cooking apple needs to be pollinated by two different types of apples as it is a triploid variety. Large green, blushed red apples are produced in mid-autumn and can be stored all winter. Ultimately 10m tall and wide (33ft **x** 33ft), although if grafted on to a dwarfing rootstock such as M.26. it may only reach 4m tall and wide (12ft **x** 12ft). Aspect Full sun.
Hardiness ❋❋❋ Zones 5–9.

M. s. var. d. 'Cox's Orange Pippin'

Enduringly popular since its introduction in the early 19th century, this reddish, orange and green apple has a distinct, sharp and sweet taste and holds its shape well when baked. If it is grafted on to a vigorous rootstock it can become quite a large and unruly tree, so it is best grafted

on to a less vigorous rootstock. On M.7. it will grow to 5m tall and wide (18ft **x** 18ft). Aspect Full sun.
Hardiness ❋❋❋ Zones 5–9.

M. s. var. d. 'Discovery'

One of the most widely planted eating apples, this is especially suitable for garden use since the fruit is best picked straight from the tree as soon as it is ripe. It is also partially self-fertile so can be pollinated easily by a crab apple or another fruiting apple. Often grafted on to an M.26. rootstock where it will grow 4m wide and tall (12ft **x** 12ft).
Aspect Full sun.
Hardiness ❋❋❋ Zones 5–9.

M. s. var. d. 'Egremont Russet'

This is the best of the russets and is grown for its strong but sweet taste, crisp and firm flesh, and because it stores relatively well. It is most often grafted on to an M.26. rootstock where it will grow 4m wide and tall (12ft **x** 12ft).
Aspect Full sun.
Hardiness ❋❋❋ Zones 5–9.

M. s. var. d. 'Golden Delicious'

This popular dessert apple is grown in warmer climates, where it is quick-growing and yields large crops of pale-yellow-skinned, light-flavoured apples. Requires additional pollinators and is often

Malus x *schiedeckeri* 'Hillieri'

Malus sylvestris var. domestica

grown on MM.106. rootstock where it will grow to 5m tall and wide (18ft **x** 18ft).
Aspect Full sun.
Hardiness ❋❋❋ Zones 5–8.

M. s. var. d. 'Golden Pippin'
An old-fashioned variety with small fruits, this has a distinct lemon aftertaste and can be used for eating, cooking and cider or juice making. Holds it shape and colour well when cooked. It is best picked in autumn and can be stored all winter. Requires another apple to pollinate it as it is not self fertile. Widely grown on MM.106. rootstock where it will grow to 5m tall and wide (18ft **x** 18ft).
Aspect Full sun.
Hardiness ❋❋❋ Zones 5–8.

M. s. var. d. 'Granny Smith'
This is one of the most famous and widely grown eating apples. Originally introduced from Australia in the 1900s, it is known for its lime green colour, tart, crisp flesh and late cropping. Requires another pollinator, and is often grown on MM.106.,

where it can grow to 4m tall and wide (12ft **x**12ft).
Aspect Full sun.
Hardiness ❋❋❋ Zones 5–8.

M. s. var. d. 'Howgate Wonder'
This apple is mainly grown for exhibition purposes since it can grow to an enormous size – up to 1.7kg (3lb 14oz).
Aspect Full sun.
Hardiness ❋❋❋ Zones 3–9.

M. s. var. d. 'Idared'
This apple is grown for both culinary and dessert use and has a sharp but sweet taste and long storability. It is an excellent garden variety, especially if it is grafted on to a dwarfing rootstock such as M.26., where it will reach 4m tall and wide (12ft **x** 12ft).
Aspect Full sun.
Hardiness ❋❋❋ Zones 4–9.

M. s. var. d. 'James Grieve'
This very sweet and juicy green apple is suitable for both dessert use and cooking. It ripens during early autumn and is best used before the end of the season. Reasonable fruit set is always

guaranteed as it is self-fertile, although fertilization by another apple will dramatically increase the yield. Grown on M.26. rootstock, it will reach 4m tall and wide (12ft **x** 12ft).
Aspect Full sun.
Hardiness ❋❋❋ Zones 5–8.

M. s. var. d. 'Laxton's Superb'
This is a late cropping 'Cox's Orange Pippin' hybrid that was bred at Laxton's Nursery, England, in 1904, and was an immediate success due to its late ripening, good flavour and reddish orange-yellow colour. Often grown on M.26. rootstock where it will grow to 4m tall and wide (12ft **x** 12ft).
Aspect Full sun.
Hardiness ❋❋❋ Zones 5–9.

M. s. var. d. 'Liberty'
A widely grown American selection, this is bred for its disease resistance, its well-balanced sweet and sharp flavour and attractive red skin. Requires additional pollinators and is often grown on MM.106. rootstock where it will grow to 5m tall and wide (18ft **x** 18ft).
Aspect Full sun.
Hardiness ❋❋❋ Zones 5–8.

M. s. var. d. 'Spartan'
This Canadian introduction has extreme cold hardiness. The tree produces apples that have a soft and sweet flesh and a crimson red skin. It makes an excellent cropping tree and one of the best cold climate apples. Best grown on M.26., where it will reach 4m tall and wide (12ft **x** 12ft).
Aspect Full sun.
Hardiness ❋❋❋ Zones 3–9.

Malus sylvestris var. domestica 'Laxton's Epicure'

MAYTENUS

The genus contains about 225 species of evergreen trees and shrubs, which are native to tropical Africa and North and South America.

Cultivation Grow in moisture-retentive but well-drained soil in full sun. Protect plants from cold, drying winds.

Pruning Early formative pruning should aim to produce a clear trunk and a balanced crown.

Propagation Seed is the main method of propagation and should be collected when fresh and sown into a container in an unheated glasshouse or cold frame until germination occurs.

M. boaria
(syn. M. chilensis)
Mayten

This fast-growing but variable tree has a beautiful weeping habit, although some plants weep more strongly than others. In addition, some forms produce a thicket of root suckers, whereas other forms do not produce any suckers at all. It has glossy, dark green leaves, up to 5cm (2in) long. In sunny areas small clusters of pale green flowers are borne in mid- to late spring, and these are followed by red-orange seedpods. Hardiness can depend on where exactly the seeds or cuttings were collected, because the species has a wide

Maytenus boaria

natural range in Chile. H 20m (65ft), S 10m (33ft).
Aspect Full sun.
Hardiness ✳✳✳ Zone 8.

MELIA

There are three to five species of deciduous or semi-evergreen trees and shrubs in the genus. They are native to India, China, South-east Asia and northern Australia and are grown as specimen trees in warm areas.

Cultivation Outdoors, grow in well-drained soil in full sun.

Pruning Formative pruning should aim to encourage a clear trunk and a balanced crown. Occasional pruning is required for the removal of dead, dying, diseased or crossing branches.

Propagation Seed should be collected when fresh and sown into a container in a heated glasshouse in a frost-free and humid environment until germination occurs.

M. azedarach
Bead tree, pride of India, Persian lilac

A fast-growing but fairly short-lived deciduous tree, it is grown for its fragrant, star-shaped, lilac-coloured flowers, which are borne from spring to early summer, and for the attractive yellow fruits that follow and that persist into winter, when they are readily distributed by birds. H 10–15m (33–50ft), S 8–10m (26–33ft). Named varieties 'Jade Snowflake' is a pretty and more compact form with creamy-white speckled leaves. H and S 8m (26ft).
Aspect Full sun.
Hardiness (Min. 7°C/45°F) Zones 7–12.

METASEQUOIA
Dawn redwood

The single species of deciduous coniferous tree in the genus is native to central China. It was originally known only from fossil records until it was discovered growing in a valley in China in 1941. Since then it has been widely grown throughout the world because of its extreme beauty and year-round interest.

Cultivation Grow in fertile, moisture-retentive but well-

Metasequoia glyptostroboides 'Gold Rush'

drained soil in full sun. Trees seem to do better in areas with warm summers.

Pruning Formative pruning should aim to produce a clear trunk and a balanced crown. Tipping the lateral branches of young trees will encourage a denser crown.

Propagation Seed is the easiest method of propagation and should be collected when fresh and sown into a container in an unheated glasshouse or cold frame until germination occurs. Semi-ripe and softwood cuttings can be rooted during summer and should be dipped in a rooting hormone and placed in a humid environment until rooting occurs. Hardwood cuttings will also root during the winter if a rooting hormone is applied to the cutting.

M. glyptostroboides

This beautiful and fast-growing tree has fern-like, bright green foliage, which turns yellow-brown or pinkish-brown in autumn. Mature trees have corrugated fluted trunks, clothed in cinnamon-brown bark. H 40m (130ft), S 10–20m wide (33–65ft).
Named varieties The fast-growing 'Emerald Feathers' has an

attractive habit, with weeping new shoots. The lime-green leaves colour well in autumn.

'Gold Rush' (syn. 'Ogon') has stunning yellow foliage in spring, and this fades to yellow-green in summer. It is slower growing than the green-leaved forms.

'National' (syn. 'Fastigiata') is a fast-growing, narrow cultivar.
Aspect Full sun.
Hardiness ✳✳✳ Zones 3–7.

METROSIDEROS
Rata, pohutakawa

There are about 50 species of evergreen trees and shrubs in the genus. They are native to South Africa, Malaysia and Australasia.

Cultivation Outdoors, grow in fertile, moisture-retentive but well-drained, neutral to acidic soil in sun. Protect plants from cold, drying winds.

Pruning Formative pruning should aim to encourage a clear trunk and a balanced crown, while tipping the lateral branches of young trees will encourage a denser crown. Occasional pruning is required for the removal of dead, dying, diseased or crossing branches.

Propagation Seed is the easiest method of propagation and should be collected when fresh and sown into a container in a heated glasshouse in a frost-free and humid environment until germination occurs. Low branches can also be layered into the soil.

M. excelsus
(syn. *M. tomentosa*)
Common pohutakawa, New Zealand Christmas tree
This tree is native to New Zealand, and in summer masses of stunning, bright scarlet, spider-like inflorescences cover the foliage as the tree explodes into bloom. (The flowers themselves are small, but the stamens are long and feathery.) The attractive leaves, up to 10cm (4in) long, are glossy, dark green above and covered with silver-white hairs beneath. H 20m (65ft), S 15m (50ft).
Aspect Full sun.
Hardiness ❀ Zone 9–11.

M. robusta
Northern rata
This tall but slender tree from New Zealand has dark green leaves, which are covered with silver-white hairs on the undersides. The inflorescences, up to 3cm (1½in) long, are matt crimson and are displayed in dense terminal clusters. H 30m (100ft), S 10–12m (33–40ft).
Aspect Full sun.
Hardiness ❀ Zones 9–11.

Metrosideros excelsa

MICHELIA
Banana shrub, port wine magnolia
There are about 45 species of evergreen or deciduous trees and shrubs in the genus, which is closely related to *Magnolia*. Like magnolias, these plants produce lovely flowers, which are often fragrant, in spring or early summer, but the flowers are borne in the leaf axils, not terminally, as on magnolias.
Cultivation Outdoors, grow in fertile, moisture-retentive but well-drained, neutral to acidic soil in semi-shade.
Pruning For a formal appearance, trim annually after flowering.
Propagation Grow from softwood cuttings or from seed. Collect ripe seeds from fruit cones as they open. Otherwise, store the fruit cones until they open naturally, but do not allow the seeds to dry out too much. Sow in a peat-based compost, cover with 6mm (¼in) grit and place in a frost-free greenhouse until they germinate.

M. doltsopa
This small, rather shrubby, evergreen tree has glossy, dark green leaves, which are covered with grey hairs beneath. In spring to early summer fragrant, creamy-white flowers, up to 10cm (4in) across, are borne. H 15m (50ft), S 5–10m (16–33ft).
Named varieties 'Silver Cloud' is a large-flowering selection, originally raised in New Zealand. Semi-evergreen in cooler climates, it is totally evergreen in milder areas. In spring it bears masses of fragrant, large, white, magnolia-like flowers.
Aspect Full sun to semi-shade.
Hardiness (Min 5°C/41°F) Zones 8–9.

MORUS
Mulberry
The genus contains 10–12 species of deciduous trees and shrubs. They are native to South and North America, Africa and Asia and are grown as specimen trees for their attractive toothed and lobed leaves and for their edible autumn fruits.
Cultivation Grow in fertile, moisture-retentive but well-drained soil in full sun. Protect

Michelia doltsopa

from cold, drying winds. Mulberries have brittle roots and should be planted and transplanted with care.
Pruning This must be done when the tree is completely dormant as if it is left until spring any wounds will bleed profusely. Pruning should aim to create an open, balanced canopy, and to remove any dying, damaged, dead or diseased branches.
Propagation Seed, grafting, or hardwood cuttings are the main methods of propagation. Sow fresh seed into a container in an unheated glasshouse or cold frame until germination occurs. Winter grafting on to seed-grown mulberries is commonly practised. Hardwood cuttings taken during the winter root easily and produce trees quickly.

M. alba
White mulberry
This spreading tree from eastern and central China is quite tolerant of drought, pollution and poor soil. It develops twisted branches as it matures. It has attractive heart-shaped, glossy, light green leaves, up to 20cm (8in) long, which turn yellow in autumn. In late spring and summer greenish-yellow catkins appear, followed in late summer by white fruits, up to 2.5cm (1in) long, which turn pink and red when they are ripe. H and S 10–15m (33–50ft).
Aspect Full sun.
Hardiness ❀❀❀ Zones 5–7.
Named varieties 'Pendula' is a low-growing weeping form.
'Russian' is very hardy and drought-resistant form, which produces good-quality fruit.

Morus alba 'Pendula'

Nothofagus dombeyi

M. nigra
Black mulberry

More compact than *M. alba*, this species, which is believed to come from south-western Asia, has coarser, mid-green leaves, up to 15cm (6in) long, which turn golden-yellow in late autumn. The oval fruits are green when they first appear but ripen to red and dark purple. H and S 10m (33ft). Aspect Full sun. Hardiness ❋❋❋ Zones 5–7.

M. rubra
Red mulberry

The species, which is native to North America, is larger than *M. alba* and *M. nigra*. It has dark green leaves, up to 12cm (5in) long, which turn yellow in autumn. The fruits are green at first, ripening to red and then purple. H 12m (40ft), S 15m (50ft). Aspect Full sun. Hardiness ❋❋❋ Zones 5–7.

MYRTUS
Myrtle

The genus contains two species of evergreen trees, which are native to Mediterranean countries, including northern Africa. They are grown for their aromatic leaves and fragrant flowers.
Cultivation Grow in moisture-retentive but well-drained soil. Protect from cold, drying winds.
Pruning Responds well to pruning in autumn or winter.
Propagation Sow seed in pots in a cold frame, or take semi-ripe cuttings in late summer.

M. communis

The glossy, dark green leaves, up to 5cm (2in) long, form a dense canopy. In mid- to late summer saucer-shaped, creamy-white flowers almost hide the foliage, followed in autumn by small black berries. H and S 3m (10ft). Aspect Full sun. Hardiness ❋❋ Zones 9–10.

NOTHOFAGUS
Southern beech

Native to the southern hemisphere, where they grow in forests in South America and Australasia, there are about 20 species of evergreen and deciduous trees in the genus. They can be grown as specimen trees or included in a woodland.
Cultivation Grow in fertile, moisture-retentive but well-drained, acidic soil in full sun. They are susceptible to damage from late spring frosts.
Pruning Early formative pruning should aim to produce a clear trunk and a balanced crown.

Myrtus communis

Occasional pruning is required for the removal of dead, dying, diseased or crossing branches as and when required.
Propagation Seed is the main method of propagation and should be collected when fresh and be sown into a container in an unheated glasshouse or cold frame until germination occurs.

N. betuloides

This is an exceptionally beautiful, broadly columnar evergreen, which is an excellent shade tree for the garden, where its toothed, glossy green leaves, to 2.5m (1in) long, produce light, dappled shade. It is quick-growing when young and can be used in screens and windbreaks as well as for upper-canopy shade. H 15–20m (50–65ft), S 6–10m (20–33ft). Aspect Full sun or semi-shade. Hardiness ❋❋ Zone 7.

N. dombeyi
Coigue, Dombey's southern beech

This columnar to conical evergreen tree is faster growing than *N. betuloides*. The finely toothed leaves, up to 4cm (1½in) long, are glossy, dark green. This may be semi-evergreen in areas with very cold winters. H 20m (65ft), S 10m (33ft). Aspect Full sun or semi-shade. Hardiness ❋❋ Zone 8.

N. obliqua
Roblé

This broadly conical deciduous species is often used in forestry because it is extremely fast-growing. The dark green leaves, up to 8cm (3in) long, are blue-green beneath and irregularly toothed. They turn yellow, orange and red in autumn. H 20m (65ft), S 15m (50ft). Aspect Full sun. Hardiness ❋❋❋ Zone 8.

NYSSA

There are approximately four or five species of deciduous trees in the genus, which are found in woodland in eastern Asia and North America. They are grown as specimen trees for their foliage and excellent autumn colour.

Cultivation Grow in fertile, moisture-retentive but well-drained, neutral to acidic soil. Protect from cold, drying winds.
Pruning Early formative pruning should aim to produce a clear trunk and a balanced crown. Occasional pruning is required for the removal of dead, dying, diseased or crossing branches as and when required.
Propagation Seed and budding are the main methods of propagation and seed should be collected when fresh and sown into a container in an unheated glasshouse or cold frame until germination occurs. Summer budding on to seed-grown sweet gums is also commonly practised.

N. sylvatica
Tupelo, black gum, sour gum

This medium-sized broadly conical to columnar tree is native to North America. It has glossy, dark green leaves, up to 15cm (6in) long, which glow yellow, orange and red in autumn. H 25m (80ft), S 10m (33ft). Numerous selections have been made for their autumn colour. 'Autumn Cascades', an excellent tree for a small garden, has a strongly weeping habit, and it is probably best trained with a straight stem and then allowed to weep. The leaves turn a beautiful red-orange in autumn.
'Jermyns' is a strongly growing form, pyramidal when young but spreading with age, with leaves that are yellow-orange in autumn.
'Red Rage' has glossy, dark green leaves that are vibrant red in autumn.
'Sheffield Park' has a broad habit; its glossy, dark green foliage turns orange-red in autumn.
'Wisley Bonfire' has slightly weeping tips and a lovely red autumn colour.
Aspect Full sun or semi-shade.
Hardiness ❋❋❋ Zone 4–9.

OLEA
Olive

The 20 or so species of evergreen trees and shrubs in the genus are found in Mediterranean countries, including northern Africa, Central Asia and Australasia. They are grown for their fruits, from which oil is extracted. In warm areas they may be grown as specimen trees.

Cultivation Olives require a fertile but free-draining soil, in a warm sunny location.

Pruning Should be undertaken when the tree is young to encourage a dome-shaped tree and an evenly balanced canopy. The only other regular pruning should be done to remove dead, dying, diseased and crossing branches.

Propagation Olives are usually propagated by semi-ripe stem cuttings taken during late autumn. T-budding is also used when faster growing specimens are required and these are grafted on to seedling-grown rootstocks.

O. europaea
European olive
This slow-growing tree from Mediterranean Europe has twisted, gnarled branches and a short trunk, eventually developing into a broad-headed tree. The small, leathery leaves, up to 8cm (3in) long, which are slightly toothed, are grey-green above and lighter, silver-green beneath. In summer clusters of small white flowers appear, and these are followed by green fruits, which ripen to black. H and S 10m (33ft).
Aspect Full sun.
Hardiness ✺✺ Zones 8–10.

Nyssa sylvatica 'Sheffield Park'

Olea europaea

OXYDENDRON
Sorrel tree, sourwood
There is a single species of deciduous tree in the genus, and it is native to North America. This is a good woodland tree, and it is grown for its autumn colour.
Cultivation Grow in fertile, moisture-retentive but well-drained, acidic soil. Protect from cold, drying winds.
Pruning Occasional pruning only is required for the removal of any dead, dying, diseased or crossing branches.
Propagation Seed should be collected when fresh and sown into a container in an unheated glasshouse or cold frame until germination occurs.

O. arboreum
This small tree or large shrub will develop into a conical or columnar plant. The dark green leaves, up to 20cm (8in) long, are glossy and toothed and turn red, yellow and purple in autumn. Clusters of creamy-white, heather-like flowers are borne in late summer to early autumn at the tips of the branches. H 15m (50ft), S 8–10m (26–33ft).
Aspect Full sun or semi-shade.
Hardiness ✺✺✺ Zones 5–9.

PARROTIA
Persian ironwood
This genus of deciduous trees is found in the Caucasus and northern Iran. Parrotia is grown as a specimen tree for its autumn colour and early spring flowers.

Oxydendron arboreum

Cultivation Grow in deep, fertile, moisture-retentive but well-drained, acidic soil in full sun or semi-shade. Trees are susceptible to damage from late spring frosts.
Pruning Formative pruning should aim to produce a clear trunk and a balanced crown. Occasional pruning only is required for the removal of any dead, dying, diseased or crossing branches.
Propagation Seed should be collected when fresh and sown into a container in an unheated glasshouse or cold frame until germination occurs. Winter grafting on to seedlings is also a good method.

P. persica
This spreading tree is tolerant of both drought and heat. It has a short trunk, and in winter the bark is a mixture of grey-brown and green flaking patterns, which reveal attractive pink, yellow and cinnamon patches underneath. The glossy green leaves, up to 12cm (5in) long, turn vivid shades of orange, red-purple and yellow in autumn. In late winter to early spring small red flowers emerge from hairy brown buds, before spring growth appears. H 8–10m (26–33ft), S 10m (33ft).
Aspect Full sun or semi-shade.
Hardiness ✺✺✺ Zones 4–8.

Parrotia persica

PAULOWNIA

The six species of deciduous trees in the genus are found throughout eastern Asia. They are handsome specimen trees, grown for their pretty flowers, which do best in hot summers.

Cultivation Grow in fertile, well-drained soil in full sun. Protect from cold winds. Young shoots are susceptible to late spring frosts.

Pruning Formative pruning should aim to produce a clear trunk and a balanced crown.

Propagation Seed should be collected when fresh and sown into a container in a protected frost-free environment until germination occurs. Hardwood cuttings can be taken in winter and planted in the ground, left for a year and then transplanted the following spring.

P. tomentosa
(syn. *P. imperialis*)
Empress tree, foxglove tree, princess tree

This stunning and fast-growing tree from China is grown for its highly prized timber, large panicles of flowers and velvety leaves. The light green leaves, 30–40cm (12–16in) long, are covered in hairs, densely beneath. In late spring fragrant, pale pink-purple flowers, up to 5cm (2in) long, are produced in upright clusters. This species is often grown as a coppiced tree, when it produces astonishingly large leaves. It is tolerant of pollution. H 15m (50ft), S 10m (33ft).

Paulownia tomentosa

Named varieties 'Lilacina' (syn. *P. fargesii*), which may be slightly hardier than the species, has paler, lilac-coloured flowers.

Aspect Full sun or semi-shade.
Hardiness ❀❀❀ Zones 6–9.

PHELLODENDRON

The genus contains ten species of deciduous trees, which are found in eastern Asia. Male and female flowers are borne on separate plants, both of which must be present to produce the round, blue-black fruits. They have aromatic, attractive foliage and make large specimen trees.

Cultivation Grow in deep, fertile, well-drained soil in full sun.

Pruning Formative pruning should aim to produce a clear trunk and a balanced crown. Occasional pruning is required to remove dead, dying, diseased or crossing branches.

Propagation Seed should be collected when fresh and sown into a container in an unheated glasshouse or cold frame until germination occurs.

P. amurense
Amur cork tree

A broadly spreading, fast-growing, medium-sized tree from north-eastern Asia, with bark that grows corky as the tree ages. The glossy, dark green leaves, up to 35cm (14in) long, are pinnate and turn yellow in autumn. H and S 12m (40ft).

Aspect Full sun or semi-shade.
Hardiness ❀❀❀ Zones 3–7.

PHOENIX
Date palm

The 17 species of palms in the genus are found in tropical and subtropical areas in the Canary Islands, Africa, and western and southern Asia. They are tender plants, which are often grown in conservatories and as houseplants in areas that are too cold for them outdoors.

Cultivation Best grown in a fertile, free-draining loam-based potting compost that retains some moisture and light shade protection in tropical climates.

Pruning Date palms require little annual pruning with the exception of the cosmetic removal of the dead fronds and fruit spikes.

Phoenix canariensis

Propagation: Seed should be collected fresh and sown in a humus-rich compost in a humid environment above 24°C (66°F).

P. canariensis
Canary Island date palm

This species is one of the most widely planted palms for tropical and Mediterranean planting. The trunk is straight with a slight taper at the base, and the arching, narrowly V-shaped, bright to mid-green fronds, which have many leaflets, may get to 6m (20ft) long. In summer bright yellow or creamy-yellow flowers are produced in clusters, up to 1.8m (6ft) long, and these ripen to edible, orange fruits. H 15m (50ft), S 12m (40ft).

Aspect Full sun.
Hardiness (Min. 10–16°C/50–61°F) Zones 8–11.

P. dactylifera
Date palm

This species is a tall, fast-growing and occasionally suckering plant. It has arching, grey-green leaves, up to 6m (20ft) long, consisting of many leaflets. The large, straw-coloured flower spikes are followed by the sweet fruits, which ripen to orange on the tree in dry conditions. H 20–30m (65–100ft), S 6–12m (20–40ft).

Aspect Full sun.
Hardiness (Min. 10–16°C/50–61°F) Zones 9–11.

PICEA
Spruce

The genus contains about 35 species of coniferous evergreen trees, which are found throughout the northern hemisphere (except Africa). They make handsome specimen trees and can also be planted to create windbreaks. Numerous cultivars have been developed, displaying a wide range of habit, size and foliage colour.

Cultivation Grow in deep, moisture-retentive but well-drained, neutral to acidic soil in full sun.

Pruning Formative pruning should aim to produce a clear trunk and a balanced crown, while tipping the lateral branches of young trees will encourage a denser crown. Occasional pruning is required to remove dead, dying, diseased or crossing branches.

Propagation Seed is the easiest method of propagation and should be collected when fresh and sown into a container in an unheated glasshouse or cold frame until germination occurs. Semi-ripe and softwood cuttings can be rooted during summer and should be dipped in a rooting hormone and placed in a humid environment until rooting occurs. Selected forms are winter grafted on to seedling-raised rootstocks.

P. abies
Norway spruce, common spruce
This highly adaptable, conical conifer, which will grow in a range of soil types, is widely grown in Europe for its timber; it is also farmed to supply Christmas trees. It has long branches, densely clothed with dark green, needle-like foliage. The needles are attached by short, woody pegs, which remain once the needles fall and give the branches a spiky appearance. Pendulous cones ripen to light brown. There are many dwarf forms, which are more suitable for gardens than the species. H 40m (130ft), S 6m (20ft).
Aspect Full sun.
Hardiness ❀❀❀ Zones 3–7.

P. breweriana
Brewer's spruce
This large, slow-growing, broadly conical tree has graceful, slightly weeping branches. The dark green, needle-like foliage, white-green beneath, is arranged on pendent side shoots. The cones are green

at first but turn purple as they mature. H 25m (80ft), S 10m (33ft).
Aspect Full sun.
Hardiness ❀❀❀ Zone 5.

P. orientalis
Caucasian spruce, oriental spruce
One of the most beautiful of the spruces, this ultimately large tree from the Caucasus and north-eastern Turkey has glossy, dark green needles that lie almost flat along the shoots. The long, brown cones hang from the foliage in winter and are highly distinctive. The stunning silhouette and slender, slightly weeping branches combine with the plant's tolerance of a range of conditions to make this a desirable addition to a large garden. H 50m (165ft), S 20m (65ft).
Named varieties 'Aurea' has an open, but graceful habit. In spring, for about six weeks, the new leaves are light creamy-gold before turning yellow-green. H 10m (33ft).
'Skylands' is similar to 'Aurea' in habit but the needles are golden-yellow throughout the year. This slender but vigorous small tree is one of the most stunning garden conifers.
Aspect Full sun.
Hardiness ❀❀❀ Zone 5.

P. pungens
Colorado spruce
This large, strongly conical tree from the north-western USA has green-grey or blue-grey

Pinus ayacahuite

needles arranged around the stem. The slender horizontal branches sweep upwards, while lower limbs may weep, often growing right down to the ground. H 35m (115ft), S 4.5m (15ft).
Named varieties The beautiful and slow-growing 'Hoopsii' has silver-blue needles and a dense conical habit. H 15m (50ft).
'Koster', a smaller but equally slow-growing form, is sometimes called the Colorado blue spruce because of its stunning silver-blue foliage. H 10m (33ft).
Aspect Full sun.
Hardiness ❀❀❀ Zones 3–7.

PINUS
Pine
This is a large genus, containing about 120 species of coniferous evergreen trees and shrubs, which are found throughout the northern hemisphere. Pines are grown as specimen trees and as windbreaks, and a vast number of cultivars have been developed, offering a range of size, habit and foliage colour.
Cultivation Grow in well-drained soil in full sun.

Pruning Early formative pruning should aim to produce a clear trunk and a balanced crown, while tipping the lateral branches of young trees encourages a denser crown.
Propagation Seed is the easiest method of propagation and should be collected when fresh and sown into a container in an unheated glasshouse or cold frame until germination occurs. Selected forms are winter grafted on to seedling-raised rootstocks.

P. ayacahuite
Mexican white pine
This broadly conical, spreading conifer is native to Mexico, Honduras and Guatemala. A five-needle pine, it has long, slender, blue-green leaves, which are borne in clusters along the stems. The light brown cones, up to 10cm (4in) long, drip a lot of white resin. Although the foliage is tolerant of heat, this pine is not drought tolerant and prefers fertile, moisture-retentive soil. H 35m (115ft), S 10m (33ft).
Aspect Full sun.
Hardiness ❀❀❀ Zone 7.

Picea breweriana

P. bungeana
Lacebark pine
Native to northern and central China, this beautiful, often multi-stemmed, three-needle pine spreads as it ages. The short, pale green needles are borne in dense clusters, giving a tufted effect to the branches. The ornamental bark flakes in patches to reveal the creamy-white, darkening to grey-green and purplish-green, bark beneath. The cones, up to 8cm (3in) long, change from yellow-brown to warm red as they mature. It prefers a warm position. H 10–15m (33–50ft), S 6m (20ft).
Aspect Full sun.
Hardiness ✿✿✿ Zones 3–7.

P. coulteri
Big-cone pine, Coulter pine
This large, three-needled pine from the south-western USA develops into a broadly spreading tree. The long grey-green or blue-green needles are borne in clusters at the tips of branches, giving a tufted appearance. The large cones, which may get up to 35cm (14in) long, are spiny and remain attached to the branches for many years, opening only in high temperatures. Mature bark is deeply furrowed with scaly ridges and is dark grey to black. They are tolerant of drought. H 25m (80ft), S 10m (33ft).
Aspect Full sun.
Hardiness ✿✿✿ Zone 7.

P. densiflora
Japanese red pine
This two-needled pine from north-eastern Asia and Japan is similar in many respects to *P. sylvestris*. It has sandy-red bark, which flakes near the top of the trunk but is grey near the base. The bright green needles are up to 12cm (5in) long, and yellow cones, up to 6cm (2½in) long, open during their second summer. This pine needs acidic soil. H 35m (115ft), S 20m (65ft).
Aspect Full sun.
Hardiness ✿✿✿ Zones 3–7.

P. palustris
Pitch pine, longleaf pine, southern yellow pine
This fast-growing, three-needled pine is native to the south-eastern USA. It has dark green needles, up to 45cm (18in) long, and reddish-brown, flaking bark. With age the lower branches die, and the crown becomes a sparse dome of tufted foliage above a clear, straight trunk. It will endure extreme summer heat. H 40m (130ft), S 15m (50ft).
Aspect Full sun.
Hardiness ✿✿ Zones 7–10.

P. patula
Mexican weeping pine, jelecote pine
A highly ornamental landscape tree for mild climates, this pine from central Mexico develops into a spreading tree. It has reddish-brown bark, and the light green needles, which are usually in threes but are occasionally in fours or even fives, are up to 30cm (12in) long. It needs acidic soil. H 20m (65ft), S 10m (33ft).
Aspect Full sun.
Hardiness ✿✿ Zone 8.

P. strobus
Eastern white pine, Weymouth pine
The species, which is native to North America, is a fast-growing, five-needled and highly resinous pine. It is grown for its attractive, slender-branched crown and blue-green foliage. The grey-green needles are up to 14m (56ft) long, and green cones, up to 15cm (6in) long, ripen to brown. H 35m (115ft), S 10m (33ft).

Pinus sylvestris

Named varieties 'Fastigiata' has upright branches clothed in dense clusters of blue-green foliage. H 20m (65ft), S 3m (10ft).
    'Pendula' has a strongly weeping habit and is often trained as a straight-trunked standard before being allowed to weep, when it produces blue-green foliage.
Aspect Full sun.
Hardiness ✿✿✿ Zones 3–7.

P. sylvestris
Scots pine
Native to Europe and temperate Asia, this two-needled species is widely grown for its timber. It is also an ornamental tree with short blue-green, twisted needles, up to 8cm (3in) long, and orange-brown bark. The green cones, up to 8cm (3in) long, mature to grey or reddish-brown. It is a broadly spreading, often flat-topped tree with a clear trunk and light 'clouds' of foliage. It does best in neutral to acidic soil. H 30m (100ft), S 9m (30ft).
Named varieties The trees in Aurea Group (syn. 'Aurea') are slower growing with golden-yellow needles in spring, turning green-yellow later in the year. H 10–15m (33–50ft).
    Trees in Fastigiata Group have twisted, upright branches clothed with blue-green foliage. They are among the most beautiful of all upright garden trees. H 8m (26ft), S 1.8m (6ft).
Aspect Full sun or semi-shade.
Hardiness ✿✿✿ Zones 3–7.

Pinus bungeana

P. wallichiana
Bhutan pine, blue pine, Himalayan pine
A beautiful, fast-growing, five-needled pine, native to the Himalayas, this develops a broadly conical habit. The smooth, grey bark ages to dark brown. The grey-green leaves, up to 20cm (8in) long, are borne in dense clusters at the ends of branches. The resinous green cones, up to 30cm (12in) long, mature to brown. H 35m (115ft), S 10–12m (33–40ft). Aspect Full sun.
Hardiness ✹✹✹ Zones 5–7.

PISTACIA
Pistachio
The genus, which contains nine to eleven species of evergreen and deciduous shrubs and small trees, is known for the nuts from *P. vera*, which is grown commercially. The species are found in warm but temperate areas of the northern hemisphere, and they are grown for their flowers, foliage and fruit. Most species are tender, but *P. chinensis* will survive in sheltered temperate gardens.
Cultivation Grow in fertile, well-drained soil. Protect from cold, drying winds.
Pruning The trees should be trained to a modified central leader with four or five main scaffold limbs branching about 1.2m (4ft) from the ground. Little subsequent pruning is needed except to remove interfering branches.

Propagation By chip-budding or grafting selected scions on to one-year rootstocks of *P. atlantica*, *P. terebinthus* and *P. integerrima*.

P. chinensis
Chinese mastic
This deciduous tree has glossy, dark green pinnate leaves, up to 25cm (10in) long, which turn golden-yellow in autumn. In mid- to late spring clusters of aromatic red flowers are borne with the new leaves, and these are followed by small, round, red fruits that mature to blue. H 15m (50ft), S 10m (33ft).
Aspect Full sun.
Hardiness ✹✹ Zones 6–10.

PITTOSPORUM
There are about 200 species of evergreen trees and shrubs in the genus, many of them from Australasia, but some from south and east Asia, southern Africa and the Pacific islands. They are grown mainly for their attractive foliage, although some pittosporums have interesting and sweetly scented flowers. Most are frost hardy to frost tender, but some varieties can be grown outdoors in mild, sheltered areas.
Cultivation Outdoors, grow in fertile, moisture-retentive but well-drained soil. Plants with purple and variegated leaves give the best colour when grown in full sun.
Pruning Only light pruning is required to maintain shape and avoid crossing branches.

Pistacia vera

Propagation By semi-hardwood cuttings. Seeds are difficult to obtain and viability is poor.

P. adaphniphylloides
This unusual species will develop into a small, round-headed tree with long, narrow, deep green leaves and delicate, cream-coloured, deliciously scented flowers, which are borne in early summer. H and S 10m (33ft).
Aspect Full sun or semi-shade.
Hardiness ✹ Zones 9–10.

P. dallii
This New Zealand tree is one of the hardiest of this group. It is a highly ornamental form, with purple shoots and long, dark green, serrated leaves up to 10cm (4in) long. Fragrant, creamy-white flowers are borne in summer. H 6m (20ft), S 4m (12ft).
Aspect Full sun or semi-shade.
Hardiness ✹✹ Zones 8–10.

P. eugenioides
Lemonwood, tarata
Also native to New Zealand, this pretty, ultimately densely crowned tree has crinkled, glossy green leaves, up to 10cm (4in) long, and honey-scented, pale yellow flowers in summer. The foliage smells pleasantly of lemons when it is crushed, and stems are widely used in the cut-flower trade. H 7–10m (23–33ft), S 3m (10ft).
Aspect Full sun or semi-shade.
Hardiness ✹ Zones 9–10.

P. tenuifolium
Kohuhu
This widely grown pittosporum is native to New Zealand, and it has been extensively hybridized to produce a range of different forms and foliage colours, including variegated, purple and mottled. The foliage is widely used in the cut-flower trade. The species, which is fast-growing, is a large shrub or small tree. The distinctive, glossy green leaves, up to 6cm (2½in) long, have wavy edges, and young shoots are black. In late spring to early summer small, fragrant, bell-shaped, black-red flowers are borne amid the leaves. H 10m (33ft), S 5m (16ft).
Aspect Full sun or semi-shade.
Hardiness ✹✹ Zones 8–10.

Pinus strobus 'Pendula'

Pittosporum tenuifolium 'Purpurea'

P. undulatum
Australian mock orange, cheesewood, Victorian box
This Australian species is a dense, rounded tree with glossy, dark green leaves, up to 15cm (6in) long, with wavy edges. In late spring to midsummer fragrant, creamy-white flowers are borne in clusters. H 14m (46ft), S 7m (23ft).
Aspect Full sun or semi-shade.
Hardiness ❋ Zones 9–10.

PLATANUS
Plane
The genus contains six species of mostly deciduous trees, which have attractive, maple-like foliage and flaking bark. They are native to North and Central America, South-east Asia and south-eastern Europe and are highly ornamental trees suitable for planting as specimen trees in large gardens. They are also tolerant of poor soil and pollution.
Cultivation Grow in fertile, well-drained soil in full sun.
Pruning Formative pruning should aim to produce a clear trunk and a balanced crown.
Propagation Collect fresh seed and sow into a pot outdoors, or in an unheated glasshouse or cold frame until germination occurs.

Platanus orientalis

P. x *hispanica*
(syn. *P.* x *acerifolia*)
London plane
This hybrid between *P. occidentalis* and *P. orientalis* is widely planted in London as a street tree, hence its common name. It is a vigorous, broadly spreading, deciduous tree, with flaking bark and palmate, bright green leaves, up to 35cm (14in) long. Clusters of green fruit, ageing to brown, are borne in autumn and last into winter. Pollard in restricted spaces.
H 30m (100ft), S 20m (65ft).
Aspect Full sun or semi-shade.
Hardiness ❋❋❋ Zones 4–9.

P. orientalis
Oriental plane
This popular and attractive spreading deciduous species originates from south-eastern Europe, but is widely planted in Asia. It has attractive flaking bark and large, deeply lobed, glossy green leaves, up to 25cm (10in) long. Clusters of up to six green fruits, which age to brown, are borne in autumn, and last into winter. It grows better in temperate areas than in the continental climate of the USA. H and S 30m (100ft).
Aspect Full sun or semi-shade.
Hardiness ❋❋❋ Zones 4–9.

Platanus x *hispanica*

PLUMERIA
Frangipani, temple tree, pagoda tree
There are seven to eight species of deciduous shrubs and trees in this genus, which is native to tropical and subtropical America. Grown for their lovely, fragrant flowers, they are popular in the tropics as they are salt-spray- and drought tolerant. Although tender, frangipani can be grown as houseplants or in a warm greenhouse or conservatory.
Cultivation Outdoors, grow in fertile, well-drained soil in sun.
Pruning Formative pruning should aim to encourage a number of clear trunks and a balanced crown, while tipping the lateral branches of young trees will encourage a denser crown.
Propagation Take softwood cuttings in early summer and place in a frost-free, humid environment until they root. Low branches can be layered.

P. rubra
Common frangipani
This rather variable large shrub or small tree develops an upright habit as it matures. The leaves are mid- to dark green, up to 40cm (16in) long, and have pale red-green midribs. In the wild the highly scented flowers, which are borne in clusters above the foliage in summer to autumn, range from white, to pink, yellow and deep pink-red. In dry regions during periods of drought the foliage will fall, but the tree will still flower. H 7m (23ft), S 5m (15ft).

Named varieties An array of vividly coloured forms have been developed, including 'Bridal White', which is a slow-growing cultivar with white flowers with reflexed petals and green foliage.
  'June Bride' bears large clusters of white flowers, tinted pink at the edges, with orange-yellow centres.
  'Royal Flush' has clusters of magenta flowers without the coloured centre.
  'Sunbathed' has yellow flowers that are white around the edge.
Aspect Full sun.
Hardiness (Min. 10–13°C/50–5°F) Zones 10–12.

PODOCARPUS
Podocarp, yellow-wood
There are 90–100 species of evergreen coniferous trees and shrubs in the genus. The leaves are usually arranged in spirals around the stems, and they have fleshy, berry-like fruits. They make excellent specimen plants and mixed border trees.
Cultivation Grow in fertile, moisture-retentive but well-drained soil. Protect plants from cold, drying winds.
Pruning Young plants often grow straight up, with no side branching. To rectify, cut them back hard, which will result in re-growth along the stem. Pinch back new growth as necessary to promote bushiness.
Propagation Plants can be started from seeds or cuttings. Seeds often sprout while still attached to the fleshy stalk on the plant. Tip cuttings take 10 to 12 weeks to root.

Plumeria rubra

P. lawrencei
This species from New Zealand is a spreading shrub or small tree with narrow green leaves, flushed with bronze, and red berries. H 10m (33ft), S 6m (20ft).
Aspect Full sun.
Hardiness ❁❁ Zone 7.

P. macrophyllus
Kusamaki, big-leaf podocarp, Japanese yew
This slow-growing conical tree, which is native to eastern China, has red-brown bark. The feathery leaves are dark green above and lighter green beneath. Red-purple fruits are borne on female plants in autumn. It requires a moist, temperate climate to thrive and long, hot, humid summers to develop into a tree. It will not survive prolonged periods of frost. H 10–15m (33–50ft), S 8–10m (26–33ft).
Aspect Full sun.
Hardiness ❁❁ Zones 9–10.

P. salignus
(syn. *P. chilinus*)
Willow-leaf podocarp
This slow-growing, graceful, small garden tree has drooping branches covered with curtains of foliage. The narrow leaves, up to 15cm (6in) long, are glossy, dark blue-green above and yellow-green beneath. Female plants produce green or purple fruits in autumn. H 15m (50ft), S 10m (33ft).
Aspect Full sun.
Hardiness ❁❁❁ Zones 9–10.

P. totara
Totara
In its native New Zealand this is a fast-growing tree, but in less favourable climates it is slower growing. It has a broadly conical habit with large, yew-like leaves, up to 2.5cm (1in) long. The brown to grey bark peels in strips. H 20m (65ft), S 10m (33ft).
Aspect Full sun.
Hardiness ❁ Zone 10.

POPULUS
Poplar, aspen, cottonwood
This genus of about 35 species of large, fast-growing deciduous trees are grown for their foliage and catkins. They make good specimens in large gardens. They are unsuitable for small gardens because their questing roots can damage foundations and drains.
Cultivation Grow in moisture-retentive but well-drained soil in sun. Poplars will not tolerate waterlogged soil.
Pruning Formative pruning should aim to produce a clear trunk and a balanced crown. Many poplars are prone to canker, so any diseased wood should be removed as it appears. Occasional pruning is required to remove dead, dying, diseased or crossing branches.
Propagation Collect fresh seed and sow in a pot in an unheated glasshouse or cold frame until germination occurs. Softwood cuttings are taken during summer and placed in a humid environment until rooting occurs. Hardwood cuttings are taken in winter.

P. x canadensis
Canadian poplar
This hybrid between *P. deltoides* and *P. nigra* is a fast-growing tree with a conical to columnar habit. The broadly triangular leaves, up to 10cm (4in) long, are glossy green, flushed bronze in summer and turn yellow in autumn. Red male catkins and yellow female catkins, both up to 10cm (4in) long, are borne in spring. H 30m (100ft), S 20m (65ft).
Named varieties 'Aurea' (syn. 'Serotina Aurea') is a columnar, male form with young leaves that are flushed with bronze, turning butter yellow in autumn. H 25m (80ft), S 10m (33ft).
Aspect Full sun.
Hardiness ❁❁❁ Zones 5–7.

P. x jackii
(syn. *P. x candicans*, *P. gileadensis*)
This columnar hybrid between *P. balsamifera* (balsam poplar) and *P. deltoides* (eastern cottonwood) has dark green, heart-shaped leaves, up to 15cm (6in) long, which are white-green beneath. Green female catkins, up to 15cm (6in) long, appear in early spring. H 25m (80ft), S 15m (50ft).
Named varieties 'Aurora' has ovate leaves that are variegated and mottled yellow along the margins and green and pink-purple in the centres. The most vivid colours are produced on the strongest growing shoots. It is often treated as a short-stemmed pollard to retain the coloured leaves. H 15m (50ft), S 6m (20ft).
Aspect Full sun.
Hardiness ❁❁❁ Zones 5–7.

Plumeria alba

Populus maximowiczii

P. lasiocarpa
Chinese necklace poplar

A graceful, medium-sized, conical tree, this has large, heart-shaped, dark green leaves, up to 30cm (12in) long. Yellow-green catkins, up to 10cm (4in) long, appear in mid-spring. H 20m (65ft), S 10m (33ft).
Aspect Full sun.
Hardiness ✱✱✱ Zones 5–7.

P. nigra
Black poplar

This fast-growing tree has very dark, deeply fissured bark. The triangular to ovate leaves, up to 10cm (4in) long, are dark green, initially bronze and turning yellow in autumn. Green female and red male catkins are borne in early to mid-spring.
Named varieties The well-known form 'Italica' (syn. *P. nigra* var. *italica*; Lombardy poplar) has been cultivated in Europe for a long time and is widely used as a windbreak tree on agricultural land. It is a beautiful, fast-growing tree with a narrow, conical shape. The close branches are erect and covered with glossy green leaves that turn yellow in autumn. H 30m (100ft), S 3m (10ft).
Aspect Full sun.
Hardiness ✱✱✱ Zones 3–9.

P. tremuloides
American aspen, quaking aspen

This adaptable, medium-sized tree, found from Canada to Mexico, has distinctive, shallowly toothed, glossy green leaves, up to 6cm (2½in) long, which are bronze when they emerge, turning yellow in autumn. The ovate leaves flutter and quiver in the lightest of winds. Green female and red-grey male catkins, both up to 6cm (2½in) long, are borne in early spring. Planted in sufficient numbers, these trees can be used to block out unwanted vehicle noise. H 15–20m (50–65ft), S 10m (33ft).
Aspect Full sun.
Hardiness ✱✱✱ Zones 3–9.

PORTLANDIA

There are over 20 species in the genus of evergreen shrubs and small trees. They are native to Central America and the Caribbean and are grown for their fragrant flowers.
Cultivation Outdoors, grow in fertile, well-drained, alkaline soil in sun or light shade.
Pruning Formative pruning should aim to encourage a clear trunk, or multiple trunks, and a balanced crown. Occasional pruning is required for the removal of any dead, dying, diseased or crossing branches.

Propagation Seed is the easiest method and should be collected when fresh and sown into a container in a heated glasshouse in a frost-free and humid environment until germination occurs. Low branches can also be layered into the soil; when rooted they should be detached from the parent tree and potted up.

P. grandiflora
Tree lily

This small tree has glossy green, magnolia-like leaves, up to 15cm (6in) or more long. The funnel-shaped flowers, up to 15cm (6in) long, are borne in summer. They are white with a reddish throat and smell of vanilla. H 6m (20ft), S 1.8m (6ft).
Aspect Full sun to light shade.
Hardiness (Min. 10°C/50°F) Zones 10–12.

PROTEA

The genus contains about 115 species of evergreen shrubs and just a few trees. They are found in Africa and are prized for their large flowerheads.
Cultivation Outdoors, grow in well-drained, neutral to acidic soil in sun. These plants will not tolerate wet winters.
Pruning Formative pruning should aim to encourage a clear trunk and a balanced crown, while tipping the lateral branches of young trees will encourage a denser crown. Occasional

pruning is required for the removal of dead, dying, diseased or crossing branches.
Propagation Seed is the easiest method of propagation and should be collected when fresh and sown into a container in a heated glasshouse in a frost-free and humid environment until germination occurs.

P. eximia

This small, upright tree from South Africa has ovate leaves, up to 10cm (4in) long. The leaves, silver-green to glaucous green, are flushed and sometimes edged with red-purple. In spring and summer, cone-shaped scarlet flowers are surrounded by large bracts, creating showy flowerheads, up to 15cm (6in) across, that resemble those of *Banksia*. H 5m (16ft), S 3m (10ft).
Aspect Full sun.
Hardiness ✱ Zones 9–11.

PRUMNOPITYS

The ten species of coniferous evergreen trees in the genus are found in Central and South America, Malaysia and New Zealand. They are similar in many respects to podocarps and have yew-like foliage. They can be grown as specimen trees or used as hedging.
Cultivation Grow in fertile, moisture-retentive but well-drained soil in sun. Protect plants from cold, drying winds.

Protea eximia

Pruning Formative pruning should aim to produce a clear trunk and a balanced crown, while tipping the lateral branches of young trees will help to encourage a denser crown. Occasional pruning is required for the removal of any dead, dying, diseased or crossing branches.

Propagation Seed is the easiest method of propagation and should be collected when fresh and sown into a container in an unheated glasshouse or cold frame until germination occurs. Semi-ripe cuttings can be taken in late summer and early autumn. The base of the cutting should be dipped in a rooting hormone before planting it and placing in a humid environment in a glasshouse until it roots.

P. andina
(syn. P. elegans, Podocarpus andinus)
Plum-fruited yew, plum yew

This species from Chile and Argentina will eventually develop into a broadly conical tree. The narrow blue-green leaves, up to 3cm (1½in) long and with two pale bands on the undersides, are arranged in whorls. The cones, up to 2.5cm (1in) long, are pale yellow, and female plants produce plum-like, yellowish fruits, up to 2cm (½in) long, which ripen to purple. H 15–20m (50–65ft), S 8–10m (26–33ft).
Aspect Full sun to semi-shade.
Hardiness ✹✹✹ Zones 8–10.

Prumnopitys andina

Prunus 'Accolade'

PRUNUS
Ornamental cherry

This enormous genus contains some 430 species of deciduous and evergreen trees and shrubs, which provide almonds, apricots, cherries, peaches and nectarines, plums and damsons and sloes. There are also many ornamental trees, grown for their delightful white, pink or red spring flowers, colourful fruits and attractive autumn colour. They are often small trees, useful for their long period of interest in gardens where space is limited. The Japanese cherries, the Sato-zakura Group, have been especially developed for their beautiful blossom, which is borne from early spring.

Cultivation Grow in fertile, moisture-retentive but well-drained soil in sun. Deciduous forms prefer full sun.

Pruning Formative pruning should aim to produce a clear trunk and a balanced crown. Many cherries are prone to canker and silver leaf, so any diseased wood should be removed as soon as it appears. Pruning should be done during summer to reduce the risk of infection from silver leaf.

Propagation Seed is used for the species while summer budding and winter grafting are the main means of propagation. Collect fresh seed and sow in a pot in an unheated glasshouse or cold frame until germination occurs. Summer budding and winter grafting are both quite popular and should be done on to disease-resistant rootstocks or on to seed-raised bird cherry stock.

P. 'Accolade'

This is an outstanding small deciduous tree, which has been developed from *P. sargentii* and *P. subhirtella*. It has dark green leaves, up to 10cm (4in) long, which turn vivid orange-red in autumn. In early spring clusters of semi-double, pale pink flowers open from dark pink buds. Like most Japanese cherries, they are best grown in moisture-retentive soils. H and S 8–10m (26–33ft).
Aspect Full sun or semi-shade.
Hardiness ✹✹✹ Zones 5–6.

Prunus sargentii

P. 'Amanogawa'
(syn. P. serrulata 'Erecta')
A small, upright, deciduous Japanese cherry, with erect branches that open with age, this has ovate leaves, up to 12cm (5in) long, which are slightly bronzed in spring. In autumn the foliage is red, yellow and green. The fragrant, semi-double, pale pink flowers, up to 4cm (1½in) across, are borne in dense clusters in mid- to late spring. H 8–10m (26–33ft), S 4m (12ft).
Aspect Full sun or semi-shade.
Hardiness ❀❀❀ Zones 5–6.

P. cerasifera
Cherry plum, myrobalan
A small deciduous tree, this is often grown as a hedge, when it will be covered with single, white flowers, up to 2.5cm (1in) across, in spring. Mature plants sometimes produce red or yellow, plum-like fruits. H and S 10m (33ft).
Named varieties The species is most often represented in gardens by the highly decorative 'Pissardii' (syn. P. pissardii; purple-leaved plum). This has reddish-purple leaves, which darken to purple as they mature. In mid-spring masses of white flowers open from pink buds. It is an adaptable, ultimately broadly spreading tree, often used as a hedge. H and S 8m (26ft).
Aspect Full sun or semi-shade.
Hardiness ❀❀❀ Zones 5–8.

P. 'Ichiyo'
This spreading deciduous tree has dark green leaves, up to 10cm (4in) long, which are tinged with bronze in spring. Double, frilly, pale pink flowers, up to 5cm (2in) across, are borne in clusters in mid- to late spring. H and S 8m (26ft).
Aspect Full sun or semi-shade.
Hardiness ❀❀❀ Zones 5–6.

P. sargentii
Sargent cherry
This spreading deciduous tree has dark green leaves, up to 12cm (5in) long, which are initially reddish then turn shades of orange, yellow and red in autumn. Pale pink flowers, up to 4cm (1½in) across, are borne in mid-spring, followed by red, cherry-like fruits. H 20m (65ft), S 15m (50ft).
Aspect Full sun or semi-shade.
Hardiness ❀❀❀ Zones 4–7.

P. serrula
(syn. P. tibetica)
This medium-sized, fast-growing deciduous tree is grown for its glossy, mahogany-red or orange-brown bark. The dark green leaves, up to 10cm (4in) long, turn yellow in autumn. White flowers, up to 2cm (¾in) across, are borne in late spring, followed by small, bright red fruits. H and S 10–15m (33–50ft).
Aspect Full sun or semi-shade.
Hardiness ❀❀❀ Zones 5–7.

P. 'Shirofugen'
This attractive, deciduous Japanese cherry develops a spreading habit. The dark green leaves, up to 12cm (5in) long, are coppery-red in spring, turning reddish-orange in autumn. The long-lasting, fragrant flowers are white, up to 5cm (2in) across, and open from pink buds in late spring, turning purple-pink before they fall. H 8m (26ft), S 10m (33ft).
Aspect Full sun or semi-shade.
Hardiness ❀❀❀ Zones 5–6.

P. 'Shirotae'
(syn. P. 'Mount Fuji')
This is a spreading, deciduous tree, which develops a slightly weeping habit. The dark green leaves, up to 12cm (5in) long, are light green when they first emerge in spring and turn vibrant red and orange in autumn. The fragrant, double, white flowers, which are up to 5cm (2in) across, are borne in pendent clusters in mid-spring. H 6m (20ft), S 8m (26ft).
Aspect Full sun or semi-shade.
Hardiness ❀❀❀ Zones 5–6.

P. 'Taihaku'
Great white cherry
This broadly spreading, vigorous, deciduous Japanese cherry has long, arching branches. The dark green, rather leathery leaves, up to 20cm (8in) long, are red-bronze when they emerge in spring and sometimes turn red-orange in autumn. The single white flowers, up to 7cm (2¾in) across, are borne in clusters in mid-spring. H 8m (26ft), S 10m (33ft).
Aspect Full sun or semi-shade.
Hardiness ❀❀❀ Zones 5–6.

PRUNUS ARMENIACA
Apricot
These are one of the most difficult of the stone fruits to grow. This is because they flower very early in the year and the delicate flowers are very easily damaged by frost. They can also be affected by peach leaf curl, especially in areas where winters are cool and wet. They are best sited in free-draining but fertile soils and in areas where summer temperatures are high.

Prunus armeniaca

Cultivation Depending on the selection, chilling requirements can vary, but these difficult trees generally require about 350 hours below 7°C (45°F). Flowers are prone to frost damage and germination can be improved by hand pollination. The best fruit is produced after hot summers, but drought conditions can cause premature fruit drop.

Pruning Fruits are borne on one-year-old shoots and on spur shoots, so regular yearly pruning is required to remove any unproductive or old shoots during winter and pruning to encourage an open-bowl-shaped tree.

Propagation Apricots are normally propagated by chip- or T-budding during summer on to a good dwarfing rootstock.

P. a. 'Goldbar'

This warm climate selection produces very large, light yellow-orange fruit with a reddish blush to the skin. The flesh is light orange, very firm, meaty and moderately juicy. It is a vigorous tree that flowers heavily and requires pollinating, but sets a light crop.
Aspect Full sun, in a moisture-retentive soil.
Hardiness ❋❋ Zones 4–8.

P. a. 'Goldstrike'

This is a free-fruiting variety that produces large and firm fruit. The skin is a light orange colour and slightly glossy. The flesh is light orange, firm, meaty and moderately juicy. 'Goldstrike' blooms heavily but fruit set is often moderate to light under natural pollination, although it will cross pollinate very well with 'Goldbar'.
Aspect Full sun, in a moisture-retentive soil.
Hardiness ❋❋ Zones 4–8.

P. a. 'Tilton'

This popular variety is widely grown in the USA. It is very good for freezing, drying and eating fresh, and is one of the tastiest of all varieties of apricot. It has a distinct appearance, with a slightly flatter shape than most varieties and a concave line that goes halfway around the fruit.

It has a light orange skin, and the flesh is firm, tender and juicy with a sweet and sour taste. It has a golden colour with a red blush. It is a vigorous tree, bearing heavy crops that are resistant to late frosts, and its fruits ripen earlier than those of many other varieties. However, since the delicate flowers are produced very early in spring they may be prone to frosts.
Aspect Full sun, in a moisture-retentive soil.
Hardiness ❋❋ Zones 4–8.

P. a. 'Tom Catt'

This variety produces very juicy, very large, orange fruits if the crop is thinned properly, and they are often the first apricots to ripen each season. One of the best cool climate varieties, it is widely grown in the UK. The firm orange flesh is delicious eaten fresh. It requires either a pollinator or hand pollination, but is one of the best of the garden varieties as it has good disease resistance.
Aspect Full sun, in a moisture retentive soil.
Hardiness ❋❋ Zones 4–8.

P. a. 'Pedigree Bush'

This variety is normally grafted on to an extreme dwarfing rootstock, which makes it suitable for growing in containers as a patio plant. Medium-sized succulent, orange-red fruits are produced late in summer on trees that are pollinated. Plants seldom exceed 2m (6ft) tall.
Aspect Full sun, in a moisture-retentive soil.
Hardiness ❋❋ Zones 4–8.

P. a. 'Wenatachee'

Synonymous with 'Moorpark', this variety bears large fruit, and is grown for its distinct light yellow fruits. The fruit is widely used in jams. Its main attraction is its self-pollination, which produces fruit annually. However, it flowers early in the spring and is prone to frost damage. It is also the least tolerant of heavy soils.
Aspect Full sun, in a moistur-retentive soil.
Hardiness ❋❋ Zones 4–8.

Prunus avium

PRUNUS AVIUM
Sweet cherry

These are generally more vigorous and adaptable to a wider range of soils than *P. cerasus*. Plant in an open location as a specimen garden tree or as part of an orchard. When selecting, it is important to note that only a few cultivars are self-fertile. Netting or bird scarers may be necessary to protect the cherry crop. H and S 7–8m (23–26ft).
Aspect Full sun, in a moisture-retentive soil.
Hardiness ❋❋❋ Zones 3–9.
Cultivation Grow in fertile, well-drained, moisture-retentive soil. Avoid soils that flood or become waterlogged in winter and spring. They do best in a sunny, warm position with some protection to maximize pollination.
Pruning Sweet cherries fruit on spurs of wood that is two years or older. Mature trees are best pruned in summer. Slow down the vegetative growth by pruning every tip back to 5–6 nodes, which encourages the tree to produce spurs.
Propagation Use chip- or T-budding in summer on an appropriate rootstock. Malling F12/1 is a vigorous rootstock that can encourage the growth of slower growing forms, and it is used on poorer, shallower soils. More vigorous rootstocks are becoming available, including

Inmil, Camil, Edabriz and the Gisela series, and these will reduce the overall size of the tree and enhance disease resistance. Trees can be raised from seed, but are often inferior and take many years to produce fruit.
Named varieties The following sweet cherries will achieve a height and spread of 5m (16ft) if they are grown on Colt rootstock.

The prolific 'Bigarreau Napoléon' bears unusual red-flushed, yellow fruits, which are quite large and very sweet. They are often referred to as 'Naps' cherries. It is not self-fertile.

'Merchant' is a well-flavoured cherry with large, dark red fruits, which are produced quite early in summer. It has reasonably good resistance to cherry canker but is not self-fertile.

The widely grown 'Merton Favourite' bears delicious fruit and is also a beautiful spring-flowering garden tree. It is not self-fertile.

'Stella' is a reliable, self-fertile, late-fruiting cultivar, which bears large, dark red fruit.

PRUNUS CERASUS
Sour cherry

Acid or sour cherries tend to be hardier than sweet cherries and can even be grown against shady walls. H and S 7–8m (23–26ft).

Pterocarya stenoptera

fruits, up to 8cm (3in) across, with pinkish flesh, which are eaten fresh and also canned and used for making jellies and juice. The white flowers are borne throughout the year. H and S 10m (33ft).
Aspect Free-draining but moisture-retentive soil in a sunny location.
Hardiness ✽ Zones 10–12.

P. littorale
Strawberry guava
This smaller plant from Brazil has bronze-red bark and pink fruits with whitish flesh. H and S 8m (26ft).
Aspect Free-draining but moisture-retentive soil in a sunny location.
Hardiness ✽ Zone 10.

PTEROCARYA
Wing nut
The genus contains about ten species of deciduous trees, which are native to Asia. They are related to the walnut and are grown for their attractive foliage and catkin-like inflorescences and for the long spikes of winged fruits that

appear in summer. They make handsome specimen trees in gardens that are large enough to accommodate them.
Cultivation Grow in fertile, deep, moisture-retentive but well-drained soil in sun. Unwanted suckers, which are an especial problem with trees growing near water, should be removed as soon as they are noticed, otherwise they will quickly develop into an almost impenetrable thicket.
Pruning Formative pruning should aim to produce a clear trunk and a balanced crown. Wing nuts are prone to both root and stem suckers and these are best removed, as and when they appear. Occasional pruning is required for the removal of dead, dying, diseased or crossing branches.
Propagation Seed, softwood and hardwood cuttings are the main methods of propagation. Seed should be collected when fresh and sown into a container in an unheated glasshouse or cold frame until germination occurs.

Softwood cuttings are taken during summer, dipped in a rooting hormone and placed in a humid environment until rooting occurs. Hardwood cuttings are taken in winter and can be rooted in the garden bed or in containers, after which they can be lifted and transplanted the following spring.

P. fraxinifolia
Caucasian wing nut
This vigorous and broadly spreading tree has glossy, dark green, pinnate leaves, consisting of about 21 leaflets and 40–60cm (16–24in) long. In autumn they turn yellow. In spring catkins appear; the small, yellowish male catkins soon fall, but the pinkish female ones, initially up to 15cm (6in) long, persist and grow to 50cm (20in) long, becoming covered with winged green fruits. H 25–30m (80–100ft), S 20–25m (65–80ft).
Aspect Full sun or semi-shade.
Hardiness ✽✽✽ Zones 5–9.

P. stenoptera 'Fern Leaf'
This beautiful cultivar of the Chinese wing nut has deeply cut, fern-like leaves, tinted purple at first and turning green in summer. It is a fast-growing tree but suckers less than other wing nuts; however, if roots are damaged by lawnmowers they may throw up suckers some way from the main trunk. H and S 25m (80ft).
Aspect Full sun or semi-shade.
Hardiness ✽✽✽ Zones 5–8.

PUNICA
Pomegranate
Of the two species of deciduous shrubs or small trees in the genus, only *P. granatum* is widely cultivated. The trees are grown for their attractive flowers and large, edible fruits. They are not hardy plants but are small enough to be grown in conservatories, and in warmer areas they can be grown as specimen trees or included in a mixed border.
Cultivation Grow in fertile, well-drained soil in sun.
Pruning Formative pruning should aim to encourage a short trunk and a balanced crown, while tipping

the lateral branches of young trees will encourage a denser crown. Occasional pruning is required for the removal of dead, dying, diseased or crossing branches.
Propagation Seed is the easiest method of propagation and should be collected when fresh and be sown into a container in a heated glasshouse in a frost-free and humid environment until germination occurs. Softwood cuttings can also be rooted during early summer and should be dipped in a rooting hormone and placed in a frost-free, humid environment until they root. Root suckers can also be carefully separated from the parent plant and potted on.

P. granatum
In tropical areas this small tree bears fruits and flowers almost all year round. The glossy green leaves, which have red veins at first, are up to 8cm (3in) long. Funnel-shaped, orange-red flowers are borne over a long period in summer to autumn and are followed by round, yellow-brown fruit. H and S 6m (20ft).
Aspect Full sun.
Hardiness ✽✽ Zones 8–10.

PYRUS
Pear
Among the 30 or so species of deciduous trees and shrubs in the genus is *P. communis*, which is

Punica granatum

Pyrus communis 'Williams' Bon Chrétien'

Pyrus communis 'Conference'

the parent of the many forms of culinary and dessert pear. However, the ornamental forms, with attractive foliage, spring flowers and good autumn colour, make excellent specimen trees, especially in small gardens.

Cultivation Grow in fertile, free-draining but moisture-retentive soil in a warm, sunny and sheltered position. If the soil does not retain enough moisture the tree will produce inferior fruit unless extra water is given as the fruits begin to develop. Quince A rootstock will grow on poor soil but does best in deep, fertile, nutrient-rich soil. Quince C is a more widely available rootstock that produces slightly smaller trees. It is less tolerant of poor soil, although it does produce earlier, if slightly smaller, fruits.

Pruning The aim is to encourage the production of fruiting spurs and to remove older, less productive wood. This should only be done during the summer or winter.

Propagation Pears are usually grafted on to rootstocks of the species, *Pyrus communis*, or on to *Cydonia* (quince) rootstock, which provide some semi-dwarfing effects. Pears can also be propagated from seed, which should be collected when fresh and be sown into a container in an unheated glasshouse or cold frame until germination occurs. Winter grafting is popular, and is done on to seedlings of species closely related to the top stock or scion material.

Pyrus calleryana
This ornamental pear has white spring flowers and good autumn colour. The two most popular forms are 'Bradford' and 'Chanticleer', both of which have a conical habit. H and S 15m (45ft). Aspect Full sun.
Hardiness ✿✿✿ Zones 4–9.

P. communis 'Blake's Pride'
This is a widely grown and hardy American pear tree. Apart from producing very reliable, heavy crops of juicy, golden russet-like fruit in early autumn, it is also very resistant to fireblight (a disease that affects members of the rose family, Rosaceae). Grafted on to the common domestic pear, *Pyrus communis*, it can be maintained at 4m tall and wide (12ft x 12ft). Aspect Full sun.
Hardiness ✿✿✿ Zones 4–9

P. c. 'Charneaux'
If planted in an orchard setting with other pears nearby, this will produce a profusion of extremely juicy sweet fruit. Grown on Quince A it can be maintained at 4m tall and wide (12ft x 12ft). Aspect Full sun.
Hardiness ✿✿✿ Zones 4–9.

P. c. 'Clapp's Favourite'
This early fruiting variety requires an additional pollinator. Fruits are large, very tasty and juicy with a distinct flavour. Grown on Quince A it can be maintained at 4m tall and wide (12ft x 12ft). Aspect Full sun.
Hardiness ✿✿✿ Zones 4–9.

P. c. 'Concorde'
This variety is an excellent garden pear that fruits regularly if a pollinator is nearby. Large, juicy fruits are produced in mid-autumn. Grown on Quince A it can be maintained at 4m tall and wide (12ft x 12ft). Aspect Full sun.
Hardiness ✿✿✿ Zones 4–9

P. c. 'Conference'
This widely grown variety is one of the best pears for cooler climates. A good pollinator for other pears, it is partially self-fertile. It is a very heavy cropping form if a suitable pollinator is nearby. The firm, yellowish fruits can be cooked or eaten fresh. Grown on Quince A it can be maintained at 4m tall and wide (12ft x 12ft). Aspect Full sun.
Hardiness ✿✿✿ Zones 4–9.

P. c. 'Jeanne De Arc'
A traditional French variety, this has been cultivated for many years. It is a very heavy cropping form if a suitable pollinator is nearby. Although fruits are slightly smaller than those of some other varieties, they are very juicy and sweet. Grown on Quince A it can be maintained at 4m tall and wide (12ft x 12ft). Aspect Full sun.
Hardiness ✿✿✿ Zones 4–9.

P. c. 'Packham's Triumph'
This smaller pear fruits late in the year. Small fruits are produced in large quantities if a suitable pollinator is grown nearby. Grown on Quince A it can be maintained at 4m tall and wide (12ft x 12ft). Aspect Full sun.
Hardiness ✿✿✿ Zones 4–9.

P. c. 'Hosui'
This is a specially selected variety of the Asian pears that are grown for their round, sweet fruits and disease resistance. 'Hosui' produces masses of round, copper-coloured fruits which are very juicy and sweet. It can be pollinated by another Asian or common pear. Grown on Quince A it can be maintained at 4m tall and wide (12ft x 12ft). Aspect Full sun.
Hardiness ✿✿✿ Zones 4–9.

QUERCUS
Oak
The genus contains about 600 species of evergreen and deciduous trees and shrubs. They vary widely in size and habit and are found in North and South

Pyrus calleryana 'Chanticleer'

Quercus suber

Q. rhysophylla
Loquat oak
This evergreen species from
Mexico is fast-growing, with a
pyramidal habit at first but
broadening with age, and dark
brown bark. The glossy, heavily
corrugated, dark green leaves, up
to 25cm (10in) long, are
shallowly lobed and tinged with
bronze-red in spring. H 20–25m
(65–80ft), S 15m (50ft).
Aspect Full sun or semi-shade.
Hardiness ✿ Zones 8–9.

Q. robur
(syn. Q. pedunculata)
Common oak, English oak,
pedunculate oak
This spreading, fast-growing
and long-lived tree from Europe
has smooth brown-grey bark,
which becomes fissured with age.
The almost stalkless leaves are
dark green, up to 15cm (6in)
long, and shallowly lobed. The
acorns have long stalks. The
species thrives in drier conditions
than *Q. petraea*. H 25m (80ft),
S 20m (65ft).
Aspect Full sun.
Hardiness ✿✿✿ Zones 4–7.

Q. rubra
(syn. Q. borealis)
Red oak, northern red oak
A fast-growing deciduous species
from North America, this
develops a smooth, grey-brown
bark. The dark green leaves, up
to 20cm (8in) long, are oval and
have lobes tipped with bristles. In

autumn the leaves turn red and
red-brown before falling. H 25m
(80ft), S 20m (65ft).
Aspect Full sun or semi-shade.
Hardiness ✿✿✿ Zones 3–9.

Q. suber
Cork oak
The distinguishing feature of this
spreading, evergreen, North
African tree is its thick, corky
bark, the source of corks for wine
bottles, for which purpose the
trees were once widely planted in
Portugal. The toothed leaves are
dark green, up to 8cm (3in) long
and covered with greyish hairs
beneath. H and S 20m (65ft).
Aspect Full sun or semi-shade.
Hardiness ✿✿ Zones 8–9.

Q. X turneri
Turner's oak
This hybrid between *Q. ilex* and
Q. robur is a fast-growing,
spreading, deciduous tree, which
may be semi-evergreen in mild
areas. The dark grey to brown-
grey bark becomes fissured with
age. The dark green leaves, up to
25cm (10in) long, are shallowly
lobed. H 20–30m (65–100ft),
S 20–25m (65–80ft).
Aspect Full sun or semi-shade.
Hardiness ✿✿✿ Zones 7–9.

Q. velutina
Black oak
Originally from North America,
this fast-growing, deciduous oak
has very dark brown, almost black
bark. The elliptic, deeply lobed,
glossy leaves, up to 25cm (10in)
long, are dark green, turning
reddish-brown or yellow-brown in
autumn. H 25–30m (80–100ft),
S 25m (80ft).
Aspect Full sun or semi-shade.
Hardiness ✿✿✿ Zones 3–9.

Q. virginiana
Live oak
This spreading evergreen species
is from the south-eastern USA.
It is fast growing and has red-
brown bark. The elliptic, round-
tipped leaves, up to 12cm (5in)
long, are glossy and dark green
above and greyish beneath. It does
well in dry, acidic soil. H and
S 15m (50ft).
Aspect Full sun or semi-shade.
Hardiness ✿ Zones 8–9.

RHAMNUS
Buckthorn
There are about 125 species of
deciduous and evergreen shrubs
and trees in the genus, most
of which are found in northern
temperate regions. Most species
are thorny, and both of the
species described below can be
used as hedges.
Cultivation Grow in moisture-
retentive soil in sun. (Note that
other species have different
cultural requirements.)
Pruning Formative pruning should
aim to encourage a single, short
trunk and a balanced crown.
Some species are best grown as
multi-stemmed specimens.
Occasional pruning may be
required for the removal of
any dead, dying, diseased or
crossing branches.
Propagation Seed is the main
method of propagation, and it
should be collected when fresh.
Sow the fresh seed into a
container in an unheated
glasshouse or cold frame until
germination occurs.

R. cathartica
Common buckthorn
This dense, thorny shrub, native
to Europe, north-west Africa and
Asia, can be grown as a small tree.
It has glossy, toothed, dark green
leaves, 6–8cm (2½–3in) long,
which turn golden-yellow in
autumn. Tiny yellow-green flowers
are borne in late spring and are
followed by shiny, black berries
in autumn. It is able to withstand
a range of difficult conditions.

H 6m (20ft), 5m (16ft).
Aspect Full sun.
Hardiness ✿✿✿ Zones 3–7.

R. frangula
Alder buckthorn
This species from Europe and
northern Africa has red autumn
colour and clusters of reddish-
black berries in late summer and
autumn. It has ovate, glossy green
leaves, up to 8cm (3in) long, and
greenish flowers in spring. It is as
adaptable and tolerant as *R.
cathartica*. H and S 5m (16ft).
Aspect Full sun.
Hardiness ✿✿✿ Zones 3–7

ROBINIA
The small genus contains about
eight species (some authorities
give four, others 20) of deciduous
trees and shrubs. These fast-
growing plants, native to the USA
and Mexico, are grown for their
pretty foliage, pea-like flowers and
autumn colour. They tolerate
atmospheric pollution.
Cultivation Grow in moisture-
retentive but well-drained soil in
full sun, although plants will also
tolerate poorer, drier conditions.
Protect from cold, drying winds.
Pruning Early formative pruning
should aim to produce a clear
trunk and a balanced crown.
Occasional pruning is required
for the removal of dead, dying,
diseased or crossing branches.
Propagation Seed, winter grafting
and summer budding are the main
methods of propagation. Sow
fresh seed into a container in an
unheated glasshouse or cold frame

Rhamnus alaternus 'Argenteovariegata'

Robinia pseudoacacia 'Frisia'

until germination occurs. Winter grafting and summer budding are done using seedling robinias.

R. x ambigua 'Bella Rosea'
(syn. R. x ambigua 'Bella-rosea', R. x ambigua 'Bellarosea')
This strongly growing cultivar, developed from a hybrid between R. pseudoacacia and R. viscosa, is a small, elegant tree, bearing large racemes of pale pink, pea-like flowers in early summer. H 12m (40ft), S 7m (23ft).
Aspect Full sun.
Hardiness ✤✤✤ Zones 3–5.

R. x ambigua 'Idaho'
(syn. R. x ambigua 'Idahoensis', R. 'Idaho')
This cultivar is widely planted in the western states of the USA. It is similar to 'Bella Rosea' but has fragrant, lavender-pink flowers. H 12m (40ft), S 10m (33ft).
Aspect Full sun.
Hardiness ✤✤✤ (borderline) Zones 3–5.

R. x margaretta 'Pink Cascade'
(syn. R. x margaretta 'Casque Rouge', R. x slavinii 'Pink Cascade')
A fast-growing form, which develops into a large, suckering shrub or small tree, this bears masses of purple-pink, pea-like flowers. H and S 10m (33ft).
Aspect Full sun.
Hardiness ✤✤✤ Zones 3–5.

R. pseudoacacia
False acacia, black locust, locust
This suckering and thorny but broadly columnar tree has deeply furrowed bark. The feathery green, pinnate leaves, up to 30cm (12in) long, have up to 23 leaflets. In warm summers fragrant white flowers are borne in long racemes, followed by dark brown seedpods. H 25m (80ft), S 15m (50ft).
Named varieties The popular 'Frisia' has butter-yellow leaves in spring and summer. In warm areas the leaves fade to yellow-green.
'Pyramidalis' (syn. 'Fastigiata'), a fastigiate form with a conical habit and thornless branches, has smaller flowers than 'Frisia'.
Aspect Full sun.
Hardiness ✤✤✤ Zones 4–8.

Roystonia oleracea

R. x slavinii 'Hillieri'
This elegant small tree, which is best planted in a sheltered spot, is an excellent choice for a small garden. It has slightly arching branches and in early summer bears clusters of lilac-pink, slightly scented flowers. H 15m (50ft), S 10m (33ft).
Aspect Full sun.
Hardiness ✤✤✤ Zones 5–8.

R. x slavinii 'Purple Robe'
(syn. R. pseudoacacia 'Purple Robe')
This tree requires a sheltered position, where it will not be buffeted by strong winds. New growth is flushed with purple in spring, and clusters of violet-purple flowers are borne in summer. H 15m (50ft), S 10m (33ft).
Aspect Full sun.
Hardiness ✤✤✤ Zones 5–8.

ROYSTONEA
Royal palm
The genus contains ten to twelve species of fast-growing, single-stemmed palms, which are found throughout the Caribbean islands and neighbouring mainlands. The upright, usually smooth grey trunks may be swollen at the base or in the centre of mature plants. Small specimens can be grown in containers in conservatories.
Cultivation Outdoors, grow in fertile, moisture-retentive but well-drained soil in sun.
Pruning Like most palms, little pruning is required apart from the occasional cosmetic removal of dead or dying leaves and spent flower clusters during early summer.
Propagation Seed is the easiest method of propagation and should be collected when fresh and sown into a container in a heated glasshouse in a humid environment at 29°C (84°F) until germination occurs.

R. oleracea
This species is widely grown in the tropics. It is a tall, slender plant with a narrow, silver trunk, the top quarter of which is green, although this is scarcely visible from the ground. The flattish, arching fronds, often up to 4m (12ft) long, consist of many narrow, dark green leaflets. H 40m (130ft), S 10m (33ft).
Aspect Full sun.
Hardiness (Min. 15°C/59°F) Zone 11.

R. regia
Cuban royal palm
A beautiful and graceful palm from Cuba, this has a silver-coloured trunk, of which the top quarter is bright green. The long leaves, up to 5m (16ft) long, consist of numerous green leaflets arranged in several ranks, giving the fronds a spiky appearance. In summer panicles, up to 1m (3ft) long, of white flowers are borne, followed by large clusters of orange, marble-like fruits. H 30m (100ft), S 10m (33ft).
Aspect Full sun.
Hardiness (Min. 15°C/59°F) Zone 11.

SABAL
Palmetto
The 14 species of palm, which may be single-stemmed or stemless, are found in southern North America, Central America and the West Indies. They are tender, but in warm areas they make fine specimen trees. Small plants can be grown in containers and kept under glass.
Cultivation Outdoors, grow in fertile, moisture-retentive but well-drained soil in sun.
Pruning Pruning is only required to remove dead leaves and spent flower clusters during early summer.

Sabal mexicana

Salix babylonica

Propagation Seed is the easiest method of propagation and should be collected when fresh and be sown into a container in a heated glasshouse in a humid environment at 29°C (84°F) until germination occurs.

S. mexicana
(syn. *S. guatemalensis*, *S. texana*)
Texas palmetto
When young, this is a beautiful palm, but as it ages it can develop a sloping, sagging trunk and the stems of the lower branches tend to remain attached for a long period, giving an untidy appearance. The bright green or yellow-green leaves, up to 1m (3ft) long, are semicircular and deeply divided to about halfway. Long panicles of creamy-white flowers are borne above the foliage in late summer. H 18m (60ft), S 4m (12ft).
Aspect Full sun.
Hardiness (Min. 10–13°C/ 50–5°F) Zones 8–10.

S. minor
Dwarf palmetto, bush palmetto, scrub palmetto
The species is often found in swampy ground in the southern USA, where it grows as an under-storey plant, developing into thickets. The stems are usually prostrate, although clear-trunk specimens occasionally occur. The fan-shaped leaves, up to 1.5m (5ft) across, are blue-green and divided into numerous spiky lobes for about two-thirds of the leaf. In summer erect panicles, up to

1.8m (6ft) long, of cream flowers are produced and are followed by blackish fruits. H 1.8m (6ft), S 3m (10ft).
Aspect Full sun.
Hardiness (Min. 3–5°C/ 37–41°F) Zones 7–11.

S. palmetto
Cabbage palmetto, common blue palmetto
This palm, which is found in swampy ground in the southern states of the USA, has a rough, erect stem. The fan-shaped leaves, to 1.8m (6ft) across, are dark green and divided into pointed lobes with thread-like filaments between them. In summer there are panicles of cream flowers. H 30m (100ft), S 7m (23ft).
Aspect Full sun to light shade.
Hardiness (Min. 5–7°C/ 41–5°F) Zones 8–11.

SALIX
Willow, osier, sallow
The 300 or so species in this genus are mostly deciduous trees and shrubs, known especially for their catkins and their thirst for water. Larger species are suitable only for large gardens, where the vigorous, questing roots can't damage drains or foundations. Smaller species make attractive focal points, and shrubby species are ideal in mixed borders.
Cultivation Grow in moisture-retentive but well-drained soil in sun. They do not do well in chalky conditions. Willows are often pollarded.

Pruning Formative pruning should aim to produce a clear trunk and a balanced crown. Most willows can be pollarded and this should be done on a regular three-year cycle during winter. Occasional pruning is required to remove dead, dying, diseased or crossing branches.
Propagation Seed should be collected when fresh and sown into a container in an unheated glasshouse or cold frame until germination occurs. Softwood cuttings are taken during summer, dipped in a rooting hormone and placed in a humid environment until rooting occurs. Hardwood cuttings can be taken in winter and then be lifted and transplanted the following spring.

S. alba
White willow
This fast-growing, vigorous tree, native to Europe, northern Africa and Asia, is often found near rivers and in water meadows. It has semi-pendulous branches and pinkish-grey to grey-brown shoots. The catkins, male ones up to 5cm (2in) long, are yellow and appear in spring. The slender leaves, up to 10cm (4in) long, are covered with silvery hairs when young, giving the plant its characteristic silver-white appearance. H 20–25m (65–80ft), S 10–m (33ft).
Named varieties *S. alba* var. *vitellina* 'Britzensis' (scarlet willow, coral bark willow) has reddish-orange winter stems. The best colour appears on shoots less than two seasons old, so prune hard back in early spring in alternate years.
Aspect Full sun.
Hardiness ✸✸✸ Zones 2–8.

S. babylonica
Chinese weeping willow
This graceful tree from northern China often grows near rivers, where the long, pendent, green-brown shoots cascade towards the water. The narrow green leaves, up to 10cm (4in) long, are grey-green beneath. Silver-green catkins, male ones up to 5cm (2in) long, appear in spring. H and S 12m (40ft).
Named varieties *S. babylonica* var. *pekinensis* 'Tortuosa' (syn. *S. matsudana* 'Tortuosa'; dragon's claw willow) has a more upright habit. The twisted shoots create a striking silhouette in winter. H 15m (50ft), S 8m (26ft).
Aspect Full sun.
Hardiness ✸✸✸ Zones 6–8.

S. caprea
Goat willow, pussy willow, great sallow
Native to Europe and north-eastern Asia, this tree is grown for its attractive spring catkins: the female catkins are the pretty, silvery flowers (pussy willow) beloved of children and flower arrangers; the yellow-green male catkins are longer and borne early in the year, sometimes in midwinter. The leaves, up to 12cm (5in) long, are dark green above and greyish beneath. The bare winter stems are yellow-purple. It is too straggly for most gardens but provides fast-growing shelter in a new garden. Unlike most willows, this will tolerate dryish ground. H 8–10m (26–33ft), S 4–6m (14–20ft).
Aspect Full sun.
Hardiness ✸✸✸ Zones 4–8.

Salix daphnoides

S. daphnoides
Violet willow
This small, conical tree from Europe and Central Asia is upright at first, spreading with age. The elliptic leaves, up to 12cm (5in) long, are dark green above and blue-green beneath. The greyish catkins, up to 4cm (1½in) long, are borne in late winter to early spring on the bare, purplish branches, which in winter have a whitish bloom. The stems are even more colourful if they are cut hard back every two years. H 8m (26ft), S 5–6m (16–20ft). Aspect Full sun. Hardiness ❊❊❊ Zones 5–8.

S. x sepulcralis
Weeping willow
This large hybrid is similar to S. babylonica, although it has a slightly less weeping habit. Its catkins are similar to those of S. alba. H and S 20m (65ft). Named varieties S. x sepulcralis var. chrysocoma (syn. S. alba 'Tristis'; golden weeping willow) has strongly arching, golden-yellow stems. In summer the stems are clothed with narrow, bright green leaves, up to 12cm (5in) long.

'Erythroflexuosa' has twisted orange and yellow stems. Both can be grown as attractive pollards or coppiced trees. Aspect Full sun. Hardiness ❊❊❊ Zones 6–8.

SASSAFRAS
The three deciduous species in the genus have aromatic foliage. They are native to China, Taiwan and North America and are grown as specimen trees for their attractive habit, small spring flowers and good autumn colour. Cultivation Grow in moisture-retentive but well-drained, acidic soil in sun. Provide shelter from cold winds. Remove suckers as soon as they appear. Pruning Formative pruning should produce a clear trunk and a balanced crown. Prune occasionally to remove dead, dying, diseased or crossing branches. Propagation Seed and natural layers or suckers are the main methods of propagation. Sow fresh seed into a container in an unheated glasshouse or cold frame until

germination occurs. Sassafras will often produce natural layers or suckers that can be lifted and removed from the parent plant during late winter or early spring.

S. albidum
This medium-sized, often suckering tree from North America has an upright trunk with grey, fissured bark. The dark green leaves, up to 15cm (6in) long, have three deep lobes and turn yellow, orange and purple in autumn; the colours are best after hot summers. H 20–25m (65–80ft), S 10–15m (33–50ft). Aspect Full sun or semi-shade. Hardiness ❊❊❊ Zones 4–9.

SCHEFFLERA
This large genus contains some 700 species of evergreen trees, shrubs and climbers. They are mostly native to South-east Asia and the islands of the Pacific and are grown for their attractive, much-divided palmate leaves. They are tender plants, which are often grown as houseplants. Cultivation Outdoors, grow in fertile, moisture-retentive but well-drained soil in shade. Protect from cold, drying winds. Pruning Formative pruning should encourage a clear trunk and a balanced crown. Prune occasionally to remove dead, dying, diseased or crossing branches. Propagation Softwood cuttings to be taken during early summer and should be dipped in a rooting hormone and placed in a frost-free, humid environment until they root.

S. actinophylla
(syn. Brassaia actinophylla)
Australian ivy palm, octopus tree, umbrella tree
In its native New Guinea and north-eastern Australia this species can be invasive. It has an upright habit. The large, glossy, bright green leaves, up to 30cm (12in) across, have 7–16 oval leaflets and are borne in dense clusters, giving the stems a tufted appearance. In spring and summer panicles, up to 80cm (32in) long, of pink to red flowers are borne at the tips of the branches, followed by small clusters of red berries.

Schefflera arboricola

H 12m (40ft), S 6m (20ft). Aspect Light shade to full sun. Hardiness (Min. 13°C/55°F) Zones 9–12.

S. elegantissima
(syn. Aralia elegantissima, Dizygotheca elegantissima)
False aralia
Small specimens of this New Caledonian plant are popular as houseplants for the long, delicate leaflets. In the wild these erect trees have leaves up to 40cm (16in) long, each deeply divided into 7–11 narrow leaflets, dark green above and brown-green beneath, with white midribs. Umbels, up to 30cm (12in) long, of yellow-green flowers are borne in autumn and early winter and are followed by round black fruits. H 15m (50ft), S 3m (10ft). Aspect Light shade to full sun. Hardiness (Min. 13–15°C/55–9°F) Zones 9–12.

SCIADOPITYS
Japanese umbrella pine
The only species is the genus, which is native to Japan and is a generally slow-growing, evergreen conifer with a graceful habit and attractive foliage and cones. It can be grown as a specimen. Cultivation Grow in moisture-retentive but well-drained, neutral to acidic soil in sun. Train the leading stem to give an upright shape. Pruning Early formative pruning should aim to produce a clear trunk and a balanced crown, while

tipping the lateral branches of young trees will encourage a denser crown. Propagation Semi-ripe and softwood cuttings can be rooted during summer and should be dipped in a rooting hormone and placed in a humid environment until rooting occurs.

S. verticillata
This distinctive conifer has a strongly conical habit and slender, glossy, dark green leaves, yellow-green beneath and up to 12cm (5in) long, which are borne in whorls of 15–25 along the stems. The leaves are often fused in pairs. The bark is red-brown and peels in ribbons. Small male cones are borne in clusters, but the large female cones, up to 8cm (3in) long, are borne singly. H 20m (65ft), S 8m (26ft). Aspect Full sun or semi-shade. Hardiness ❊❊❊ Zones 5–7.

Sciadopitys verticillata

Sequoiadendron giganteum

SEQUOIA
Coast redwood, Californian redwood

The single species in the genus is a fast-growing, evergreen conifer, native to California and Oregon. These trees are among the tallest in the world. They do best in areas with moist, cool summers, when they can be used as handsome specimens. They tolerate pollution well.
Cultivation Grow in fertile, moisture-retentive but well-drained soil in sun or semi-shade. This is one of the few conifers that will re-shoot from old wood.
Pruning Early formative pruning should aim to produce a clear trunk and a balanced crown, while tipping the lateral branches of young trees will encourage a denser crown.

Propagation Seed is the easiest method of propagation. Sow fresh seed into a container in an unheated glasshouse or cold frame until germination occurs.

S. sempervirens
This columnar conifer has horizontal or slightly downturned branches and deeply ridged, red-brown bark. The dark green leaves, up to 2cm (½in) long, are borne in pairs, pointing forwards along the shoots. Cones, up to 4cm (1½in) long, ripen to brown. H 35m (115ft), S 10m (33ft). Named varieties 'Cantab' is a fast-growing form with needles that are adpressed (flattened against the stem), light green when young and dark when older.
Aspect Full sun or semi-shade.
Hardiness ❋❋❋ Zones 7–9.

SEQUOIADENDRON
Sierra redwood, giant redwood, wellingtonia

The single species is an evergreen conifer from California, which makes a striking specimen, attaining heights of 80m (260ft) or more in the wild (less in gardens). It has a more columnar habit than the closely related *Sequoia sempervirens* and prefers a drier climate.
Cultivation Grow in fertile, moisture-retentive but well-drained soil.
Pruning Early formative pruning should aim to produce a clear trunk and a balanced crown, while tipping the lateral branches of young trees will encourage a denser crown.
Propagation Seed is the easiest method of propagation and should be collected when fresh and sown into a container in an unheated glasshouse or cold frame until germination occurs. Semi-ripe and softwood cuttings can be taken during summer and should be dipped in a rooting hormone and placed in a humid environment until rooting occurs.

S. giganteum
This fast-growing redwood is distinguished by its massive trunk, covered with thick, spongy red-brown bark. The long branches often sweep down to the ground. The tiny pointed leaves are scale-like and blue-green. H 30m (100ft), S 10m (33ft). Named varieties 'Glaucum' is a bold narrowly conical form with intense blue-green foliage.
Aspect Full sun.
Hardiness ❋❋❋ Zones 6–8.

SOPHORA
The 50 or so species in the genus are evergreen and deciduous trees and shrubs. They have attractive leaves and fragrant flowers and can be successfully grown as specimen plants.
Cultivation Grow in well-drained soil in sun.
Pruning Early formative pruning should aim to produce a clear trunk and a balanced crown.
Propagation Seed, winter grafting and summer budding are the main methods of propagation. Seed

should be collected when fresh and sown into a container in an unheated glasshouse or cold frame until germination occurs. Winter grafting and summer budding can be carried out using seedling rowans or whitebeams.

S. japonica
Japanese pagoda tree
This graceful deciduous tree from China and Korea is not dissimilar to *Robinia pseudoacacia*, but it is thornless and smaller. The dark green leaves, up to 25cm (10in) long, are divided into up to 17 narrow leaflets, which turn yellow in autumn. In late summer to early autumn pea-like, fragrant, white flowers are borne in panicles. H 30m (100ft), S 20m (65ft).
Named varieties The cultivar 'Regent' is popular in the USA for its speed of growth, good summer and autumn foliage and ability to flower from a young age. 'Violacea' has white flowers, flushed with rose-violet, which are borne amid the green, fern-like foliage in early autumn.
Aspect Full sun or semi-shade.
Hardiness ❋❋❋ Zones 3–9.

SORBUS
Mountain ash
The genus contains about 100 species of deciduous trees and shrubs, which are found throughout the northern hemisphere. These are some of the finest ornamental trees for

Sequoia sempervirens

small gardens, providing an attractive habit together with flowers, variously coloured berries and good autumn foliage.
Cultivation Grow in fertile, moisture-retentive but well-drained soil in sun or light shade. Rowans prefer moister soil than whitebeams do.
Pruning Early formative pruning should aim to produce a clear trunk and a balanced crown. Fireblight can be a problem and any infected branches should be removed as soon as symptoms appear back to healthy tissue.
Propagation Seed, winter grafting and summer budding are the most common methods of propagation. Seed should be collected when fresh and sown into a container in a cold frame until germination occurs. Winter grafting and summer budding are done using seedling rowans or whitebeams.

S. alnifolia
Korean mountain ash, alder whitebeam
This medium-sized tree, native to eastern Asia, is broadly conical. It has toothed, dark green leaves, up to 10cm (4in) long, which turn yellow-orange and purple in autumn. Dense clusters, up to 8cm (3in) across, of small white flowers are borne in spring and are followed by pretty dark pink to red berries, up to 1cm (⅓in) across. H 20m (65ft), S 10m (33ft).

Sophora microphylla

Named varieties 'Skyline' has an upright habit and orange-yellow autumn colours.
Aspect Full sun or semi-shade.
Hardiness ❋❋❋ Zone 5.

S. aria
Whitebeam
A broadly columnar tree from Europe, this has toothed, glossy, dark green leaves, up to 12cm (5in) long, which are covered with silver-white hairs on the undersides and turn yellow in autumn. In late spring clusters, up to 8cm (3in) across, of white flowers are borne, and these are followed by dark red berries, up to 1cm (⅓in) across. H 15–20m (50–65ft), S 8–10m (26–33ft).
Aspect Full sun or semi-shade.
Hardiness ❋❋❋ Zone 5.

S. aucuparia
Common mountain ash, rowan
A small tree from Europe, this species has ferny, dark green leaves, 20cm (8in) long, which have 9–15 sharply toothed leaflets. The leaves turn red or yellowish in autumn. Clusters, up to 12cm (5in) across, of white flowers are borne in spring and are followed by orange-red berries. H 15m (50ft), S 7–8m (23–26ft).
Named varieties 'Cardinal Royal' is an upright form with masses of beautiful scarlet berries, which persist long into winter.
Aspect Full sun or semi-shade.
Hardiness ❋❋❋ Zones 3–6.

Sorbus aucuparia

S. cashmiriana
Kashmir rowan
This is a good tree or large shrub for a small garden. It is native to the western Himalayas, has a spreading habit and dark green, pinnate leaves, up to 20cm (8in) long and with 17–21 leaflets. In spring it bears clusters, up to 12cm (5in) across, of pink or white flowers, and these are followed by white berries. The berries remain on the tree long after the leaves have fallen. H 8m (26ft), S 5–7m (16–23ft).
Aspect Full sun or semi-shade.
Hardiness ❋❋❋ Zone 4.

S. commixta
(syn. S. discolor, S. reflexipetala)
Scarlet rowan
A broadly conical tree, this species from Japan and Korea has dark green, pinnate leaves, up to 20cm (8in) long and consisting of 17 leaflets. The leaves turn yellow-red and purple in autumn. In late spring the tree bears clusters, up to 15cm (6in) across, of creamy-white flowers, which are followed by bright orange-red berries. H 10m (33ft), S 5–7m (16–23ft).
Aspect Full sun or semi-shade.
Hardiness ❋❋❋ Zone 6.

S. folgneri
Chinese whitebeam
Native to China, this graceful if rather variable small garden tree

has toothed, dark green leaves, white beneath and up to 10cm (4in) long. White flowers are borne in dense clusters, to 10cm (4in) across, in spring and are followed by clusters of dark red or purple-red berries. H and S 8m (26ft).
Named varieties 'Lemon Drop' has orange-yellow berries and brownish-yellow autumn colour.
Aspect Full sun or semi-shade.
Hardiness ❋❋❋ Zone 6.

S. hupehensis
(syn. S. glabrescens)
Hubei rowan
This spectacular, small, round-headed tree from China has pinnate, blue-green leaves, up to 15cm (6in) long and with up to 15 leaflets. The leaves turn vivid red in autumn. In late spring pyramidal clusters, to 12cm (5in) across, of white flowers are borne and are followed by small white, occasionally pink-tinged, berries. H 8–12m (26–40ft), S 8m (26ft).
Named varieties 'Coral Fire' has reddish stems, scarlet berries and good autumn colour.
'Pink Pagoda' (syn. 'November Pink') has pink-tinged fruits, which slowly whiten in autumn before turning pink and persisting well into winter.
Aspect Full sun or semi-shade.
Hardiness ❋❋❋ Zone 6.

Sorbus vilmorinii

S. intermedia
Swedish whitebeam
A neat, round-headed tree, this whitebeam, which is native to north-western Europe, has toothed, glossy, dark green leaves, up to 12cm (5in) long, which are covered with grey-white hairs on the undersides. Dense clusters, up to 12cm (5in) across, of white flowers are borne in late spring and are followed by oval, bright red berries. H and S 12m (40ft).
Aspect Full sun or semi-shade.
Hardiness ✹✹✹ Zone 5.

S. 'Joseph Rock'
This widely planted tree has bright green, pinnate leaves, up to 15cm (6in) long, with 15–19 leaflets, which turn red, orange, purple and copper in autumn. White flowers are borne in clusters, up to 10cm (4in) across, in late spring, and these are followed by masses of yellow berries, which turn bright orange-yellow. It is susceptible to fireblight. H 10m (33ft), S 7m (23ft).
Aspect Full sun or semi-shade.
Hardiness ✹✹✹ Zones 3–6.

S. megalocarpa
A small garden tree or large shrub, this species from China has a spreading habit. The toothed, dark green leaves, up to 25cm (10in) long, are reddish as they emerge in spring and again in autumn. Clusters, up to 15cm (6in) across, of highly pungent, creamy-white flowers are borne in early spring and are followed in

late summer by edible, yellow-brown fruits. H 8m (26ft), S 10m (33ft).
Aspect Semi-shade.
Hardiness ✹✹✹ Zone 6.

S. 'Sunshine'
This small cultivar has dark green, pinnate leaves, each with 14–18 leaflets, which turn vivid orange and yellow in autumn. Large clusters of golden-yellow berries follow the white flowers which appear in spring. H 10m (33ft), S 7m (23ft).
Aspect Full sun or semi-shade.
Hardiness ✹✹✹ Zones 3–6.

S. thibetica
A broadly conical tree from south-western China, this has dark green leaves, up to 12cm (5in) long, which are covered with white hairs when they first emerge, remaining hairy on the undersides. White flowers are borne in clusters, up to 6cm (2½in) across, in late spring and are followed by greenish berries. H 20m (65ft), S 15m (50ft). Named varieties 'John Mitchell', an attractive small tree, has large green leaves, silvery on the underside. Small, creamy-white flowers are followed by clusters of large, orange-yellow berries. H and S 15m (50ft).
Aspect Full sun or semi-shade.
Hardiness ✹✹✹ Zone 5.

S. vilmorinii
Vilmorin's rowan
This outstandingly beautiful small garden tree, which is native

to south-western China, has low, spreading branches. The glossy, dark green, pinnate leaves, up to 15cm (6in) long, have 11–31 leaflets. Creamy-white flowers are borne in clusters, up to 10cm (4in) across, from late spring to early summer and are followed by dark red fruits. H and S 5–8m (16–26ft).
Aspect Full sun or semi-shade.
Hardiness ✹✹✹ Zone 5.

S. 'Wilfred Fox'
This upright tree has glossy, dark green leaves, up to 12cm (5in) long, which are covered with white hairs beneath. The white flowers, borne in clusters, up to 10cm (4in) across, in late spring, are followed by red-flushed, yellowish berries. H 12–15m (40–50ft), S 10–12m (33–40ft).
Aspect Full sun or semi-shade.
Hardiness ✹✹✹ Zone 5.

SPATHODEA
African tulip tree
The single species in the genus is a usually evergreen tree from tropical Africa. It is tender and needs to be grown under glass where the temperature falls below 13°C (55°F). In warm areas it can be grown as a specimen tree.
Cultivation Grow in fertile, moisture-retentive soil in full sun.
Pruning Formative pruning should produce a clear trunk and a balanced crown. Prune dead, diseased or crossed branches.
Propagation Sow fresh seed in a pot at 18–24°C (64–75°F) in spring, or air-layer in summer.

S. campanulata
The fast-growing species is grown for its bright red, azalea-like flowers, which are borne in large clusters in spring and autumn. The glossy, dark green, pinnate leaves, up to 45cm (18in) long, have 9–19 leaflets, arranged in pairs down a central stem. The quick growth produces brittle branches, which are easily damaged. H 25m (80ft), S 18m (60ft).
Aspect Full sun.
Hardiness (Min. 13–15°C/ 55–9°F) Zones 10–12.

STAPHYLEA
Bladdernut
There are 11 species of deciduous shrubs and small trees in the genus, which are found in temperate areas of the northern hemisphere. They can be used in shrub borders and woodland gardens.
Cultivation Grow in moisture-retentive but well-drained soil in sun or semi-shade.
Pruning Early formative pruning should aim to produce a clear trunk and a balanced crown. Occasional pruning is required for the removal of dead, dying, diseased or crossing branches.
Propagation Collect fresh seed and sow in a pot in an unheated glasshouse or cold frame. Softwood cuttings are taken during summer and placed in a humid environment until rooting occurs. Bladdernuts will often produce natural layers or suckers that can be lifted and removed from the parent plant during late winter or early spring.

Spathodea campanulata

Staphylea trifolia

Stewartia pseudocamellia

S. holocarpa
Chinese bladdernut
This spreading shrub or small tree has blue-green leaves with three leaflets, up to 10cm (4in) long. In late spring white to pink bell-shaped flowers, up to 15mm (½in) long, are borne in clusters and are followed by greenish fruits, up to 5cm (2in) long. H 10m (33ft), S 6m (20ft).
Named varieties 'Rosea' is a large, shrub-like plant, which can be easily trained to grow as a small standard tree. In spring it has beautiful dangling clusters of pale pink flowers. Its blue-green leaves are tinged with bronze in spring and pale yellow in autumn.
Aspect Full sun or semi-shade.
Hardiness ✽✽✽ Zone 6.

STEWARTIA
(syn. Stuartia)
The 15–20 species in the genus are related to *Camellia*. They are deciduous and evergreen trees and shrubs from eastern Asia and the south-eastern USA, grown for their attractive foliage and flowers. They make good specimen trees.
Cultivation Grow in fertile, moisture-retentive but well-drained, neutral to acidic soil in full sun or semi-shade.
Pruning Formative pruning should aim to produce a clear trunk and a balanced crown. Prune occasionally to remove dead, dying, diseased or crossing branches.
Propagation Collect fresh seed and sow in a pot in an unheated glasshouse or cold frame. Take softwood cuttings in summer.

Winter grafting on to seedlings is practised on those that are hard to root.

S. malacodendron
Silky camellia
This small, deciduous tree makes a lovely garden tree. The glossy, dark green, ovate leaves are up to 10cm (4in) long, toothed and covered with hairs on the undersides; they turn orange-yellow in autumn. In midsummer white flowers, streaked and centred with purple, up to 10cm (4in) across, are borne along the stems. H 6–7m (20–23ft), S 6m (20ft).
Aspect Semi-shade.
Hardiness ✽✽ Zones 6–9.

S. monadelpha
Tall stewartia
This deciduous tree has a broadly columnar habit, which spreads with age, and attractive grey and red-orange, peeling bark. The dark green, ovate leaves, up to 10cm (4in) long, are glossy and toothed, turning orange and red in autumn. Yellow-centred, white flowers, up to 4cm (1½in) across, are borne in summer. H 25m (80ft), S 20m (65ft).
Aspect Semi-shade.
Hardiness ✽✽✽ Zones 5–8

S. pseudocamellia
Japanese stewartia
This small, deciduous tree from Japan has a tight, upright habit. In autumn the toothed, dark green leaves turn russet-orange and the winter bark is a brownish silver and green. In summer white,

yellow-centred flowers, up to 6cm (2½in) across, are produced in abundance. H 20m (65ft), S 8–10m (26–33ft).
Named varieties The semi-weeping form 'Cascade' has long, arching shoots.
Plants in Koreana Group (syn. *S. koreana*, *S. pseudocamellia* var. *koreana*; Korean stewartia) are grown for their large flowers, which open wide in late summer. They have an upright habit and silver, green and brown bark. In autumn the dark green leaves turn orange-yellow.
Aspect Semi-shade.
Hardiness ✽✽✽ Zones 5–8.

S. serrata
This small deciduous tree has orange-brown bark and reddish shoots. The leaves, up to 8cm (3in) long, turn orange-yellow in autumn. In early summer purple-tinged, white flowers, up to 6cm (2½in) across and with yellow centres, are borne singly on branches. H 4m (12ft), S 3m (10ft).
Aspect Semi-shade.
Hardiness ✽✽ Zone 6.

S. sinensis
(syn. S. gemmata)
Chinese stewartia
This small deciduous tree has peeling reddish-brown bark. The dark green leaves, up to 10cm (4in) long, turn crimson in autumn. Fragrant white flowers, to 5cm (2in) across, are borne singly in midsummer. H 20m (65ft), S 5m (16ft).
Aspect Full sun or semi-shade.
Hardiness ✽✽✽ Zones 5–7.

S. 'Skyrocket'
(syn. S. x henryae)
This fast-growing hybrid between *S. monadelpha* and *S. pseudocamellia* has flaking bark. The dark green leaves turn orange-yellow in autumn, and yellow-centred, white flowers are borne in midsummer. H 25m (80ft), S 8m (26ft).
Aspect Semi-shade.
Hardiness ✽✽✽ Zones 5–8.

STYRAX
Snowbell, silverballs
This genus comprises 100 or so species of evergreen and deciduous shrubs and trees grown

for their lovely spring and summer flowers. They do best in a woodland setting.
Cultivation Grow in fertile, moisture-retentive but well-drained, neutral to acidic soil in sun or semi-shade.
Pruning Formative pruning should produce a clear trunk and a balanced crown. Prune occasionally to remove dead, dying, diseased or crossing branches.
Propagation Sow fresh seed in a pot in an unheated glasshouse or cold frame until germination occurs. Softwood cuttings are taken during summer. Winter grafting on to seedling snowbell trees can also be done.

S. japonicus
Japanese snowbell
This small, deciduous garden tree has wide-spreading branches with drooping tips. The glossy green leaves, up to 10cm (4in) long, turn yellow or red in autumn. In early summer clusters of white, yellow-centred flowers hang from the undersides of the branches. H 10m (33ft), S 8m (26ft).
Named varieties Benibana Group 'Pink Chimes' has an upright habit and pink flowers.
'Crystal' is an upright, vigorous form with dark purple-green foliage and white flowers, faintly tinted purple.
'Emerald Pagoda' has large white, fragrant flowers, an attractive vase-shaped habit and good heat tolerance.
Aspect Full sun or semi-shade.
Hardiness ✽✽✽ Zones 5–8.

Styrax japonicus

SYZYGIUM

There are about 500 species of evergreen trees and shrubs in the genus. They are closely related to myrtles and have aromatic foliage. The most widely grown member of the genus is *S. aromaticum* (clove). They are tender plants, mostly native to tropical areas of South-east Asia and Australasia, where they can be grown in mixed borders or, in cold areas, in containers under glass.
Cultivation Outdoors, grow in moisture-retentive but well-drained soil in sun or semi-shade.
Pruning Early formative pruning should aim to encourage a clear trunk and a balanced crown. Occasional pruning is required for the removal of dead, dying, diseased, or crossing branches.
Propagation Sow fresh seed in a pot in a heated glasshouse in a frost-free and humid environment. Low branches can also be layered.

S. pycnanthum
Wild rose

This dainty, highly ornamental tree from Java, Sumatra and Borneo has glossy green leaves and dense clusters of pink flowers in spring and occasionally also in autumn. The flowers are followed by pale pink or purple fruits.
H 15m (50ft), S 10m (33ft).
Aspect Full sun.
Hardiness ✤ Zones 10–12.

TABEBUIA

This genus of evergreen and deciduous trees includes about 100 species, which are found in the West Indies and in Central and South America. They are grown for their attractive foliage and the clusters of bell-shaped flowers that appear on mature trees. They are tender plants, suitable for specimen trees or for growing in a mixed border in mild areas or in containers under glass.

Cultivation Outdoors, grow in fertile, moisture-retentive but well-drained soil in sun.
Pruning Formative pruning should aim to encourage a clear trunk and a balanced crown. Occasional pruning is required for the removal of dead, dying, diseased, or crossing branches.
Propagation Sow fresh seed into a container in a heated glasshouse until germination occurs.

T. chrysantha

This fast-growing, generally deciduous tree from Central America is widely grown in the tropics. The palmate green leaves, up to 18cm (7in) long, are mid-green and covered with hairs beneath. In spring and throughout the season large clusters of yellow, azalea-like flowers are produced. H 30m (100ft), S 20m (65ft).
Aspect Full sun.
Hardiness (Min. 8°C/46°F) Zones 10–12.

T. heterophylla
White cedar, pink trumpet flower

This wonderful, fast-growing landscape tree from Cuba and Puerto Rico is well adapted to dry soils. The flowers, up to 8cm (3in) long, can vary in colour from rosy-pink to pale pink or white, but all have a pink throat. Flowering usually follows rain, followed by a period of drought, at which point the tapered, glossy green leaves fall and the flowers open. H 15m (50ft), S 8m (26ft).
Aspect Full sun.
Hardiness (Min. 10–15°C/ 50–9°F) Zones 10–12.

T. impetignosa

This species from Central and South America is the least drought-tolerant species in the genus, needing moist, fertile soil to do prosper. In spring it produces a spectacular display of flowers. The dense clusters of spectacular, trumpet-shaped dark pink flowers are borne before the leaves and continue until the leaves emerge. H 10m (33ft), S 8m (26ft).
Aspect Full sun.
Hardiness (Min. 8°C/46°F) Zones 9–11.

Syzygium aromaticum

T. rosea
(syn. T. pentaphylla)
Pink poui, pink tecoma, rosy trumpet tree

This vigorous tree, which is native to Central America, has pink, yellow-throated flowers, produced in great numbers in spring on almost leafless branches. The lower branches are often shed, leaving a clear trunk. H 25m (80ft), S 10m (33ft).
Aspect Full sun.
Hardiness (Min. 10–15°C/ 50–9°F) Zones 10–12.

TAXODIUM
Bald cypress

The genus contains two to three species of deciduous or semi-evergreen coniferous trees from the USA and Central America. When grown in wet ground they produce pneumatophores (hollow tubes known as 'knees'), which allow the exchange of oxygen and carbon dioxide in times of flooding or when the roots are below water level. They make handsome specimen trees.
Cultivation Grow in moist, acidic soil in sun or semi-shade.
Pruning Formative pruning should aim to produce a clear trunk and a balanced crown, while tipping the lateral branches of young trees will encourage a denser crown. Occasional pruning may be required to remove dead, dying, diseased or crossing branches.

Taxodium distichum

Propagation Seed is the easiest method of propagation. Collect it when it is fresh and sow into a container in an unheated glasshouse or cold frame until germination occurs. Softwood cuttings can be taken during summer and should be dipped in a rooting hormone and placed in a humid environment until rooting occurs.

T. distichum
Swamp cypress
This slow- to medium-growing tree is native to the south-eastern USA. It is found growing in wet ground near, on or even in rivers and swamps. The sturdy trunk is wide and fluted at the base in order to withstand the force of moving water. Young trees are conical, and they develop flat tops with age. The pale green, needle-like foliage turns rusty brown in autumn before falling. H 20–40m (65–130ft), S 6–9m (20–30ft).
Named varieties The naturally occurring form *T. distichum* var. *imbricarium* (syn. *T. ascendens*) (pond cypress) is one of the most widely seen trees in the South Georgia swamps and Florida Everglades. A slow-growing tree when grown in water, it has narrow, needle-like, slightly twisted foliage. When it is growing in water the tree produces pneumatophores, but in ordinary soil these are rarer. The tops of the trees become flatter with age. H 20m (65ft), S 9m (30ft).

Taxus baccata

T. distichum var. *imbricatum* 'Nutans' has a conical habit and twisted stems, and the foliage weeps slightly on the branches. **Aspect** Full sun. **Hardiness** ✽✽✽ Zones 4–11.

TAXUS
There are ten species of evergreen coniferous shrubs and trees in the genus, mainly from northern temperate areas. They are fairly slow growing, but are highly adaptable plants, suitable for use as small, under-storey garden trees, as informal screens or formal hedges or as specimens.

They are unusual among conifers in that they will re-grow from old wood, which makes them popular for topiary. Most are spreading trees or large shrubs, although some forms have a strongly upright habit, and others have been developed for their bronze-coloured foliage.

They have male and female flowers in spring, usually on different trees, and the female flowers develop a single, fleshy, brightly coloured fruit, which contains a poisonous seed. The foliage is poisonous to animals, apart from deer. The leaves, borne in two opposite ranks, are long and narrow, dark green above and with two light green bands beneath. **Cultivation** Grow in fertile, well-drained soil in sun or shade. **Pruning** Formative pruning should produce a clear trunk and a balanced crown, while tipping the lateral branches of young trees will encourage a denser crown. Occasional pruning is required to remove dead, dying, diseased or crossing branches. **Propagation** Seed should be collected when fresh and be sown into a container in an unheated glasshouse or cold frame until germination occurs. Semi-ripe cuttings can be taken in late summer and early autumn. The base of the cutting should be dipped in a rooting hormone and placed in a humid environment in a glasshouse until the cuttings root.

T. baccata
Common yew, English yew
This is one of the three conifers native to the UK, where it

naturally occurs on chalky, alkaline soil. It is a broadly spreading tree with ascending branches, and the gnarled trunk is covered with shredding, dark red-brown bark, which may become hollow on old trees. The foliage is very dark green, and the berries are red. H 20m (65ft), S 10m (33ft). **Named varieties** Many garden-worthy forms have been developed from the species. The female form 'Adpressa' has short, stumpy needles, which are pressed flat to the stems. It is a small tree or spreading shrub, with bright red berries in autumn. H 6m (20ft), S 4m (12ft).

'Adpressa Variegata' is a non-fruiting male form with the same tightly pressed foliage and habit as 'Adpressa', but the new leaves have bright yellow margins, which age to old gold.

Plants in Aurea Group have golden-yellow or gold-edged foliage. Their yellow colouration is brightest in spring and fades by the time the needles are two years old. Members of this group eventually develop into small but broadly spreading trees.

'Dovastoniana' (West Felton yew) is a broadly spreading or vase-shaped tree with long, horizontal branches, dressed with hanging foliage. Although a fruitless male form exists, the distinctive fruiting female form is more commonly grown.

Young specimens of the female 'Fastigiata' (syn. 'Hibernia'; Irish yew) have a narrow, tightly columnar habit, and although they spread a little as they age, they remain columnar and densely leaved. The foliage is black-green, and the berries are red. H 10m (33ft), S 6m (20ft).

'Lutea' (syn. 'Fructu Lutea') is grown for its unusual, pale yellow berries. It is ultimately a spreading tree.

'Washingtonii' is a freely fruiting, spreading, female form with slightly upright branches clothed with bright yellow foliage, which fades to green-yellow. When winter temperatures are sufficiently cold the foliage turns a delightful bronze-yellow. **Aspect** Full sun or semi-shade. **Hardiness** ✽✽✽ Zones 5–7.

Taxus baccata 'Fastigiata'

T. chinensis
Chinese yew
The species is less widely planted than the common yew (*T. baccata*). It is an elegant if slow-growing tree. The glossy needles, which are larger than those of other yews, are greenish-yellow, and it produces abundant, red, fleshy fruits. H 12m (40ft), S 10m (33ft).
Aspect Full sun or semi-shade. **Hardiness** ✽✽✽ Zones 5–7.

T. cuspidata
Japanese yew
The species is native to north-eastern China and Japan. It is hardier than *T. baccata* and can be planted where that species would not survive. It is a medium-sized tree with greenish-yellow foliage and bright red fruits. H 15m (50ft), S 8m (26ft).
Aspect Full sun or semi-shade. **Hardiness** ✽✽✽ Zones 4–7.

T. x media
This hybrid of *T. baccata* and *T. cuspidata* arose in Massachusetts in 1903 and is now widely planted in place of *T. baccata* in colder parts of the USA, for which purpose a number of named forms have been developed. These exhibit similar habits and needle colour to the cultivars of *T. baccata*, although some forms develop curiously twisted branches. It is intermediate between both parents, with

dark green foliage in two ranks, H and S 20–25m (65–80ft).
Aspect Full sun or semi-shade.
Hardiness ✿✿✿ Zones 4–7.

TECOMA

There are about 12 species of evergreen trees and shrubs in the genus, and they are native to southern Africa and to the southern USA and Central and South America. They are grown for their large, colourful flowers and attractive foliage. They are not hardy and in cold areas can be grown in large containers under glass. In mild areas they can be grown as specimens.
Cultivation Outdoors, grow in fertile, moisture-retentive but well-drained soil in sun.
Pruning Formative pruning should aim to encourage a clear trunk and a balanced crown. Occasional pruning is required for the removal of dead, dying, diseased or crossing branches.

Propagation Seed should be collected when fresh and sown into a container in a heated glasshouse in a frost-free and humid environment until germination occurs.

T. stans
(syn. *Bignonia stans*, *Stenolobium stans*)
Yellow elder, trumpet bush, yellow bells
A beautiful, small tree or large, multi-stemmed shrub, this species from the southern USA to Argentina, produces bright yellow, trumpet-shaped flowers in dense clusters over a long period from late winter to summer. The pinnate leaves, up to 35cm (14in) long, are bright green and have 5–13 leaflets. The flowers are followed by cylindrical seedpods. H 8–9m (26–30ft), S 3–5m (10–16ft).
Aspect Full sun.
Hardiness (Min. 7–10°C/ 45–50°F) Zones 10–12.

THUJA
Arborvitae
The six species in the genus are coniferous evergreen trees native to eastern Asia and North America. They have a conical or broadly columnar habit and small, overlapping leaves. They make handsome specimens and can also be used in hedges.
Cultivation Grow in fertile, moisture-retentive but well-drained soil in sun. Protect young plants from cold, drying winds.
Pruning Formative pruning should produce a clear trunk and a balanced crown, while tipping the lateral branches of young trees will encourage a denser crown.
Propagation Seed is the easiest method of propagation. It should be collected when fresh and sown into a container in an unheated glasshouse or cold frame until germination occurs. Semi-ripe and softwood cuttings can be taken during summer and should be dipped in a rooting hormone and placed in a humid environment until rooting occurs.

T. koraiensis
(syn. *Thujopsis koraiensis*)
Korean arborvitae
This small tree from China and Korea has a conical habit and flattened, fern-like leaves, which are bright green above and silvery beneath. When the leaves are crushed they emit a pungent aroma. The bark is reddish-brown. H 10m (33ft), S 3–5m (10–16ft).
Aspect Full sun or semi-shade.
Hardiness ✿✿✿ Zones 5–7.

T. plicata
Western red cedar
A tall, beautiful conifer, this fast-growing species from western North America has strongly weeping and billowing lower branches and reddish, shredding bark. The flattened, scale-like leaves are mid- to dark green and smell of pineapple when crushed. H 25–35m (80–115ft), S 10m (33ft).
Named varieties A huge number of selections have been made from the species, and these vary from dwarf forms to those with brightly coloured foliage.

Tecoma stans

'Atrovirens', probably the most widely grown form in Europe, is often used for hedging because it is fast-growing and has dense, glossy, dark green foliage.
'Fastigiata' is a slow-growing, narrow form with tightly upright branches and green foliage that weeps at the tips.
'Green Giant' is widely grown in the USA as a screening or hedging plant because it is quick-growing and heat tolerant. The foliage occasionally turns bronze in winter.
Aspect Full sun or semi-shade.
Hardiness ✿✿✿ Zones 4–7.

THUJOPSIS
Hiba
The only species in the genus is a slow-growing evergreen conifer from Japan. It is closely related to *Thuja* but has larger leaves. These trees make good specimens.
Cultivation Grow in fertile, moisture-retentive but well-drained soil in sun. Protect plants from cold, drying winds.
Pruning Formative pruning should aim to produce a clear trunk and a balanced crown, while tipping the lateral branches of young trees encourages a denser crown.
Propagation Seed is the easiest method of propagation. It should be collected when fresh and be sown into a container in an unheated glasshouse or cold frame until germination occurs. Semi-ripe and softwood cuttings can be taken during summer and should be dipped in a rooting hormone and placed in a humid environment until rooting occurs.

Thuja plicata

T. dolabrata

This broadly conical tree has shredding, reddish-brown bark. The scale-like leaves are borne in dense sprays and are dark green above and marked with silver-white beneath. H 20m (65ft), S 6–10ft (20–33ft).

Named varieties The cultivar 'Aurea' is a large shrub or small tree with stunning yellow-green foliage, strongest in spring and dulling with age.

Aspect Full sun or semi-shade.
Hardiness ✴✴✴ Zones 5–7.

TILIA
Lime, linden

There are about 45 species of deciduous trees in the genus. They come from Europe, Asia and North America, where they are found in woodlands, and are grown for their fragrant flowers and attractive foliage. They are traditionally used in landscape avenues or as specimen trees, although they can also be pleached and pollarded.

Cultivation Grow in moisture-retentive but well-drained soil in sun or semi-shade.

Pruning Early formative pruning should aim to produce a clear trunk and a balanced crown. Trunk suckers are common on many lime trees and should be removed during late spring or early summer.

Propagation Seed and budding are the main methods of propagation. Seed should be collected when fresh and be sown into a container in an unheated

Tilia cordata

glasshouse or cold frame until germination occurs. Summer budding on to seed-grown limes is commonly practised. Trunk suckers can also be rooted if a cage frame is built around the trunk and the cages filled with compost during spring. The cage is removed a year later in winter and the rooted suckers are removed.

T. cordata
Small-leaved lime

This broadly conical tree from Europe has small, heart-shaped leaves, up to 8cm (3in) long, which are glossy, dark green above and blue-green below. In late summer it bears clusters of scented, cream-white flowers with the typical lance-shaped, grey-green bract. It is not as tolerant of heat as some species. H 25–30m (80–100ft), S 15–20m (50–65ft).

Named varieties 'Corinthian' is a compact, pyramidal form, with dark green, but smaller leaves.

The fast-growing 'Greenspire' is one of the most widely grown of the cultivars. It develops into a straight-trunked tree, with an open, oval crown, dark green foliage and orange shoots. H 15m (50ft), S 7m (23ft).

'Rancho' is a free-flowering form with smaller than average leaves and an upswept habit. H 15m (50ft), S 8m (26ft).

Best grown as a pollard, 'Winter Orange' has red buds and orange shoots. It is particularly attractive when it is in flower and in autumn.

Aspect Full sun or semi-shade.
Hardiness ✴✴✴ Zones 4–7.

T. × europaea
(syn. *T. intermedia*, *T. × vulgaris*)
Common lime, European lime

This widely grown hybrid between *T. cordata* and *T. platyphyllos* often produces suckers.. The dark green leaves, up to 10cm (4in) long, are heart-shaped and pale green beneath; they turn yellow in autumn. In summer clusters of pale yellow flowers are produced. H 35m (115ft), S 15m (50ft).

Named varieties 'Goldcrown' is a beautiful cultivar with leaves that are yellow when they first emerge, fading to yellow-green in summer.

Thujopsis dolabrata

'Pallida' (Kaiser linden) is a form with ascending branches and broadly conical crown. The stems are reddish-brown.

Aspect Full sun or semi-shade.
Hardiness ✴✴✴ Zones 3–7.

T. platyphyllos
Broad-leaved lime, large-leaved lime

This stately tree, which is native to Europe and is often planted in parks, develops a broadly conical crown. The trunk is covered with suckering shoots. The dark green leaves, 8–15cm (3–6in) long, are covered with dense hairs on the underside and turn yellow in autumn. Clusters of fragrant, pale yellow flowers are borne in late summer. H 30m (100ft), S 15–20m (50–65ft).

Named varieties 'Aurea' has attractive bright yellow shoots, turning olive-green as they mature.

'Fastigiata' (syn. 'Erecta') is an initially strongly upright form that becomes more open with age. H 13m (43ft).

'Prince's Street', a widely grown street tree, has an upright habit and reddish shoots.

Aspect Full sun or semi-shade.
Hardiness ✴✴✴ Zones 4–6.

T. tomentosa
European white lime, silver lime

This lovely tree from south-eastern Europe and south-western

Asia has a broadly conical habit. The dark green leaves, up to 10cm (4in) long, are covered with silvery hairs on the undersides. In summer fragrant white flowers are borne in clusters. H 25–30m (80–100ft), S 20m (65ft).

Named varieties The conical 'Brabant' is widely planted as a street tree. Its dark green leaves turn yellow in autumn.

'Green Mountain' is a fast-growing cultivar with dark green leaves, which are silvery beneath. It has reliable autumn colour, good drought and heat tolerance and a conical habit.

The beautiful 'Petiolaris' develops a clear central leader, and the strongly weeping branches, covered with dark green leaves, silver beneath, hang like curtains. The fragrant white flowers are borne in late summer. H 30m, S 20m (65ft).

Aspect Full sun or semi-shade.
Hardiness ✴✴✴ Zones 4–7.

TRACHYCARPUS

There are six species of evergreen palm trees in the genus. They are single-stemmed or clustering plants from tropical Asia and are grown for their divided, fan-shaped leaves and flower clusters.

Cultivation Outdoors, grow in fertile, well-drained soil in sun or light shade. Protect from cold, drying winds.

Trachycarpus fortunei

Pruning Like most palms, little pruning is required apart from the cosmetic removal of dead leaves and spent flower clusters during early summer.
Propagation Seed is the easiest method of propagation. It should be collected when fresh and be sown into a container in a heated glasshouse in a humid environment at 29°C (84°F) until germination occurs.

T. fortunei
(syn. *Chamaerops excelsa, T. excelsa*)
Chusan palm, windmill palm
This popular species is of unknown origin. It is probably the hardiest of the palms, and can be grown in mild maritime regions or sheltered gardens in cooler areas, as long as it is not exposed to cold winds or frost. It develops a single, unbranched trunk, covered with brown fibre and the remains of dead stems, which should be removed to keep the trunk neat.

The dark green leaves, up to 75cm (30in) long, are fan-shaped and deeply cut into numerous sharply pointed leaflets. The leaves are arranged spirally around the main trunk. In early summer pendent panicles of yellow flowers, up to 60cm (24in) long, are borne just below the leaves from the trunk, and are followed by small brown fruits. H 12m (40ft), S 2.4m (8ft).
Aspect Full sun or semi-shade.
Hardiness ✹✹ Zones 7–11.

T. wagnerianus
This slow-growing species has a fatter and squatter trunk than *T. fortunei*, and the leaves grow up to 45cm (18in) long. They are white-green when they first emerge. Although the species was discovered in Japan, it is not native to the region and is known only through having been cultivated in Japan and China. H 7–9m (23–30ft), S 2.4m (8ft).
Aspect Full sun or semi-shade.
Hardiness ✹✹ Zones 7–11.

TSUGA
Hemlock
The 10–11 species in the genus are evergreen coniferous trees from the forests of eastern Asia and North America. They are grown for their elegant habit and make fine specimen trees.
Cultivation Grow in fertile, moisture-retentive but well-drained, acidic to slightly alkaline soil in sun or semi-shade. In poor soils protect plants from cold, drying winds.
Pruning Formative pruning should aim to produce a clear trunk and a balanced crown, while tipping the lateral branches of young trees to encourage a denser crown.
Propagation Seed should be collected when fresh and be sown into a container in an unheated glasshouse or cold frame until germination occurs. Semi-ripe and softwood cutting can be taken during summer and should be dipped in a rooting hormone and placed in a humid environment until rooting occurs. Selected forms are winter grafted on to seedling-raised rootstocks.

T. canadensis
Eastern hemlock
This spreading conifer from eastern North America is an excellent tree for a shady position, and it can also be used as an under-storey tree. It has arching new growth, and dark green, small needles with silvery-white undersides. The needles are arranged in two ranks at opposite sides of the stems. It is a fast-growing tree, often grown for its timber. It makes a beautiful hedge. H 25m (80ft), S 10m (33ft).

Named varieties 'Golden Splendor' is a fast-growing, narrow form with yellow foliage that is less prone to sun scorch than some golden conifers. The new growth is bright yellow, which turns yellow-green as it ages.

'Pendula' is a slow-growing, strongly arching, small tree, often trained up a short trunk before being allowed to weep. H 4m (12ft), S 8m (26ft).
Aspect Full sun or semi-shade.
Hardiness ✹✹✹ Zones 3–7.

T. mertensiana
Mountain hemlock, blue hemlock
This columnar to conical tree from western North America is one of the most ornamental of the genus. It has purple to red-brown bark and spiky, grey-green or blue-grey foliage. H 15m (50ft), S 6m (20ft).
Aspect Full sun or semi-shade.
Hardiness ✹✹✹ Zones 5–6.

ULMUS
Elm
The genus contains 45 species of deciduous or semi-evergreen trees and a few shrubs. They are native to northern temperate areas and are grown for their habit and attractive foliage. Until the outbreak of Dutch elm disease (DED) in the 1930s, followed by a second outbreak in the 1970s, elms were widely planted as city, street, hedgerow and parkland trees in Europe and the USA. DED, a fungal disease spread by beetles, is usually fatal and, for this reason, elms are not suitable for long-term planting as

Tsuga mertensiana

specimen trees, although they are still grown in areas free of the disease. Some elms have been found to show varying degrees of resistance, including *U. parvifolia* and its cultivars, *U. pumila* and *U.* 'Sapporo Autumn Gold'. Some other cultivars that are believed to be resistant to DED are noted below.
Cultivation Grow in well-drained soil in sun or semi-shade.
Pruning Early formative pruning should aim to produce a clear trunk and a balanced crown. Some elms produce tight branch angles and these should be removed when the tree is young.
Propagation Seed and summer budding are the main methods of propagation. Seed should be collected when it is fresh and be sown into a container in an unheated glasshouse or cold frame until germination occurs. Summer budding can be done using seed-grown elms.

U. 'Accolade'
This vase-shaped tree, a hybrid between two Asiatic species, *U. japonica* and *U. wilsoniana*, has glossy green foliage that turns yellow in autumn. It has good resistance to DED. H 18m (60ft), S 12m (40ft).
Aspect Full sun.
Hardiness ✹✹✹ Zone 3.

U. americana
American white elm
A graceful, spreading tree from the eastern USA, the species is often multi-stemmed with large, V-shaped trunks covered with silver bark. The dark green leaves, up to 15cm (6in) long, are heavily toothed and turn butter yellow in autumn. It is still widespread in the USA, although it is not resistant to DED. H 25m (80ft), S 20m (65ft).
Named varieties The cultivar 'American Liberty' has an upright habit; it shows good resistance to DED.

In tests 'Valley Forge', which has good autumn colour, has been shown to have the greatest resistance to DED of all American elms.
Aspect Full sun.
Hardiness ✹✹✹ Zones 3–9.

U. x hollandica
Dutch elm
This naturally occurring hybrid, probably between *U. glabra* (wych elm) and *U. minor* (European field elm), appears wherever the parents meet. It is a broadly columnar tree, with toothed, dark green leaves, up to 12cm (5in) long, which turn yellow in autumn. Small red flowers are borne in spring, followed by winged fruits. H 30–35m (100–115ft), S 20–25m (65–80ft).
Named varieties The cultivar 'Christine Buisman' has a tight vase shape and has shown good disease resistance.
   'Dampieri Aurea' (syn. 'Wredei') is a narrowly conical tree with beautiful yellow leaves up to 6cm (2½in) long, and with some resistance to DED. H 10m (33ft), S 1m (3ft).
Aspect Full sun.
Hardiness ✱✱✱ Zones 3–9.

U. 'New Horizon'
This hardy hybrid elm, arising from *U. japonica* and *U. pumila*, is a vigorous tree with dark green foliage, an upright habit and vivid autumn colour. It has good resistance to DED. H 18m (60ft), S 10m (33ft).
Aspect Full sun.
Hardiness ✱✱✱ Zone 3.

U. parvifolia
Chinese elm
This spreading tree has glossy, dark green leaves, up to 6cm (2½in) long, which can turn orange-yellow in autumn, but which often persist into winter.

Ulmus

The grey-brown bark flakes to reveal the light brown underbark. The species does not appear to be affected by DED. H 15–18m (50–60ft), S 12–15m (40–50ft).
Named varieties 'Allee' has an upright, vase-shaped habit. The flaking bark is green-grey, silver-green and orange-brown. The leaves turn yellow in autumn. H 20–25m (65–80ft), S 20m (65ft).
   'Athena' has a rounded habit with green foliage and exfoliating bark, grey-silver-green and brown.
   The US form 'Golden Ray' has leaves that are gold-coloured in summer, turning yellow in autumn.
Aspect Full sun.
Hardiness ✱✱✱ Zone 4.

U. 'Patriot'
This narrow form, derived from *U.* 'Urban' and *U. wilsoniana*, has good autumn colour and high resistance to DED. H 18m (60ft), S 12m (40ft).
Aspect Full sun.
Hardiness ✱✱✱ Zone 3.

U. pumila
Siberian elm
This rather variable tree has toothed, dark green leaves, up to 10cm (4in) long, which are covered with hairs beneath. Small red flowers are borne in spring and are followed by winged fruits. H 30m (100ft), S 12m (40ft).
Aspect Full sun.
Hardiness ✱✱✱ Zone 3.

U. 'Sapporo Autumn Gold'
This hardy and fast-growing cultivar, a hybrid between *U. pumila* and *U. japonica*, is a broadly conical tree with upright branches. The glossy leaves, up to 8cm (3in) long, are tinged with red in spring, turning dark green and then yellow-green in autumn. H 18m (60ft), S 12m (40ft).
Aspect Full sun.
Hardiness ✱✱✱ Zone 3.

U. 'Urban'
The parents of this hardy, drought-resistant form include *U. x hollandica* var. *vegeta*, *U. minor* and *U. pumila*. It has a spreading habit and dark green leaves. H 18m (60ft), S 12m (40ft).
Aspect Full sun.
Hardiness ✱✱✱ Zone 3.

WASHINGTONIA
Fan palm
There are two species of single-stemmed palms in the genus. They are native to dry areas in the southern USA and northern Mexico.
Cultivation Outdoors, grow in fertile, well-drained soil in full sun.
Pruning Little pruning is required apart from the removal of dead leaves and spent flower clusters.
Propagation Sow fresh seed into a container in a heated glasshouse in a humid environment at 29°C (84°F) until germination occurs.

W. filifera
Desert fan palm
This is a medium to large palm tree with 2m (6ft) wide and long leaves that have a spiky petiole. The clusters of stunning white flowers are up to 5m long and drupe from the foliage. H 20m (70ft) S 6m (20ft).
Aspect Full sun.
Hardiness ✱ Zones 8–11.

W. robusta
Thread palm
A fast-growing, slender palm, this has sharply toothed leaf stalks, and less fibre hanging from the leaves. The trunk is quite tapered at the base and the palm-like foliage grows to 1m wide and long (3ft x 3ft). The flowers are creamy-white. H 25m (80ft) and S 5m (15ft).
Aspect Full sun.
Hardiness ✱ Zones 9–11.

ZELKOVA
The genus contains five or six species of deciduous trees, which are grown for their habit and foliage. The genus is closely related to *Ulmus*. Zelkovas may be distinguished by their round fruits.
Cultivation Grow in fertile, moisture-retentive, well-drained soil in sun or semi-shade. Protect plants from cold, drying winds.
Pruning Early formative pruning should aim to produce a clear trunk and a balanced crown. Occasional pruning is required for the removal of dead, dying, diseased or crossing branches.
Propagation Fresh seed should be sown into a container outside in an unheated glasshouse or cold

Zelkova carpinifolia

frame until germination occurs. Summer budding on to seed-grown zelkovas is also quite commonly practised.

Z. serrata
(syn. Z. keaki)
Japanese zelkova
This spreading, fast-growing tree, from Korea, Taiwan and Japan, has upswept branches, which create a rounded crown. The bark is grey, flaking to reveal orange underbark. The narrow, ovate leaves, up to 12cm (5in) long, are toothed, dark green, turning yellow, orange and red in autumn. H 30m (100ft), S 18m (60ft).
Named varieties 'Autumn Glow' is smaller than the species and has a compact habit and stunning purple leaves in autumn.
   The vigorous and fast-growing 'Green Vase' has dark green leaves that turn orange-yellow and bronze-red in autumn.
   'Green Veil' is often grown as a graft on the species to make an unusual weeping standard tree.
   The fast-growing, pollution-tolerant and apparently disease-resistant 'Village Green' has orange-yellow and purple-red autumn colour.
Aspect Full sun.
Hardiness ✱✱✱ Zones 5–8.

Glossary

Acid soil Soil with a pH lower than 7.
Adventitious Occurring in an unusual location.
Alkaline soil Soil with a pH higher than 7.
Amendments/Amelioration Organic or mineral materials, such as garden compost and perlite, that are used to improve the soil.
Angiosperms Trees with seeds enclosed within a protective ovary capsule or fruit.
Anther Part of the male organ found inside the flower that releases the pollen.
Apical The furthest point referring often to a shoot.
Apical dominance The ability to produce a single main leader in the form of a dominant stem which suppresses other shoots.
Arboriculture The care and maintenance of trees.
Aril A fleshy seed coat that protects the seed.
Bloom A white waxy or bluish-white powder or covering.
Bract A modified paper-like leaf, usually located at the base of a flower, a fruit, or a cluster of flowers or fruits.
Buttress Extensive widening of the base of the stem to provide additional structural support, often found on tropical trees that grow in poor soils.
Calcicole Trees that prefer alkaline soils.
Calcifuge Trees that dislike alkaline soils.
Callus Tissue produced around a wound of a tree.
Cambium A thin layer of cells that divide and produce the annual growth in the stems of trees.
Canopy The area made up of the branches and leaves.

Aesculus carnea

Catkin Pendulous cluster of flowers or bract that is usually male or female.
Chlorophyll Green pigment that enables trees to produce energy from sunlight.
Clay soil Soil with small, flat particles that tend to pack together tightly, which hardens when dry, and drains poorly without organic amendments.
Clone Offspring that is genetically identical to its parent.
Compost (garden) Organic material composed of decaying plant and animal matter.
Cone The reproductive organ of a conifer.
Cordate Heart-shaped leaves.
Cross Term used to describe a hybrid.
Crown The upper part of a tree usually forming the canopy of the tree.
Cultivar A tree that has arisen or been selected for its distinct characteristics, produced and maintained by vegetative propagation.
Cuttings Stems, roots or leaves taken from plants for propagation.
Dead-heading Removing blooms that have died.
Deciduous Without leaves for part of the year.
Dormant Plants which are in a resting state, most often during low or high temperatures. Usually refers to deciduous trees when without leaves.
Double Refers to flowers when they have more than the average number or a different arrangement of petals.
Endemic Only found in a particular region or country.
Epicormic Describes shoots that appear out of the trunk or branches.
Ericaceous Referring to members of the heather family (Ericaceae); ericaous compost is potting compost (soil mix) suitable for calcifuge (acid-loving or lime-hating) plants.
Evergreen A tree that retains its leaves for longer than a year.
Exposure The intensity, duration and variation in sun, wind and temperature that can affect the growth of a tree.
Fastigiate Trees with very upright growth that is often parallel to the main trunk.
Filament The stalk that holds up and supports the anther.
Germination The sprouting of a shoot and root from a seed.
Glaucous Blue-white in colour; it often refers to the leaves.
Gymnosperm A tree with its seed naked in its ovary and often within a protective cone.

Hardiness The level of cold temperatures that a tree can survive.
Hardiness zones Locations in the United States defined by the coldest winter temperatures.
Heat zone A location in the United States determined by the average annual number of days its temperature climbs above 30°C (86°F).
Humus Decomposed vegetable matter, an important element of soil.
Hybrid A tree produced by cross-breeding between two different parents.
Invasive species A species of tree that spreads quickly, to the detriment of other flora and fauna in the area; often non-native, introduced species.
Juvenile Describes the foliage produced by certain plants on young growth, when different in form from the mature foliage.
Leaching The removal of nutrients from the soil caused by high rainfall or overwatering.
Lenticel A corky area of the trunk or stem that indicates an opening in the bark to allow for air or gas exchange.
Loam A soil type containing an equal balance of sand, silt and clay.
Microclimate The influence of sun, shade, wind, drainage and other factors that affect a tree's growth in a small area of the garden.
Monotypic A tree that is the only member of that particular plant family.
Mulch Any material spread over the soil surface to retain soil moisture, moderate soil temperature, and suppress the growth of weeds.
Mycorrhizal Beneficial symbiotic fungus that grows on tree roots.
Native A tree that occurs naturally in a particular region and was not introduced from another country or region.
Naturalized Introduced by humans and acclimatized and thriving in that particular country or region.
Nectar A sweet tasting liquid produced by the flower to attract pollinators.
Neutral soil A soil having a pH value of 7.0 that is neither acid nor alkaline.
Node The location on the stem where buds, leaves and branches are attached.
Nutrients Nitrogen, phosphorus, potassium, calcium, magnesium, sulphur, iron and other essential elements required to allow for the healthy growth of trees.

Caryota mitis

Ovary The female reproductive part of the flowers that protects the seeds.
Palmate Leaves with three or more leaflets.
Palm-like With leaves similar to a palm tree.
Pea-like With flowers similar to that of a sweet pea (*Lathyrus odoratus*).
Pedicel The stalk supporting the fruit or flower.
pH A measure of soil acidity or alkalinity on a scale of 1 to 14 Neutral is 7. A pH below 7 is acidic; above 7 is alkaline.
Pistil The female reproductive organ of a flower, consisting of an ovary, style and stigma.
Rootball The clump of roots and soil on a plant when removed from its pot.
Seed heads Pods or clusters of seeds on mature plants at the end of the growing season.
Shrub Term used to describe a woody perennial plant that grows multiple stems and does not appear to have a clear single trunk.
Species Plants which are genetically similar and which breed true to type from seed.
Stamen The male reproductive organ of a flower, consisting of a filament and a pollen-containing anther.
Subsoil A light-coloured soil of varying consistencies below the topsoil.
Tap root The main root of a tree.
Tepal Term used when a petal or sepal cannot be differentiated.
Tipping The practice of pruning the tips of branches that is used to control the size of tree crowns.

Index

A

Abelia x *grandiflora* 168
Abeliophyllum distichum (white
   forsythia) 168
Abies (silver fir) 412
   A. alba (European silver fir,
     common silver fir) 267, 412
   A. 'Aurea' 412
   A. bracteata (Santa Lucia fir,
     bristlecone fir) 276, 412
   A. 'Brilliantissimum' 305
   A. 'Columnare' 417
   A. concolor (white fir, Colorado
     white fir) 412
   A. var. *dissectum* Atropurpureum
     Group 267
   A. firma (Japanese fir, momi fir)
     412
   A. nebrodensis (Sicily fir) 412
   A. pinsapo (Spanish fir, hedgehog
     fir) 412
Abutilon (Chinese lantern) 168
   A. megapotamicum (Brazilian bell-
     flower, trailing abutilon) 169
Acacia (wattle) 412–3
   A. auriculaeformis (black wattle)
     413
   A. baileyana (Cootamundra wattle)
     413
   A. confusa (false koa) 413
   A. dealbata (mimosa, silver wattle)
     413
   A. longifolia (Sydney golden
     wattle) 413
   A. melanoxylon (blackwood wattle)
     413
   A. pravissima (Oven's wattle) 413
Acer spp. (maple) 19, 48, 169, 346
   357
   A. buergerianum (trident maple,
     three-toothed maple) 413
   A. campestre (field maple, hedge
     maple) 413
   A. capillipes 269
   A. cappadocicum (Cappadocian
     maple, Caucasian maple) 414
   A. x *conspicuum* 361
   A. davidii (Père David's maple,
     snakebark maple) 269, 414–15
   A. x *freemanii* (Freeman's maple,
     hybrid red maple) 415
   A. 'Ginger Bread' 415
   A. griseum (paperbark maple,
     Chinese paperbark maple) 269,
     312, 361, 402, 415
   A. grosseri var. *hersii* (syn. *A. davidii*
     subsp. *grosseri*, *A. grosseri*, *A.*
     hersii) (Hersii maple) 269, 415
   A. japonicum (full moon maple,
     Japanese maple) 328, 415
   A. macrophyllum (Oregon maple,
     big-leaf maple) 416
   A. negundo (box elder, ash-leaved
     maple) 416
   A. palmatum (Japanese maple) 22, 23,
     36, 49, 169–70, 312, 328, 416

   A. palmatum 'Osakazuki' (Japanese
     maple) 170, 416
   A. palmatum 'Sango-kaku'
     (Japanese maple, coral bark
     maple) 170
   A. pensylvanicum (striped maple,
     moosewood, snakebark maple)
     269, 416
   A. 'Phoenix' 402, 414
   A. platanoides (Norway maple)
     390, 397, 416–17
   A. pseudoplatanus (sycamore, plane
     tree maple, great maple) 417
   A. pycnanthum (Japanese red
     maple) 417
   A. rubrum (red maple, scarlet
     maple, swamp maple) 310,
     390, 396, 417
   A. rufinerve (red-vein maple, grey-
     budded snakebark maple) 412
   A. saccharinum (syn. *A. dasycarpum*)
     (silver maple) 412
   A. saccharum (sugar maple, rock
     maple) 412
   A. 'Silver Cardinal' 414
   A. maple) 312, 416
   A. sterculiaceum (syn. *A. villosum*)
     (Himalayan maple) 412–13
   A. 'White Tigress' 361, 419
Aceraceae 266
Actinidia kolomikta (kolomikta
   vine) 132, 232
Aesculus (horse chestnut, buckeye)
   345, 346, 419
   A. x *carnea* (red horse chestnut)
     419
   A. hippocastanum (horse chestnut)
     419
   A. indica (Indian horse chestnut)
     419
   A. x *neglecta* 'Erythroblastos'
     (sunrise horse chestnut) 420
   A. turbina (Japanese horse
     chestnut) 420
African tulip tree (*Spathodea*) 492
Agathis (kauri pine, dammar pine) 420
   A. australis (kauri pine) 420
   A. robusta (Queensland kauri, bark
     kauri) 420
Agrobacterium tumefaciens 348
Ailanthus 420
   A. altissima (syn. *A. glandulosa*)
     (tree of heaven) 420
air-layering 388–9
Akebia (chocolate vine) 232
   A. quinata 25, 35, 66, 134, 232
Albizia (silk trees) 361, 421
   A. julibrissin (syn. *Acacia julibrissin*)
     421
alder (*Alnus*) 349, 350, 386, 421
alder buckthorn (*Rhamnus frangula*)
   486
Aleurites 421
   A. moluccana (candlenut) 421
Alexandrian laurel (*Calophyllum*

   inophyllum) 429
Allegheny serviceberry (*Amelanchier
   laevis*) 422
almond (*Prunus dulcis*) 346, 480–1
Alnus spp. (alder) 386, 421
   A. cordata (Italian alder) 421
   A. glutinosa (common alder) 421
   A. 'Imperialis' 421
   A. incana (grey alder) 422
Aloysia triphylla (lemon verbena) 170
Alpine snow gum (*Eucalyptus
   pauciflora* subsp. *niphophila*) 267
Amelanchier (juneberry, snowy
   mespilus, shadbush) 170, 388,
   422
   A. laevis (Allegheny serviceberry)
     422
   A. lamarckii 22–23, 44, 170, 422
   A. x *grandiflora* 170, 422
American aspen (*Populus tremuloides*)
   476
American beech (*Fagus grandifolia*) 448
American holly (*Ilex opaca*) 453
American hornbeam (*Carpinus
   caroliniana*) 430
American persimmon (*Diospyros
   virginiana*) 445
American plane trees 346
American smoke tree (*Cotinus
   obovatus* (syn. *C. americanus*, *Rhus
   cotinoides*)) 441
American sweet chestnut (*Castanea
   dentata*) 431
American sycamore 350
American white elm (*Ulmus
   americana*) 498
Ampelopsis 232
   A. aconitifolia 232
   A. glandulosa var. *brevipedunculata*
     134, 232
   A. megalophylla 233

amur cork tree (*Phellodendron
   amurense*) 470
angiosperms 278

angled staking 332, 333
annual climbers 75, 77, 79
Aphidoletes 349
Aphiduis 349
apple (*Malus sylvestris* var. *domestica*)
   278, 279, 328, 345, 346, 349,
   341, 347, 376
apricot (*Prunus armeniaca*) 278, 346,
   478–9
Araucaria 422–3
   A. araucana (syn. *A. imbricata*)
     (monkey puzzle, Chilean pine)
     423
   A. heterophylla (syn. *A. excelsa*)
     (Norfolk Island pine) 423
arboreta 295, 296, 297, 299, 363
arborvitae (*Thuja*) 388, 496
Arbutus (strawberry tree, madroño)
   346, 423
   A. andrachne (Grecian strawberry
     tree) 423
   A. x *andrachnoides* 423
   A. 'Elfin King' 275, 423
   A. 'Marina' 423
   A. unedo (strawberry tree) 423
arches 74–5, 95
   supporting plants 100–3
Aristolochia (Dutchman's pipe) 134,
   233
   A. littoralis 233
   A. macrophylla 233
Armillaria 346
Artocarpus (breadfruit) 424
   A. altilis (syn. *A. communis*)
     (breadfruit) 424
ash (*Fraxinus*) 346, 282, 401, 405,
   450
aspen (*Populus tremens*) 475
Atlantic cedar (*Cedrus atlantica*)
   (syn. *C. libani* subsp. *atlantica*)) 433
Aucuba japonica (Japanese laurel) 171
Australian eucalyptus (*Eucalyptus
   regnans*) 263
Australian fan palm (*Livistona
   australis*) 459
Australian ivy palm (*Schefflera
   actinophylla* (syn. *Brassaea
   actinophylla*)) 489
avenues, landscaping for 388–9
autumn 36–7, 150–1, 256–7
Azalea 27, 41
   evergreen azaleas 216–17
Azara dentata 171

B

Bacillus thuringiensis 349, 350
backdrops, trees as 402–3
bald cypress (*Taxodium*) 494–5
Ballota acetabulosa 171
banana shrub (*Michelia*) 467
Banksia
   B. baxteri 424
   B. coccinea (scarlet banksia) 172,
     424
   B. integrifolia (coast banksia) 424

Abutilon x *suntense*

Buddleja davidii 'Dartmoor'

Acer palmatum 'Osakazuki'

Cistus x cyprius

Pittosporum tenuifolium 'Variegatum'

Rosa 'Mountbatten'

Philodendron scandens

Clematis 'Mrs Cholmondeley'

Aesculus x *carnea*

Betula alleghaniensis

Cedrus atlantica

Licuala grandis

Malus 'Striped Beauty'

This edition is published by Lorenz Books
an imprint of Anness Publishing Ltd
Hermes House, 88–89 Blackfriars Road
London SE1 8HA
tel. 020 7401 2077; fax 020 7633 9499

www.lorenzbooks.com; www.annesspublishing.com

If you like the images in this book and would like to investigate using them
for publishing, promotions or advertising, please visit our website
www.practicalpictures.com for more information.

UK agent: The Manning Partnership Ltd
tel. 01225 478444; fax 01225 478440; sales@manning-partnership.co.uk

UK distributor: Grantham Book Services Ltd
tel. 01476 541080; fax 01476 541061; orders@gbs.tbs-ltd.co.uk

North American agent/distributor: National Book Network
tel. 301 459 3366; fax 301 429 5746; www.nbnbooks.com

Australian agent/distributor: Pan Macmillan Australia
tel. 1300 135 113; fax 1300 135 103; customer.service@macmillan.com.au

New Zealand agent/distributor: David Bateman Ltd
tel. (09) 415 7664; fax (09) 415 8892

Publisher: Joanna Lorenz
Editorial Director: Helen Sudell
Project Editors: Clare Hill and Lucy Doncaster
Designer: Nigel Partridge
Production Controller: Don Campaniello

A CIP catalogue record for this book is available from the British Library.

Previously published in two separate volumes,
The Gardener's Guide to Shrubs & Climbers and
The Gardener's Guide to Planting & Growing Trees

ETHICAL TRADING POLICY
Because of our ongoing ecological investment programme,
you, as our customer, can have the pleasure and reassurance of
knowing that a tree is being cultivated on your behalf to naturally replace the
materials used to make the book you are holding. For further information
about this scheme, go to www.annesspublishing.com/trees

Acknowledgements

The publishers would like to thank Peter Anderson for his work on the
original photography. Unless listed below, photographs are © Anness
Publishing Ltd. t = top; b = bottom; l = left; r = right; c = centre.
Garden World Images: 171tr, br; 174tr; 181bl; 182tr, tc; 190tr; 197tr;
200tr; 203br; 204tr; 211br; 214bl; 215br; 224bl, br; 225tr; 226tl; 233tl,
tr; 240tl; bl; 241bl; 242bl; 245t, b; 247tc; 250bl; 293t (J. Need); 293b
(C. Hawes); 420br (Bot. Images Inc.); 427br (K. Jayaram); 452t (P. Lane);
453tr (Bot. Images Inc.); 456bl (Bot. Images Inc); 457t (M. Keal); 460t
(G. Harland); 467bl (L. Stock); 467tr; 469tr; 473tr; 476br (J. Swithinbank);
480br (T. McGlinchey); 482b (L.Claeys-Bouuaert); 489tr (Bot. Images Inc.)
Andrew Lawson Photography: 83b; 138–9; 156-7; 170bl; 171tl; 176bl;
179tr, b; 184tl, tr; 185tl; 187bl; 190bl; 193tl; 196tr; 210b; 215bl; 250br.

Plant hardiness zones

Hardiness symbols
❋ = half-hardy (down to 0°C)
❋❋ = frost hardy (down to -5°C)
❋❋❋ = fully hardy (down to -15°C)

Zone entries
Plant entries in this book have been given zone numbers.
These zones relate to their hardiness. The zonal system
used (shown below) was developed by the Agricultural
Research Service of the US Department of Agriculture.
According to this system, there are 11 zones, based on the
average annual minimum temperature in a particular
geographical zone. When a range of zones is given for a
plant, the smaller number indicates the northern-most
zone in which a plant can survive the winter. The higher
number gives the most southerly in which it will perform
consistently. As with any system, this one is not hard and
fast. It is simply a rough indicator, as many factors other
than temperature play an important part where hardiness
is concerned. These factors vary across the same state and
include altitude, wind exposure, proximity to water, soil
type, the presence of snow, the existence of shade, night
temperature and the amount of water received by the
plant. These factors can easily alter a plant's hardiness by
several zones.

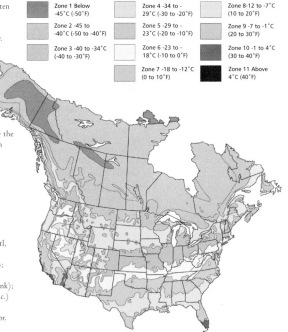

Zone 1 Below -45°C (-50°F)
Zone 2 -45 to -40°C (-50 to -40°F)
Zone 3 -40 to -34°C (-40 to -30°F)
Zone 4 -34 to -29°C (-30 to -20°F)
Zone 5 -29 to -23°C (-20 to -10°F)
Zone 6 -23 to -18°C (-10 to 0°F)
Zone 7 -18 to -12°C (0 to 10°F)
Zone 8-12 to -7°C (10 to 20°F)
Zone 9 -7 to -1°C (20 to 30°F)
Zone 10 -1 to 4°C (30 to 40°F)
Zone 11 Above 4°C (40°F)